Access to Medicines and Vaccines

Carlos M. Correa • Reto M. Hilty
Editors

Access to Medicines and Vaccines

Implementing Flexibilities Under Intellectual Property Law

Springer

Editors
Carlos M. Correa
South Centre
Geneva, Switzerland

Reto M. Hilty
Max Planck Institute for Innovation and Competition
München, Bayern, Germany

ISBN 978-3-030-83113-4 ISBN 978-3-030-83114-1 (eBook)
https://doi.org/10.1007/978-3-030-83114-1

This Springer imprint is published by the registered company Springer Nature Switzerland AG.
The registered company address is: Gewerbestrasse 11, 6330 Cham, Switzerland

Preface

This book is an outcome of a partnership between the Max Planck Institute (MPI) for *Innovation* and Competition and the South Centre, which jointly organized a Global Forum on Intellectual Property, Access to Medicine and Innovation in Munich on 9–10 December 2019.

The MPI is more than 50 years old, but it was less than 20 years ago that its research focus began to change quite fundamentally. In the first decades after its foundation, the Institute academically supported and accompanied efforts to achieve a certain standard of protection on the international level. At that time, there was hardly any consideration of the implications of the intellectual property system for countries at different levels of technological and economic development.

Much changed in the 1990s, however—not least with the creation of the WTO and the entry into force of the Agreement on Trade Related Aspects of Intellectual property Rights (the TRIPS Agreement) in 1994. One year later, in 1995, the South Centre was launched and began its work, at a time when it was becoming increasingly doubtful whether high standards of intellectual property protection would produce comparable benefits for all countries, regardless of their level of development. The South Centre published in 1997 '*The TRIPS Agreement. A Guide for the South. The Uruguay Round Agreement on Trade-Related Intellectual Property Rights*', one of the first analysis of the 'flexibilities' allowed by the TRIPS Agreement, the main theme of the Global Forum referred to above.

It took a little more time before a differentiated view began to gain ground at the MPI, but a new era began in 2002 with a change in the management of the Institute. The question of how to avoid dysfunctional effects of IP rights in certain areas and contexts became more and more important.

Naturally, these perspectives brought into focus countries whose development depended much more on policies other than strong intellectual property protection. How little their own industries benefitted from high protection standards became particularly obvious when primarily foreign rather than local companies used the domestic intellectual property system to protect their own inventions, creations, or trademarks.

While in earlier years, the MPI's activities in Asia or Latin America, for instance, were targeted at explaining the meaning and rationale of high standards of IP protection, the view became much more cautious under the new perspective. In the first instance, the Institute tried to understand the socio-economic context of a country, and supported local academics, but also legislators and national policymakers in the analysis and assertion of their specific needs.

This cautious approach to research activities and target-oriented support meanwhile has become a tradition of the MPI, especially in Southeast Asia and partly in Africa. A new and special focus, however, now lies on Latin America. An initiative started there a few years ago with 'Smart IP for Latin America'. Its purpose above all is to promote cooperation among the states concerned, but also to increase awareness for specific interests these countries may have and commonly defend. The topic of the Global Forum—access to medicine—is just one of many examples.

The South Centre, on its part, has worked extensively on intellectual property, particularly but not only in relation to access to medicines. As an intergovernmental organization of developing countries, it has focused on the analysis of the intellectual property system as it may affect development strategies, including the disciplines of the TRIPS Agreement and the standards of protection established pursuant to free trade agreements. A key area of work has been the extent to which that Agreement leaves policy space to implement intellectual property policies suited to different national scenarios in the developing world. The Global Forum jointly convened with the MPI gave the South Centre an opportunity to gather scholars and professionals of developed and developing countries to review current trends and advance in the understanding of the issues at stake with a focus in the area of intellectual property and medicines.

In this context, this book examines topics of particular relevance for shaping intellectual property regimes that take into account public health concerns. It provides not only deep analyses but options for the interpretation of existing regulations or the adoption of new legislation that, being consistent with the TRIPS Agreement, can allow the judiciary and policy makers to take such concerns into account. In different chapters, the book addresses various dimensions of the flexibilities allowed under the TRIPS Agreement. Although there is a significant literature and statements on the subject, such as the 'Declaration on Patent Protection. Regulatory Sovereignty under TRIPS' elaborated under the auspices of the MPI,[1] the book contains new reflections and examines recent developments in case law and legislation.

The covered issues include how the TRIPS Agreement can be interpreted to implement its flexibilities, the use of competition law to promote access to medicines, the role of cooperation in the examination of patent applications, patentability requirements, the impact of TRIPS plus provisions (such as the linkage between patents and drug regulatory approvals), the patentability in the area of CRISPR genome editing technologies, as well as an analysis of the scope of exceptions and limitations to exclusive rights provided for by the Agreement, such as the exhaustion

[1] Available at https://www.mpg.de/8132986/Patent-Declaration.pdf.

of rights and parallel imports, compulsory licenses, the 'Bolar exemption', and procedural mechanisms like pre-grant oppositions. The implications of the protection of test data are also examined.

While celebrating the opportunity of working together in organizing the Global Forum, we hope that this book will assist policy makers and judges and provide new inputs for academic research. While, as mentioned, there is a differentiated impact of intellectual property rights depending on the level of development of the country where it applies, the reconciliation of such rights with public health interests, particularly in relation to access to medicines, is a matter of concern for all countries.

Geneva, Switzerland — Carlos M. Correa
München, Germany — Reto M. Hilty

Contents

Interpreting the Flexibilities Under the TRIPS Agreement

Carlos M. Correa

Abstract While the TRIPS Agreement provides for minimum standards of protection of intellectual property, it leaves certain degree of policy space for WTO members, whether developed or developing countries, to implement the Agreement's provisions in different manners, to legislate in areas not subject to the minimum standards under the Agreement, and to develop legal interpretations of such provisions to determine the scope and content of the applicable obligations. This paper focuses on some aspects of how panels and the Appellate Body of the WTO have interpreted said provisions. The paper also draws general conclusions for the implementation of TRIPS flexibilities, which are of crucial importance for the design of a pro-competitive intellectual property system and, in particular, for achieving public health objectives, as specifically recognized by the Doha Declaration on TRIPS and Public Health.

1 Introduction

While the Agreement on Trade-Related Aspects of Intellectual Property Rights ('the TRIPS Agreement') has had a major impact in framing national laws on intellectual property rights (IPRs)—notably in developing countries—and has led to some degree of harmonization of such laws, it is not a uniform law on IPRs.

One the one hand, the TRIPS Agreement provides for *minimum* standards, thereby allowing the members of the World Trade Organization (WTO) to adopt broader protections.[1] Many such 'TRIPS-plus' protections have been established through free trade agreements signed by the US and the European Union with

[1] Article 1.1 of the TRIPS Agreement makes it clear, however, that no WTO member is obliged to grant such a broader protection. See, e.g., Correa (2020b), p. 21.

C. M. Correa (✉)
South Centre, Geneva, Switzerland
e-mail: director@southcentre.int

C. M. Correa, R. M. Hilty (eds.), *Access to Medicines and Vaccines*,
https://doi.org/10.1007/978-3-030-83114-1_1

developing country partners.[2] Examples of such TRIPS-plus protections include (in the area of patents) the extension of the patent term in order to compensate for delays in the grant of a patent or the marketing approval of a pharmaceutical product,[3] data exclusivity,[4] and what is known as 'patent linkage',[5] among others.

On the other hand, the TRIPS Agreement leaves some room for WTO members, whether developed or developing countries, to *implement* the Agreement's provisions in different manners, to *legislate in areas not subject to the minimum standards* under the Agreement, and to develop legal *interpretations* of such provisions to determine the scope and content of the applicable obligations.

The possibility, and admissibility, of differences in the implementation of the provisions of the TRIPS Agreement are expressly recognized in Article 1.1 of the Agreement: "Members shall be free to determine the appropriate method of implementing the provisions of this Agreement within their own legal system and practice." Competition law, which may be applied to control the acquisition or exercise of IPRs, is an example of the second situation in which the Agreement does not provide a binding standard.[6] The room for different interpretations may result from the absence of definitions. One example is the lack of a definition of the concept of 'invention,' which differs among countries and allows WTO members not to grant patents, for instance, on developments without a technical effect (such as under European law), or to grant or not grant patents on genetic materials.[7] In many cases, the space for different interpretations derives from general expressions or ambiguities in the text resulting from compromises reached in the negotiation of the Agreement. An outstanding example is the WTO members' right to grant compulsory licenses due to lack of working of a patent, an issue indirectly referred to in Article 27.1 of said Agreement.[8] The task of the interpreter is particularly daunting when the text includes general terms such as "reasonably," "unreasonably,"[9] "unjustifiable,"[10] or "unjustifiably."[11]

The actual policy space available under the TRIPS Agreement—beyond those areas not covered under the Agreement—depends, in the last instance, on the

[2] See, e.g., Morin and Surbeck (2020).

[3] See, e.g., The Law Library of Congress, Global Legal Research Center (2016). Available from: https://www.loc.gov/law/help/patent-terms/patent-term-extensions-adjustments.pdf.

[4] Shaikh (2016).

[5] Son et al. (2018). Available from: https://doi.org/10.1186/s12992-018-0423-0.

[6] UNDP (2015b). Available from: https://www.undp.org/content/undp/en/home/librarypage/hiv-aids/using-competition-law-to-promote-access-to-medicine.html.

[7] Minn (2016).

[8] Article 27.1 in fine: "...patents shall be available and patent rights enjoyable without discrimination as to the place of invention, the field of technology and whether products are imported or locally produced." See, e.g., Correa (2005). See also below.

[9] A large number of provisions in the TRIPS Agreement uses these terms, e.g., Articles 8.2, 13, 15.5, 25.5, 26.2, 30. 31(b), 31(l), 34.2, 37, 1, 39.2(c), 41, 43.

[10] Article 4(d) of the TRIPS Agreement.

[11] Article 20 of the TRIPS Agreement.

interpretation of the Agreement's provisions. This paper focuses on some aspects of how panels and the Appellate Body of the WTO have interpreted said provisions. It discusses, first, the concept of 'TRIPS flexibilities' and the possible types of such flexibilities as found in the legislation of developing and developed countries. Second, the paper discusses the references to such flexibilities in WTO jurisprudence. Third, it briefly refers to some of the principles of interpretation that are relevant for the use of TRIPS flexibilities, including the value of dispute settlement rulings, the search for the ordinary meaning of the terms used, the context, and the object and purpose of the treaty. Fourth, it discusses the legal status of the Doha Declaration on the TRIPS Agreement and Public Health adopted at the 4th WTO Ministerial Conference in November 2001.[12] There is no attempt in this paper to analyze the specific content of the rulings in TRIPS-related disputes; however, the paper does draw some general conclusions for the implementation of such flexibilities, which are of crucial importance for the design of a pro-competitive intellectual property system and, in particular, for achieving public health objectives (as specifically recognized by the Doha Declaration).[13]

2 Defining the TRIPS Flexibilities

The terminology used to refer to the policy space available for the implementation of the TRIPS Agreement has evolved. Expressions such as "room to maneuver," "margins of freedom," "safeguards," and "margin of discretion" were used in the early studies and reports that identified various aspects of such space.[14] Currently, the diversity of legislative options available under said Agreement is generally known as 'TRIPS flexibilities.'

The term 'flexibility' appears in the Preamble (sixth paragraph) and in Article 66.1 of the TRIPS Agreement but it is used there with a broader meaning. It indicates that least-developed countries (LDCs) are not bound to comply with the TRIPS Agreement obligations (except Articles 3 through 5) during the transition period:

> In view of the special needs and requirements of least-developed country Members, their economic, financial and administrative constraints, and their need for *flexibility* to create a viable technological base, such Members shall not be required to apply the provisions of this Agreement, other than Articles 3, 4 and 5, for a period of ...[15]

---

[12] Available from: https://www.who.int/medicines/areas/policy/tripshealth.pdf?ua=1. Hereinafter, "the Doha Declaration."

[13] See, e.g., Velásquez et al. (2020). https://www.southcentre.int/book-by-the-south-centre-2020/#more-14014.

[14] Germán Velásquez (2013), p. 5. https://www.southcentre.int/wp-content/uploads/2013/05/RP47_WTO-role-in-IP-and-access-to-medicines_EN.pdf.

[15] Emphasis added.

The terminology 'TRIPS flexibilities' does include the *exemption* for LDCs, but it also encompasses possible variations *in the manner* in which the TRIPS Agreement's provisions are interpreted and implemented as they are applied to countries actually subject to them. Such terminology was used for the first time with this latter meaning in the context of the WTO in paragraph 4 of the Doha Declaration.[16] Said paragraph states:

> 4. We agree that the TRIPS Agreement does not and should not prevent Members from taking measures to protect public health. Accordingly, while reiterating our commitment to the TRIPS Agreement, we affirm that the Agreement can and should be interpreted and implemented in a manner supportive of WTO Members' right to protect public health and, in particular, to promote access to medicines for all. In this connection, we reaffirm the right of WTO Members to use, to the full, the provisions in the TRIPS Agreement, which provide *flexibility* for this purpose.[17]

The Declaration confirmed the availability of a number of flexibilities. Its adoption was a response to the concerns of developing countries about the obstacles they faced when seeking to implement measures to promote access to affordable medicines, without limitation to certain diseases, in the interest of public health.[18]

Since the adoption of the Doha Declaration, the concept of 'TRIPS flexibilities' has been referenced in a vast body of literature, especially (but not only) in relation to access to medicines,[19] and in numerous resolutions of UN agencies[20] and bodies, including the World Health Organization (WHO), the Human Right Council (HRC),[21] and the UN Assembly, as well as in reports of the UN Special Rapporteur

[16] Paragraph 17 of the general Doha Ministerial Declaration states: "We stress the importance we attach to implementation and interpretation of the Agreement on Trade-Related Aspects of Intellectual Property Rights (TRIPS Agreement) in a manner supportive of public health, by promoting both access to existing medicines and research and development into new medicines and, in this connection, are adopting a separate Declaration." https://www.wto.org/english/thewto_e/minist_e/min01_e/mindecl_e.htm.

[17] Emphasis added.

[18] The Council for TRIPS convened special sessions (which were held in June, August, and September of 2001) to deal with the relationship between health and TRIPS. See, e.g., the submissions made by the European Communities and their Members States on the relationship between the provisions of the TRIPS Agreement and access to medicines, IP/C/W/280 (12 June 2001); and submissions by the African Group, Barbados, Bolivia, Brazil, Cuba, Dominican Republic, Ecuador, Honduras, India, Indonesia, Jamaica, Pakistan, Paraguay, Philippines, Peru, Sri Lanka, Thailand, and Venezuela on TRIPS and public health, IP/C/W/296 (29 June 2001). See also Council for TRIPS Special Discussion on Intellectual Property and Access to Medicines, IP/C/M/31 (10 July 2001).

[19] See, e.g., Velásquez et al. (2020). https://www.southcentre.int/book-by-the-south-centre-2020/#more-14014.

[20] One of the first studies on TRIPS flexibilities was published by the UNCTAD (1996). https://unctad.org/en/docs/ite1_en.pdf.

[21] On the relationship between the TRIPS Agreement and the human right to health, see, e.g., Sellin (2015). https://link.springer.com/article/10.1007/s40802-015-0047-5#Abs1.

on the Right to Health.[22] For instance, the World Health Assembly (WHA) urged member states "to consider, whenever necessary, adapting national legislation in order to use to the full the flexibilities contained in the Agreement on Trade-Related Aspects of Intellectual Property Rights (TRIPS)".[23] The Global Strategy and Plan of Action on Public Health, Innovation and Intellectual Property[24] explicitly referred to the flexibilities reaffirmed by the Doha Declaration, including the research exception (Element 2.4e), the transitional period for least-developed countries (LDCs) (Element 6.1b), and the regulatory exception or "Bolar exception" (Element 6.3a). A 2011 resolution adopted by the HRC, and subsequent resolutions on the matter, also noted the governments' right to use, to the fullest extent, the provisions of the TRIPS Agreement, the Doha Declaration, and the WTO General Council Decision of 30 August 2003 in the context of the HIV/AIDS epidemic.[25] Importantly, Goal 3. Target 3.b of the Sustainable Development Goals (SDGs), as adopted by the UN General Assembly, also refers to the TRIPS flexibilities:

> Goal 3. Target 3.b: Support the research and development of vaccines and medicines for the communicable and noncommunicable diseases that primarily affect developing countries, provide access to affordable essential medicines and vaccines, in accordance with the Doha Declaration on the TRIPS Agreement and Public Health, which affirms the right of developing countries to use to the full the provisions in the Agreement on Trade-Related Aspects of Intellectual Property Rights regarding flexibilities to protect public health, and, in particular, provide access to medicines for all.[26]

There is no agreed-upon definition of 'TRIPS flexibilities.' In accordance with a WIPO document, the term "flexibilities" means that there are "different options through which TRIPS obligations can be transposed into national law so that national interests are accommodated and yet TRIPS provisions and principles are complied with."[27] That concept implies that the legislative options made are compatible with the TRIPS Agreement and, hence, fully *legitimate*. Although this remark may be deemed trite , it is important to make it in view of the reluctance of some developed countries to accept the use of such flexibilities, and even to exert pressures on or apply retaliatory trade sanctions against countries that do comply with the Agreement's obligations. This position is well reflected in the continuous

[22] See, e.g., WHO, WIPO, and WTO (2012). https://www.wipo.int/edocs/pubdocs/en/global_challenges/628/wipo_pub_628.pdf.

[23] WHA 56.27, "Intellectual property rights, innovation and public health" (28 May 2003). Available from: https://apps.who.int/gb/archive/pdf_files/WHA56/ea56r27.pdf?ua=1. For a list of WHO resolutions referring to intellectual property, see Germán Velásquez, Carlos M. Correa, and Vitor Ido, op. cit., pp. 73–75.

[24] Available from: https://www.who.int/phi/implementation/phi_globstat_action/en/. See, Germán Velásquez (2019).

[25] See, https://www.ohchr.org/EN/Issues/HIV/Pages/Documents.aspx.

[26] Resolution adopted by the General Assembly on 25 September United Nations General Assembly (2015), A/RES/70/1. https://www.un.org/ga/search/view_doc.asp?symbol=A/RES/70/1&Lang=E.

[27] WIPO (2010), p. 11. https://www.wipo.int/meetings/en/doc_details.jsp?doc_id=142068.

use by the US of the Special Section 301 of the US Trade Act 1974,[28] and in the European Commission Staff Working Document on the protection and enforcement of intellectual property rights in third countries.[29]

There are different types of TRIPS flexibilities. Some refer to the scope and extent of the substantive rights to be recognized under the Agreement,[30] and others to the ways in which such rights can be enforced. One way of grouping flexibilities is also to take into account "the point in time at which Members may resort to them: (i) in the process of the acquisition of the right; (ii) defining the scope of the right; and (iii) when enforcing the right."[31] As noted in one report, those flexibilities

> …sometimes are made very explicit (as in the right of each WTO Member to choose its national regime of exhaustion of IP rights, hence allowing parallel imports), and in other instances follow from the use of general and open terms in TRIPS provisions (such as legitimate interests, justifiability, *ordre public* and morality) that WTO Member can – within the limits of accepted principles of treaty interpretation in public international law – interpret and implement in accordance with their public policy preferences.[32]

Given the possible variations in national regimes in interpreting and implementing the TRIPS Agreement, it would be an impossible task to identify all flexibilities. They can be found in *all the areas* covered by the Agreement, and they can be identified as new circumstances arise. Thus, the exception to copyright protection, which is of particular importance to ensure access to knowledge and preserve a robust public domain,[33] needs to be considered in light of technological developments.[34] WIPO's Database on Flexibilities in the Intellectual Property System[35] provides information on just fourteen TRIPS flexibilities as provided for in the national laws of some countries, but the list is certainly much longer and their use in national laws and regulations more extensive. As noted, the type and use of such flexibilities have been widely explored, most particularly in relation to public health policies and access to medicines,[36] in academic literature, numerous reports, and

[28] See, e.g., Correa (2020a).

[29] European Commission (2020). https://trade.ec.europa.eu/doclib/docs/2020/january/tradoc_158561.pdf.

[30] The 'scope' of a right delimits the boundaries and defines its content; the 'extent' refers to the legal limitations on the exercise of the right.

[31] WIPO (2010), op. cit., p. 12.

[32] Ruse-Khan and Puutio (2017), p. 10. Available from: https://www.unescap.org/sites/default/files/IPR%20Handbook.pdf.

[33] See, e.g., Geiger et al. (2013). https://digitalcommons.wcl.american.edu/cgi/viewcontent.cgi?article=1041&context=research.

[34] Eger and Scheufen (2012). https://www.researchgate.net/publication/280043122_The_past_and_the_future_of_copyright_law_technological_change_and_beyond.

[35] Available from: https://www.wipo.int/ip-development/en/agenda/flexibilities/database.html.

[36] See, e.g., Germán Velásquez, Carlos M. Correa, and Vitor Ido, op. cit.

other sources of information.[37] Box 1 includes references to some of the flexibilities available in the field of public health.

Box 1 Public health-related TRIPS flexibilities

(1) ***Flexibility in the choice of patentability criteria, including for chemical entities and biologics***—WTO members have considerable policy space to define what an 'invention' is and to apply rigorous standards of patentability to avoid the grant of patents that, without making a genuine technical contribution, may distort market competition.

(2) ***Compulsory license***—Widely recognized in the legislation of developed and developing countries—and granted since the adoption of the TRIPS Agreement by administrations or courts in countries such as Thailand, Ecuador, Indonesia, India, USA, Italy, and Germany—compulsory licenses may be necessary to correct market distortions (abuses of market power, unfair pricing, refusal to license, etc.).

(3) ***Government use***—In many cases governments may decide, consistently with the TRIPS Agreement, to use patented inventions for non-commercial purposes, such as for ensuring the supply of essential medicines.

(4) ***Compulsory licenses for the supply of medicines to countries with a lack of or insufficient manufacturing capacity***—Compulsory licenses exclusively for the export of medicines can be granted under the amendment introduced to the TRIPS Agreement in 2017 and the waiver adopted by WTO in 2003.

(5) ***Test data protection***—The TRIPS Agreement (Article 39.3) requires WTO members to protect test data against unfair competition, which does not create exclusive rights. The Agreement is complied with if legislation on unfair competition is implemented to protect such data.

(6) ***Exemptions) for LDCs***—LDCs need not grant patents for pharmaceuticals and test data protection at least until 2033 under the extended transition period provided for under Article 66.1 of the TRIPS Agreement.

(7) ***Parallel importation***—Importing protected medicines from any country where they can be purchased cheaper than locally is consistent with the TRIPS Agreement.

(8) ***Pre and post patent grant opposition***—Procedures before patent offices provide for the possibility for third parties to contribute to the

(continued)

[37] See, e.g., Medicines Law & Policy, The TRIPS Flexibilities Database. Available from: http://tripsflexibilities.medicineslawandpolicy.org/. See also, The Graduate Institute Geneva, Knowledge Portal on Innovation and Access to Medicines. https://www.knowledgeportalia.org/.

Box 1 (continued)

examination process through 'observations' or 'oppositions,' whether before or after the grant of a patent, or both.

(9) ***Use of competition law to address the misuse of IPRs***—Competition law may be applied to correct market distortions created through the abuse of IPRs.

(10) ***Bolar exception***—'Bolar exceptions' are important to accelerate the entry of generic products and promote a dynamic market for medicines.

(11) ***Research or experimentation exception***—This exception allows research to be conducted by third parties on patented inventions, for instance, to improve on them or derive new inventions.

(12) ***Disclosure requirement, particularly for biologics***—The full and precise disclosure of an invention is crucial for the patent system to perform its informational function. This is particularly relevant for biologicals, which cannot be described in the same way as medicines produced by chemical synthesis

(13) ***Flexibilities in enforcement of IP***—Measures to enforce IPRs—such as reversal of the burden of proof, determination of infringement by equivalence and damages, and border measures—if overly broad, may distort competition by discouraging or preventing market entry and the availability of generic medicines. Provisional injunctions need to be cautiously granted so as not to distort the market dynamics, generally after giving the alleged infringer an opportunity to articulate his defense. Permanent injunctions may be denied for public health reasons under certain circumstances.

(14) ***Security exception***—Compliance with obligations under the TRIPS Agreement can be suspended, inter alia, in cases of emergency in international relations, such as in the case of a pandemic (Article 73 (b) of the Agreement).

Source: adapted from South Centre, "A Public Health Approach to Intellectual Property Rights: Public Health Related Flexibilities in the TRIPS Agreement," available from: https://ipaccessmeds.southcentre.int/wp-content/uploads/2018/12/Public-Health-Related-Flexibilities-in-the-TRIPS-Agreement.pdf.

Any WTO member can make use of the TRIPS flexibilities, as applicable, in order to attain public health or other public objectives and, in fact, both developed and developing countries have done so. Thus, the flexibility in the TRIPS Agreement permitted the US to maintain a double-novelty standard depending on whether the disclosure of the invention had taken place within or outside the territory of the US

(35 USC section 102 (a)).[38] In defending this flexibility, which has allowed for the misappropriation of genetic resources and traditional knowledge,[39] the US held that in the TRIPS Agreement there was "no prescription as to how WTO Members define what inventions are to be considered 'new' within their domestic systems" and, hence, that its legislation was "perfectly consistent with the provisions of the TRIPS Agreement."[40] Another example in the US is the doctrine that allows US courts not to grant a permanent injunction despite the proven existence of an infringement of IPRs, in accordance with the precedent set by the US Supreme Court in the *eBay vs. MercExchange* case.[41] There are also many examples in Europe[42] where, for instance, the European Parliament's Resolution of 2 March 2017 on EU options for improving access to medicines (2016/2057(INI)) emphasized "that the European Patent Office (EPO) and the Member States should only grant patents on medicinal products that strictly fulfil the patentability requirements of novelty, inventive step and industrial applicability, as enshrined in the European Patent Convention" (paragraph 48).[43] More recent examples are the amendments to the patent laws in Canada and Germany to address the COVID-19 emergency. Bill C 13 2020 of Canada,[44] for instance, added a new section to the Patent Act implementing a new type of compulsory license for patents:

> 19.4 **(1)** The Commissioner shall, on the application of the Minister of Health, authorize the Government of Canada and any person specified in the application to make, construct, use and sell a patented invention to the extent necessary to respond to the public health emergency described in the application.

---

[38] According to this section, "[a] person shall be entitled to a patent unless the invention was known or used by others in this country, or patented or described in a printed publication in this or a foreign country, before the invention thereof by the applicant for patent, or the invention was patented or described in a printed publication in this or a foreign country or in public use or on sale in this country, more than one year prior to the date of the application for patent in the United States." This rule was amended by the Leahy-Smith America Invents Act (2011). http://www.wipo.int/edocs/lexdocs/laws/en/us/us219en.pdf.

[39] Reid (2019). https://digitalcommons.law.ou.edu/cgi/viewcontent.cgi?article=1121&context=ailr.

[40] See, Document IP/Q3/USA/1 (1 May 1998). As a result of the relative novelty requirement of the US, several patents were granted to researchers or firms relating to or consisting of genetic materials or traditional knowledge acquired in developing countries. See, e.g., Mgbeoji (2006). https://books.google.fr/books?id=q4MIoBKy88MC&pg=PA121&lpg=PA121&dq=biopiracy+us+patents&source=bl&ots=-ZBMOhXLLn&sig=ACfU3U0DslCI-lxiwQuSmN-jeuuC-fafLQ&hl=en&sa=X&ved=2ahUKEwitsrmu8N_pAhUSx4UKHe1_DHYQ6AEwEnoECAkQAQ#v=onepage&q=biopiracy%20us%20patents&f=false.

[41] eBay Inc. v. MercExchange, L.L.C., 547 U.S. 388 (2006), https://www.supremecourt.gov/opinions/05pdf/05-130.pdf.

[42] For the use of TRIPS flexibilities in relation to plant patents, see, e.g., Correa (2014). https://www.southcentre.int/wp-content/uploads/2014/11/RP55_Patent-Protection-for-Plants_EN.pdf. See also, Prifti (2015).

[43] Available from: https://www.europarl.europa.eu/doceo/document/TA-8-2017-0061_EN.html.

[44] Available from: https://www.parl.ca/DocumentViewer/en/43-1/bill/C-13/royal-assent.

In Germany, an amendment to the Patent Act provided that an invention relating to medicinal products, including narcotics; the active ingredients, starting materials, and auxiliary materials for these products; medical devices; laboratory diagnostics; aids; personal protective equipment; and products for disinfection of the products shall be used in the interest of public welfare ("öffentliche Wohlfahrt") or in the interest of the security of the Federation.[45]

3 TRIPS Flexibilities in WTO Jurisprudence

Despite the TRIPS Agreement being one of the most controversial components of the WTO system, and that it has given rise to a large number of proceedings under the Dispute Settlement Understanding, a relatively small number of cases has reached the phase of a panel or Appellate Body intervention.

Paradoxically, although the adoption of the TRIPS Agreement essentially was aimed at disciplining developing countries, who have been forced to make massive legislative changes to adapt to the Agreement's high minimum standards,[46] most disputes leading to the establishment of a panel have been against developed countries (two against the US,[47] two against the European Communities and their Member States,[48] two against Canada,[49] and one against Australia[50]). Only two developing countries were subject to such procedures:[51] India (two complaints

---

[45] Fuchs (2020). https://www.twobirds.com/en/news/articles/2020/germany/covid-19-new-german-legislation-to-fight-pandemic-may-affect-granted-patents.

[46] See, e.g., Correa (2011a).

[47] See, DS 160 Panel Report *United States — Section 110(5) of US Copyright Act* (2010); Appellate Body report DS 176 *United States — Section 211 Omnibus Appropriations Act of 1998* (2002).

[48] See, DS 174 Panel Report *European Communities — Protection of Trademarks and Geographical Indications for Agricultural Products and Foodstuffs* (2005); DS 290 Panel Report, *European Communities — Protection of Trademarks and Geographical Indications for Agricultural Products and Foodstuffs* (2005).

[49] See, Report of the WTO Panel, *Canada—Patent Protection for Pharmaceutical Products*, WT/DS114/R; Report of the Appellate Body, *Canada—Term of Patent Protection*, WT/DS170/AB/R (2000).

[50] See Panel Report in DS435, 441, 458, 467, *Australia — Certain Measures Concerning Trademarks, Geographical Indications and Other Plain Packaging Requirements Applicable to Tobacco Products and Packaging* (2018) (hereinafter, "*Australia—Tobacco Plain Packaging*"). The panel report was appealed by Honduras and the Dominican Republic (see, https://www.wto.org/english/tratop_e/dispu_e/cases_e/ds441_e.htm). The report of the Appellate Body was issued on June 9, 2020 (WT/DS435/AB/R WT/DS441/AB/R). On the situation of the Appellate Body as a result of the US blockade to the appointment of new members, see, e.g., Danish and Aileen Kwa (2019). Available from: https://www.southcentre.int/wp-content/uploads/2019/12/PB69_Crisis-at-the-WTO%E2%80%99s-Appellate-Body-AB-Why-the-AB-is-Important-for-Developing-Members_EN-1.pdf.

[51] A violation to the TRIPS Agreement was incidentally invoked in the *Indonesia-Autos* case in relation to the protection of trademarks. The panel, however, found that the United States had not

concerning the implementation of Article 70.8, the so called "mailbox" provision)[52] and China (criminal sanctions for copyright infringement and other issues).[53] Only four developing countries (Indonesia, Cuba, Honduras, and the Dominican Republic) have been complaining parties (against Australia in the tobacco plain packaging case) in WTO disputes under the TRIPS Agreement that have reached such stage.[54]

In other cases of disputes initiated against developing countries, no panel was established. One example was a complaint by the US against Argentina on patents and test data protection.[55] A mutually agreed-upon solution was communicated to the Dispute Settlement Body (DSB) on 20 June 2002. However, the parties did not reach a common understanding on the interpretation of Article 39.3 of the TRIPS Agreement, nor on the application of Article 70.7.[56] Argentina has not to date introduced the data exclusivity regime that the US claimed would remedy the (unproven) violation of Article 39.3. Another example, further discussed below, was the US challenge in January 2001 against Brazilian legislation that authorizes the granting of compulsory licenses and parallel imports in instances when patents are not worked.[57] The dispute ended several months later when the US complaint was withdrawn.[58]

The panel and Appellate Body reports produced in relation to the disputes mentioned above have, in practice, addressed the policy space available under the TRIPS Agreement, but they have only occasionally referred to the concept of 'flexibilities.' In *China—Intellectual Property Rights*, for instance, third parties

---

demonstrated that Indonesia was in breach of its TRIPS obligations (Report of the WTO Panel, *Indonesia—Certain Measures Affecting The Automobile Industry*, WT/DS 54/R, WT/DS 55/R, WT/DS 59/R, WT/DS 64/R (1998), para. 11.1–11.43).

[52] *See* Report of the Appellate Body, *India-Patent Protection for Pharmaceutical and Agricultural Chemical Products*, WT/DS50/AB/R (1998) and Report of the WTO Panel, *India—Patent Protection for Pharmaceutical and Agricultural Chemical Products*, WT/DS79/R (1998) (hereinafter, "*India—Patents (US)*").

[53] See Panel Report in IDS362, *China—Measures Affecting the Protection and Enforcement of Intellectual Property Rights* (2009) (hereinafter, "*China—Intellectual Property Rights*").

[54] Brazil requested the US consultations with regard to provisions of US legislation that limits the right to use or sell any federally-owned invention only to a licensee that agrees that any products embodying the invention or produced through the use of the invention will be manufactured substantially in the United States. See, *United States—US Patents Code*, WT/DS224/1 (7 February 2001). In DS 408, India complained about border measures imposed on the transit of medicines. See, *European Union and a Member State—Seizure of Generic Drugs in Transit (*2010*)*. These cases were not ultimately pursued.

[55] *Argentina—Patent Protection for Pharmaceuticals and Test Data Protection for Agricultural Chemicals*, WT/DS171 (6 May 1999) and *Argentina-Certain Measures on the Protection of Patents and Test Data*, WT/DS196 (30 May 2000).

[56] See, *Notification of Mutually Agreed Solution According to the Conditions Set Forth in the Agreement* (IP/D/18/Add.1, IP/D/22/Add.1).

[57] See, *Brazil—Measures Affecting Patent Protection, Request for the Establishment of a Panel by the United States*, WT/DS199/3 (9 January 2001).

[58] *Brazil—Measures Affecting Patent Protection, Notification of Mutually Agreed Solution*, WT/DS199/4, G/L/454, IP/D/23/Add.1 (19 July 2001).

alluded to the 'flexibility' allowed by the TRIPS Agreement in relation to the definition of 'commercial scale.'[59] The US noted, with respect to Article 1.1 of the Agreement, that the provision "only offers flexibility in how a Member implements TRIPS obligations and does not exempt a Member from full compliance with TRIPS obligations."[60] In this case the panel confirmed that the TRIPS Agreement does not mandate specific forms of legislation.[61] In relation to the US claim that China did not comply with Article 61 of the TRIPS Agreement, it stated:

> The Panel may not simply assume that a Member must give its authorities wide discretion to determine what is on a commercial scale in any given case, and may not simply assume that thresholds, including numerical tests, are inconsistent with the relative benchmark in the first sentence of Article 61 of the TRIPS Agreement. As long as a Member in fact provides for criminal procedures and penalties to be applied in cases of wilful trademark counterfeiting or copyright piracy on a commercial scale, it will comply with this obligation. If it is alleged that a Member's method of implementation does not so provide in such cases, that allegation must be proven with evidence. . .(para. 7.602).

A few references to the 'flexibilities' allowed by the prohibition contained in Article 20 of the TRIPS Agreement can be found in the panel report in *Australia—Tobacco Plain Packaging*. For instance, the panel stated:

> On their face, the explicit prohibitions contained in Article 20 of the TRIPS Agreement and Article 2.2 of the TBT Agreement respectively must be read and, absent a conflict, applied together. The principle of harmonious reading dictates that the flexibilities implicitly left by those prohibitions also need to be viewed together, without a priori giving precedence to one over, and to the exclusion of, the other.[62]

The panel in the same case also referred, as discussed below, to the Doha Declaration as a "re-affirmation by Members of the flexibilities provided in the TRIPS Agreement in relation to measures taken for the protection of public health";[63] the concept of TRIPS flexibilities was also alluded to, for example, by Brazil and Thailand as third parties[64] and by the panel itself (para. 7.2407 and 7.2408). Interestingly, the Appellate Body in *Australia—Tobacco Plain Packaging* referred to the concept of Members' 'regulatory autonomy' in encumbering the use of trademarks by special requirements under Article 20.[65]

---

[59] See, *China—Intellectual Property Rights*, para. 7.484, 7.493, 7.597, and 7.678.

[60] Idem, para. 7.199.

[61] Para 7.602.

[62] *Australia—Tobacco Plain Packaging*, para. 7.100.

[63] Idem, para. 7.2408.

[64] Idem, para. 7.2391 and 2387.

[65] Appellate Body Report, op. cit., para. 6.697.

4 Interpretation of the TRIPS Agreement[66]

This section considers some principles for and aspects of the interpretation of the TRIPS Agreement particularly relevant for the application of the TRIPS flexibilities.

4.1 *Precedential Value of GATT/WTO Jurisprudence*

Neither the GATT nor the WTO jurisprudence have precedential value; however, even if unrelated to intellectual property, such jurisprudence may influence and provide guidance for future rulings on the TRIPS Agreement.[67] One issue of particular relevance is whether jurisprudence on subjects other than those covered by this Agreement should be used to interpret it. The panel in *India—Patent Protection for Pharmaceutical and Agricultural Chemical Products,* for instance, held that although the TRIPS Agreement has a "relatively self-contained, *sui generis* status within the WTO," it also was "an integral part of the WTO system, which itself builds upon the experience of over nearly half a century under the GATT 1947."[68] In *United States—Section 110(5) of the U.S. Copyright Act*, while the panel noted that caution was required when interpreting the TRIPS Agreement provisions in the light of precedents developed in GATT dispute settlement practice, it stated that

> given that the agreements covered by the WTO form a single, integrated legal system, we deem it appropriate to develop interpretations of the legal protection conferred on intellectual property right holders under the TRIPS Agreement which are not incompatible with the treatment conferred to products under the GATT, or in respect of services and service suppliers under the GATS, in the light of pertinent dispute settlement practice.[69]

The application of general GATT and WTO jurisprudence to cases involving the TRIPS Agreement would ignore the specificity of intellectual property issues and one major difference between the TRIPS Agreement and other WTO covered agreements: the former provides for disciplines on intellectual property rights, which are *private rights*,[70] the exercise of which may restrain rather than facilitate international trade (as in the case of other WTO agreements). The private rights nature of intellectual property rights was highlighted in the panel report in *China—Intellectual Property Rights*:

---

[66] This section is partially based on Carlos Correa, op. cit., 2005, which examines other aspects, such as the role of the negotiating history and the application of prior intellectual property conventions incorporated into the TRIPS Agreement;—,; see also Kennedy (2016).

[67] See, e.g., Flowers (2019), pp. 90–104. See also, Howse (2000). Available from: https://onlinelibrary.wiley.com/doi/abs/10.1111/j.1747-1796.2000.tb00139.x.

[68] Para. 7.19.

[69] Para. 6.185.

[70] See, the Preamble to the TRIPS Agreement, fourth paragraph.

> Viewed in context, the phrase "shall have the authority" does not require Members to take any action in the absence of an application or request. Therefore, a condition that authority shall only be available upon application or request seems to be assumed in much of Sections 2, 3 and 4 of Part III. This is consistent with the nature of intellectual property rights as private rights, as recognized in the fourth recital of the preamble of the TRIPS Agreement. Acquisition procedures for substantive rights and civil enforcement procedures generally have to be initiated by the right holder and not *ex officio*.[71]

One corollary of this, for instance, is that in contrast to the general GATT/WTO jurisprudence, the exceptions in the TRIPS Agreement need not to be read narrowly, but instead with the aim of achieving the objectives as defined in Article 7 (see below). Notably, intellectual property rights constitute exceptions in terms of Article XX(d) of GATT and, hence, their restrictive effects should not be augmented but mitigated through the interpretation of the scope and extent of the conferred exclusive rights.[72] The exceptions to exclusive rights are crucial to preserve market dynamics and achieve a diversity of public interests; they are a key component of the TRIPS flexibilities.[73]

4.2 Ordinary Meaning

The GATT and WTO panels, as well as the WTO Appellate Body, have relied on the interpretive method codified by the Vienna Convention on the Law of the Treaties (VCLT). One of the basic steps for interpretation under Article 31 of the VCLT is the determination of the 'ordinary meaning' of the terms employed in the treaty, provided that "a special meaning shall be given to a term if it is established that the parties so intended" (Article 31.4). Many WTO panel and Appellate Body reports clearly indicate that such ordinary meaning is searched in the dictionary in order to clarify the scope and content of the relevant texts.[74] Thus, the Appellate Body in *EC – Chicken Cuts* states: "The Appellate Body observed that dictionaries

> are a useful starting point" for the analysis of 'ordinary meaning' of a treaty term, but they are not necessarily dispositive. The ordinary meaning of a treaty term must be ascertained according to the particular circumstances of each case. Importantly, the ordinary meaning

[71] Panel Report, lDS362, *China—Measures Affecting the Protection and Enforcement of Intellectual Property Rights*, op. cit., para 7.247. See also, para. 7.135. See also, para. 7.247, 7.135, 7.241, and 7.530; and *Australia—Tobacco Plain Packaging*, footnote 4472.

[72] See, e.g., Okediji (2017).

[73] Rodrigues Jr. (2012). https://www.researchgate.net/publication/288719106_The_general_exception_clauses_of_the_TRIPS_agreement_Promoting_sustainable_development.

[74] See, e.g., the elaboration DS 160 Panel Report, *United States — Section 110(5) of US Copyright Act* (2010); Appellate Body report DS 176, *United States — Section 211 Omnibus Appropriations Act of 1998* (2002).

of a treaty term must be seen in the light of the intention of the parties "as expressed in the words used by them against the light of the surrounding circumstances."[75]

In *China—Intellectual Property Rights*, the panel observed that

> the general rule of treaty interpretation in Article 31 of the Vienna Convention refers in paragraph 1 to the ordinary meaning of the terms of the treaty, read in context. Where the terms are a single term, or ordinarily used together, then the treaty interpreter should refer to the ordinary meaning of that single term, or of each term in the particular context of each other. This is a distinct exercise from that in paragraph 4 of Article 31 of the Vienna Convention which requires a "special meaning" to be given to a term if it is established that the parties so intended. No party to this dispute considers that a "special meaning" should be given to the phrase "on a commercial scale," and nor does the Panel.[76]

While the rule regarding the ordinary meaning seems clear, an important question relates to the temporal aspect of the interpretation, that is, whether panels and Appellate Body should rely on the meaning of a term at the time of negotiation or adoption of an agreement, or whether they would be authorized to apply an evolutionary approach, that is, to rely on the meaning of a term at the time of its interpretation. Two approaches exist on this issue:

> ...the **principle of contemporaneity**, according to which the terms of a treaty are to be interpreted according to the meaning which they possessed, or which would have been attributed to them, and in the light of current linguistic usage, at the time when the treaty was originally concluded. Opposed to that is the **dynamic approach**, very often also labelled 'evolutionary' interpretation, which seeks to establish the meaning of a treaty at the time of its interpretation.[77]

In *Canada—Patent Protection for Pharmaceutical Products,* the panel examined the status of the legislation at the time of the negotiation of the Agreement to determine the concept of "legitimate interest" as contained in Article 30:

> Moreover, the Panel believed that it was significant that concerns about regulatory review exceptions in general, although well known at the time of the TRIPS negotiations, were apparently not clear enough, or compelling enough, to make their way explicitly into the recorded agenda of the TRIPS negotiation. The Panel believed that Article 30's "legitimate interests" concept should not be used to decide, through adjudication, a normative policy issue that is still obviously a matter of unresolved political debate.[78]

---

[75] Appellate Body Report in *EC – Chicken Cuts*, para. 175, quoting Appellate Body Report in *US – Softwood Lumber IV*, para. 59, and referring to Appellate Body Reports in *US – Offset Act (Byrd Amendment)*, para. 248, and *US – Gambling*, para. 166, and quoting McNair (1961), p. 365.

[76] Para 7.558.

[77] Dörr and Schmalenbach (2012). Available from: https://link.springer.com/chapter/10.1007%2F978-3-642-19291-3_34, para. 58 (emphasis in the original), para. 23 (emphasis in the original). On the importance of the principle of "contemporaneity" in treaty interpretation, see also, Brownlie (1998), p. 627.

[78] *Canada—Patent Protection for Pharmaceutical Products*, para. 7.82.

The WTO jurisprudence has adopted in some cases the evolutionary method of interpretation.[79] In *United States—Section 110(5) of the US Copyright Act*, reference was made to the WIPO Copyright Treaty (WCT) adopted in 1996, 2 years after the TRIPS Agreement. The panel stated that the WCT should be viewed as "relevant to seek contextual guidance ... when developing interpretations that avoid conflicts within the overall multilateral copyright framework . . ."[80] Although it noted that the statement concerning WCT's Article 10 adopted by the signatory parties did not fall under the Vienna Convention rules on a subsequent agreement on the same matter or subsequent practice, the recourse to a post-TRIPS treaty to interpret a provision of the TRIPS Agreement constitutes a troubling precedent as long as it may lead to interpretations unduly expanding the Agreement's obligations. This is particularly the case in the light of technological developments and the increase of the level of protection beyond the standards of the TRIPS Agreement resulting from free trade agreements.[81]

It is also worth noting that article 71 of the TRIPS Agreement specifically provides for the TRIPS Council to review the Agreement "in the light of any relevant new developments, which might warrant modification or amendment of this Agreement," thereby suggesting that any further 'developments' in intellectual property law need to be incorporated on the basis of WTO members' consensus, rather than via interpretation.

4.3 Context

In accordance with Article 31 of the VCLT, the terms in a treaty need to be considered taking their context into account. The preambles of WTO agreements have often been considered as the relevant context for the interpretation of particular provisions.[82] In *India–Patents (US)*, the Appellate Body referred to the Preamble of the TRIPS Agreement for the interpretation of Article 70.8(a): "The Panel's interpretation here is consistent with the object and purpose of the TRIPS Agreement." According to the Appellate Body, the object and purpose of the Agreement is, *inter alia*, "the need to promote effective and adequate protection of intellectual property rights."[83] References to the preamble were also made in *China—Intellectual*

[79] In *United States – Import Prohibition of Certain Shrimp and Shrimp Products*, WT/DS58/AB/R, para. 130 (1998), the Appellate Body held that certain terms in the WTO Agreements are not "static" but evolutionary, in relation to the term "exhaustible natural resources" as it appears in GATT Article XX(g) (para. 127, 130).

[80] *United States—Section 110(5) of the U.S. Copyright Act*, para. 6.70.

[81] See, e.g., Ruse-Khan (2017) (forthcoming, Netherlands Yearbook of International Law); Max Planck Institute for Innovation & Competition Research Paper, No. 18-02; University of Cambridge Faculty of Law Research Paper, No. 3/2018. https://ssrn.com/abstract=3082718.

[82] See, e.g. Carlos Correa, op. cit., 2020, Chapter 1.

[83] See, https://www.wto.org/english/docs_e/legal_e/27-trips_02_e.htm.

Property Rights.[84] The Preamble of the Agreement on Technical Barriers to Trade was largely invoked as well by the panel in *Australia—Tobacco Plain Packaging*.[85]

The appropriate choice of treaty provisions that provide the context for interpreting other provisions is crucial. One example is the interpretation of Article 27.1 *in fine*. As noted above, the US initiated a case against Brazil arguing that Article 68 of the Brazilian patent law, which authorizes the government to grant a compulsory license if the patent owner fails to work the patent, was inconsistent with Article 27.1 *in fine* of the TRIPS Agreement. In accordance to this provisions, "patents shall be available and patent rights enjoyable without discrimination as to the place of invention, the field of technology and whether products are imported or locally produced." Key to addressing the US argument is identifying the context for the interpretation of this phrase in Article 27.1. In fact, this text incorporated a compromise reached, at the final stages of the negotiation of the Agreement, between developed and developing countries since the latter wanted to preserve the possibility of granting compulsory licenses for the lack or insufficient working of a patent.[86]

Developing countries expressed the concern that Article 27.1 could be read in a way that restricts the use of compulsory licenses, for instance, on the grounds of lack of working, as specifically provided for under Article 5A of the Paris Convention for the Protection of Industrial Property. In fact, the "patent rights" referred to in Article 27.1 are defined in Article 28.1, which only requires the granting of *negative* rights with regard to the exploitation of the invention, that is, the right to prevent third parties from using (without authorization) the patented invention. Hence, a proper interpretation of Article 27.1 read in conjunction with Article 28.1, based on the rules of the Vienna Convention, indicates that the products mentioned in Article 27.1 are *infringing* products, not the products of the patent owner itself, since patents only confer exclusionary and not positive rights. In other words, Article 27.1—if read in the context of Article 28 of the Agreement—forbids discrimination between *infringing* imported and *infringing* locally-made products, but it does not prevent the establishment of differential obligations with regard to non-infringing imported and locally-made products (i.e., products made or imported by the patent owner or with his/her consent). Hence, it does not outlaw compulsory licenses for lack of working.

The principle of "effective interpretation" (or "l'effet utile") requires that a treaty must be interpreted in such a way as to give meaning and effect to all the terms of the treaty. This is certainly possible with respect to Article 27.1 *in fine*. This non-discrimination clause may apply, for instance, to a case in which the rights enjoyed by patent owners differ depending on whether the alleged infringing goods have been locally produced or imported. For instance, Section 337 of the U.S. Tariff Act was found inconsistent with the GATT in *United States—Section 337 of the*

[84] See, para. 7.135.

[85] See, e.g., para. 7.2398.

[86] UNCTAD and ICTSD (2005), p. 467. https://unctad.org/en/PublicationsLibrary/ictsd2005d1_en.pdf.

Tariff Act of 1930, since it accorded less favorable treatment to imported products challenged as infringing on US patents than the treatment accorded to similarly challenged products of United States origin.[87]

Another example in which the correct identification of the context for a provision may have decisive effects relates to Article 39.3, which has been interpreted by the US and the European Commission as requiring the grant of exclusive rights ('data exclusivity') with respect to test data for pharmaceuticals and agrochemical products. This interpretation is clearly inviable in light of Article 39.1 which provides an essential contextual element and only requires protection against unfair commercial practices, which does not entail such exclusive rights.[88]

In engaging in the difficult task of clarifying the meaning of 'unjustifiably' in Article 20 of the TRIPS Agreement, the panel in *Australia—Tobacco Plain Packaging* elaborated on the context of that provision. It specifically alluded to the Preamble and Articles 7 and 8 of the Agreement:

> We first note that the first recital of the preamble to the TRIPS Agreement expresses a key objective of the TRIPS Agreement, namely to "reduce distortions and impediments to international trade" and takes into account the need, on one hand, "to promote effective and adequate protection of intellectual property rights" and, on the other, "to ensure that measures and procedures to enforce intellectual property rights do not themselves become barriers to legitimate trade" (para. 7.2398).
>
> We also consider that Article 7 entitled "Objectives" and Article 8 entitled "Principles" provide relevant context (para 7.2399).
>
> Articles 7 and 8, together with the preamble of the TRIPS Agreement, set out general goals and principles underlying the TRIPS Agreement, which are to be borne in mind when specific provisions of the Agreement are being interpreted in their context and in light of the object and purpose of the Agreement. As the panel in Canada – Pharmaceutical Patents observed in interpreting the terms of Article 30 of the TRIPS Agreement, "[b]oth the goals and the limitations stated in Articles 7 and 8.1 must obviously be borne in mind when doing so as well as those of other provisions of the TRIPS Agreement which indicate its object and purposes" (para. 7.2402).

The panel further elaborated on the 'balance' suggested by Articles 7 and 8.1 of the TRIPS Agreement and, in particular, on the fact that the Agreement did not intend to prevent WTO members from adopting measures to protect public interests, such as public health. It stated:

> Article 7 reflects the intention of establishing and maintaining a balance between the societal objectives mentioned therein. Article 8.1, for its part, makes clear that the provisions of the TRIPS Agreement are not intended to prevent the adoption, by Members, of laws and regulations pursuing certain legitimate objectives, specifically, measures "necessary to protect public health and nutrition" and "promote the public interest in sectors of vital importance to their socio-economic and technological development," provided that such measures are consistent with the provisions of the Agreement (para. 7.2403).

[87] See, e.g., Haedicke (2000), p. 1774.

[88] See, e.g., Correa (2011b).

> Article 8 offers, in our view, useful contextual guidance for the interpretation of the term "unjustifiably" in Article 20. Specifically, the principles reflected in Article 8.1 express the intention of drafters of the TRIPS Agreement to preserve the ability for WTO Members to pursue certain legitimate societal interests, at the same time as it confirms their recognition that certain measures adopted by WTO Members for such purposes may have an impact on IP rights, and requires that such measures be "consistent with the provisions of the [TRIPS] Agreement" (para. 7.2404).
>
> The specific objectives expressly identified in Article 8.1 do not, in our view, necessarily exhaust the scope of what may constitute a valid basis for the "justifiability" of encumbrances on the use of trademarks under Article 20. However, their identification in Article 8.1 may shed light on the types of recognized "societal interests" that may provide a basis for the justification of measures under the specific terms of Article 20, and unquestionably identify public health as such a recognized societal interest (para. 7.2406).

In summary, while the Preamble and Articles 7 and 8 of the TRIPS Agreement provide the context for the interpretation of all its provisions, as suggested by the examples above, the careful choice of other specific provisions to examine the scope and extent of particular obligations is key to preserving the flexibilities under that agreement.

4.4 Object and Purpose

As noted, the interpretative method codified by the VCLT—as spelled out in Articles 31 and 32 of the VCLT—relies on the *textual* interpretation of treaty provisions. The reference, however, to the 'object and purpose' of the treaty as one of the elements for interpretation has been understood by some courts as leaving room to consider the 'intention' of the negotiating parties or to apply a teleological approach.[89] It has been noted, for instance, that the European Court of Human Rights, "has developed its own version of these rules of interpretation—a version that tracks the three traditional approaches to treaty interpretation: the textual approach, the subjective approach, and the teleological approach.[90] However, as noted by two commentators,

> The consideration of object and purpose finds its **limits in the ordinary meaning of the text** of the treaty. It may only be used to bring one of the possible ordinary meanings of the terms to prevail and cannot establish a reading that clearly cannot be expressed with the words used in the text.[91]

The quoted authors note in this regard the opinion in the *Iran-US Claims* Tribunal which pointed out:

> Even when one is dealing with the object and purpose of a treaty, which is the most important part of the treaty's context, the object and purpose does not constitute an element

[89] Linderfalk (2007), p. 205. https://www.corteidh.or.cr/tablas/r32592.pdf.

[90] See, e.g., Dothan (2019), p. 765; iCourts Working Paper Series, No. 141. https://ssrn.com/abstract=3241331.

[91] Oliver Dörr and Kirsten Schmalenbach, op. cit., para 58.

> independent of that context. The object and purpose is not to be considered in isolation from the terms of the treaty; it is intrinsic to its text. It follows that, under Article 31 of the Vienna Convention, a treaty's object and purpose is to be used only to clarify the text, not to provide independent sources of meaning that contradict the clear text.[92]

In the case of the WTO agreements, adherence to the treaty text and avoiding 'activism' in the interpretation of their provisions is of utmost importance—as shown by recent debates on the functioning of the Appellate Body[93]—so as not to expand the Members' obligations or create new ones, and to provide certainty to their trade relations.

Notably, under Article 4.2 of the Dispute Settlement Understanding ("DSU"), panels and the Appellate Body are mandated to 'clarify' the various WTO agreements, and in doing so they cannot add to or diminish the rights and obligations provided in such agreements. Moreover, Article 4.9 provides that the DSU does not prejudice a government's right to seek an 'authoritative interpretation' of any of those agreements from the Ministerial Conference or General Council of the WTO. Hence, the WTO attempts to introduce a difficult distinction between 'clarification' and 'interpretation.' The panels and Appellate Body reports regularly note, however, that they 'interpret' the provisions invoked by the members in accordance to the VLCT rules. This has indeed been the case in those disputes referring to the TRIPS Agreement.[94]

However, although the literal interpretation is the basic rule of interpretation under Article 31 (1) of the VCLT as recognized in the Convention itself, in some cases the textual reading of a provision or a term thereof in its context may still leave ambiguity as to the legal meaning of a text. At this point, the identification of the 'object and purpose' of the treaty, conceived as part of the literal interpretation and not as a separate step, acquires particular importance. It is difficult to think of judgments that are absolutely neutral in terms of the policy objectives enshrined in the treaty.

Identifying the object and purpose of the TRIPS Agreement is different from characterizing the purpose of intellectual property rights, as the objectives pursued by governments with these rights, as well as the way of implementing them, may differ significantly, even while they comply with the standards of the Agreement and other applicable international treaties). There is no global, uniform system of intellectual property protection.

In *Canada—Patent Protection for Pharmaceutical Products*, the panel elaborated on the policy objective of patent laws. It stated:

> The normal practice of exploitation by patent owners, as with owners of any other intellectual property right, is to exclude all forms of competition that could detract significantly from the economic returns anticipated from a patent's grant of market exclusivity . . . Patent laws

[92] Iran-United States Claims Tribunal, *Federal Reserve Bank of New York v. Bank Markazi* (n 19) para 58.

[93] See, e.g., Danish and Aileen Kwa, op. cit.

[94] See, e.g., M. Kennedy, op. cit., 2016.

> establish a carefully defined period of market exclusivity as an inducement to innovation, and the policy of those laws cannot be achieved unless patent owners are permitted to take effective advantage of that inducement once it has been defined.[95]

This view seems to suggest that obtaining 'economic returns' as an 'inducement to innovation' is what underpins patent policies. It is not consistent with the purpose of the TRIPS Agreement as reflected in Articles 7 and 8. This approach overlooks that patents, as well as other intellectual property rights, can and should be designed and implemented to achieve public rather than private interests, including the diffusion of technical knowledge, technological progress, and access to the outcomes of innovation.[96] Thus, in 1917, the US Supreme Court noted that "the primary purpose of that [patent] law is not to create private fortunes, but is to promote the progress of science and the useful arts."[97]

Articles 7 ('Objectives') and 8 ('Principles') of the TRIPS Agreement are key for the determination of the object and purpose of the Agreement, in conjunction, as discussed below, with the Doha Declaration as a subsequent agreement among the parties. Importantly, those provisions are not just hortatory provisions[98] but have been incorporated—upon the demand of developing countries during the negotiations[99]—among the prescriptive provisions of the Agreement.

In *Canada–Patent Term*, the Appellate Body referred to the need to interpret Article 70.1 of the Agreement as having particular regard to the object and purpose of the treaty, but it eluded an interpretation and application of Articles 7 and 8:

> [W]e note that our findings in this appeal do not in any way prejudge the applicability of Article 7 or Article 8 of the TRIPS Agreement in possible future cases with respect to measures to promote the policy objectives of the WTO Members that are set out in those Articles. Those Articles still await appropriate interpretation.[100]

The Panel Report in *Canada—Pharmaceutical Patents* dealt more specifically with the question of the 'object and purpose' of the TRIPS Agreement. It relied to this end on Articles 7 and 8 for that determination, but in conjunction with other provisions of the Agreement. It stated:

> Article 30's very existence amounts to a recognition that the definition of patent rights contained in Article 28 would need certain adjustments. On the other hand, the three limiting conditions attached to Article 30 testify strongly that the negotiators of the Agreement did not intend Article 30 to bring about what would be equivalent to a renegotiation of the basic balance of the Agreement. Obviously, the exact scope of Article 30's authority will depend on the specific meaning given to its limiting conditions. The words of those conditions must

[95] *Canada—Patent Protection for Pharmaceutical Products, supra* note 23, para. 7.55.

[96] See, paragraph 4 of the Doha Declaration.

[97] *Motion Picture Patents Co. v. Universal Film Co.* [1917] 243 U. S. 502.

[98] See, e.g., "TRIPS provisions as interpreted by the WTO dispute settlement organs", *Law Explorer*. https://lawexplores.com/trips-provisions-as-interpreted-by-the-wto-dispute-settlement-organs/.

[99] See, Carlos Correa, op. cit., 2020, pp. 83–95.

[100] Appellate Body Report, *Canada – Term of Patent Protection*, WT/DS170/AB/R (18 September 2000), para. 101. https://www.wto.org/english/tratop_e/dispu_e/170abr_e.pdf.

> be examined with particular care on this point. Both the goals and the limitations stated in Articles 7 and 8.1 must obviously be borne in mind when doing so as well as those of other provisions of the TRIPS Agreement which indicate its object and purposes.[101]

It is unclear what "other provisions of the TRIPS Agreement which indicate its object and purposes" are suggested by the panel. While there might be different perceptions about the object and purpose of the TRIPS Agreement—as the debates between developed and developing countries have shown during the negotiation and after the adoption of the TRIPS Agreement[102]—the panels and Appellate Body need to be guided by the text of the Agreement and not by the individual views of the members of those bodies.

Paragraph 5(a) of the Doha Declaration confirmed the importance of Articles 7 and 8 for the interpretation of the TRIPS Agreement:

> Accordingly and in the light of paragraph 4 above, while maintaining our commitments in the TRIPS Agreement, we recognize that these flexibilities include:
>
> a. In applying the customary rules of interpretation of public international law, each provision of the TRIPS Agreement shall be read in the light of the object and purpose of the Agreement as expressed, in particular, in its objectives and principles.

The wording of this paragraph ("in particular") suggests that while Articles 7 and 8 are determinant in defining the object and purpose of the Agreement, other provisions of the Agreement, as well as the preambular provisions, can also contribute to the determination of its object and purpose. Such may be the case, for instance, of Article 41.2 which states: "Procedures concerning the enforcement of intellectual property rights shall be fair and equitable . . ." This provision makes it clear that one purpose of the Agreement is to ensure that the enforcement of intellectual property rights (as mandated in Part III of the Agreement) is 'fair and equitable' to all the parties concerned, and that it does not provide undue advantages to the right holders over third parties in judicial or administrative procedures, or vice versa.

An interesting elaboration on the object and purpose of the TRIPS Agreement based on Articles 7 and 8 was undertaken by the panel in *Australia—Tobacco Plain Packaging*.[103] The panel largely relied on the Doha Declaration to address this issue. It noted:

> We note in this respect that the Doha Declaration, adopted by Ministers on 14 November 2001, provides that, "[i]n applying the customary rules of interpretation of public international law, each provision of the TRIPS Agreement shall be read in the light of the object and purpose of the Agreement as expressed, in particular, in its objectives and principles" (para. 7.2407).
>
> While this statement was made in the specific context of a re-affirmation by Members of the flexibilities provided in the TRIPS Agreement in relation to measures taken for the protection of public health, we note that paragraph 5 of the Doha Declaration is formulated in

---

[101] See, *Canada—Patent Protection for Pharmaceutical Products*, *supra* note 23, para. 7.26.

[102] Shadlen (2004). Available from: https://link.springer.com/article/10.1007%2FBF02686283.

[103] Romero (2020b). Available from: https://www.southcentre.int/policy-brief-79-june-2020/.

> general terms, inviting the interpreter of the TRIPS Agreement to read "each provision of the TRIPS Agreement" in the light of the object and purpose of the Agreement, as expressed in particular in its objectives and principles. As described above, Articles 7 and 8 have central relevance in establishing the objectives and principles that, according to the Doha Declaration, express the object and purpose of the TRIPS Agreement relevant to its interpretation (7.2408).

The Appellate Body essentially followed the panel's views on this matter. It clarified, however, that the conclusions reached regarding the purpose of the TRIPS Agreement are supported by Articles 7 and 8, and that the analysis of the Doha Declaration reconfirmed the panel's findings. It held:

> The Panel also remarked that the societal interests referred to in Article 8 may provide a basis of the justification of measures under Article 20. Thus, we agree with Australia that, in any event, the reliance on the Doha Declaration was not of decisive importance for the Panel's reasoning since the Panel had reached its conclusions about the contextual relevance of Articles 7 and 8 of the TRIPS Agreement to the interpretation of Article 20 before it turned to the Doha Declaration. The Panel relied on the Doha Declaration simply to reconfirm its previous conclusions regarding the contextual relevance of Articles 7 and 8 of the TRIPS Agreement (6.658).

This analysis and the observations above show that the WTO case law has considered Articles 7 and 8, both as part of the context for interpretation and as defining elements of the object and purpose of the TRIPS Agreement. It confirms the relevance of said provisions for the interpretation of other provisions in the Agreement.

4.4.1 Legal Weight of the Doha Declaration

In order to give authority to its argument regarding the relevance of Articles 7 and 8 for the interpretation of the TRIPS Agreement's provisions, the panel in *Australia—Tobacco Plain Packaging* specifically elaborated on the legal weight of the Doha Declaration. This is one of the most distinct (and welcome) contributions of this panel's report, as it is the first time in which the normative effects of that Declaration have been considered in WTO jurisprudence.

In some WTO disputes prior to the Australia tobacco case, the issue of subsequent practices as an element for interpretation of the TRIPS provisions was very cautiously considered. Thus, in *Canada—Patent Protection for Pharmaceutical Products,* the panel considered comparative law in order to determine whether the interest claimed as "legitimate" by the EC was a "widely recognized policy norm."[104] In *United States—Section 110(5) of the US Copyright Act*, the panel confirmed its conclusion with reference to examples of "state practice" of members of the Berne Union and WTO, but it warned that it "did not wish to express a view on whether these are sufficient to constitute 'subsequent practice' within the meaning of Article

[104] Para.7.77.

31(3)(b) of the Vienna Convention."[105] In *China—Intellectual Property Rights*, the panel rejected certain material submitted by China to prove a "subsequent practice" in the application of the TRIPS Agreement within the meaning of Article 31(3) of the Vienna Convention. The panel considered that it lacked "the breadth to constitute a common, consistent, discernible pattern of acts or pronouncements" and that "the content of the material does not imply agreement on the interpretation of Article 61 of the TRIPS Agreement."[106]

A key panel assertion in the referenced case against Australia is that the Doha Declaration must be considered a 'subsequent agreement' as defined in the VCLT.[107] In accordance with Article 31.3(a) of the VCLT, "any subsequent agreement between the parties regarding the interpretation of the treaty or the application of its provisions" shall be taken into account, together with the context.[108] It is worth noting that the International Law Commission adopted in its 2018 report "Draft Conclusions on Subsequent Agreements and Subsequent Practice in Relation to the Interpretation of Treaties"[109] which, in accordance with one commentator, suggests a "subtle elevation of subsequent agreement and subsequent practice," which would thereby become an integral part of the main rule of interpretation.[110]

In making reference to the Appellate Body ruling in *US – Clove Cigarettes* (para. 262), the panel stated:

> This paragraph of the Doha Declaration may, in our view, be considered to constitute a "subsequent agreement" of WTO Members within the meaning of Article 31(3)(a) of the Vienna Convention. As the Appellate Body has clarified:
>
> Based on the text of Article 31(3)(a) of the Vienna Convention, we consider that a decision adopted by Members may qualify as a "subsequent agreement between the parties" regarding the interpretation of a covered agreement or the application of its provisions if: (i) the decision is, in a temporal sense, adopted subsequent to the relevant covered agreement; and (ii) the terms and content of the decision express an agreement between Members on the interpretation or application of a provision of WTO law (para. 7.2409).

The panel's view rebuts the United States Trade Representative' (USTR) opinion expressed upon the conclusion of the Doha Conference that the Doha Declaration merely was a "political declaration."[111] As noted by a commentator, "[d] istinguishing legal claims from non-legal or political claims, such as access to

---

[105] See, *United States—Section 110(5) of the U.S. Copyright Act*, para. 6.55, n. 68.

[106] Para. 7.581.

[107] For an early analysis on this subject, see, Correa (2002), p. 45. https://apps.who.int/iris/handle/10665/67345.

[108] See, e.g., Stefan Kadelbach (2018). http://www.qil-qdi.org/international-law-commission-and-role-of-subsequent-practice-as-a-means-of-interpretation-under-articles-31-and-32-vclt/.

[109] United Nations (2018). https://legal.un.org/ilc/reports/2018/english/a_73_10_advance.pdf.

[110] Tladi (2018). https://www.ejiltalk.org/is-the-international-law-commission-elevating-subsequent-agreements-and-subsequent-practice/.

[111] USTR Fact Sheet Summarizing Results from WTO Doha Meeting, 15 November 2001.

essential medicines, can deprive them of their status as rights and thereby serve to legitimize an unjust status quo."[112]

The panel further explored the legal status of the Doha Declaration under WTO law, noting that although being a 'declaration,' it was adopted by a consensus decision at the WTO Conference. The panel argued as follows:

> In this instance, the instrument at issue is a "declaration," rather than a "decision." However, the Doha Declaration was adopted by a consensus decision of WTO Members, at the highest level, on 14 November 2001 on the occasion of the Fourth Ministerial Conference of the WTO, subsequent to the adoption of the WTO Agreement, Annex 1C of which comprises the TRIPS Agreement. The terms and contents of the decision adopting the Doha Declaration express, in our view, an agreement between Members on the approach to be followed in interpreting the provisions of the TRIPS Agreement. This agreement, rather than reflecting a particular interpretation of a specific provision of the TRIPS Agreement, confirms the manner in which "each provision" of the Agreement must be interpreted, and thus "bears specifically" on the interpretation of each provision of the TRIPS Agreement (7.2410).

This paragraph reiterates the characterization of the Doha Declaration as a 'subsequent agreement' under the VCLT and adds two important elements: its adoption 'at the highest level' and an agreement 'on the approach' to be followed in interpreting each provision of the Agreement. This 'approach' is reflected in paragraph 5(a) of the Declaration quoted above but also in the rest of the Declaration, particularly as it makes a clear case for protecting public health, a key public interest and a matter of respect and realization of human rights, in implementing the TRIPS Agreement.[113]

The panel's analysis on the Doha Declaration does not aim, however, at asserting its legal value *per se* but its role as a confirmation that Articles 7 and 8 of the TRIPS Agreement provide both the context and define the object and purpose of the Agreement. The panel stated in this regard:

> The guidance provided by the Doha Declaration is consistent, as the Declaration itself suggests, with the applicable rules of interpretation, which require a treaty interpreter to take account of the context and object and purpose of the treaty being interpreted, and confirms in our view that Articles 7 and 8 of the TRIPS Agreement provide important context for the interpretation of Article 20 (7.2411).

The analysis of the legal status of the Doha Declaration is one of the most significant contributions by the panel in *Australia—Tobacco Plain Packaging*. It supported the panel's conclusion with respect to the justifiability of the plain packaging measures adopted by that country and, hence, their consistency with Article 20 of the TRIPS Agreement.[114]

---

[112] Gathii (2002), p. 315. https://pdfs.semanticscholar.org/a3a6/65016915476d1088fea2e7f4e97baf2f0f03.pdf.

[113] See, e.g., Carlos Correa, op cit., 2002; Velasquez, Correa, and Ido, op. cit, 2020; UNDP (2015a). https://www.undp.org/content/undp/en/home/librarypage/hiv-aids/doha10yearson.html.

[114] Romero (2020a). https://www.southcentre.int/research-paper-108-april-2020/.

5 Conclusions

The notion that the TRIPS Agreement is not a uniform law and that it allows WTO members some room to maneuver in interpreting and implementing the Agreement's obligations is well established in the literature and numerous resolutions by UN agencies and bodies. The adoption of the Doha Declaration, and several rulings by panels and the Appellate Body, point in the same direction. An evolution is perceptible in the WTO jurisprudence on the matter. In particular, the most recent panel report in *Australia—Tobacco Plain Packaging* shows the explicit acceptance of the concept of TRIPS flexibilities in WTO case law and their role in preserving the required policy space to pursue public policies such as public health. This is an important development that could provide the basis for a further step in that jurisprudence: the integration of human rights law, as a component of international law, in the analysis of the obligations imposed by that Agreement and of the leeway that states should preserve for the realization of such rights.[115]

The extent to which the TRIPS flexibilities can be implemented at the national level without the risk of trade retaliations depends on the way the Agreement's provisions are interpreted by panels and the Appellate Body. Several issues need to be addressed in considering how such provisions should be interpreted, consistently with the interpretive method codified by the VCLT. While the search for the ordinary meaning of the terms used is a well-established methodology, divergences may exist with regard to whether they should be deemed as 'static' or 'evolutionary.' An evolutionary approach creates the risk of unduly expanding the obligations under the Agreement, as actively promoted by some developed countries through free trade agreements. The adequate determination of the context—beyond the Preamble and Articles 7 and 8—for interpretation of a particular provision is also important, as it may decisively influence the determination of the scope and extent of the obligation under the Agreement. Similarly, the understanding on the object and purpose of the Agreement plays an important role. The WTO jurisprudence seems to have firmly admitted that such a determination is to be based on said Articles 7 and 8.

The impact of the TRIPS Agreement on public health and, particularly, access to medicines has been one of the most sensitive issues since its adoption. This issue has been key in promoting debates and analyses on the TRIPS flexibilities (although they are also important in relation to other public interests, such as access to knowledge or food security). In this regard, the panel ruling in the case against Australia on plain packaging has confirmed the legal status of the Doha Declaration—seen by some as a merely political instrument—as a 'decision' taken by consensus that constitutes a 'subsequent agreement' among the WTO members. This is also an important development as it suggests that a pro-public health interpretation is not only tenable but also mandated, and confirms the room that

[115]See, e.g., Sellin (2015), pp. 445–473. https://link.springer.com/article/10.1007/s40802-015-0047-5.

governments have to confidently adopt pro-public health measures without fearing the risk of costly and burdensome litigation under the DSU.

References

Brownlie I (1998) Principles of public international law. p. 627
Correa C (2002) Implications of the Doha Declaration on the TRIPS agreement and public health. World Health Organization, Geneva, p 45. Available from https://apps.who.int/iris/handle/10665/67345
Correa C (2005) The TRIPS Agreement from the perspective of developing countries. In: Macrory P, Appleton A, Plummer M (eds) The World Trade Organization: legal, economic and political analysis. Springer, Berlin, p 2005
Correa C (2011a) Globalisation and intellectual property rights. The struggle of developing countries to influence TRIPS. In: Alam S, Klein N, Overland J (eds) Globalisation and the quest for social and environmental justice: the relevance of international law in an evolving World Order. Routledge, Milton Park
Correa C (2011b) Test data protection: rights conferred under the TRIPS Agreement and some effects of TRIPS-plus standards. In: Dreyfuss RC, Strandburg KJ (eds) The law and theory of trade secrecy. A handbook of contemporary research. Edward Elgar, Cheltenham
Correa C (2014) Patent protection for plants: legal options for developing countries. Research Paper No. 55. South Centre, Geneva. Available from https://www.southcentre.int/wp-content/uploads/2014/11/RP55_Patent-Protection-for-Plants_EN.pdf
Correa C (2020a) Special Section 301: US interference with the design and implementation of National Patent Laws. Research Paper 115. South Centre, Geneva. Available from https://www.southcentre.int/research-paper-115-july-2020/
Correa C (2020b) Trade Related Aspects of Intellectual Property Rights. A commentary on the TRIPS Agreement, 2nd edn. Oxford University Press, p 21
Danish and Aileen Kwa (2019) Crisis at the WTO's Appellate Body (AB): why the AB is important for developing members. Policy Brief No. 69. South Centre, Geneva. Available from https://www.southcentre.int/wp-content/uploads/2019/12/PB69_Crisis-at-the-WTO%E2%80%99s-Appellate-Body-AB-Why-the-AB-is-Important-for-Developing-Members_EN-1.pdf
Dörr O, Schmalenbach K (2012) Article 31. General rule of interpretation. In: Vienna Convention on the law of treaties – a commentary. Springer, Berlin. Available from https://link.springer.com/chapter/10.1007%2F978-3-642-19291-3_34
Dothan S (2019) The three traditional approaches to treaty interpretation: a current application to the European Court of Human Rights. Fordham Int Law J 42:765; iCourts Working Paper Series, No. 141. Available from: https://ssrn.com/abstract=3241331
Eger T, Scheufen M (2012) The past and the future of copyright law: technological change and beyond". In Liber Amicorum Boudewijn Bouckaert. Die Keure. Available from https://www.researchgate.net/publication/280043122_The_past_and_the_future_of_copyright_law_technological_change_and_beyond
European Commission (2020) Report on the protection and enforcement of intellectual property rights in third countries. Commission staff working document. Available from https://trade.ec.europa.eu/doclib/docs/2020/january/tradoc_158561.pdf
Flowers Z (2019) The role of precedent and stare decisis in the World Trade Organization's dispute settlement body. Int J Legal Information 47(2):90–104
Fuchs S (2020) COVID-19: New German legislation to fight pandemic may affect granted German patents. Available from https://www.twobirds.com/en/news/articles/2020/germany/covid-19-new-german-legislation-to-fight-pandemic-may-affect-granted-patents

Gathii JT (2002) The legal status of the Doha Declaration on TRIPS and public health under the Vienna Convention of the Law of Treaties. Harv J Law Technol 15(2):315. Available from https://pdfs.semanticscholar.org/a3a6/65016915476d1088fea2e7f4e97baf2f0f03.pdf
Geiger C, Gervais D, Senftleben M (2013) The three-step test revisited: how to use the test's flexibility in national copyright law. PIJIP Research Paper Series. Available from https://digitalcommons.wcl.american.edu/cgi/viewcontent.cgi?article=1041&context=research
Germán Velásquez (2013) Access to medicines and intellectual property: the contribution of the World Health Organization. Research Paper No. 47. South Centre, Geneva, p 5. Available from https://www.southcentre.int/wp-content/uploads/2013/05/RP47_WTO-role-in-IP-and-access-to-medicines_EN.pdf
Germán Velásquez (2019) Medicines and intellectual property: 10 years of the WHO global strategy. Research Paper No. 100. South Centre, Geneva
Haedicke M (2000) U.S. imports, TRIPS and Section 337 of the Tariff Act of 1930. Int Rev Indus Property Copyright Law 31(7/8):1774
Howse R (2000) The Canadian medicine panel: a dangerous precedent in dangerous times. J World Intellectual Property 3(4). Available from https://onlinelibrary.wiley.com/doi/abs/10.1111/j.1747-1796.2000.tb00139.x
Kadelbach S (2018) The International Law Commission and role of subsequent practice as a means of interpretation under Articles 31 and 32 VCLT. Questions of International Law. Available from http://www.qil-qdi.org/international-law-commission-and-role-of-subsequent-practice-as-a-means-of-interpretation-under-articles-31-and-32-vclt/
Kennedy M (2016) WTO dispute settlement and the TRIPS agreement: applying intellectual property standards in a trade law framework. Cambridge University Press, Cambridge
Linderfalk U (2007) On the interpretation of treaties: the modern international law as expressed in the 1969 Vienna Convention on the Law of Treaties. Springer, Berlin, p 205. Available from https://www.corteidh.or.cr/tablas/r32592.pdf
McNair (1961) The law of treaties. Clarendon Press, Oxford, p 365
Mgbeoji I (2006) Global biopiracy: patents, plants, and indigenous knowledge. UBC Press, Vancouver. Available from https://books.google.fr/books?id=q4MIoBKy88MC&pg=PA121&lpg=PA121&dq=biopiracy+us+patents&source=bl&ots=-ZBMOhXLLn&sig=ACfU3U0DslCI-lxiwQuSmN-jeuuC-fafLQ&hl=en&sa=X&ved=2ahUKEwitsrmu8N_pAhUSx4UKHe1_DHYQ6AEwEnoECAkQAQ#v=onepage&q=biopiracy%20us%20patents&f=false
Minn M (2016) Patenting of genetic research in Europe and the U.S.: a questionable future for diagnostic methods and personalized medicines. Biotechnology Law Report 38(2). Available from https://www.liebertpub.com/doi/10.1089/blr.2019.29108.mm
Morin J-F, Surbeck J (2020) Mapping the new frontier of international IP law: introducing a TRIPs-plus dataset. World Trade Rev 19(1)
Okediji RL (ed) (2017) Copyright law in an age of limitations and exceptions. Cambridge University Press, Cambridge. Available from https://books.google.fr/books?id=3lpEDgAAQBAJ&pg=PA241&lpg=PA241&dq=copyright+exception+interpretation+article+30+ruth&source=bl&ots=7MCIdWRbq7&sig=ACfU3U2kCly0QaU-zPXhb83gb8QcSF8Utw&hl=en&sa=X&ved=2ahUKEwjU4NCby-zpAhURnxQKHXg0AtoQ6AEwBHoECAkQAQ#v=onepage&q=copyright%20exception%20interpretation%20article%2030%20ruth&f=false
Prifti V (2015) The breeder's exception to patent rights – analysis of compliance with article 30 of the TRIPS Agreement. Springer, Berlin
Reid J (2019) Biopiracy: the struggle for traditional knowledge rights. Am Indian Law Rev 34(1). Available from https://digitalcommons.law.ou.edu/cgi/viewcontent.cgi?article=1121&context=ailr
Rodrigues EB Jr (2012) The general exception clauses of the TRIPS agreement: promoting sustainable development. Cambridge University Press, Cambridge. Available from https://

www.researchgate.net/publication/288719106_The_general_exception_clauses_of_the_TRIPS_agreement_Promoting_sustainable_development
Romero T (2020a) Public health and plain packaging of tobacco: an intellectual property perspective. Research Paper No. 108. South Centre, Geneva. Available from: https://www.southcentre.int/research-paper-108-april-2020/
Romero T (2020b) Articles 7 and 8 as the basis for interpretation of the TRIPS Agreement. Policy Brief No. 79. South Centre, Geneva. Available from https://www.southcentre.int/policy-brief-79-june-2020/
Ruse-Khan HG (2017) From TRIPS to FTAs and back: re-conceptualising the role of a multilateral IP framework in a TRIPS-plus world. Forthcoming, Netherlands Yearbook of International Law; Max Planck Institute for Innovation & Competition Research Paper, No. 18-02; University of Cambridge Faculty of Law Research Paper, No. 3/2018. Available from: https://ssrn.com/abstract=3082718
Ruse-Khan HG, Puutio TA (2017) A handbook on negotiating development oriented intellectual property provisions in trade and investment agreements. UNESCAP, Bangkok, p 10. Available from https://www.unescap.org/sites/default/files/IPR%20Handbook.pdf
Sellin JA (2015) Does one size fit all? Patents, the right to health and access to medicines. Netherlands Int Law Rev 62:445–473. Available from https://link.springer.com/article/10.1007/s40802-015-0047-5
Shadlen K (2004) Patents and pills, power and procedure: the north-south politics of public health in the WTO. St Comp Int Dev 39, 76–108. Available from https://link.springer.com/article/10.1007%2FBF02686283
Shaikh OH (2016) Access to medicine versus test data exclusivity – Safeguarding flexibilities under international law. Springer, Berlin
Son KB, Lopert R, Gleeson D, Lee TJ (2018) Moderating the impact of patent linkage on access to medicines: lessons from variations in South Korea, Australia, Canada, and the United States. Globalization and Health vol. 14. Available from https://doi.org/10.1186/s12992-018-0423-0
The Graduate Institute Geneva, Knowledge Portal on Innovation and Access to Medicines. Available from: https://www.knowledgeportalia.org/. Last accessed 12 Feb 2021
The Law Library of Congress, Global Legal Research Center (2016) Patent Term Extensions and Adjustments
Tladi D (2018) Is the International Law Commission elevating subsequent agreements and subsequent practice? EJIL:Talk! Available from https://www.ejiltalk.org/is-the-international-law-commission-elevating-subsequent-agreements-and-subsequent-practice/
UNCTAD (1996) The TRIPS agreement and developing countries. Available from https://unctad.org/en/docs/ite1_en.pdf
UNCTAD & ICTSD (2005) Resource book on TRIPS and development. Cambridge University Press, Cambridge, p 467. Available from https://unctad.org/en/PublicationsLibrary/ictsd2005d1_en.pdf
UNDP (2015a) The Doha Declaration 10 years on and its impact on access to medicines and the right to health. Available from https://www.undp.org/content/undp/en/home/librarypage/hiv-aids/doha10yearson.html
UNDP (2015b) Using competition law to promote access to medicine. Available from https://www.undp.org/content/undp/en/home/librarypage/hiv-aids/using-competition-law-to-promote-access-to-medicine.html
United Nations (2018) Report of the International Law Commission (A/73/10, 2018). Available from https://legal.un.org/ilc/reports/2018/english/a_73_10_advance.pdf

United Nations General Assembly (2015) A/RES/70/1. Available from https://www.un.org/ga/search/view_doc.asp?symbol=A/RES/70/1&Lang=E

Velásquez G, Correa CM, Ido V (2020) Intellectual property, human rights and access to medicines: a selected and annotated bibliography, 3rd edn. South Centre, Geneva. Available from https://www.southcentre.int/book-by-the-south-centre-2020/#more-14014

WHO, WIPO, and WTO (2012) Promoting access to medical technologies and innovation - intersections between public health, intellectual property and trade. Available from https://www.wipo.int/edocs/pubdocs/en/global_challenges/628/wipo_pub_628.pdf

WIPO (2010) Patent related flexibilities in the multilateral legal framework and their legislative implementation at the national and regional levels, p 11. Available from https://www.wipo.int/meetings/en/doc_details.jsp?doc_id=142068

Intellectual Property Exhaustion and Parallel Imports of Pharmaceuticals: A Comparative and Critical Review

Irene Calboli

Abstract This Chapter addresses the topic of intellectual property (IP) exhaustion in the context of the parallel trade of pharmaceuticals. These imports, which are controversial in general, are more complex with respect to pharmaceuticals, which require additional marketing and import authorizations. Nevertheless, individual countries remain free to accept these imports under the flexibility of Article 6 of the Agreement on Trade Related Aspects to Intellectual Property Rights (TRIPS Agreement). This Chapter reviews several national approaches—in developed, developing, and least developed countries (LDCs)—from the perspective of the exhaustion of patent rights as well as other IP rights. Through this review, it highlights that several countries today accept parallel trade. A large number of these countries are, however, developed countries, whereas several developing countries and LDCs instead prohibit parallel imports. This finding is perplexing, and the reasons for this restrictive approach are unclear as developing countries and LDCs need flexible policies and can largely benefit from parallel trade. In addition, despite the claim by the pharmaceutical industry that parallel trade would increase the price of medicines in these countries—as originator would increase prices due to the fear of parallel imports—medicines are sold at lower prices mostly because of governments' pricing or after the expiration of patent protection. Based on this review, this Chapter concludes that national legislations, which are not taking advantage of the flexibility in Article 6 of the TRIPS Agreement, may consider reviewing their policies and allow parallel imports.

I. Calboli (✉)
Texas A&M University School of Law, Fort Worth, TX, USA

Nanyang Business School, Nanyang Technological University, Singapore, Singapore

C. M. Correa, R. M. Hilty (eds.), *Access to Medicines and Vaccines*,
https://doi.org/10.1007/978-3-030-83114-1_2

1 Introduction: The Relevance (and Resilience) of the Principle of Intellectual Property Exhaustion and Its Application to Pharmaceuticals

In this chapter, I explore the application of the principle of intellectual property (IP) exhaustion to the parallel imports of pharmaceuticals and the impact that different policies on exhaustion can have on these imports across selected jurisdictions. The legal treatment of IP exhaustion continues to represent one of the most debated and unresolved issues in international trade.[1] In addition, the debate regarding IP exhaustion and pharmaceuticals reflects the more complex debate on access to medicines and public health, and how domestic policies on IP exhaustion can be used to implement the existing IP-related flexibilities provided in the international system.[2] Several commentators have addressed this debate before, yet disagreements and uncertainty continue to characterize this important area of IP and international trade.

Moreover, domestic policies on IP exhaustion are not the only barrier to parallel imports of pharmaceuticals, as these imports are also subjected to national marketing approvals, import authorizations, and other formalities. In addition, in many instances, national governments exert price control on the sale of pharmaceuticals, in particular prescription medications. In other words, as commentators have noted, pharmaceuticals are traded, and parallel traded, in "distorted" markets due to the additional regulatory schemes and price control policies that apply to these products. National competition laws are also important in the context of parallel imports of pharmaceuticals, for example regarding excessive pricing or the validity of contractual clauses to block the products' redistribution after they have first been put into the market by the IP holders. Because of its limited scope, this Chapter only mentions and does not analyzes in detail this complex ecosystem of parallel trade in pharmaceuticals.[3] In practice, however, these factors remain very relevant, perhaps even more relevant than domestic policies on IP exhaustion in certain instances. In particular, in some countries, the actual impact of IP exhaustion on the admissibility of parallel imports of pharmaceuticals is certainly minimal, if not irrelevant due to the additional regulatory requirements and possible contractual limitations against these imports.

---

[1]For a detailed analysis and summary of the relevant debates, see the contributions in Calboli and Lee (2016). *See also* Ghosh and Calboli (2018); Fink 2004, p. 174); Maskus (2000), p. 1269; Abbott (1998), pp. 607–636; Abbott 2000) http://ssrn.com/abstract=1921856; Heath (1997), p. 623; Jehoram (1996), p. 280; Hilke (1988), p. 75.

[2]For a discussion of the flexibilities and applications to pharmaceuticals and health care, *see* El-Said (2010).

[3]For a comprehensive review of all these aspects, *see* Abbott (2016), p. 145 [hereinafter Abbott, *Parallel Trade in Pharmaceuticals*]. *See also* Kyle (2007), p. 88 and Maskus (2001).

In light of this, why then writing a chapter on this topic, if IP exhaustion may not matter, or matter considerably less than originally thought, for the admissibility of parallel imports of pharmaceuticals into national markets?

As I mentioned, the debate in this area remains complex and, even though domestic policies on IP exhaustion are not the only aspect to consider, these policies are still relevant, in particular when national governments are in favor of parallel imports and grant the pharmaceuticals the necessary marketing approvals and import authorizations. It is difficult to predict how often, in practice, national governments would approve these imports, but certainly in these instances domestic policies on exhaustion would make the difference in the legal treatment of the imports. Would these be treated as legitimate imports or IP infringements? Moreover, domestic policies on exhaustion not only can affect the imports of patented pharmaceuticals, but also generics. In particular, national rules on trademark exhaustion can be used to block parallel imports including of generics. While this may not affect countries with the ability to produce generics domestically, it could affect countries without manufacturing capacity. Instead, domestic policies favoring parallel imports could facilitate the supply of medicines at lower prices than branded versions, or even the supply of certain medicines altogether as originator companies often not directly distribute certain medicines in some countries.

The chapter proceeds as follows. Section 2 presents an overview of the principle of exhaustion in the context of international trade. This background leads to the discussion on the legal treatment of parallel imports of pharmaceuticals. Section 3 explores the domestic policies on patent exhaustion in selected developed and developing countries and elaborates on how different solutions—national, international, or regional exhaustion—impact the parallel trade of pharmaceuticals in these countries. Section 4 focuses on the impact of overlapping IP rights—notably trademarks and copyrights in addition to patents—to the parallel trade of pharmaceuticals. This Section highlights how parallel imports can be affected by these overlaps, in particular when a country adopts international patent exhaustion, but practices national exhaustion for copyrights or trademarks. It also highlights that overlapping rights can block parallel imports when the imported products, albeit genuine, carry small quality differences from the products distributed into the importing countries by IP holders.[4] Section 5 concludes and highlights that several developed countries adopt today more liberal policies on IP exhaustion, notably international exhaustion, than several developing and least developed countries (LDCs), which follow instead national exhaustion. This is certainly problematic for the latter countries and their access to pharmaceuticals.

[4]*See, e.g.* Calboli (2014a), p. 151 [hereinafter Calboli, *Avoidable Effects*]; Calboli (2011), p. 1241 [hereinafter Calboli, *Market Integration*] (addressing in details the legal treatment of quality differences in the context of trademark exhaustion).

2 Intellectual Property Exhaustion and Paralle Trade: General Considerations and Application to Pharmaceuticals

The doctrine of IP exhaustion is crucial in IP theory, as it limits the rights of IP holders to control the distribution of the products they have put in the market after their first lawful release.[5] This doctrine was developed in the nineteenth century to balance the rights of IP holders and to prevent the use of their IP rights against the lawful rights of retailers, second-hand dealers, and consumers to freely display, advertise, and resell the products they lawfully purchased in the market, even if those actions directly compete with the IP holders' business activities in the same market.[6] Generally, there are not major controversies regarding the application of this doctrine within national markets, at least regarding products whose quality has not been changed and are resold nationally.[7] In contrast, controversy has traditionally characterized the debate over the application of the doctrine of exhaustion in the context of international trade. In particular, the legal treatment of the phenomenon of parallel imports—the imports of genuine products, imported into a country from unauthorized third party importers after their first authorized sale by the IP holders abroad[8]—is one of the few aspect of IP that has never been internationally harmonized and discussion over the admissibility into national markets of these products continue to date. The tension between the application of the principle IP exhaustion and the movement of products across national border, in general and in the context of pharmaceuticals, is addressed in this Section.

2.1 The Principle of Intellectual Property Exhaustion in International Trade: An Overview

Professor Ghosh and I have extensively addressed the debates over the exhaustion doctrine and cross-border trade in our recent book, *Exhausting Intellectual Property Rights: A Comparative Law and Policy Analysis*.[9] The surge in global trade over the past century has heightened these debates, driven primarily by the concerns

---

[5] *See, e.g.*, Ghosh and Calboli (2018), pp. 22–40.

[6] *See* Kohler (1900), p. 452. An English translation of Josef Kohler's passages on exhaustion can be found in Heath (2014a), p. 419, 424.

[7] With the exception of the transfer of digital goods and self-replicating technologies—two recent phenomena that have been addressed by courts in several jurisdictions. *See, e.g.*, *Capitol Records, LLC v. ReDigi Inc.*, 934 F. Supp. 2d 640 (S.D.N.Y 2013); Case C-128/11, UsedSoft GmbH v. Oracle Int'l Corp., 2012 E.C.R. I-00000; *Bowman v. Monsanto Co.*, 133 S.Ct. 1761 (2013); Case No. C-428/09, Monsanto v. Cefetra, 2010 E.C.R. I-09961.

[8] Ghosh and Calboli (2018), pp. 41–64.

[9] *Id.*

expressed against and in favor of the arbitrage of consumer goods from low-cost to high-cost jurisdictions.[10] Although IP holders are interested in the benefits of free trade in reducing manufacturing costs and decreasing tariffs, quotas, and other trade restrictions, they generally oppose parallel imports because of the competition the imports create in the high cost domestic markets and the resulting loss of profits in those markets.[11] On the other side, supporters of parallel imports, including this author, point specifically to the inconsistency of the international IP system, which seeks harmonizing the IP system to eliminate barriers to trade and facilitate the registration and enforcement of IP rights worldwide, yet does not equally harmonize the free movement of products across jurisdictions to the same—in essence allowing IP rights to possibly operate as an invisible barrier to otherwise legitimate trade.[12]

The issue of IP exhaustion is not addressed in any of the agreements administered by the World Intellectual Property Organization (WIPO). Exhaustion, or lack of agreement thereof, is mentioned explicitly only in Article 6 of the Agreement on Trade Related Aspects to Intellectual Property Right (TRIPS Agreement), adopted under the auspices of the Word Trade Organization (WTO). The provision famously states that "nothing in this Agreement shall be used to address the issue of the exhaustion of intellectual property rights."[13] Accordingly, the choice of exhaustion regimes depends on national decisions about desirable economic outcomes based on specific economic and trade-related factors, the size of national markets, the level of development, and possibly the pressure exerted foreign governments. Essentially, cross-border trade remains a form of national strategy, which may or may not include economic integration, and in which nation states maintain their political independence, while economic agents are permitted to engage in trade crossing their respective countries.[14]

---

[10] Parallel imports can be divided into two specified categories: passive and active parallel imports. *See* Fink (2004), pp. 171–188. The first category relates to the situation in which third party importers purchase products in one country and sell them in another. The second identifies the case of a foreign licensee, or authorized distributor abroad, who sell into the national market of the IP holders without her consent. The latter case is less frequent and is often prohibited through specific clauses in licensing agreements.

[11] For an excellent review of the economic studies on parallel imports, *see* Maskus (2016), p. 106 [hereinafter Maskus, *Economic Perspective*]. *See also* Saggi (2013), p. 131; Valletti and Szymanski (2006), p. 499; Valletti (2006), p. 314; Chen and Maskus (2005), p. 1; Malueg and Schwartz (1994), p. 187.

[12] *See* Ghosh and Calboli (2018), pp. 41–64. *See also* Calboli (2002), p. 47 (advocating for a change to international exhaustion in the EU).

[13] Agreement on Trade-Related Aspects of Intellectual Property Rights, April 15, 1994, Marrakesh Agreement Establishing the World Trade Organization, Annex 1C, Legal Instrument—Result of the Uruguay Rounds Vol. 31, 33 I.L.M. 83, 1869 U.N.T.S. 299 (1994), art. 6 [hereinafter TRIPS]. On the drafting of Article 6 of TRIPS, *see* Jehoram (1999), pp. 495, 508 (noting that this provision represents a compromise between two opposite approaches: "[t]he US Proposal [to introduce its own national system,] national exhaustion[,] and the [pleas of] developing countries . . . for the opposite," international exhaustion). *See also* Yusuf (2016) p. 23, 26; Taubman et al. (2012), pp. 18–20; Verma (1998), pp. 534, 539.

[14] Ghosh and Calboli (2018), pp. 44–48.

As it is generally known, countries follow one of three systems: national, regional, or international exhaustion.[15] Under the principle of *national* exhaustion, IP holders' rights are exhausted after the first sale of a good or batch of goods, but only if this first sale has occurred in the national territory.[16] This regime is the least friendly for international trade and permits IP holders to stop parallel imports at the border or legitimately seize products after importation as IP infringements, even though these are genuine goods.[17] Instead, under the principle of *regional* exhaustion, a compromising solution between the international and regional exhaustion, the rights of IP holders are exhausted after the first sale of a good or batch of goods, but only if the sale has occurred in one of the member countries of a regional organization following this principle as a common rule for all members.[18] Under this system, the import of products originating from third countries from outside the region remains unlawful and can be stopped as infringement.[19] Finally, under the principle of *international* exhaustion, IP holders' rights to control the further distribution of a good or batch of goods exhaust after the first sale of the goods regardless of the country where this first sale has occurred.[20] Undoubtedly the friendliest approach for international trade, under this system parallel imports are considered lawful in the country of importation, even though the country from which the goods are imported may well apply a different system, i.e. national or regional exhaustion.[21]

National exhaustion should be contrasted with regional exhaustion, the rule that is currently established in the European Union (EU as extended to the European Economic Area, EEA)[22] and the *Organization Africaine pour la Propriete Intellectuelle* (OAPI).[23] What contrasts regional from national exhaustion is that regional exhaustion stems from the economic union of regions, but not necessarily the political union. Still, the principle is often the product of courts, treaties, or legislation.[24] In the EU, for example, much of the credit for the system's development is due to the EU Commission and the Court of Justice of the EU (CJEU).[25]

[15] *Id.* at 10–11.

[16] *See* Rothchild (2016), p. 226. *See also* Ghosh and Calboli (2018), pp. 10–11.

[17] Ghosh and Calboli (2018), pp. 10–11.

[18] On the development of this principle in the EU, *see* Beier (1990), p. 131; Jehoram (1992), p. 622.

[19] *See, e.g.*, Calboli (2002), p. 47 [hereinafter Calboli, *Trademark Exhaustion in the EU*] (discussing the debate on the geographical extent of trademark exhaustion in the EU); Shea (1995), p. 463.

[20] Ghosh and Calboli (2018), pp. 10–11.

[21] *Id.*

[22] For a review, *see* Calboli (2019a), p. 22 [hereinafter Calboli, *Comparing IP Exhaustion*].

[23] *See Accord portant révision de l'Accord de Bangui du 2 mars 1977 instituant une Organisation Africaine de la Propriété Intellectuelle (Bangui (République centrafricaine), le 24 février 1999)* [hereinafter Bangui Agreement].

[24] Ghosh and Calboli (2018), pp. 63–64.

[25] *See* Jehoram (1992), p. 622; *see also* Beier (1990), p. 131. For example, the role of the Court of Justice of the EU (CJEU) was crucial in clarifying and enforcing the rule of regional trademark exhaustion in the EU. *See* Case C-335/96, Silhouette Int'l Schimed Gmbh & Co. KG v. Hartlauer Handelsgesellschaft mbH, 30 I.I.C. 920 (1998); Case-173/98, Sebago, Inc. v. GB-Unic SA,

Moreover, economic integration within the regional area generally arises prior to the decision among member states to adopt the rule of regional exhaustion.[26] It could be argued (and this author believes) that, in a harmonized international trade system, in which international organizations administer treaties, international exhaustion could be the logical step following from national and regional exhaustion. However, the TRIPS Agreement—and accordingly international trade construct supervised by the WTO—makes exhaustion a matter of territoriality and national choice.[27]

In our book, Professor Ghosh and I discuss at length the complex set of policy debates in this area.[28] We also highlight how a meaningful assessment of exhaustion policy needs to take into consideration economic implications, possibly through empirical analysis of the relationships among exhaustion policy, international trade, and IP. In this respect, we refer to several economic studies analyzing the effects of parallel importation on market prices, consumers, producers, and importers.[29] Through empirical studies, prominent economists found that in some instances, price differences are due to marketing decisions by IP holders.[30] These decisions reflect the seeking of price differences across countries to attract licensees and distributors in various jurisdictions that can take advantage of market conditions. In this scenario, parallel importers seek to take advantage of arbitrage possibilities arising from the ability to buy products at a low price and sell them at a high price, depending on the legal regime.[31] In other instances, however, price differences can arise from decisions in separate countries independent from the marketing decisions of the IP holders, for example because of higher product demand due to consumer tastes or regulatory differences that translate into higher or lower prices depending on the nature of the regulation.[32] The latter consideration is relevant regarding the

2 C.M.L.R. 1317 (1999); Joined Cases C-414-416/99, Zino Davidoff SA v. A & G Imports Ltd., Levi Strauss & Co. v. Tesco Stores Ltd., and Levi Strauss & Co. v. Costco Wholesale UK Ltd., 2001 E.C.R. I-8691.

[26]The principle of free movement of goods, for example, predates the adoption of the principle of regional exhaustion in the EU and was already enshrined into the Treaty of Rome in 1957. *See* Consolidated Version of the Treaty on the Functioning of the European Union, Mar. 30, 2010, 2010 O.J. (C 83) [hereinafter TFEU] as amended following the entering into force of the Treaty of Lisbon on December 1, 2009. Treaty of Lisbon, Dec. 13, 2007, 2007 O.J. (C 306). Several decisions were issued by the CJEU regarding the free movement of goods and the exercise of IP rights, before the official adoption of the principle of regional exhaustion. *See* Joined Cases 56 & 58/64, Costen & Grunding v. EC Comm'n, 1966 E.C.R. 299; Case 24/67, Parke Davis v. Centrafarm, 1968 E.C.R. 55; Case 40/70, Sirena v. Eda, 1971 E.C.R. 69; Case15/74, Centrafarm v. Sterling Drugs, [1974] E.C.R. 1147; Case 187/80, Merck & Co. v. Stephar, [1981] E.C.R. 2063. *See also* Saggi (2014), p. 125.

[27]Ghosh and Calboli (2018), pp. 63–64.

[28]*Id.* at 41–64.

[29]*See* Ganslandt and Maskus (2008), pp. 267–268; Ganslandt and Maskus (2004), p. 1035 [hereinafter Ganslandt and Maskus (2004)]; Roy and Saggi (2012), p. 262.

[30]Ganslandt and Maskus (2004), p. 29.

[31]*Id.*

[32]*Id. See also* Ghosh and Calboli (2018), pp. 48–51.

discussion of parallel imports in pharmaceuticals, which are subject to non IP-related regulations and whose price is often negotiated by governments and not private economic agents.[33]

Overall, looking at the spectrum of national solutions adopted on exhaustion and the various interests at stake, two observations can be derived from the existing studies. First, it seems the price differences of parallel imported products can be a social benefit for importers and, in several instances, for the importing countries. This could also be the case for parallel imported pharmaceuticals.[34] Price differences do matter for how national legal regimes on exhaustion are implemented both in a particular country or region—that is, whether a country chooses national, regional, or international exhaustion.[35] This first observation has implications for the second, notably that parallel importation is largely the result of price arbitrage arising from differences in prices. Importers see a profit-making opportunity and respond by buying low(er) and selling high(er). Here again, as empirical studies indicate, IP holders can nonetheless respond strategically to these importers either by pre-empting importation before it occurs through contractual clauses they can enforce through litigation[36] or marketing strategies—such as applying small differences in product quality in different countries or appealing to national tastes with varied products. IP holders can also lobby for changes in national laws favoring national exhaustion. Because of various strategic behaviors, the analysis of exhaustion is complicated and the policy responses become more challenging, as one size does not fit all. The approach under Article 6 of the TRIPS Agreement attempts to allows flexibility for individual national responses within this complexity.[37] However, as explained in the next Section, a system of international exhaustion does promote free trade. In turn, this can lead to access to lowered prices products, or access to products that would not be sold in certain countries altogether.[38]

[33] *See* discussion *infra* Part 2.2.

[34] Ghosh and Calboli (2018), p. 49.

[35] *Id.*

[36] *Id.*, at 49–50.

[37] *Id.* at 63–64. *See also* Maskus (2016), p. 106; Chiappetta (2016), p. 125.

[38] For a relevant empirical study of the impact of parallel imports (although limited in geographical scope), *see* National Economic Research Associates, The Economic Consequences of the Choice of Regime in the Area of Trademarks: Final Report for DG XV of the European Commission 76-100 (1999). *But see* Kanavos et al. (2004) (finding neutral welfare effects as most of the benefits from producers went to the parallel importers and not to consumers). *See also* Kanavos and Costa-i-Font (2005), pp. 758, 772–775. A similar conclusion is supported by Ganslandt and Maskus (2004), p. 1035 (finding the actual cost savings were small in a study of Sweden because the wholesale price reductions were not passed on to hospitals and patients, instead the retailers and parallel importers made larger margins).

2.2 *Patent Exhaustion and the Debate on Parallel Trade of Pharmaceuticals*

Unlike most products, pharmaceuticals "are developed, approved, manufactured, traded, and used under complex and demanding regulatory schemes."[39] For strictly regulated markets such as the U.S. or the EU, these regulatory schemes apply all the way from the time of production of the active pharmaceutical ingredients.[40] Still, in all countries today, also developing countries, regulators must issue an official marketing approval before the pharmaceuticals are put in the market.[41] This approval may vary in standards for "new" pharmaceuticals and "generic" versions of previously approved pharmaceuticals.[42] For new medicines, elaborate lists of documents, including clinical trials and manufacturing, are necessary, while applicants for generics need to present details of the "bioequivalence" of the compound and manufacturing. Additionally, importers and distributors of pharmaceuticals are generally subject to import regulations and procedures for product recalling and other safety requirements.[43]

It is old news that bringing a new medicine to market is a costly and lengthy processes. On average, a successful drug costs over $1 billion to develop, and only one in several thousand compounds reaches the final approval stage.[44] Since it is relatively uncomplicated and inexpensive to copy the molecules of a new drug, patents are a fundamental part of the industry for the exclusive rights granted through patents. One of the main factors for the industry to obtain the maximum profitability is also the possibility to sell the medicines at differentiated prices across different countries. However, price setting for pharmaceuticals does not depend entirely on the industry international pricing strategy. Instead, many national governments control the prices pharmaceuticals are sold at nationally and later control these prices within hospitals, pharmacies, and other distributors.[45] Because of these negotiations, in countries offering national healthcare schemes, prescription medications are considerably less expensive than in other countries, while pricing of over the counter medications are left more to the market rules.[46] In some instances, national competition authorities have also determined when pricing was "excessive."[47] As noted before, this complex regulatory ecosystem makes it even more important, from the

---

[39] Abbott (2016), p. 145.

[40] *Id.* at 148–149.

[41] *Id.*

[42] *Id.* For the process of developing generics, see the contributions in Shargel and Kanfer (2014).

[43] Abbott (2016), pp. 149–150.

[44] The Drug Development Process, United States Food and Drug Administration, https://www.fda.gov/patients/learn-about-drug-and-device-approvals/drug-development-process.

[45] Abbott (2016), p. 150; Wasserman Rajec (2016), pp. 271, 283; Grabowski (2002), p. 533, 535.

[46] Abbott (2016), p. 150.

[47] *See* Abbott (2014), pp. 78–79.

pharmaceutical industry's viewpoint, that producers are able to prevent parallel trade from lower priced into higher priced markers.[48]

A rule of national patent exhaustion is the most effective rule to facilitate national price discrimination and block parallel imports of pharmaceuticals on the basis of national patent enforcement.[49] Representatives of the industry strongly support this rule. To justify their support, they have argued that price discrimination is advantageous not only for pharmaceutical producers, but also for developing countries, as this rule allows producers to set higher prices in more affluent markets while lowering prices in less affluent ones. This position has been supported by several economists.[50] Supporters of this view have argued that parallel imports could lead to a price increase, and not a price reduction, in lower priced markets (and possibly to a reduction of the supply of pharmaceuticals altogether) precisely to prevent possible trade diversion by parallel importers of pharmaceuticals first sold in these markets.[51] The industry also likes to point to the losses that parallel imports can bring to pharmaceutical companies and the fact that these losses would inevitably lead to less investments in R&D with consequential damage for pharmaceutical innovation.[52] The argument has been made that parallel imports also harbour counterfeited products, which are certainly a growing threat for public health, especially in developed countries.[53]

These positions have been largely rebutted, however, by proponents of international patent exhaustion and convincingly.[54] Supporters of international exhaustion have highlighted that it is difficult to assess whether price discrimination effectively benefits low income countries since many drugs are not sold at all in these countries[55] or they are sold for a small section of the affluent population at the same price as in higher-priced markets. Simply put, the assertions of the industry in this respect are speculative, as there are no data comparing the prices of the same pharmaceuticals in developed and developing countries, on a large scale and for a considerable number of products. Similarly, it has been correctly stressed that the industry has not presented compelling evidence that it would suffer severe losses and, in turn, these losses would affect reinvestment in R&D. Instead, supporters of international exhaustion noted that the industry spends large sums on the advertising and

---

[48] *See* Bale Jr (1999), p. 637 (arguing for the pharmaceutical industry).

[49] *See supra* Sect. 2.1.

[50] *See* Bale Jr (1999), p. 648 (noting that "[t]he threat of parallel trade takes away any incentive of vaccine and pharmaceutical patent holders to make significant concessions to poorer countries"). *See also* Varian (1985), p. 870; *see also* Schwartz (1990), p. 1259; Singham (2000), pp. 363, 407.

[51] Bale Jr (1999), p. 637.

[52] *Id. See also* Danzon (1998), p. 293.

[53] *See, e.g.*, Delepierre et al. (2012), p. 247; Kelesidis et al. (2007), p. 214; Harper and Gellie (2006).

[54] *See, e.g.* Abbott (2007) (providing of a detailed and very convincing rebuke to the various arguments called by the pharmaceutical industry in favour of national exhaustion and price discrimination) [hereinafter Abbott, *Economic and Social Welfare*]. *See also* Owoeye (2015), p. 359; Kumar Rai and Jagannathan (2012), p. 53.

[55] Abbott (2007), p. 8.

promotion of "lifestyle" (highly profitable) drugs rather than reinvesting all their profits in R&D.[56] The argument about fake medicines is increasingly important as the size of counterfeited medicines in developing countries has become a true issue.[57] This argument is not directly related to parallel imports, however, and again no evidence has been brought that parallel importers—who are subject to strict import controls and regulations no less than other imported medicines—are necessarily linked to the increase of counterfeited medical products in national markets.[58]

Accordingly, despite the pressure against parallel imports on the part of the industry, it cannot be disputed that parallel imports of pharmaceuticals can have beneficial effects for importing countries in terms of prices and access to pharmaceuticals. In particular, imports of lower priced pharmaceuticals can increase access to medicines and, in turn, assist both patients and national governments in saving costs, as several pharmaceuticals are provided through publicly funded health programs.[59] Certainly, for this advantage to be true, the cost savings from the lower point price of the medicines should be shared between importers, retailers, hospitals, and ultimately patients and cannot be pocked only by the importers and the distributors.[60] In this respect, the role of national governments remains crucial, as governments retain regulatory control on the importation of paralleled imported pharmaceuticals. Governments should (and generally do) exercise price control for these pharmaceuticals in order to impose that importers share the savings obtained through the arbitrage of the pharmaceuticals across different national markets.[61] It is thus advisable that individual countries—above all developing countries and LDCs—use the flexibility provided under Article 6 of the TRIPS Agreement and practice the type of domestic exhaustion that best suits national needs in terms of access to pharmaceuticals, thus international exhaustion.[62]

Opponents of parallel imports tried to argue soon after the adoption of the TRIPS Agreement that Article 28 grants patent holders the right to "prevent third parties from making, using, offering for sale, selling or importing" a product and thus it

[56] *Id.*, at 8-9 (noting that "[this argument is based on the premise that higher levels of income will lead to increased investments in R&D ... [but] originator companies on average invest about 15% of their gross income on R&D.]" Instead, it is noted that "[t]he industry spends a substantially higher percentage of income on advertising, promotion and administration. Much of the advertising and promotion costs are spent on "lifestyle" drugs such as Viagra. Considerable R&D spending is directed to lifestyle products and minor variations on existing therapies (so-called "me too" drugs).").

[57] United Nations Interregional Crime and Justice Research Institute, Counterfeit Medicines and Organised Crime (2012).

[58] Abbott (2007), pp. 9–10.

[59] *See* Ho (2011), p. 91.

[60] *But see* Kanavos and Costa-i-Font (2005), pp. 772–775; Ganslandt and Maskus (2004), p. 1035.

[61] Abbott (2007), pp. 9–10.

[62] *See* Musungu and Cecilia (2006).

limits the application of Article 6.[63] This argument was rebuked, however, and a footnote in Article 28 confirms explicitly that the provision of Article 28 is subject to Article 6.[64] This point was further addressed by the Declaration on the TRIPS Agreement and Public Health at the WTO Ministerial Conference held in Doha in 2001.[65] The Doha Declaration focused on accessed to health and reinforced the right of WTO members to take measures to protect public health, including issuing compulsory licenses. In particular, paragraph 5(d) of the Doha Declaration clarified that countries can adopt international exhaustion to allow the parallel importation of lower-priced medicines for public health purposes under Article 6 of the TRIPS Agreement and this cannot be challenged under the WTO dispute settlement system.[66]

One controversial point remained after the Doha Declaration: whether pharmaceuticals produced under compulsory licences could be imported into foreign countries. These imports may represent the only option for access to medicines for some of the LDCs, which cannot effectively avail themselves of compulsory licensing for lack of manufacturing capacity. In fact, most LDCs are still not obliged to implement pharmaceutical patents and clinical trial data protection, as the TRIPS Council agreed in 2015 to extend the waiver, which was set to expire on January 1, 2016, until 2033.[67] Hence, manufacturing capacity is the highest barrier in these countries. However, Article 31(f) of the TRIPS Agreement does not explicitly allow parallel imports of compulsory licensed medicines. Instead, the provision allows compulsory

[63] TRIPS, *supra* note 13, Art. 28. *See* Bale Jr (1999), pp. 641–648. *See also* Kodak SA v Jumbo-Markt AG, 4C. 24/1999/rnd, Dec. 7, 1999 (the Swiss Federal Supreme Court stated that: "Article 28 of the TRIPS Agreement gives the patent holder the right to prevent third parties from selling and importing patented products".).

[64] TRIPS, *supra* note 13, Art. 28 fn 6 ("this right [i.e. the right of importation], like all other rights conferred under this Agreement in respect of the use, sale, importation or other distribution of goods, is subject to the provisions of Article 6."). De Carvalho (2010), p. 173.

[65] *See* Abbott (2002), p. 469. For a detailed review of the TRIPS Agreement and public health, *see* Musungu (2016), p. 489. *See also* t'Hoen (2002), p. 27; Coriat and Orsenigo (2014); Velásquez et al. (2020).

[66] Declaration on the TRIPS Agreement and Public Health (14 November 2001), Doc. WT/ MIN (01)/DEC/2 (20 Nov. 2001) ("5(d)The effect of the provisions in the TRIPS Agreement that are relevant to the exhaustion of intellectual property rights is to leave each Member free to establish its own regime for such exhaustion without challenge, subject to the MFN and national treatment provisions of Articles 3 and 4.").

[67] Council for TRIPS, Extension of the Transitional Period Under Article 66.1 of the TRIPS Agreement for Least Developed Country Members for Certain Obligations With Respect to Pharmaceutical Products, IP/C/73 (Nov. 6, 2015). *See also* Daniel Benoliel & Timothy John Chirwa, *The Impact of Pharmaceutical Patents on Health Expenditures in Least-Developed Countries*, unpublished paper available at http://law.haifa.ac.il/images/Publications/BenolielChirwa.pdf (comparing LDCs in OAPI with other LDCs and noting that patents are not a primary obstacle to access to medicines in LDCs, as opposed to several other factors such as: rational selection and use of drugs, affordable prices, unsustainable and inadequate funding, and Reliable health and supply systems).

licencing to be granted "predominantly" for the domestic market.[68] Finally, in 2003, WTO members agreed to facilitate LDCs to import medicines made under compulsory licensing if they are unable to manufacture the medicines themselves. This resulted in the adoption of Article 31*bis* of the TRIPS Agreement in 2005.[69] The provision became effective in January 2017, after a sufficient number of countries ratified the provision,[70] even though the provision has not been invoked by any LDCs in the context of parallel imports of compulsory licensed pharmaceuticals to date.

3 National Solutions to Patent Exhaustion and Parallel Trade of Pharmaceuticals

Because of the flexibility of Article 6 of the TRIPS Agreement, countries worldwide can decide their national policy on patent exhaustion autonomously between national, international, or regional exhaustion. Some countries also apply a differentiated approach to the exhaustion of pharmaceuticals. In the following Section, I review the domestic policies of selected countries in various continents.[71] This information is necessarily limited due to the impossibility to comprehensively address all countries' policies in this Chapter. In addition, as mentioned above, the analysis does not extend to the national requirements each country applies regarding the regulatory schemes for the marketing approval and import authorization for the parallel imports of pharmaceuticals, which again remain a fundamental aspect of imports of medicines (both by originator companies and parallel importers).

3.1 Selected Jurisdictions in Asia

Several countries in Asia[72] follow a regime of international exhaustion related to patent rights. This choice can be explained by the fact that several countries in Asia are still developing countries or LDCs. For example, the two largest countries in Asia, India and China, both practice international patent exhaustion. India's

[68] TRIPS Agreement, *supra* note 13, Art. 31(f).

[69] *Id.*, Art. 31*bis*. *See* Abbott (2005), p. 317; Abbott and Reichman (2007), p. 921.

[70] Zaheer Abbas and Riaz (2017), p. 451.

[71] For detailed overview in this respect, *see* World Intellectual Property Organization, Standard Committee on Patents Electronic Forum, Questionnaire on Exceptions and Limitations of Patent Rights, the database administered by the WIPO's Standing Committee on Patents https://www.wipo.int/scp/en/exceptions/ [hereinafter WIPO, Questionnaire on Patent Exceptions].

[72] Even if partially outdate now, a relevant resource for Asia is still Parallel Imports in Asia (Heath 2004).

approach is based on Section 107A of the Indian Patent Act, as amended in 2002, which provides that "[f]or the purpose of this Act, (b) importation of patented products by any person from a person who is duly authorized under the law to produce and sell or distribute the product, shall not be considered as an infringement of patent rights".[73] In China, Article 69 of the Chinese Patent Law provides that the following shall not be deemed to be patent right infringement "(1) after a patented product or a product directly obtained by using the patented method is sold by the patentee or sold by any unit or individual with the permission of the patentee, any other person uses, offers to sell, sells or imports that product."[74] Previously, under the rule of the Patent Law of China of 1985, the applicable rule was national patent exhaustion. This was changed, however, with the entry into force of new 2008 Patent Law, which provides for international patent exhaustion.[75]

Out of the ten members of the Association of South East Asian Nations (ASEAN),[76] three countries also practice international exhaustion. In particular, Cambodia follows international patent exhaustion under its Law on the Patents, Utility Model Certificates and Industrial Designs,[77] even though Cambodia does not currently provide patent protection for pharmaceuticals under the TRIPS Council's waiver for LDCs. International exhaustion is also adopted under the Patents Act of Malaysia[78] and the Intellectual Property Law of Vietnam.[79] Other ASEAN countries, such as Brunei,[80] Lao PDR[81] (also an LDC), and Thailand[82] do not have a specific rule on patent exhaustion. In these countries, whether the parallel importation of genuine products sold overseas with the proprietors' consent constituted infringement may depend on the contents of the contracts signed between the parties concerned. In Myanmar, a new Patent Law has been adopted in 2019, which is currently pending for approval, even though it remains unclear how the principle of

[73] Patents (Amendment) Act, 2002, No. 38, Acts of Parliament, 2002 (India). *See also* Ghosh and Calboli (2018), pp. 108–109; Pai (2016), pp. 324, 327; Gopalakrishnan and Agitha (2012), p. 229; Basheer and Kochupillai (2009), p. 63.

[74] Patent Law of the People's Republic of China (promulgated by the Standing Comm. Nat'l People's Cong., Dec. 27, 2008, effective Oct. 1, 2009) CN028 (China). *See also* Yu (2004), pp. 25–38.

[75] *See* Yu and Yin (2016), pp. 308, 311. *See also* Ghosh and Calboli (2018), p. 109.

[76] For a discussion on ASEAN, including the principle of exhaustion and free movement, *see*Calboli (2019b), pp. 363–391.

[77] Law on Patents, Utility Models and Industrial Designs, Art. 44 (Cambodia).

[78] Patents Act 1983, as amended by the Patents (Amendment) Act 2006, § 58A (Malay.).

[79] Law on Intellectual Property (No. 50/2005/QH11 of Nov. 29, 2005), art. 125(2)(b) (Viet.).

[80] Constitution of Brunei Darussalam, Patents Order, Art. 83(3) (2011) (Brunei).

[81] Lao People's Democratic Republic Intellectual Property Laws (Law No. 01/NA of 20 Dec. 2011) (Lao PDR) [hereinafter Lao PDR Law].

[82] Patent Act B.E. 2522, as amended by the Patent Act (No. 2) B.E. 2535 and the Patent Act (No. 3) B.E. 2542 (Thai.).

patent exhaustion is addressed in the new law. Myanmar can also be exempted from implementing patent protection for pharmaceuticals until 2033 (as an LDC).[83]

Other Asian countries follow a hybrid system. In particular, the 2016 Patent Law of Indonesia[84] grants patent owners the exclusive right to prohibit other parties from "importing" the patented products or the products derived from the patented products.[85] Yet, this provision does not apply, explicitly, to the imports of patented pharmaceuticals that have been lawfully marketed outside Indonesia and have been imported into Indonesia by third parties.[86] Similarly, the Philippine Intellectual Property Code[87] includes the right to oppose unauthorized imports,[88] but again this provision does not apply to the imports of pharmaceuticals.[89] Singapore also follows a hybrid approach, but opposite to the approach adopted by Indonesia and the Philippines. Notably, Singapore does not allow imports of patented pharmaceuticals if the products have not been previously sold or distributed in Singapore by the patent owner or with her consent.[90] After the products have been marketed in Singapore by the originator companies, then parallel imports are theoretically allowed. However, also after the first released in the Singaporean market by the patent holders, imports can still be blocked when the pharmaceuticals have been parallel imported because of a breach in the contract between the patent holder and her licensees, including outside Singapore.[91] As parallel imports are often the results of genuine products diverted from their original distributors into the distribution channels of parallel importers, this principle effectively nullifies the possibility to parallel imports pharmaceuticals into Singapore. This principle was introduced after the US-Singapore trade agreement. On the other side, Singapore practices international patent exhaustion for all other products.[92]

The remaining largest economies in Asia, Japan and Korea, do not have a specific statutory policy on patent exhaustion, and their respective case law has led to diverging position. In Japan, courts have largely recognized international patent exhaustion.[93] In particular, the Supreme Court stated that enforcing Japanese patents would not be consistent with international trade, even though the Court did not

---

[83] At this time, the author could not locate the pending draft of the 2019 Patent Law (Myanmar), as the draft is not published not available in any known database.

[84] Law of the Republic of Indonesia No. 13 of July 28, 2016, on Patents (Indon).

[85] *Id.* at art. 19(1)-(2) and art. 160.

[86] *Id.* at art. 167. This exception is based directly on the need to "to ensure a reasonable price and satisfy the justice of a pharmaceutical product is necessary for human health." *Id.* at Explanation to art. 167.

[87] Intellectual Property Code, Rep. Act 8293, as amended by Rep. Act 10372 (Phil).

[88] *Id.* at § 72.

[89] *Id.*

[90] Patents Act (Ch. 221, 2005 Rev. Ed.) § 66(3)(a) (Sing.).

[91] *Id.* at §§ 66(3)(b) & (c).

[92] *Id.* at § 66(2)(g).

[93] Heath (2004), p. 51.

directly acknowledge that Japan practices international exhaustion. The Court recognized the patent owner could prohibit the importation of goods through contractual restrictions and by indicating on the product that the patented item is not intended for sale in Japan.[94] In Korea, the Patent Act also does not elaborate on the issue of patent exhaustion and judicial decisions led to an opposite interpretation—national exhaustion. This position makes of Korea one of the few Asian countries choosing national patent exhaustion and it probably consistent with the level of technological development of the country[95] (even though the same could be said for Japan). However, in 1981, precisely in a case related to the imports of Italian pharmaceuticals from Switzerland into Korea, the Seoul District Court said the foreign sale had also exhausted the rights in Korea.[96] Still, the court fell short of explaining the reasoning for the decision in that case and no later case confirmed nor denied this position. It thus remains unclear if this decision changed the general view in favor of national patent exhaustion in Korea, or if it could be supported that also Korea decided through caselaw to follow a differentiated regime for the exhaustion of pharmaceuticals (international) versus other patented products (national).[97]

3.2 Canada, United States, Australia, and New Zealand

Today, international patent exhaustion is the system of choice also in Canada and the U.S., based on judicial precedents.[98] Specifically in Canada, in the 1998 decision in *Eli Lilly & Co v Novopharm Ltd.*, the Supreme Court confirmed that, when a patentee sells a patented product, the rights of the products exhaust as long as the seller did not impose any restrictions on the subsequent distribution.[99] Thus, the key inquiry in Canada is today not where the goods were first sold, whether in or outside Canada, but whether the products were sold with or without restrictions.[100]

The U.S. follows a very similar position. Notably, the traditional interpretation on patent exhaustion was recently changed in favor of international exhaustion by the 2017 Supreme Court decision *Impression Products v. Lexmark.*[101] Like in several other countries, the U.S. Patent Act does not elaborate on the geographical extent of the exhaustion of a patented product, or a product embodying patented process, after

[94] *Id.* at. 52–58.

[95] Byung-Il (2004), p. 73.

[96] *Id.* at 76–77 (citing the decision of the Seoul District Court in the case *Ildong Pharmacie v. Farmatalia Carlo Erba S.p.A.*, Mar. 14, 1981).

[97] *Id.* at 77.

[98] *See* Calboli, *Comparing IP Exhaustion, supra* note 22, at 32.

[99] Eli Lilly & Co. v. Novopharm Ltd., [1998] 2 S.C.R. 129.

[100] *Id.*

[101] *Impression Prods., Inc. v. Lexmark Int'l, Inc.*, 581 U.S. 1523 (2017). *See* Ghosh and Calboli (2018), pp. 88–102.

the first sale of the products. In the past decades, several decisions by U.S. courts adopted the position that the sale of an article in a foreign country does not exhaust the U.S. patent.[102] In its February 2016 decision in the *Lexmark* case, the U.S. Court of Appeals for the Federal Circuit repeated this position. However, to the disbelief of many in the U.S., the Supreme Court reversed and stated that the first sale of products anywhere in the world exhausted the rights also in the U.S. Still, the Court did not exclude that contractual restrictions could prevent the import of gray market goods after the decision in *Lexmark*.[103] Thus, also in the U.S., the key inquiry may still be whether the products were sold with or without restrictions. Moreover, regardless of the change in national policy, the imports of pharmaceuticals remain subjects to the US regulatory schemes and the impact of *Lexmark* on these imports is, in practice, non-existing.

On the other side, Australia follows a less trade friendly national policy and favors national patent exhaustion. Also in Australia, however, the Patents Act does not specifically address the issue.[104] Notably, the Patent Act states that patent holders have exclusive rights to exploit their inventions in Australia.[105] The definition of "exploitation" is provided in the Patent Act and includes importation, similar to the TRIPS Agreement and other national laws.[106] This leads to the interpretation that Australia practices national exhaustion. Patent law in Australia is also constrained by the obligations under the Australia–United States trade agreement, whose Article 17.9.4 states that "Each Party shall provide that the exclusive right of the patent owner to prevent importation of a patented product, or a product that results from a patented process, without the consent of the patent owner shall not be limited by the sale or distribution of that product outside its territory, at least where the patentee has placed restrictions on importation by contract or other means."[107]

Similarly to Australia, also New Zealand does not allow parallel importation of patented products.[108] Here again, we have a hybrid system, however, as the Crown has the authority to order parallel importation of pharmaceuticals under the Medicines Act of 1981, notwithstanding the Patents Act.[109] Of course, provided that the products are in line with the requirements imposed under the country's regulatory schemes and import authorizations.

---

[102] *See* Ghosh and Calboli (2018), at 88-102 (citing *Boesch v. Graff*, 133 U.S. 697 (1890); *Jazz Photo Corp. v. Int'l Trade Comm'n*, 264 F.3d 1094 (Fed. Cir. 2001); *Lexmark Int'l, Inc. v. Impression Prods. Inc.*, 816 F.3d 721, 771 (Fed. Cir. 2016)).

[103] *Impression Products, Inc. v. Lexmark Int'l, Inc.*, 581 U.S. 1523 (2017).

[104] *See* Ghosh and Calboli (2018), pp. 107–108.

[105] *Patents Act* 1990 s 13 (Austl.).

[106] *Id.* at Schedule 1 (Austl.).

[107] Free Trade Agreement, U.S.-Austl., May 18, 2004, art. 17.9.4.

[108] *See* Ghosh and Calboli (2018), pp. 107–108; Susy Frankel, Test Tubes for Global Intellectual Property Issues: Small Market Economies 178 (2015).

[109] Frankel, *supra* note 108, at 178 (citing Section 32A of the Medicines Act 1981, introduced by the Medicines Amendment Act 1989). *See also* Patents Act, pt 2 (N.Z.).

3.3 Selected Jurisdictions in Latin America

Like in Asia, most countries in Latin America follow the principle of international patent exhaustion. There are important exceptions, however, to this rule.

The first exception is Mexico, which is surprising as both its partner members in the North American Free Trade Agreement (NAFTA), Canada and the U.S., follow now international patent exhaustion. Instead, Mexico practices national exhaustion. Also, in Mexico, no specific language related to the exhaustion of patent rights is found under the Mexican law. The Mexican Industrial Property Law clarifies, however, that the rights conferred by a patent cannot be asserted against "any person who markets, acquires or uses the patented product or the product obtained by means of the patented process, after said product has been lawfully placed on the market."[110] In the absence of a provision stating the opposite, the majoritarian interpretation of the wording "the market" is that it only includes "national market."[111]

National patent exhaustion is also the system adopted in Brazil. This position is particularly perplexing in light of Brazil's role in the parallel importation of pharmaceuticals in the 1990s. Notably, Article 43 of Law 9.279 of 1996 provides national exhaustion for patent and trademark rights regarding products "manufactured in accordance with a process or product patent that has been placed on the internal market directly by the patent holder or with his consent."[112] However, under Article 68(4) of the same law, if the exploitation of the patent (and use of the trademark) is made through importation of the product—that is, in the case where the products are not manufactured in Brazil, third parties are allowed to import these products after they have put them into the "market", which is interpreted in this instance as anywhere in the world.[113] Accordingly, in this case, parallel imports are admitted in Brazil.[114]

On the other side, Chile follows a system of international patent exhaustion as per Article 49(5) of Law No. 19.039, according to which a "patent shall not confer the right to prevent third parties from marketing the patent protected product, which such parties have acquired lawfully after that product has been lawfully introduced into the market of any country by the right owner or by a third party with the owner's

---

[110]Mexican Industrial Property Law, art. 22. Ley de la Propiedad Industrial, Diario Oficial de la Federación [D.O.F.] 27-06-1991, amended by D.O.F. 02-08-1994 (Mex.).

[111]*See* Correa and Correa (2016), p. 206.

[112]Lei No. 9.279, de 14 de Mayo de 1996, art. 43(4) (Braz.) [hereinafter Brazilian IP Law].

[113]*Id.*, at art. 68(4). *See also* Correa and Correa (2016), p. 206.

[114]This provision finds its origin of the requirement of "local manufacture obligation" for patent holders that was originally provided under Brazilian law. As this requirement could have been challenged as incompatible with Article 27(1) of the TRIPS Agreement, the 1996 Law abolished the rule. Yet, Article 68(1), under the rubric "Compulsory Licensing," provides that the following can grant a decision of issuing compulsory licensing: "I. failure to work the subject matter of a patent on the territory of Brazil, failure to manufacture or incomplete manufacture of the product or failure to completely use a patented process, except for failure to work due to lack of economic viability, in which case importing shall be admitted. Brazilian IP Law, *supra* note 112, at art. 68(1).

consent."[115] As reported, legislative debates found this solution necessary "to provide a balance between the ... right holders and ... the citizens"[116] Argentina also adopts international exhaustion, according to Article 36(c) of Law No. 24.481 (consolidated text, 1996) on Patents and Utility Models and subsequent amendments "The right conferred by a patent shall not have any effect against: (c) Anyone acquiring, using, importing or in any way marketing the patented product or the product obtained by means of the patented process, after said product has been lawfully placed on the market in any country."[117]

The four members of the Andean Community—Bolivia, Ecuador, Colombia, and Peru—also practice international exhaustion.[118] Article 54 of Decision 486 of the Commission of the Andean Community establishes that the patent shall not confer the right "to proceed against a third party making commercial use of a product protected by a patent once that product has been introduced into the commerce of any country by the owner or another person authorized by the right holder or with economic ties to that patent owner."[119] Notwithstanding, the imports of these products can be further restricted by national laws providing for the import authorizations and other formalities.

3.4 European Union and Switzerland

Free movement of goods, including of pharmaceuticals, is allowed in the EU/EEA under the rule of regional exhaustion. Articles 34 and 36 of the Treaty on the Functioning of the European Union (TFEU)—originally then the Treaty Establishing the European Economic Community (EEC Treaty)—are the applicable provisions to the exhaustion of patented goods within the EU. Notably, the distribution of a patented good by the consent of the patent owner into the market of any EU Member State exhausts the rights of distribution within the EU.[120] Exhaustion does not apply, however, if the product is a patented pharmaceutical manufactured

---

[115]Law No. 19.039 on Industrial Property of 1991, art. 49(5) (Chile). This provision has not been modified in the various amendment and updates of Law 19.039 that have been adopted since 1991.

[116]World Intellectual Property Organization, Standard Committee on Patents Electronic Forum, Questionnaire on Exceptions and Limitations of Patent Rights, Chile, Exhaustion of Rights, https://www.wipo.int/scp/en/exceptions/replies/chile.html#Q8.

[117]Law No. 24.481, Oct. 23, 1995, art. 36(c), [LV-C] A.D.L.A. 2948 (as amended by Law No. 24.572 [LV-E] A.D.L.A. 5892 (Arg.) [hereinafter Argentine Patent Law]. *See also* Correa and Correa (2016), p. 202.

[118]Decision No. 486 Establishing the Common Industrial Property Regime, Sept. 14, 2000, art. 54, WIPO CAN012, https://wipolex.wipo.int/en/text/223717 (Andean Community).

[119]*Id.*

[120]*See* Stothers (2007); Case15/74, Centrafarm v. Sterling Drugs, [1974] E.C.R. 1147; Case 187/80, Merck & Co. v. Stephar, [1981] E.C.R. 2063.

for the purpose of marketing approval rather than for commercialization.[121] Articles 34 and 36 also apply regardless of possible contractual limitations against further distribution of patented products. In particular, these limitations may be in conflict with Article 34 if they restrict or prevent importation into and distribution in another Member State.

An additional exception to the principle of free movement is found in the Act of Accession 2003[122] of new members from Eastern Europe, which provides that IP holders can rely on the "Specific Mechanism" and prevent the import and marketing of pharmaceuticals from new EU Member States into other EU Members States in which they have protection.[123] The reason for this exception was because patent protection and supplementary protection certificate (SPC) for pharmaceuticals was implemented later in time in these countries and at the time of accessions, several drugs were patented in the Western EU Member States but could no longer be patented in these countries. The "Specific Mechanism" additionally provides importers should demonstrate to the authorities in charge of issuing the permission to import they have notified the patent or SPC holder no less than a month earlier.[124] In 2005, the "Specific Mechanism" was later extended to Bulgaria and Romania, and in 2012 to Croatia.[125]

The only case in this area, *Merck v. Sigma*,[126] confirmed nonetheless a pro-exhaustion stance by the CJEU's interpretation of the provision. In particular, even though the Court accepted the Specific Mechanism provides for a specific derogation to the principle of free movement, it also stated that importers do not have "an obligation to obtain the express prior consent" from the rights holders.[127] Instead, rights holders have one month to oppose the imports and if they do not "take advantage of that period," importers "may legitimately apply to the competent authorities for authorisation to import the product and, where appropriate, import

[121] Case C-316/95, Generics v. Smith Kline & French Laboratories, [1997] E.C.R. I-3929.

[122] Act of Accession of Cyprus, the Czech Republic, Estonia, Hungary, Latvia, Lithuania, Malta, Poland, Slovenia and Slovakia, Apr. 16, 2003, 2003 O.J. (L236) 33 [hereinafter Specific Mechanism]. *See* Heath (2014b), p. 399; Stothers (2016), pp. 169, 178.

[123] Specific Mechanism, *supra* note 122.

[124] *Id.* Critically, in general, over this type of differentiated systems, see Jerome Reichman, Ruth Okediji, Ioannis Lianos, Robin Jacob, Christopher Stothers, The WTO Compatibility of a Differentiated International Exhaustion Regime Proposed by the Eurasian Economic Community, A Consultancy Report, Research Paper Series, Skolkovo-HSE International Laboratory for Law & Development (on file with author).

[125] Act of Accession of Bulgaria and Romania, 2005 O.J. (L157) 203, Annex V.1; Act of Accession of Croatia 2012 O.J. (L112) 21, Annex IV.1.

[126] Case C-539/13, Merck Canada Inc. v. Sigma Pharmaceuticals plc, [2015] R.P.C. 30. The importer provided advanced notification to Merck of its intention to import pharmaceuticals from Poland, where protection did not apply. Merck did not respond and the products were imported into the U.K. Merck objected and parallel imports were blocked. When Merck also sought damages, the issue was referred to the CJEU. *See* Stothers (2016), at 179.

[127] *Case C-539/13, Merck Canada,* ¶ 28.

and market it."[128] This should not be read as the rights holders have "forfeited the right to rely on the Specific Mechanism."[129] They simply cannot "obtain compensation for the loss" due to the imports "which he failed to oppose" in time,[130] but remain "free to oppose future importation and marketing of the pharmaceutical product protected by the patent or SPC."[131]

Not an EU Member State, Switzerland's example is worth noting as part of the European region. Until 2008, Swiss law applied national exhaustion to patents. The rule was then changed in favour of regional patent exhaustion and Switzerland now practices regional exhaustion with the countries members of the EU/EEA.[132] However, pharmaceuticals are still subject to national patent exhaustion in Switzerland, and parallel imports of pharmaceuticals first put into the market in a foreign country, including in the EU/EEA, cannot enter into the country. To be precise, Article 9 (a) paragraph 5 indicates that the principle of regional exhaustion does not apply and the consent of the holder of the patent of a product "is reserved" in the instances in which the price the product "in Switzerland or in the country in which they are placed" has been "fixed by the state."[133] This principle applies directly to prescription pharmaceuticals and all the medicines that are subjected to price control by national government. However, in the law, this principle is not directly referred to pharmaceuticals, but to all patented products that could be subject to price control.

3.5 *Selected Jurisdictions in Africa*

Access to medicines is a priority for most countries in Africa, the continent with the largest number of LDCs worldwide,[134] all of which are users of pharmaceuticals coming from foreign countries.[135] National practice on patent exhaustion varies

---

[128] *Id.* at ¶ 31.

[129] *Id.* at ¶ 32.

[130] *Id.*

[131] *Id.*

[132] Federal Act on Patents for Inventions (SR 232.14 LBI) art. 9a (inserted by No I of the Federal Act of June 22, 2007 (AS 2551 (2009); BBl 1 (2006)), *as amended by* No I of the Federal Act of Dec. 19, 2008, in force since July 1, 2009 (AS 2615 (2009); BBl 303 (2008)) (Switz.).

[133] *Id.* at art. 9a, ¶ 5 LBI ("Irrespective of the provisions of paragraphs 1–4, the consent of the proprietor of the patent for the placing on the market of patent-protected goods is reserved if their price in Switzerland or in the country in which they are placed on the market is fixed by the state."). *See also* Kyle (2009), p. 339, 345 (noting that, on the other side, "Switzerland treats copyrights and trademarks as internationally exhausted.").

[134] *See* United Nations, Committee for Development, List of Least Developed Countries, https://www.un.org/development/desa/dpad/wp-content/uploads/sites/45/publication/ldc_list.pdf (listing the 47 countries currently categorized as LDCs).

[135] Vawda and Shozi (2020); dos Santos and Lowé Gnintedem (2018), pp. 592, 593–594; Ncube (2016), p. 110.

across countries in the continent, however, with some countries practicing international exhaustion, while others national or regional exhaustion. The laws of several countries also remain silent on the issue.[136]

For example, the following countries do not seem to have a clear position on the issue as of today: Congo, Egypt, Nigeria, Swaziland, Angola, Lesotho, and Malawi.[137] South Africa's position is also unclear, even though several commentators support it following international exhaustion. In the late 1990s, South Africa implemented regulations authorizing parallel importation of medicines protected by patents and trademarks,[138] but the South African Patents Act remains unclear as to whether the doctrine of exhaustion of rights applies nationally or internationally.[139] Well-known by experts in this area, South Africa wanted to authorize parallel importation of retroviral pharmaceuticals for AIDS in the 1990s.[140] It was precisely in this occasion that patent holders argued that international exhaustion was precluded by Article 28 of the TRIPS Agreement.[141] The case was eventually dropped, but the ensuing criticism led to the adoption of the Doha Declaration.[142]

International patent exhaustion is instead directly adopted in the law of several countries in Africa. These countries include Ghana, which changed its previous regime of national patent exhaustion with the revision of the Patent Act in 2003, whose Section 11(4)(a) now states that "[t]he rights conferred under the patent shall not extend to acts in respect of articles which have been put on the market in any country by the owner of the patent or with the owner's consent."[143] Similarly, Article 43(1) of the 2012 Industrial Property Act of Namibia provides that "[t]he following acts do not constitute an infringement of the rights under a patent, namely: a) acts of importation of patented inventions which have been put on the market in any territory or country by the owner of the patent or with his or her authorization."[144] Kenya also explicitly permits the parallel imports of patented pharmaceuticals under the Industrial Property Act 2001, replacing the Industrial Property Act 1989, which prohibited parallel imports. Notably, Article 58(2) now recites, "[t]he rights under the patent shall not extend to acts in respect of articles which have been put on the market in Kenya or in any other country or imported into Kenya."[145] Additional

---

[136] *Id.* at 31–32. In general, *see also* McKeith (2013), p. 287.

[137] *See* WIPO, Questionnaire on Patent Exceptions (in which the respective countries may indicated that there is no clear national position of the issue).

[138] Abbott (2016), pp. 146–147.

[139] *Id.*

[140] *See* (Tayler 2004, p. 117).

[141] *See supra* Section 1.2.

[142] *Id.*

[143] Patents Act No. 657 (2003), § 11(4)(a) (Ghana). Vawda and Shozi (2020), p. 32.

[144] Industrial Property Act No. 1 (2012), § 42(1)(a) (Namibia). Vawda and Shozi (2020), p. 32.

[145] Industrial Property Act No. 3 (2001), § 58(2), *as amended* up to Act No. 11 (2017) (Kenya).

countries that explicitly follow international patent exhaustion are: Botswana,[146] Burundi,[147] Liberia,[148] Seychelles,[149] Sierra Leone,[150] Zambia,[151] Zanzibar,[152] and Zimbabwe.[153]

To the contrary, the following countries provide for national exhaustion: Madagascar, Mozambique, Rwanda, Sao Tome and Principe, South Sudan, and Uganda.[154] This choice is, at best, puzzling as all the countries in this list are LDCs.[155] Even though these countries may not protect pharmaceuticals with patents at this time because of the TRIPS Council's waiver—thus the impact of a national exhaustion regime ultimately does not affect imports of pharmaceuticals—this system can affect parallel imports of other products currently patented in these countries. Moreover, a system of national exhaustion may protect the business interests of the foreign patent holders more than the national interests, as most patents are filed by foreigners in the countries in question.[156] Another country practicing national exhaustion is Morocco under Article 55(d) of the Patent Law of 2000.[157] The provision was repeated in the US-Morocco FTA in 2004,[158] in which both the U.S. and Morocco subscribed to this position. As the U.S. later changed its national rule to international patent exhaustion,[159] Morocco could also consider a change in policy for public health reasons.

Finally, regional exhaustion is the system practiced by the seventeen members of the Organisation Africaine de la Propriété Intellectuelle (OAPI): Benin, Burkina Faso, Cameroon, Central African Republic, Chad, Comoros, Congo, Côte d'Ivoire, Gabon, Guinea, Equatorial Guinea, Mali, Mauritania, Niger, Guinea Bissau, Senegal, and Togo. Its seat is in Yaoundé, Cameroon. In particular, OAPI operates a

---

[146] Industrial Property Act No. 8 (2010), § 25(1)(a) 2010 (Botswana). Vawda and Shozi (2020), p. 32 (recounting that Botswana utilized this flexibility when it declared HIV/AIDS a national emergency in 2000 and began importing cheaper ARV drugs).

[147] Industrial Property Law No. 1 (2009), art. 57 (Burundi).

[148] Liberia Intellectual Property Act, § 13.11(b) (2016) (Liberia).

[149] The Patents and Industrial Design Act, § 19 (2012) (Seychelles).

[150] Patents and Industrial Design Act, § 23(1)(a) (2012) (Sierra Leone).

[151] Patents Act No. 40 (2016) § 76 (Zam).

[152] Industrial Property Act No. 4 (2008) § 11(4)(a)(i) (Zanzibar).

[153] Patents Act [Chapter 26:03], § 24A (amended by Act 9 of 2002) (Zimbabwe).

[154] Vawda and Shozi (2020), p. 32.

[155] *See* United Nations, *supra* note 134.

[156] *See* Graff and Pardey (2019) (for a survey of patent filing by foreigner and local inventors in Africa).

[157] Law No. 17-97 on the Protection of Industrial Property, art. 55 (Morocco).

[158] United States-Morocco Free Trade Agreement, 15 June 2004, 44 I.L.M. 544, art. 15.9 ("4. Each Party shall provide that the exclusive right of the patent owner to prevent importation of a patented product, or a product that results from patented process, without the consent of the patent owner shall not be limited by the sale or distribution of that product outside its territory").

[159] *Impression Prods., Inc. v. Lexmark Int'l, Inc.*, 581 U.S. 1523 (2017). *See* Ghosh and Calboli (2018), pp. 88–102.

unitary system for patents and OAPI member states do not have individual national laws. The Revised Bangui Agreement of February 1999 is the applicable patent law for all member states.[160] Article 8(1)(a) of Annex I provides that "The rights deriving from the patent shall not extend: (a) to acts in relation to subject matter brought on to the market on the territory of a member State by the owner of the patent or with his consent."[161] It should be noted, however, that even though thirteen of OAPI members states (excluding Cameroon, Congo, Côte d'Ivoire, and Gabon) are LDCs, the rights granted under the Bangui Agreement include pharmaceutical patents (as per Article 27 of the TRIPS Agreement).[162] Accordingly, LDCs in OAPI are de facto excluded from taking advantage of the existing TRIPS Council's waiver for patent protection for pharmaceuticals.[163] Moreover, these countries are bound by a system of regional exhaustion and not international exhaustion, whereas international exhaustion could likely a more favorable approach for all OAPI member states.[164]

4 Overlapping Intellectual Property Rights and Parallel Trade of Pharmaceuticals

In addition to patents, other IP rights can affect parallel trade, even when countries practice international patent exhaustion. This situation can arise when countries practice national exhaustion for trademark, copyright, or design rights.[165] In general, overlapping IP rights can apply to a product in its entirety or to different parts or features of it.[166] An example of the former is the overlapping trademark and copyright protection that can apply to the shape of a perfume bottle, the décor of a store, or the pictorial logo affixed to the packaging of consumer products, including pharmaceuticals.[167] An example of the latter is the cumulation of patent, trademark, and copyright protection that can cumulate on a pharmaceutical, the first protecting the compound/product and/or process of making the compound, the second protecting the shape and/or color of the pill made with the patented compound and

---

[160] Bangui Agreement, *supra* note 23.

[161] *Id.* at Art. 8(1)(a). *See also* Kongolo (2000), p. 717.

[162] Bangui Agreement, *supra* note 23, art. 2.

[163] Deere (2008), p. 240.

[164] Vawda and Shozi (2020), pp. 32–33. In addition, the same regime of regional exhaustion applies to trademarks, which may result in blocking, as possible trademark infringement, also trademarked generic medicines from foreign countries. *See* Calboli and Visser (2020), p. 102.

[165] *See* Calboli, *Avoidable Effects*, *supra* note 3; Ginsburg and Calboli (2020), p. 434. In this chapter, I do not focus on design rights, which nonetheless may remain a relevant area of investigation, even this overlap may be less relevant, in practice, due to the limited duration of design rights, which is generally comparable, or shorter in time than patents rights.

[166] Ginsburg and Calboli (2020), p. 434; Derclaye and Leistner (2011); Moffat (2004), p. 1473.

[167] Ginsburg and Calboli (2020), p. 434.

through the patented process, and the third being the written instructions accompanying the medicines' packaging, or the decoration of the packaging itself.[168] The problematic effects of these overlaps and their application to parallel imports is addressed in this Section.

4.1 *Overview of Overlapping Rights and Enforcement of Copyright to Parallel Imports*

Overlapping IP protection can apply simultaneously or sequentially. In the first case, two or more rights protect the same product at the same time. For example, a pictorial logo or the shape or color of a product—be this product a chocolate, liquor, or a pharmaceutical—can simultaneously enjoy trademark protection as distinctive signs and possibly copyright protection as independent artistic works, in addition to the protection the product may enjoy under patent or design law.[169] Likewise, the labels, instructions, and other literary parts of a products could be protected under copyright in addition to the protection that the products enjoys under patent law. Instead, in the second case, two or more types of protection apply to the same product at different times. For instance, the patent or design granted on a product, or copyright protection on its shape or logo, are set to be limited in time. Instead, trademark protection on a product's logo and possibly shape or color can continue without time limits.[170] Whether they are used simultaneously or sequentially, overlapping rights can prolog and/or enhance the scope of protection of the interested products.

In the context of pharmaceuticals, overlapping protection is often sought for different parts of the medicines or their packaging during or after patent protection. For example, in addition to protecting the names of the pharmaceuticals as marks, trademark registrations are often granted for the shape, colors, and other distinctive features of the medicines.[171] Similarly, logos and decorative or distinctive elements

---

[168] *Id.*

[169] *Id.* For a detailed list of examples, *see* Calboli (2014b), p. 52 [hereinafter Calboli, *Overlapping Rights*]. For examples of overlapping protection between trademarks and patents, in particular applied to pharmaceuticals, see the cases cited *infra* in Part IV.B. *See also* Calboli (2020), p. [hereinafter Calboli, *Trademark Protection for Medicines*]. *See also* the contributions in Overlapping Intellectual Property Rights (Neil Wilkof & Shamnad Basheer eds., 2012.

[170] Ginsburg and Calboli (2020), p. 434. For famous cases in the U.S., *see Frederick Warne & Co. v. Book Sales, Inc.*, 481 F. Supp. 1191, 1196 (S.D.N.Y. 1979); *Walt Disney Prods. v. Air Pirates*, 581 F.2d 751 (9th Cir. 1978) (finding that both copyright and trademark permissible on Disney comic book characters); *Universal City Studios v. J.A.R. Sales, Inc.*, 216 U.S.P.Q. 679 (C.D. Cal. 1982) (discussing the protection of the "E.T." motion picture character).

[171] For several relevant examples in the U.S., *see* U.S. Trademark Registration Nos. 2,593,407 (Pfizer Inc.; Viagra pill; diamond shape and color blue); 2,625,335 (Glaxo Group; Flovent HFA inhaler; tethered cap, mouthpiece covering shape, edge shapes); 2,679,181 (Gilead Sciences, Inc.; Viread pill; almond shape and color blue); 3,812,561 (Glaxo Group; Advair diskus inhaler; unique

applied to the packaging, or the labels, product instructions, or similar features of the pharmaceuticals could be protected as copyrighted works.[172]

The justification for overlapping IP rights rests on several elements: the broad definition of protectable subject matter (the item to be protected and the individual scope of protection of the type of products or individual product features); the lack of a comprehensive normative system prohibiting the possibility to cumulate separate types of IP protection in the same product, or different features of the same product; and the lack of a comprehensive system prohibiting, as misuse or abuse of rights, the enforcement of IP protection outside the traditional scope of protection.[173] Even though national variations subsist regarding the treatment of overlapping rights in individual nations, overlapping IP protection is generally accepted.[174] Some exclusions apply regarding the protection of the functional elements and additional protection under trademarks or copyright.[175] Still, in most countries, there are no

round design, color purple, color white, and wave patterns); 5,018,105 (Gilead Sciences, Inc.; Harvoni pill; diamond shape, light-orange color, and identification number); 5,018,106 (Gilead Sciences, Inc.; Sovaldi pill; oval shape, light-yellow color, and identification number); 5,030,567 (Gilead Sciences, Inc.; Truvada pill: oblong shape, color blue, word engraving); 5,298,494 (Eli Lilly and Co.; Olumiant pill; color light pink, oval/oblong shape, and word engraving); 5,435,196 (Teva Respiratory; AirDuo RespiClick inhaler; colors yellow and white); 5,614,245 (Glaxo Group; Seretide evohaler; color purple Pantone Matching System 2587). *See also* Calboli, *Trademark Protection for Medicines, supra* note 170.

[172]In the U.S., for example, the following are registered: U.S. Copyright Registration Nos. TX0004141715 (Pfizer, Inc.; Zyrtec (certirizine Hydrochloride) tablets for oral use; copyright registration for the product label); TX0004065039 (Abbott Laboratories; Advera, Specialized, complete nutrition, clinically proven effective nutritional management; copyright registration for the product label); TX0004068652 (Abbott Laboratories: Pedialyte oral electrolyte maintenance solution; copyright registration for the product label); TX0004862188 (Novartis Crop Protection, Inc.: AAtrex 4L herbicide : CGA 7L38BB 052 : 2/12 gallons, US standard measure: copyright registration for the directions for use and conditions of sale and warranty); TX0001650844 (Merck & Company, Inc.: Clinoril (selindac/ M S D:), copyright registration for the product information summary); TX0001135773 (Merck & Company, Inc.: Cosmegen (dactinomycin, M S D), actinomycin D, injection; copyright registration for the product label).

[173]*See* Calboli (2014b), p. 58.

[174]For example, in 2013, the United Kingdom eliminated the prohibition of cumulating copyright and design protection. The Enterprise and Regulatory Reforms Act 2013 extended copyright protection also to artistic works that have been reproduced more than 50 times. *See* Enterprise and Regulatory Reforms Act 2013, § 74 (U.K.) http://www.legislation.gov.uk/ukpga/2013/24/section/74/enacted.

[175]In the U.S., *see TrafFix Devices v. Mktg. Displays*, 532 U.S. 23, 32 (2001); see also McKenna (2012), pp. 823, 824 (advocating for a broader application of the doctrine of functionality and prohibiting overlaps). In the EU, *see* Case C-299/99, Philips v. Remington, 2002 E.C.R. I-05475, ECLI:EU:C:2002:377; Case C-48/09, Lego Juris v. OHIM, 2010 E.C.R. I-08403, ECLI:EU:C:2010:516; Case C-30/15, Simba Toys v. European Union Intellectual Property Office (EUIPO), 2016 EUR-Lex-62014TJ0687, ECLI:EU:C:2016:849. *See also* the contributions in The Protection of Non-Traditional Trademarks: Critical Perspectives (Irene Calboli & Martin Senftleben eds., 2018).

bright line rules also in this respect and the decision frequently falls with the courts.[176]

To date, several national decision related to overlapping rights in the context of parallel imports have focused on the mutual overlap between copyright or trademark rights, the use of copyright for incidental product features,[177] and the overlap between patent and trademark rights.[178] In the reminder of this section, I address the overlap between copyright and trademarks and the use of copyright on incidental feature, including the use copyright protection against generic pharmaceuticals. The use of copyright in this context is particularly pernicious. Copyright protection applies without the need of registration or other formalities across all members of the Berne Convention for the Protection of Literary and Artistic Works, which makes its enforcement with respect to pharmaceuticals both inexpensive and applicable worldwide without the need to market the product in the countries where protection is sought. Trademark protection is also useful, but is based on national registration and/or national use. Moreover, marks are deemed abandoned after a few years of non-use. Still, trademark protection's primary advantage remains the potential for perpetual protection as trademarks can be renewed for an unlimited number of times while copyright also expires.[179]

The overlap between trademark and copyright protection came to the attention of the courts first in Australia, a country practicing international trademark exhaustion but national copyright exhaustion.[180] In 1986, however, this strategy went too far when the parallel imports of liqueur bottles were stopped based on infringement of the copyright in the labels affixed to the bottles.[181] Considerable criticism followed this decision, and in turn the Australian Parliament deliberated to introduce Section 44C into the Copyright Act to prevent similar situations in the future. The new provision specifically prohibits against invoking copyright protection (and national copyright exhaustion) in the context of parallel imports. The provision reads that "[t]he copyright in a work a copy of which is, or is on, or embodied in, a non-infringing accessory to an article is not infringed by importing the accessory with the article"[182]—"accessory" being defined as: labels, packaging, containers,

---

[176] Australia, Singapore, and other parts of the Commonwealth practice a demarcation between copyright and design protection regarding artistic works that are reproduced in series. In particular, creators generally lose copyright protection in artistic works when the works are industrially applied (more than 50 copies of the work are made) or when the work is registered, or could be registered, as a design (the owner must then rely on the Designs Act). *See, e.g.*, Copyright Act 1968 (Cth) §§ 75, 77, and 77A (Austl.); Singapore Copyright Act of 1987, §§ 69, 70, and 74 (2006) (Sing.).

[177] *See* Calboli (2014b).

[178] *See infra* discussion and cases cited in Part IV.B.

[179] Ginsburg and Calboli (2020), p. 434.

[180] *See, e.g.*, Calboli and LaFrance (2013), p. 1.

[181] R A & A Bailey & Co. Ltd. v. Boccaccio Pty. Ltd. (1986) 6 IPR 279.

[182] *Copyright Amendment Act (No. 1) 1998* (Cth.) [Austl.] (amending § 10(1) and adding ss. 44C, 112C).

instructions, warranties, "or other information," as well as instructional sound recording or films, "provided with the article."[183]

IP holders played a similar game in the U.S. and Canada, until the respective Supreme Courts called it off. In the U.S., the 2013 decision in *Kirtsaeng v. Wiley and Sons*[184] clarified that the Copyright Act provides for a system of international exhaustion. Previously, however, the majority of courts supported that the combined reading of Section 109(a) and Section 602(a)(1) of the Copyright Act prescribed national copyright exhaustion.[185] Before *Kirtsaeng*, IP holders used copyright protection to block parallel imports of otherwise legitimate products—famous examples were shampoos bottles[186] and sports watches.[187] Similarly, Canada practices international trademark exhaustion and national copyright exhaustion.[188] In *Euro-Excellence, Inc. v. Kraft Canada*, Kraft sued an importer for copyright infringement for the importation of chocolate bars.[189] The Supreme Court found the imports to be lawful, however, even though it reached its decision "on contractual grounds."[190] In 2013, Professor Mary LaFrance and I[191] proposed a legislative provision be implemented in the U.S. similar to the amendment approved in Australia in order to prohibit the enforcement of a claim for copyright infringement on "accessory copyright."[192] A revision of copyright law to this extent would prevent misuses of copyright law to block the parallel imports of otherwise legitimate products, in particular when the claim for copyright infringement refers to accessories or nonessential parts of the products.[193] Even though the US currently applies international exhaustion both for patents and copyrights, a similar

---

[183] *Id.* In 2003, the Australian legislature expanded this list, and added that a "computer program," "electronic literary or music item," or "sound recording" that is part of or combined with imported articles are also "accessories. *Copyright Amendment (Parallel Importation) Act 2003* (Cth.) [Austl.]. *See* Polo/Lauren Co. LP v. Ziliani Holdings Pty. Ltd. [2008] 75 I.P.R. 143 (F.C.A.) (applying the provisions and finding that parallel imports of polo shirts were not infringing). *See* Ghosh and Calboli (2018), pp. 148–152.

[184] *Kirtsaeng v. John Wiley & Sons, Inc.*, 133 S. Ct. 1351, 1358 (2013).

[185] For a detailed reconstruction of doctrine of copyright exhaustion in the U.S., *see* Calboli (2014c), p. 75; Ghosh and Calboli (2018), p. 116.

[186] *Quality King Distribs., Inc. v. L'Anza Research Int'l, Inc.*, 523 U.S. 135 (1998).

[187] *Costco Wholesale Corp. v. Omega, S.A.*, 131 S. Ct. 565 (2010).

[188] *See* Ghosh and Calboli (2018), p. 122.

[189] Euro-Excellence Inc. v. Kraft Canada Inc., [2007] 3 S.C.R. 20, 2007 SCC 37.

[190] *Id.*

[191] Calboli and LaFrance (2013), p. 1.

[192] *Id.* at 266-72 (referring also to the relevant case law in Australia).

[193] *See supra* note 172 listing examples of copyright registration for medicines in the U.S. For an example of attempt to enforce copyright against a generic pharmaceuticals producer, see SmithKline Beecham Consumer Healthcare, L.P. v. Watson Pharms., Inc. 211 F.3d 21 (2d Cir. 2000) (holding that copyright liability does not attach to the use by the seller of a generic medicine of the label of the same medicine by the originator company, the Nicorette gum, after the generic seller had obtained FDA approval to sell the medicine).

amendment would prevent the opportunity for future strategic overlaps, should the law again be amended toward a system of national exhaustion.

Attempts by the pharmaceutical industry to use copyright law have been acknowledged in the U.S. and Australia, for example, even though this use was not with respect to parallel imports of genuine products but to block the introduction to market of generics nationwide. In 2000, the U.S., an originator company attempted to block the distribution of a generic claiming copyright infringement on the FDA-approved labelling that the generic manufactured used. This claim was rejected by the court based on the fact that the Hatch-Waxman Act requires the use of the "same" labelling and accordingly this requirement trumps the possibility to claim copyright infringement on pharmaceutical labels. Still, the court stated that copyright protection could be used, not regarding labels, but other materials such as advertising.[194] Similarly, in Australia, in 2008, an originator company claimed copyright infringement against a generic producer because of the reproduction of the legally required product information of the medicine. This claim was eventually also rejected and led to adoption of another amendment in Australia: the Therapeutic Goods Legislation Amendment (Copyright) Bill 2011, which was passed in 2001 and introduced Section 44BA to the Copyright Act.[195]

In Norway, however, the pharmaceutical industry attempted to claim copyright infringement against parallel imports within the EU/EEA. This attempt was also rejected.[196] Notably, the Norwegian Medicines Control Agency had provided notice to the industry that it would allow parallel importers to use the official Summaries of Product Characteristic (SPCs) given by originator companies for the purpose of seeking the importing authorization for intra EEA parallel imports. Astra Norge sued the Norwegian government on the claim that this infringed its copyright in the SPCs. The court of first instance ruled in favor of Astra Norge, but the court of appeal referred asked to the EFTA court if this decision would violate the EU Directive on marketing authorizations.[197] In conclusion, the EFTA Court ruled that indeed a finding of copyright infringement would represent a measure having equivalent

[194] *SmithKline Beecham*, 211 F.3d 21. *See* Tsien (2014), p. 334, 366.

[195] *Therapeutic Goods Legislation Amendment (Copyright) Bill 2011 (Cth)* [Austl.] (adding s. 44BA). According to the new provision the copyright infringement cannot be invoked: "2 ...: (a) supplying, in Australia, some or all of any product information that is approved... in relation to medicine; (b) reproducing, in Australia, [this] information ...; (c) publishing, in Australia, [this] information ...; (d) communicating, in Australia, [this] information ...; (e) adapting, in Australia, [this] information ...; to the extent that the supply, reproduction, publication, communication or adaptation is for a purpose related to the safe and effective use of the medicine referred to in paragraph (a)." Moreover, "3. An act done in Australia that is ancillary or incidental to a supply, reproduction, publication, communication or adaptation referred to in subsection (2) is not an infringement of any copyright ..." I am grateful to Luigi Palombi for pointing me to this specific amendment.

[196] This is reported by Stothers (2007), p. 426 (citing the decision Case E-1/98 Norway v. Astra Norge [1998] EFTA Court Reports 140).

[197] *Id.*

effect to a quantitative restriction and a disguised restriction to EU/EEA trade.[198] Once again, the principle of free movement in the EEA prevailed over the attempt to use copyright (or other IP rights) to block intra EU/EEA parallel trade. Ultimately these various attempts demonstrate that IP holder always try to use multiple avenues to pursue their interests, the enforcement of copyright to features of the packaging or information annexed to the medicines being also one of these avenues.

4.2 Enforcement of Trademark Rights to Parallel Imports of Pharmaceuticals

In addition to (attempting to) enforce copyright protection, an additional avenue to attempt to block the parallel imports of pharmaceuticals, and products in general, is the enforcement of trademark protection for products that may still be protected by patents or whose patent protection has expired.

The advantage of this overlap is obvious when the country of importation practices international exhaustion for patents but national exhaustion for trademarks, as the imports can then be blocked as a trademark infringement. For example, amongst the countries analyzed in Part III, several of the countries practicing international patent exhaustion have no clear policy in the area and apply instead national trademark exhaustion.[199] This is the case, for example in LDCs in ASEAN, Cambodia and Lao PDR,[200] which block parallel imports under trademark law. Also in Thailand, which does not have an express position on trademark exhaustion in general, it has been noted that trademark law can be invoked to block the imports of pharmaceuticals not imported directly by the trademark holders.[201] Another country practicing national trademark exhaustion is Brazil, with the exception of the instance where the trademark holder has not restricted in licensing agreements against parallel imports into Brazil or does not have a licensee in Brazil.[202] Unfortunately,

---

[198] *Id.*

[199] Ghosh and Calboli (2018), p. 65. *See also* Grigoriadis (2014).

[200] *See* Law Concerning Marks, Trade Names and Acts of Unfair Competition of the Kingdom of Cambodia, Art. 11(c) (Cambodia); Lao PDR Law, *supra* note 81, at art. 57(3) lit. 1.

[201] *See* Lifescience Asia-Pacific Network, A Comparative Overview of Distribution and Marketing of Drugs in Asia-Pacific:, p. 49. https://corrs.com.au/site-uploads/images/PDFs/Insights/article-IP-comparative-overview-of-distribution-and-marketing-of-drugs-across-asia-pacific.pdf (noting that, in Thailand, "parallel imports are not permitted in the pharmaceutical sector because it is mandatory for a company to preliminarily obtain an import license and product registration locally" and that "the FDA will not accept an application for a product with a trademark that is identical to other products in the Thai market, unless this product has the same manufacturer and the manufacturer has given its authorization to use and sell the product.").

[202] Brazilian IP Law, *supra* note 112, Art. 132 (III). *See also* Grigoriadis (2014), pp. 457–458 (highlighting that Brazil practices national trademark exhaustion even though it is a Member State of Mercosur, which establishes the principle of international exhaustion under Article 13 of the

information is not readily available at this time regarding the position several African countries, in particular LDCs, adopt on trademark exhaustion. Still, there are no doubts the effect of the limitations invoked under a system of national exhaustion are very relevant, as they can contribute to effectively blocking medicines from entering the countries allowing these imports under patent law.

IP holders have invoked trademark law to block the parallel imports also within regions that practice regional exhaustion, notably in the EU. However, the CJEU resisted the IP overlaps game and, in most instances, ruled in favor of parallel imports. As mentioned above, free movement of goods is one of the fundamental freedoms of the EU, and the CJEU long made it clear that the exercise of IP rights cannot trump free movement. Moreover, the CJEU designed the principle "mutual recognition" according to which Member States should accept "the sale in [their] territory of a product lawfully produced and marketed in another Member" even when the "technical or quality requirements ... differ from those imposed on [their] domestic products."[203] In other words, genuine products of materially different quality cannot be blocked within the EU/EEA as long as they comply with national standards, which today have largely been replaced with EU standards. However, in the EU cases in question, parallel importers repackaged the pharmaceuticals—thus, the products carried differences in quality not because the trademark holder had produced them as such, but because the importers had altered the quality of the packaging. Yet, the CJEU still allowed the imports.[204]

In particular, the CJEU supported trademark rights could not be enforced against repackaged parallel imported medicines when "the repackaging did not adversely affect the original condition of the product" and that "the trade mark owner receives prior notice of the marketing of the repackaged product."[205] In *Bristol-Myers Squibb v. Paranova*,[206] the Court created a specific list of conditions for the repackaging and stated that: (1) it should be necessary to market the product in the country of importation; (2) does not affect the original condition of the product inside the packaging; (3) clearly states who repackaged the product and the name of the manufacturer; (4) does not damage the reputation of the trademark or of its holder; and (5) the importer gives notice to the trademark holder before the repackaged

Protocol on Harmonization of Norms on Intellectual Property in Mercosur in Matters of Trademarks, Indications of Source and Appellations of Origin adopted in 1995).

[203] Commission Communication No. C 256/2, Communication from the Commission concerning the consequences of the judgment given by the Court of Justice on 20 Feb. 1979 in Case 120/78, 1980 O.J. (C 256) 2, 2–3 (EC). The CJEU developed the principle of "mutual recognition" in Case 120/78, Rewe-Zentral AG v. Bundesmonopolverwaltung fur Branntwein, 1979 E.C.R. 649 (*Cassis de Dijon*).

[204] *See* Stothers (2016), pp. 171–175.

[205] Hoffmann-La Roche v Centrafarm, 1978 E.C.R at 1166. *See* Stothers (2016), pp. 171–172.

[206] Joined Cases 427, 429 & 436/93, Bristol-Myers Squibb v. Paranova 1996 E.C.R. I-3457. *See* Stothers (2016), pp. 172–173.

product is put for sale, and, on demand, supplies her with a specimen.[207] In addition, the CJEU ruled that even changing the mark on the packaging (with the mark used by trademark holders in the country of importation) was not grounds to prohibit parallel imports if the trademark holders deliberately used different marks in different EU countries.[208] This constituted, according to the Court, a "disguised restriction on trade between Member States" under the rule of Article 36 of the Treaty[209] as long as[210] the mark's replacement is "objectively necessary"[211] and not only for "the parallel importer . . . to secure a commercial advantage."[212] Still, despite these supportive rulings regarding parallel imports of pharmaceuticals, the CJEU also ruled a decade ago the unauthorized repackaging and relabeling of genuine products may constitute "legitimate reasons" against parallel trade within the EU/EEA when this may lead to consumer confusion or provoke unfair detriment to a mark's reputation.[213]

Using trademark protection can prove useful to block parallel imports not only when a country practices national exhaustion but also when it follows a system of international trademark exhaustion.[214] Notably, under the rule of several national trademark laws—the U.S., Canada, India, China, Korea, Singapore, amongst others—IP holders can oppose parallel imports under a regime of international exhaustion when the quality of the imported products is different of those sold nationally, even if the products are genuine and were first marketed by IP holders in foreign markets.[215] This principle is based on the idea trademarks indicate to

[207] Several cases followed from these "BMS conditions," which frequently were resolved in favor of parallel importers. *See* Stothers (2016), p. 172 (citing C-143/00, Boehinger Ingelheim v. Swingward, 2002 E.C.R. I-3759; Case C-348/04, Boehinger Ingelheim v. Swingward, 2002 E.C.R. I-3759, as applied by the English Court of Appeal in [2008] EWCA (Civ) 83; Joined Cases C-400/09 and C-207/10, Orifarm v. Merck Sharp & Dohme, 2011 E.C.R. I-7063). As we have seen in Section III regarding the Specific Mechanism, the requirement to notify the originator of the pharmaceuticals remains, however, an important condition to fulfil by parallel importers. Courts have rules that failure to notify will result in finding of infringement. *See Id.* at 173 (citing Hollister v. Medik Ostomy Supplies, [2012] EWCA (Civ) 1419, [2012] W.L.R 327 (Eng.)).

[208] Case 3/78, Centrafarm BV v. American Home Prods. Co., 1978 E.C.R. 1823.

[209] *Id.* at 1841–1842.

[210] Case C-379/97, Pharmacia & Upjohn v. Paranova, 1999 E.C.R. I-6927.

[211] *Id.* at I – 6967–6969.

[212] *Id. See* Stothers (2016), pp. 174–175 (citing Specialty Euro. Pharm. v. Doncaster Pharms. Ltd., [2015] EWCA (Civ) 54, [69], [2015] W.L.R.).

[213] Case C-59/08, Copad, SA v. Christian Dior Couture SA, 2009 E.C.R I- 03421 (stating that a trademark owner may oppose the unauthorized sale of luxury goods to discount stores by a licensee if the sale could damage the reputation of the mark). *See* Calboli, *Reviewing Trademark Exhaustion*, *supra* note 10, at 261–262.

[214] *See, e.g.*, Calboli (2011), p. 1241; LaFrance (2013), p. 45.

[215] Ghosh and Calboli (2018), p. 65; Grigoriadis (2014).

consumers origin and consistent quality.[216] Accordingly, consumers could be confused when they rely on the mark affixed to the paralleled imported products, but these products are "materially different" in quality.[217] Small quality differences often apply to products marketed in different countries because of national standards or producers' choices (or marketing partitioning strategy by IP holders).[218] In some countries, like the U.S. and Singapore, this rule is mitigated by the use of disclaimers—in other words, the products can still be lawfully imported as long as the importers properly labels the products indicating their origin and quality dispelling the risk of consumer confusion.[219] Yet, in an action for infringement, it is up to national courts to decide the extent they could find these disclaimers weigh against a likelihood of consumer confusion. Courts in the U.S., for example, have interpreted the concept of "material differences" broadly, to include a large set of product features and accessories and have blocked parallel imports accordingly.[220]

In summary, it is not surprising that the pharmaceutical industry considers trademark protection as an important avenue to block parallel imports even though the courts have frequently denied their claims. Considering the expansion of trademark protection, that can protect today the packaging but also the color and shape of several pharmaceuticals, and the length that this protection grants due to the possibility to renew the protection indefinitely, we will certainly continue to see more activity in this respect.

---

[216] *See* Landes and Posner (1987), pp. 265–266 ("[T]rademark law . . . can best be explained on the hypothesis that the law is trying to promote economic efficiency."); *see also* Economides (1988), p. 523, 526; Kratzke (1991), pp. 199, 205.

[217] *See* Schechter (1927), p. 813, 818 ("The true functions of the trademark are, then, to identify a product as satisfactory and thereby to stimulate further purchases by the consuming public."); Sanders and Maniatis (1993), p. 406.

[218] Calboli (2011), p. 1271.

[219] Tariff Act, 19 U.S.C. § 1307 (1930). "This product is not a product authorized by the United States trademark owner for importation and is physically and materially different from the authorized product." The disclaimer must be "designed to remain on the product until the first point of sale to a retail customer in the United States." 19 C.F.R. § 133.23(b).

[220] In the US, for example, *see Societe Des Produits Nestle S.A. v. Casa Helvetia, Inc.*, 982 F.2d 633, 639 n.7 (1st Cir. 1992) ; *Lever Bros. Co. v. U.S.*, 877 F.2d 101, 103, 108 (D.C. Cir. 1989); *Dial Corp. v. Encina Corp.*, 643 F. Supp. 951, 952 (S.D. Fla. 1986); *Ferrero U.S.A., Inc. v. Ozak Trading, Inc.*, 753 F. Supp. 1240, 1243, 1247 (D.N.J.), *aff'd*, 935 F.2d. 1281 (3rd Cir. 1991); *El Greco Leather Prods. Co. v. Shoe World, Inc.*, 806 F.2d 392 (2d Cir. 1986).

5 Conclusion: A Call for a Wider Application of the Flexibility of Article 6 of the TRIPS Agreement in Developing and Least Developed Countries

In the light of the above, what conclusions could be derived from the comparative review offered by this chapter regarding domestic policies on patents exhaustion and the application of overlapping IP right to the parallel imports of pharmaceuticals?

At the outset, the analysis elaborated in this chapter confirms that the national treatment of the principle of IP exhaustion remains a highly complex legal question across different jurisdictions. This is even more true regarding pharmaceuticals considering how many countries apply differentiated rules or have recently changed their national laws to address these imports. As I anticipated in the Introduction, this review also confirms that the principle of IP exhaustion remains a relevant tool for countries' international trade policies, including for trade in pharmaceuticals. In turn, it is still important to engage in scholarly discussions on this area, even though other factors—from marketing approvals, to import authorizations, or contractual restrictions—can affect the admissibility of these imports into national markets. For example, domestic policies providing for national exhaustion can become the ultimate barrier against parallel imports of pharmaceuticals in the instances in which national governments do grant the necessary regulatory approvals (or recognize specific foreign approvals) to these products. To the contrary, domestic policies on international exhaustion would become the decisive factor to permit these imports into national markets. In addition to patent exhaustion, domestic policies on trademark or copyright exhaustion can also be used as effective barrier to the parallel imports of pharmaceuticals, including generics.

More specifically, the comparative review presented in this chapter highlights that, twenty-five years after the adoption of the TRIPS Agreement, a number of national governments are using more actively the flexibility offered by Article 6 of the TRIPS Agreements in order to frame national solutions on the application of the principle of IP exhaustion in ways that best fit their international and domestic trade-related interest. Several countries, developing and developed countries, have undergone specific revisions of their national laws in this respect, and the interpretation of the principle of exhaustion has been debated at large by national courts in the past several decades. In general, both national legislators and judges seem to have acquired a better understanding of the possible applications of this principle. National and international economic studies have also been prepared to assist policy makers in determining the economic implications of legislative choices in this area. Interestingly, several developed countries, including the US and Canada, have changed their national policies from national to international patent exhaustion—even though parallel imports may still be blocked in several countries through (enforceable) contractual restrictions and, with respect to pharmaceuticals, by the mentioned regulatory requirements.

To the contrary, legislative or judicial reforms in favour of more liberal policies on IP exhaustion are still not the case for several developing countries and LDCs.

Instead, as noted in this chapter, several of these countries continue to follow a system of national patent exhaustion. For example, this position is followed by several LDCs in Africa. Several developing countries and LDCs even allow for the enforcement of overlapping IP rights in their jurisdictions. As noted in this chapter, the LDCs countries members of OAPI follow a system of regional exhaustion, which remains more restrictive than international exhaustion. These findings, and the limited use of the flexibility of Article 6 of the TRIPS Agreement in these countries, are the most problematic conclusions from the comparative review in this chapter. The reasons for these choices are difficult to identify as the legislative history of these laws cannot be easily reconstructed, but most likely range from the lack of expertise of national legislators, to the lack of economic studies regarding these countries, or the absence of, or low quality technical assistance, or the pressure of foreign governments and business interests, including trade-offs accepted as part of trade agreements or foreign direct investments. Regardless of the reasons, these national policies are problematic as they undermine the possibility, for these countries, to import less costly products, including pharmaceuticals. In the case of pharmaceuticals, these national policies could essentially amount to block these countries from accessing life saving medicines for their citizens.

Simply put, it is almost paradoxical, and quite problematic, that several developed countries currently apply less restrictive IP exhaustion policies than a number of developing countries and LDCs, whereas the former have larger economic capabilities and access to products than the latter.

The last conclusion that can be derived from the comparative review in this chapter is the relevance of IP overlaps in this debate, in particular when countries practice different type of exhaustion—national instead of international. In particular, it is clear that only when countries practice international exhaustion for all IP rights overlapping IP protection cannot interfere with the general admissibility of parallel imports in that country—at least from the perspective of the enforcement of IP rights. As a result, pharmaceutical companies have attempted to invoke copyright and trademark rights to block the further circulation of their products or to block the introduction to market of generics. In the EU, in particular, companies have invoked both copyrights, and most frequently trademark protection to try to block the parallel trade of their products within the EU since the late 1970s. As mentioned in this chapter, copyright could be used to protect the packaging, the logos, and the instructions of the medicine. Likewise, trademark rights are granted today not just for the marks affixed to the pharmaceutical packaging, but also on the pills, the devices necessary to inhale the medicines, etc.

This finding, certainly not new but not frequently raised in the debate of scholars, which are experts on patents and pharmaceuticals, is also problematic. In particular, the enforcement of these additional rights can easily nullify the effects of domestic policies on international patent exhaustion, should countries practice national trademark or copyright exhaustion. The same applies, as this chapter illustrates, when IP holders can invoke differences in the quality of the products, even in the case of domestic policies providing for international exhaustion. Again, calling upon these rights may become a last resort for the pharmaceutical industries—which still heavily relies on regulatory schemes to control the international distribution of pharmaceuticals—and courts seem to have rarely supported these claims. Yet, these disputes may not be representative of the number of claims actually used in cease and desists letters to parallel importers and distributors of these products nationally. As it is known, very few disputes reach the courts, due to the time and legal fees involved. Instead, most disputes are settles in highly secretive and nontransparent out-court proceedings where dubious claims and weak rights—such as copyright and trademark protection for pharmaceuticals—can be validated by the parties in the settlements. Ultimately, this large numbers of rights simply offers more arrows that IP holders to throw against parallel imports, and we can be sure that, should the occasion arise, the arrows will be used with full force.

References

Abbott FM (1998) First report (final) to the Committee on International Trade law of the international law association on the subject of parallel importation. J Int Econ Law 1(4):607–636

Abbott FM (2000) Second Report (Final) to the Committee on International Trade Law of the International Law Association on the Subject of the Exhaustion of Intellectual Property Rights and Parallel Importation. 69th Conference of the International Law Association. http://ssrn.com/abstract=1921856

Abbott FM (2002) The Doha declaration on the TRIPS agreement and public health: lighting a dark corner at the WTO. J Int Econ Law 5:469

Abbott FM (2005) The WTO medicines decision: world pharmaceutical trade and the protection of public health. Am J Int Law 99(2):317

Abbott FM (2007) Parallel importation: economic and social welfare dimensions. International Institute for Sustainable Development

Abbott FM (2014) Anti-competitive behaviours and the remedies available for redress. UNDP Competition Guidelines, pp 78–79

Abbott FM (2016) Parallel trade in pharmaceuticals: trade therapy for market distortions. In: Calboli I, Lee E (eds) Research handbook on intellectual property exhaustion and parallel imports. Edward Elgar, Cheltenham, p 145

Abbott FM, Reichman J (2007) The Doha round public health legacy: strategies for the production and diffusion of patented medicines under the amended TRIPS provisions. J Int Econ Law 10 (4):921

Agreement on Trade-Related Aspects of Intellectual Property Rights, April 15, 1994, Marrakesh Agreement Establishing the World Trade Organization, Annex 1C, Legal Instrument—Result of the Uruguay Rounds Vol. 31, 33 I.L.M. 83, 1869 U.N.T.S. 299 (1994)

Bale HE Jr (1999) The conflicts between parallel trade and product access and innovation: the case of pharmaceuticals. J Int Econ Law 1:637

Basheer S, Kochupillai M (2009) TRIPS, patents and parallel imports in India: a proposal for amendment. Indian J Intell Prop Law 2:63

Beier F-K (1990) Industrial property and the free movement of goods in the internal European market. I.I.C. 21(4):131

Benoliel D, Chirwa TJ. The Impact of Pharmaceutical Patents on Health Expenditures in Least-Developed Countries, unpublished paper available at http://law.haifa.ac.il/images/Publications/BenolielChirwa.pdf

Byung-Il K (2004) Parallel imports in Korea. In: Heath C (ed) Parallel Imports in Asia. Kluwer Law International, p 73

Calboli I (2002) Trademark exhaustion in the European Union: community-wide or international? The Saga continues. Marq Intell Prop Law Rev 6:47
Calboli I (2011) Market integration and (the limits of) the first sale rule in North American and European Trademark Law. Santa Clara Law Rev 51:1241
Calboli I (2014a) The (avoidable) effects of territorially different approaches to trademark and copyright exhaustion. In: Calboli I, Lee E (eds) Trademark protection and territoriality challenges in a global economy. Edward Elgar, p 151
Calboli I (2014b) Overlapping rights: the negative effects of trademarking creative works. In: Gervais DJ, Frankel S (eds) The evolution and equilibrium of copyright in the digital age, p 52
Calboli I (2014c) The United States Supreme Court's decision in Kirtsaeng v. Wiley & Sons: an "Inevitable" step in which direction? Int Rev Intell Prop Compet Law 45:75
Calboli I (2019a) The intricate relationship between intellectual property exhaustion and free movement of goods in regional organizations: comparing the EU/EEA, NAFTA, and ASEAN. Queen Mary J Intell Prop 9(1):22
Calboli I (2019b) The ASEAN way or no way? A closer look at the absence of a common rule on intellectual property exhaustion in ASEAN and the impact on the ASEAN market. Univ Pa Asian Law Rev 14(363):363–391
Calboli I (2020) Beyond patents: the problems of non-traditional trademark protection for medicines and heath technologies. Int Rev Intell Prop Compet Law 51:1
Calboli I, LaFrance M (2013) The case for a legislative amendment against "accessory copyright" for Gray market products: what can the U.S. learn from Singapore and Australia?, Singapore J Legal Stud 2013:1
Calboli I, Lee E (eds) (2016) Research handbook on intellectual property exhaustion and parallel imports. Edward Elgar
Calboli I, Senftleben M (eds) (2018) The protection of non-traditional trademarks: critical perspectives. Oxford University Press
Calboli I, Visser C (2020) Regional trademark protection: comparing regional organizations in Europe, Africa, South East Asia, and South America. In: Calboli I, Ginsburg JC (eds) Cambridge handbook on international and comparative trademark law. Cambridge University Press, p 102
Chen Y, Maskus KE (2005) Vertical pricing and parallel imports. J Int Trade Econ Dev 14:1
Chiappetta V (2016) Working towards international harmony on intellectual property exhaustion (and substantive law). In: Calboli I, Lee E (eds) Research handbook on intellectual property exhaustion and parallel imports. Edward Elgar, p 125
Coriat B, Orsenigo L (2014) IPRs, Public Health and the Pharmaceutical Industry: Issues in the Post-2005 TRIPS Agenda. In: Cimoli M, Dosi G, Maskus KE, Okediji RL, Reichman JH (eds) Intellectual property rights legal and economic challenges for development
Correa CM, Correa JI (2016) Parallel imports and the principle of exhaustion of rights in Latin America. In: Calboli I, Lee E (eds) Research handbook on intellectual property exhaustion and parallel imports. Edward Elgar, p 206
Council for TRIPS, Extension of the Transitional Period Under Article 66.1 of the TRIPS Agreement for Least Developed Country Members for Certain Obligations With Respect to Pharmaceutical Products, IP/C/73 (Nov. 6, 2015)
Danzon PM (1998) The economics of parallel trade. Pharmacoeconomics 13:293
De Carvalho NP (2010) The TRIPS Regime of Patents Rights 173
Declaration on the TRIPS Agreement and Public Health (14 November 2001), Doc. WT/ MIN(01)/ DEC/2 (20 Nov. 2001)
Deere C (2008) The Implementation Game: the TRIPS Agreement and the Global Politics of Intellectual Property Reform in Developing Countries 73, 240
Delepierre A et al (2012) Update on counterfeit antibiotics worldwide; Public health risks. Medecine et Maladies Infectieuses 42:247
Derclaye E, Leistner M (2011) Intellectual property overlaps: a European perspective. Hart

dos Santos F, Lowé Gnintedem PJ (2018) Regional frameworks for protection of intellectual property in Africa. In: Oyewunmi A et al (eds) Intellectual property law, practice and management: perspectives from Africa, pp 592, 593–594
Economides NS (1988) The economics of trademarks. Trademark Rep 78(523):526
El-Said MK (2010) Public Health Related TRIPS-plus Provisions in Bilateral Trade Agreements: A Policy Guide for Negotiators and Implementers in the WHO Eastern Mediterranean Region 200–04
Enterprise and Regulatory Reforms Act 2013, § 74 (U.K.). http://www.legislation.gov.uk/ukpga/2013/24/section/74/enacted
Federal Act on Patents for Inventions (SR 232.14 LBI) art. 9a (inserted by No I of the Federal Act of June 22, 2007 (AS 2551 (2009); BBl 1 (2006)), *as amended by* No I of the Federal Act of Dec. 19, 2008, in force since July 1, 2009 (AS 2615 (2009); BBl 303 (2008)) (Switz.)
Fink C (2004) Entering the jungle of intellectual property rights exhaustion and parallel imports. In: Fink C, Maskus KE (eds) Intellectual property rights and development: lessons from recent economic research, p 174
Ganslandt M, Maskus KE (2004) Parallel imports and the pricing of pharmaceutical products: evidence from the European Union. J Health Econ 23:1035
Ganslandt M, Maskus KE (2008) Intellectual property rights, parallel imports, and strategic behavior. In: Maskus KE (ed) Intellectual property, growth, and trade. pp 267–268
Ghosh S, Calboli I (2018) Exhausting intellectual property rights: a comparative law and policy analysis. Cambridge University Press
Ginsburg JC, Calboli I (2020) Overlapping copyright and trademark protection in the United States: more protection and more fair use? In: Ginsburg JC, Calboli I (eds) Cambridge handbook on international and comparative trademark law. Cambridge University Press, p 434
Gopalakrishnan NS, Agitha TG (2012) Indian patent system: the road ahead. In: Shimanami R (ed) The future of the patent system, p 229
Grabowski H (2002) Patents and New Product Development in the Pharmaceutical and Biotechnology Industries. In: Smith CG, O'Donnell JT (eds) The process of new drug discovery and development, 2nd edn. p 533, 535
Graff GD, Pardey PG (2019) Inventions and patenting in Africa: empirical trends from 1970 to 2010. J World Intell Prop 23(4)
Grigoriadis LG (2014) Trade marks and free trade: a global analysis. Springer
Harper J, Gellie B (2006) Counterfeit Medicines: Survey Report
Heath C (1997) Parallel imports and international trade. I.I.C. 28:623
Heath C (2004) Parallel Imports in Japan. In: Heath C (ed) Parallel Imports in Asia. Kluwer Law International, p 51
Heath C (2014a) Exhaustion and patent rights. In: Bagley M, Okediji R (eds) Patent law in global perspective. Oxford University Press, p 419, 424
Heath C (2014b) Patent rights and the "Specific Mechanism" to prevent parallel imports. I.I.C 45:399
Hilke JC (1988) Free trading or free-riding: an examination of the theories and available empirical evidence on Gray market imports. World Compet Law Econ Rev 31:75
Ho CM (2011) Access to Medicine in the Global Economy: Intnational Agreements on Patents and Related Rights 91
Jehoram HC (1992) Harmonising intellectual property law within the European community. I.I.C. 23:622
Jehoram HC (1996) International exhaustion versus importation right: a murky area of intellectual property law. G.R.U.R. Int 4:280
Jehoram HC (1999) Prohibition of parallel imports through intellectual property rights. I.I.C. 30:495, 508
Kanavos P et al (2004) The economic impact of pharmaceutical parallel trade in European Union Member States: a stakeholder analysis, Special Research Paper, London School of Economics

Kanavos P, Costa-i-Font J (2005) Pharmaceutical parallel trade in Europe: stakeholder and competition effects. Econ Policy 758:772–775
Kelesidis T et al (2007) Counterfeit or substandard antimicrobial drugs: a review of the scientific evidence. J Antimicrobial Chemotherapy 60:214
Kohler J (1900) Handbuch des Deutschen Patentrechts. Mannheim, p 452
Kongolo T (2000) The new OAPI agreement as revised in February 1999: complying with TRIPS. J World Intell Prop 3:717
Kratzke WP (1991) Normative economic analysis of trademark law. Memphis State Univ Law Rev 21(199):205
Kumar Rai R, Jagannathan S (2012) Parallel imports and unparallel laws: an examination of the exhaustion doctrine through the lens of pharmaceutical products. Info Comms Technol Law 21:53
Kyle M (2009) Parallel trade in pharmaceuticals: firm responses and competition policy. In: Hawk BE (ed) International antitrust law & policy: Fordham competition law, Juris Publishing, pp 339, 345
Kyle MK (2007) Pharmaceutical price controls and entry strategies. Rev Econ Stat 89:88
LaFrance M (2013) Wag the dog: using incidental intellectual property rights to block parallel imports. Mich Telecomm Technol Law Rev 20:45
Landes WM, Posner RA (1987) Trademark law: an economic perspective. J Law Econ 30 (265):265–266
Malueg DA, Schwartz M (1994) Parallel imports, demand dispersion, and international price discrimination. J Int Econ 37:187
Maskus KE (2000) Parallel imports. World Econ 23:1269
Maskus KE (2001) Parallel imports in pharmaceuticals: implications for competition and prices in developing countries: final report. World Intellectual Property Organization
Maskus KE (2016) Economic Perspectives on Exhaustion and Parallel Imports. In: Calboli I, Lee E (eds) Research handbook on intellectual property exhaustion and parallel imports. Edward Elgar, p 106
McKeith S (2013) Pharmaceutical patents in developing nations: parallel importation and the doctrine of exhaustion. Afr J Legal Stud 6:287
McKenna M (2012) (Dys)functionality. Houston Law Rev 48:823, 824
Moffat VR (2004) Mutant copyrights and backdoor patents: the problem of overlapping intellectual property protection. Berkeley Technol Law J 19:1473
Musungu S, Cecilia Oh (2006) The use of flexibilities in TRIPS by developing countries: can they promote access to medicines?, WHO Study on IPRs, Innovation and Public Health
Musungu SF (2016) The TRIPS agreement and public health. In: Correa CM, Yusuf AA (eds) Intellectual property and international trade: trips agreement, 3rd edn. Kluwer Law International, p 489
National Economic Research Associates, The Economic Consequences of the Choice of Regime in the Area of Trademarks: Final Report for DG XV of the European Commission 76-100 (1999)
Ncube CB (2016) Intellectual property policy, law and administration in Africa. Exploring Continental and Sub-regional Co-operation, p 110
Overlapping Intellectual Property Rights (2012) Wilkof N, Basheer S (eds)
Owoeye O (2015) Access to medicines and parallel trade in patented pharmaceuticals. E.I.P.R. 37 (6):359
Pai Y (2016) The hermeneutics of the patent exhaustion Doctrine in India. In: Calboli I, Lee E (eds) Research handbook on intellectual property exhaustion and parallel imports. Edward Elgar, pp 324, 327
Reichman J, Okediji R, Lianos I, Jacob R, Stothers C. The WTO Compatibility of a Differentiated International Exhaustion Regime Proposed by the Eurasian Economic Community, A Consultancy Report, Research Paper Series, Skolkovo-HSE International Laboratory for Law & Development (on file with author)

Rothchild JA (2016) Exhaustion of intellectual property rights and the principle of territoriality in the United States. In: Calboli I, Lee E (eds) Research handbook on intellectual property exhaustion and parallel imports. Edward Elgar, p 226
Roy S, Saggi K (2012) Equilibrium parallel imports and international market structure. J Int Econ 87:262
Saggi K (2013) Market power in the global economy: the exhaustion and protection of intellectual property. Econ J 123:131
Saggi K (2014) Regional exhaustion of intellectual property. Int J Econ Theory 10:125
Sanders AK, Maniatis SM (1993) A consumer trade mark: protection based on origin and quality. E.I.P.R. 11:406
Schechter FI (1927) The rational basis of trademark protection. Harv Law Rev 40(813):818
Schwartz M (1990) Third-degree price discrimination and output: generalizing a welfare result. Am Econ Rev 80:1259
Shargel L, Kanfer I (eds) (2014) Generic drug product development: solid oral dosage forms, 2nd edn. CRC Press
Shea N (1995) Does the first trade marks directive allow international exhaustion of rights?, E.I.P.R. 10:463
Singham SA (2000) Competition policy and the stimulation of innovation: TRIPS and the interface between competition and patent protection in the pharmaceutical industry. Brooklyn J Int Law 26:363, 407
Stothers CM (2007) Parallel Trade in Europe: Intellectual property. Competition and Regulatory Law
Stothers CM (2016) The European internal market: exhaustion plus. In: Calboli I, Lee E (eds) Research Handbook on intellectual property exhaustion and parallel imports. Edward Elgar pp 169, 178
t'Hoen E (2002) TRIPS, pharmaceutical patents, and access to essential medicines: a long way from Seattle to Doha. Chicago J Int Law 3:27
Taubman A, Wager H, Watal J (2012) A handbook on the WTO TRIPS Agreement, pp 18–20
Tayler Y (ed) (2004) Battling HIV/AIDS: a decision maker's guide to the procurement of medicines and related supplies, World Bank, p 117
The Drug Development Process, United States Food and Drug Administration, https://www.fda.gov/patients/learn-about-drug-and-device-approvals/drug-development-process. Accessed 10 March 2021
Tsien AY (2014) Legal and legislative hurdles to generic drug development approval, and marketing. In: Shargel L, Kanfer I (eds) Generic drug product development: solid oral dosage forms, 2nd edn. 334, 366
United Nations, Committee for Development, List of Least Developed Countries, https://www.un.org/development/desa/dpad/wp-content/uploads/sites/45/publication/ldc_list.pdf
United Nations Interregional Crime and Justice Research Institute, Counterfeit Medicines and Organised Crime (2012)
Valletti TM (2006) Differential pricing, parallel trade, and the incentive to invest. J Int Econ 70:314
Valletti TM, Szymanski S (2006) Parallel trade, international exhaustion and intellectual property rights: a welfare analysis. J Indus Econ 54:499
Varian HR (1985) Price discrimination and social welfare. Am Econ Rev 75:870
Vawda YA, Shozi B (2020) Eighteen years after Doha: an analysis of the use of public health TRIPS flexibilities in Africa. South Centre
Velásquez G, Correa CM, Pinto Ido VH 2020) Intellectual property, human rights and access to medicines: a selected and annotated bibliography, 3rd edn
Verma SK (1998) Exhaustion of intellectual property rights and free trade—Article 6 of the TRIPS agreements. I.I.C. 29:534, 539
Wasserman Rajec SR (2016) Regulatory Responses to International Patent Exhaustion. In: Calboli I, Lee E (eds) Research handbook on intellectual property exhaustion and parallel imports. Edward Elgar, pp 271, 283

WIPO, Questionnaire on Patent Exceptions (in which the respective countries may indicated that there is no clear national position of the issue)

World Intellectual Property Organization, Standard Committee on Patents Electronic Forum, Questionnaire on Exceptions and Limitations of Patent Rights, the database administered by the WIPO's Standing Committee on Patents. https://www.wipo.int/scp/en/exceptions/

World Intellectual Property Organization, Standard Committee on Patents Electronic Forum, Questionnaire on Exceptions and Limitations of Patent Rights, Chile, Exhaustion of Rights, https://www.wipo.int/scp/en/exceptions/replies/chile.html#Q8

Yu X (2004) Exhaustion and Parallel Imports in China. In: Heath C (ed) Parallel Imports in Asia. Kluwer Law International, pp 25–38

Yu X, Yin C (2016) Development of Patent Exhaustion in Mainland China. In: Calboli I, Lee E (eds) Research handbook on intellectual property exhaustion and parallel imports. Edward Elgar, pp 308, 311

Yusuf AA (2016) TRIPS: background, principles and general provisions. In: Correa CM, Yusuf AA (eds) Intellectual property and international trade: trips agreement, 3rd edn. Kluwer Law International, pp 23, 26

Zaheer Abbas M, Riaz S (2017) Compulsory licensing and access to medicines: TRIPS amendment allows export to least-developed countries. J Intell Prop Law Prac 12(6):451

Compulsory Licenses and Government Use: Challenges and Opportunities

Yousuf A. Vawda

Abstract The compulsory licensing and government use flexibility is potentially the most powerful tool available under the TRIPS Agreement, as amplified by the Doha Declaration, to advance public health objectives. Yet, many lower and middle income countries have shown an apparent reluctance to both incorporate them into their national legislation and then utilise them—except in a relatively small number of cases. This contribution analyses the circumstances surrounding this phenomenon. It outlines the context, historical roots of compulsory licensing and its inclusion on the TRIPS Agreement, recent examples of its utility including in two sub-Saharan countries affected by HIV/AIDS, and offers some recommendations. Among the propositions advanced are that the use of such flexibilities is not an insurmountable problem (as the case of Zimbabwe illustrates) and that in the longer term, public health objectives are best advanced by, among others, amending the TRIPS Agreement to exempt health technologies from the ambit of intellectual property protection, and new, alternative models for rewarding innovation in this field of technology being introduced.

1 Introduction

This paper is a contribution to the debate on the role of compulsory licensing and government use to promote access to medicines, and is situated within the context of the universally accepted right of access to health care and medicines.[1] These are two types of authorisation issued to either third parties or the government itself to make use of a patented invention without the consent of the patent holder, under defined circumstances.

[1]For present purposes, the term 'medicines' includes pharmaceutical and biologic products, vaccines, diagnostics and related technologies.

Y. A. Vawda (✉)
School of Law, University of KwaZulu-Natal, Durban, South Africa
e-mail: vawday@ukzn.ac.za

C. M. Correa, R. M. Hilty (eds.), *Access to Medicines and Vaccines*,
https://doi.org/10.1007/978-3-030-83114-1_3

Despite the fact that international law unequivocally establishes access to healthcare as a fundamental right,[2] this right has achieved recognition mostly in theory. The consistent prioritisation by states and multinational corporations of enforcement of intellectual property (IP) rights over promoting access to medicines, has resulted in health technologies becoming increasingly inaccessible. This is largely because of the monopoly pricing of many life-saving medicines—which has rendered them unaffordable and endangered public goods.[3] Such an indictment has been met by the proponents of strong IP protection with the counterclaim that certain provisions in international instruments secure IP protection as a human right. They often cite, in support, the recognition in the ICESCR of the right to the 'protection of the moral and material interests resulting from any scientific, literary or artistic production of which he is author'.[4] However, this sub-article must not be read in isolation, and is counterbalanced by another, which recognises everyone's right 'to enjoy the benefits of scientific progress and its applications'[5] which, it is argued, must trump any IP claims.

This tension between IP protection and access to health has been the subject of a number of international commissions and, most recently, the UN Secretary-General's High Level Panel on Access to Medicines in 2016.[6] One of the Panel's key recommendations directly references the need for adoption and use of compulsory licensing legislation:

> Governments should adopt and implement legislation that facilitates the issuance of compulsory licenses. Such legislation must be designed to effectuate quick, fair, predictable and implementable compulsory licenses for legitimate public health needs, and particularly with regards to essential medicines. The use of compulsory licensing must be based on the provisions found in the Doha Declaration and the grounds for the issuance of compulsory licenses left to the discretion of governments.[7]

It is in this context that compulsory licences and government use provisions in IP law are advanced as both important safeguards against abusive practices by IP rights holders, and enablers of the public's right to access medicines at affordable prices.

In theory, the compulsory licence and government use flexibility is one of the most powerful tools available under the 1994 WTO Agreement on Trade Related

[2]For example, in the Universal Declaration of Human Rights https://www.ohchr.org/EN/UDHR/Documents/UDHR_Translations/eng.pdf (UDHR), the International Covenant on Economic Social and Cultural Rights https://www.ohchr.org/Documents/ProfessionalInterest/cescr.pdf (ICESCR), and a host of other international and regional instruments.

[3]Vawda and Baker (2013). http://www.scielo.org.za/scielo.php?script=sci_arttext&pid=S1996-20962013000100004#top119.

[4]UDHR, art 27(2) and ICESCR art 15(1)(c).

[5]ICESCR, art 15(1)(b).

[6]United Nations (2016), http://www.unsgaccessmeds.org/final-report.

[7]United Nations (2016), recommendation 2.6.1 (b). In addition, recommendation 2.6.1 (c) urges the revision and adoption of the paragraph 6 decision.

Aspects of Intellectual Property Rights (TRIPS Agreement)[8] (as amplified by the Doha Declaration[9]) to advance public health objectives. This is because is removes the patent holder's exclusive right to work the patent. Despite these options having been recognised internationally since as far back as the Paris Convention in 1883[10] (as elaborated below), and more recently in Article 31 of the TRIPS Agreement, and with increasing use particularly in the wake of the HIV/AIDS pandemic, many lower and middle income countries (LMICs) have shown an apparent reluctance to fully engage with these mechanisms. They have firstly, not universally incorporated these and other flexibilities into their national legislation and, secondly, where they are available in their legislation, failed or refused to utilise them—except in a relatively small number of cases.[11]

"The lack of appropriate national legislation for the full implementation of such flexibilities remains one of the greatest difficulties for some developing countries. At the international level, there is a need to improve the legal and technical assistance offered to these countries with respect to intellectual property and public health. In the 16 years since the Doha Declaration, technical assistance has been insufficient or inappropriate."[12] This comment highlights the twin problems of the failure to incorporate the flexibilities in national legislation, and the lack of sufficient and, importantly, appropriate technical assistance.

There are of course multiple other difficulties to be surmounted. They include: political and economic pressures by countries which house IP-rich industries not to use the flexibilities;[13] the lack of political will by the governments of LMICs, as well as of some regional IP organisations;[14] the lack of technical, legal and regulatory capacity to process such applications; and the legal and judicial culture existent in

[8] Trade-Related Aspects of Intellectual Property Rights [WTO] https://www.wto.org/english/docs_e/legal_e/27-trips_03_e.htm.

[9] Declaration on the TRIPS agreement and public health [WTO] https://www.wto.org/english/thewto_e/minist_e/min01_e/mindecl_trips_e.htm.

[10] As elaborated below in Sect. 2.

[11] See, for example, Ellen 't Hoen, *The Global Politics of Pharmaceutical Monopoly Power. Drug patents, access, innovation and the application of the WTO Doha Declaration on TRIPS and Public Health* (2009) https://www.msfaccess.org/sites/default/files/MSF_assets/Access/Docs/ACCESS_book_GlobalPolitics_tHoen_ENG_2009.pdf.

[12] Correa and Velasquez (2019) South Centre Research Papers 85 https://www.southcentre.int/wp-content/uploads/2019/04/RP85_Access-to-Medicines-Experiences-with-Compulsory-Licenses-and-Government-Use-The-Case-of-Hepatitis-C_EN.pdf.

[13] This problem was most recently highlighted in the case of Colombia's attempts to issue a compulsory licence on *imatinib*, as indicated by its Minister of Health to a meeting of the World Health Assembly. See WIPO (2017) WIPO Standing Committee on the Law of Patents https://www.wipo.int/edocs/mdocs/scp/en/scp_27/scp_27_6.pdf, 3.

[14] Sangeeta Shashikant, "The African Regional Intellectual Property Organization (ARIPO) Protocol on Patents: Implications for Access to Medicines" [2014] South Centre Research Paper No 56, 6.

many countries whose intellectual property law has its genesis in the period of colonialism.[15]

This paper's sights are more modest. It reviews the distinct responses of two countries caught in the epicentre of the HIV/AIDS pandemic in sub-Saharan Africa (namely Zimbabwe and South Africa), to understand their respective approaches to the use of compulsory licensing and government use and the barriers that need to be confronted, and to explore some future directions for policy and legal reform in this thematic area.

2 Historical and Conceptual Roots

A compulsory licence is an authorisation granted by a government allowing third parties to produce a patented product or to utilise a patented process without the consent of the patent holder, and which use will not amount to an infringement of the patent. The grant of a compulsory licence constitutes a proactive governmental intervention when market forces result in a disequilibrium between the objectives of rewarding innovation and ensuring social and economic welfare.[16] They 'ensure an efficient operation of innovation markets by avoiding the risk that patents themselves become barriers to invention and innovation ... (and) ... (a)s policy tools, compulsory licences help to ensure that patent protection remains properly balanced with other socio-economic interests.'[17]

The first iteration of the term 'compulsory licence' in an international instrument is to be found in the Paris Convention of 1883[18] which, although it does not itself define the term, provides for its grant 'to prevent the abuses which might result from the exercise of the exclusive rights conferred by the patent, for example, failure to work.'[19] The earliest recorded references to compulsory licences are found in the Venice Patent Law of 1474.[20] This was followed by the UK Statute of Monopolies of 1623 and has, over the past few centuries, been received into the national laws of many jurisdictions.[21] In similar vein, 'government use' or 'crown use' is a grant by

[15] Vawda (2018) South Centre Research Papers 90, 16–18.

[16] For a history of the evolution of intellectual property, compulsory licences and related issues, see May and Sell (2006).

[17] Max Planck Institute (2014), p. 9 https://www.mpg.de/8133454/Patent-Declaration1.pdf.

[18] Paris Convention for the Protection of Industrial Property of March 20, 1883 https://www.wipo.int/edocs/lexdocs/treaties/en/paris/trt_paris_001en.pdf.

[19] Paris Convention for the Protection of Industrial Property of March 20, 1883, art 5A(2).

[20] See Editorial (2012) http://thailawforum.com/articles/Trips-and-access-to-medicines-India-and-Thailand-2.html.

[21] Correa (1999) Trade-Related Agenda, Development and Equity, Working Papers https://www.iatp.org/sites/default/files/Intellectual_Property_Rights_and_the_Use_of_Co.pdf. accessed 26 January 2020. For a background of the use of compulsory licensing in other jurisdictions, see Ellen 't Hoen, *The Global Politics of Pharmaceutical Monopoly Power. Drug patents, access,*

the government, to itself or other entities or contractees acting on behalf of government, to make use of a patented product or process without the consent of the patent holder. Its origin is frequently attributed to UK law.[22] In both instances of compulsory licences and government use, a royalty is required to be paid to the patent holder.[23] In the case of compulsory licences, prior negotiation for a voluntary licence on reasonable commercial terms and within a reasonable period of time is also a requirement.[24] This requirement is waived in cases of national emergency or other circumstances of extreme urgency, or in cases of public non-commercial use (government use)[25] or to remedy a practice that has been determined after a judicial or administrative process to be anti-competitive.[26]

The availability and use of compulsory licensing in the pharmaceutical sector was apparently limited during the early twentieth century, as many countries excluded such products from patentability.[27] Nonetheless, there are examples of its use in industrialised countries, for example, early instances of use in Canada[28] resulted in some of the lowest prices for medicines, while in the UK[29] the 'crown use' provisions have been effectively deployed to secure generic medicines for the National Health Service. The US,[30] too, has a long history of government use licences under 28 U.S.C. section 1498, especially for federal programmes involving defence equipment as well as medicines. In terms of this expeditious provision, the government was able to procure cheaper generic drugs in the 1960s at less than 1% of their list price together with a reasonable royalty.[31] And recently, during the 2001 anthrax

innovation and the application of the WTO Doha Declaration on TRIPS and Public Health (2009), 41–44.

[22] Patents, Designs, and Trade Marks Act of 1883, s 27(2) https://archive.org/stream / patentsdesignsa01britgoog/patentsdesignsa01britgoog_djvu.txt.

[23] Trade-Related Aspects of Intellectual Property Rights [WTO], art 31(h) requires the payment of 'adequate remuneration'.

[24] Trade-Related Aspects of Intellectual Property Rights [WTO], art 31(b).

[25] Trade-Related Aspects of Intellectual Property Rights [WTO], art 31(b).

[26] Trade-Related Aspects of Intellectual Property Rights [WTO], art 31(k).

[27] Ellen 't Hoen, *The Global Politics of Pharmaceutical Monopoly Power. Drug patents, access, innovation and the application of the WTO Doha Declaration on TRIPS and Public Health* (2009), 40.

[28] Ellen 't Hoen, *The Global Politics of Pharmaceutical Monopoly Power. Drug patents, access, innovation and the application of the WTO Doha Declaration on TRIPS and Public Health* (2009), 41.

[29] Ellen 't Hoen, *The Global Politics of Pharmaceutical Monopoly Power. Drug patents, access, innovation and the application of the WTO Doha Declaration on TRIPS and Public Health* (2009), 42.

[30] Ellen 't Hoen, *The Global Politics of Pharmaceutical Monopoly Power. Drug patents, access, innovation and the application of the WTO Doha Declaration on TRIPS and Public Health* (2009), 43.

[31] Brennan et al. (2016) "A Prescription for Excessive Drug Pricing: Leveraging Government Patent Use for Health (2016), p. 275 https://yjolt.org/sites/default/files/kapczynski_18yjolt275_gk_0_0.pdf.

scare, Canada and the US were willing to consider invoking this flexibility, as has Italy on a number of occasions on anti-trust grounds.[32]

3 The TRIPS Framework

Article 31 (a) to (l) of the TRIPS Agreement provides for the grant of compulsory licences provided certain conditions are satisfied and procedures followed. These are:

- Each case must be considered on its individual merits;
- The proposed user must have made a prior attempt to obtain a voluntary licence from the right holder on reasonable commercial terms, which attempt has not been successful within a reasonable period of time. This requirement is waived (1) in the cases of national emergency or other circumstances of extreme urgency, or in cases of public non-commercial use, although the right holder must be notified; and (2) where a compulsory licence has been granted to remedy anti-competitive practices;
- The scope and duration of use is limited to the purpose for which the use was authorised and such authorisation shall be terminated if and when the circumstances which led to the use cease to exist and are unlikely to recur, subject to the legitimate interests of the licensee being protected;
- The use is non-exclusive, and is non-assignable except with that part of the enterprise or goodwill which enjoys such use;
- The use is to be predominantly for the supply of the domestic market, except when the compulsory licence is issued to remedy anti-competitive practices. (There is now an additional exception for countries with little or no manufacturing capacity under Article 31*bis*);
- The patent holder must be paid adequate remuneration for such use taking into account the economic value of the authorisation, but compensation may be adjusted downwards when a compulsory licence is issued to remedy anti-competitive practices;
- The legal validity of any decision relating to the authorisation of the use, as well as the amount of remuneration, is subject to judicial or other independent review by a "distinct higher authority" in that country; and
- The right holder of a second patent that cannot be exploited without infringing the first patent may receive a licence if the second invention involves an important technical advance of considerable economic significance in relation to the first invention. In such instances, the owner of the first patent shall be entitled to a cross-licence to the second invention on reasonable terms, and the use authorised

[32]Ellen 't Hoen, *The Global Politics of Pharmaceutical Monopoly Power. Drug patents, access, innovation and the application of the WTO Doha Declaration on TRIPS and Public Health* (2009), 41–42.

in the licence on the first invention shall not be assigned without assignment of the second patent.

Article 31 of the TRIPS Agreement does not specify or otherwise limit the grounds upon which licences can be granted. This clarification was one of the key outcomes of the Doha Declaration, namely that each country has the right to grant compulsory licences, to determine the grounds on which to grant them, and to determine what constitutes an emergency or other circumstances of extreme urgency, notably public health crises with no restrictions as to disease coverage or frequency of use.[33] In addition, the TRIPS Council was mandated to find a solution to the problem encountered by countries with insufficient or no manufacturing capacity in their potential use of the compulsory licensing provisions of Article 31.[34] Finally, the Declaration reiterated the freedom of countries to adopt the exhaustion regime of their choice (in order to facilitate parallel importation).[35]

In the wake of the HIV/AIDS pandemic, and buoyed by the Doha Declaration's pro-public health interpretation of the TRIPS Agreement, a significant number of developing countries and LDCs afflicted by this crisis issued a combination of compulsory licences and government use orders to facilitate the acquisition of antiretroviral medicines (ARVs) and, occasionally, medicines for other conditions. Such countries include Brazil, Ecuador, Eritrea, Ghana, India, Indonesia, Malaysia, Mozambique, Thailand, Zambia and Zimbabwe.[36] Further discussion of such use is undertaken below.

Compulsory licences are generally available on a variety of grounds, most notably in relation to patents where the patentee is found to have abused its rights in one manner or another, for example, by excessive pricing, refusals to license, or failure to work, but also where the government wants to ensure alternate sources of medicines supply, to facilitate co-formulations, or even to promote local production. Countries might also consider including judicial licences as an alternative remedy to interdicts in claims of infringement.[37]

[33] Doha Declaration paragraphs 4b and 4c.

[34] The solution proposed and now codified in Article 31*bis* entails onerous procedural requirements on both importing and exporting countries, and has been used only once. See Correa (2019) South Centre Policy Brief N0 57 https://www.southcentre.int/wp-content/uploads/2019/01/PB57_Will-the-Amendment-to-the-TRIPS-Agreement-Enhance-Access-to-Medicines_EN-1.pdf.

[35] Doha Declaration paragraph 4d.

[36] See Khor (2014), p. 24.

[37] See, for example, United Nations Development Programme (2013), p. 39 https://www.undp.org/content/dam/undp/library/hivaids/English/using_law_to_accelerate_treatment_access_in_south_africa_undp_2013.pdf accessed 26 January 2020. This option is discussed in some detail below in the section 'The South Africa case'. (See also, further discussion on judicial licences below).

Table 1 Use of flexibilities against type. Adapted from Medicines Law and Policy (note 38)

Flexibility utilised or intended	Number of uses
TRIPS Art 31 (compulsory licensing, public non-commercial use)	105
Doha Declaration Para 7 (LDC pharmaceutical transition period provision)	46
TRIPS Art 30 (patent exception)	3
Doha Declaration Para 5(d) (parallel importation)	1
TOTAL	155

4 A Scan of the Use of TRIPS Flexibilities

The most comprehensive data currently available on the use of flexibilities are those compiled by Medicines Law and Policy.[38] It records some 155 instances of the use of various TRIPS flexibilities since 2001 in 82 countries across the spectrum of WTO classification (least developed countries, developing countries, high-income countries).

In terms of the relevant flexibility invoked, the majority (105) were in respect of compulsory licensing and government use, followed by the LDC pharmaceutical transition period provision (46), which provides a total waiver from recognizing or enforcing pharmaceutical patents and data protections (Table 1).

A recent update by the South Centre records further uses of compulsory licensing in Russia, in 2019, and Israel, in 2020, the latter in the wake of the COVID-19 pandemic.[39]

It is evident that the compulsory licensing and government use flexibility is most favoured by countries seeking to enhance access to medicines, with some of them invoking a public health emergency as the basis for their decision.[40]

Thailand and Ecuador feature as the countries which have made the most frequent use of TRIPS flexibilities, in some 11 instances each. Thailand's example of government use licences is instructive for the manner in which it marshalled the synergies among evidence-based research and analysis, public mobilisation by civil society, and leadership by politicians and policy makers to 'move the mountain'.[41] The effects of the licences issued between 2006 and 2007 on the prices of various medicines have been substantial. The price for the ARV efavirenz dropped by more than 7 times, and lopinavir/ritonavir by 3 times; for the anti-platelet clopidogril by 50 times; and for the anti-cancer drugs docetaxel and letrazole by 24 and 70 times

[38] Medicines Law and Policy, "The TRIPS Flexibilities Database" http://tripsflexibilities.medicineslawandpolicy.org/.

[39] See South Centre, "Compulsory Licences and Government Use of Patented Medicines: Precedents Relevant to Address COVID-19" https://ipaccessmeds.southcentre.int/covid-19-pandemic/.

[40] See Khor (2014). Of the 12 countries surveyed Ghana, Mozambique, Eritrea and Zimbabwe premised their licences on the emergency ground.

[41] Wibulpolprasert et al. (2011) https://www.ncbi.nlm.nih.gov/pmc/articles/PMC3180369/.

respectively.[42] Indonesia is another country with multiple uses, having issued compulsory licences for the supply of ARVs on 3 occasions.[43]

According to the TRIPS Flexibilities Database, 40 of the 46 instances of the use of flexibilities by LDCs related to the LDC transition provision. With the exception of Bangladesh[44] there does not appear to be any instances of the use of this flexibility prior to the Doha Declaration. It is therefore significant that there has been a surge in the use of this flexibility post-Doha. Additionally, in terms of the most recent extension of the waiver until 2033, the exemption relates not only to pharmaceutical patents, but also to data protection, mailbox obligations and market exclusivity.[45]

Reference has been made to the lack of appropriate technical advice to countries, when formulating their IP laws, in relation to their use of public health flexibilities. In this regard, the situation of the African Regional Intellectual Property Organisation (ARIPO) is instructive. A 2014 study on the ARIPO Protocol on Patents[46] revealed that the effective use of TRIPS flexibilities by countries in the East African Community (EAC), for example, has been constrained by the workings of ARIPO, which processes the majority of patent applications for that region. Further, that its current *modus operandi* 'does not facilitate the full use of TRIPS flexibilities and instead erects patent barriers to the importation and local production of affordable medicines.'[47] A recent analysis by Baker of the ARIPO-commissioned 'Comparative Study of the Industrial Property Laws of ARIPO Member States' (Comparative Study) criticises it for 'its failure to address the vast majority of TRIPS flexibilities' that are available to its members.[48] These include, among others: the lack of substantive discussion on stringent patentability standards; on the full range of allowable non-inventions and exclusions; on research and education, as well as other exceptions permitted under TRIPS Article 30; on disclosure requirements; on the prerogative of governments to define the grounds for compulsory licences; and on the use of competition policy to address abuse of patents.

---

[42] Khor (2014), p. 13.

[43] Medicines Law and Policy, "The TRIPS Flexibilities Database".

[44] See Gay (2018) https://www.researchgate.net/publication/325206579_Pharmaceutical_Dreams_TRIPS_and_drugs_policy_in_Bangladesh.

[45] UN Committee for Development Policy (2015) https://www.un.org/ldcportal/wto-drugs-patent-waiver-for-ldcs-extended-until-2033/.

[46] Shashikant (2014) South Centre Research Paper No 56 https://www.southcentre.int/wp-content/uploads/2014/11/RP56_The-ARIPO-Protocol-on-Patents_ENl.pdf.

[47] Shashikant (2014) South Centre Research Paper No 56, 45.

[48] Baker (n.d.) "A Full description of WTO TRIPS Flexibilities Available to ARIPO Member States and a Critique of ARIPO's Comparative Study Analyzing and Making Recommendations Concerning Those Flexibilities [2019] http://kelinkenya.org/wp-content/uploads/2019/05/ARIPO-Member-States-obligations-and-flexibilities-under-the-WTO-TRIPS-Agreement-March-2019.pdf.

5 A Tale of Two Countries

This section will focus on two case examples from Southern Africa, regarding neighbouring countries heavily affected by the HIV/AIDS pandemic, and their respective approaches to the use of compulsory licensing and government use for access to medicines.

5.1 The Zimbabwean Case

Zimbabwe's compulsory licensing regime presents an interesting legal framework. The primary statute is the Patents Act,[49] which has undergone three rounds of amendments (in 2001, and twice in 2002) to make it TRIPS-compliant. The Act contains, in addition to provisions for compulsory licensing and government use, special provisions for government use during particular emergencies.

In addition, there is extensive resort to secondary legislation, such as statutory letters or instruments, to support this framework. Statutory instruments are a form of legislation which allow the provisions of an Act of Parliament to be subsequently brought into force without Parliament having to pass a new Act. They are derived from UK law, Zimbabwe having been a former British colony. The Statutory Instrument or Government Notice is thus a form of delegated or subsidiary legislation.[50] In Zimbabwe, an Act of Parliament may delegate power to a relevant Minister to make statutory instruments[51] within the scope, and for the purposes, of the particular Act, provided they are consistent with that Act, as well as the Declaration of Rights in Chapter 4 of the country's Constitution.[52]

It should be noted that the range of flexibilities incorporated into the Patents Act includes provisions for: compulsory licensing[53] and government use;[54] parallel importation;[55] early working exception ('test batches');[56] pre-grant opposition to

[49] Patents (Amendment) Act, 1987 Chapter 26:03 (amended by Acts 26/1971, 39/1973 (ss. 39 and 52), 42/1976 (s. 15), 39/1979, 15/1981, 29/1981, 41/1983, 12/1986 (s. 13), 11/1991 (s. 17), 20/1994 (s. 7), 22/2001, 9/2002, 14/2002.)

[50] Statutory Instruments (2008), UK House of Commons Information Office Factsheet L7 Legislative Series https://www.parliament.uk/documents/commons-information-office/l07.pdf.

[51] Delegated or Subsidiary Legislation (undated) Zimbabwe Legal Information Institute https://zimlii.org/content/delegated-or-subsidiary-legislation.

[52] Constitution of Zimbabwe Amendment (No 20) Act (2013). See also, Declaration of Rights (2013), Zimbabwe Human Rights Commission. http://www.zhrc.org.zw/your-rights/.

[53] Patents (Amendment) Act, 1987 Chapter 26:03, ss 30A and 31.

[54] Patents (Amendment) Act, 1987 Chapter 26:03, ss 34 and 35.

[55] Patents (Amendment) Act, 1987 Chapter 26:03, s 24A.

[56] Patents (Amendment) Act, 1987 Chapter 26:03, s 24B.

patents on a wide range of grounds;[57] and revocation on substantially the same grounds as those for opposition to the grant of a patent.[58]

Exemptions are granted from patenting of diagnostic, therapeutic or surgical methods of treatment; plants, animals, micro-organisms, and essentially biological processes for their production.[59]

The requirements of novelty, inventive step and industrial applicability for the grant of a patent are included as grounds for pre-grant opposition should they not be satisfied, but the Act does not address the patentability criteria in any detail, and does not specifically exclude new uses, or new compounds, combinations or admixtures of a known substance from patenting. Neither are there any exceptions for educational, research, experimental and other uses. A 'relative novelty' standard is applicable, as the Act requires that the invention was 'not known or used in Zimbabwe.'[60]

5.1.1 Compulsory Licences

The grounds for compulsory licences are limited to: (1) dependent patents,[61] and (2) several grounds for 'abuse of patent', such as: non-working; failure to meet demand on reasonable terms; refusal to license; and any anti-competitive abuse.[62] In the second set of instances, an applicant has to demonstrate that he or she has not been able to obtain a licence on reasonable terms within 6 months of a request for a voluntary licence, and on the ground that the reasonable requirements of the public with respect to the invention have not been or will not be satisfied.[63] The circumstances which will satisfy the latter criterion are deemed to have occurred if:

- the invention, though capable of being worked in Zimbabwe, is not being worked on a commercial scale and there is no satisfactory reason for non-working;
- such working is being prevented by the importation of the patented article by the patentee or associated persons, namely, persons claiming under him, or directly or indirectly purchasing from him, or against whom he is not taking legal action for infringement;
- the demand for the patented article in Zimbabwe is not being met to an adequate extent and on reasonable terms;[64]

[57] Patents (Amendment) Act, 1987 Chapter 26:03, s 17.

[58] Patents (Amendment) Act, 1987 Chapter 26:03, s 45.

[59] Patents (Amendment) Act, 1987 Chapter 26:03, s 2A.

[60] Patents (Amendment) Act, 1987 Chapter 26:03, s 2(2)(a).

[61] Patents (Amendment) Act, 1987 Chapter 26:03, s 30A.

[62] Patents (Amendment) Act, 1987 Chapter 26:03, s 31.

[63] Patents (Amendment) Act, 1987 Chapter 26:03, s 31(1).

[64] See also footnote 84, and accompanying text. In this regard, it is submitted that the reference to 'reasonable terms' could well include 'unreasonable pricing' of a medicine, particularly in the context of the socio-economic conditions in a particular country.

- by the refusal to grant a licence on reasonable terms, trade or industry in Zimbabwe, or that of any persons trading or the establishment of any new trade or industry in Zimbabwe is being prejudiced, and it is in the public interest that licence(s) be granted;
- trade, industry, or any person(s) engaged therein are being prejudiced by unfair conditions attached by the patentee to the purchase, hire, license or use of the patented article or use or working of the patented process;
- any restrictive condition (such as being in restraint of trade or contrary to public policy) has been inserted into a licensing contract for the sale, lease or use of any article or process protected by the patent; and
- a practice by the patent holder has been determined after a judicial or administrative process to be anti-competitive, in which case the requirement for prior negotiation for a voluntary licence is waived.[65]

The procedure for the application for a compulsory licence is relatively workable. It entails a fully motivated application to the Registrar of Patents in the manner prescribed by the Act; permits the patentee or other person to oppose it; and after consideration of all the submissions, the Registrar may grant the application on appropriate terms, or refuse it.[66] Decisions of the Registrar may be appealed before the Intellectual Property Tribunal.[67] This entails an essentially administrative procedure with recourse to appeal before a quasi-judicial Tribunal.

In addition, the Act apparently also permits a presumptive licence where a patent is in force in respect of a substance capable of being used as food or medicine or in their production.[68] This 'necessity' premise is plausible where the invention is a medicine or other public necessity that is not available to the general public or a significant group of patients. The relevant tribunal shall on application, grant a presumptive licence subject to payment of a reasonable and affordable royalty. Other inventions falling into this category include the process for producing such substances, inventions capable of being used as surgical or curative devices, or in the protection of the environment, or those capable of substantially improving the technological, social and economic development of the country.[69]

5.1.2 Government Use

By far the strongest flexibility in the Act relates to government use and the special provisions as to State use during an emergency. The essence of this use provision is that 'any department of state or any person authorized in writing by the Minister

[65] Patents (Amendment) Act, 1987 Chapter 26:03, ss 31(1), 31(6) and 31(6a).
[66] Patents (Amendment) Act, 1987 Chapter 26:03, ss 31(1) to 31(5).
[67] Patents (Amendment) Act, 1987 Chapter 26:03, s 69.
[68] Patents (Amendment) Act, 1987 Chapter 26:03, s 32(1)(a).
[69] Patents (Amendment) Act, 1987 Chapter 26:03, s 32(1).

(of Justice, Legal and Parliamentary Affairs) may make, use or exercise any invention disclosed in any specification lodged at the Patent Office for the service of the State in accordance with this section.'[70] Section 34(1) is TRIPS-plus to the extent it requires agreement with the patent holder on the terms and conditions of the use,[71] and appears to contradict section 34(5) (which requires that the patent holder need only be informed). It elaborates that the authority may be given either before or after the patent grant, or either before or after the acts for which the authority is given are done, that is, the authority is retrospective in this regard, presumably with an emergency in mind. Secondly, the authority may be given to any person, whether or not he or she is authorised directly or indirectly by the patentee to make, use, exercise or vend the invention.[72] The patentee need only be informed timeously and be furnished with any information required, unless it would be contrary to the public interest to do so.[73]

The Act additionally includes 'Special provisions as to State use during emergency'[74] in terms of which the State and authorised parties shall have the power to make, use, exercise and vend the invention for purposes deemed by the Minister necessary or expedient to achieve a number of identified public interest purposes. In the case of access to pharmaceutical inventions, the relevant provisions relate to the following needs: the maintenance, and securing a sufficiency, of supplies and services essential to both the life and well-being of the community; promoting the productivity of industry, commerce or agriculture; fostering and directing exports and reducing imports of any classes, from all or any countries and for redressing the balance of trade; or generally, ensuring that the whole resources of the community are available for use, and are used, in a manner best calculated to serve the interests of the community.[75]

Employing this framework, the Zimbabwean government issued what appears to be the first government use licence on medicines in the post-Doha era.[76] The licence invokes the following legal provisions:

1. Section 34 of the Patents Act which is the enabling provision for the government use licence (Use of patented inventions for service of the State).

[70] Patents (Amendment) Act, 1987 Chapter 26:03, s 34(1).

[71] Patents (Amendment) Act, 1987 Chapter 26:03, s 34(2). TRIPS Article 31(b) waives this condition in cases of national emergency or other circumstances of extreme urgency, or of public non-commercial use.

[72] Patents (Amendment) Act, 1987 Chapter 26:03, ss 34(4)(a) and (b).

[73] Patents (Amendment) Act, 1987 Chapter 26:03, s 34(5).

[74] Patents (Amendment) Act, 1987 Chapter 26:03, s 35.

[75] Patents (Amendment) Act, 1987 Chapter 26:03, ss 35(1)(b), (c), (d), (e) and (f).

[76] Cecilia (2006) Int. J Intellectual Property Management Vol 1 Nos 1/2, 22-36 https://www.researchgate.net/publication/247835566_Compulsory_licences_Recent_experiences_in_developing_countries.

2. Section 35 of the Patents Act which enables the declaration of an emergency to override, in this case, antiretroviral patents (Special provisions as to State use during emergency).
3. General Notice 240 of 2002: Declaration of Period of Emergency for an initial period of 6 months commencing 24 May 2002 (reproduced below).
4. Statutory Instrument 32 of 2003, extending the period of emergency for a further 5 years (from January 2003 to December 2008).

General Notice 240 of 2002
PATENTS ACT [CHAPTER 26:03]

Declaration of Period of Emergency (HIV/AIDS) Notice 2002

IT is hereby notified that the Minister of Justice, Legal and Parliamentary Affairs has, in terms of section 34 as read with section 35 of the Patents Act [Chapter 26:03] made the following notice:

1. This notice may be cited as the Declaration of Period of Emergency (HIV/AIDS) Notice, 2002.

2. In view of the rapid spread of HIV/AIDS among the population of Zimbabwe, the Minister hereby declares an emergency for a period of six months, with effect from the date of promulgation of this notice, for the purpose of enabling the State or a person authorised by the Minister under section 34 of the Act

(a) to make or use any patented drug, including any antiretroviral drug, used in the treatment of persons suffering from HIV/AIDS or HIV/AIDS related conditions;

(b) to import any generic drug used in the treatment of persons suffering from HIV/AIDS or HIV/AIDS-related conditions.

P. A. CHINAMASA Minister of Justice, Legal and Parliamentary Affairs.

24-5-002

Once the extended period of emergency had been proclaimed, several companies applied for authorisation to supply antiretrovirals, with a locally-registered company Varichem Pharmaceuticals [Pvt] Ltd being granted authority to 'produce antiretroviral or HIV/AIDS-related drugs and supply three-quarters of its produced drugs to State-owned health institutions' at prices that 'shall be fixed subject to price control mechanisms to be determined by the Minister.'[77] Subsequently, another local company Datlabs, and a local agent Omahn, were authorised to import ARVs from Indian companies Ranbaxy and Cipla, respectively. The authorisation did not

[77] As quoted in Cecilia (2006), p. 26.

specify the rate of royalty payable, but it appears that the rate offered was 4% of the value of the generic medicines actually delivered.[78]

5.1.3 Lessons

The provisions discussed above represent an expeditious mechanism to enable access to medicines in the context of a declared public health emergency. A number of important lessons may be drawn from this example.

Firstly the importance of effective enabling legislation, so that clear guidelines are available in the law to institute the use of this flexibility, supplemented by detailed mechanisms in the regulations.

Secondly, an expedient administrative rather than judicial procedure, both for the issuance of a compulsory licence, as well as the operation of the government use licence. It is vital that such a procedure is time-saving and cost-effective.

Thirdly, various other access-friendly considerations were tied in with this public health flexibility, namely: advancing the industrial policy objective of promoting local production; cost-saving measures such as the use of generic medicines; and the employment of price controls to make the medicines affordable to the State.

However, medicines prices generally continue to be high in both the private and public sectors in Zimbabwe, with one study showing that public sector prices were higher than average prices for medicines in seven other African countries,[79] although subsequent public sector prices for essential medicines have declined.[80] Since the establishment of the Unitaid Medicines Patent Pool, and the inclusion in its coverage of all WHO-recommended ARVs, all sub-Saharan African countries are included in the category of eligible countries, rendering the use of flexibilities superfluous for such medicines. However, as there are no such licensing arrangements for a range of other highly-priced essential medicines, the need to utilise TRIPS flexibilities continues to exist.[81]

---

[78] Ibid.

[79] See Gavaza et al. (2009), https://www.researchgate.net/publication/51704733_The_prices_people_pay_for_medicines_in_Zimbabwe.

[80] Marume et al. (2018), https://www.ajol.info/index.php/cajm/article/view/164302.

[81] Hoen et al. (2018), https://joppp.biomedcentral.com/articles/10.1186/s40545-018-0157-7.

5.2 *The South African Case*

5.2.1 Legal Framework

Despite the existence of relevant provisions in over a century of patent legislation,[82] not a single compulsory licence has been granted on a pharmaceutical-related patent in South Africa.[83] The existing legislation provides for compulsory licences in cases of (1) dependent patents,[84] and (2) abuse of patents. In the latter case, the following permissible grounds are enumerated:

- The patented invention is not being worked in the country on a commercial scale or to an adequate extent;
- The demand for the patented article is not being met to an adequate extent and on reasonable terms; (One proposed policy option available in this regard is that 'a price charged by the patent holder that bears no reasonable relation to the marginal or average variable cost of manufacturing the item shall be deemed unreasonable.')[85]
- The refusal to license on reasonable terms prejudices trade, industry or agriculture in the country, and it is in the public interest that a licence be granted; and
- The demand is being met by importation and the price charged is excessive in relation to the price charged in countries of manufacture.[86]

The government use provision states that 'a Minister of State may use an invention for public purposes on such conditions as may be agreed upon with the patentee, or in default of agreement on such conditions as are determined by the commissioner (of patents) on application by or on behalf of such Minister and after hearing the patentee.'[87] The requirement of 'on such conditions as may be agreed upon with the patentee' is, of course, TRIPS-plus in that TRIPS Article 31 (b) expressly waives this requirement in certain circumstances, in particular for public non-commercial use.

For reasons that are explored more fully below, which include the problem of AIDS denialism, pressure from the US government and the legal difficulties of

[82] Patents Act No 57 of 1978, s 56 provides a limited number of grounds for the issuance of compulsory licences, and s 4 permits government use (albeit still requiring prior agreement on the terms).

[83] See, for example: Vawda (2018), https://www.southcentre.int/wp-content/uploads/2018/12/RP90_Compulsory-Licensing-Jurisprudence-in-South-Africa-Do-We-Have-Our-Priorities-Right_EN-1.pdf; Yousuf A Vawda (2013), "Country Case Study: South Africa. In Correa (2013) https://www.southcentre.int/wp-content/uploads/2016/05/Bk_2013_Pharmaceutical-innovation_EN.pdf.

[84] Patents Act 57 of 1978, s 55.

[85] See United Nations Development Programme (2013), p. 68.

[86] Patents Act 57 of 1978, ss 56(a), (c), (d) and (e) respectively.

[87] Patents Act, s 4.

succeeding in compulsory licensing applications,[88] advocates of access to medicines have had to seek other flexibilities to advance their cause.

It has been said that the key to successful rights litigation is both the framing of access issues as human rights claims, as well as having this framing embedded in domestic law.[89] Although South African treatment activists have been successful in framing their access to health care and medicines campaigns in terms of human rights norms, they have been less successful in having this paradigm inserted in IP contests in the courts.[90] Sometimes presented as the use of compulsory licensing in South Africa,[91] the most successful use of a TRIPS flexibility in the country was the invocation of competition law and policy to challenge excessive prices and refusal to licence key ARVs. In the first 2002 *Hazel Tau* case, after the Competition Commission found probable violations and prior to the Competition Tribunal considering the Commission's request to grant anti-competition compulsory licences, the patent holders settled by granting licences to multiple generic companies allowing sales throughout the region, thus increasing affordable access to medicines.[92] The second case, in 2007, involved a complaint against another company on the grounds of refusal to licence.[93] Here again, the company negotiated voluntary licences, with similar results.[94]

In this instance, not only was the general framing in terms of human rights norms evident, but the legislation in terms of which the complaint had been lodged was expressly grounded in transformative and rights-based terms:

> The people of South Africa recognise:
>
> That apartheid and other discriminatory laws and practices of the past resulted in excessive concentrations of ownership and control within the national economy, weak enforcement of anti-competitive trade practices. and unjust restrictions on full and free participation in the economy by all South Africans.
>
> That the economy must be open to greater ownership by a greater number of South Africans.

---

[88] See Sects. 5.2.2, 5.2.3 and 5.2.4 below.

[89] See, for example: Land (2013) https://www.academia.edu/10455316/Human_Rights_Frames_in_IP_Contests?email_work_card=view-paper; and Berger and Kapczynski (2009) Human Rights Advocacy Stories https://papers.ssrn.com/sol3/papers.cfm?abstract_id=1323522.

[90] See discussion below in respect of the approach of South African courts to employing a human rights lens in IP disputes, despite having a strong Bill of Rights in its Constitution.

[91] See Medicines Law and Policy, "The TRIPS Flexibilities Database".

[92] *Hazel Tau and Others v GlaxoSmithKline and Boehringer Ingelheim* (Competition Commission) Case No 2002Sep226, in which patients and civil society organisations complained to the Competition Commission that the named pharmaceutical companies had abused their dominant position in the ARV market, refused to license an essential facility, and engaged in excessive pricing. The Commission found against the companies, and its request to the Competition Tribunal was to order compulsory licences. As indicated, the dispute was settled prior to this hearing with the companies agreeing to grant several voluntary licences for the medicines involved.

[93] *Treatment Action Campaign v MSD (Pty) Ltd & Another* (November 2007) Competition Commission of South Africa.

[94] United Nations Development Programme (2013), pp. 93–95.

> That credible competition law, and effective structures to administer that law are necessary for an efficient functioning economy.
>
> **That an efficient, competitive economic environment, balancing the interests of workers, owners and consumers and focussed on development, will benefit all South Africans.**[95]

This legal text is significant in that it situates competition law in the context of South Africa's history, distorted by apartheid, and outlines a developmental path to the application of competition law in the country.

5.2.2 AIDS Denialism

The unfortunate chapter of AIDS denialism in South Africa's lack of response to the pandemic and the resultant avoidable and unnecessary deaths has now been well documented.[96] In the context of the government's questioning of the connection between HIV and the resulting disease syndrome as well as the efficacy of ARVs and other medicines having rendered the question of treatment highly controversial, prospects for the use of compulsory licences were remote.

5.2.3 US Pressure

Early legal challenges and threats against South Africa, Brazil and Thailand on proposed and purported use of compulsory licences have also been well documented.[97] In addition, over the past two decades, the US has threatened many countries contemplating such use and routinely placed them on its Special 301 Reports under the US Trade Act of 1974. As commentators have noted, while such threats are usually bluster, it has not stopped some countries (such as India and Brazil) from backing down.[98] No doubt, such threats have a chilling effect on countries seeking to preserve their trade relations with the US.

The use of TRIPS flexibilities has increasingly come under attack in recent bilateral and regional trade agreements involving the US. In particular, the US has sought to constrain the use of compulsory licensing by, for example, limiting the

---

[95] Competition Act No 89 of 1998, Preamble. The emphasis here is on the final sentence.

[96] See, for example, Nattrass (2005) https://www.sahistory.org.za/sites/default/files/nattrass_hivaids_policy.pdf; and Geffen and Cameron (2009) Centre for Social Science Research Aids and Society Research Unit, CSSR Working Paper No 257 https://open.uct.ac.za/bitstream/item/22585/Geffen_deadly_hand_denial_2009.pdf?sequence=1.

[97] See, for example: Oxfam (2001), https://oxfamilibrary.openrepository.com/bitstream/handle/10546/620381/bn-access-to-medicines-south-africa-010201-en.pdf?sequence=1&isAllowed=y; Ooms and Hanefeld (2019) https://www.bmj.com/content/bmj/365/bmj.l2098.full.pdf; and Reichman (2009) https://www.ncbi.nlm.nih.gov/pmc/articles/PMC2893582/.

[98] Baker (2018) https://healthgap.org/dont-be-afraid-of-compulsory-licenses-despite-us-threats-special-301-reports-1998-2017-listing-concerns-but-taking-little-action/.

grounds to: remedying anti-competitive practices, or in cases of public non-commercial use, or of national emergency or other circumstances of extreme urgency (as in the Australia-US Free Trade Agreement).[99] This strategy 'has been characterised by a progressive "ratcheting up" of IP protections for pharmaceuticals, with provisions intended to prolong monopolies, support high prices and frustrate market entry of generic medicines—all of which undermine access to affordable medicines.'[100]

In South Africa, neither the government nor the judiciary appears to have had any appetite for compulsory licences, despite the declarations of its representatives at global fora.[101]

Previous calls by civil society and generic manufacturers on the government to implement the provisions of the Patents Act to this end have gone unheeded.[102] Currently, patient groups are again engaging the government to issue compulsory licences in respect of newer ARVs, and drugs for use in the treatment of cancer and tuberculosis.[103]

5.2.4 Judicial Deference

An analysis of compulsory licence applications on pharmaceutical and chemical products before the Commissioner of Patents (High Court) or the Supreme Court of Appeal of South Africa during the period 1978 - 2018 revealed that not a single compulsory licence had been issued, nor has one been issued since the advent of patent legislation in the country in the early twentieth century.[104]

In summary, the case analysis highlighted the following lines of reasoning adopted by the courts in rejecting such applications:

- The failure on the part of the applicant to discharge the evidentiary burden that the patent had been abused.[105]
- The concept of working a patent included exploitation, which was interpreted widely enough to entail working by importation.[106]

[99] See Lopert and Gleeson (2013), pp. 199–223 http://onlinelibrary.wiley.com/doi/10.1111/jlme.12014/abstract.

[100] Lopert and Gleeson (2013), p. 199.

[101] See, for example, WIPO (2016) https://www.wipo.int/edocs/mdocs/scp/en/scp_25/scp_25_6.pdf.

[102] See, for example, Oxfam (2001), pp. 2–3.

[103] See Medicins Sans Frontieres (2015) https://www.msf.org/south-africa-should-override-patent-key-hiv-medicine-after-widespread-stock-out-problem; and Fix the Patent Laws Campaign (2019) https://www.fixthepatentlaws.org/.

[104] Vawda (2018), p. 90.

[105] *Syntheta (Pty) Ltd v Janssen Pharmaceutica NV & Another* 1999 (1) SA 85 SCA.

[106] *Sanachem (Pty) Ltd v British Technology Group PLC* 1992 BP 276 (CP).

- With regard to the amount of remuneration, that it was not unreasonable to charge a royalty which the trade would carry.[107]
- Regarding negotiating reasonable terms for a licence, the court required evidence indicating, with reasonable precision, what reasonable terms are.[108]
- That a charge of unreasonable terms is not established merely on proof that the compulsory licensing applicant can sell the same sort of article at a lower price.[109]

Absent from this formalistic reasoning were any considerations of the level of development of the country, the socio-economic status of the majority of it population, or the impact of the price of the medicines on access to health care.

Of significance is the manner in which the courts have approached the dispute between the patent holder and patent challenger. Thus, in an application *(Aventis)*[110] for, among others, a temporary interdict (injunction) based on an infringement claim against a generic drug manufacturer, the court refused, despite being requested, to consider the impact of the interdict on the supply of medicines and adjudicate the case through the lens of the Constitution and its Bill of Rights.[111] It further took a rather narrow view on the question of awarding damages (royalties) as an alternative to the interdict, holding that this would be tantamount to granting a compulsory licence. Article 44.2 of the TRIPS Agreement permits this option and there is now strong precedent for the granting of judicial, royalty-bearing licences instead of injunctions from the US Supreme Court.[112] Even though the court in *Aventis* acknowledged that the issue of patent validity (which had been challenged) still stood to be determined in revocation proceedings, it refused to accept this less restrictive means of resolving an interim dispute, and appears to have disregarded the social value of the alleged infringing product in its considerations.

There are several other instances of what appear to be deference towards the interests of patent holders. One relates to the anomalous practice in infringement proceedings that, even if it were found that the invention was not patentable, it would remain valid absent a counterclaim for revocation.[113] The effect of this approach is that in infringement proceedings, even if the defence of invalidity is successful thereby defeating an infringement claim, the patent remains on the register, and the proprietor can sue others on the patent.

Another instance where the prerogatives of the patent holder are prioritised are the so-called interlocutory applications for amendments to patent specifications, where the court has relieved the applicant (the patent holder) of the burden of

[107] *Sanachem (Pty) Ltd v British Technology Group PLC* 1992 BP 276 (CP).

[108] *Afitra (Pty) Ltd and Another V Carlton Paper of SA (Pty) Ltd* 1992 BP 331 (CP).

[109] *Afitra (Pty) Ltd and Another V Carlton Paper of SA (Pty) Ltd* 1992 BP 331 (CP).

[110] *Cipla Medpro v Aventis Pharma (139/12); Aventis Pharma SA v Cipla Life Sciences* (138/12) [2012] ZASCA 108 (26 July 2012).

[111] Constitution of the Republic of South Africa (1996).

[112] *eBay Inc. v MercExchange, L.L.C. 547 U.S. 388* (2006). See also the Indian High Court decision of *Hoffman La Roche v. Cipla & Anr,* IA No. 642/2008 in CS (OS) No, 89.2008.

[113] *Strix Ltd v Nu-World Industries (Pty) Ltd* 2016 (1) SA 387 (SCA).

providing full reasons for the amendment.[114] The *Bateman* judgment cites with approval another decision (*Kimberly-Clark*),[115] despite the fact that the latter decision in fact adopts the opposite approach. In addition, this court adopted the approach that 'it is in the public interest that patents should be rectified or validated by way of amendment'[116] without having regard to the impact of the continuing validity of the patent on the broader public interest. Any appreciation of the notion of 'access' as a public interest in relation to an essential product, facility or service is absent.

It is therefore contended that the very architecture of the patent landscape, the rather limited grounds on which an application for a compulsory licence may be brought, combined with the overly formal approach to judicial interpretation and adjudication, including an apparent deference to patent holders over the general public, may be responsible for the dearth of such applications, and hence the lack of their grant. It must be noted in passing that generic manufacturers are unlikely to apply for compulsory licences unless there are sufficient commercial prospects, given that the South African pharmaceuticals market is relatively small. And, as regards those medicines covered by the Medicines Patent Pool, South Africa is already benefiting from this initiative.[117]

5.2.5 New IP Policy Phase I

In 2018 after a protracted civil society-led campaign,[118] the South African Cabinet approved a new IP policy, premised on public health,[119] in recognition of the abject failure of the present system to adequately meet the need of the general public to access affordable medicines. The IP Policy draws its inspiration from the Constitution of South Africa, and recognises that 'there is a need for a comprehensive IP Policy that will promote a holistic, balanced and coordinated approach to IP that is mindful of the many obligations mandated under the South African Constitution.' The policy expressly recognises the need to reform the regime as it relates to compulsory licences, both in terms of their scope and procedure for application, as well as for the establishment of guidelines for expedited government use.[120]

---

114 *Bateman Equipment Ltd and Another v The Wren Group (Pty) Ltd* 2000 (1) SA 649 (SCA).

115 *Kimberly-Clark of South Africa (Pty) Ltd formerly Carlton Paper of South Africa (Pty) Ltd v Proctor & Gamble (Pty) Ltd* (A488/96) [1998] ZASCA 39.

116 *Bateman Equipment Ltd and Another v The Wren Group (Pty) Ltd* 2000 (1) SA 649 (SCA).

117 See footnote 80 and accompanying text.

118 Baker (2015-16), pp. 309–343 documents the origins of such a campaign.

119 Republic of South Africa (2018) https://www.thedti.gov.za/news2018/IP_Policy2018-Phase_I.pdf.

120 Republic of South Africa (2018), p. 28.

6 Compulsory Licensing Options Under TRIPS

As indicated,[121] the TRIPS Agreement does not limit the grounds upon which licences can be granted. The robust discourse over the last two decades around the use of TRIPS flexibilities and, in particular compulsory licensing, had provided policy-makers, legislators and advocacy groups with a panoply of options to consider[122] in relation to various aspects of this flexibility: broad grounds, easy-to-use procedures, and royalty guidelines and rates that are not so onerous that they frustrate generic competition and hence access to affordable medicines.

6.1 Expanded Grounds for Compulsory Licences

The expanded grounds for the issuance of compulsory licences that may be considered are:

- The patent is not worked or not fully worked in the country by the patent holder including that the invention is not available to the public at a reasonably affordable price; or that it has not been worked locally other than by importation and the patent holder fails to demonstrate that it is not economically or technologically feasible to manufacture it in whole or in part in the country;
- The patent is worked by the patent holder or licensee in a form and by means that are harmful to or abusive of the public interest;
- The price charged by the patent holder bears no reasonable relation to the marginal or average variable cost of manufacturing the item and is deemed to be unreasonable;
- The patent can be worked locally on a feasible economy of scale and may benefit the general public; or through a licence granted for importation where it is considered advantageous to do so;
- There is an emergency or other urgent matter of national interest, in which case prior negotiation for a licence on reasonable commercial terms is not required;
- There is a risk of supply interruptions of essential products such as medicines;
- There is a need to promote local production and technology transfer;
- There is any other public interest or public health need;
- The patent holder has been found to have engaged in an anti-competitive practice;
- Where the invention, being a medicine or other public necessity, is not available to the general public or a significant group of patients, the relevant tribunal is

[121] See Sect. 3 above.

[122] These options are drawn primarily from United Nations Development Programme (2013), pp. 57–71; Baker and Vawda (2017), pp. 40–60 https://www.fixthepatentlaws.org/submission-by-university-of-kwazulu-natal-affiliated-academics-on-sa-draft-intellectual-property-policy/.

enabled to grant, on application, a presumptive licence subject to a reasonable and affordable royalty;

- Where the country lacks sufficient capacity to produce a medicine patented in that country, a compulsory licence may be issued for the importation of the product; and conversely for a compulsory licence to be issued in the manufacturing country where that medicine is under patent, for the purpose of supplying a country with insufficient manufacturing capacity, in terms of a streamlined, easy-to-use procedure. Alternatively, to adopt Article 31*bis* of the TRIPS Agreement and the Annex to it;
- The grant of a judicial licence in cases alleging infringement, as a satisfactory and less restrictive alternative to the grant of an interdict or injunction;
- Where it is not possible to execute the licence granted on any of the foregoing grounds based on patent disclosures alone, a compulsory licence may be granted on otherwise confidential manufacturing know-how, subject to prior negotiation, payment of reasonable royalty, and non-exclusivity and non-assignability; and
- Where a product is already on the market while the patent application regarding a needed invention (such as a medicine to respond to an epidemic) is still pending, a provisional compulsory licence may be granted to take effect when the relevant patent/s are granted.

6.2 *Government Use*

With regard to government use licences, these need to be expeditious and easy to implement. The following formulation has been proposed:[123]

- Any properly designated public official or government contractor, domestic or foreign, receiving the authorisation or consent of the government of a country, may make public, non-commercial use of a patent.
- No prior negotiation with the patent holder is required, it being necessary only to promptly notify the holder of such use.
- For the purposes of this provision, the use or manufacture of an invention described in and covered by a patent granted in the country by a contractor, sub-contractor, or any person, firm or corporation for the government and with the authorisation or consent of the government, shall be construed as use for that country.

[123] Baker and Vawda (2017), pp. 47–49.

6.3 Adequate Remuneration

As regards remuneration of the right holder, TRIPS Article 31(f) requires adequate remuneration based on the economic value of the licence in the country issuing it. The following formulation has been proposed:[124]

- Remuneration Guidelines shall specify a normal royalty of 4% of wholesale cost, with an upward adjustment of no more than 2% based on disclosed, extraordinary research and development costs or therapeutic breakthrough in the case of pharmaceuticals. The rate could be adjusted downwards by the same margin based on the use of public funds in the research, or if the holder has already recovered significantly more than its research and development costs as adjusted for risk and opportunity costs.

6.4 Procedures for Compulsory Licensing Applications

As indicated, procedures for compulsory licensing should be expeditious and easy-to-use. Expedited administrative procedures, rather than judicial processes, which are both more time-consuming and expensive, should be used. The TRIPS Agreement requires judicial process only in relation to independent administrative review in respect of the legal validity of a licence and the amount of remuneration.[125] The following formulation has been proposed:[126]

- Examination of an application for a compulsory licence shall be conducted by the relevant authority or tribunal.
- The relevant authority or tribunal shall by notice summon the patent holder and applicant to hear their evidence and opinions, and shall stipulate time periods for the submission of evidence, opinions and other matter.
- Should the patent holder not respond to the notice within 2 months, the patent holder will be presumed to have no objection to the issuance of the compulsory licence.

6.5 Collaboration and Cooperation in the Issuance of CLs

Finally, there are significant benefits to cooperation between countries on the issuance of compulsory licences. Groups of developing countries could, for example, pool their procurement needs and coordinate the proposed use of compulsory

[124]Baker and Vawda, "Submission by University of KwaZulu-Natal-Affiliated Academics", 56–58.
[125]TRIPS Agreement, art 31(i) and (j).
[126]Baker and Vawda (2017), pp. 58–60.

licences for selected medicines, thereby generating sufficient economies of scale to make it viable for generic manufacturers to enter those markets.[127]

An interesting variant of this approach is that permitted by Article 31*bis* of TRIPS:

> With a view to harnessing economies of scale for the purposes of enhancing purchasing power for, and facilitating the local production of, pharmaceutical products: where a developing or least developed country WTO Member is a party to a regional trade agreement . . . at least half of the current membership of which is made up of countries presently on the United Nations list of least developed countries, the obligation of that Member under Article 31(f) shall not apply to the extent necessary to enable a pharmaceutical product produced or imported under a compulsory licence in that Member to be exported to the markets of those other developing or least developed country parties to the regional trade agreement that share the health problem in question. It is understood that this will not prejudice the territorial nature of the patent rights in question.[128]

Thus, for example, all member states of the Southern African Development Community can benefit from this collaborative and pooled procurement mechanism, as 9 of the 15 members are LDCs,[129] or those of the East African Community as well, with 4 of its 5 WTO-member states being LDCs.

A strong case has been made that, for African countries to make optimal use of compulsory licensing, they must develop strong manufacturing capacity in the pharmaceutical sector. This is imperative because, as the emerging economies in Asia have begun 'to implement a more protectionist intellectual property framework, Africa is ill-advised to continue relying on generic manufacturers in Asia for access to affordable pharmaceuticals.'[130] The African Union's Pharmaceutical Manufacturing Plan for Africa[131] has increasingly been promoting national and regional collaboration in order to achieve greater self-sufficiency and a sustainable supply of pharmaceuticals for the continent.

6.6 A Compulsory Licensing Facility

Another novel proposal to address the inadequate and uncoordinated use of compulsory licensing is that of the establishment of a compulsory licensing facility or consortium (CL Facility).[132] In a submission to the UN Secretary-General's High

---

[127] See Reichman (2009), pp. 247–263.

[128] TRIPS Agreement, art 31*bis* 3.

[129] Hoen et al. (2018).

[130] Owoeye (2014), pp. 92, 217 http://www9.who.int/bulletin/volumes/92/3/13-128413/en/.

[131] African Union (2012), https://apps.who.int/medicinedocs/documents/s20186en/s20186en.pdf.

[132] See Baker (2016a) http://www.unsgaccessmeds.org/inbox/2016/2/27/brook-baker?rq=brook%20baker; Baker (2016b) http://www.unsgaccessmeds.org/inbox/2016/2/26/z73kpodxk4jw96mhqe2tivq0sd1g3v.

Level Panel on Access to Medicines, the aims of the proposed CL Facility are stated as being to:

- undertake a series of analyses on all possible options for compulsory licences, the conditions and circumstances of their use, and their implications for access to medicines;
- develop and support the implementation of model legislation effectuating the optimal use of compulsory licences and government use orders; provide technical and advocacy assistance for their adoption and use both nationally and regionally (to enable aggregated markets to sustain production and access to medicines).

7 Conclusion

Developing countries and LDCs, particularly, face many challenges with both the domestication and also the implementation of TRIPS flexibilities, including compulsory licences and government use. Many of these are not insurmountable, such as the need for political will, the ability to resist trade and political pressures, and the engagement of appropriate technical assistance. In some instances, such as in South Africa, there is the additional reluctance of the judicial system to apply access-friendly interpretations of IP law in line with its Constitution and Bill of Rights.

In the two case studies presented here, the prospects for the use of compulsory licensing and government use are not encouraging. Although Zimbabwe used this flexibility in the instances cited more than 10 years ago, it has not done so since then. In South Africa, it has never been used despite many compelling circumstances and strong appeals. There is great expectation that the new IP Policy, once legislated, ought to clear the path for easy use of these forms of licensing. Thereafter it will be entirely up to the political will of government to act on the legislation.

The current COVID-19 pandemic has brought into sharp relief the inequality that exists both among countries of the world, and within them. Access to any vaccines and other therapies that may be developed cannot be guaranteed, because they are likely to be protected by various forms of intellectual property rights, and hence only be available at a high cost. In this context, compulsory licensing and government use remain an important option for, particularly, developing and least developed countries to ensure access to such health technologies.

References

Cases

South Africa

Afitra (Pty) Ltd and Another V Carlton Paper of SA (Pty) Ltd 1992 BP 331 (CP)
Bateman Equipment Ltd and Another v The Wren Group (Pty) Ltd 2000 (1) SA 649 (SCA)
Cipla Medpro v Aventis Pharma (139/12); Aventis Pharma SA v Cipla Life Sciences (138/12) [2012] ZASCA 108 (26 July 2012)
Hazel Tau and Others v GlaxoSmithKline and Boehringer Ingelheim (Competition Commission) Case No 2002Sep226
Kimberly-Clark of South Africa (Pty) Ltd formerly Carlton Paper of South Africa (Pty) Ltd v Proctor & Gamble (Pty) Ltd (A488/96) [1998] ZASCA 39
Sanachem (Pty) Ltd v British Technology Group PLC 1992 BP 276 (CP)
Strix Ltd v Nu-World Industries (Pty) Ltd 2016 (1) SA 387 (SCA)
Syntheta (Pty) Ltd v Janssen Pharmaceutica NV & Another 1999 (1) SA 85 SCA
Treatment Action Campaign v MSD (Pty) Ltd & Another (November 2007) Competition Commission of South Africa

USA

eBay Inc. v MercExchange, L.L.C. 547 U.S. 388 (2006)

India

Hoffman La Roche v. Cipla & Anr, IA No. 642/2008 in CS (OS) No. 89.2008 (India)

Statutes and Statutory Instruments

International

Declaration on the TRIPS agreement and public health [WTO]. https://www.wto.org/english/thewto_e/minist_e/min01_e/mindecl_trips_e.htm. Accessed 23 Feb 2021
International Covenant on Economic Social and Cultural Rights. https://www.ohchr.org/Documents/ProfessionalInterest/cescr.pdf. Accessed 23 Feb 2021
Paris Convention for the Protection of Industrial Property of March 20, 1883. https://www.wipo.int/edocs/lexdocs/treaties/en/paris/trt_paris_001en.pdf. Accessed 23 Feb 2021
Trade-Related Aspects of Intellectual Property Rights [WTO]. https://www.wto.org/english/docs_e/legal_e/27-trips_03_e.htm. Accessed 23 Feb 2021
Universal Declaration of Human Rights. https://www.ohchr.org/EN/UDHR/Documents/UDHR_Translations/eng.pdf. Accessed 23 Feb 2021

United Kingdom

Patents, Designs, and Trade Marks Act of 1883, s 27(2) https://archive.org/stream / patentsdesignsa01britgoog/patentsdesignsa01britgoog_djvu.txt. Accessed 23 Feb 2021
Statutory Instruments (2008) UK House of Commons Information Office Factsheet L7 Legislative Series https://www.parliament.uk/documents/commons-information-office/l07.pdf. Accessed 23 Feb 2021

South Africa

Constitution of the Republic of South Africa, 1996
Patents Act No 57 of 1978

Zimbabwe

Constitution of Zimbabwe Amendment (No 20) Act, 2013
Declaration of Rights (2013) Zimbabwe Human Rights Commission. http://www.zhrc.org.zw/your-rights/. Accessed 23 Feb 2021

Books

Correa CM (ed) (2013) Pharmaceutical innovation, incremental patenting and compulsory licensing. South Centre, Geneva. https://www.southcentre.int/wp-content/uploads/2016/05/Bk_2013_Pharmaceutical-innovation_EN.pdf. Accessed 23 Feb 2021
Khor M (2014) Compulsory license and "Government Use" to promote access to medicines: some examples. Third World Network 24
May C, Sell SK (2006) Intellectual property rights: a critical history. Lynne Rienner Publishers, Boulder

Contributions to Edited Books

Vawda YA (2013) Country case study: South Africa. In: Correa CM (ed) Pharmaceutical innovation, incremental patenting and compulsory licensing. South Centre, Geneva. https://www.southcentre.int/product/pharmaceutical-innovation-incremental-patenting-and-compulsory-licensing/. Accessed 23 Feb 2021

Journal Articles

Baker BK (2015-16) International collaboration on IP and access to medicines: the birth of the S. Africa fix the patents law campaign. NYLS Law Rev 60:309–343
Brennan H et al (2016) A prescription for excessive drug pricing: leveraging

Cecilia O (2006) Compulsory licences: recent experiences in developing countries. Int. J Intellect Property Manag 1(1/2):22–36. https://www.researchgate.net/publication/247835566_Compulsory_licences_Recent_experiences_in_developing_countries. Accessed 23 Feb 2021
Government Patent Use for Health (2016) Yale J Law Technol 18: 275 https://yjolt.org/sites/default/files/kapczynski_18yjolt275_gk_0_0.pdf. Accessed 23 Feb 2021
Hoen E't et al (2018) Patent challenges in the procurement and supply of generic new essential medicines and lessons from HIV in the Southern African Development Community (SADC) region. J Pharm Policy Practice. https://joppp.biomedcentral.com/articles/10.1186/s40545-018-0157-7. Accessed 23 Feb 2021
Lopert R, Gleeson D (2013) The high price of 'Free' trade: US trade agreements and access to medicines. J Law Med Ethics 41(1):199–223. http://onlinelibrary.wiley.com/doi/10.1111/jlme.12014/abstract. Accessed 23 Feb 2021
Ooms G, Hanefeld J (2019) Threat of compulsory licences could increase access to essential medicines. BMJ. https://www.bmj.com/content/bmj/365/bmj.l2098.full.pdf. Accessed 23 February 2021
Reichman JH (2009) Compulsory licensing of patented pharmaceutical inventions: evaluating the options. J Law Med Ethics. https://www.ncbi.nlm.nih.gov/pmc/articles/PMC2893582/. Accessed 23 Feb 2021
Vawda YA, Baker BK (2013) Achieving social justice in the human rights/intellectual property debate: Realising the goal of access to medicines. Afr Human Rights Law J. http://www.scielo.org.za/scielo.php?script=sci_arttext&pid=S1996-20962013000100004#top119. Accessed 23 Feb 2021

Online Journals

Berger JM, Kapczynski A (2009) The story of the TAC case: the potential and limits of socio-economic rights litigation I South Africa. Human Rights Advocacy Stories. https://papers.ssrn.com/sol3/papers.cfm?abstract_id=1323522. Accessed 23 Feb 2021
Correa CM (1999) Intellectual property rights and the use of compulsory licences: options for developing countries. South Centre, Geneva, Trade-Related Agenda, Development and Equity, Working Papers https://www.iatp.org/sites/default/files/Intellectual_Property_Rights_and_the_Use_of_Co.pdf. Accessed 23 Feb 2021
Correa CM (2019) Will the amendment to the TRIPS agreement enhance access to medicines?" South Centre Policy Brief N0 57 https://www.southcentre.int/wp-content/uploads/2019/01/PB57_Will-the-Amendment-to-the-TRIPS-Agreement-Enhance-Access-to-Medicines_EN-1.pdf. Accessed 23 Feb 2021
Correa CM, Velasquez G (2019) Access to medicines: experiences with compulsory licenses and government use – the case of Hepatitis C. South Centre Research Papers 85. https://www.southcentre.int/wp-content/uploads/2019/04/RP85_Access-to-Medicines-Experiences-with-Compulsory-Licenses-and-Government-Use-The-Case-of-Hepatitis-C_EN.pdf. Accessed 23 Feb 2021
Editorial (2012) Compulsory licensing: background. Thailand J Law Policy. http://thailawforum.com/articles/Trips-and-access-to-medicines-India-and-Thailand-2.html. Accessed 26 Jan 2020
Gavaza P et al (2009) The prices people pay for medicines in Zimbabwe. Central Afr J Med. https://www.researchgate.net/publication/51704733_The_prices_people_pay_for_medicines_in_Zimbabwe. Accessed 23 Feb 2021
Gay D (2018) Pharmaceutical dreams: TRIPS and drugs policy in Bangladesh" https://www.researchgate.net/publication/325206579_Pharmaceutical_Dreams_TRIPS_and_drugs_policy_in_Bangladesh. Accessed 23 Feb 2021

Geffen N, Cameron E (2009) The deadly hand of denial: Governance and politically-instigated denialism in South Africa", Centre for Social Science Research Aids and Society Research Unit, CSSR Working Paper No 257 https://open.uct.ac.za/bitstream/item/22585/Geffen_deadly_hand_denial_2009.pdf?sequence=1. Accessed 23 Feb 2021

Land M (2013) Human Rights Frames in IP Contests (uncorrected proof). Oxford University Press, Oxford. https://www.academia.edu/10455316/Human_Rights_Frames_in_IP_Contests?email_work_card=view-paper . Accessed 23 Feb 2021

Marume A et al (2018) Price and availability survey of essential medicines in the Harare province, Zimbabwe. Central African J Med. https://www.ajol.info/index.php/cajm/article/view/164302. Accessed 23 Feb 2021

Shashikant S (2014) The African Regional Intellectual Property Organization (ARIPO) Protocol on patents: implications for access to medicines" South Centre Research Paper No 56 https://www.southcentre.int/wp-content/uploads/2014/11/RP56_The-ARIPO-Protocol-on-Patents_ENl.pdf. Accessed 23 Feb 2021

Vawda YA (2018) Compulsory licensing jurisprudence in South Africa: do we have our priorities right?" South Centre Research Papers 90 https://www.southcentre.int/wp-content/uploads/2018/12/RP90_Compulsory-Licensing-Jurisprudence-in-South-Africa-Do-We-Have-Our-Priorities-Right_EN-1.pdf. Accessed 23 Feb 2021

Wibulpolprasert S, et al (2011) Government use licences in Thailand: The power of evidence, civil movement and political leadership" https://www.ncbi.nlm.nih.gov/pmc/articles/PMC3180369/. Accessed 23 Feb 2021

Command Articles and Law Commission Reports

African Union (2012) Pharmaceutical Manufacturing Action Plan for Africa Business Plan, https://apps.who.int/medicinedocs/documents/s20186en/s20186en.pdf. Accessed 23 Feb 2021

Max Planck Institute (2014) Declaration on Patent Protection: Regulatory Sovereignty under TRIPS, 9 https://www.mpg.de/8133454/Patent-Declaration1.pdf. Accessed 23 Feb 2021

Oxfam (2001) South Africa vs. the Drug Giants – A Challenge to Affordable Medicines. Oxfam Background Briefing February 2001 https://oxfamilibrary.openrepository.com/bitstream/handle/10546/620381/bn-access-to-medicines-south-africa-010201-en.pdf?sequence=1&isAllowed=y. Accessed 23 Feb 2021

Republic of South Africa (2018) Intellectual Property Policy of the Republic of South Africa Phase I https://www.thedti.gov.za/news2018/IP_Policy2018-Phase_I.pdf. Accessed 23 Feb. 2021

UN Committee for Development Policy (2015) WTO drugs patent waiver for LDCs extended until 2033 https://www.un.org/ldcportal/wto-drugs-patent-waiver-for-ldcs-extended-until-2033/. Accessed 23 Feb 2021

United Nations (2016) Secretary-general's high level panel on access to medicines report: promoting innovation and access to health technologies. http://www.unsgaccessmeds.org/final-report. Accessed 23 Feb 2021

United Nations Development Programme (2013) Using law to accelerate treatment access in South Africa: an analysis of patent. Compet Med Law 39. https://www.undp.org/content/dam/undp/library/hivaids/English/using_law_to_accelerate_treatment_access_in_south_africa_undp_2013.pdf. Accessed 23 Feb 2021

WIPO (2016) Standing Committee on the Law of Patents, Twenty-Fifth Session. https://www.wipo.int/edocs/mdocs/scp/en/scp_25/scp_25_6.pdf. Accessed 23 Feb 2021

WIPO (2017) Constraints Faced by Developing Countries and Least Developed Countries (LDCs) in Making Full Use of Patent Flexibilities and Their Impacts on Access to ffordable Especially Essential Medicines for Public Health Purposes in Those Countries: Supplement to Document

SCP/26/5 WIPO Stnding Committee on the Law of Patents https://www.wipo.int/edocs/mdocs/scp/en/scp_27/scp_27_6.pdf, 3. Accessed 23 Feb 2021

Websites and Blogs

Baker B (2016a) Health gap submission to the UNSG's high level panel on access to medicines (1) (unsgaccessmeds.org) http://www.unsgaccessmeds.org/inbox/2016/2/27/brook-baker?rq=brook%20baker. Accessed 23 Feb 2021

Baker B (2016b) Submission to UN Secretary-General's High Level Panel on Access to Medicines"(2) (unsgaccessmeds.org) http://www.unsgaccessmeds.org/inbox/2016/2/26/z73kpodxk4jw96mhqe2tivq0sd1g3v. Accessed 23 Feb 2021

Baker B (2018) Don't Be Afraid of Compulsory Licenses Despite US Threats: Special 301 Reports 1998-2017 – Listing Concerns But Taking Little Action" (*HealthGap*) https://healthgap.org/dont-be-afraid-of-compulsory-licenses-despite-us-threats-special-301-reports-1998-2017-listing-concerns-but-taking-little-action/. Accessed 23 Feb 2021

Baker BK (n.d.) A Full Description of WTO TRIPS Flexibilities Available to ARIPO Member States and a Critique of ARIPO's Comparative Study Analyzing and Making Recommendations Concerning Those Flexibilities. https://www.bu.edu/gdp/files/2020/05/ARIPO-Member-States-obligations-andflexibilities-under-the-WTO-TRIPS-Agreement-March-2019.pdf

Baker BK, Vawda YA (2017) Submission by University of KwaZulu-Natal-Affiliated Academics on The Draft Intellectual Property Policy of the Republic of South Africa Phase 1", 40–60. https://www.fixthepatentlaws.org/submission-by-university-of-kwazulu-natal-affiliated-academics-on-sa-draft-intellectual-property-policy/. Accessed 23 Feb 2021

Fix the Patent Laws Campaign (2019) Minister Mkhize must ensure access to cancer medicine that WHO now considers 'essential'". https://www.fixthepatentlaws.org/. Accessed 23 Feb 2021

Medicines Law and Policy, "The TRIPS Flexibilities Database" http://tripsflexibilities.medicineslawandpolicy.org/. Accessed 23 February 2021

Medicins Sans Frontieres (2015) South Africa should override patent on key HIV medicine after widespread stock out problem: Press Release https://www.msf.org/south-africa-should-override-patent-key-hiv-medicine-after-widespread-stock-out-problem. Accessed 23 Feb 2021

Nattrass N (2005) "AIDS Policy in Post-Apartheid South Africa" (SA History Online) https://www.sahistory.org.za/sites/default/files/nattrass_hivaids_policy.pdf. Accessed 23 Feb 2021

Owoeye OA (2014) Compulsory patent licensing and local drug manufacturing capacity in Africa". Bulletin of the WHO, 92, 217 http://www9.who.int/bulletin/volumes/92/3/13-128413/en/ Accessed 23 Feb 2021

Recommendations Concerning Those Flexibilities (2019). http://kelinkenya.org/wp-content/uploads/2019/05/ARIPO-Member-States-obligations-and-flexibilities-under-the-WTO-TRIPS-Agreement-March-2019.pdf. Accessed 23 Feb 2021

South Centre, "Compulsory Licences and Government Use of Patented Medicines: Precedents Relevant to Address COVID-19" https://ipaccessmeds.southcentre.int/covid-19-pandemic/. Accessed 23 Feb 2021

Zimbabwe Legal Information Institute, "Delegated or Subsidiary Legislation" (undated) https://zimlii.org/content/delegated-or-subsidiary-legislation. Accessed 23 Feb 2021, Chapter 4

Access to CRISPR Genome Editing Technologies: Patents, Human Rights and the Public Interest

Duncan Matthews

Abstract While detailed debates are underway about the scientific and ethical implications of genome editing, this chapter argues that greater attention should be paid to the patent policy issues that these technologies raise. The chapter argues that WTO Members need to consider urgently the implications of patenting genome editing inventions for human rights and the public interest, taking into account Article 27.2 of the TRIPS Agreement, which provides that Members may exclude from patentability inventions, the prevention within their territory of the commercial exploitation of which is necessary to protect *ordre public* or morality. Furthermore, while genome editing has great potential to transform healthcare and the wellbeing in society across a broad range of scientific fields, the granting of patent rights for these technologies will have profound implications for affordability and access, particularly for people living with chronic lifelong illnesses and for future generations not yet born who are at risk of inheriting preventable medical conditions from their parents. The chapter argues that WTO Members need to consider carefully the impact of granting of genome editing patents, balancing the need to reward inventorship while at the same time having regard to implications for affordability, acccss and thc cnjoymcnt of fundamcntal human rights.

1 Introduction

Genome editing technologies hold great potential for scientific research and society. They provide fast, efficient, precise and relatively inexpensive tools to modify the cells of any living organism. Using genome editing techniques, cells of the body (somatic cells) can be modified, potentially curing patients of chronic, lifelong illnesses. Editing the genome of human embryos can also modify the germline identity of human beings, eradicating hereditary diseases in new-born babies and creating resistance to life-threatening conditions for future generations. There is also

D. Matthews (✉)
Queen Mary University of London, London, UK
e-mail: d.n.matthews@qmul.ac.uk

C. M. Correa, R. M. Hilty (eds.), *Access to Medicines and Vaccines*,
https://doi.org/10.1007/978-3-030-83114-1_4

great potential for non-human uses of genome editing technologies. New varieties of plants can be developed that are disease resistant or have a higher crop yield, while new breeds of farmed animals or marine life can be introduced into the food system in order to offer a broader range of options to consumers and to contribute positively to food security.

The great potential of genome editing is due to the fact that it offers a relatively simple tool to change any organism's deoxyribonucleic acid (DNA). This allows genetic material to be added, removed or altered in particular locations in the genome. Genome editing technologies can be divided into four types: zinc finger nucleases (ZFNs), transcription activator-like effector nucleases (TALENs), meganucleuses and CRISPR (Clustered Regularly Interspaced Short Palindromic Repeats). All four work by inducing a natural cellular repair mechanism designed to repair breakages in DNA but the first three are considered more difficult, less precise and more time-consuming process than CRISPR.

Since 2012, CRISPR has been used in combination with Cas9 (CRISPR associated protein number 9, which plays a vital role in the natural immunological defence system of the body) to guide and cut DNA, and therefore alter, a cell's genome. It does not fundamentally differ from the previously known genome editing technologies but the additional advantages of the CRISPR-Cas9 system lie in its ability to provide a faster, cheaper, more accurate and more efficient method than other previously known genome editing techniques.[1] For instance, if there is a mutation in the genome, CRISPR-Cas9 makes it possible to search, delete and even replace it.[2] A simple analogy would be with a word processor document, whereby the author can search for, delete and replace a typographical error.[3]

Yet genome editing raises new challenges in terms of how governance systems regulate technologies and involves key public policy imperatives, particularly those of human rights, fair and equitable access to the benefits of this new technologies' use, and how governance systems can act in the public interest.

In the patent policy debate on genome editing technologies thus far, preliminary studies have already been undertaken into the patentability of CRISPR-Cas9 inventions under United States (U.S.) law,[4] while claims have been made that patent law in Europe is already fit for purpose.[5] Elsewhere, various studies have examined the extent that licensing practices can enable or impede research,[6] how patent-holding

---

[1] See also National Institutes of Health (NIH), U.S. National Library of Medicine, Your Guide to Understanding Genetic Conditions: What Are Genome Editing and CRISPR-Cas9? https://ghr.nlm.nih.gov/primer/genomicresearch/genomeediting

[2] The human genome is about 300 billion letters long and, so far, scientists have identified approximately 6000 mutations.

[3] This analogy with word processing was used, for example, in the presentation by Feng Zhang (Broad Institute) at the Program on Science, Technology and Society Workshop on Editorial Aspirations: Human Integrity at the Frontiers of Biology, 26–28 April 2017, Harvard University.

[4] Deborah (2017), p. 408; Hannah Mosby (2018), p. 579.

[5] All European Academies (ALLEA) (2016).

[6] Sherkow (2017a), p. 565; McMahon (2020) op. cit. n 6.

universities grant exclusive licences to private companies which stand in as surrogates for the institutions themselves,[7] and how ethical licensing can be used as a tool of privately driven governance,[8] with evidence that the private governance function of patents is often overlooked.[9] Other studies have advocated using international law to facilitate agreement on the governing principles,[10] particularly to identify appropriate limitations to the CRISPR toolkit.[11] Elsewhere research exemptions have been advocated as mechanisms to guarantee freedom to operate alongside patent pools, clearing houses and compulsory licences in order to help to facilitate access to patented genome editing technologies.[12]

Rather less attention has been paid to the extent that patents for genome editing technologies can be considered barriers to affordable healthcare that infringe the fundamental rights, particularly the right to health.[13] Greater attention needs to be paid to the extent that the patent issues that CRISPR-based therapies raise can have adverse implications for public health.[14]

Fair and equitable access to healthcare in the context of the right to health is underpinned by the fundamental principle that everyone should have access to the health services they need, when and where they need them, without suffering financial hardship.[15] This principle takes as its legal basis Article 25.1 of the Universal Declaration of Human Rights, 1948, which states explicitly that "([E] veryone has the right to a standard of living adequate for the health and well-being of himself and his family, including food, clothing, housing and medical care..." and by Article 12.1 of the United Nations International Covenant on Economic, Social and Cultural Rights, which states that "[T]he States parties to the present Covenant recognize the right of everyone to the enjoyment of the highest attainable standard of physical and mental health".[16]

This chapter will argue that, in debates about the inter-relationship between patents, fair and equitable access to human genome editing, greater attention needs to be paid to human rights approaches, taking into account the public interest. As such the patent system needs to be considered carefully from a human rights perspective when the governance of genome editing is scrutinised. This human

---

[7] Contreras and Sherkow (2017), p. 698.

[8] Guerrini et al. (2017), p. 22.

[9] McMahon (2020), p. 161.

[10] Tsung-Ling (2019), p. 1.

[11] Sadie (2019), p. 1.

[12] Van Overwalle et al. (2006), p. 143.

[13] For a general discussion see on the relationship between patents, access to healthcare and the right to health see Matthews (2015), pp. 496–512.

[14] For a preliminary study see Sherkow (2017b), p. 667.

[15] *Health is a fundamental human right.* Statement by Dr Tedros Adhanom Ghebreyesus, WHO Director-General, 10 December 2017: https://www.who.int/mediacentre/news/statements/fundamental-human-right/en/.

[16] For further discussion see Matthews (2010), pp. 118–139.

rights approach to the study of patents for genome editing technologies is underdeveloped and, the chapter will argue, must take place if governance institutions are to understand fully the impact of granting of genome editing patents, balancing the need to reward inventorship with affordability, access and the enjoyment of fundamental human rights.

In order to address these issues, the chapter will first provide an explanation of the human genome and how CRISPR-Cas9 genome editing works, highlighting the huge potential genome editing of the germline identity of humans for individuals and for society. The chapter will then turn attention to recent patenting controversies, highlighting the genome editing patent disputes that have already taken place in the U.S. and Europe.

Observed through the lens of recent patent disputes in the U.S. and Europe, the chapter will argue that World Trade Organisation (WTO) Members need to pay greater consideration of the patent policy implications of genome editing. Such consideration is imperative in order to ensure that the granting of private rights can be accommodated on an equitable basis, balanced alongside the need to avoid unnecessary risk (including *ordre public* and morality exceptions under patent law), taking into account human rights principles, meeting public expectations, ensuring fair and equitable access, and acting in the public interest with regard to these potentially transformational healthcare technologies.

By way of limitation, it should be stated from the outset that this chapter is concerned primarily with editing the human germline, given that this specific application of genome editing technologies accords most closely with (and has most immediacy for) concerns about the patent policy implications in terms of the impacts on society outlined above. While it should be acknowledged that many of the issues considered in this chapter apply equally to somatic therapeutic uses (the cells of the body that are not involved in reproduction) and to agricultural or fisheries food production, germline applications will remain the chapter's primary focus.

2 The Human Genome

The human genome is contained in 23 pairs of chromosomes (22 autosomes and 1 pair of sex chromosomes) in a sequence of paired chemical bases that are held together in the long molecules of DNA that are present in almost all the cells of the body. The genome is the complete set of genes—regions of the DNA molecule of varying length that usually encode proteins that perform distinct biological functions—together with interspersed non-coding regions that regulate when the genes are expressed.[17]

[17] Nuffield Council on Bioethics, Genome Editing and Human Reproduction: Social and Ethical Issues (2018), p. 7.

Although all people have similar sets of genes, no two people have exactly the same genome. Even the genomes of "identical" (monozygotic) twins may differ owing to errors in DNA replication and somatic mutations, as well as acquired differences in their epigenomes.[18] Some of the genomic differences between people produce differences in their appearance or in their physiology (known as their "phenotype"), while others have no observable effects. Although genomic differences can be highly significant for the expression of disease-related and other characteristics, many of the differences between people that are observable or medically significant arise from the combined effects of genetic, environmental and biographical factors. The Nuffield Council on Bioethics, for instance, has pointed out that environmental factors can cause changes in genes that may increase susceptibility to cancers.[19]

From time to time, inherited genomic variations result in disease or confer a predisposition to disease. This usually comes about due to small changes in the genome, which may be transmitted to future generations. These changes can affect the production of proteins in cells, as well as the regulatory regions of genes or genes that encode a ribonucleic acid (RNA) product. Inherited genetic conditions include life-limiting conditions such as Duchenne muscular dystrophy and cystic fibrosis. Genetic conditions are also significant causes of infertility, pregnancy loss and neonatal death.[20] Additionally, even the same genetic mutation can differ significantly in terms of the way it is manifested in the people affected (their "phenotype") and the consequences that this may have for the length or quality of their lives. This is because the function of some genes can be modified by other genes, as well as by environmental factors. In the case of single gene disorders, such as Huntingdon's Disease, it is therefore possible that multiple variants in the same genome affect the associated phenotype. These are sometimes referred to as "modifier genes".[21]

Thus far, over 10,000 single gene disorders have been identified which are associated with an alteration in a region of a single gene that affects the biological function of that gene product. Individually, single gene disorders are usually rare, but collectively they affect at least one in every hundred people born worldwide. Since they can be inherited and because of the way humans have evolved, migrated and

[18] The epigenome is a multitude of chemical compounds that can tell the genome what to do. The human genome is the complete assembly of DNA (deoxyribonucleic acid)-about 3 billion base pairs—that makes each individual unique. DNA holds the instructions for building the proteins that carry out a variety of functions in a cell. The epigenome is made up of chemical compounds and proteins that can attach to DNA and direct such actions as turning genes on or off, controlling the production of proteins in particular cells. When epigenomic compounds attach to DNA and modify its function, they are said to have "marked" the genome. These marks do not change the sequence of the DNA. Rather, they change the way cells use the DNA's instructions. The marks are sometimes passed on from cell to cell as cells divide. They also can be passed down from one generation to the next. Source: National Human Genome Research Institute, Epigenomics Fact Sheet: https://www.genome.gov/about-genomics/fact-sheets/Epigenomics-Fact-Sheet.

[19] Nuffield Council on Bioethics (2018), op. cit. n 17, 7.

[20] Zorrilla and Yatsenko (2013), p. 1; Hyde and Schust (2015), p. 5; Wojcik et al. (2018), p. 20.

[21] Nuffield Council on Bioethics (2018), op. cit. n 17, 8.

mixed or, in some cases, become geographically isolated, some genetic disorders tend to be associated with particular ethnic groups.

An example is the blood disorder beta thalassaemia, which occurs more commonly among people of Mediterranean origin; another is sickle cell disease, which is more prevalent in Afro-Caribbean groups. In Europe, one of the most widely known single gene disorders is cystic fibrosis, which arises in children of parents who each have an altered copy of the cystic fibrosis transmembrane conductance regulator gene when the child inherits both mutated alleles. While many genetic disorders are now well understood, many rare genetic disorders have not yet been defined in terms of the genetic mutation responsible.[22]

The Nuffield Council on Bioethics has highlighted the practical consequences of the diffusion of genomics. On the one hand, there will be increasing emphasis in health care on prevention and public health and, on the other, the development of increasingly 'personalised' (and therefore differentiated) medicine. This suggests that, as greater awareness of individuals' susceptibility to illness becomes known through the diffusion of genomics, new obligations will arise for public authorities to provide improved societal conditions (for example, higher-quality environmental standards, such as improved air quality, and equitably provided healthcare). Importantly, knowledge about genomics also raises the question of responsibility on individuals not only for adapting their *own* behaviour and choosing a suitable lifestyle and a suitable material and social environment, but also, potentially, for selecting a genotype that will be expressed in their future children.[23]

Debates about "designer babies" resulting from genetic interventions into pre-implantation embryos in an attempt to influence the traits that resulting children will have are not new.[24] However, these debates have been brought more sharply into focus by the relative ease with which CRISPR genome editing techniques can alter the germline identity of human beings. The National Academies of Sciences, Engineering and Medicine 2017 Report on Human Genome Editing, for instance, draws the distinction between restorative intervention that can alleviate suffering caused by genetically inherited diseases on the one hand, and interventions that improve bodily condition or function beyond what is needed to restore or sustain health, such as enhanced sports prowess, on the other hand.[25]

---

[22] Nuffield Council on Bioethics (2018), op. cit. n 17, 8.

[23] Nuffield Council on Bioethics (2018), op. cit. n 17, 13.

[24] See, for instance, Bonnie Steinbock, Designer babies: choosing our children's genes, *The Lancet* (11 October 2008); Jonietz (2003).

[25] The National Academies of Sciences, Engineering and Medicine, Human Genome Editing: Science, Ethics and Governance, 2017, Consensus Study Report, 145.

3 The CRISPR-Cas9 Genome Editing Technique

The transformative potential of CRISPR-Cas9 first came to public attention in 2012 following the publication of a seminal paper published in *Science* by Jennifer Doudna of University of California Berkeley, Emmanuelle Charpentier, at that time based at Umeå University in Sweden, and their collaborators.[26] The *Science* paper demonstrated that CRISPR-Cas9 can be used to cut and (possibly) edit DNA *in vitro*. Doudna and Charpentier, and also Feng Zhang and George Church at the Broad Institute (an independent research institute that evolved from a decade of research collaborations among scientists at Harvard University and the Massachusetts Institute of Technology), became the names most closely associated with CRISPR-Cas9, while the parallel work of Virginijus Šikšnys was also recognised along with that of Doudna and Charpentier with their joint award of the Kavli Prize in Nanoscience in 2018.

CRISPR-Cas9 was adapted from a naturally occurring genome editing in the bacterial immune system. The bacterial immune system captures snippets of DNA from invading viruses and uses them to create DNA segments known as CRISPR arrays.[27] The CRISPR arrays allow the bacteria to remember the viruses and, if the viruses attack again, the bacteria produce RNA segments from the CRISPR arrays to target virus DNA. The bacteria then use Cas9 or a similar enzyme to cut the DNA apart, which disables the virus.[28]

In the context of CRISPR-Cas9 gene editing in the laboratory, bio-scientists are able to create a small piece of RNA with a short "guide" sequence that attaches (binds) to a specific target sequence of DNA in a genome. The RNA also binds to the Cas9 enzyme and guides it to the targeted location. The Cas9 enzyme then cuts the DNA at the targeted location so that the genome editing can take place.[29] As such, CRISPR-Cas9 has enabled precisely targeted alterations to be performed on DNA sequences in living cells. Working like genetic scissors, the Cas9 nuclease opens both strands of the targeted sequence of DNA to introduce the modification to knock-out the mutation. In this way, genome editing is in effect the ability to develop one-shot genome editing medical treatments.[30] It is being explored in research on a wide variety of diseases, including single-gene disorders such as cystic fibrosis, haemophilia, Huntingdon's disease and sickle cell anaemia, with possible

[26] Jinek et al. (2012), p. 816.

[27] National Institutes of Health (NIH), op. cit. 1.

[28] National Institutes of Health (NIH), op. cit. 1.

[29] The underlying mechanism of CRISPR had also been described previously in Archaea by Francisco Mojica in 1993, who is later said to have coined the term 'CRISPR' in correspondence with a colleague (see: Mojica et al. 1993, pp. 613–621; Davies and Mojica 2018, p. 5) and earlier in bacteria by Ishino and colleagues (see: Ishino et al. 1987, pp. 5429–5433), while the conjunction of CRISPR and CRISPR associate nucleases (CRISPR-Cas) was identified as a proto-immune system from 2007 (see: Barrangou et al. 2007, pp. 1709–1712).

[30] Feng Zhang (Broad Institute), op. cit. n 3.

applications including plant, microbial, animal and human genetic interventions.[31] Genome editing also holds promise for the treatment and prevention of complex diseases such as cancer, heart disease, mental illness and human immunodeficiency virus (HIV) infection.[32]

In order to allow access to embryos for the purpose of editing them, these would be created in a laboratory using a method of in vitro fertilisation (IVF). Perhaps the most plausible application for this would be cases in which the variant predisposed whoever had it to a clinically recognised disease. In this case, it would be necessary to know before the embryo was created that there was a likelihood of it inheriting the disease-causing variant, such as by screening the prospective parents. For instance, individuals might have been alerted to the possible presence of the variant through having an affected relative and through screening.

However, it is important to recognise the uncertainty that continues to exist about the technical efficacy of the procedures currently available. Of particular concern in this regard is whether CRISPR-Cas9 systems faithfully cleave their intended genomic target without uncontrolled cutting of other sequences ("off-target events") in ways that would make them unsafe for clinical use. The Nuffield Council on Bioethics has also pointed to uncertainty over whether the HDR pathway can be recruited to produce the desired genome change at sufficiently high frequencies for effective clinical use or, if so, how.[33]

There are widespread concerns that CRISPR-based genome editing may result in unintended effects in terms of both off-target effects and mutations of human embryos and of incidental editing.[34] Kosicki, Tomberg and Bradley, for example, found DNA damage that included deletions of thousands of DNA bases, including at spots far from the edit.[35] In some instances deletions can silence genes that should be active and, in other instances, activate genes that should be silent, including cancer-causing genes.[36]

[31] See also Nordberg et al. (2018), pp. 36–83: 37.

[32] National Institutes of Health (NIH), op. cit., n 1.

[33] Nuffield Council on Bioethics (2018), op. cit. n 17, 36. Homology directed repair (HDR) is a naturally occurring nucleic acid repair system that can be used to modify genomes in many organisms, including humans. HDR is initiated by the presence of double strand breaks (DSBs) in DNA.

[34] For the US Food and Drug Administration (FDA), off-target effects would usually be assessed in relation to toxicity of a drug. How the off-target effects of gene editing can be assessed is less clear, given that mutations will perhaps occur two or three generations later.

[35] Kosicki et al. (2018), p. 765.

[36] Sharon Begley, 'Potential DNA damage from CRISPR has been "seriously underestimated" study finds', 16 July 2018, STAT News: https://www.statnews.com/2018/07/16/crispr-potential-dna-damage-underestimated/.

4 Lulu and Nana: The Chinese Genome-Edited Twins "Immune from HIV"

Widespread public awareness of the possible negative implications and controversies associated with the use of genome editing to edit the human germline identity became the focus of global attention in November 2018 when a Chinese researcher at the Southern University of Science and Technology of China in Shenzhen, Dr. He Jiankui, revealed at the Second International Summit on Human Genome Editing in Hong Kong that, as a result of his research, he had implanted into a female patient embryos that had been edited to disable the genetic pathway HIV uses to infect cells and twins had been born whose embryonic genomes had been edited.[37] Dr. He claimed to have disabled a gene called CCR5, which encodes a protein that allows HIV to enter cells. Dr. He was seeking to mimic a mutation that is present in about 6–8% of the population and which helps to protect them from HIV infection.

Concerns were raised in the scientific community that Dr. He might have inadvertently caused mutations in other parts of the genome, which could have unpredictable health consequences.[38] If the gene has been disabled, the twin girls born with CCR5 disabled could be vulnerable to other diseases. CCR5, for instance, is already thought to help people fight off, for example, the effects of West Nile virus.[39]

Dr. He was widely condemned by the global scientific community for violating long-standing scientific principles and ethical norms through the application of his research. Subsequently, on 21 January 2019, the Southern University of Science and Technology in Shenzhen announced that Dr. He had been dismissed from his post following an investigation by the Guangdong Health Ministry.[40] By the end of 2019 a court in Shenzhen had found He and two collaborators guilty of conducting illegal medical practices when they had forged ethical review documents and misled doctors into unknowingly implanting gene-edited embryos into two women.[41]

[37] Cyranoski and Ledford (2018), pp. 607–608, https://www.nature.com/articles/d41586-018-07545-0.

[38] Most recently, see Antonio Regalado, *MIT Technology Review*, December 3, 2019: https://www.technologyreview.com/s/614764/chinas-crispr-babies-read-exclusive-excerpts-he-jiankui-paper/.

[39] Cyranoski and Ledford (2018) op. cit. 37.

[40] Cyranoski and Ledford (2018) op. cit. 37.

[41] Normile (2019).

5 Patenting the CRISPR-Cas9 Genome Editing Breakthrough

Doudna, Charpentier and their collaborators were named as co-inventors for U.S. Patent Application No. 13/842,859, filed by the University of California, the University of Vienna and Charpentier on 15 March 2013, with a priority date of 25 May 2012 when the original provisional application was filed at the US Patent and Trademark Office (USPTO). The patent application was particularly broad in scope, listing 155 claims to the general CRISPR technology.[42]

Zhang and Church's Broad Institute patent application to the USPTO, US Patent No. 8,697,359, was filed later with a priority date of 12 December 2012, seven months after the Doudna, Charpentier and collaborators' priority date. The Broad Institute patent was nevertheless deemed eligible for a special accelerated examination track and the patent was issued by the USPTO on 15 April 2014.[43]

The USPTO granted the key patent over the foundational CRISPR technology to the Broad Institute following interference proceedings with the University of California.

The outcome of the USPTO Patent Trial and Appeal Board (PTAB), rendering judgment that there was no interference-in-fact between the claims in interference between the University of California and the Broad Institute.[44] Broad persuaded the PTAB that the parties claim patentably distinct subject matter, rebutting the presumption of interference. Broad convinced the PTAB that its claims, which were all limited to CRISPR-Cas9 systems in a eukaryotic environment, are not drawn to the same invention as the University of California's, the latter which were all directed to CRISPR-Cas9 systems not restricted to any environment.

Specifically, the evidence showed the PTAB that the invention of such systems in eukaryotic cells would not have been obvious over the invention of CRISPR-Cas9 systems in any environment, including in prokaryotic cells or *in vitro*, because the ordinary skill in the art would not have reasonably expected a CRISPR-Cas9 system to be successful in a eukaryotic environment.[45]

The PTAB terminated interference proceedings upon accepting Broad's argument that its claims pertaining to eukaryotic cells are sufficiently distinct from the University of California's claims for use in any environment, meaning there was no "interference in fact," a threshold requirement rooted in 37 C.F.R. § 41.203(a).

---

[42] See also Feldman (2016), p. p. 401.

[43] See also Jacob S. Sherkow, The CRISPR Patent Interference Showdown Is on: How Did We Get Here and What Comes Next? Stanford Law School Law and Biosciences Blog: https://law.stanford.edu/2015/12/29/the-crispr-patent-interference-showdown-is-on-how-did-we-get-here-and-what-comes-next/.

[44] USPTO Patent Interference No. 106,048. Decisions on Motions 37 C.F.R. § 41.125(a).

[45] Cyranoski and Ledford (2018) op. cit. 37, 2. See also Kevin Noonan, 'CRISPR Interference Parties Propose Motions', Patent Docs Patent Law Blog, 1 August 2019: https://www.patentdocs.org/2019/08/crispr-interference-parties-propose-motions.html.

The University of California's claims had been based on inventions made by Doudna, Charpentier and their collaborators. As discussed above, their breakthrough research in 2012 had demonstrated that CRISPR-Cas9 can be used to cut and (possibly) edit DNA *in vitro*. However, the USPTO decided that this did not extend to editing genomes in advanced, or eurkaryotic cells, and as such the Broad Institute's invention was not obvious having regard to the prior art.

Though the PTAB did not cancel or finally refuse any claims when terminating the interference, its decision triggered speculation that UC might eventually take U.S. rights to use in prokaryotes, with Broad taking them in eukaryotes.

The equivalent application by the Broad Institute for European patent was filed at the European Patent Office (EPO) but, on 23 March 2018, the EPO Opposition Division (OD) found that the priority claim is not valid and revoked the patent for lack of novelty. The case was then referred to the EPO Board of Appeal (BoA), which issued its preliminary comments in preparation for Oral Proceedings on 4 November 2019 (T 0844/18).

The key issues for the Oral Proceedings were whether the priority claim of the Broad Institute patent EP2771468 was valid and whether the EPO had the power to decide on entitlement to priority. The patentees appealed the OD Decision and the Oral Proceedings before EPO Board of Appeal 3.3.08 on this critical issue commenced on 13 January 2020.

The opponents to the Broad Institute argued successfully that the EPO is competent to priority and bound to do so by Article 87 of the European Patent Convention (EPC), and that the OD decision was in line with the large body of EPO case law on priority. The EPO case law provides that the right to claim priority from an earlier application according, as set out in Article 87 EPC which itself is derived from Article 4 of the Paris Convention on the Protection of Industrial Property (1967), is afforded to the applicant of the earlier application and to no other party. As such, the applicant (or applicants) must be the same as the original filing. The Broad Institute's European patent EP2771468 was based on a Patent Cooperation Treaty (PCT) filing (WO2014204729) claiming priority from a number of US provisional applications. One of the US provisionals named an inventor-applicant who was not named on the PCT application.

The two earliest priority documents that the Broad Institute was seeking to rely on at the EPO from 12 December 2012 and 2 January 2013 named Luciano Marraffini of Rockefeller University as an inventor-applicant. Marraffini was not an applicant on the later patent and had not assigned priority rights to the Broad Institute. In fact, until mid-2017 the Broad Institute and Rockefeller University were in an inventorship dispute over a number of early CRISPR patents.[46] The '468 patent was thus revoked in view of an invalid priority claim.

---

[46] Allen & Overy, Broad Institute CRISPR-Cas9 Patent Revoked in Europe, https://www.allenovery.com/en-gb/global/news-and-insights/publications/broad-institute-crispr-cas9-patent-revoked-in-europe.

Of particular note in this case, was the impressive array of prominent experts who provided expert opinions on behalf of the Broad Institute, including former UK Supreme Court President The Rt. Hon. Lord Neuberger, former UK Lord of Appeal in Ordinary judge The Rt. Hon. Lord Hoffmann, Matrix Chambers barrister Philippe Sands, Emeritus Scientific Member of the Max-Planck-Institute for Innovation and Competition Prof. Dr. Joseph Straus, former chair of an EPO Board of Appeal Dr. Ursula Kinkeldey and Swiss Federal Patent Court Judge Dr. Tobias Bremi.[47] This list of experts attests to the significance that the Broad Institute placed on the value of the patent at stake and the significance of the legal issue in question.

Despite expectations that the Board of Appeal would refer questions on priority arising in the case to the EPO Enlarged Board of Appeal, in fact the Board of Appeal decided it could sufficiently answer all questions on priority and, as such, upheld the findings of the Opposition Division and dismissed the case on grounds that there was already substantial and consistent body of EPO case law on the matter of priority under Article 87 EPC. Broad will also face further oppositions to EP3009511, which is directed to CRISPR-Cpf1 (now called Cas12a) systems.[48]

At the time of writing, the EPO has so far granted three European patents, all to the University of California, the University of Vienna and Emmanuelle Charpentier, and related to “Methods and compositions for RNA-directed target DNA modification and for RNA-directed modulation of transcription”.

The first European patent granted to the Regents of the University of California, the University of Vienna and Emmanuelle Charpentier (EP2800811), concerning the basic CRISPR method, was granted on 7 April 2017.[49] It claims a DNA-targeting RNA that comprises a targeting sequence and, together with a modifying polypeptide, provides for site-specific modification of a target DNA and/or a polypeptide associated with the target DNA. Opposition Proceedings at the EPO were filed subsequently by seven parties, with oral proceedings taking place on 5–7 February 2020. The outcome of the EPO Opposition Proceedings was, taking account of the amendments made by the patent proprietor during the opposition proceedings, the patent and the invention to which it relates were found to meet the requirements of the EPC.[50]

---

[47] Amy Sandys, EPO Revokes Broad Institute Patent – But it’s just the beginning for CRISPR-cas, JUVE Patent, 17 January 2020.

[48] Jef Akst, UC Berkeley Receives CRISPR Patent in Europe, Scientist (March 24, 2017), https://www.the-scientist.com/?articles.view/articleNo/48987/title/UC-Berkeley-Receives-CRISPR- Patent-in-Europe/.

[49] EP2800811: https://register.epo.org/application?number=EP13793997&tab=main (accessed 1 December 2019).

[50] Art. 53(c) and Rule 28 objection raised by only one of several opponents against EP2800811. The Opposition Division’s provisional opinion was fairly dismissive of the Article 53(c) and Rule 28 objections.

The second European patent, with claims that are directed to compositions and uses of a chimeric version of the Cas9 protein, most often associated with use in regulation of gene expression as opposed to direct editing of the genetic code itself, was granted on 26 January 2018.[51] Opposition proceedings against the grant of the second European patent have been initiated by four parties, while the most recent European patent for a CRISPR-related invention, which claims methods and compositions of using CRISPR-Cas9 to modify DNA and regulate gene activity in eukaryotic cells, including kits to carry out such work, was granted on 1 March 2019, with the first opponent filing an EPO Opposition almost immediately on 1 April 2019.[52] At the time of writing, the date for oral proceedings relating to the second and third European patents granted to the Regents of the University of California *et al* has yet to be set and, overall, this is likely to be a lengthy process.

6 Excluding Genome Editing Technologies from Patentability

What is surprising about the cases related to CRISPR-Cas9 genome editing that have been considered thus far at the USPTO and EPO is the lack of consideration of the necessity test in decisions to grant patents on these foundational technologies. The Agreement on Trade-Related Aspects of Intellectual Property (the TRIPS Agreement) introduces a "necessity test" to assess whether protection of an overriding social interest is justified.[53] Specifically, Article 27.2 permits World Trade Organisation (WTO) Members to "exclude from patentability inventions, the prevention within their territory of the commercial exploitation of which is necessary to protect *ordre public* or morality, including to protect human, animal or plant life or health or to avoid serious prejudice to the environment, provided that such exclusion is not made merely because the exploitation is prohibited by their law".

As is often stressed, a patent is a grant of exclusive rights but not in itself an authorisation to exploit the patented invention. The latter can be regulated by separate legislation provided this is consistent with Article 27.2, including on grounds that it is necessary to protect human, animal or plant life or health or to avoid serious prejudice to the environment.[54] The flexibility of WTO Members to exclude patents, for example on inventions related to genome editing technologies, therefore is provided for explicitly in the TRIPS Agreement.

The TRIPS flexibilities contained in Article 27.2 reflect the "necessity test" under the evolving jurisprudence of the WTO whereby the national regulatory autonomy constitutes a core principle for WTO Members which are entitled to pursue their

---

[51] EP3241902: https://register.epo.org/application?number=EP17163434&tab=main.

[52] EP3401400: https://register.epo.org/application?number=EP18152360.

[53] See also UNCTAD-ICTSD Project on IPRs and Sustainable Development (2005), p. 378.

[54] Ibid., page 382–383.

domestic policy objectives and choose the means for their fulfilment, provided they do not entail protectionist ends.[55] The necessity test also underpins the principles set out in Article 8.1 of the TRIPS Agreement, whereby "Members may, in formulating or amending their laws and regulations, adopt measures necessary to protect public health and nutrition, and to promote the public interest in sectors of vital importance to their socio-economic and technological development, provided that such measures are consistent with the provisions of this Agreement."

The scope of Article 8.1 was elaborated on by the WTO Dispute Settlement Panel Report in *Canada—Patent Protection of Pharmaceutical Products*, whereby the prohibition on discrimination as to the field of technology contained in Article 27.1 of TRIPS "does not limit the ability to target certain products in dealing with certain of the important national policies referred to [in Article 8.1]."[56] The Panel therefore confirmed that there is considerable scope for WTO Members to include in national legislation exclusions based on measures necessary to protect health and to promote the public interest as set out in the permissible *ordre public* or morality exceptions set out in Article 27.2 of TRIPS.

With regard to the application of the TRIPS flexibilities available under Articles 8.1 and 27.2 of TRIPS in the U.S., it is widely understood that there are no restrictions on patentable subject matter under Section 101 of the U.S.C., and hence no immediate grounds for the USPTO to refuse CRISPR-Cas9 genome editing patents using Article 27.2 type *ordre public* or morality exceptions to patentability. This legal position was subject to confirmatory judgment by the U.S. Supreme Court in Diamond v. Chakrabarty, with the seminal conclusion that statutory subject matter under 101 includes "everything under the sun that is made by man".[57]

The situation differs in Europe, where the patentability of inventions related to the editing of germline genomes is already restricted in EPC countries, exceptions to patents being directly linked and based on the logic of inserting public policy mechanisms in patent law.[58] When these public policy mechanisms are applied to the grant of patents in the field of the life sciences, and particularly in reproductive medicine and genetic engineering, the debate has been controversial for decades.[59]

Article 53(a) of the EPC sets out a general *ordre public* and morality exception whereby "European patents shall not be granted in respect of ... inventions the publication or exploitation of which would be contrary to 'ordre public' or morality, provided that the exploitation shall not be deemed to be contrary merely because it is prohibited by law or regulation in some or all of the Contracting States".

The meaning of *ordre public* in the context of Article 53(a) EPC has since been elaborated by the EPO Technical Board of Appeal in the T356/93 decision as

[55] Kapterian (2010), pp. 89–127; Salinas Alcaraz (2015), pp. 77–99.

[56] Canada – Patent Protection of Pharmaceutical Products, Report of the Panel, WT/DS114/R, 17 March 2000, paragraph 7.92.

[57] Diamond v. Chakrabarty 447 U.S. 303 (1980).

[58] Nordberg et al. (2018) op. cit. n 31, 40.

[59] For a wider discussion see Ingrid SchneiderLL (2019), pp. 263–287.

follows: "It is generally accepted that the concept of *'ordre public'* covers the protection of public security and the physical integrity of individuals as part of society. This concept encompasses also the protection of the environment. Accordingly, under Article 53(a) EPC, inventions the exploitation of which is likely to breach public peace or social order (for example, through acts of terrorism) or to seriously prejudice the environment are to be excluded from patentability as being contrary to 'ordre public'."[60]

In the same T 356/93 decision, the EPO Technical Board of Appeal elaborated on the meaning of "morality" under Article 53(a) EPC as follows: "The concept of *morality* is related to the belief that some behaviour is right and acceptable whereas other behaviour is wrong, this belief being founded on the totality of the accepted norms which are deeply rooted in a particular culture. For the purposes of the EPC the culture in question is the culture inherent in European society and civilisation. Accordingly, under Article 53(a) EPC, inventions the exploitation of which is *not* in conformity with the conventionally accepted standards of conduct pertaining to this culture are to be excluded from patentability as being contrary to morality."

The EPO Guidelines for Examination on Article 53(a) EPC also elaborate on how the test should be applied: "Any invention the commercial exploitation of which would be contrary to 'ordre public' or morality is specifically excluded from patentability. The purpose of this is to deny protection to inventions likely to induce riot or public disorder, or to lead to criminal or other generally offensive behaviour ... Anti-personnel mines are an obvious example. This provision is likely to be invoked only in rare and extreme cases. A fair test to apply is to consider whether it is probable that the public in general would regard the invention as so abhorrent that the grant of patent rights would be inconceivable. If it is clear that this is the case, objection should be raised under Art. 53(a); otherwise not...".[61]

In the EU law context there are explicit links with the *ordre public* and morality exceptions of Article 53(a) EPC by means of the 1998 Biotechnology Directive.[62] The Directive includes, in Articles 5 and 6, provisions which can be interpreted as having the aim of preserving European fundamental values and human rights norms in patent law.[63]

Article 5 of the Biotechnology Directive focuses on the human body which, at various stages of its formation and development, and the simple discovery of one of its elements, including the sequence or partial sequence of a gene, cannot constitute patentable inventions. Nevertheless, Article 5 goes on to state that an element isolated from the human body or otherwise produced by means of a technical process, including the sequence or partial sequence of a gene, may constitute a

[60] EPO Technical Board of Appeal in *Plant Genetic Systems/Glutamine synthetase inhibitors* T356/93 [1995] EPOR 357.

[61] Guidelines for Examination in the EPO C-IV, 4.1.

[62] Directive 98/44 of the European Parliament and of the Council of 6 July 1998 on the Legal Protection of Biotechnological Inventions.

[63] Schneider, op. cit. n 58.

patentable invention, even if the structure of that element is identical to a natural element, provided that the industrial application of a sequence or a partial sequence of a gene is disclosed in the patent application.

The sixteenth recital to the Biotechnology Directive indicates that the logic of Article 5 is "respect for the fundamental principles safeguarding the dignity and integrity of the person", asserting that "it is important to assert the principle that the human body, at any stage in its formation or development, including germ cells and the simple discovery of one of its elements or one of its products, including the sequence or partial sequence of the human gene, cannot be patented".[64]

Article 6(1) of the Biotechnology Directive then goes on to require that "inventions shall be considered unpatentable where their commercial exploitation would be contrary to *ordre public* or morality", while Article 6(2) sets out a non-exhaustive list of examples of biotechnological inventions that are excluded from patentability on moral grounds, including (a) "processes for cloning human beings", (b) "processes for modifying the germ line genetic identity of human beings", and (c) "uses of human embryos for industrial or commercial purposes".

Nevertheless, Article 6(1) of the Biotechnology Directive should be read in conjunction with Recital 42, which states that "... in any case such exclusion does not affect inventions for therapeutic or diagnostic purposes which are applied to the human embryo and are useful to it". Whether genome editing techniques comprising processes for modifying the germline genetic identity of human beings constitute inventions for "therapeutic" purposes within the meaning of Recital 42 therefore remains uncertain and is yet to be clarified by the EPO or its Boards of Appeal.

In this regard, it should be noted that although the EPO, as an organisation constituted by the EPC, is not subject to the treaties and legislation of the EU, the EPO Administrative Council adopted all the articles of the Biotechnology Directive into its own legal order via the implementing rules of the EPC, with Articles 5 and 6 of the Biotechnology Directive comprising Rules 28 and 29 of the EPC.[65]

Consequently, Rule 28 of the Implementing Regulations to the EPC imports the Article 6(2)(b) provision of the Biotechnology Directive into EPO examination practice whereby "Under Article 53(a) EPC European patents shall not be granted in respect of biotechnological inventions which, in particular, concern: ... (b) processes for modifying the germ line genetic identity of human beings...". The possibility that Recital 42 of the Biotechnology Directive could over-ride the exception to the patentability of genome editing technologies for processes related to modifying the germline genetic identity of human beings therefore remains remote before the EPO.

---

[64] See also Schellekens and Vantsiouri (2013), p. 190: https://www.tandfonline.com/doi/abs/10.5235/17579961.5.2.190, who elaborate on the concept of human dignity and refer to Marco Olivetti's commentary on Article 1 of the EU Charter of Fundamental Rights, in which he 'discerns human beings becoming mere objects in medical or biological practices as an example of an affront to dignity' (Olivetti 2010, p. 7).

[65] See also Schneider, op. cit., n 58, 264.

Rule 29 of the Implementing Regulations is also directly relevant to genome editing technologies relating to the human germline given that it states, in Rule 29.1, that "[t]he human body, at the various stages of its formation and development, and the simple discovery of one of its elements, including the sequence or partial sequence of a gene, cannot constitute patentable inventions".

Nevertheless, the debate remains ongoing as to whether the exclusions to patentability encompassed in Articles 5 and 6 of the Biotechnology Directive and, by association, Rules 28 and 29 of the Implementing Regulations to the EPC embody the precautionary principle as enshrined in Article 191 of the Treaty on the Functioning of the European Union (TFEU) which aims at ensuring a higher level of environmental protection through preventative decision-taking in the case of risk. In practice, the scope of the principle is far wider and covers also consumer policy, as well as EU legislation concerning food and human, animal and plant health.[66] Whether the precautionary principle should (or could) also be taken into account by patent granting authorities when determining whether a European patent should be issued remains, as yet, unresolved.[67]

As demonstrated by the foregoing discussion, the European patent system therefore comprises a fairly comprehensive toolkit to enable patent examiners to assess what types of inventions should be excluded from patentability on grounds that they are considered socially undesirable and/or violate human dignity.[68] This has a perceptible impact on the drafting of CRISPR-related patent applications to the EPO, with disclaimers such as "non-human', "human germline not modified" or "wherein the cells are not germ cells".[69]

Specifically, although European patent claims to the "composition" or "vector system" (that is to say a DNA molecule used as a vehicle to artificially carry foreign genetic material into another cell) are regularly being granted by the EPO, on grounds that they are considered to fall outside the Rule 28(b) exception, there is significant evidence of amendments to the claims in genome editing European patent applications which explicitly exclude use of a process for modifying the germline genetic identity of human beings.[70]

---

[66] European Commission, Communication (COM(2000) 1 final) on the Precautionary Principle: https://eur-lex.europa.eu/legal-content/EN/TXT/?uri=LEGISSUM%3Al32042.

[67] See, for instance, Reynolds (2013), p. 95; Nordberg et al. (2018), op. cit. 31, 49–50, noting that in its most simple formulation the Precautionary Principle may seem to ignore the costs of not continuing a line of research and development and finding that, while a broadly precautionary approach to regulation of gene editing is justified, it is important that it is interpreted in a way that avoids a disproportionate (and potentially incoherent) focus on possible harm. Nordberg et al. (2018) op. cit. n 31, sum up that CRISPR-Cas9 and the future of gene-editing technology can potentially produce enormous benefits to humans, but the uncertainty about possible harm that may result from large-scale gene editing means that a precautionary approach is advisable to policy decisions that respect a proportionality constraint on acceptable precautions.

[68] See also Schneider, op. cit. n 58, 267.

[69] See also Schneider, op. cit. n 58, 283.

[70] Sherkow and Thomas Scott (2019), p. 97 North Carolina Law Review 1497, discusses the strategy of keeping some of the most significant information about vectors secret while patenting only certain aspects.

A practical example of limitations to claim language introduced by the EPO Examining Division is the aforementioned Broad Institute European patent EP2771468, which was subject to Oral Proceedings at the EPO in January 2020. The Broad Institute patent contained amended claim language relating to "Use of the composition of claim 1, or the vector system of claim 2 or any claim dependent thereon for genome engineering, provided that said use is not a method for treatment of the human or animal body by surgery or therapy, *and provided that said use is not a process for modifying the germline genetic identity of human beings*" [emphasis added]. This amended claim language is, of course, consistent with both Rule 28 of the Implementing Regulations to the EPC and Article 6(2)(b) the Biotechnology Directive.

Indications that limiting claim language into European patents for CRISPR technologies is being established as office practice at the EPO is supported by closer examination of the Regents of the University of California, University of Vienna, Emmanuelle Charpentier European patent EP2800811. The University of California *et al* patent contains similar amended language to the Broad Institute '468 patent. Specifically, the '811 patent at claims 20 and 21 states: "*provided that said method is not a method of modifying the germ line identity of a human being*" [emphasis added], this wording being upheld during EPO Oral Proceedings on 5-7 February 2020.

It is certainly significant that the limiting claim language to the '468 and '811 patents are very similar, indicating a practice for the EPO Examining Division to insert Rule 28 type language in all such cases. The approach taken in the '468 and '811 patents is also consistent with findings of the All European Academies (ALLEA) Statement on Patent-Related Aspects of CRISPR-Cas Technology which, in 2016, considered the principles enshrined in the EU Biotechnology Directive and the Implementing Regulations of the EPC, as applied in the patent grant practice of the EPO to inventions related to CRISPR technology, fit for purpose and flexible enough to take account of future regulatory developments.

Such limitations on patent claims (or refusal to grant a patent based on morality exceptions) have raised concerns that such a policy may result in a chain reaction of overall reduction in the various types of incentives to innovate and invest in the areas of research concerned.[71] No doubt such concerns will continue to be raised and limitations to claim language for European patents related to genome editing technologies will remain under close scrutiny in the future.

[71] See, for instance, Nordberg et al. (2018), op. cit. n 31, 51.

7 International Human Rights Law and Genome Editing

We now turn in this chapter to the implications of granting patents relating to genome editing in terms of the enjoyment of internationally binding human rights. The applicable international and legally binding instrument dealing specifically with the protection of human rights in the biomedical field is the Oviedo Convention.[72]

The Oviedo Convention draws on the principles established by Article 1 of the Universal Declaration on Human Rights (UDHR) of 1948, which affirms that "[a]ll human beings are born free and equal in dignity and rights."

As the Nuffield Council on Bioethics has acknowledged, dignity is an important concept that links human beings to the possession of a human genome and, at the same time, elevates the being of individual humans above the given.[73] Dignity also plays a restraining role. For example, the UNESCO Declaration on Science and the Use of Scientific Knowledge affirms specifically that both "scientific research and the use of scientific knowledge should respect human rights and the dignity of human beings."[74]

The Oviedo Convention aims to protect the dignity and identity of all human beings and guarantee everyone, without discrimination, respect for their integrity and other rights and fundamental freedoms with regard to the application of biology and medicine. It set out fundamental principles applicable to daily medical practice and is regarded as establishing basic patient's rights. It also deals with biomedical research, genetics and transplantation of organ and tissues.[75]

Specifically, Article 13 of the Oviedo Convention (entitled 'Interventions on the human genome') prohibits germline modification: "An intervention seeking to modify the human genome may only be undertaken for preventive, diagnostic or therapeutic purposes and only if its aim is not to introduce any modification in the genome of any descendants."

Article 13 therefore establishes two key principles. First, that any genome modification (in research or in treatment) should have as its aim a benefit for human health. It does not permit genome modifications that are for other purposes. For example, it does not permit attempts to enhance human characteristics beyond normal functioning or for welfare purposes not related to health. For those states in which the Oviedo Convention is in force, Article 13 therefore limits, but does not prohibit, genome editing involving human embryos for research purposes. Second,

---

[72] *Convention for the Protection of Human Rights and Dignity of the Human Being with regard to the Application of Biology and Medicine: Convention on Human Rights and Biomedicine (ETS No 164).*

[73] Nuffield Council on Bioethics (2018), op. cit. n 17, 124.

[74] UNESCO Declaration on Science and the Use of Scientific Knowledge (1999), Preamble, para. 19. The UNESCO Declaration on Bioethics and Human Rights asserts that the "ethical issues raised by the rapid advances in science and their technological applications should be examined with due respect to the dignity of the human person...".

[75] Oviedo Convention and its Protocols, Council of Europe, opened for signature on 4 April 1997, Oviedo, Spain: https://www.coe.int/en/web/bioethics/oviedo-convention.

the aim must not be to introduce changes that can be passed on to future generations; that is, interventions that lead to the birth of children with a modified genome.[76]

On the face of it, Article 13 of the Oviedo Convention appears to prohibit heritable genome editing interventions although, according to the Nuffield Council on Bioethics, not without some ambiguity.[77] However, it has been argued persuasively that the Convention does not veto genetic editing for basic research purposes, but only its clinical application on human embryos to be transferred into the womb.[78] This argument is supported by the strict textual interpretation of the Convention, given that Article 13 states explicitly that "An intervention seeking to modify the human genome may only be undertaken for preventive, diagnostic or therapeutic purposes and *only if its aim is not to introduce any modification in the genome of any descendants*" [emphasis added].

The prohibition introduced by Article 13 of the Oviedo Convention therefore appears limited to interventions seeking to modify the human genome only where this introduces modifications into the genome of descendants. As such, the wording of Article 13 can be interpreted as giving sufficient room for basic research into preventive, diagnostic or therapeutic purposes.[79] Nevertheless, it should also be borne in mind that the explanatory report to the Convention refers explicitly to the need to "protect the dignity and identity of all human beings",[80] underpinned by the guiding principle of the primacy of the human being.[81]

Although the Oviedo Convention is the only international legal instrument that explicitly addresses heritable genetic modification, even those countries that have not signed or ratified the Convention, including the UK and Germany, have taken it into account in framing their domestic provisions in many areas of biomedicine such as patient rights, consent and privacy, the protection of biomedical research participants or living donors and in relation to applications of biomedicine such as genetics.[82]

[76] See also Nuffield Council on Bioethics (2018), op. cit. n 17, 117.

[77] Nuffield Council on Bioethics (2018), op. cit. 17, 124.

[78] de Mignuel Beriain et al. (2019), p. 226.

[79] Ibid, 229.

[80] 'In every case, any intervention which aims to modify the human genome must be carried out for preventive, diagnostic or therapeutic purposes. Interventions aimed at modifying genetic characteristics not related to a disease or to ailment are prohibited. As long as somatic cell gene therapy is currently at the research stage, its application can be allowed only if it complies with the standards of protection provided for in Article 15 and the following Articles'. Paragraph 90, Explanatory Report to the Convention for the Protection of Human Rights and Dignity of the Human Being with regard to the Application of Biology and Medicine: Convention on Human Rights and Biomedicine', Oviedo, 4.IV.1997, European Treaty Series No. 164, Council of Europe: https://rm.coe.int/16800ccde5. See also Nordberg (2018), pp. 54–92: 77.

[81] The whole Convention, the aim of which is to protect human rights and dignity, is inspired by the principle of the primacy of the human being, and all its articles must be interpreted in this light'. Paragraph 22, Explanatory Report to the Convention, ibid.

[82] See also Nuffield Council on Bioethics (2018) op. cit. n 17, 116.

Elsewhere, in the scientific community, the wider debate on whether there should be a complete ban on gene editing technologies continues and remains largely polarised.[83] Central to this wider debate are arguments that the Oviedo Convention, as currently worded, prioritises human rights and human dignity over the interests of scientific endeavour and technological needs.[84] This emphasis on human rights and human dignity is consistent with Article 3 of the EU Charter of Fundamental Rights, which protects the right to respect for a person's physical and mental integrity.[85] Paragraph 1 of the Charter asserts that "everyone has the right to respect for his or her physical and mental integrity", while paragraph 2 sets out a not exhaustive list of acts that must be respected in particular in the fields of medicine and biology, namely: (a) the free and informed consent of the person concerned, according to the procedures laid down by law; (b) the prohibition of eugenic practices, in particular those aiming at the selection of persons; (c) the prohibition on making the human body and its parts as such a source of financial gain; and (d) the prohibition of the reproductive cloning of human beings.

8 International Initiatives on the Regulation and Governance of Gene Editing

International initiatives lead by the scientific community have also played an important role to play in framing the debate on access to gene editing technologies and allaying fears of a eugenic future.[86] Persistent calls have been made for an international moratorium on gene editing.[87] In March 2015, many of the eminent scientists working at the cutting-edge of CRISPR research co-authored a statement published in *Science* magazine calling for a moratorium on germline cell editing.[88]

Elsewhere, the US National Academies of Science and National Academy of Medicine Human Gene-Editing initiative, designed to inform decision-making related to recent advances in human genome-editing research, has been a particularly

---

[83] See, for example, the counter arguments in Sykora and Caplan (2017), pp. 1871–1872, who argue that the debate cannot occur while scientists and clinicians forge ahead with germline modifications and disregard the views, interests and concerns of the many communities to whom germline modification matters; and Baylis and Ikemoto (2017), pp. 2084–2085.

[84] Baylis and Ikemoto (2017) ibid 2084.

[85] Charter of Fundamental Rights of the European Union (2010/ C 83/389: https://eur-lex.europa.eu/LexUriServ/LexUriServ.do?uri=OJ:C:2010:083:0389:0403:en:PDF.

[86] Nordberg et al. (2018), op. cit. n 31, 39.

[87] See, for example, Schneider, above, n 58, 281, citing Baltimore et al. (2015a), pp. 36–38; Lanphier et al. (2015), pp. 410–411; Leopoldina Nationale Akademie der Wissenschaften, *The Opportunities and Limits of Genome Editing* (2015): https://www.leopoldina.org/en/publications/detailview/publication/chancen-und-grenzen-des-genome-editing-2015/; Reich et al. (2015).

[88] Baltimore et al. (2015b), pp. 365–338: https://www.ncbi.nlm.nih.gov/pmc/articles/PMC4394183/.

valuable venue for international dialogue.[89] The First International Summit on Gene Editing took place in Washington DC on 1-3 December 2015, hosted by the National Academy of Sciences and the National Academy of Medicine and co-hosted by the Chinese Academy of Sciences and the UK Royal Society. The Summit convened experts from around the world to discuss the scientific, ethical, and governance issues associated with human gene-editing research. A Second International Summit on Human Genome Editing took place in Hong Kong on 27–29 November 2018, hosted by the Academy of Sciences of Hong Kong in collaboration with the UK Royal Society, the US National Academy of Sciences and the US Academy of Medicine.

Subsequently, on 13 August 2019, the first public meeting on the International Commission on the Clinical Use of Human Germline Genome Editing took place in Washington DC, hosted by the National Academy of Sciences, with the second meeting of the Commission taking place in London on 14–15 November 2019 and hosted by the Royal Society.

The World Health Organization (WHO) is also playing an increasing active role in coordinating global policy responses to CRISPR genome editing worldwide. On 14 December 2018 the WHO announced the establishment of an 18-member multi-disciplinary Expert Advisory Committee on the Governance and Oversight of Human Genome Editing to examine the scientific, ethical, social and legal challenges associated with human genome editing (both somatic and germ cell).[90] The committee sought to identify regulatory and governance gaps, concerns about inappropriate use of human genome editing technologies and concerns regarding rogue clinics exploiting regulatory gaps in some parts of the world. On 29 August 2019 the WHO expert advisory committee announced that it had approved the first phase of a new global registry to track research on human genome editing, using the International Clinical Trials Registry Platform (ICTRP), a WHO entity.[91]

On 12 July 2021 the WHO Expert Advisory Committee on the Governance and Oversight of Human Genome Editing published its final reports entitled Human Genome Editing: A Framework for Governance and Recommendations. The Committee's Framework for Governance elaborates why a governance role for patents can be significant, acknowledging that patent holders may find themselves with a reasonable amount of influence over how a technology develops. Likewise, the Committee's Recommendations recognise the practical considerations in terms of relevant patent holders perhaps being unwilling to limit the use of their inventions, and the unequal geographic distribution of patent holders given the location of current patent applications relevant to human genome editing. To implement these

[89] National Academies of Sciences Human Genome Editing Initiative: https://nationalacademies.org/gene-editing/index.htm.

[90] Global health ethics: Human Genome editing, World Health Organization: https://www.who.int/ethics/topics/human-genome-editing/en/.

[91] WHO Launches Global Registry on Human Genome Editing, World Health Organization, 29 August 2019: https://www.who.int/news-room/detail/29-08-2019-who-launches-global-registry-on-human-genome-editing.

actions, the specific Recommendations of the Committee are: first, in collaboration with other international institutions, such as the World Intellectual Property Organization (WIPO), the WTO and its TRIPS Agreement, that the WHO should encourage relevant patent holders to help ensure equitable access to human genome editing interventions; second, that the WHO should encourage industry to work with resource-constrained countries to build capacity to take advantage of human genome interventions; and, third, that the WHO should convene a meeting of those holding or applying for patents relevant to human genome editing, industry bodies, international organisations such as WIPO and the WTO, and those involved in establishing or running relevant patent pools to explore the potential for the adoption of appropriate ethical licensing requirements.

WHO Expert Advisory Committee's Recommendations on intellectual property comprise one of eight core themes on the governance of human genome editing and have been subject to careful analysis by patent scholars (including the author of this chapter). This patent scholars' analysis builds upon and elaborates the Committee's work, in particular by calling for wider public debate about the role of "ordre public" or morality exceptions to patentability in the area of genome editing or considering promoting post-grant governance through the use of research exceptions or compulsory licences.[92]

The WHO has also called for a moratorium, emphasising that countries should not allow any further work on human germline genome editing in human clinical applications until the technical and ethical implications have been properly considered.[93] Such further work is considered, at this time, to be inconsistent with the principle of responsible stewardship of science.[94]

9 Concluding Remarks

CRISPR genome editing interventions have great potential to edit the germline human identity in a manner which will eliminate diseases, improve public health and contribute positively to welfare in society. Yet genome editing also poses unique and unprecedented challenges: scientific, regulatory and ethical. The potential uses of these technologies to alter the human germline raise a number of fundamental issues for society. Editing of the human genome will influence the characteristics of

---

[92] Matthews et al. (2021).

[93] WHO Launches Global Registry on Human Genome Editing, World Health Organization, 29 August 2019: https://www.who.int/news-room/detail/29-08-2019-who-launches-global-registry-on-human-genome-editing.

[94] Presentation by Robin Lovell Badge (Francis Crick Institute, UK), member of the WHO expert advisory committee on developing global standards for governance and oversight of Human Genome editing at the Second Meeting of the International Commission on the Clinical Use of Human Germline Genome Editing, London, 14 November 2019. Available at: https://royalsociety.org/topics-policy/projects/genetic-technologies/international-commission/.

future generations in ways that may well be considered ethically unacceptable given the unknown risks of off-target effects. Ensuring that institutions are appropriately equipped to accommodate this new technology is essential for the future governance and regulation of gene editing technologies, of which the patent system forms a crucial component part.

The risks, benefits and ethical reasoning for exclusions to patentability need to be considered carefully by the policy community, based on inputs from all stakeholders, including patient groups, the scientific community and also those engaged in patent law and policy. As has been argued convincingly, it is only through public policy engaging multiple stakeholders and the interdisciplinary academic community that dialog proceeds in a manner that is conducive to the future development of this ground-breaking technology.[95] This imperative applies to the patent system as much as it does to other levers of governance and regulation.

In this context, WTO Members should pay careful attention to the patent policy implications of genome editing technologies, particularly for inventions relating to altering the germline identity of human beings. Strong arguments can be made in favour of encouraging such inventions in terms of eradicating hereditary diseases in new-born babies and creating resistance to life-threatening conditions for future generations. Such uses of genome editing technologies may well be considered consistent with fundamental human rights, particularly the right to dignity, of future generations under Article 13 of the Oviedo Convention.

Nonetheless, WTO Members must balance decisions about permitting the patenting of this transformational technology and the possibilities of eradicating, for example certain hereditary diseases from society, with the possibilities of negative impacts when deciding to permit patents on altering the germline identity of human beings. The extent of off-target effects for future generations, effects that are ancillary to the intended genome alteration, are not yet known or fully understood. The shadow of eugenics experiments conducted in Europe during the middle of the last century remains strong. Human rights, particularly those enshrined in Article 13 of the Oviedo Convention, must be given primacy at all costs.

The patent system can, and should, play an important role in this process. As we have seen in this chapter, Article 27.2 of the TRIPS Agreement establishes a "necessity test" and encompasses the TRIPS flexibility that WTO Members may exclude from patentability within their territory inventions, the commercial exploitation of which could be considered contrary to *ordre public* and morality, including to protect human animal or plant life or to avoid serious prejudice to the environment, provided that such exclusion is not made merely because the exploitation is prohibited by their law.

The approach now being taken by the EPO is instructive in this respect. By eschewing an approach based on rejecting CRISPR-based patent applications outright in favour of a more nuanced approach when considering the European patent claim language of genome editing technologies with the potential to alter the

---

[95] Nordberg et al. (2018) op. cit. n 31, 46.

germline identity of human beings, the EPO has retained limits on patentability within the established EPC norms on exclusions to patentability. This chapter has set out how the European patent tradition of exclusions to patentability based on *ordre public* and morality is well-established by virtue of Article 53(a) EPC, Articles 5 and 6 of the Biotechnology Directive and Rule 28 of the Implementing Regulations to the EPC. The chapter has also demonstrated how the EPO is now paying due regard to these provisions by requiring amended claim language for European Patents relating to genome editing technologies. Other WTO Members should take note of this approach and, it is suggested by this chapter, follow suit. This is imperative in order to ensure that the granting of private patent rights can be accommodated on an equitable basis, balanced alongside the need to avoid unnecessary risk (including the morality exception under patent law), take account of human rights, meet public expectations, and act in the public interest with regard to this potentially transformational healthcare technology.

This chapter has set out some of the risks, advantages, ownership issues, ethics and access problems related to genome editing. We saw in this chapter that the right to health carries with it the expectation that everyone should have access to the health services they need, when and where they need them, without suffering financial hardship. This is particularly pertinent given the global context in which access to health care technologies needs to be evaluated. Different IP regimes and the national legislation of different countries express different ethical values.[96] The world is now only at the beginning of this new healthcare debate and patent systems will be central to how we conceptualise and resolve these public policy problems. Without doubt, given the rapid pace of genome editing science and its wide applications, greater consideration of these crucial issues within the global patent policy community is urgently required if governance institutions are to adequately take into account the impact of granting of genome editing patents, balancing the need to reward inventorship with affordability, access and the enjoyment of fundamental human rights in the public interest.

Acknowledgements With thanks to Emanuela Gambini for invaluable research assistance and insights, and to Phil Hinchliffe, Abbe Brown, Jacob S Sherkow and two anonymous referees for their helpful comments and suggestions. The opinions and any errors in the chapter remain the author's own.

References

Akst J (2017) UC Berkeley Receives CRISPR Patent in Europe. Scientist (March 24, 2017), https://www.the-scientist.com/?articles.view/articleNo/48987/title/UC-Berkeley-Receives-CRISPR-Patent-in-Europe/ (Last accessed 16 February 2021)

[96] Nuffield Council on Bioethics (2018), op. cit. 17, xvi.

All European Academies (ALLEA) (2016) Statement on Patent-Related Aspects of CRISPR-Cas Technology

Allen & Overy (2021) Broad Institute CRISPR-Cas9 Patent Revoked in Europe, https://www.allenovery.com/en-gb/global/news-and-insights/publications/broad-institute-crispr-cas9-patent-revoked-in-europe (Last accessed 16 February 2021)

Baltimore D et al (2015a) A prudent path forward for genomic engineering and germline gene modification. Science 348:36–38

Baltimore D, Berg P, Botchan M, Dana Carroll R, Charo A, Church G, Corn JE, Daley GQ, Doudna JA, Fenner M, Greely HT, Jinek M, Martin GS, Penhoet E, Puck J, Sternberg SH, Weissman JS, Yamamoto KR (2015b) A prudent path forward for genomic engineering and germline gene modification. Science 348(6230):365–338: https://www.ncbi.nlm.nih.gov/pmc/articles/PMC4394183/ (Last accessed 17 February 2021)

Barrangou R, Fremaux C, Deveau H et al (2007) CRISPR provides acquired resistance against viruses in prokaryotes. Science 315(5819):1709–1712

Baylis F, Ikemoto L (2017) The Council of Europe and the prohibition on germline genome editing. EMBO Report 18(12):2084–2085

Begley S (2018) Potential DNA damage from CRISPR has been "seriously underestimated" study finds. 16 July 2018, STAT News: https://www.statnews.com/2018/07/16/crispr-potential-dna-damage-underestimated/ (Last accessed 16 February 2021)

Canada – Patent Protection of Pharmaceutical Products, Report of the Panel, WT/DS114/R, 17 March 2000, paragraph 7.92

Charter of Fundamental Rights of the European Union (2010/ C 83/389: https://eur-lex.europa.eu/LexUriServ/LexUriServ.do?uri=OJ:C:2010:083:0389:0403:en:PDF (Last accessed 16 February 2021)

Contreras J, Sherkow JS (2017) CRISPR, surrogate licensing, and scientific discovery. Science 355:(6326)698

Convention for the Protection of Human Rights and Dignity of the Human Being with regard to the Application of Biology and Medicine: Convention on Human Rights and Biomedicine (ETS No 164)

Cyranoski D, Ledford H (2018) Genome-edited baby claim provokes international outcry. Nature 563:607–608, 26 November: https://www.nature.com/articles/d41586-018-07545-0 (Last accessed 16 February 2021)

Davies K, Mojica F (2018) Crazy about CRISPR: an interview with Francisco Mojica. CRISPR J 1:5

de Mignuel Beriain I, Armaza EA, Sánchez AD (2019) Human Germline editing is not prohibited by the Oviedo convention: an argument. Med Law Int 19(2–3):226–232, 226

Deborah K (2017) The patentability of the Crispr-Cas9 genome editing tool. Chicago-Kent J Intell Prop 16:408

EP2800811: - Methods and Compositions for RNA-Directed Target DNA Modification and for RNA-Directed Modulation of Transcription. https://register.epo.org/application?number=EP13793997&tab=main (Last accessed 16 February 2021)

EP3241902 – Methods and Compositions for RNA-Directed Target DNA Modification and for RNA-Directed Modulation of Transcription. https://register.epo.org/application?number=EP17163434&tab=main (Last accessed 16 February 2021)

EP3401400 – Methods and Compositions for RNA-Directed Target DNA Modification and for RNA-Directed Modulation of Transcription. https://register.epo.org/application?number=EP18152360 (Last accessed 16 February 2021)

EPO Technical Board of Appeal in *Plant Genetic Systems/Glutamine synthetase inhibitors* T356/93 [1995] EPOR 357

European Commission, Communication (COM(2000) 1 final) on the Precautionary Principle: https://eur-lex.europa.eu/legal-content/EN/TXT/?uri=LEGISSUM%3Al32042 (Last accessed 16 February 2021)

Feldman R (2016) The CRISPR revolution: what editing human DNA reveals about the patent system's DNA. UCLA Law Rev Discourse 392:401

Global health ethics: Human Genome editing, World Health Organization: https://www.who.int/ethics/topics/human-genome-editing/en/ (Last accessed 17 February 2021)

Guerrini C, Curnette M, Sherkow JS, Scott C (2017) The rose of ethical license. Nat Biotechnol 35:22

Hannah Mosby H (2018) Biotechnology's great divide: strengthening the relationship between patent law and bioethics in the age of CRISPR-Cas9. Minnesota J Law Sci Technol 19, 2, 565–604:579

Health is a fundamental human right. Statement by Dr Tedros Adhanom Ghebreyesus, WHO Director-General, 10 December 2017.: https://www.who.int/mediacentre/news/statements/fundamental-human-right/en/ (last accessed 16 February 2021)

Hyde KJ, Schust DJ (2015) Genetic considerations in recurrent pregnancy loss. Cold Spring Harb Perspect Med, p 5

Ishino Y, Shinagawa H, Makino K et al (1987) Nucleotide sequence of the *iap* gene, responsible for alkaline phosphatase isozyme conversion in *Escherichia coli* and identification of the gene product. J Bacteriol 169:5429–5433)

Jinek M, Chylinski K, Fonfara I et al (2012) A programmable dual-RNA-guided DNA endonuclease in adaptive bacterial immunity. Science 337(6096):816

Jonietz E (2003) Choosing our children's genetic futures. Technol Rev (1 February 2003)

Kapterian G (2010) A critique of the WTO jurisprudence of 'necessity. Int Comp Law Q 59 (1):89–127

Kosicki M, Tomberg K, Bradley A (2018) Repair of double-strand breaks induced by CRISPR-Cas9 leads to large deletions and complex rearrangements. Nat Biotechnol 36:765

Lanphier E et al (2015) Don't edit the human germ line. Nature 519(7544):410–411; Leopoldina Nationale Akademie der Wissenschaften, *The Opportunities and Limits of Genome Editing* (2015) https://www.leopoldina.org/en/publications/detailview/publication/chancen-und-grenzen-des-genome-editing-2015/ (Last accessed 16 February 2021)

Matthews D (2010) Intellectual property rights, human rights and the right to health. In: Grosheide W (ed) Intellectual property rights and human rights: a paradox. Edward Elgar Publishing, pp 118–139

Matthews D (2015) The right to health and patents. In Geiger C (ed) Research handbook on human rights and intellectual property. Edward Elgar Publishing pp 496–512

Matthews D, Brown A, Gambini E, McMahon A, Minssen T, Nordberg A, Sherkow JS, Wested, J, van Zimmeren E (2021) The role of patents and licensing in the governance of human genome editing: a white paper. Response to the WHO Expert Advisory Committee on Developing Global Standards for Governance and Oversight of Human Genome Editing Reports, Queen Mary Law Research Paper No. 354/2001

McMahon A (2020) Biotechnology, health and patents as private governance tools: the good, the bad and the potential for ugly? Intellect Prop Q 161

Mojica FJM, Juez G, Rodrıguez-Valera F (1993) Transcription at different salinities of *Haloferax mediterranei* sequences adjacent to partially modified *Pst*I sites. Mol Microbiol 9(3):613–21

National Academies of Sciences Human Genome Editing Initiative.: https://nationalacademies.org/gene-editing/index.htm (Last accessed 17 February 2021)

National Human Genome Research Institute, Epigenomics Fact Sheet: https://www.genome.gov/about-genomics/fact-sheets/Epigenomics-Fact-Sheet (Last accessed 16 February 2021)

National Institutes of Health (NIH), U.S. National Library of Medicine, Your Guide to Understanding Genetic Conditions: What Are Genome Editing and CRISPR-Cas9? https://ghr.nlm.nih.gov/primer/genomicresearch/genomeediting (Last accessed 16 February 2021)

Noonan K (2019) CRISPR Interference Parties Propose Motions. Patent Docs Patent Law Blog, 1 August 2019: https://www.patentdocs.org/2019/08/crispr-interference-parties-propose-motions.html (Last accessed 16 February 2021)

Nordberg A (2018) Patentability of human enhancement: from ethical dilemmas to legal (un)-certainty. In: Pistorius T (ed) Intellectual property perspectives on the regulation of new technologies. Edward Elgar, pp 54–92: 77

Nordberg A, Minssen T, Holm S, Horst M, Mortensen K, Møller BL (2018) Cutting edges and weaving threads in the gene editing (r)evolution: reconciling scientific progress with legal, ethical and social concerns. J Law Biosci 36–83:37

Normile D (2019) Chinese scientist who produced genetically altered babies sentenced to 3 years in jail. Science (December 30, 2019) https://www.sciencemag.org/news/2019/12/chinese-scientist-who-produced-genetically-altered-babies-sentenced-3-years-jail. Accessed 22 Aug 2021

Nuffield Council on Bioethics (2018) Genome Editing and Human Reproduction: Social and Ethical Issues 7

Olivetti M (2010) Article 1: dignity. In: Mock W, Demuro G (eds) Human Rights in Europe: commentary on the charter of fundamental rights of the European Union. Carolina Academic Press, p 7

Oviedo Convention and its Protocols, Council of Europe, opened for signature on 4 April 1997, Oviedo, Spain: https://www.coe.int/en/web/bioethics/oviedo-convention (Last accessed 16 February 2021)

Presentation by Feng Zhang (Broad Institute) at the Program on Science, Technology and Society Workshop on Editorial Aspirations: Human Integrity at the Frontiers of Biology, 26-28 April 2017, Harvard University

Presentation by Robin Lovell Badge (Francis Crick Institute, UK), member of the WHO expert advisory committee on developing global standards for governance and oversight of Human Genome editing at the Second Meeting of the International Commission on the Clinical Use of Human Germline Genome Editing, London, 14 November 2019. Available at: https://royalsociety.org/topics-policy/projects/genetic-technologies/international-commission/ (Last accessed 17 February 2021)

Regalado A (2019) MIT Technology Review, December 3, 2019: https://www.technologyreview.com/s/614764/chinas-crispr-babies-read-exclusive-excerpts-he-jiankui-paper/ (Last accessed 16 February 2021)

Reich J et al (2015) Human genome surgery – towards a responsible evaluation of a new technology. Berlin-Brandenburg Academy of Sciences and Humanities (BBAW)

Reynolds G (2013) The precautionary principle and its application in the intellectual property context: towards a public domain assessment. In: Courtney Doaygoo B et al (eds) Intellectual property for the 21st century: interdisciplinary approaches. Irwin Law, Toronto, p 95

Sadie G (2019) CRISPR's creatures: protecting wildlife in the age of genomic editing. J Environ Law 37:1

Salinas Alcaraz IC (2015) The concept of necessity under the GATT and national regulatory autonomy. Revista Virtual Via Inveniendi et Iudicandi (VIeI) 10(2):77–99

Sandys A (2020) EPO Revokes Broad Institute Patent – But it's just the beginning for CRISPR-cas. JUVE Patent, 17 January 2020

Schellekens M, Vantsiouri P (2013) Patentability of human enhancements. Law Innov Technol 5 (2):190–213: 190 https://www.tandfonline.com/doi/abs/10.5235/17579961.5.2.190 (Last accessed 16 February 2021)

Schneider I (2019) Patent governance, ethics and democracy: how transparency and accountability norms are challenged by patents on stem cells, gametes and genome editing. In: Berg TC, Cholij R, Ravenscroft S (eds) Patents on life: religious, moral and social justice aspects of biotechnology and intellectual property. Cambridge University Press, pp 263–287

Sherkow JS (2017a) Patent protection for CRISPR: an ELSI review. J Law Biosci 565

Sherkow JS (2017b) CRISPR, patents, and the public health. Yale J Biol Med 90:667

Sherkow JS (2021) The CRISPR patent interference showdown is on: how did we get here and what comes next? Stanford Law School Law and Biosciences Blog: https://law.stanford.edu/2015/12/29/the-crispr-patent-interference-showdown-is-on-how-did-we-get-here-and-what-comes-next/ (Last accessed 16 February 2021)

Sherkow JS, Thomas Scott C (2019) The pick-and shovel play: bioethics for gene-editing vector patents. North Carolina Law Rev 97:1497

Steinbock B (2008) Designer babies: choosing our children's genes. The Lancet (11 October 2008)

Sykora P, Caplan A (2017) The Council of Europe should not reaffirm the ban on germline genome editing in humans. EBMO Report 18(11):1871–1872

The National Academies of Sciences, Engineering and Medicine, Human Genome Editing: Science, Ethics and Governance, 2017, Consensus Study Report, 145

Tsung-Ling L (2019) Two Minutes to Midnight – What International Law Can Do About Genome Editing, 1

UNCTAD-ICTSD Project on IPRs and Sustainable Development (2005) Resource book on TRIPS and development. Cambridge University Press, p 378

UNESCO Declaration on Science and the Use of Scientific Knowledge (1999), Preamble, para. 19

Van Overwalle G, van Zimmeren E, Verbeure B, Matthijs G (2006) Models for facilitating access to patents on genetic inventions. Nat Rev Genet 7:143

WHO Launches Global Registry on Human Genome Editing, World Health Organization, 29 August 2019.: https://www.who.int/news-room/detail/29-08-2019-who-launches-global-registry-on-human-genome-editing (Last accessed 17 February 2021)

Wojcik MH, Schwartz Inbar Yamin TS, Edward HL, Genetti CA, Towne MC, Agrawal PB (2018) Genetic disorders and mortality in infancy and early childhood: delayed diagnosis and missed opportunities. Genet Med, p 20

Zorrilla M, Yatsenko AN (2013) 'The Genetics of Infertility' Current Status in the Field, Current Genetic Medicine Reports, 1

Bolar Exception

Viviana Munoz Tellez

Abstract This chapter discusses the exemption from liability of patent infringement for activities related to regulatory approval for medicines, also known as the "regulatory review" or "Bolar" exception. The Bolar exception supports the market entry of generics by allowing the use of a patented invention by a third party without the consent of the patent holder for the sole purpose of obtaining regulatory approval. This constitutes an important defense for generic manufacturers when undertaking activities such as studies and trials to provide the information required by regulatory agencies. In this regard, the Bolar exception can respond to a public policy objective of facilitating market entry of generics to support competition and exerting downward pressure on prices for medicines. The Bolar exception is included in many country patent laws and is compatible with international legal instruments regarding patent law.

1 Exceptions to Patent Rights

A patent grants the patent holder the exclusive right to exclude others from making, using, importing, and selling the patented innovation for a limited period of time.[1] Most, if not all, patent laws exclude certain matter from patentability, and also limit the rights of patent holders by way of exceptions.[2] These have the important function

[1] The TRIPS Agreement states that the available term of protection must expire no earlier than 20 years from the date of filing the patent application. In some jurisdictions the term may be extended, for example in the United States through Patent Term Adjustment (PTA) and Patent Term Extension (PTE). The extended exclusivity delays generic competition that can negatively affect access to medical products in the trading partners, and pressures patent offices to examine patent applications more expediously. Patent term extensions are often requirements in regional trade agreements involving the United States and European Union. See Correa (2017).

[2] Bently (2011), pp. 315–347.

V. Munoz Tellez (✉)
South Centre, Geneva, Switzerland
e-mail: Munoz@southcentre.int

C. M. Correa, R. M. Hilty (eds.), *Access to Medicines and Vaccines*,
https://doi.org/10.1007/978-3-030-83114-1_5

of defining spaces of freedom of action, wherein obtaining permission from patent right holders is not required.

International patent law as regulated by the World Trade Organization (WTO) Agreement on Trade Related Aspects of Intellectual Property Rights (TRIPS)[3] contains an overall obligation for members of the WTO to grant patents for inventions that meet the criteria of patentability[4] in all fields of technology. Nonetheless, certain exclusions from patentable inventions are permitted.[5]

Exceptions allow activities that would otherwise be considered patent infringement. They may remove liability for infringing patent rights, by deeming certain acts as non-infringing (as is the case of the Bolar exception analysed in this chapter). WTO members have greater freedom to introduce exceptions to the rights of patent holders in their legal systems, as compared to exclusions from patentable subject matter. Rather than defining the exceptions, the TRIPS Agreement allows Members to develop limited exceptions so long as these comply with certain conditions.[6] Exceptions that can be found in many jurisdictions are exceptions for private, non-commercial use, or to promote research or experimentation.[7] Generally, the Bolar exception can be considered to be a specific type of experimental use exception.

Members have discretion to decide what exceptions to establish, consistent with the TRIPS Agreement. This has the advantage of allowing countries to determine what exceptions are most relevant to their evolving domestic priorities and various policy considerations. These may include, to confine the patent right for the subject matter that it was intended, and for protecting third party rights and the public interest.[8] Exceptions to patent rights may be stipulated in legislation or judicially created—developed through case law. Domestic exceptions can however be challenged under the WTO Dispute Settlement Understanding (DSU). There has so far been a single instance of a challenge to exceptions that limit patent rights, in the

[3] Agreement on Trade-related Aspects of Intellectual Property Rights of 1994; being Annexe 1C to the Agreement Establishing the World Trade Organization, April 15, 1994 (hereafter "TRIPS Agreement").

[4] TRIPS Article 27.1 states that "...patents shall be available for any inventions...in all fields of technology, provided that they are new, involve an inventive step and are capable of industrial application." The TRIPS Agreement does not define "invention" and "technology" and does not determine how patentability requirements should be applied. This is an important area of policy space for WTO members to define the appropriate contours of their patent laws in accordance to meeting the objectives of the patent system and against other objectives such as public health policy. See Correa (2014).

[5] The permissible exclusions are defined in the TRIPS Article 27.2 and Article 27.3.

[6] TRIPS Article 30 states that "Members may provide limited exceptions to the exclusive rights conferred by a patent, provided that such exceptions do not unreasonably conflict with a normal exploitation of the patent and do not unreasonably prejudice the legitimate interests of the patent owner, taking account of the legitimate interests of third parties."

[7] See Correa (2005).

[8] Dreyfuss (2018), p. 8.

panel *Canada-Pharmaceutical Patents* case.[9] The panel decision is not a binding precedent for Members in developing their exceptions that are compatible with the TRIPS Agreement. Moreover, given that the decision was not appealed, the Appellate Body did not provide its own interpretation.[10]

2 Rationale for the Bolar Exception

When the patent monopoly expires, the patent ceases be a legal obstacle for a competitor to produce and commercialize the protected product or use the protected process. However, other market barriers may remain. Pharmaceutical products must meet regulatory requirements for authorization to be placed on the market. The patent status of the originator product can impede the competitor from being able to start work to meet regulatory requirements in order to be able to place the product on the market once the originator patent expires. Unless such work is permitted during the patent term, by an exception. Without the Bolar exception, or a broad experimental use exception that includes acts to provide information for regulatory approval, the competitor will not be able to prepare for regulatory approval until the patent expiry. This means that, as obtaining the marketing approval for a generic[11] medicine takes time, the patent monopoly for the originator is practically extended further in time than originally conceived. In recognition of this problematic, the Bolar exception is present in many national jurisdictions.

A review of the process of market authorization for medical products is presented below, prior to discussing in more detail examples of how the Bolar exception is crafted in various jurisdictions.

[9] World Trade Organization (2000)

[10] Mercurio and Tyagi note that the Appellate Body has supported a broad interpretation of exceptions based on the Appellate Body Report, European Communities—Measures Concerning Meat and Meat Products (Hormones), ¶ 104, WT/DS26/AB/R, WT/DS48/AB/R (Jan. 16, 1998), ("[M]erely characterizing a treaty provision as an 'exception' does not by itself justify a 'stricter' or 'narrower' interpretation of that provision than would be warranted by examination of the ordinary meaning of the actual treaty words, viewed in context and in the light of the treaty's object and purpose, or, in other words, by applying the normal rules of treaty interpretation."). Mercurio and Tyagi (2010), 262, footnote 68.

[11] In this chapter the term generics is used to describe chemical, small molecule medicinal products that are structurally and therapeutically equivalent to an originator product. Generics are interchangeable with an originator product.

2.1 Marketing Authorization of Medical Products

Governments have an important role in formulating laws and regulations to define and control the national market in medical products in the interest of public health.[12] The national medicine regulatory authority aims to protect public health by ensuring that a product is safe, efficacious and of good quality before it reaches a patient. Thus, national medicine regulatory authorities around the world subject pharmaceutical products to premarketing evaluation and marketing authorization to ensure that they conform to required standards.[13] The marketing approval system is applied in accordance to national law. All medicines have to be authorized before they can be marketed. The manufacturers of any medicine, whether it is a brand-name originator or a generic,[14] need to comply with the requirements. A granted marketing authorization is valid in the geographical territory in which it is applied for.[15]

The specific regulatory requirements for a medical product to be marketed may vary. For chemically synthesized pharmaceuticals, regulatory authorities generally require that generic products demonstrate the same bioavailability and often bioequivalence of the generic medicine to a reference product. Producing a full dossier, including showing the results of pre-clinical tests and clinical trials to show safety and efficacy of the product, can require significant investment and time. In the case of requests for approval for local production of medicines or import of medicines already marketed and approved in third countries, requirements of local clinical trials may be waived. Hence, if a medical product is a generic of a reference medical product, it may receive an abridged process for compliance with the premarketing evaluation and marketing authorization.

Marketing approval or licensure of biologics—referring to medical products that are made from living organisms-, and biosimilars[16] may be subject to specific and more stringent requirements. There is significant divergence on approaches being

[12] See World Health Organization (1999).

[13] See World Health Organization (2011).

[14] A generic medicine is an equal substitute for an already marketed brand-name drug and is not protected by a patent in force. Generics are generally commercialized under a non-proprietary name. Pharmaceutical substances and active pharmaceutical ingredients are given unique, non-proprietary, generic International Nonproprietary Names (INN). A generic may also be marketed under its own brand name.

[15] However, many national regulatory authorities have entered into harmonization initiatives or mutual recognition agreements. For example, in the European Union there are different authorization routes and some medicines go through a centralised marketing authorisation valid in all EU member States.

[16] Another term used for example by the WHO is "similar biotherapeutic products", to refer to a biological product which is similar in terms of quality, safety and efficacy to an already licensed reference biotherapeutic product.

taken by regulatory agencies in this area and debate are ongoing on the current guidance by the World Health Organization (WHO) on the matter.[17]

2.2 *Relationship of Patent Protection, Marketing Authorization and Supplementary Legal Protection*

The relationship between patent protection and marketing authorization of medical products at first would appear to be very weak. All medical products are subject to regulatory requirements, regardless of their patent status. Moreover, in accordance to patent law, once patent protection expires, competitors should have free entry. However, in practice, questions of marketing authorization and patent protection for medical products have become more intertwined, as policy makers juggle in balancing between innovation and competition incentives, under pressure from a wide range of stakeholders.

In principle, the patent status of the originator medical product should be irrelevant for purposes of the regulatory requirements for approval of generics or biosimilars. However, some countries have adopted a patent linkage regime to link the grant of marketing approval by a regulatory authority with the patent status of an originator medical product.[18] This system poses the additional burden on the regulatory authority to review whether there may be a patent infringement before it will issue marketing approval for a new product and creates new restrictions for the registration of generic and biosimilar products.

In addition, patent term extensions may be available in some jurisdictions under the rationale of compensating for delays in examination or simply because the product is subject to regulatory review. These provisions, generally incorporated in free trade agreements entered into by the USA and the European Union,[19] result in further delays of generic and biosimilar market entry.

The increased laxity in the criteria applied in patent examination in some jurisdictions also enables the pharmaceutical industry to employ strategic patenting tactics such as "evergreening" to artificially extend the patent term for profitable medical products.[20] Moreover, in some jurisdictions, the patent incentive for innovation is now supplemented with other legal exclusivities that support the originator

[17] See Velásquez (2018). See also on challenges on advancing biosimilars, Vaca and Gómez (2020), Kang et al. (2020).

[18] Patent linkage is not an international obligation, but often requested by the United States in free trade agreement negotiations and as part of unilateral trade pressures. See Mercurio (2017), pp. 97–122, and Correa (2020).

[19] See Daniel Opoku Acquah, Revisiting the Question of Extending the Limits of Protection of Pharmaceutical Patents and Data Outside the EU – The Need to Rebalance, Research Paper 127, December 2020, South Centre, https://www.southcentre.int/wp-content/uploads/2020/12/RP-127.pdf.

[20] See Ducimetière (2019). Gurgula (2019). I-Mak (2018).

in delaying entry of generics or biosimilars after the patent term expiry, including data and market exclusivity[21] and supplementary protection certificates.[22]

On the other hand, in order to promote competition, regulatory authorities may provide abbreviated pathways for the approval of generics and more recently, for biosimilars. The policy rationale of the Bolar exception, where available in national patent laws, also aims to lower product development costs, expedite regulatory approval and ease market entry.

In this sense, the balance between innovation and competition no longer rests solely on the design and implementation of the patent system—but on the myriad of other related instruments that are crafted to respond to the variety of interests involved and overall complex ecosystem of medical product development, procurement and supply.

2.3 Role of Generic and Biosimilar Competition in Promoting Access

Medicine prices decrease significantly after patent expiry.[23] The increased use of generic medicines is an important measure for cost-containment in pharmaceutical procurement. Generics increase competition and lower prices for medicines that improve access and lower medicine purchase expenditures for governments, to sustain their healthcare systems. This is of particular relevance today in the context of rising drug spending, affected by high prices for some medicines, in particular of biologics such as monoclonal antibodies, notably in low and middle income countries where in addition to limited government budgets for public procurement, out-of-pocket purchases are high.

In the United States, the top twelve grossing medicines, mostly biologicals, have increased by 68% from 2012 to 2018 and cost $96 billion to health insurers, government payers, and consumers in 2017 alone.[24] A recent US FDA report from December 2019 compared medicines that had initial generic entry between 2015 and 2017 and found that the median price of generics relative to brands is 40%.[25] In Europe, pioneer in biosimilar registration and the largest market for global biosimilar

---

[21] See Correa (2013), pp. 16-/173.

[22] The experience with these new exclusivities or sui generis IPRs for regulated products has also led to the adoption of new exceptions. See Seuba (2019), pp. 876–886, https://doi.org/10.1093/jiplp/jpz108.

[23] Vondeling et al. (2018), pp. 653–660. https://doi.org/10.1007/s40258-018-0406-6 pmid:30019138.

[24] I-Mak Report, Overpatented, Overpriced: how excessive pharmaceutical patenting is extending monopolies and driving up drug prices, 2018. http://www.i-mak.org/wp-content/uploads/2018/08/I-MAK-Overpatented-Overpriced-Report.pdf.

[25] The calculations use average manufacturer prices. Conrad and Lutter (2019).

sales, biosimilar competition has significantly reduced prices for biologicals.[26] Nonetheless, the overall market penetration of biosimilars remains low, though expiration of patent and exclusivities of the originator biologics is increasing opportunities for further savings.[27] Currently 61 biosimilars have been approved in Europe since the establishment of the regulatory framework for registration of biosimilars in 2005.[28] India is the largest provider of generic medicines globally, occupying a 20% share in global supply by volume, and with increasing capacity for production of biosimilars.[29]

The extent of the cost-saving potential from switching from originators to generic products may nonetheless vary among countries depending on, among other factors, differences in the timing of patent expiries, the type of generic medicine pricing policies they apply,[30] dispensing practices, the market share of generic medicines. Expanding biosimilar uptake presents additional challenges, including the extensive litigation actions by biopharmaceutical manufacturers, the need for greater acceptance by physicians and patients of biosimilars as safe and effective alternatives to reference-biologic products.

On a more global level, the role of generics in increasing access is evident in relation the HIV/AIDS pandemic. The decline in mortality rates between the mid 1990s to early 200s is attributable in large part to the expanded access to generic antiretrovirals (ARVs), mostly produced in India, that greatly reduced prices and allowed for treatment expansion. In Brazil, with the production of local generic ARVs, the prices fell by more than 70% in four years. By 2000, AIDS mortality rate in Brazil had been halved and HIV-related hospital admissions had fallen by 80%.[31]

3 History of the Bolar Exception

Patents and other exclusivities constitute barriers to market access for generics and biosimilars. The Bolar exception is a tool within patent law that supports market entry of generics and biosimilars, by allowing manufacturers to prepare these products in advance of the expiration of the originators' patents.

The history of the Bolar Exception is well documented. It stems from US Congress reaction to the US Court of Appeals Federal Circuit 1984 decision in

[26] Gabi Journal Editor Biosimilars Markets (2020), pp. 90–92. https://doi.org/10.5639/gabij.2020.0902.015.

[27] OECD/European Union (2018), https://doi.org/10.1787/health_glance_eur-2018-en.

[28] European Medicines Agency, https://www.ema.europa.eu/en/medicines/.

[29] https://www.investindia.gov.in/sector/pharmaceuticals.

[30] The various policies include free-pricing systems (i.e. US) versus price-regulated systems (i.e. EU), reference pricing, price competition and discounts, and tendering procedures. Reimbursement policies may also affect final generic price.

[31] UNAIDS (2008), p. 113.

Roche Products v Bolar Pharmaceutical Co. where it was held that the experimental use doctrine did not protect the "limited use of a patented drug for testing and investigation strictly related to US Food and Drug Administration (FDA) drug approval requirements" and found that Bolar's experimental use in this case had definite, cognizable, and not insubstantial commercial purposes.[32] The Generic Pharmaceutical Industry Association (GPIA) had shown in its *amicus curiae* that various generics had been tested prior to patent expiry, and argued that the decision essentially allowed originator manufacturers to retain market exclusivity for their products beyond the duration of the patent terms because generic manufacturers could not even start developing and seeking approval for competing generic products until after the originator patent expired.[33] Soon after, the US Congress passed the Drug Price Competition and Patent Term Restoration Act of 1984, better known as the Hatch-Waxman Act, 35 U.S.C. § 271(e) (2003). The Hatch-Waxman Act made significant changes to US patent law with the aim to encourage innovation in the pharmaceutical industry while facilitating the speedy introduction of lower-cost generic medicines, thereby attempting to get a compromise between the interests of the research based and generic segments of the industry. Among the changes introduced, was the Bolar exception codified as 35 U.S.C. § 271(e)(1) that reversed Roche v Bolar court of appeals decision:

> It shall not be an act of infringement to make, use or sell a patented invention . . . solely for uses reasonably related to the development and submission of information under a Federal law which regulates the manufacture, use, or sale of drugs or veterinary biological products.

Judicial interpretations of 271(e)(1) have given a broad reading of the subject matter (i.e. originators, biologics, generics, biosimilars, medical devices) and permitted the coverage of a range of activities under the exemption.[34]

Many countries have subsequently introduced a similar regulatory review exception in their patent laws, as will be discussed further in section 5 below.

4 Consistency with Article 30 of the TRIPS Agreement

A WTO dispute settlement panel examined the regulatory review provision of the Patent Act of Canada in the *Canada–Pharmaceuticals Patent* case[35] and confirmed that it conforms with the TRIPS Agreement. The panel found that there was no conflict with a normal exploitation of the patent (Article 28.1 of the TRIPS

---

[32] *Roche Products v Bolar Pharmaceutical Co.*, 733 F.2d.858 (Fed.Cir.1984) at 863.

[33] Krulwich (1985), pp. 519–525. Retrieved December 20, 2020, from http://www.jstor.org/stable/26658803.

[34] See Noonan (2015), p. a020800. Published 2015 Mar 16. https://doi.org/10.1101/cshperspect.a020800.

[35] Ibid, at 9.

Agreement) and that it was justified under Article 30 of the TRIPS Agreement (exceptions).

The Canada Patent Act, Section 55.2(1) reads: "It is not an infringement of a patent for any person to make, construct, use or sell the patented invention solely for uses reasonably related to the development and submission of information required under any law of Canada, a province or a country other than Canada that regulates the manufacture, construction, use or sale of any product."

The panel held that the provision was justified under Article 30 by meeting all of the three cumulative criteria: it is a "limited" exception, not unreasonably interfering with the normal exploitation of the patent, and not unreasonably prejudicing the rights of the patent holder, taking into account the legitimate interests of third parties.[36]

In the WTO Council for Trade Related Aspects of Intellectual Property Rights (TRIPS Council)[37] and at the World Intellectual Property Organization,[38] countries have continued to exchange on the rationale for inclusion of the exception in their laws as a mean to balance the private interests of patent right holders and public interest, and experiences in its use.

5 Crafting National Legal Frameworks for the Bolar Exception

The Bolar Exemption is recognized in various national patent laws, generally with the aim to support entry of competitor products upon patent expiry of the originator product. A WIPO study from 2018 indicates that at least 65 countries and two regional instruments provide for a Bolar exception.[39] While the objective of the Bolar exception is the same—to avoid delays in market entry for competitor products—there can be significant divergences among national approaches, including on scope and implementation.

In fact, for the design of a Bolar exception, there can be numerous alternative approaches. Professor Correa has advanced that "the broader the formulation of the exception in terms of covered products, sources of samples, type of trials allowed,

---

[36] The panel found that the stockpiling provision in the Canadian Patent Act is inconsistent with TRIPS Agreement Article 28.1, as it did not satisfy the first condition of TRIPS Agreement Article 30 because it is not a "limited exception."

[37] WTO document IP/C/M/88/Add.1, Minutes of the TRIPS Council, 12 April 2018, Agenda item 12: Intellectual Property and Public Interest, Regulatory Review exception, https://docs.wto.org/dol2fe/Pages/SS/directdoc.aspx?filename=q:/IP/C/M88A1.pdf&Open=True.

[38] WIPO draft reference document on the exception regarding acts for obtaining regulatory approval from authorities (second draft), document SCP/28/3, https://www.wipo.int/edocs/mdocs/scp/en/scp_28/scp_28_3.pdf. The document is kept open for future discussion by the Standing Committee on Patents.

[39] Ibid, at 35.

time to undertake them, and geographical scope, the more competitive environment is ensured that will benefit consumers, health providers and other public agencies."[40] The policy choice for designing a broader Bolar exception is more favourable to the objective of promoting competition.

Several countries, such as the United Kingdom and Ireland, have in recent years amended their patent laws to broaden the scope of the Bolar exception. The extension of the Bolar exception has also been under consideration in the EU[41] given the divergences in current implementation throughout the member States and in the context of how a future Unified Patent Court (UPC) may apply the Bolar exception.[42] A study by the Max Planck Institute for Innovation and Competition prepared for the European Commission recommended that the EU member States adopt a broader than the minimum standard currently provided for under Art. 27 (d) UPCA, in following the national Bolar exceptions in Germany, Ireland, Italy, France, among other EU member States.[43] The economic impacts of extending the Bolar exception in the EU to cover any medicines (not limited to products following an abridged marketing authorisation only), have been estimated as cost savings from patent screening of up to €23-€34.2 million per year.[44]

In order to well define the Bolar exception, it may be preferable to design it as a specific exception, as opposed to inclusion as part of a general research or experimental exception.

The Bolar exception can be crafted to cover all regulated products, including but not limited to health-related products for human use, such as medicines and medical devices. Other regulated products covered in some Bolar exceptions include veterinary medicines and plant protection products.

The scope of the activities should be clearly defined. These should relate to obtaining marketing approval for generics and biosimilars, but may also extend for acts relating to medical devices (as provided for in the US) and innovative medicines (for example to carry out health technology assessments as in the Bolar exception in the UK Patents Act).

It is not necessary to restrict the user of the Bolar exception to the party that would be requesting the marketing authorization. It can also include acts by third parties involved in supplying materials to a company to run tests and trials related to obtaining marketing authorization for a generic or biosimilar.

---

[40] Correa (2016).

[41] The Bolar exception was introduced in Article 10(6) of the Directive 2004/27/EC of 31 March 2004, https://eur-lex.europa.eu/legal-content/EN/TXT/?uri=CELEX:32004L0027.

[42] The establishment of the unitary patent system and UPC may follow if the Agreement on a Unified Patent Court (UPCA) enters into force. The UPCA Article 27(d) contains the Bolar Exception: "The rights conferred by a patent shall not extend to . . .the acts allowed pursuant to Article 13(6) of Directive 2001/82/EC or Article 10(6) of Directive 2001/83/EC in respect of any patent covering the product within the meaning of either of those Directives".

[43] Max Planck Institute for Innovation and Competition, Study on the legal aspects of supplementary protection certificates in the EU, European Union, 2018, pp. 338–361.

[44] Charles River Associates (2016).

A clear definition of the scope of the permitted acts is one of the critical aspects of a Bolar exception so as to provide legal certainty of the safeguards it provides against patent infringement and to the rights of patent holders. Acts that are related to obtaining marketing approval that should be covered include studies, trials and experiments required for obtaining marketing approval in the country, as well as for obtaining marketing approval in other countries. As noted earlier, third party activity for the company seeking marketing approval, such as delivery of an Active Pharmaceutical Ingredient (API) to carry out tests or trials when the company is unable to produce the API in-house, can also be included.[45]

6 India Bolar Exception: Recent Developments

The design and implementation of the Bolar exception is of particular relevance in countries that have domestic production capacity for generics and biosimilars. The Bolar exception in Indian legislation is of special interest, as India, as noted, is a global leader in the global supply of affordable generic and biosimilar products. The Bolar exception contributes to a favorable environment for the generic and biosimilar industry in India to develop and expand.

The Indian patent act in Section 107A includes a broad Bolar exception. It reads: "any act of making, using, selling or importing a patented invention solely for uses reasonably related to the development and submission of information required under any law in India, or in a country other than India, shall not be considered as infringement of patent rights."[46]

The exception applies to any regulated sector, and extends to acts done for submission of information not only in India but in any other country. The scope of acts covered can include the manufacture of the patented protected product, export of an API or finished formulation by a generic company, conduct of clinical trials, or import of the API or formulation by a third party to support relevant regulatory approvals in India or other countries.

While the Section. 107A is clearly worded, there has been significant litigation with respect to this provision, and, accordingly the Indian judiciary has provided important interpretation of its scope. A recent case tested in particular the definition of "selling" and determined that it allows export of a patented product for generation or submission of information for seeking regulatory approval in India or other countries, without such export constituting an act of patent infringement. A Division Bench of the Delhi High Court held that export for the purpose of conducting development/clinical studies and trials is within the ambit of the Indian Bolar

---

[45] The Dusseldorf Court of Appeal in 2013 (docket no. I-2 U 68/12, Astellas v Polharma) referred a preliminary ruling on this question to the European Court of Justice (ECJ), but the ECJ did not issue a judicial pronouncement as Astellas withdrew action against Polpharma.

[46] https://indiankanoon.org/doc/151051886/.

exception.[47] The Court established an indicative list of factors to determine whether the export is 'reasonably related' to the research purpose or not.

The court also clarified that section 107A is not to be treated as an exception to section 48 of Indian Patent Act: "*Its history of interpretation by TRIPS, the discussion in the Parliamentary Joint Committee Report, all clearly point to its being a special provision that deals with the rights of the patented invention for research purposes.*"[48]

The relationship of the Bolar exception with the terms of a compulsory license was also considered by the court. As noted by Indian delegation to the WTO, "Bolar exceptions have an important link with compulsory licensing. The absence of the Bolar exceptions can severely affect the ability of a country to effectively utilize compulsory license provisions when considered necessary."[49]

In Bayer Corporation and Ors. v. Union of India and Ors., Bayer had filed a suit for infringement of Patent against Natco, a generic producer. During the pendency of the suit, Natco obtained a compulsory license for the same patent for the territory of India. Bayer filed a writ petition in the High Court of Delhi seeking a direction to the Custom Authorities to seize the consignments for export of the products covered by the compulsory license (CL) manufactured by Natco, on grounds that the export violated the terms of the CL. The Court passed an interim order to restrain Natco from the export. In parallel, Natco requested and obtained permission to export 1 kg of API to China to conduct clinical studies and trials for regulatory purposes. Bayer considered that the API sale was an infringement of the patent in violation of the CL terms. Natco argued that it was covered by the Bolar exemption as the export was for regulatory purposes.[50] In its decision the Court noted that "it is..of the opinion that Natco's status as compulsory licensee did not place it under any additional statutory bar from exporting the product, as long as the underlying condition in Section 107A was satisfied".[51]

7 Conclusions

Policy makers can apply different approaches to address the competing interests of promoting innovation and the discovery of new medicines while at the same time fostering competition through the development and market entry of lower cost

---

[47] Delhi High Court decision pronounced on 22 April 2019 on Bayer Corporation vs Union Of India & Ors. and *Bayer Intellectual Property GMBH & Anr. v. Alembic Pharmaceuticals Ltd.*RFA(OS) (COMM) 6/2017, https://indiankanoon.org/doc/85364944/.

[48] Ibid, *para 89.*

[49] Ibid at 35, para 435, page 53.

[50] For further analysis of the arguments made by Bayer and Natco, see Rathod (2017), available at https://doi.org/10.2139/ssrn.2971521.

[51] Ibid at 45, para 94.

generic and biosimilar products. The policy approach should be in line with public health policies, i.e. to support access to medicines for all, and informed by the domestic context of the pharmaceutical industry.

Without the regulatory review or "Bolar" exception, competitive products such as generics and biosimilars would not be able to enter the market for prolonged periods following patent expiry of originator products. The safeguard against patent infringement for acts covered by the Bolar exception supports the regulatory approvals for generics and biosimilars without delay. Policy choices to expand the term of patent protection, introduce test data exclusivity or patent linkage can have the effect of increasing barriers for generic and biosimilar market entry.

A broad and well-defined Bolar exception, as described in this chapter, is suited to the objective of promoting timely regulatory approval for generics and biosimilars to lower costs for health systems and improve access to medicines.

References

Agreement on Trade-related Aspects of Intellectual Property Rights of 1994; being Annexe 1C to the Agreement Establishing the World Trade Organization, 15 April 1994

Bently L (2011) Exclusions from patentability and exceptions to patentees' rights: taking exceptions seriously. Curr Leg Probl 64:315–347

Charles River Associates (2016) Assessing the Economic Impacts of the exemption provisions during patent and SPC protection in Europe, European Commission

Conrad R, Lutter R (2019) U.S. Food and Drug Administration Generic Competition and Drug Prices: New Evidence Linking Greater Generic Competition and Lower Generic Drug Prices. https://www.fda.gov/media/133509/download

Correa C (2005) The international dimension of the research exception. SIPPI (Project on Science and Intellectual Property in the Public Interest), The American Association for the Advancement of Science, Washington, DC. http://sippi.aaas.org/Pubs/Correa_International%20Exception.pdf

Correa C (2013) Protection of data submitted for the registration of pharmaceutical products: trips requirements and "TRIPS-Plus" provisions. In: Intellectual Property and Access to Medicines. South Centre and World Health Organization, pg. 16-/173. https://www.southcentre.int/wp-content/uploads/2016/05/Bk_2013_IP-and-Access-to-Medicines_EN.pdf

Correa CM (2014) Tackling the Proliferation of Patents: How to avoid undue limitations to competition and the public domain. Research Paper 52, South Centre, 2014 https://www.southcentre.int/wp-content/uploads/2014/09/RP52_Tackling-the-Proliferation-of-Patents-rev_EN.pdf

Correa CM (2016) The Bolar exception: legislative models and drafting options. Research Paper 66, South Centre. https://www.southcentre.int/wp-content/uploads/2016/03/RP66_The-Bolar-Exception_EN1.pdf

Correa CM (2017) Intellectual Property in the Trans-Pacific Partnership: Increasing the Barriers for the Access to Affordable Medicines. Research Paper 62R, South Centre

Correa CM (2020) Special Section 301:US Interference with the Design and Implementation of National Patent Laws, Research Paper 115. South Centre, July 2020. https://www.southcentre.int/research-paper-115-july-2020/

Delhi High Court decision pronounced on 22 April 2019 on Bayer Corporation vs Union Of India & Ors. and Bayer Intellectual Property GMBH & Anr. v. Alembic Pharmaceuticals Ltd.RFA(OS) (COMM) 6/2017. https://indiankanoon.org/doc/85364944/

Dreyfuss RC (2018) Justine Pila intellectual property law: an anatomical overview. In: The Oxford handbook of intellectual property law. Oxford University Press, p 8

Ducimetière C (2019) Second Medical Use Patents – Legal Treatment and Public Health Issues, Research Paper 101. South Centre, December 2019. https://www.southcentre.int/research-paper-101-december-2019/

European Medicines Agency., https://www.ema.europa.eu/en/medicines/

Gabi Journal Editor Biosimilars Markets: US and EU compared, Generics and Biosimilars Initiative Journal (GaBI Journal). 2020;9(2):90–92. https://doi.org/10.5639/gabij.2020.0902.015

Gurgula O (2019) The 'obvious to try' method of addressing strategic patenting: How developing countries can utilise patent law to facilitate access to medicines. Policy Brief 59, April 2019, South Centre. https://www.southcentre.int/policy-brief-59-april-2019/#more-12341

I-Mak, Overpatented, overpriced: how excessive pharmaceutical patenting is extending monopolies and driving up drug prices, 2018. http://www.i-mak.org/wp-content/uploads/2018/08/I-MAK-Overpatented-Overpriced-Report.pdf

I-Mak Report Overpatented, Overpriced: How Excessive Pharmaceutical Patenting is Extending Monopolies and Driving up Drug Prices. http://www.i-mak.org/wp-content/uploads/2018/08/I-MAK-Overpatented-Overpriced-Report.pdf

Kang HN, Thorpe R, Knezevic I et al (2020) Regulatory challenges with biosimilars: an update from 20 countries. Ann N Y Acad Sci. https://pubmed.ncbi.nlm.nih.gov/33222245/

Krulwich A (1985) Statutory reversal of Roche v. Bolar: what you see is only the beginning of what you get. Food Drug Cosmetic Law J 40(4):519–525. http://www.jstor.org/stable/26658803

Max Planck Institute for Innovation and Competition (2018) Study on the legal aspects of supplementary protection certificates in the EU. European Union, pp 338–361

Mercurio B (2017) Patent linkage regulations. In Mercurio B, Kim D (eds) Contemporary issues in pharmaceutical patent law. Routledge, pp 97–122

Mercurio B, Tyagi M (2010) Treaty interpretation in WTO dispute settlement: the outstanding question of the legality of local working requirements. Minnesota J Int Law. 262, footnote 68

Noonan KE (2015) The role of regulatory agencies and intellectual property: Part I. Cold Spring Harb Perspect Med. 5(7):a020800. Published 2015 Mar 16. https://doi.org/10.1101/cshperspect.a020800

OECD/European Union (2018) Health at a Glance: Europe 2018: State of Health in the EU Cycle. OECD Publishing, Paris/European Union, Brussels. https://doi.org/10.1787/health_glance_eur-2018-en

Panel Report Canada – Patent Protection of Pharmaceutical Products WT/DS114/R, 17 March 2000. https://www.wto.org/english/tratop_e/dispu_e/7428d.pdf

Rathod S (2017) The Curious Case of India's Bolar Provision. SSRN https://doi.org/10.2139/ssrn.2971521

Roche Products v Bolar Pharmaceutical Co., 733 F.2d.858 (Fed.Cir.1984) at 863

Seuba X (2019) The export and stockpiling waivers: new exceptions for supplementary protection certificates. J Intellect Prop Law Pract 14(11):876–886. https://doi.org/10.1093/jiplp/jpz108

UNAIDS: The First Ten Years, Joint United Nations Programme on HIV/AIDS (UNAIDS) 2008, p 113

Vaca C, Gómez C (2020) The Controversy around technical standards for similar biotherapeutics: barriers to access and competition. Pharmacoepidemiol Drug Safety. https://doi.org/10.1002/pds.5100

Velásquez G (2018) The international debate on generic medicines of biological origin, Policy Brief No. 50, South Centre, https://www.southcentre.int/wp-content/uploads/2018/08/PB50_The-International-Debate-on-Generic-Medicines-of-Biological-Origin_EN.pdf

Vondeling GT, Cao Q, Postma MJ, Rozenbaum MH (2018) The impact of patent expiry on drug prices: a systematic literature review. Appl Health Econ Health Policy 16:653–660. https://doi.org/10.1007/s40258-018-0406-6 pmid:30019138

WIPO. draft reference document on the exception regarding acts for obtaining regulatory approval from authorities (second draft), document SCP/28/3, https://www.wipo.int/edocs/mdocs/scp/en/

scp_28/scp_28_3.pdf. The document is kept open for future discussion by the Standing Committee on Patents

World Health Organization (1999) Marketing authorization of pharmaceutical products with special reference to multisource (generic) products: a manual for a drug regulatory authority. World Health Organization. https://apps.who.int/iris/handle/10665/65175

World Health Organization (2011) Marketing authorization of pharmaceutical products with special reference to multisource (generic) products: a manual for National Medicines Regulatory Authorities (NMRAs), 2nd edn. World Health Organization. https://apps.who.int/iris/handle/10665/44576

World Trade Organization (2000) Canada – Patent Protection of Pharmaceutical Products, Report of the Panel, WT/DS114/R, 17 March 2000

WTO document IP/C/M/88/Add.1, Minutes of the TRIPS Council, 12 April 2018, Agenda item 12: Intellectual Property and Public Interest, Regulatory Review exception. https://docs.wto.org/dol2fe/Pages/SS/directdoc.aspx?filename=q:/IP/C/M88A1.pdf&Open=True

Patent Oppositions in India

Sandeep Kanak Rathod

Abstract Pre-grant and post-grant oppositions filed in India by civil society and generic companies have been instrumental in visibly increasing access of drugs to the public—both in terms of earlier generic entry and also cheaper prices due to such generic competition. This paper looks at the significant pharmaceutical patent oppositions in India during the last 15 years. It focuses on some unique aspects connected to each of these oppositions and tracks how these oppositions helped in securing earlier access to generic drugs. The last part of the paper analyses patent opposition pendency statistics and notes that increasing pendency numbers, over the last few years, is a matter of deep concern as it could impact access to drugs, in future.

1 Introduction

Patent oppositions by civil society organisations and generic pharmaceutical companies have been instrumental in increasing access of drugs to the public—by preventing patent evergreening and bringing in earlier generic drug entry as well as increasing competition in the pharmaceutical sector leading to cheaper prices due to such generic entry. Over the years, various commentators have written on Indian patent oppositions—from different legal and policy perspectives.[1]

In this paper, the author analyses key pharmaceutical patent oppositions in the last one and half decade and shares certain lesser discussed angles of these oppositions. The paper is divided in two parts. The first part discusses important pharmaceutical patent oppositions pertaining to drugs across disease categories and looks at how legal arguments have progressed moving beyond the simplistic statutory arguments as well as how certain strategies that are beyond the opposition framework can lead to successful results even when an opposition is not filed.

[1] Below are some papers that have looked at patent oppositions in India from different perspectives: Amin (2010); Ho (2011); Ali (2016); Serrano and Burri (2019), pp. 275–294.

S. K. Rathod (✉)
Mumbai, India

C. M. Correa, R. M. Hilty (eds.), *Access to Medicines and Vaccines*,
https://doi.org/10.1007/978-3-030-83114-1_6

The second part of the paper looks at the current opposition pendency statistics and what these statistics mean for oppositions for the times to come. Before proceeding further, it is important to note that India, like many developing countries, has a healthcare system where individuals pay a very large proportion of healthcare expenses from their pocket.[2] This reality combined with a large population, means that the drug access mechanism becomes that much more strained and every attempt at increasing drug access needs to be seen not only in the limited framework of intellectual property (IP) but in the broader framework of living in a resource constrained country.

India has a long history of patent law, going back to the 1850s.[3] The present patents regime in India is enshrined within the Patents Act, 1970[4] ('the 1970 Act') that was enacted after repealing the Indian Patents and Designs Act 1911. After independence in 1947, India set up committees to look at the 1911 Act and these committees noted the stage of economic development in India, the relevance of patents to a country that was then not an industrially developed nation and what possible changes could be made to the 1911 Act. The *Ayyangar* Committee Report[5] also noted the disparities resulting from the 1911 Act and how certain steps were necessary to completely rewrite the statute. Importantly, this Report recommended moving to a 'process claims' only regime for certain sectors[6] and was the foundation for the 1970 Act.

The 1970 Act allowed only process patents within the drug/pharmaceuticals and food domain, until 2005. Changes were made in stages to the 1970 Act in 1999, 2002 and 2005 as a part of India's commitments to the Trade Related Aspects of Intellectual Property Agreement (TRIPs Agreement) and India restarted issuing product patents for pharmaceuticals and allied sectors from 2005.

---

[2] As per the National Health Accounts (NHA) estimate for 2014–15, Out-of-Pocket Expenditure (OPE) per person, per year in India, is Rs. 2394, which comes out to be 63% of the total health expenditure.

Reference: <https://www.downtoearth.org.in/dte-infographics/india_s_health_crisis/index.html>.

The World Bank data also gives a similar figure (of 62.4% as OPE—latest data pertained to year 2017): <https://data.worldbank.org/indicator/SH.XPD.OOPC.CH.ZS?end=2017&locations=IN&start=2000&view=chart>.

[3] The 'background' section has been adopted from author's earlier article: *Compulsory licences on pharmaceutical patents in India: A short article. Journal of Generic Medicine, 13(3), 108–113.* doi:10.1177/1741134317691804.

[4] A copy of the statute is available at the Indian Patent Office' website: <http://www.ipindia.nic.in/acts-patents.htm>.

[5] '*Report on the revision of the patents law*' by Justice N. Rajagopala Ayyangar; released in September 1959 and available at <http://www.ipindia.nic.in/writereaddata/Portal/Images/pdf/1959-_Justice_N_R_Ayyangar_committee_report.pdf>.

[6] The Report discussed the background and rationale for moving from product claims to a process claims only regime for certain sectors, extensively—Refer Paragraphs 56 through 102 of the Report.

Originally, oppositions came in the prosecution framework only once—i.e. after a patent application had already been examined and accepted by the Patent Office i.e. India allowed filing oppositions against 'applications accepted for grant'. India modified its patent opposition system in 2005 and created provisions for two types of oppositions—pre-grant opposition against a published application and post-grant opposition against a granted patent. In the earlier system, oppositions came in the prosecution framework only once—i.e. after a patent application had already been examined and accepted by the Patent Office. The modification thus allowed an opposition to be filed at an earlier stage of the prosecution framework as well as after the grant of patent.

Accordingly, a patent application can now be opposed under section 25(1) by filing a representation with the Patent Office. This is also normally called as a 'pre-grant opposition'. A granted patent can be opposed under section 25(2) by filing an opposition. This is normally called as a 'post-grant opposition'. It needs to be filed within 12 months from the date of publication of such grant. A patent can also be sought to be revoked under section 64 and the Government can revoke patents on policy considerations under section 66.

There are four main players within the patent opposition framework as applied to pharmaceutical inventions:

- The Government—Ministry of Commerce & Industry, Government of India (which is ultimately responsible for the functioning of the Patent Office and grant of patents), the Ministry of Health and Family Welfare (responsible for health framework) and the Ministry of Chemicals and Fertilizers (that houses the Department of Pharmaceuticals);
- Innovator companies filing patents for their products (Applicants);
- Generic companies seeking to launch drugs as soon as possible (Opponents); and
- Civil society/Non-governmental organisations (also termed as 'NGOs') working at the grassroots on access to medicines and patient rights and who oppose patent applications/patents for ensuring drug access (hence, also Opponents).

Each of these players are important stakeholders and have different priorities/goals within the patent system but each of them must play their roles with integrity and efficiency to create a system that balances drug access and health with encouraging an intellectual property (IP) rights framework to reward innovators.

The paper discusses 14 oppositions (both pre-grant and post-grant) that relate to important drugs that are needed by a large patient population. Oppositions for niche drugs are excluded. In most of the cases, companies had launched a generic version of the product, while the opposition proceedings were on-going and hence if the oppositions would have failed, it would have negatively impacted generic drug access.

As we trace these pharmaceutical oppositions, we note that many of the early oppositions filed in 2005–2015 were centered mainly around the statutory arguments from S.3[7] (which excludes from patentability certain inventions and is titled 'What are not inventions') and mostly around S.3(d) of the Patents Act (that bars grant of patents to new form of known substances or mere use of known processes).

Opponents have, over the years, moved beyond basing their case on S.3(d) alone and have gone to draft and win oppositions based on more complex arguments like lack of inventive step, obvious to try, anticipatory disclosures from *markush* claim[8] filings etc. Just like the opposition arguments moved beyond 3(d), so have the patent examiners, for examination of pharmaceutical claims.

Published empirical research[9] covering patent applications having priority dates between 2000 and 2012 advises that while examiners are invoking S. 3(d) more over time, but when they do so, it still tends to be in conjunction with novelty and inventive step objections. But effective use of S.3 and its implementation is an open question. A later paper[10] covering pharmaceutical patents granted between 2009 and 2016 argues that the Examiners at the Patent Office have not been implementing S.3 framework to its fullest and that more than 70% of such patents were in contravention of the anti-evergreening framework of S.3.

Hence, while one can try and imagine what would have happened in these 13 cases in absence of these oppositions; the undeniable fact is these pharmaceutical oppositions have expanded drug access for multiple important drugs—not just for Indian patients but also for patients from other countries that are dependent on Indian generic drugs.

Within this scenario, increasing pendency statistics for oppositions, over the last few years, is a matter of deep concern as it could negatively impact drug access.

2 Patent Oppositions in India

2.1 Gleevec Opposition

Any paper on Indian patent oppositions can move forward only by starting from the Imatinib Mesylate Beta polymorph form opposition. Imatinib (brand name *Gleevec*)

[7] Section 3 of the Patents Act, 1970, is titled—'What are not inventions'. Section 3 is a 'deeming' fiction—it prohibits grant of patents to certain categories of inventions and is part of the chapter titled 'Inventions not patentable'. Thus, these inventions, in absence of this section would have been patentable. Text of S.3 is available at https://indiankanoon.org/doc/874310/. Within S.3, S. 3(d), 3 (e) and 3(i) have special importance as they relate to pharmaceutical inventions.

[8] A '*Markush*' claim recites a list of alternatively useable members and can cover millions of compounds in a single claim. This can, at times, go much beyond actual embodiments exemplified in the patent specification. For a general discussion on what are *markush* claims, please refer https://www.uspto.gov/web/offices/pac/mpep/s2117.html.

[9] Sampat and Shadlen (2018), p. e0194714.

[10] Ali et al. (2018).

Table 1 Imatinib opposition

Drug:	Imatinib
Therapeutic area:	Anti-cancer/Oncology
Nature of patent filing in India:	Beta crystalline polymorph of drug—Imatinib Mesylate
Application #	1602/MAS/1998
Date & links to opposition decision:	25/Jan/2006 Natco: <https://indiankanoon.org/doc/1352538/> Cipla: <https://indiankanoon.org/doc/1740470/> Hetero: <https://indiankanoon.org/doc/1629598/> CPAA: <https://indiankanoon.org/doc/994049/>
Expiry, if patent would have been granted:	17/July/2018
Opponent(s):	Cancer Patients Aid Association (CPAA) Companies: Hetero, Cipla, Natco
Unique points:	Evidence submission, obviousness, disclosure versus claim scope and S.3(d)

is a Novartis drug used in treatment of certain cancers (such as acute lymphoblastic leukemia, chronic myeloid leukemia, gastrointestinal stromal tumors etc.).

This opposition battle went all the way up to the Supreme Court of India[11] where besides looking at the S.3(d) interpretation, the Court also made way for some very interesting case-law on inventive step, rejecting Novartis' arguments on disclosure v/s claim scope.

Filing details in Table 1:

The Indian Imatinib opposition saga starts after the grant of an exclusive marketing right (EMR) in December 2003 by the Patent Office to Novartis on its application for Beta polymorph of Imatinib Mesylate.

EMRs[12] were the predecessors of 'pharmaceutical product patent claims'. EMRs were brought into the statute book in 1999 as an interim mechanism to afford product patent type protection, after the United States' filed an action against India at the World Trade Organisation's Dispute Settlement Body in 1997.[13] These EMRs could be granted only upon satisfying certain criteria and were to cease upon grant of product patent to the EMR holder, in due course.

The drug 'Imatinib', including its salts forms was invented at Novartis in 1993 and patents were filed for it in many countries. This patent was not filed in India since India did not allow product patent status for pharmaceutical products, in 1993.

---

[11] *Novartis AG v. Union of India & Ors.* [2013] INSC 369. https://www.globalhealthrights.org/wp-content/uploads/2013/04/SC-2013-Novartis-AG-v.-Union-of-India.pdf.

[12] EMRs were bought in via the 1999 amendment and covered in Chapter IVA (Sections 24A through F) of the Patents Act. The EMR chapter was removed in the 2005 amendment that reintroduced product patents for pharmaceuticals.

[13] *Refer Nupur Maithani and Priyanka Vyas, 'India: Exclusive Marketing Rights Revisited in India' available at* https://www.mondaq.com/india/patent/73894/exclusive-marketing-rights-revisited-in-india.

Novartis' own experiments in 1996 had shown that there was no difference in efficacy between Imatinib and Imatinib Mesylate salt. It filed the Indian patent application for the Beta crystalline polymorph of Imatinib Mesylate in July 1998 and sought an EMR for the same from the Indian Patent Office, in March 2002. This 1998 patent filing was two steps away from the original 1993 invention—a move from Imatinib base to Imatinib Mesylate and then a move from Imatinib Mesylate to making a Beta crystalline polymorph of the same.

Meanwhile, Novartis had launched the drug in United States in 2001 and in India in April 2002. It got the EMR in December 2003. Some generic companies also launched the drug in India after Novartis' launch, but before the grant of EMR. There was a huge difference between Novartis' price and the price charged by generic companies.

Based on this EMR, in early 2004, Novartis went ahead with filing of infringement suits at two Courts—the Madras High Court (seven cases) and the Bombay High Court (three cases). The Madras High Court granted injunction(s) in favour of Novartis against such generic launches but the Bombay High Court did not grant injunctions. Multiple generic companies and civil society groups filed pre-grant oppositions against the pending application.

While journal articles have discussed nuances of the later court battles that came after the pre-grant opposition—including the Madras High Court[14] decision(s), the Intellectual Property Appellate Board decision[15] (IPAB) and the Supreme Court's decision,[16] but there is very little written material on the actual pre-grant decision.

While the Opponents raised multiple grounds, two key questions raised were related to (i) S.3(d) and (ii) assessment of obviousness. S.3(d) brings in an additional question of examination when claims relate to new forms of known substances—in this case, claimed 'beta polymorph of imatinib mesylate' was a new form of known substance—Imatinib and its salts and would be eligible for patent only if the beta polymorph passed the framework of S.3(d) i.e. a patent could be granted only if the beta polymorph differed significantly in properties with regard to efficacy when compared to Imatinib or its known salts. The obviousness assessment for these claims was focused on the question of how making polymorphs of a known drug or its salt forms could be considered obvious to a person skilled in the art.

There is a notion that the opposition proceeding was superficial and did not give Novartis a fair chance to adduce evidence/data that it could not have put in the original patent specification. This notion is not based on facts. Actually, the Patent Controller (Mr. Rengaswamy), at first instance, had afforded an opportunity to Novartis to show the merits of the beta polymorphic form. Novartis could only show that there was a 30% improvement in bioavailability—i.e. the relative

---

[14] Basheer and Reddy (2008), pp. 131–155.

[15] The IPAB's decision was analysed here: https://spicyip.com/2009/07/breaking-news-novartis-loses-glivec.html.

[16] The Supreme Court decision has been discussed below: (i) Ragavan (2013). http://works.bepress.com/srividhya_ragavan/156/. (ii) Attaran (2014), pp. 477–479. (iii) Grebe and Low (2017).

bioavailability of Imatinib Mesylate in the beta crystalline form versus Imatinib free base (and not Imatinib Mesylate salt)—but could not show any specific therapeutic advantage of the beta crystalline form over Imatinib Mesylate itself. A salt form of a drug (regardless of its polymorphic form) would normally have increased bioavailability over a drug in its base form.

Importantly, in his decision, the Controller noted that '. . . also the difference in bioavailability may be due to the difference in their solubility in water' and he held:

> . . . As regards efficacy, the specification itself states that wherever ß-crystals are used the imatinib free base or other salts can be used. The present patent specification does not bring out any improvement in the efficacy of the ß-crystal form over the known substances rather it states the base can be used equally in the treatment of diseases or in the preparation of pharmacological agents wherever the ß-crystal is used. Even the affidavit submitted on behalf of the Applicant does not prove any significant enhancement of known efficacy. It is found that this patent application claims only a new form of a known substance without having any significant improvement in efficacy. Hence I conclude that the subject matter of this application is not patentable. . .

Had these oppositions not been filed and Controller Rengaswamy not considered these key questions viz. (i) S.3(d) framework for assessing patentability arguments for new forms of a known substance and (ii) the law of obviousness for pharmaceutical inventions—then theoretically, the EMR and subsequent product patent would have sustained and possibly blocked generic launch until July 2018. While this opposition used S.3(d) extensively, the jurisprudence that developed from the Patent Office all the way up to the Supreme Court went a lot beyond the plain S.3 (d) argument.

Let's focus on some things that had their genesis from this set of pre-grant opposition(s). The filing of the pre-grant oppositions became the foundation for the later battles that led to the following important consequences:

- Securing earlier and consistent availability of generic version—from 2003 onwards and much before July 2018 (which would have been the expiry for the granted patent—thus earlier generic availability by a margin of 15 years);
- Bringing in a framework for examining obviousness while assessing pharmaceutical inventions;
- Creating jurisprudence on the concept of efficacy in pharmaceutical inventions and the difference between bioavailability and therapeutic efficacy (S.3(d));
- Laid the foundation for the Supreme Court to note that there cannot be a difference between what is disclosed in the patent specification versus what is claimed in the patent' claims.

This last point will again be in focus in the coming years—as Markush disclosures versus specific compound patent claim invalidation litigations are now pending the Indian Courts.

As noted earlier, literature has discussed extensively about the later high court, IPAB and Supreme Court battles of Imatinib. However, it is Controller Rengaswamy who was the first adjudicator/judge and made an important contribution that later

Table 2 Valganciclovir opposition

Drug:	Valganciclovir
Therapeutic area:	Anti-viral
Nature of patent filing in India:	Compound (L-valinate ester of Ganciclovir)
Patent/Application #	IN207232 (from 959/MAS/1995)
Dates of decision(s):	2nd Pre-grant: 30/Jan/2009 Post-grant: 30/April/2010 and again on 01/July/2015
Expiry, if patent remained granted:	27/July/2015
Opponent(s):	Indian Network of People Living with HIV/AIDS (INP+); Companies: Matrix; Ranbaxy; Cipla and Bakul Pharma.
Unique points:	Ambit of 'Person interested' to file post-grant opposition, Obvious to try and S.3(d).

became the cornerstone for India's pharmaceutical patent opposition/drug access saga.

2.2 *Valcyte Opposition*

Ganciclovir was approved as a drug in 1988. Roche later filed a patent application for a modification of Ganciclovir—i.e. it claimed the L-valinate ester of Ganciclovir (Valganciclovir, brand name: Valcyte). This drug is used in the treatment of adults in preventing infection with cytomegalovirus (CMV) that may occur after an organ transplant (heart, kidney, or pancreas). It is also used to treat CMV infection of the eye in adults with acquired immunodeficiency syndrome (AIDS). See Table 2.

This application saw the opposition fight in multiple rounds at the pre-grant stage and then a strongly contested post-grant opposition stage as well. And in the midst of this, there were rounds to the Madras High Court and the Supreme Court too.

In the first round, only a single short pre-grant opposition was filed by civil society groups (NGOs) in July 2006. The Controller rejected this opposition in November 2007 summarily and proceeded to process the grant of the patent. The civil society groups then moved the Madras High Court (HC) challenging this patent arguing that their pre-grant opposition was not heard by the patent controller. In December 2008, the HC asked the Patent Office to review its decision.

Roche decided to move the Supreme Court contesting the HC order[17] which then directed the Patent Controller to consider the pre-grant opposition and dispose the case by 31/Jan/2009. The Patent Controller heard the matter again and through his decision dated 30/Jan/2009, rejected the NGOs' pre-grant opposition. Accordingly, the first set of pre-grant oppositions (in 2 rounds) did not succeed and a patent was granted to Roche.

[17] https://economictimes.indiatimes.com/industry/healthcare/biotech/pharmaceuticals/sc-asks-chennai-patent-office-to-hear-roche/printarticle/4213952.cms.

Meanwhile, Cipla had launched a generic version of the product in September 2008 and Roche filed a patent infringement suit. Subsequently, NGOs and multiple generic companies filed post-grant oppositions.

While the post-grant opposition was fought on multiple grounds including (a) S.3 (d) barred patenting of 'new' ester form of a known substance 'ganciclovir', in absence of enhanced efficacy and (b) an important obviousness argument was also bought in by a generic company (Matrix) which argued that making a valinate ester of a drug like Ganciclovir was obvious when seen from prior art construct of making a valinate ester of a drug like Aciclovir (an 'obvious to try' framework→Acicyclovir to its valinate ester—Valacyclovir approach would prompt a person to attempt to make the valinate ester—Valganciclovir—from Ganciclovir since these are similar drugs chemically and the underlying problem to be solved was similar)—this obviousness argument was eventually accepted by the Controller.

Apart from the science aspects noted above, a lesser known but key aspect in the post-grant stage was whether civil society groups had a 'standing' ('locus') to file a post-grant opposition as the Patents Act states that only a 'person interested' could file a post-grant opposition. Hence whether a non-manufacturing entity (like a civil society group) could come within the scope of 'person interested', thus having 'locus-standi' to file a post-grant opposition was, till then, an open question. To this question, the Controller specifically ruled that civil society groups came within the ambit of 'person interested'. This ruling expanded the scope of entities that could file a post-grant opposition and consequently civil society groups were now free to file post-grant oppositions.

The Controller, in the final Valcyte decision, not only revoked the granted patent and secured generic production, but also helped in expanding the ambit of the term 'person interested' and demonstrated how an 'obvious to try' argument could be effectively implemented for assessing patentability of alternative forms of known substances.

Roche appealed the post-grant rejection from the Patent Office to the IPAB, which remanded the matter back to the Controller. In July 2015, the Controller revoked this patent a second time,[18] which reconfirmed the earlier decision, including 'obvious to try' framework and the standing of civil society organisations to file post-grant oppositions as 'person interested'.

2.3 Herceptin Opposition

Trastuzumab (brand name: Herceptin) is a biologic drug (a monoclonal antibody) from Roche/Genentech, used primarily in the treatment of breast cancer. Roche had one Indian patent that covered a particular formulation of this drug. Roche had—over the years—filed multiple divisional applications from this original filing,

[18] https://spicyip.com/2015/07/valganciclovir-patent-revoked.html.

creating a series of pending divisional filings—each of which would have normally required filing separate oppositions, to secure launch of any generic product. Each of the three divisional filings suffered from individual procedural defects which meant that these were incorrect filings and should have not been allowed to remain in the system, in the first place.

A generic company (Glenmark) had filed a post-grant opposition against the granted patent, but that opposition never saw any traction at the Patent Office. Glenmark had also filed a pre-grant opposition against the first divisional application (1638), but this opposition too never reached the stage of a formal hearing.

Since late 2012, an NGO ('Campaign for Affordable Trastuzumab') had been working to increase access to Trastuzumab and was talking to the Government for the same.[19] In March 2013, the Health Ministry had even recommended issuance of a compulsory license against the formulation patent[20] but no compulsory license was issued on this patent.

In February 2013, a generic company had (Mylan Laboratories) bought the issue of all three divisional filings being incorrect in law, to the notice of the Patent Office by means of detailed letters. Consequently, the Patent Office invited Roche to explain its divisional filings. Roche did not attend the meetings in July 2013 and subsequently the Patent Office rejected the divisional filings.[21] Roche had kept all of above Indian filings, active, from 2000 through July 2013.

In August 2013, Roche also abandoned its main patent[22] (by opting to not pay renewal fee), but not before asserting[23] that "This decision takes into account the strength of the particular rights and the IP (intellectual property) environment in India in general." Roche statement excluded any mention about Roche's rationale for originally filing and then abandoning these divisional filings or why it suddenly abandoned its main granted patent, for no specific reason.

Global media reports around the matter—led the Indian Patent Office to do something that it had never done (and has not done since). The Patent Office put out a press release (noted in Table 3) which systematically mentioned the defects in each of the Roche' divisional filings.

Roche's decision to originally prosecute and later abandon the Indian formulation patent as well as file and later abandon the multiple divisional applications (all of which it had kept alive for many years)—must be also seen in a broader context of corresponding filings outside India. While the above actions were going in India during 2012–13, Roche had been fighting an intense battle with Hospira (a generic company) first at the EPO (since 2006) and later also at the UK Courts for

[19]http://www.pharmabiz.com/NewsDetails.aspx?aid=77303&sid=1.

[20]Refer Compulsory Licenses article, noted earlier, at pages 111 and 113.

[21]https://www.livemint.com/Companies/TBQxokHyVTMGozu78o6CSL/India-partly-revokes-Roche-cancer-drug-patent.html.

[22]https://www.ft.com/content/b8c9cf06-0676-11e3-9bd9-00144feab7de.

[23]https://www.reuters.com/article/us-roche-herceptin-india/roche-gives-up-on-india-patent-for-breast-cancer-drug-idUSBRE97F08220130816.

Table 3 Trastuzumab opposition

Drug:	Trastuzumab
Therapeutic area:	Oncology (Breast cancer)
Nature of patent filing in India:	Formulation for Trastuzumab
Patent/Application #	1. Original: IN/PCT/2000/391/KOL (matured into a patent IN205534) 2. 1638/KOLNP/2005—first divisional application (child); 3. 3272/KOLNP/2008—second divisional application (i.e. first grandchild); 4. 3273/KOLNP/2008—third divisional application (i.e. second grandchild)
Date & Link:	Government Press Release dated 05/Aug/2013 (Krishnan 2013)
Expiry date, for the granted patent:	03/May/2019
Unique points:	Filing of multiple divisional applications; Patent Office dismissed the applications on procedural grounds

counterpart of this formulation patent. In October 2010, the EPO, in a first instance ruling, ruled this formulation patent (EP1308455), invalid. As of 2013, when Roche abandoned the Indian patent, its appeal against the invalidity decision, was pending at the EPO. In April 2014,[24] the UK Patents Court, ruled the UK counterpart of the formulation patent as being invalid.

The author submits that while these abandonment/rejection results were achieved outside of the standard 'oppositions' framework, it must be noted that 'out of the box' actions/petitions can also achieve path-breaking results, even before/without filing an opposition. The Patent Office's decision of removing these incorrect divisional application filings and Roche' abandonment of the sole granted patent removed the need for filing multiple oppositions to thc applications as well as the granted patent and thus cleared the way for launch of the world's first biosimilar Trastuzumab, in India in early 2014.[25]

2.4 *Zykadia Opposition*

Ceritinib (brand name: Zykadia) is a Novartis drug used for treatment of lung cancer. This relatively recent post-grant opposition decision against Ceritinib compound patent is a short and interesting decision. See Table 4.

Natco had launched an 'at risk' generic version of Ceritinib in India, prior to this opposition decision. Novartis also has a patent infringement suit pending against

[24] [2014] EWHC 1094 (Pat), https://www.bailii.org/ew/cases/EWHC/Patents/2014/1094.html.

[25] https://www.thehindubusinessline.com/companies/mylan-launches-first-trastuzumab-biosimilar-in-india/article23122107.ece.

Table 4 Ceritinib opposition

Drug:	Ceritinib
Therapeutic area:	Oncology
Patent/Application #	IN276026 (from 3951/DELNP/2009)
Opponent:	Natco Pharma
Dates of decision(s):	16/Aug/2019
Expiry, if patent remains standing:	08/Dec/2026
Unique points:	Anticipation—*Markush* disclosure versus specific compound; Lack of inventive step and S.3(d)

Natco at the Delhi High Court. The opposition decision allowed Natco to continue to be present in market, but with the risk of payment of damages in future.

For the opposition, Natco used 3 main arguments—lack of novelty (anticipation), lack of inventive step and not an invention u/s 3(d).

For anticipation, Natco argued that two separate prior document(s): IN232653 (application # 2241/CHENP/2005, coming from WO2004080980) and IN240560 (application # 553/CHENP/2006, coming from WO2005016894)—both disclosed Markush[26] group of compounds which individually destroyed novelty for Ceritinib molecule i.e. one would get/find the Ceritinib molecule in either of these documents, if one used the right substitutions. WO2005016894 had been cited in the original prosecution but the Controller, at that time, had allowed the claims during examination.

The Opponent also used these 2 documents and additionally 4999/KOLNP/2007 (coming from WO2007006926) to argue that the Ceritinib molecule lacked an inventive step.

Finally, the Opponent also argued that the Patentee did not provide any in vivo efficacy data for Ceritinib in comparison to compounds disclosed in these 2 documents and hence it failed the threshold of S.3(d) as Ceritinib would be a new form of known compounds in either of these filings.

The Controller's approval of the Markush filing destroying the novelty of later specific compounds in his decision is very interesting to this author since there are many other compound patent filings which fall in this template of an earlier Markush patent disclosing a large number of compounds and a later specific patent filing for the compound. This decision could potentially imply that the earlier broad Markush patent disclosures can be used to invalidate later specific compound patent filings.

Note: The Patentee filed an appeal against the Controller's revocation decision, at the IPAB. In July 2020, the IPAB has issued a 'stay' on the Controller's revocation order[27] as an interim order in the appeal proceedings.

[26] Refer earlier note for definition of 'Markush' claims.

[27] A copy of the IPAB Order is available at https://ipab.gov.in/ipab_orders/delhi/MP.NO.8.2019-OA.20.2019.PT.DEL.pdf.

2.5 The Viread Oppositions

Tenofovir Disoproxil Fumarate (brand name: Viread) is used in treatment of AIDS and Hepatitis B. Gilead had filed a bunch of patent applications related to its Viread IP portfolio for—Tenofovir Disoproxil (ester) and the final product—Tenofovir Disoproxil Fumarate (salt form of the ester). Tenofovir had been invented years earlier by a Czech scientist[28] and later Gilead + UC San Francisco carried out additional work. Finally, Gilead developed the salt form that finally became the block-buster HIV drug.

Some interesting facets to the Gilead Viread Indian patent portfolio:

- Gilead filed a large number of divisional filings from the 2 original filings—eventually turning into multiple 'children'/'grandchildren' filings.
- Multiple companies, civil society and patient groups filed pre-grant oppositions in 2006 and onwards against most of these filings, over the years, including the divisional filings.
- Gilead secured a process patent in 2004 (IN190780 from the 1998 Fumarate filing) and later went on to complete a series of bilateral licenses with multiple Indian generic companies for making and supplying Tenofovir and its combination products for HIV for multiple countries, including India.

While many Indian companies went ahead with the royalty bearing license agreements around 2007, companies like Cipla did not take the license and continued with the opposition. It is worth nothing that except the original process grant, Gilead lost out in the compound oppositions—on both the ester and salt patent application series. Gilead also modified the license structure when it was argued that the original bilateral license template covered language that would stop companies from opposing Gilead' patents—a position that was specifically barred in Indian patent law. Table 5 summarizes the tenofovir opposition.

Over the years, Gilead has transformed its TDF licensing program from bilateral licenses to eventually moving onto the Medicine Patent Pool (MPP) multi-lateral license platform. The number of countries has also modified over the years with some critics arguing that the licenses exclude important middle income countries from the license ambit.[29]

It must always be remembered that Gilead' first interaction in India was the genesis of many later developments—mass pharmaceutical patent licensing, market segmentation and targeted exclusion of generics from middle income countries,

[28] https://www.latimes.com/business/la-fi-gilead-timeline-20160527-snap-story.html.

[29] https://www.bizjournals.com/sanfrancisco/blog/biotech/2011/07/gilead-hiv-aids-quad-india-africa.html.

Table 5 Tenofovir opposition

Drug:	Tenofovir
Therapeutic area:	HIV
Nature of patent filings in India:	Prodrug of Tenofovir & Salt of above prodrug
Patent/Application #	(a) Tenofovir Disoproxil—an ester prodrug of tenofovir (2076/DEL/1997) (b) Tenofovir Disoproxil Fumarate (TDF)—a salt form of Tenofovir Disoproxil (896/DEL/2002—this itself came as a divisional application from 2174/DEL/1998)
Opponents:	Indian Network of People Living with HIV/AIDS (INP+) Delhi Network of People Living with HIV/AIDS (DNP+) Cipla Ltd.
Expiry, if granted:	25/July/2017 for the ester form and 24/July/2018 for the salt form
Unique points:	Filing of multiple divisional applications, S.3(d)

expanding license program for later drugs to gain market acceptance (Gilead loaded a lot of its later drugs onto the TDF license).

Observers opine that the Gilead licensing program is a fairly successful program for most stakeholders. The MPP platform's[30] status today as the major licensing platform covering HIV, Hepatitis and other drugs—is arguably due to Gilead's early move to that platform. The MPP platform has now become a template for most of later HIV drug licenses and Gilead and many other companies extensively license their IP across multiple drug categories, mostly for developing and least developed countries.

2.6 *Kaletra Opposition*

We now look at another opposition worth noting—this too was not a routine opposition against compounds, salts or polymorphs. This was an opposition against Abbotts' (now Abbvie) application covering its formulation technology platform to make heat stable tablets of various HIV drugs (see Table 6). Abbott's product (brand name Kaletra) was originally a soft gelatin capsule containing a fixed-dose of 2 drugs—Lopinavir and Ropinavir, used in the treatment of HIV. The new platform made it possible to make solid oral tablet formulation, instead of the earlier soft gelatin capsules. The earlier capsule had some limitations in terms of storage/handling etc.

This opposition is extremely significant from a drug access perspective since the underlying technology platform is the basis for supply of heat stable formulations of

[30] For list of available drug patent licenses on the MPP platform, visit: https://medicinespatentpool.org/what-we-do/global-licence-overview/licences-in-the-mpp/.

Table 6 Ritonavir and Lopinavir opposition

Drug:	Ritonavir and Lopinavir
Brand:	Kaletra
Therapeutic area:	Anti HIV
Nature of filings in India:	Formulation platform to make heat stable tablets of various drugs
Application #	1. 339/MUMNP/2006 and its 2 divisionals: 2. 726/MUMNP/2009 and 3. 2474/DELNP/2009.
Date of decision:	30/Dec/2010
Opponents:	Matrix Laboratories Limited, I-MAK, Cipla Ltd. and Okasa Pvt. Ltd.
Expiry, if granted:	23/Aug/2024
Unique points:	Filing of multiple divisional applications, obviousness.

various HIV drugs—which is how multiple drugs can be given in tablet form across many high temperature countries (especially as the African countries have a very high presence of HIV-AIDS). This technology platform allowed making heat stable tablets of the drug Ritonavir (and additional drugs) dissolved within a polymer versus the earlier generation soft gelatin capsules that were not heat stable and hence, had this application been granted in India, it would have given Abbott/Abbvie a monopoly on the entire heat stable platform which today covers all Ritonavir based combinations—e.g., Ritonavir + Lopinavir, Ritonavir + Atazanavir etc. Abbvie also uses this platform today for its Hepatitis drug tablets.

Companies had launched generic versions of combination tablet in India and other countries during the time the opposition was going on. So, the opposition paved the way for securing continued marketing of multiple heat stable drug formulations in India and other developing countries.

There were multiple arguments used including anticipation (including Abbott's own poster presentations and previous patent filings as anticipating the claimed tablet invention). While the opponents lost out arguments under S.3(d), S.3 (e) [admixture of known substances] and insufficient description, the Patent Office went ahead and rejected the application on the grounds of anticipation and lacking an inventive step, in late 2010.

One key fact that is not well known publicly is that the Applicant also filed multiple divisionals during the prosecution—including on the day of the parent application's opposition hearing. Interestingly, the Applicant filed not one divisional but two divisionals—at two different branches of the Patent Office in two different cities. Eventually, these divisionals were abandoned but not before the fact of the divisional filings in different cities was highlighted to the Controller.[31]

[31] For more information on the various divisional filings, refer:"Ever-greening: A status check in selected countries" (Journal of Generic Medicines (2010) 7, 227–242. DOI: 10.1057/jgm.2010.14).

Table 7 Atazanavir Sulphate opposition

Drug:	Atazanavir Sulphate
Therapeutic area:	Anti HIV
Nature of filing in India:	Process to make the Sulphate salt/crystals from Atazanavir
Application #	6425/DELNP/2006
Date of decision	20/Dec/2010
Expiry, if granted:	03/May/2015
Opponents:	Matrix Laboratories, Cipla Ltd.
Unique points:	Obvious to try, insufficiency of disclosure and S.3(d)

2.7 *Reyataz Opposition*

The next opposition is worth noting against a Bristol Myers' patent application for a commercially relevant process to make the Sulphate salt of Atazanavir. Bristol Myers' sells an oral formulation of Atazanavir Sulphate under the brand name: Reyataz.

This decision is important because it highlights the position that generic companies keep a keen watch on not only the product/salt applications but also track and file detailed and strong oppositions against commercially sensitive process invention claims. Indian companies had launched generic version of this drug much before the opposition was finally adjudicated.

Apart from the standard approach for arguing obviousness (i.e. the process to make unique crystals of Atazanavir Sulphate from Atazanavir) based on prior art of Atazanavir and state of art, an interesting obviousness argument used here was that a process to make the Sulphate salt of an anti-coagulant drug (Clopidogrel to Clopidogrel Bisulphate) could lead to claims for making the Sulphate salt of Atazanavir, as lacking an inventive step. This was another 'obvious to try' argument by bringing in analogous prior art related to a different drug, but from overall field of developing synthetic processes for crystals of drugs. This 'obvious to try' argument, along with the other arguments, succeeded at the Patent Office. See Table 7.

2.8 *Combivir Opposition*

Combivir is Glaxo's brand product for an oral fixed-dose combination of Lamivudine and Zidovudine, used in the treatment of HIV infection. NGOs had filed a pre-grant opposition (see Table 8) this filing in March 2006[32] at the Kolkata Patent Office, stating the drug was not a new invention.

[32] https://www.msf.org/patent-application-aids-drug-opposed-first-time-india.

Table 8 Combivir opposition

Drug:	Fixed dose combination of two existing drugs: Zidovudine and Lamivudine
Therapeutic area:	Anti-HIV
Application #	2044/CAL/1997
Link	A copy of the opposition as filed, is available here
Expiry, if granted:	29/Oct/2017
Opponents:	Indian Network for People Living with HIV/AIDS and the Manipur Network of Positive People
Unique point:	Applicant abandoned after civil society opposition

After this opposition, Glaxo withdrew its patent application in Aug 2006[33] in India and Thailand[34] and this removed the threat of a patent infringement suit against generic companies, in these 2 countries. The withdrawal meant that further oppositions were not required. Combivir was not the only Glaxo HIV/AIDS medical product that was opposed and this later resulted in more patent application(s) being abandoned by Glaxo.

2.9 *Trizivir Opposition*

Trizivir is an oral fixed-dose combination of 3 drugs—Lamivudine, Zidovudine and Abacavir Sulphate by Glaxo, used for the treatment of HIV infection. In October 2007, Glaxo withdrew its Indian application for Trizivir, after an opposition (see Table 9) was filed. Glaxo stated[35] that "the company's move is in public interest and is part of its policy of routine review of patent applications."

2.10 *Ziagen Opposition*

Ziagen is a Glaxo product for the treatment of HIV, consisting Abacavir Sulphate. Glaxo abandoned its patent application for the Hemisulphate salt of Abacavir, after an opposition (see Table 10) was filed.

Per the author's checks, Indian companies had launched generic version of the above 3 Glaxo' medicines even before the abandonment actions by Glaxo.

[33] https://economictimes.indiatimes.com/industry/healthcare/biotech/pharmaceuticals/gsk-withdraws-patent-application-for-aids-drug/articleshow/1912871.cms.

[34] http://www.twn.my/title2/intellectual_property/info.service/twn.ipr.info.090603.htm.

[35] https://www.livemint.com/Home-Page/kx90Ckvbspy4ApeAOxPFZP/GSK-withdraws-Trizivir-patent-application-8216in-public-i.html.

Table 9 Trizivir opposition

Drug:	Combination of 3 drugs: Lamivudine, Zidovudine and Abacavir Sulphate
Therapeutic area:	Anti-HIV
Application #	IN/PCT/00/00521
Expiry, if granted:	26/April/2019
Opponent:	Cipla Ltd.
Unique point:	Applicant abandoned after pre-grant opposition

Table 10 Abacavir Sulphate opposition

Drug:	Abacavir Sulphate
Therapeutic area:	Anti-HIV
Application #	872/CAL/98
Opponent:	Indian Network of People Living with HIV/AIDS (INP+)
Expiry, if granted:	14/May/2018
Copy of decision:	Image, here.
Unique point:	Applicant abandoned after civil society opposition

2.11 Isentress Opposition

Merck had filed a patent application for the Potassium salt of Raltegravir. Merck sells this product under the brand 'Isentress'.

Cipla has been selling a generic version of Raltegravir in India, for the last few years. Three separate pre-grant oppositions (see Table 11) were filed against this application. The first opposition was filed in 2011 and the last one in late 2018. The oppositions did not see any traction for many years. When the Patent Office finally called all parties for a hearing in Aug 2020, Applicant (Merck) sent a letter—less than a week before hearing date—stating that they were not interested in pursuing the application, any further.

2.12 Sanofi TB Drugs Oppositions

Sanofi had filed two patent applications in India pertaining to anti-tuberculosis drug formulations for therapies known as 3HP and 3RH. The two applications covered two different formulations of known TB 2 drugs (Isoniazid and Rifapentine). One application covered a film coated formulation and the other application covered a dispersible (pediatric) formulation of the 2 drugs.

Civil society groups have been advocating to Sanofi on these patents. They filed oppositions (see Tables 12 and 13) in November 2019—first in India and then in

Table 11 Raltegravir Potassium opposition

Drug:	Raltegravir Potassium
Therapeutic area:	Anti HIV
Nature of filing in India:	Potassium salt of Raltegravir; crystals of the salt
Application #	4187/DELNP/2007
Expiry, if granted:	02/Dec/2025
Opponents:	Indian Network for People Living with HIV/AIDS, Delhi Network of Positive People and Mylan Laboratories Limited
Unique point:	Applicant abandoned after civil society opposition

Table 12 Isoniazid and Rifapentine opposition

Drug:	Dispersible combination formulation of Isoniazid and Rifapentine
Therapeutic area:	Anti-Tuberculosis
Application #	IN201637002758
Expiry, if granted:	22/July/2034
Opponent:	Delhi Network of People Living with HIV/AIDS (DNP+)

Table 13 Isoniazid and Rifapentine opposition (different formulation)

Drug:	Film coated combination formulation of Isoniazid and Rifapentine
Therapeutic area:	Anti-Tuberculosis
Application #	IN201637002757
Expiry, if granted:	22/July/2034
Opponent:	Delhi Network of People Living with HIV/AIDS (DNP+)

Thailand[36] and have also written letters asking Sanofi to abandon the patent families. After the oppositions were filed, Sanofi withdrew both application families in many countries. The application families were first withdrawn at the EPO, then Indonesia[37] and later in India[38] (February 2020). In August 2020, Sanofi formally confirmed that it was abandoning all patent filings relating to these 2 applications.[39]

As noted in the multiple instances above, many patent applicants, especially from the HIV domain, abandon their secondary patent applications (i.e. those related to process, salt or crystal forms) once they face pre-grant oppositions or once civil society groups start a public action on such drugs. It can be argued that the such later

[36] https://www.treatmentactiongroup.org/statement/sanofi-withdraws-two-patent-applications-on-life-saving-tuberculosis-prevention-drugs-in-europe-and-in-indonesia/.

[37] https://www.rouse.com/magazine/news/sanofis-tb-patents-dispute-overflows-to-indonesia/?tag=indonesia.

[38] Refer information tweeted at: <https://twitter.com/achayansz/status/1245229743521370112>.

[39] Refer Sanofi's letter dated 04/August/2020, to Treatment Action Group, available at: <https://www.treatmentactiongroup.org/wp-content/uploads/2020/08/tag_otmeds_sanofi_patent_withdrawals_RESPONSE.pdf>.

Table 14 Remdesivir opposition

Drug:	Remdesivir
Therapeutic area:	CoVid-19
Patents #	IN275967 (from 7068/DELNP/2010) IN332280 (from IN201727012821)
Petitioner(s)	(i) Cancer Patients Aid Association (CPAA) (ii) Campaign for Access to Affordable Medicines, Diagnostics and Devices, India (CAMeD-India) + Third World Network (India)
Opponent:	(iii) LowCost Standard Therapeutics
Copy of request letter:	Copy of the Request letter dated 09/April/2020 is available at the CPAA website Copy of the Third World Network letter dated 13/May/2020 is available at their website.

abandonment action is due to the patent applicant assessing the strength of its filing versus the legal arguments put forth by the pre-grant opponents [e.g. obviousness and S.3(d)] and the potential negative press related to drug access issues.

2.13 Veklury Opposition

The CoVid-19 pandemic has bought many drugs and issues surrounding drug access and patents, in the public limelight, at a scale, hitherto unseen. Gilead has at least 4 patents/patent applications pertaining to Remdesivir (Gilead brand: Veklury), in India. Amidst the global medical crisis, in April 2020, the Cancer Patients Aid Association ('CPAA') and later Third World Network (both being civil society organizations) asked the Government of India to revoke Gilead's granted Indian patent(s).

A post-grant opposition under section 25(2) was filed by a not-for-profit civil society organisation—LowCost Standard Therapeutics—on the patent (IN332280) in June 2020 (see Table 14). The petitions/letters did not opt for filing the standard post-grant opposition(s) under S.25(2) but sought revocation of the patent(s) under S.66 ('Revocation of patent in public interest'[40]).

CPAA filed the request for revoking one patent (IN332280) with the Ministry of Chemicals and Fertilizers as well as the Health Secretary for the Government of India.

[40]Text of S.66 is available at <https://indiankanoon.org/doc/441313/>. It states:

66 Revocation of patent in public interest. –

Where the Central Government is of opinion that a patent or the mode in which it is exercised is mischievous to the State or generally prejudicial to the public, it may, after giving the patentee an opportunity to be heard, make a declaration to that effect in the Official Gazette and thereupon the patent shall be deemed to be revoked.

The Campaign for Access to Affordable Medicines, Diagnostics and Devices, India (CAMD-India) and Third World Network (India) jointly wrote a separate request calling for revocation of two patents (IN275967 and IN332280) with the Department of Promotion of Industry and Internal Trade (DPIIT) (within the Ministry of Commerce & Industry, Government of India).

The DPIIT supervises the functioning of the Patent Office. None of the Government ministries/departments have made any public statement on these letters as of end July, 2020. In July 2020, the Patent Office asked Gilead to respond to the LowCost Standard' opposition. Gilead filed its reply in Oct 2020. A final hearing on the Opposition has not yet been scheduled.

Starting May 2020, Gilead has signed voluntary licenses for manufacture and sale of Remdesivir in 127 countries (including India), with multiple companies (nine companies as of end July 2020[41]) on a 'zero royalty' basis, until the disease remains a pandemic. These bilateral licenses are a change in Gilead's strategy from the HIV multi-lateral licenses on the MPP platform. The Remdesivir license text is not available in the public domain.

3 Pendency of Oppositions in the Indian Patent Office

Oppositions can only help in increasing access if they are adjudicated in a timely and transparent fashion. So, while in the earlier section, we saw the monumental impact that pre-grant and post-grant oppositions had on drug access, it would be remiss if we do not look at some current ground realities.

The Government has over the last few years, multiple times, shown that it is focused towards higher number of patent grants[42] but the author believes that adjudication of oppositions has been very slow at the Indian Patent Office, over the years.

We have two sources for numbers—the first are the annual reports published by the Patent Office. The Report for year ending March 2020 is not available on IPO site as of end December 2020. The CIPAM website[43] is the second source for some of the numbers. A few years ago, Prashant Reddy (an Indian IP lawyer) tried to find out[44] the exact number of oppositions pending at the Indian Patent Office, using the information request pathway, but the exercise did not yield relevant results. The 2020 Numbers are courtsey SpicyIP website.

[41] Gilead's website discusses its Remdesivir licensing program here: <https://www.gilead.com/purpose/advancing-global-health/covid-19/voluntary-licensing-agreements-for-remdesivir>.

[42] https://m.economictimes.com/news/economy/indicators/grant-of-patents-up-12-per-cent-during-april-december-fy19-dpiit/articleshow/68317795.cms.

[43] http://cipam.gov.in/iptrends/#patent.

[44] For a detailed article on his exercise, do read his note at the SpicyIP blog, available here: <https://spicyip.com/2017/12/rtis-reveal-tardy-record-keeping-practices-at-the-ipo-no-records-of-pending-patent-oppositions-113857-trademark-oppositions-pending-5533-rectifications.html>.

The Patent Office has done a commendable job in terms of increasing the size of the Examiner cadre, increasing the number of applications examined, reducing the pendency of period taken to examine and grant a patent, but a deeper check reveals the potential opposition pendency numbers and that presents an alarming picture.

As will noted, the data is not complete. And even for items where the IPO releases numbers, there are internal inconsistencies.

3.1 Pre-grant Oppositions

- Post 2008–09, specific data for cumulative pre-grant oppositions pending at end of every year is not given in the Patent Office' Annual Reports. Hence, we do not know the number pre-grant oppositions pending on a cumulative basis, as per the IPO.
- For the latest 12-year period (FY 2007–8 through FY 2019–20), cumulatively ~3600 pre-grant oppositions have been filed while the cumulative disposal number is ~950 oppositions. This means, potentially, 64% pre-grant oppositions are, as yet, undecided as per my calculations (see Fig. 1).
- The number of 'new' pre-grant oppositions filed annually for last few years has been below 300 (with a sudden upward spike from FY 2018–19: 426 and going to a massive 800 in FY 2019–20). This trend, when considered with the larger increase in number of patent applications filed each year, would still imply that on a percentage basis, a lesser number of applications are now being opposed, each year.
- The annual pre-grant opposition disposal rate has not kept pace with trend of increased patent application filings or the number of examiners inducted, nor has

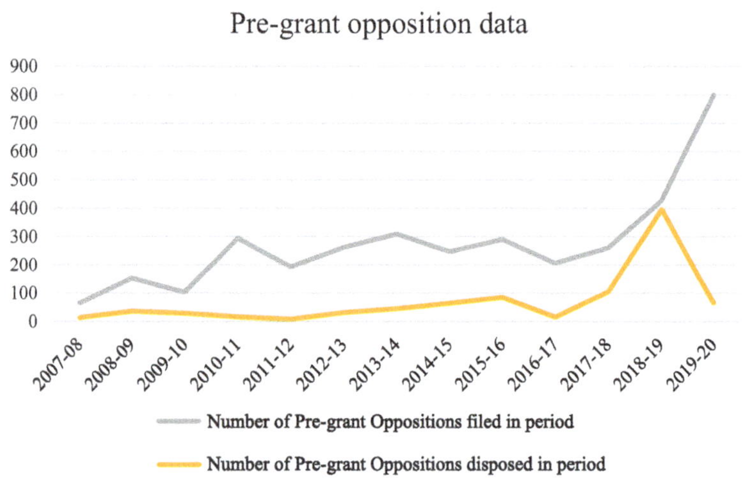

Fig. 1 Pre-grant opposition data 2007–2020

it matched the pace of increase in new opposition filings. The disposal rate for year 2018–19 shows a sudden, huge upward unexplained spike: 399 and then a fall back to 67. This fall is in line with earlier trend of close to 100 or less pre-grant disposals annually. The one-time surprise figure of 399 pre-grant disposals in FY 2018–9 is an unexplainable mystery.

- For the same period, upon adding the numbers for pre-grant oppositions filed and reducing the annual pre-grant oppositions disposed (3607 less 947 equals 2660) and assuming that at least some of the pre-grant oppositions are duplicates against a single patent application or some oppositions may have been withdrawn, I believe that at least 1300+ unique pre-grant total oppositions are still pending.

3.2 *Post-grant Oppositions*

- As at end of FY 2019–20, per the IPO, only 99 post-grant oppositions are pending on a cumulative basis. This differs drastically from my calculation (184)—which is based on simple addition/subtraction.
- For the latest 12 year period (FY 2007–8 through FY 2019–20), based on my calculation, cumulatively 310 post-grant oppositions have been filed while the cumulative disposal number is 126 oppositions (see Fig. 2).
- Around 10 post-grant oppositions are being disposed, annually for the last few years.
- The number of 'new' post-grant oppositions filed annually for last few years has been below 20 (with a sudden upward rise in last 2 years—28 each for last

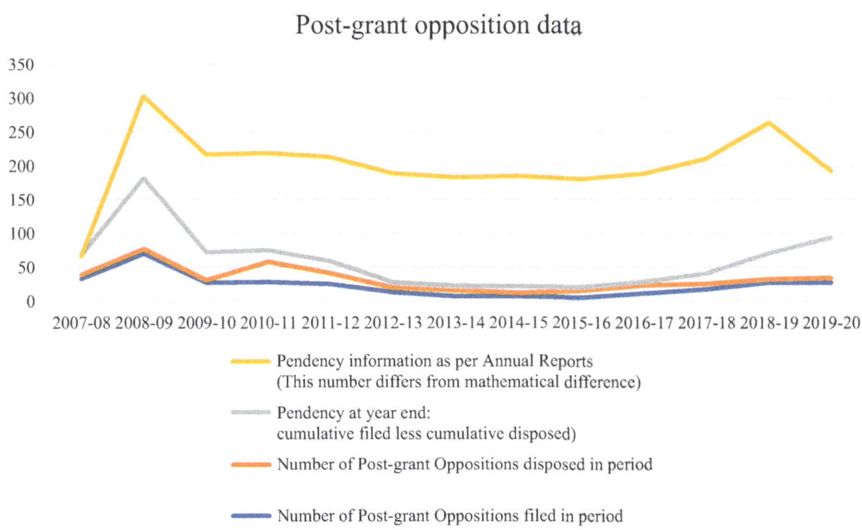

Fig. 2 Post-grant opposition data 2007–2020

2 years)—which when considered with the large increase in number of patents granted, would again imply that on a percentage basis, comparatively lesser number of post-grant oppositions are now being filed every year.
- As per IPO annual report data, annual post-grant opposition pendency figure was below 170 for last few years. This high pendency number is also a cause of concern. However, the IPO data for pending post-grant opposition at year end is not completely understanding. For instance, for FY 2019-18: 193 pending and then for 2019–20 only 99 pending, but the IPO did not dispose 100 odd post-grant oppositions in FY 2019–20—so there is some confusion as to how the 193 pendency figure went down to only 99.
- The difference in the calculated pending cumulative post-grant oppositions 184 at end of FY 2019–20 versus the pending cumulative post-grant oppositions as per IPO (99)—cannot be easily explained but could possibly be due to some cases of multiple oppositions to a single patent or expiry of some patents before disposal, where no disposal decision was issued.

The number of patents granted has moved to approx. 25,000 grants for year ending March 2020 while the number of applications examined moved impressively by approx. 7 times (from ~11,700 to ~80,000+), with an approx. 3 times increase in the Examiner cadre (163 to 449). Within these numbers, the contentious proceedings disposal pendency as mentioned by IPO (from 23 in 2007–8 (17 pre-grants + 6 post-grants) to ~74 in 2019–20 (67 pre-grants + 7 post-grants) continues to remain a cause of concern.

3.3 Pendency at the Intellectual Property Appellate Board (IPAB)

Appeals from IPO (for most items) needed to be filed at the IPAB. As of mid-2019, approx. 617 Patent cases were pending with IPAB.[45] Even after starting various advertising initiatives on the importance of IP, it is glaring that the Government was consistently not able to keep the requisite bench strength at the IPAB, including the chairperson or the technical member (patents) at the IPAB.

As per a calculation done on SpicyIP, an Indian IP blog, 'in its 17 years of existence, the IPAB has not had a Chairperson for a cumulative total of 1130 days'.[46]

The position of the Chairperson of the IPAB (i.e. the judicial member) was vacant for quite a long time and so the Supreme Court granted a fresh term in December

[45] Year wise pendency data is not available for the IPAB. These numbers have come from a court case: refer para 7 in Mylan Laboratories Limited v. Union of India <https://indiankanoon.org/doc/58294410/>.

[46] https://spicyip.com/2020/04/the-case-for-shutting-down-the-intellectual-property-appellate-board-ipab.html.

2019 to the already retired judicial member.[47] In a similar pattern, the position of the technical member (patents) was vacant since May 2016 and so, in July 2019, the Delhi High Court had then asked the technical member (plant variety protection) to look at the patent responsibilities.[48]

These judicial interventions show that recruitment of the senior-most IPAB functionaries was not done in time even when the government was aware of the normal tenure of such functionaries. Note: A new technical member (patents) was finally appointed in July 2020 and the process of recruiting a new chairperson (judicial member) to replace the current chairperson's whose extended term was to end in September 2020, had started.[49]

3.4 Impact of Pendency

The pendency number and dismal disposal for each component—pre-grant oppositions, post-grant oppositions and IPAB cases—is very worrying. The adjudication of pending oppositions (both pre-grant oppositions and post-grant oppositions) is a continuing challenge for the Patent Office. The rise in pre-grant disposals for 2018–19 needs to be understood and expanded upon. While the number of examiners at the Patent Office has trebled in the 3-year period, the numbers of controllers becoming Assistant or Deputy Controllers has not jumped by that percentage. It is the Controller who is at the center of managing the pre-grant and post-grant opposition process and finally adjudicating on the opposition and this could also be a reason for slower disposal.

The IPAB pendency position, for both proceedings and personnel, brings in a bigger question on the Government's willingness to work towards a quick and efficient IP dispute disposal system. Undecided oppositions/IPAB revocations mean that generic companies may not have the confidence to undertake at risk launches, due to the threat of damages. Likewise, delay in clearing pre-grant oppositions also hurts patent applicants as it chips away at the term of any future patent available to the applicant and at same time, keeps a sword hanging on opponents for years. The IPO's leadership must examine the pendency and should incentivize examiners and Controllers for faster adjudication of contentious proceedings. Examiners and Controllers today are assessed based on examinations and grants and if opposition adjudication can be kept as an independent performance target which can lead to faster professional growth inside the IPO, it could act as an incentive for proceedings being completed faster.

---

[47] https://images.assettype.com/barandbench/2019-12/829f572d-5ff5-421d-8a2ba10cc8d07727/Supreme_Court___IPAB_Chairman_Order.pdf.

[48] Mylan, Ibid.

[49] Refer SpicyIP post: https://spicyip.com/2020/08/breaking-news-controller-generals-office-agrees-with-our-petition-for-scrapping-the-intellectual-property-appellate-board.html.

Clearly, the present system for managing and adjudicating oppositions/IPAB matters, including timely recruitment, needs a major overhaul with time-bound proceedings and decision issuance being implemented for faster adjudication of oppositions. Urgent and immediate actions need to be undertaken by the Government to bring in requisite personnel, reduce pendency and increase disposal of oppositions and IPAB matters.

4 Conclusion

The pre-grant and post-grant oppositions filed by civil society organisations and generic companies—over the years have been instrumental in earlier launch of drugs, thereby increasing access of drugs not only for the Indian population—but also allowed export of drugs to other countries.

The filing (and winning) of these oppositions have been the pivot for earlier generic entry of many life-saving drugs. Oppositions have been instrumental in competitively priced generics. These oppositions not only led to generic products in India but also in a whole host of developing and least developed countries.

As we saw, the Indian oppositions have moved beyond the simple arguments of S.3(d) to more complex arguments and have seen fair bit of success.

Finally, the increasing pendency of oppositions over the last few years is a matter of deep concern and the current trend seems to imply that unless the Government strengthens the system by bringing in requisite number of personnel, the pendency numbers will not come down, substantially, in the near term.

Author's Note

The Indian opposition saga has been one of achieving path-breaking results through sheer advocacy and fighting spirit of the civil society organisations (NGOs). The massive efforts undertaken by these NGOs over the years in litigating against corporates with huge budgets must to be applauded, for the results achieved.

The author is deeply indebted to friends from the civil society and generic companies who willingly shared anecdotes and facts from these opposition battles. Most of them chose to remain anonymous for the purposes of this paper. The author thanks (in alphabetical order)—Swaraj Barooah, (Late) Shamnad Basheer, Adv. Julie George, Adv. Rajeshwari Hariharan, Adv. Feroz Ali Khader, Ms. Leena Menghaney, Adv. Guruswamy Nataraj and

(continued)

Prof. Bhaven Sampat for discussions over the years and friends who have reviewed draft versions of this paper.

The present paper is based on a talk given by the author at the invitation of the South Centre and the Max Planck Institute for Innovation and Competition at the 'Global Forum on Intellectual Property, Access to Medicines and Innovation' held at Munich in Dec 2019. The author thanks the South Centre (and its wonderful team—Dr. Carlos Correa, Dr. German Velasquez, Dr. Viviana Munoz and Mr. Nirmalya Syam) and Professor Dr. Reto M. Hilty at the Max Planck Institute for Innovation and Competition, for the opportunity.

Conflict Declaration/Disclaimer

The author has been employed within the generic pharmaceutical industry for 18 plus years and was professionally involved in some of the opposition cases, discussed in this paper. The paper is based on information available in public domain as of 31/Dec/2020 and discussions with multiple stakeholders, over many years. All website links have been last accessed on the same date.

Errors, if any, are the sole responsibility of the author. The views, observations and submissions presented in this paper are entirely personal and should not be attributed or construed to reflect the views of the author's present or past employer(s).

Annex: Opposition Pendency Data for the Period 2007–08 to 2019–2020

Year	Number of pre-grant oppositions filed in period	Number of pre-grant oppositions disposed in period	Pendency at year end: cumulative filed less cumulative disposed	Number of post-grant oppositions filed in period	Number of post-grant oppositions disposed in period	Pendency at year end: cumulative filed less cumulative disposed	Pendency information as per annual reports[a]	Patent examiners	Applications examined	Patents granted
2007–08	64	17	47	34	6	28	Pendency data was not given in the IPO' annual report	163	11,751	15,316
2008–09	153	39	161	71	7	92	122 post-grant cases and 337 pre-grant cases remained pending		10,296	16,061
2009–10	103	32	232	28	4	116	146 post-grant cases pending; pre-grant pendency—not mentioned		6069	6168
2010–11	294	19	507	29	30	115	145 post-grant cases pending: pre-grant—not mentioned		11,028	7509
2011–12	193	11	689	26	16	125	155 post-grant cases pending; pre-grant pendency—not mentioned		11,031	4381

(continued)

Year	Number of pre-grant oppositions filed in period	Number of pre-grant oppositions disposed in period	Pendency at year end: cumulative filed less cumulative disposed	Number of post-grant oppositions filed in period	Number of post-grant oppositions disposed in period	Pendency at year end: cumulative filed less cumulative disposed	Pendency information as per annual reports[a]	Patent examiners	Applications examined	Patents granted
2012–13	262	34	917	14	7	132	162 post-grant cases pending; pre-grant pendency—not mentioned		12,268	4126
2013–14	309	48	1178	8	9	131	161 post-grant cases pending; pre-grant pendency—not mentioned		18,615	4227
2014–15	247	67	1358	8	5	134	164 post-grant cases pending; pre-grant pendency—not mentioned		22,631	5978
2015–16	290	88	1560	6	10	130	160 post-grant cases pending; pre-grant pendency—not mentioned	132	16,851	6326
2016–17	206	18	1748	12	12	130	160 post-grant cases pending; pre-grant pendency—not mentioned	458	28,967	9847
2017–18	260	108	1900	18	8	140	170 post-grant cases pending; pre-grant pendency—not mentioned	572	60,330	13,045

(continued)

Year	Number of pre-grant oppositions filed in period	Number of pre-grant oppositions disposed in period	Pendency at year end: cumulative filed less cumulative disposed	Number of post-grant oppositions filed in period	Number of post-grant oppositions disposed in period	Pendency at year end: cumulative filed less cumulative disposed	Pendency information as per annual reports[a]	Patent examiners	Applications examined	Patents granted
2018–19	426	399	1927	28	5	163	193 post-grant opposition cases remained pending. NOTE: Pre-grant opposition pendency figures are not given separately in the annual reports since 2008–09.	449	85,426	15,283
2019–20	800	67	2660	28	7	184	As per IPO, only 99 oppositions remained pending at the end of March 2020. There is a noticeable difference between the calculated number of 184 and IPO data of 99—it could be on account of patents having expired, oppositions being withdrawn etc.		80,088	24936

[a]This number differs from mathematical difference—but data cannot be reconciled as we do not method of calculation for IPO—whether it is cumulative or merely mathematical.

References

Ali F (2016) Open prosecution: towards ex ante validation of patents. Available at SSRN: https://ssrn.com/abstract=2755189 or https://doi.org/10.2139/ssrn.2755189

Ali F, Rajagopal S, Raman VS, John R (2018) Pharmaceutical patent grants in India: how our safeguards against evergreening have failed, and why the system must be reformed. Available at <https://accessibsa.org/media/2018/04/Pharmaceutical-Patent-Grants-in-India.pdf>

Amin T (2010) Re-visiting the patents and access to medicines dichotomy: an evaluation of TRIPS implementation and public health safeguards in developing countries. In: Aginam O, Harrington J, Yu P (eds) Global governance of HIV/AIDS: intellectual property and access to essential medicines. Edward Elgar. SSRN: https://ssrn.com/abstract=1573723 or https://doi.org/10.2139/ssrn.1573723

Attaran A (2014) A modest but meaningful decision for Indian Drug Patents (August 9, 2014). Lancet 384:477–479. Available at SSRN: https://ssrn.com/abstract=2747623

Basheer S, Reddy P (2008) "Ducking" TRIPS in India: a saga involving Novartis and the legality of Section 3(d). Natl Law School India Rev 20(2):131–155

EWHC 1094 (Pat), available at https://www.bailii.org/ew/cases/EWHC/Patents/2014/1094.html

Financial Times, Roche drops patent for Herceptin in India. https://www.ft.com/content/b8c9cf06-0676-11e3-9bd9-00144feab7de

Gilead, Voluntary Licensing Agreements for Remdesivir. <https://www.gilead.com/purpose/advancing-global-health/covid-19/voluntary-licensing-agreements-for-remdesivir>

Grant of patents up 12 per cent during April-December FY'19: DPIIT, 8 March 2019. https://m.economictimes.com/news/economy/indicators/grant-of-patents-up-12-per-cent-during-april-december-fy19-dpiit/articleshow/68317795.cms

Grebe E, Low M (2017) The global movement around the Imatinib Mesylate case and its roots in the AIDS movement (April 23, 2017) Revised version of CSSR Working Paper No. 349. Available at SSRN: https://ssrn.com/abstract=2546392

Ho CM (2011) Freedom under TRIPS: India as an example. In: Access to medicine in the global economy: international agreements on patents and related rights. Oxford University Press, Loyola University Chicago School of Law Research Paper No. 2011-025. Available at SSRN: https://ssrn.com/abstract=1921583

Krishnan V (2013) Roche lost Herceptin patent due to procedural problems, 13 Aug 2013. https://www.livemint.com/Companies/TBQxokHyVTMGozu78o6CSL/India-partly-revokes-Roche-cancer-drug-patent.html

Melody Petersen A history of Gilead's biggest HIV drug, 29 May 2016. https://www.latimes.com/business/la-fi-gilead-timeline-20160527-snap-story.html

MSF, Patent application for AIDS drug opposed for first time in India, Press Release 30 March 2006. https://www.msf.org/patent-application-aids-drug-opposed-first-time-india

Mylan Laboratories Limited v. Union of India. https://indiankanoon.org/doc/58294410/

Mylan launches first Trastuzumab biosimilar in India, 4 February 2014. https://www.thehindubusinessline.com/companies/mylan-launches-first-trastuzumab-biosimilar-in-india/article23122107.ece

Nick Redfearn Sanofi's TB patents dispute overflows to Indonesia, Rouse, 29 January 2020. https://www.rouse.com/magazine/news/sanofis-tb-patents-dispute-overflows-to-indonesia/?tag=indonesia

Novartis AG v. Union of India & Ors. [2013] INSC 369. Available at: <https://www.globalhealthrights.org/wp-content/uploads/2013/04/SC-2013-Novartis-AG-v.-Union-of-India.pdf>

Ragavan S (2013) The patent failure of Novartis with Gleevec, Note on Novartis v. Union of India Judgment. Wegner's Writings (Blog by Hal Wegner). Available at: http://works.bepress.com/srividhya_ragavan/156/

Rathod SK (2010) Ever-greening: a status check in selected countries. J Generic Med 7(3):227–242. https://doi.org/10.1057/jgm.2010.14

'Report on the revision of the patents law' by Justice N. Rajagopala Ayyangar; released in September 1959 and available at <http://www.ipindia.nic.in/writereaddata/Portal/Images/pdf/1959-_Justice_N_R_Ayyangar_committee_report.pdf>

Reuters, Roche gives up on India patent for breast cancer drug, 16 August 2013. https://www.reuters.com/article/us-roche-herceptin-india/roche-gives-up-on-india-patent-for-breast-cancer-drug-idUSBRE97F08220130816

Sampat BN, Shadlen KC (2018) Indian pharmaceutical patent prosecution: the changing role of Section 3(d). PLoS ONE 13(4):e0194714. https://doi.org/10.1371/journal.pone.0194714

Serrano O, Burri M (2019) TRIPS implementation in developing countries: likely scenarios to 2025. In: Elsig M, Hahn M, Spilker G (eds) The shifting landscape of global trade governance. Cambridge University Press, pp 275–294. Available at SSRN: https://ssrn.com/abstract=3380246

The Business Journals, Gilead boosts low-cost HIV drug deal in developing countries, 12 July 2011. https://www.bizjournals.com/sanfrancisco/blog/biotech/2011/07/gilead-hiv-aids-quad-india-africa.html

The Economic Times, GSK withdraws patent application for AIDS drug, 21 August 2006. https://economictimes.indiatimes.com/industry/healthcare/biotech/pharmaceuticals/gsk-withdraws-patent-application-for-aids-drug/articleshow/1912871.cms

The Economic Times, SC asks Chennai patent office to hear Roche, https://economictimes.indiatimes.com/industry/healthcare/biotech/pharmaceuticals/sc-asks-chennai-patent-office-to-hear-roche/printarticle/4213952.cms

The Office of the Controller General off Patents, Designs, Trade Marks And Geographical Indications, Annual Report 2018-19. http://www.ipindia.nic.in/writereaddata/Portal/Images/pdf/IP_India_Annual_Report_2019_Eng.pdf

Third World Network, GSK withdraws Combivir patent application from India and Thailand, 12 September 2006. http://www.twn.my/title2/intellectual_property/info.service/twn.ipr.info.090603.htm

Treatment Action Group Sanofi Withdraws Two Patent Applications on Life-Saving Tuberculosis Prevention Drugs in Europe and in Indonesia, 22 January 2020. https://www.treatmentactiongroup.org/statement/sanofi-withdraws-two-patent-applications-on-life-saving-tuberculosis-prevention-drugs-in-europe-and-in-indonesia/

USPTO, Markish Claims https://www.uspto.gov/web/offices/pac/mpep/s2117.html

Protection of Clinical Test Data and Public Health: A Proposal to End the Stronghold of Data Exclusivity

Ellen 't Hoen

Abstract Test data demonstrating the efficacy, safety and quality of a medicine is required by drug regulatory agencies before a new treatment obtains marketing approval and can be made available to patients. Because test data can be costly and time-consuming to produce, certain countries have 'data exclusivity' regimes that restrict use of test data to the originator company for a period of time. Generic and biosimilar companies rely on originator test data to obtain marketing approval for generic products, so data exclusivity periods can delay entry of lower-cost treatments to the market. While data exclusivity is not required by the World Trade Organization, countries such as the United States and the European Union often push their stronger data exclusivity provisions on other countries through free trade agreements (FTAs). While a small number of countries have waivers to data exclusivity for cases of emergency or other public health need, most do not. This can hamper the timely and affordable availability of needed medicines. Waivers to data exclusivity should be included in legislation to protect public health, and other ways to protect test data against unfair commercial use should be explored.

1 Introduction: Test Data and Efficacy, Safety and Quality of Medicines

Assuring the efficacy, safety and quality of medicines—be it of originator products or generic medicines—is an important public function meant to protect the health of consumers and patients. This function is performed by national or regional medicines regulatory agencies, such as the US Food and Drug Administration (FDA) and the European Medicines Agency (EMA), using the data that is submitted to the agency by companies that seek to obtain a marketing authorisation for a medicinal product. For new medicines, medicines regulatory agencies require drug companies to submit test data that demonstrates efficacy, safety and quality of the medicine

E. 't. Hoen (✉)
Medicines Law & Policy, Amsterdam, The Netherlands
e-mail: ellenthoen@medicineslawandpolicy.net

C. M. Correa, R. M. Hilty (eds.), *Access to Medicines and Vaccines*,
https://doi.org/10.1007/978-3-030-83114-1_7

before granting marketing authorisation. Generating such data can be time-consuming and costly, particularly when it involves a new chemical entity or a new biologic medicine. As a result, test data is often protected against use by others. The TRIPS Agreement (Article 39.3) requires the protection of certain kinds of test data against unfair commercial use but does not require to provide exclusive rights to such data. In certain jurisdictions the protection of test data takes the form of data exclusivity; data exclusivity means that the use of the test data is exclusive to the originator company for a certain period of time. In practical terms, this means that during the data exclusivity period a generic version of the product cannot be registered by the regulatory agency.

2 Generic and Biosimilar Medicine Marketing Approval and the Use of Test Data

A generic company applying for marketing authorisation for a generic product has to demonstrate that its product is bioequivalent to the originator product. Importantly, the generic applicant is not required to generate its own clinical efficacy and safety data. The generic applicant can rely on the clinical test data that was submitted by the original applicant, and which is on file with the regulatory agency. Applicants for biosimilar medicines (generic biologic medicines) have to demonstrate biosimilarity (analogue to bioequivalence for biologic medicines) and can also rely on the safety and efficacy experience gained with the reference medicine.[1] This avoids unnecessary repetition of clinical trials already carried out with the reference medicine.

Data exclusivity regimes delay the use of existing test data by generic and biosimilar companies in seeking marketing approval for their medicines for as long as the data exclusivity period holds.[2]

Data exclusivity does not prohibit the generic or biosimilar company from generating its own clinical efficacy data, but this is costly and, in most cases, would raise serious ethical issues. Such tests would involve carrying out randomised controlled clinical trials in which an already proven effective treatment is withheld from part of the study participants who receive the comparator or placebo product. In reality, generic companies do not carry out such trials. Therefore, a data exclusivity regime creates strong monopolies that are automatically granted, quietly enforced by the medicines regulatory system and often without exceptions or limitations.

---

[1] European Medicines Agency and the European Commission, *Biosimilars in the EU: Information guide for healthcare professionals* (European Medicines Agency, 2019) https://www.ema.europa.eu/en/documents/leaflet/biosimilars-eu-information-guide-healthcare-professionals_en.pdf.

[2] Technopolis (15 June 2018a). https://www.technopolis-group.com/report/effects-of-supplementary-protection-mechanisms-for-pharmaceutical-products/.

3 Rationale for Data Exclusivity

The notion behind data exclusivity is that the production of clinical test data—by running, for example, clinical trials—requires significant investments. Protecting such test data against use by generic and biosimilar companies is thus seen as a means to encourage medical research and development (R&D). The rationale behind data exclusivity is similar to the rationale behind patents and other pharmaceutical market exclusivities: the assumption that the protection of the research and development investments that companies make by providing exclusive rights is needed and sufficient to stimulate innovation.

3.1 Data Exclusivity and Patents

There are important differences between data exclusivity regimes and patents. Data exclusivity is granted automatically and enforced through the regulatory system; the holders of the rights, mostly drug companies, do not have to apply or provide evidence of eligibility. Patent applications, by contrast, are examined before market exclusivities are granted; rights holders must demonstrate their product meets patentability criteria such as novelty, usefulness and inventive step. Most medicines laws that provide for data exclusivity do not provide for a waiver of it should it be necessary for public interest grounds to suspend the exclusivity. For patents, compulsory licences and other measures to circumvent exclusivity can be sought when there is a public health need (see also Sect. 6).

Data exclusivity rights exist independently of patents, can overlap with patents and can also exist where patents do not. Data exclusivity is also different from patents in that there is no international obligation to provide data exclusivity.

3.2 Data Exclusivity's Effectiveness in Stimulating Innovation

Whether data exclusivity is an effective or necessary measure to stimulate innovation is questionable at best. A publication by Dutch research group Technopolis, prepared upon request of the Dutch government that looked at pharmaceutical exclusivity incentives available to industry in the EU[3] concluded "this study cannot provide any evidence on whether, or to what extent, the impacts of these exclusivities and protections align with the intended objectives." In 2009, the US Federal Trade Commission (FTC) concluded that a lengthy exclusivity period of

[3]Technopolis (May 2018b) http://www.technopolis-group.com/wp-content/uploads/2018/06/2718-Technopolis-report-on-supplementary-protection-mechanisms.pdf.

12–14 years is unnecessary to promote innovation by biologic drug manufacturers. The FTC considered existing incentives (patents and market-based pricing) to be sufficient to support biologic innovation.[4] In 2016, the EU Council decided to carry out an assessment of the various pharmaceutical incentive mechanisms contained in EU regulations with a view "to strengthen the balance in the pharmaceutical systems in de EU and its Member States." This review is ongoing but preliminary reports indicate that evidence is ambiguous at best.[5,6,7]

4 History of Data Exclusivity

4.1 Data Exclusivity in the United States

Data exclusivity was first introduced in the US in 1984 when the "*Drug Price Competition and Patent Term Restoration Act of 1984*," also known as the "*Hatch-Waxman Amendments*" was adopted. The act provided several types of exclusivities to innovators, in addition to patents, as a trade-off for provisions to make market entry of generics easier and quicker.[8] The US provides 5 years of data exclusivity for small molecule new chemical entities; 3 years for a new indication of a previously approved medicine; and 4 years for biologics, complemented by a parallel 12-year market exclusivity.[9]

4.2 Data Exclusivity in the European Union

The EU introduced data exclusivity in 1987. Directive 87/21/EEC initially provided for 6 years of data exclusivity for most medicines, and 10 years for biotechnology products, both measured from the date of first marketing approval. Member states

---

[4]Federal Trade Commission (June 2009) https://www.ftc.gov/sites/default/files/documents/reports/emerging-health-care-issues-follow-biologic-drug-competition-federal-trade-commission-report/p083901biologicsreport.pdf.

[5]Council of the EU, 'Council conclusions on strengthening the balance in the pharmaceutical systems in the EU and its Member States' (17 June 2016) https://www.consilium.europa.eu/en/press/press-releases/2016/06/17/epsco-conclusions-balance-pharmaceutical-system/.

[6]Copenhagen Economics, *Study on the economic impact of supplementary protection certificates, pharmaceutical incentives and rewards in Europe* (European Commission, May 2018) https://ec.europa.eu/health/sites/health/files/human-use/docs/pharmaceuticals_incentives_study_en.pdf.

[7]https://medicineslawandpolicy.org/useful-resources/briefs/.

[8]Lietzan (2016), p. 91 https://pdfs.semanticscholar.org/2fdb/0784f6fb314cf99063933cb6bfbfae6a7091.pdf.

[9]U.S. Federal Trade Commission (*FTC*, June 2009). https://www.ftc.gov/reports/emerging-health-care-issues-follow-biologic-drug-competition-federal-trade-commission-report.

could extend data exclusivity to 10 years if they considered this was "in the interest of public health." Member states had different views as to when an extension to 10 years was justified, which led to a variation in exclusivity periods throughout the EU. In 2004, the EU data exclusivity rules were further harmonised and extended to 8 years of data exclusivity, plus two additional years of market exclusivity during which generic companies can prepare and apply for their marketing approval using test data but not market the product. An additional 1 year of market exclusivity can be obtained by the originator company for a new indication with significant added clinical benefit.[10] The new EU exclusivity regime became known as the 8+2+1 rule. The EU data exclusivity regime is the most generous in the world.

4.3 Protection of Test Data and the Rules of the World Trade Organization

During the Uruguay Round negotiations on intellectual property, the option of making data exclusivity an explicit obligation under the Agreement on Trade-Related Aspects of Intellectual Property Rights (TRIPS Agreement)[11] was discussed, but the TRIPS negotiators explicitly rejected language that would have required granting exclusive rights to test data, opting for the more general text of Article 39.3,[12] which reads as follows:

> Members, when requiring, as a condition of approving the marketing of pharmaceutical or of agricultural chemical products which utilize new chemical entities, the submission of undisclosed test or other data, the origination of which involves a considerable effort, shall protect such data against unfair commercial use. In addition, Members shall protect such data against disclosure, except where necessary to protect the public, or unless steps are taken to ensure that the data are protected against unfair commercial use.

The WTO TRIPS Agreement contains an obligation of WTO members to protect certain kinds of test data against unfair commercial use, but does not create an obligation to provide data exclusivity. TRIPS data protection against unfair commercial use is required only where that data is related to a new chemical entity and required as a condition of marketing approval, was previously undisclosed, and required considerable effort to generate. Importantly, TRIPS does not stipulate a time period for this protection. This is further evidence of the absence of a data exclusivity obligation.

---

[10] Directive 2004/27/EC on the Community code relating to medicinal products for human use [2004] OJ L136/34.

[11] Agreement on Trade-Related Aspects of Intellectual Property Rights (Apr. 15, 1994) (hereinafter TRIPS Agreement).

[12] The World Health Organization (WHO), the World Intellectual Property Organization (WIPO) and the World Trade Organization (WTO), WHO (2012), p. 64. https://www.wipo.int/policy/en/global_health/trilateral_cooperation.html.

TRIPS also does not preclude the use of test data for the regulatory approval of a competing product, which, as some have argued, does not fall within the definition of 'unfair commercial use'.[13,14,15] This position was reiterated by the developing country members of the WTO in 2001 at the Doha Ministerial Conference, where they stated that article 39.3 of TRIPS "does not require granting 'exclusive rights' to the owner of the data" and that it "does permit a national competent authority to rely on data in its possession to assess a second and further applications, relating to the same drug, since this would not imply any 'unfair commercial use'."[16] TRIPS also does not require WTO members to extend protection to data that is in the public domain.[17]

The obligation to protect test data against 'unfair commercial use' does not yet apply to least developed country members (LDCs) of the WTO, who do not need to implement pharmaceutical-related aspects of the TRIPS agreement until 2033 or until they cease to be LDCs.[18]

Today, most WTO members, outside the EU or the United States, do not provide data exclusivity. A survey of MedsPaL,[19] a database of select medicines patent and exclusivity status, shows that only around 16 middle-income countries provide data exclusivity. Data exclusivity regimes often find their origin in trade agreements with the EU or the US that were negotiated outside of the WTO (see Sect. 5).

In conclusion, the TRIPS Agreement gives countries considerable latitude as to how they want to implement test data protection.

[13] Reichman (2009), p. 17.

[14] Timmermans (2007), p. e2.

[15] Commission on Intellectual Property Rights, Innovation and Public Health, *Public Health, Innovation and Intellectual Property Rights* (World Health Organization, 2006).

[16] 'TRIPS Council Discussion on Access to Medicines: Developing Country Group's Paper' (World Trade Organization, 20 June 2001) IP/C/W/296, paras 39–40. https://www.wto.org/english/tratop_e/trips_e/paper_develop_w296_e.htm.

[17] Correa (2002). https://www.southcentre.int/wp-content/uploads/2019/02/Bk_2002_Protection-of-Data-Submitted-for-Pharmaceuticals-Registration_EN.pdf.

[18] The Council for Trips Extension of the Transition Period Under Article 66.1 of the Trips Agreement for Least Developed Country Members for Certain Obligations with Respect to Pharmaceutical Products (6 November 2015), World Trade Organization IP/C/73.

[19] 'MedsPaL: The Medicines Patents and Licences Database'. https://www.medspal.org.

5 Data Exclusivity in Free Trade Agreements (FTAs)

The obligation to grant data exclusivity to the originator company in the US and the EU goes beyond the requirement of the TRIPS Agreement[20] for the protection of undisclosed test data against unfair commercial use. Both the US and the EU seek to globalise their data exclusivity norms through trade agreements, including in WTO accession agreements with other countries or in bilateral agreements or trading blocs, by demanding from their trading partners that they introduce or expand data exclusivity.

In recent FTAs there has been some roll back of the demands related to data exclusivity. In 2018, after the withdrawal of the US, the 11 remaining parties to the Comprehensive and Progressive Agreement for Trans-Pacific Partnership (CPTPP, formerly the TPP) suspended the IP chapter, including its various market exclusivity obligations. The US-Mexico-Canada Agreement (USMCA) initially contained a provision that bound parties to 5-year exclusivity for small molecules, 3 years for new clinical information (new use of a known medicine), and 10-years for biologics. In 2019, driven by the debate on high drug prices in the US, the provision for 10-year exclusivity for biologics was removed from the USMCA.

6 Data Exclusivity and TRIPS Flexibilities

The TRIPS Agreement includes a number of flexibilities that are relevant for public health. Data exclusivity can form a serious barrier to the effective use of such flexibilities for the purpose of accessing lower priced medicines. In particular, the effectiveness of compulsory licensing—a mechanism whereby a government grants third parties or itself the right to use a patented innovation without the consent of the patent holder—may be muted by data exclusivity.

6.1 Compulsory Licensing and Government Use in Drug Procurement

When a government grants itself the right to make use of a patented innovation through a compulsory licence, this is often called 'government use', or 'public non-commercial use'.[21] Such compulsory licences can be particularly useful in

[20] During the Uruguay Round negotiations, the option of making data exclusivity an explicit obligation under the TRIPS Agreement was discussed, but negotiators instead adopted the general wording of the current Article 39.3. See: WTO, WIPO, and the WHO (n 10).

[21] This chapter will further use the term 'compulsory licence' to refer to both compulsory licences and government use or public non-commercial use of a patent.

public procurement of medicines to access lower-priced medicines from generic competitors.

The government is free to determine the grounds for granting a compulsory licence. Some countries' domestic laws include specific provisions such as 'high prices' of medicines, or a 'lack of access to medicines'. For example, French patent law authorises government use upon request by the minister of health when medicines are 'only available to the public in insufficient quantity or quality or at abnormally high prices.'[22]

In 2001 the WTO Doha Declaration on the TRIPS agreement and Public Health[23] provided a welcome clarification of the flexibilities[24] contained in the TRIPS Agreement for the purpose of public health and specifically 'to promote access to medicines for all'.[25] Against the background of trade pressure on low- and middle-income countries that contemplated the use of compulsory licensing and other TRIPS-flexibilities, the Doha Declaration took away any doubts about the legality of such measures. Subsequently, low- and middle-income countries have used TRIPS flexibilities on a large scale in particular but not exclusively to facilitate the supply of low-cost generic medicines used for the treatment of HIV.[26]

6.2 *Data Exclusivity and Compulsory Licensing*

Countries that have a data exclusivity regime may find providing more affordable access to a patent-protected medicine through a compulsory licence is hindered if the originator company's product benefits from data exclusivity. While a compulsory licence may open the possibility of providing generic versions of a medicine that is still patent protected, data exclusivity may prevent the registration of such generic medicines and therefore still block their entry into the market.

[22] Code de la propriété intellectuelle (version consolidée au 9 octobre 2016) *Article L613-16.*

[23] Declaration on the TRIPS agreement and public health (14 November 2001) WT/MIN(01)/DEC/2. https://www.wto.org/english/thewto_e/minist_e/min01_e/mindecl_trips_e.htm (hereinafter Doha Declaration).

[24] The term 'flexibilities' is used to describe limitations and exceptions to exclusive rights that countries can deploy for reasons of public interest. See also: WIPO, 'Meaning of Flexibilities'. http://www.wipo.int/ip-development/en/agenda/flexibilities/meaning_of_flexibilities.html.

[25] Doha Declaration (n 22).

[26] Hoen (2016).

6.3 *Remedies to Data Exclusivity Barriers and Compulsory Licensing*

Some countries have introduced waivers to data exclusivity, which can be invoked to ensure that the regulatory authority can proceed with the registration of a generic product produced or imported under a compulsory licence. Countries that have such data exclusivity waivers include Malaysia, Chili and Colombia.[27]

Section 5 of the **Malaysia** 2011 Directive of Data Exclusivity,[28] entitled Non-Application of Data Exclusivity, provides that Nothing in the Data Exclusivity shall:

(i) apply to situations where compulsory licenses have been issued or the implementation of any other measures consistent with the need to protect public health and ensure access for all; or
(ii) prevent the Government from taking any necessary action to protect public health, national security, non-commercial public use, national emergency, public health crisis or other extremely urgent circumstances declared by the Government.

In **Chile**, Article 91 of Law 19.996, as amended in 2012,[29] provides that test data exclusivity shall not be applied:

(b) Where, for reasons of public health, national security, public non-commercial use, national emergency or other circumstances of extreme urgency declared by the competent authority, it is justified to terminate the protection referred in Article 89' [on test data exclusivity].
(c) The pharmaceutical or agrochemical product is the subject of a compulsory license in conformity with the provisions of this law.

In **Colombia**, Article 4 of Decree 2085 of 2002 on data exclusivity provides that, 'The protection referred to in this Decree does not apply in the following cases [...] c) where necessary to protect the public, as qualified by the Ministry of Health'.

In the absence of such a waiver, countries have found it difficult to make effective use of compulsory licensing. See Box 1.

Box 1: Case of Romania and Malaysia

In 2015 the World Health Organization (WHO) set the target of eliminating hepatitis C (HCV) as a public health threat by 2030. To reach this goal, prevention and treatment are necessary. People infected with HCV need a 12-week course of antiviral treatment. In countries that cannot access generic supply of HCV medicines, the price of the originator product may be a barrier to reaching the elimination target.

In 2016, the government of Romania contemplated use of a compulsory licence for sofosbuvir, an essential medicine for the treatment of HCV.

(continued)

[27] Hoen et al. (2017). https://joppp.biomedcentral.com/articles/10.1186/s40545-017-0107-9.

[28] https://npra.gov.my/images/reg-info/DataEx/Directive_on_DE.pdf.

[29] http://www.wipo.int/edocs/lexdocs/laws/en/cl/cl042en.pdf.

Box 1 (continued)
Sofosbuvir was only available from the originator company at a price of around 50,000 euro for a 12-week treatment.[30] However, EU data exclusivity for the product will not expire before 2022. This means that, even with a compulsory licence, the registration of a generic version of sofosbuvir would be prohibited until that date.[31] Further, the EU market exclusivity for sofosbuvir expires at the earliest in 2024. Romania, like any other EU Member State, cannot give effect to a compulsory licence during the data and market exclusivity terms.

In contrast, when Malaysia issued a compulsory licence for sofosbuvir in 2017[32] it was not hampered to register the generic product due to its legal waiver to data exclusivity (see Sect. 6.3).

6.4 Data Exclusivity Waivers in FTAs

The US does not have an explicit exception to data exclusivity for medical products. However, the consequence of data exclusivity for the effective use of TRIPS flexibilities was recognised in 2007 when the New Trade Policy in the US explicitly authorised a public health exception to data/market exclusivity in the event of a compulsory licence or other public health need. This flexibility in implementing data exclusivity was included in several US developing-country FTAs, including with Colombia, Panama, and Peru. This implementation flexibility reads:

> For pharmaceutical products, Article 16.10.2(e)(i) provides an exception to the data exclusivity obligations for measures to protect public health in accordance with the Declaration on the TRIPS Agreement and Public Health (WT/MIN(01)/DEC/2) (the 'Doha Declaration'). Thus, where a Party issues a compulsory licence in accordance with Article 31 of the TRIPS Agreement and the Doha Declaration, the data exclusivity obligations in Chapter Sixteen will not prevent the adoption or implementation of such a public health measure. In addition, in a case in which there is no patent on the pharmaceutical product, and, therefore, no need to issue a compulsory licence, the data exclusivity obligations in Chapter Sixteen will not prevent the adoption or implementation of such a measure.[33]

Certain trade agreements the EU is a party to establish that, in regard to test data, parties may provide exceptions to exclusivity for reasons of public interest and for

[30] Paun (2016) http://www.politico.eu/pro/high-drug-prices-romania-changes-patents-hepatitis/.

[31] European Medicines Agency, 'Marketing authorization' *Europa* http://www.ema.europa.eu/ema/index.jsp?curl=pages/regulation/general/general_content_001595.jsp&mid=WC0b01ac0580b18a3d#.

[32] Hoen (2018) https://medicineslawandpolicy.org/2018/04/the-power-of-trips-flexibilities-in-medicines-procurement/.

[33] Office of the U.S. Trade Representative, Statement of Administration Action (2007) https://ustr.gov/archive/assets/Trade_Agreements/Bilateral/Peru_TPA/PTPA_Implementing_Legislation_Supporting_Documentation/asset_upload_file194_15341.pdf.

emergency situations. An example is the EU–Peru Agreement. Article 231 (4) provides that '[t]he Parties may regulate exceptions for reasons of public interest, situations of national emergency or extreme urgency, when it is necessary to allow access to those data to third parties.'[34] The implication of this is that the EU and Peru, both party to this agreement, may provide and use data exclusivity waivers to ensure effective use of compulsory licence. The waiver may also be relevant for non-patented products that still have a monopoly in the market because of data exclusivity. To take advantage of this provision, the party countries would need to provide for a data exclusivity waiver in their regulations.

6.5 EU Medicines Regulation and Compulsory Licensing

EU law does not yet provide a safety valve to data exclusivity to allow registration of a competitor product in the EU. This became apparent during the h5n1 virus (avian influenza) outbreak in 2006, when the threat of a shortage of the antiviral oseltamivir (Tamiflu) signalled the need for an emergency compulsory licence in countries that wanted to ensure sufficient stockpile of the antiviral medicine. The European Generic Association had inquired as to the options under EU law to provide generic oseltamivir for epidemic preparedness purposes, but the European Commission informed them that:[35]

> National emergency provisions in an EU Member State may allow the granting of a compulsory patent licence which would allow a generic or other company to use the patented product in the Member State in question.
>
> However, the Community pharmaceutical acquis does not currently contain any provision allowing the waiver of the rules on data exclusivity and marketing protection periods described above in the case of a national or an EU-wide emergency.
>
> Before expiry of the data exclusivity and marketing protection periods provided for by the European pharmaceutical legislation, applicants for a generic marketing authorisation have to either (1) *provide* the relevant authority with the required documentation on *pre-clinical tests and clinical trials or (2) confirm that the marketing authorisation holder has consented* to the use of the required documentation by the applicant.

The Commission response confirms the lack of public health safeguards in European pharmaceutical legislation. Even in cases of an urgent need or emergency situations, no data exclusivity waiver exists that can be applied by EU member states.

---

[34] Trade Agreement between the European Union and its Member States, of the one part, and Colombia and Peru, of the other part [2012] L354/3.

[35] European Commission, 'Letter from the European Commission to Mr. Greg Perry, EGA-European Generic Medicines Association on the subject of Tamiflu application and data exclusivity in an emergency compulsory license situation' (Brussels, 2006) http://www.cptech.org/ip/health/dataexcl/ec-de-tamiflu.pdf.

6.6 EU Data Exclusivity Waiver and Compulsory Licence for Export

The one waiver to data exclusivity in the EU is only foreseen in cases of compulsory licensing for manufacturing a product for export outside the EU but not to enable effective use of compulsory licensing or other measures to protect public health within EU member states.[36,37] Article 18 of the EU Regulation addresses the situation in which the applicant for a compulsory licence to manufacture medicines in an EU Member State for export outside the EU may use the scientific opinion procedure of the European Medicines Agency[38,39] or any similar national procedures intended exclusively for markets outside the EU. These scientific opinions provide a benefit/risk analysis of a medicine, designed to facilitate registration in importing countries.[40] The procedure provides waivers to data exclusivity rules necessary to obtain such opinions from the EMA or national authorities.[41]

6.7 Data Exclusivity Waivers in Voluntary Patent Licences

The need to provide data exclusivity waivers to ensure effective availability of generic medicines is often recognised in voluntary licences. For example, all Medicines Patent Pool[42] (MPP) licences include a data exclusivity waiver to facilitate

---

[36] Regulation 816/2006 on Compulsory Licensing of Patents Relating to the Manufacture of Pharmaceutical Products for Export to Countries with Public Health Problems [2006] OJ L157/1.

[37] This regulation implements the WTO 'August 30, 2003 decision', which provided a waiver to the TRIPS Article 31(f) requirement that production under a compulsory licence be predominantly for the domestic market. This restriction hampered the use of compulsory licensing by countries that were dependent on the importation of medicines. The 30 August 2003 waiver became a permanent amendment of the TRIPS Agreement in 2017 (see: WTO, 'WTO Members Welcome Entry Into Force of Amendment to Ease Access to Medicines' (30 January 2017) https://www.wto.org/english/news_e/news17_e/heal_30jan17_e.htm.

[38] Article 58 of Regulation (EC) No 726/2004.

[39] Committee for Medicinal Products for Human Use (CHMP) (European Medicines Agency, 17 November 2005). http://www.ema.europa.eu/docs/en_GB/document_library/Scientific_guideline/2009/09/WC500003883.pdf.

[40] European Medicines Agency, 'Medicines for use outside the European Union'. https://www.ema.europa.eu/en/human-regulatory/marketing-authorisation/medicines-use-outside-european-union.

[41] Regulation (EC) No 816/2006 of the European Parliament and of the Council of 17 May 2006 on compulsory licensing of patents relating to the manufacture of pharmaceutical products for export to countries with public health problems. Article 18(2) reads: "If a request for any of the above procedures concerns a product which is a generic of a reference medicinal product which is or has been authorised under Article 6 of Directive 2001/83/EC, the protection periods set out in Article 14 (11) of Regulation (EC) No 726/2004 and in Articles 10(1) and 10(5) of Directive 2001/83/EC shall not apply".

[42] Medicines Patent Pool http://www.medicinespatentpool.org/.

regulatory approval of generics manufactured by MPP licensees in the territories that grant test data exclusivity. For instance, Guatemala is included in the territory of the MPP licences with ViiV Healthcare for paediatric formulations of dolutegravir (DTG) and for adult formulations of DTG and abacavir (ABC), both treatments for HIV. The licences specifically state that:

> ViiV shall provide any Sublicensee with NCE [New Chemical Entity] exclusivity or other regulatory exclusivity waivers to the extent required by the applicable regulatory authorities in order to manufacture or sell Product in the Territory in accordance with the terms of the Sublicence. ViiV shall further provide to any Sublicensee such consents which it has the legal capacity to give as are necessary to enable such Sublicensee to perform its obligations.[43]

Box 2: Data Exclusivity Waiver in Voluntary Licences: The Case of Guatemala

The HIV treatment formulations of DTG 50 mg and ABC/DTG/3TC 600/50/300 mg are protected by test data exclusivity in Guatemala until 11 November 2020 and 29 November 2021 respectively.[44] However, MPP licensees will be able to register and market generic versions of these formulations in Guatemala before the expiration of these rights, based on the waiver included in the MPP licence agreements.

Drug company Gilead has included the following waiver of data exclusivity in its licence agreements for HCV treatment sofosbuvir:

> Gilead agrees to provide Licensee with NCE Exclusivity, or other regulatory exclusivity, waivers as may be required by the applicable regulatory authorities in order to manufacture or sell Product in the Territory, provided such manufacture and sale by Licensee is compliant with the terms and conditions of this Agreement. Licensee agrees not to pursue or obtain regulatory exclusivity on any Product in any country within the Territory.[45]

Even though Gilead obtained test data exclusivity for sofosbuvir 400 mg until 14 July 2021 in Guatemala, for instance, Gilead licensees should not be barred from registering and selling generic versions of sofosbuvir 400mg during this data exclusivity period in Guatemala, which is included in the license territory.

[43] Medicines Patent Pool, 'Products Licensed: ViiV' https://medicinespatentpool.org/what-we-do/global-licence-overview/licences-in-the-mpp/?patent_holder=2718 Link Does Not Work.

[44] Medicines Patent Pool, 'MedsPaL The Medicines Patent and Licences Database'. https://www.medspal.org.

[45] Gilead Sciences (15 September 2014) https://www.gilead.com/~/media/files/pdfs/other/2014_original_hcv_licensing_agreement.pdf?la=en.

6.8 *Public Health Measures, Data Exclusivity and Competition Law*

Some scholars have argued that the issuance of a compulsory licence for public interest reasons creates the obligation for the patent holder to provide a waiver to data exclusivity.[46] A company holding a dominant position in the market that denies access to the data held by the regulatory authority in the case of a compulsory licence is likely to be viewed as abusive under competition law since national authorities have already decided that the public interest requires an additional product on the market. However, enforcing this position will likely lead to protracted legal procedures and delays in the availability of the medicine for which the compulsory licence was requested.

6.9 *EU Law Needs an Explicit Data Exclusivity Waiver*

It would be desirable to introduce explicit data and market exclusivity waivers in national legislation. This is particularly important in the EU, now that European countries have indicated that they lack the negotiating power to obtain good results in price negotiations with pharmaceutical companies concerning patented products and several EU countries are exploring the use of compulsory licensing to strengthen this position.[47]

The following amendment to the EU medicines regulation would introduce a waiver to data exclusivity similar to the one contained in the Regulation on compulsory licensing for export:[48,49]

> The protection periods set out in article 14 (11) of Regulation 726/2004 shall not apply in cases where it is necessary to allow access to and the use of pharmaceutical test data to register a generic of a reference medicinal product, which is or has been authorised under article 6 of Directive 2001/83/EC, for reasons of public interest including public health, in case of compulsory licensing of patents, including for public non-commercial use, and in situations of national emergency or extreme urgency.

[46] Junod (29 January 2019) https://www.publiceye.ch/fileadmin/doc/Medikamente/ValerieJunod_Legal-Analysis-CL_20190129.pdf.

[47] Rumney (*Public Finance International*, 16 January 2017). https://www.publicfinancefocus.org/news/2017/01/drug-manufacturers-have-too-much-power-price-negotiations-says-oecd.

[48] *Regulation* (EC) No 816/2006 of the European Parliament and of the Council of 17 May 2006 on *compulsory licensing* of patents relating to the manufacture of pharmaceutical products for *export* to countries with public health problems.

[49] Hoen et al. (2017).

7 Conclusion and Recommendations

The TRIPS Agreement provides much flexibility for WTO members to design a test data protection regimes conducive to public health.

Where possible, countries should refrain from implementing data exclusivity and instead use the flexibility offered to them in the TRIPS agreement to provide data protection for certain types of data only and without granting exclusive rights to the originator of the data.

Safeguards need to be in place to ensure that data remains available for legitimate public health functions including the assessment of efficacy and safety of needed products. Countries that have a data exclusivity regime should have the option to use waivers to data (and market) exclusivity for effective use of measures such as compulsory licensing, to protect public health.

There are different ways in which undisclosed test data can be protected, including: protecting it against dishonest commercial practices, but allowing its use to register a generic product,[50] permitting generic reliance on the test data but with compensation to the entity that originally generated the data.[51] Countries should consider replacing data exclusivity regimes with data protection regimes that acknowledge the investment made to generate data but do not allow the investor to exclude others from using the data. Under a *data compensation regime*, the registration of a generic medicine or biosimilar medicine is considered fair commercial use. The originator company that made the investment that was needed to generate the data will receive adequate remuneration for the use of the data but cannot prevent its necessary use by the medicines agency to perform its public health duties. The data compensation regime could be proposed as an alternative to data exclusivity demands in trade negotiations.

References

Agreement on Trade-Related Aspects of Intellectual Property Rights (Apr. 15, 1994) Marrakesh Agreement Establishing the World Trade Organization, Annex 1C, The Legal Texts: The Results of the Uruguay Round of Multilateral Trade Negotiations 320 (1999), 1869 U.N.T.S. 299, 33 I.L.M. 1197 (1994)

Code de la propriété intellectuelle (version consolidée au 9 octobre 2016) Article L613-16

Commission on Intellectual Property Rights, Innovation and Public Health, Public Health, Innovation and Intellectual Property Rights (World Health Organization, 2006)

Committee for Medicinal Products for Human Use (CHMP), 'Guideline on Procedural Aspects Regarding a CHMP Scientific Opinion in the Context of Cooperation with the World Health Organisation (WHO) for the Evaluation of Medicinal Products Intended Exclusively for Markets Outside the Community' (European Medicines Agency, 17 November 2005). http://www.

[50] Correa (2002).

[51] For example, in the US, Knowledge Ecology International has proposed a cost sharing model. See for details: Sanjuan et al. (2006), p. 1.

ema.europa.eu/docs/en_GB/document_library/Scientific_guideline/2009/09/WC500003883.pdf. Last accessed 23 Feb 2021

Copenhagen Economics, Study on the economic impact of supplementary protection certificates, pharmaceutical incentives and rewards in Europe (European Commission, May 2018). https://ec.europa.eu/health/sites/health/files/human-use/docs/pharmaceuticals_incentives_study_en.pdf. Last accessed 22 Feb 2021

Correa CM (2002) Protection of data submitted for the registration of pharmaceuticals: implementing the standards of the TRIPS Agreement. South Centre, Geneva. http://apps.who.int/medicinedocs/en/d/Jh3009ae/. Last accessed 23 Feb 2021

Council of the EU (17 June 2016) Council conclusions on strengthening the balance in the pharmaceutical systems in the EU and its Member States. https://www.consilium.europa.eu/en/press/press-releases/2016/06/17/epsco-conclusions-balance-pharmaceutical-system/. Last accessed 22 Feb 2021

Declaration on the TRIPS agreement and public health (14 November 2001) WT/MIN(01)/DEC/2 https://www.wto.org/english/thewto_e/minist_e/min01_e/mindecl_trips_e.htm

European Commission, 'Letter from the European Commission to Mr. Greg Perry, EGA-European Generic Medicines Association on the subject of Tamiflu application and data exclusivity in an emergency compulsory license situation' (Brussels, 2006). http://www.cptech.org/ip/health/dataexcl/ec-de-tamiflu.pdf. Last accessed 23 Feb 2021

European Medicines Agency, 'Marketing authorization' Europa http://www.ema.europa.eu/ema/index.jsp?curl=pages/regulation/general/general_content_001595.jsp&mid=WC0b01ac0580b18a3d#. Last accessed 23 February 2021

European Medicines Agency, 'Medicines for use outside the European Union' https://www.ema.europa.eu/en/human-regulatory/marketing-authorisation/medicines-use-outside-european-union. Last accessed 23 Feb 2021

European Medicines Agency and the European Commission, Biosimilars in the EU: Information guide for healthcare professionals (European Medicines Agency, 2019). https://www.ema.europa.eu/en/documents/leaflet/biosimilars-eu-information-guide-healthcare-professionals_en.pdf. Last accessed 22 Feb 2021

Federal Trade Commission (June 2009) Emerging health care issues: follow-on biologic drug competition. https://www.ftc.gov/sites/default/files/documents/reports/emerging-health-care-issues-follow-biologic-drug-competition-federal-trade-commission-report/p083901biologicsreport.pdf. Last accessed 22 Feb 2021

Gilead Sciences, 'Licence Agreement' (15 September 2014). https://www.gilead.com/~/media/files/pdfs/other/2014_original_hcv_licensing_agreement.pdf?la=en. Last accessed 23 Feb 2021

Hoen E't (2016) private patents and public health: changing intellectual property rules for access to medicines. AMB Press, Health Action International, The Netherlands

Hoen E, 'The Power of TRIPS Flexibilities in Medicines Procurement' (Medicines Law & Policy, 9 April 2018). https://medicineslawandpolicy.org/2018/04/the-power-of-trips-flexibilities-in-medicines-procurement/. Last accessed 23 Feb 2021

Hoen E't FM, Boulet P, Baker BK (2017) Data exclusivity exceptions and compulsory licensing to promote generic medicines in the European Union: a proposal for greater coherence in European pharmaceutical legislation. JOPPP 10. https://joppp.biomedcentral.com/articles/10.1186/s40545-017-0107-9. Last accessed 23 Feb 2021

Junod V, 'Legal analysis: the interface between patent protection and data exclusivity – the issue of compulsory licensing in the public interest under Swiss Law' (Public Eye, 29 January 2019). https://www.publiceye.ch/fileadmin/doc/Medikamente/ValerieJunod_Legal-Analysis-CL_20190129.pdf. Last accessed 23 Feb 2021

Law No. 19.996 revising Law No. 19.039 on Industrial Property. http://www.wipo.int/edocs/lexdocs/laws/en/cl/cl042en.pdf. Last accessed 23 February 2021

Lietzan E (2016) The myths of data exclusivity (University of Missouri School of Law). Lewis Clark Law Rev 20:91. https://pdfs.semanticscholar.org/2fdb/0784f6fb314cf99063933cb6bfbfae6a7091.pdf. Last accessed 22 February 2021

Medicines Law & Policy, How the 'Oxford' Covid-19 vaccine became the 'AstraZeneca' Covid-19 vaccine. https://medicineslawandpolicy.org/useful-resources/briefs/. Last accessed 22 February 2021

Medicines Patent Pool, MedsPaL: The Medicines Patents and Licences Database https://www.medspal.org. Last accessed 23 February 2021

Medicines Patent Pool. http://www.medicinespatentpool.org/. Last accessed 23 February 2021

Medicines Patent Pool 'Products Licensed: ViiV'. https://medicinespatentpool.org/what-we-do/global-licence-overview/licences-in-the-mpp/?patent_holder=2718. Link Does not Work

Office of the U.S. Trade Representative, Statement of Administration Action (2007). https://ustr.gov/archive/assets/Trade_Agreements/Bilateral/Peru_TPA/PTPA_Implementing_Legislation_Supporting_Documentation/asset_upload_file194_15341.pdf. Last accessed 23 Feb 2021

Paun C (16 March 2016) 'Skyhigh drug prices made Romania mull unusual path' Politico, http://www.politico.eu/pro/high-drug-prices-romania-changes-patents-hepatitis/. Last accessed 23 Feb 2021

Regulation 816/2006 on Compulsory Licensing of Patents Relating to the Manufacture of Pharmaceutical Products for Export to Countries with Public Health Problems [2006] OJ L157/1

Reichman JH (2009) The international legal status of undisclosed clinical trials data: from private to public goods? Marquette Intellect Property Law Rev 13:17

Rumney E, 'Drug manufacturers have too much power in price negotiations, Says OECD' (Public Finance International, 16 January 2017). https://www.publicfinancefocus.org/news/2017/01/drug-manufacturers-have-too-much-power-price-negotiations-says-oecd. Last accessed 23 Feb 2021

Sanjuan JR, Love J, Weissman R (2006) Protection of pharmaceutical test data: a policy proposal' KEI Research Paper 2006:1

Technopolis (15 June 2018a) Effects of supplementary protection mechanisms for pharmaceutical products. https://www.technopolis-group.com/report/effects-of-supplementary-protection-mechanisms-for-pharmaceutical-products/. Last accessed 22 Feb 2021

Technopolis (May 2018b) Effects of supplementary protection mechanisms for pharmaceutical products. http://www.technopolis-group.com/wp-content/uploads/2018/06/2718-Technopolis-report-on-supplementary-protection-mechanisms.pdf. Last accessed 22 Feb 2021

The Council for Trips Extension of the Transition Period Under Article 66.1 of the Trips Agreement for Least Developed Country Members for Certain Obligations with Respect to Pharmaceutical Products (6 November 2015), World Trade Organization IP/C/73

Timmermans K (2007) Monopolizing clinical trial data: implications and trends. PLoS Med 4:e2

U.S. Federal Trade Commission, 'Emerging Health Care Issues: Follow-on Biologic Drug Competition' (FTC, June 2009). https://www.ftc.gov/reports/emerging-health-care-issues-follow-biologic-drug-competition-federal-trade-commission-report. Last accessed 22 Feb 2021

WHO (2012) WTO, WIPO Trilateral Study Promoting Access to Medical Technologies and Innovation, 64 https://www.wipo.int/policy/en/global_health/trilateral_cooperation.html. Last accessed 22 February 2021

WIPO, 'Meaning of Flexibilities' http://www.wipo.int/ip-development/en/agenda/flexibilities/meaning_of_flexibilities.html. Last accessed 23 February 2021

WTO, 'WTO Members Welcome Entry Into Force of Amendment to Ease Access to Medicines' (30 January 2017). https://www.wto.org/english/news_e/news17_e/heal_30jan17_e.htm. Last accessed 23 Feb 2021

WTO 'TRIPS Council Discussion on Access to Medicines: Developing Country Group's Paper' (World Trade Organization, 20 June 2001) IP/C/W/296, paras 39–40. https://www.wto.org/english/tratop_e/trips_e/paper_develop_w296_e.htm. Last accessed 23 Feb 2021

Courts and Pharmaceutical Patents: From Formalist Positivism to the Emergence of a Global Law

Calixto Salomão Filho and Vitor Henrique Pinto Ido

Abstract This article seeks to repurpose the relation between courts and IP law, avoiding describing them as a purely neutral and unidimensional process whereby 'courts apply IP law'. Based on two cases from Brazil (Trastuzumab and Sofosbuvir), the article argues that the role of courts in implementing TRIPS flexibilities is in itself a factor that determines or at least influences the behavior of actors in the field. As such, courts are not arenas, but actors that influence competition and restructure markets. This pushes for the recognition that patent use and patent abuse, including practices in patent filings such as evergreening and sham litigation, are legal phenomena that ought to be regulated differently by law. Instead of formalist positivism, law should be more thoughtful of socio-economic consequences and of existing contexts. This aims at addressing economic structures rather than reinforcing them in cases pertaining to pharmaceutical patents.

The article concludes by proposing an interpretation of IP law which is integrated with competition law principles, both oriented towards, and based on, public interest provisions. Overall, the article posits that this is a better framework than regarding IP and competition law as 'complementary' and to address issues of how courts may be misused by economic actors due to fragmentation of the two legal fields. Furthermore, such endeavors are part of an emerging body of what some could even call "global law"; in this case, it means a nod for the transnational implications of national IP cases beyond its original realm.

C. S. Filho (✉) · V. H. P. Ido
Faculty of Law, University of São Paulo, São Paulo, Brazil

South Centre, Geneva, Switzerland

C. M. Correa, R. M. Hilty (eds.), *Access to Medicines and Vaccines*,
https://doi.org/10.1007/978-3-030-83114-1_8

1 Introduction

Courts are prominent actors in the implementation of intellectual property (IP) law. [1] Apart from being enforcers of the existing law, they also delineate the contours of IP protection, including the definition of patentability criteria, scope of protection of IPRs, exclusions of patentable subject and conditions for enactment of injunctions. [2] This is an intrinsic characteristic of how IP law is conceived and how it operates, rather than a process of politicization of courts or an expansion of their role beyond their competence. [3] By doing so, courts inevitably affect competition and play a major role in the implementation of TRIPS in national jurisdictions, often with transnational consequences.

Scholarship's attention on the role of judicial and quasi-judicial courts in IP has risen, [4] including advocates for courts to be the best suited for balancing IP policies [5] and ample discussions on specialized IP courts. [6] Judicial enforcement of IP has become a common, yet very questionable, variable for assessing what is understood as the level of IP protection in a given country. [7] It has also deserved emerging

[1] While judges in some jurisdictions may be typically more prominent in such role—such as common law systems, which give more importance on precedents—, the last decades saw an unquestionable rise in the number of courts dealing with IP. This process has both a geographical dimension and an institutional one. Geographically, there has been a "globalization" of jurisdictions deciding upon IP and pharmaceutical cases. Institutionally, there has been a stark expansion of actors deciding IP cases, such as quasi-judicial independent IP appellate bodies, competition authorities' decisions and IP specialized courts.

[2] They are not the only relevant actors, as administrative border agents, police officers and others all concretely decide on issues such as what is a counterfeit. Nonetheless, courts have a specifically defining role as they provide the basis for the applicability of laws and regulations "on the ground".

[3] In this sense, when adjudicating IP cases, judges do not *create,* but rather apply, law. The issue is that this process is by default not a mere formalistic endeavor, and the exact details of IP law necessarily depend upon such interpretation. In many jurisdictions, where public considerations are directly embedded into IP law, this adjudication cannot be dissociated from a broader spectrum of public principles, including health and socio-economic development. Acknowledging this particular feature of IP law is *not* the same as advocating for courts to disregard precedents, decide against the law or over-expanding their own competence. As this paper will point out in more detail, the refusal to acknowledge such role, including when courts do not rule, is in itself a factor that impacts competition, generates judicial uncertainty and compromises the whole IP system. Also please see Sect. 2 of this article for a more comprehensive argument on the role of courts in IP.

[4] For a comprehensive overview of developed countries, see Geiger et al. (2018).

[5] Burk and Lemley (2013) (on the specific case of the USA, acknowledging its failures and considering that courts are the most suitable for patent law reform by adopting different interpretations according to different industries).

[6] de Werra (2016). Published in: Specialised Intellectual Property Courts - Issues and Challenges, Global Perspectives for the Intellectual Property System, Issue Number 2: CEIPI-ICTSD. 2016, p. 15-41. Available at SSRN: https://ssrn.com/abstract=2761209 (drawing positive and negative arguments for their implementation, noting that they cannot be recommended in all circumstances).

[7] In those cases, "judicial enforcement" simply means the enforcement of pro-IP holder interests, without the inclusion of public interest provisions. As such, these rankings may wrongly give the impression that enforcement of IP means exclusively the protection of private rights. It is not a

importance by the WIPO, the South Centre and other international organizations as key players in implementing IP norms, each with a distinct approach. [8]

In particular, the consequences of court rulings to access to medicines is a sensitive topic, particularly if decisions are taken prioritizing exclusively IP holder interests. A single court ruling (or sometimes lack thereof) may have huge consequences for public policies and the realization of rights, as IPRs may pose major barriers to competition and access to essential products. As such, it makes sense to craft a more comprehensive analysis of the role of courts in implementing or not the in-built TRIPS flexibilities [9] across jurisdictions.

This article seeks to repurpose the relation between courts and IP law, avoiding describing them as a purely neutral and unidimensional process whereby 'courts apply IP law'. According to this view, the main issue of concern would be how to provide specific technical knowledge on IP for judges. Instead, this article aims at exposing that jurisdictional practices are *themselves* an element to interpret TRIPS flexibilities, as courts reshape markets and the extension of patent monopolies even when they decide not to take action. In this sense, courts apply IP and by doing so define markets; they are also mutually influenced by the market structures.

---

surprise that they are used as pressure tools for developing countries to adopt more stringent standards of protection. In reality, the process of enforcement is supposed to be a balancing between private and public interests and should be seen as an important policy space for countries to enact IP policies that are coherent with other goals such as public health and industrial development (see Li and Correa (2009). For the use of rankings, see, for instance, *"create"*, the U.S. Chamber International IP Index, which includes numerous indicators on enforcement. The 2018 edition included new indicators, which "cover important evolving areas of IP rights, such as injunctive-style relief through the disabling of infringing content online, as well as the practical operation of a given national IP system. As the Index evolves, it is only natural that a greater focus be placed on the operational aspects of a national IP system. The new indicators seek to measure national efforts at coordinating IP rights enforcement", among others (https://www.theglobalipcenter.com/wp-content/uploads/2018/02/GIPC_IP_Index_2018.pdf). Similarly, the International Property Rights Index (associated to the Property Rights Alliance, an explicitly pro-property organization) includes indicators such as "judicial independence", "rule of law", "protection of intellectual property rights" and "perception of IP protection" (https://www.internationalpropertyrightsindex.org/about). These rankings also find a notable echo in older and criticizable views of the "Law and Finance literature", which evaluated jurisdictions according to their capacity to secure private rights (See La Porta et al. (1998), pp. 1113–155).

[8] The World Intellectual Property Organization (WIPO), for instance, has created its WIPO Judicial Institute (https://www.wipo.int/about-wipo/en/activities_by_unit/index.jsp?id=1022). Technical assistance provided by many multilateral institutions, including the European Patent Office (EPO), the European Commission, the United States Patent and Trademark Office (USPTO) and the JPO (Japanese Patent Office) have reportedly increased attention to judges, offering trainings that often mirror their understandings of IP law to other jurisdictions. An example is the internationalization of doctrines that are originally European, such as the "Swiss claims" or the need to protect "Markush claims" for pharmaceuticals. Other institutions seek an alternative approach, such as the South Centre, which focuses its activities on the full implementation of TRIPS flexibilities in relation to IP law (https://ipaccessmeds.southcentre.int/).

[9] For an overview of the notion of TRIPS flexibilities and their implementation, see Correa (2016); see also Deere (2008).

Furthermore, other actors play crucial roles, including civil society organizations and lobbying economic pressures,[10] and dealing with them is another important dimension of the role of courts. In summary, it means a broader understanding of their role, which is embedded in certain structures of thinking and socio-economic implications and pressures. As we wish to propose, this framework allows a different legal assessment of what in practice courts do and what economic consequences their own behavior bear. For instance, when a court does not rule or takes too long to rule an IP case, this in itself likely generates more judicial uncertainty than the content of the decision. Despite differences in how this understanding reverberates in concrete IP cases, a general takeaway is that this requires a different interpretation of IP law, as per below.

The structure of the article is as follows: after this overview, it provides some inputs for the reasons why courts, while implementing TRIPS flexibilities, can be considered to be channels of "structural change". This serves as a theoretical premise to the analysis. It is followed by an assessment of the consequences of the legal utilization—both directly and indirectly—of a narrative that treats intellectual property protection as necessary for innovation.[11] This normative argument serves as a *de facto* tool for impeding evidence-based discussions on the competitive implications of IP in concrete cases. In short, the threat of decreased innovation is used, even if sometimes implicitly, to impede a more balanced and real consideration of rights and interests involved in IP law.

It then exemplifies the overall argument above through the comparison of two cases in Brazil. They share the similarity of dealing with access to medicines curbed by high prices (due to, among other reasons, intellectual property rights), albeit with different profiles, courts and arguments. In both, the role of courts is paramount, not only as the ones defining the interpretation of legal principles and rules in IP law with regards to demands of access to medicines, but also as setters of expectations for competitors and society at large. Both medicines have been subject to patent disputes in the country, in a way that IP is not necessarily the only issue to be considered, but certainly a relevant one. The first case refers to a litigation that questioned prices on the selling of cancer biological medicine Trastuzumab to Brazilian public entities, particularly in light of a stark price discrimination between regular public purchases

[10] The number of institutions, arenas and players engaging with the topic of IP has grown immensely since the TRIPS Agreement was enacted. In the IP and public health field, key actors include civil society organizations (such as Médécins sans Frontières—MSF Access Campaign) and industry representatives (International Federation of Pharmaceutical Manufacturers & Associations—IFPMA). New organizations (such as the Medicines Patent Pool—MPP) have been created and also shape and influence the very interpretation and implementation of IP. The existing framework of global IP law and access to medicines is in many senses dependent on the work of these organizations. See Hein and Moon (2013) and Matthews (2011).

[11] While the specialized literature has a lot of divergence, the transplantation of this discussion into a legal argument in IP cases tends to over-expand the scope of protection of patents in particular. Therefore, by shedding light on the possibility of another kind of relation, that of innovation that arises precisely from more *access* (to knowledge), and not from more monopolies (patents and other IPRs), it is possible to reassess the role of IP in legal rulings.

and purchases to enforce judicial decisions. The second case deals with the procurement of hepatitis C medicine Sofosbuvir and the price differentiation after a patent was granted and later suspended, which is evidence for possible anti-competitive excessive pricing and/or abuse of dominant position.

Finally, the text provides some theoretical conclusions on the relation between courts and IP. It firstly proves that the role of courts in implementing TRIPS flexibilities is in itself a factor that determines or at least influences the behavior of actors in the field. As such, courts are not arenas, but actors that influence competition and restructure markets. This pushes for the recognition that patent use and patent abuse, including practices in patent filings such as evergreening and sham litigation, are legal phenomena that can be at least partly regulated differently by law. In fact, by shedding light and putting all pieces of this interaction together, there is a need for a different interpretation of IP law. Theoretically, it means a law that is more thoughtful of socio-economic consequences and of existing contexts, which aims at addressing economic structures rather than reinforcing them.

The article concludes by proposing an interpretation of IP law which is *integrated* with competition law principles, both oriented towards, and based on, public interest provisions. Overall, we argue that this is a better framework than regarding IP and competition law as 'complementary' and to address issues of how courts may be misused by economic actors due to fragmentation of the two legal fields. Moreover, this interpretation is derived from international law, from the theoretical foundations of IP and competition laws, and from the historical development of substantive national provisions—and not a mere theoretical speculation. Furthermore, such endeavors are part of an emerging body of what some could even call "global law"; in this case, it means a nod for the transnational implications of national IP cases beyond its original realm.

2 Assessing the Role of Courts in TRIPS Flexibilities As Forms of Structural Change

In previous works, the authors have argued that the strong interplay between economic power and law are so pervasive that structural interventions are needed in order to prevent law from becoming a mere instrument of economic interests, and to instead promote broader societal goals. [12] A "neo-structuralist" approach [13] means that individual, moral(istic), and even institutional explanations are insufficient and even sometimes misleading. Therefore, efforts to ensure the full implementation of TRIPS flexibilities need to rely on a legal interpretation that is structural in the sense of taking into account the role of economic structures of pharmaceutical monopolies and ready to counter their negative consequences when needed. The approach

[12] Salomão Filho (2013a) and Salomão Filho and Ido (2019).

[13] Salomão Filho (2015).

generally proposes that, willingly or not, legal interpretation will either be accepting of the *status quo* (adopting compensatory mechanisms at most) or transformative in a structural way. This analysis provides some inputs for a legal proposal for the role of courts to be less formalistic—in its intimate, self-referred and negative connotation—and more mindful about structural intervention through the application of public values. Whether courts wish to acknowledge this role or not, adjudicators will invariably perform it.

Specifically on the topic of TRIPS flexibilities, achieving broad access to medicines for all knowingly demands structural reforms in the current R&D model for pharmaceuticals, a high-level policy commitment by governments to act boldly, and a major rethinking in the behavior of companies. [14] None of this is primarily a task of any courts around the world; none is exclusively a legal enterprise. Indeed, judges and decision-makers should operate within the realm of existing laws and have, in the majority of circumstances, a limited role for structural change. This is all true. However, it should equally be stressed that structural change is a task that *includes* courts and *includes* legal thinking. Legal interpreters need to rely, even if partly, on philosophical foundations and legal theories for the interpretation of concrete cases. Judges and adjudicators reflect certain viewpoints and distinct ideologies even if they do not acknowledge so. [15]

Both considerations seem particularly relevant to IP and access to medicines, where notions of innovation, public interest and limits of monopolies are deeply intertwined and even part of ordinary legal arguments on IP. [16] Considering how the implementation of IP norms around the world since the TRIPS Agreement has been the result of a push by developed countries and their industries, [17] courts that adopt a formalist and limited approach will invariably reproduce the notion that IP needs to be expanded at all costs. This disregards that TRIPS flexibilities, including a focus on technological development and public health, are all primarily *legal* and *legitimate* tools. As such, if courts would strictly "follow the law", they should enforce the

[14] For a critical overview of the current R&D model, see Velásquez (2020).

[15] For a compelling general critique, see Kennedy (1997); for an example of how courts may incorporate neoliberal values despite claims of impartiality, see Sanghera (2015), available at: https://www.opendemocracy.net/en/odr/unmasking-central-asias-neoliberal-judges/; for how a community of adjudicators and lawyers defines certain arguments in international arbitration and assumes a central role for a transnational legal order, see Dezalay and Garth (1996).

[16] Examples would include the interpretation of the common clause on exception of patentability due to "public order", dependent not only on an understanding of what "public order" means, but also how it is applicable in an analysis of a patent application. For an overview, see Bently (2011), pp. 315–347. Real cases show the need for courts to decide on multiple elements at once when faced with concrete cases, from patentability of living organisms to the limits posed by religious and morality laws to alleged obscene patent applications (see, for instance, Pankhuri and Shamnad (2018), available at: https://spicyip.com/2018/08/the-morality-of-sexual-pleasure-patent-office-training.html).

[17] Sell (2003).

validity of TRIPS flexibilities, and be particularly aware of the socio-consequences to the public interest of patents and other intellectual property rights.[18] In other words, courts have the potential of *de facto* limiting the policy space of a country, and it is no surprise that so much effort is now given to the role of courts as part of the international economic architecture.[19]

In developing countries, these considerations are even more evident for two reasons: on one hand, the material conditions of access to medicines are generally worse;[20] on the other, the majority of such countries contain constitutional and legal provisions that advocate for implementation of socio-economic rights (such as health) and development goals, often in more directive and transformative ways than the counterparts in industrialized economies.[21]

Therefore, courts' stance on TRIPS flexibilities is of utmost importance, such as the position towards the validity of stringent patentability criteria for pharmaceuticals and the use of competition law to address anti-competitive practices in IP and health cases. Courts do not need to be "advocates" nor political actors to applying IP

[18] This can be traced back to the very foundation of intellectual property law scholarship, such as that of Italian Tulio Ascarelli, with profound repercussions to Brazilian commercial law, among others. For Ascarelli (1970), p. 276.

[19] Apart from intellectual property and TRIPS flexibilities, such considerations could be extended to multiple realms, such as international investment law (particularly investor-state dispute settlement—ISDS) and business and human rights litigation for environmental disasters, in which both pro-private biases and formalist views on jurisdictions and conflict of laws effectively lead to transnational economic deregulation. For notes on the impact of courts' rulings in international economic governance, see Muir-Watt et al. (2019) (for a compilation of cases that redefine the boundaries of public and private, and highlight the increasing interdependence between national and international jurisdictions); and for a more theoretical account, Muir-Watt (2016), pp. 347–428. ("despite the contemporary juridification of international politics, private international law has contributed very little to the global governance debate, remaining remarkably silent before the increasingly unequal distribution of wealth and authority in the world. [...] According to the genealogy of private international law depicted here, the discipline has developed, under the aegis of the liberal divides between law and politics and between the public and the private spheres, a form of epistemological tunnel-vision, actively providing immunity and impunity to abusers of private sovereignty.); see also Zumbansen (2012), pp. 899–925.

[20] See the final report of the United Nations Secretary-General High-Level Panel on Access to Medicines (2016) for some considerations. The language agreed as part of the Sustainable Development Goals (SDGs), especially SDG 3 on health, should also be stressed: "Target 3.b.Support the research and development of vaccines and medicines for the communicable and non-communicable diseases that primarily affect developing countries, provide access to affordable essential medicines and vaccines, in accordance with the Doha Declaration on the TRIPS Agreement and Public Health, which affirms the right of developing countries to use to the full the provisions in the Agreement on Trade-Related Aspects of Intellectual Property Rights regarding flexibilities to protect public health, and, in particular, provide access to medicines for all.". There is broad consensus on the need of specific, and often bolder action, in the context of developing countries.

[21] See, for instance, the constitutional provisions that have been deemed, among other terms, "transformative" and "social", including those of Brazil (1988), South Africa, (1996), Colombia (1991), Bhutan (2008) and India (1950), just to name a few remarkable examples. See, for theoretical discussions: Uprimny (2011); Bonilla Maldonado (2013); Mendes (2013), 272p; Iyer (2019), pp. 359–385; Hailbronner (2017), pp. 527–565.

law in a manner that is consistent with broader societal goals such as ensuring access to medicines. However, they sometimes refrain from doing so on such grounds. As we have noted before, the mere lack of decision is also a crucial feature in the lack of their implementation.[22] In this context, advocates for judicial adjudication as a purely neutral and technical process do not address the negative impact this very stance has or might have on access to medicines.

3 Access and Innovation in Legal Discourse: From Opposition to Coexistence

There is one economic narrative that has profoundly influenced the debate on IP and access to medicines: the rhetoric whereby IP is an enabler of innovation, to the extent which it provides incentives for inventors, and therefore is also a prerequisite for access to future technologies.[23] In short, no access without IP. Importantly, this has been often converted into a self-standing *legal* argument, either underpinned or explicitly referred to, in multiple cases, without further consideration of historical and empirical circumstances of the real markets they address.

The objective of this section is not to delve deeply into the broader debate on IP and innovation, and how IP affects access to the outcomes of future and existing

[22] The argument is also valid in the other direction: sometimes, measures taken by courts (such as investigations) have an indirect effect that is sufficient for social results. For instance, in the Hazel Tau case (2003), when the South African Competition Commission publicly announced that would sanction pharmaceutical company Glaxo-Smith-Klein (GSK) for the abuse of the exercise of its patent rights by charging excessive prices, a settlement was reached and no decision was taken. For an overview, see Knowledge Ecology International (KEI). CPTech's 2003 reports for the RSA Competition Commission, in Hazel Tau et al. v GSK, Boehringer, et al. Available at: https://www.keionline.org/competition/2003-hazel-tau-tac.

[23] For example, the director-general of the International Federation of Pharmaceutical Manufacturers & Associations (IFPMA), Thomas Cueni, noted in a Financial times article on 17 May 2020 that "Patents, and IP more generally, are the main reason that there is such a strong innovation base to work from to find solutions" (Cueni, Thomas. Intellectual property is not a hindrance but a help to end Covid-19, Financial Times, available at: https://www.ft.com/content/e82dd07c-95c5-11ea-899a-f62a20d54625). Another example of the utilization of this rhetoric is found in the official stance of the United States Trade Representative (USTR)'s Special 301 report of April 2020 *"To promote affordable healthcare for American patients today and innovation to preserve access to the cutting-edge treatments and cures that they deserve tomorrow, USTR has been engaging with trading partners to ensure that U.S. owners of IP have a full and fair opportunity to use and profit from their IP, including by promoting transparent and fair pricing and reimbursement systems"*, available at: https://ustr.gov/sites/default/files/2020_Special_301_Report.pdf. Similarly, in a publication by the International Federation of Pharmaceutical Manufacturers & Associations (IFPMA), it is noted that *"A robust, time-limited system of patent protection is proven to facilitate development of, and access to, innovative pharmaceutical products and processes. In particular, a well-functioning patent protection system is a prerequisite for attracting finance for costly pharmaceutical research, given its high failure rates, by ensuring that successful innovation is rewarded"*. Gawel (2016), pp. 45–53.

innovation, but to note how the conversion of this narrative into a legal argument is highly problematic. According to this view, less IP protection would necessarily lead to less innovation and therefore less access. This means that protecting IP would always be, according to this particular narrative, in the public interest.[24] Accordingly, if IPRs are to be anyhow limited or restricted—even when they were wrongfully granted in the first place—this argument will consider that innovation will be hampered and, as a final result, access will be compromised.[25]

However, this assumption is remarkably questionable. For one, the role of IP in fostering innovation is far from clear.[26] Some markets are innovative and creative despite the lack of exclusivity rights,[27] and in many cases, IP is simply detrimental to innovation. A number of evidence-based studies propose that the barriers created

[24] In this sense, it performs the same functional role that theories on IP as natural rights once had. Treating IP as a natural right tends to maximize its protection. Conversely, treating IP as a temporary monopoly granted by the State requires a public interest justification based on the incentives provided by it. The "IP as channel of innovation" argument leads to the same maximization of IP as natural rights without needing to give away the notion that IP only exist to provide market incentives. It creates an overarching and somehow incontestable argument to consider that IP should always be expanded (in order to "achieve innovation"). This leads to very pragmatic consequences on the role of courts in IP law. When courts adopt fully this latter myth, the balancing of private and public interests in IP becomes a *de facto* imbalance gearing towards the private interest only. It becomes a tool for an adjudication that is incapable of properly taking into account public needs in the protection of IP. For a comprehensive critical analysis of patent law and history, which could include a reflection on the very adequacy of the "public and private balancing in IP", see Pottage and Sherman (2010).

[25] One such example is found among opposers of compulsory licensing, despite their recognition as a legal and legitimate tool under multiple international law instruments, including the WTO Doha Declaration on Public Health (2001). For instance, in a preliminary ruling on a class action in Brazil requesting the compulsory licensing of medicine Kaletra (lopinavir/ritonavir) due to high prices, the judge considered that "*issuing a compulsory license would trigger retaliation by the developed world and possible shortages of the drug, while the very capacity of domestic industry to produce the medicine in Brazil was also called into question*". See Costa et al. (2008). In a similar sense: "*Patents benefit society in a number of ways, and although their specific role in each industry is unique, they are generally recognized for their ability to spur innovation. In the pharmaceutical industry, for example, patents are essential to motivating and directing future innovation, which generates new and better medicines for all. [. . .] The promise of immediate and improved access to brand name HIV/AIDS drugs is definitely alluring, but issuing or threatening a compulsory license has consequences. Compulsory licenses not only reduce foreign investment, they also impose costs related to litigation, safety, and efficacy.*" Borowski (2009). http://ir.law.fsu.edu/lr/vol36/iss2/6.

[26] Boldrin and Levine have famously argued against patents: "The case against patents can be summarized briefly: there is no empirical evidence that they serve to increase innovation and productivity, unless productivity is identified with the number of patents awarded – which, as evidence shows, has no correlation with measured productivity". Boldrin and Levine (2013), pp. 3–22. Moreover, the importance given to the number of patents as a measure of innovation has been challenged not only as inaccurate, but also representative of a process of financial speculation of patents as credits and even as financial assets. For such critique, see Kang (2020).

[27] For an overview, see Darling and Perzanowski (2017). For a specific case, see Lemos and Castro (2012), on the tecnobrega music style in Northern Brazil as an example of an open business model which relies its success on the sharing of music without enforcement of copyrights.

by IP serve not as catalysts, but hinderances, of innovation.[28] Notions of "patent trolls" and "patent thickets", where strategic patenting filing leads to an overlap of multiple IP rights that unfairly block competition, have become a major issue for contemporary markets.[29] As economist Joseph Stiglitz noted, following the US Supreme Court Myriad Genetics case (2013), which defined that isolated genes cannot be patented, "*innovation has been accelerated, leading to better diagnostic tests [...] at much lower costs.*"[30] Accordingly, it is possible to argue that markets without patents may be equally or even more innovative than those with IP protection and simultaneously also conducive to better access conditions.

Furthermore, for many accounts, IP has been historically an inefficient incentive at best.[31] The development processes of the overwhelming majority of now industrialized countries were based on copying strategies, national industrialization and the creation of innovation ecosystems that include know-how and skilled professionals. In fact, IP has been deemed a limitation to development and innovation in most cases.[32] The innovation landscapes of highly innovative countries in current

[28] See Heller (2010); Heller et al. (1998), pp. 698–701. For some, this means an IP system that does not deliver what it originally promises: "Intellectual Property rights are becoming increasingly badly configured in the developed world, leading to a stifling of innovation, distortions in the direction of innovation, and a reduction in the benefits which accrue from any innovation that occurs. Many of these failures arise because there is, especially under currently prevalent IPR regimes, no clear relationship between the social returns to innovation and the private returns. The proliferation of me-too drugs, the increase in patent hold-ups and similar excesses buttress the argument that the IPR system in the developed world is poorly configured." Baker et al. (2017), available at: http://ip-unit.org/wp-content/uploads/2017/07/IP-for-21st-Century-EN.pdf.

[29] See Matthews and Gurgula (2016). Queen Mary School of Law Legal Studies Research Paper No. 233/2016. Available at SSRN: https://ssrn.com/abstract=2779014.

[30] Stiglitz (2017), available at: https://www.theguardian.com/business/2017/oct/18/intellectual-property-laws-demand-a-21st-century-solution.

[31] "Both theory and the preponderance of historical evidence suggest that development, at least in its initial stages, is best promoted by a weaker intellectual property regime than reflected in TRIPS, or at the minimum a markedly different regime." Baker et al. (2017), available at: http://ip-unit.org/wp-content/uploads/2017/07/IP-for-21st-Century-EN.pdf.

[32] See, for instance, the landmark book Schiff (1971). Irregular or protection exclusively for nationals was also a feature in the United States, Germany and the United Kingdom. The studies on the socio-economic transformation of Japan, and then the Asian Tigers and more recently China, also prominently play a crucial role in a developmental State process that had little to do with the protection of foreign IP, relying instead on imitation and adaptation processes, at least in its earlier stages. For instance, Japan provided protection for national applicants but low protection for foreigners in the decades after WW2—a strategy later emulated by other late industrializing regions with high levels of innovation, such as South Korea and Taiwan. This is all relatively well-known and increasingly defended as means to assess even current practices by the very same players that actively put pressure in the international arena for developing countries to adopt higher standards of IP protection against what they have done in the past and also what they continue on doing. See, for instance, Chang (2002) and Amsden (2001).

times are also not reliant on IP alone, [33] even if the extent of its impact is debatable. In fact, even among its strong defenders, there is a general consensus that IP is not necessarily conducive to innovation at all times, [34] and that in particular the effects of patents differ between industrialized and developing countries. [35] An example of the detrimental consequences to access without accruing any benefits of innovation is the early implementation of the TRIPS Agreement in Brazil in 1996, which can be contrasted with the relative positive experience of India. [36]

[33] Highly innovative countries do not adopt a *laissez-faire* approach and contain enormous funding for basic research, different research grants and direct investments alike. Examples include massive investments by DARPA and BARPA US agencies. For an assessment of the role of the State in innovation and the economy more broadly, see Mazzucato (2013).

[34] See, for instance, Fink and Raffo (2019).

[35] IP may possibly serve as an incentivizing mechanism in industrialized countries with a robust pharmaceutical industry already in place, with proper financial mechanisms, large public grants in early stages of research and research institutions and universities with large capacity and expertise. It will however not produce such an effect in countries with different profiles, and the historical global evidence in developing countries seems very clear in that regard. In summary, the already contested effects of IP towards innovation are even less compelling in the Global South, precisely where issues of access have been the most pressing and negative. The fact that HIV treatments were effectively rendered available in African countries around 10 years after they were available, leading to the unnecessary death of literally millions of lives, is no overstatement. For some broad considerations, see Cimoli et al. (2014). For a defense of the idea that prices should necessarily be lower in developing countries, and dissociated from any notion of compensation for investments, see Salomão Filho (2007), pp. 160–161.

[36] Brazil and India are among the very few countries in the Global South which have developed solid national generic industries (public and private). In both countries, the creation and consolidation of national pharmaceutical industries took place in the absence of IP incentives in the mid-twentieth century. In fact, similarly to the majority of the Global South, laws had been amended as to remove pharmaceutical patents from its national laws, a clear industrial and developmental policy measure. While the lack of IP was definitely not the only element that enabled the rise of pharmaceutical industries, they were seen as a clear barrier to the development of emerging industries. In Brazil, public laboratories such as Farmanguinhos and Butantã Institute play a crucial role in ensuring manufacturing of vaccines and medicines at affordable prices, as well as world-known R&D and public health research. India was able to consolidate the largest generic pharmaceutical market of the world and is still lauded as a prime example of success, deemed the "pharmacy of the [developing] world". Nonetheless, despite relatively comparable benchmarks, the implementation of TRIPS led Brazil and India to remarkably different paths. While Brazil opted to enact an Industrial Property Law in 1996, not fully enjoying the crucial TRIPS flexibility to only recognize pharmaceutical patents in 2001, India used it fully until the latest possible deadline in its case (2005). A major promise of the proponents of the Industrial Property Law of 1996 in Brazil was the need to "modernize" the national system and "promote investments and innovation". Yet, the granting of pharmaceutical patents in Brazil is overwhelmingly composed of foreign applicants, and combined with the lack of other policy incentives for the national industry, the result was a major negative impact in terms of its industrial capacity. It also has no signs of innovation output growth at all in the pharmaceutical sector. In fact, the new patent system created *disincentives* for generic companies due to their legal risks: as almost all of those benefitting from patents were foreign applicants, the investment in R&D in Brazil for pharmaceuticals actually declined and many generic firms are said to have become particularly conservative in their business practices, delaying competition even further. Even if the majority of the Indian companies are not lead innovators in the

Finally, there are also particular issues with any direct association between IP and innovation in legal thinking. The TRIPS Agreement and many national laws note that IP requires a constant balancing between public and private, the public value pertaining to access to medicines being one of paramount importance.[37] Patents are granted taking into account the public interest related to the disclosure of the invention and competition; they are an exceptional, limited and temporary legal bundle of exclusivity rights granted by the State solely in, and to the extent which it favors, the public interest.[38] As a consequence, the impediments created by IP as barriers to access should always be taken into account in the interpretation of concrete cases more prominently.

Indeed, the pharmaceutical sector is a particular and very sensitive case. On one hand, R&D investments are higher than most other industries, and risks are larger, with few successful products out of a much larger pipeline of candidates. On the other, in this field, there is much more public investment in R&D (in many cases the main investment is public not private) because its products are or at least should be essential goods, as they directly relate to health, sometimes as a life or death dilemma. Perhaps curiously, these arguments have been utilized to sustain opposite views: both the need for less or no patents (prioritizing access) and for more patents (prioritizing innovation). In light of the overview above, the problem with the debate framed in such a way is that it reinforces a questionable direct relation between IP, innovation and access.

Many have empirically exposed, for instance, that the enactment of compulsory licensing has not had detrimental effects to foreign investment and has not undermined innovation overall,[39] and successful cases have drastically reduced prices and therefore enhanced access to medicines. Additionally, the global community increasingly acknowledges that a model based only on patent protection is

---

pharmaceutical field, they have proven remarkably successful in ensuring access to medicines worldwide. Its economic importance to the country is also huge. See, for comparisons and analyses of the political economy of such countries, Shadlen (2017) and Vanni (2020).

[37] Articles 7 and 8, TRIPS Agreement: "Article 7 Objectives.The protection and enforcement of intellectual property rights should contribute to the promotion of technological innovation and to the transfer and dissemination of technology, to the mutual advantage of producers and users of technological knowledge and in a manner conducive to social and economic welfare, and to a balance of rights and obligations Article 8. Principles 1. Members may, in formulating or amending their laws and regulations, adopt measures necessary to protect public health and nutrition, and to promote the public interest in sectors of vital importance to their socio-economic and technological development, provided that such measures are consistent with the provisions of this Agreement. 2. Appropriate measures, provided that they are consistent with the provisions of this Agreement, may be needed to prevent the abuse of intellectual property rights by right holders or the resort to practices which unreasonably restrain trade or adversely affect the international transfer of technology". For the effective implications of this tension in various countries and situations, see Dreyfuss and Rodríguez-Gavarito (2014).

[38] In light of these considerations, it makes sense to conceive IP in terms of bundles of rights instead of an absolute and unitary right.

[39] For example, Inthira et al. (2011), p. 7:28.

not the best incentive for innovation in the pharmaceutical sector, and alternatives exist.[40] For example, Amy Kapczynski compellingly describes the open science network of the Global Influenza Surveillance and Response System (GISRS), where *"a global influenza virus-sharing network that has for decades produced critically important information goods, at significant expense, and in a loose-knit group—all without recourse to IP"*,[41] which both responds better to societal health needs and does not treat innovation and access as a trade-off.

The global initiatives seeking the development and subsequent "equitable and affordable" access to Covid-19 vaccines and treatment, treating them as "global public goods" and as a "people's vaccine",[42] with support by key actors such as the European Union and China, have highlighted the needs for collaborative efforts. Unprecedented funding and multiple actions have been taken, including the creation of the voluntary WHO Covid-19 Technology Access Pool on the basis of a proposal by Costa Rica,[43] public international pledges for more resources,[44] as well as private pledges for making IP-protected technologies related to Covid-19 free of charge.[45] It highlights a possible new approach to global pharmaceutical R&D, not based on competition, but rather on intense sharing of information, which may produce faster and much more accessible outcomes in terms of health products.

[40] It is not a surprise that calls for a renewed R&D model for pharmaceuticals are a constant demand in international discussions. See, for instance, Velásquez and Seuba (2011) (calling for a mandatory international agreement on pharmaceutical R&D at the World Health Organizaation); Stiglitz and Jayadev (2010), pp. 217–226 ("promoting prizes over patents; directing innovation toward socially beneficial outputs by adopting some form of value-based pricing; publicly funding clinical trials to reduce conflicts of interest while reducing costs; and actively managing frontier technologies to maximize positive social spillovers"). Proposals on prizes are among the most common alternative, at least in academia. See, for instance, the proposed Health Impact Fund—HIF (https://healthimpactfund.org/). Nowadays, alternative R&D models do exist for neglected diseases, such as the successful non-profit organization Drugs for Neglected Diseases Initiative (DNDi), which has already achieved approved medicines for neglected diseases under substantially lower R&D costs if compared to large transnational pharmaceutical firms for most diseases (https://www.dndi.org/). CEPI—Coalition for Epidemic Preparedness Innovation (https://cepi.net/), founded in 2017, may also serve as an alternative model for financing future vaccines, including for Covid-19. It is currently funded by industrialized countries and charities such as Bill and Melinda Gates Foundation and the Wellcome Trust. Unlike DNDi, the exact access conditions in case of a successful candidate are however yet unclear and subject to debates.

[41] Kapczynski (2017) Available at: https://scholarship.law.cornell.edu/clr/vol102/iss6/3.

[42] For an analysis of the debate and how it has been partly incorporated (albeit with major limitations) into the 73rd World Health Assembly Resolution "Response to Covid-19" in 2020, see Syam et al. (2020).

[43] See WHO COVID-19 Technology Access Pool (C-TAP): https://www.who.int/emergencies/diseases/novel-coronavirus-2019/global-research-on-novel-coronavirus-2019-ncov/covid-19-technology-access-pool.

[44] See European Commission Press Release. "Coronavirus Global Response: €7.4 billion raised for universal access to vaccines". 4 May 2020, available at: https://ec.europa.eu/commission/presscorner/detail/en/ip_20_797.

[45] See Open Covid Pledge: https://opencovidpledge.org/.

Again, in this sense, a more efficient approach that may achieve more innovation *and* broader access.[46]

Finally, a caveat to the association between IP and innovation refers to the real costs of R&D, which are deeply non-transparent, and where, as noted before, the role of public funding is pivotal.[47] It challenges once again the assumption of a necessary trade-off, rendering explicit instead the possibility of achieving a coexistence between access and innovation. More transparency on the pharmaceutical sector could enable courts to rely not on the general, abstract notion that IP is conducive to innovation, and instead make an empirical assessment of, for instance, how much public funding the medical product received or not, how the final net pricing has been fixed, and the exact socio-economic repercussions of a patent or other IP to the market. This would mean a better balance between private and public interest in IP and access to medicines.

In summary, this section aimed at presenting two important points for adjudicators dealing with IP and access to medicines to consider:

1. arguments that entangle the protection of IP with innovation and access are an improper interpretation legal technique, which disregards the socio-economic and developmental implications of IP as much as it tends to limit the role of the public interest in IP.[48]
2. access and innovation are not a necessary trade-off: under many (and perhaps most) circumstances, collaborative and deeply competitive markets are more inventive and also provide better access conditions.

As a conclusion, adjudication in IP and access to medicines calls for an evidence-based and thoughtful analysis of what is really at stake in a particular case. From a legal point of view, the broader pharmaceutical sector regulation can be interpreted

[46] For a proposal, see Mazzucato and Torreele (2020), available at: https://www.project-syndicate.org/commentary/universal-free-covid19-vaccine-by-mariana-mazzucato-and-els-torreele-2020-04.

[47] While pharmaceutical companies may insist some of this information is trade secret (therefore legally protected), much of this data is actually not. A landmark Resolution at the 72nd World Health Assembly (WHA/72.8) agreed on the need for more transparency in the pharmaceutical industry, including net prices, but falling short of including specific commitments to the transparency of R&D costs. Moreover, much attention has been given to the role of public funding in pharmaceutical innovation, particularly in earlier stages, which is neither recognized nor reflected in safeguards in terms of affordability and accessibility for the very public that financed it in the first place. For an overview of existing literature, see Vieira and Moon (2019), available at: https://www.knowledgeportalia.org/public-funding-of-r-d; Vieira and Moon (2020), available at https://www.knowledgeportalia.org/cost-of-r-d.

[48] Rather than conclusive remarks on the relation between intellectual property and innovation—or more precisely, the multiple relations between IP, access and innovation—, the crucial point to be made is that courts have no clear evidence to decide based only on the premise that IP is a necessary element to achieve innovation. However, this is exactly how many courts are inclined to argue; or, at least, by exacerbating the role of IP in innovation without a proper balance with public interests related to access, courts will also be inclined to maximize IP protection in the detriment of all other stakeholders, patients included. Therefore, as a conclusion, it is necessary to disentangle IP and innovation as separate categories, with a direct impact to legal interpretation.

in a way that secures *both* access and innovation, and not as a trade-off as a departing point. The following section attempts to exemplify how a legal rationale in that sense could take place, and what may happen when this is not taken into account. By doing so, it will also be possible to reflect on what role do courts have in TRIPS flexibilities' implementation.

4 Trastuzumab High Price Litigation in Brazil

Trastuzumab (sold under brand name Herceptin) is a groundbreaking medicine for the treatment of breast cancer, listed as essential medicines by the World Health Organization (WHO).[49] Breast cancer is a disease that kills thousands of persons, especially women, yearly around the world. In Brazil alone, 53.680 cases were reported in 2013, and more than 56.000 in 2014. Trastuzumab was developed by Genentech, a pharmaceutical company based in San Francisco, United States, which later licensed to Swiss pharmaceutical[50] company F. Hoffmann-La Roche (henceforth Roche) for US$40 million upfront, later sharing royalties with Genentech.[51] In practice, Roche is the owner of patents related to the drug and manages them. According to a Forbes article on 28 August 2019, Trastuzumab "is the leader in the breast cancer drugs space with annual sales of around $7 billion", accounting for about 15% of the overall profits of Roche yearly.[52]

Given how essential the medicine is[53] and its very high prices overall, various concerns about access to Trastuzumab have been highlighted in multiple jurisdictions around the world by civil society organizations. The production cost of the medicine is reported to be around US$240 for a 1-year supply.[54] Nonetheless, as reported by Médécins sans Frontières in 2017, Trastuzumab's annual prices were set at around US$ 38 365 for the private sector and US$ 15 735 for the public sector in

[49] World Health Organization (2019).

[50] Grupo Direito e Pobreza (Law and Poverty Group) (2014).

[51] Hu et al. (2020).

[52] Forbes (2019), available at: https://www.forbes.com/sites/greatspeculations/2019/08/28/can-roches-blockbuster-drug-herceptins-sales-grow/#62da696a42e5.

[53] In fact, from a competition perspective, all cancer drugs are essential in terms of the demand side, given the severity of the disease. As it is literally a matter of death or life, the equilibrium point between offer and demand is drastically influenced by a hugely inelastic demand. This means that structurally such drugs tend to be highly priced under purely market conditions, and therefore particular attention to potential competitive abuses is necessary. In other words, this means a careful assessment of pricing and how offer takes place.

[54] See Hoen (2019) Strong call for transparency on medicine prices, cost of R&D at WHO Fair Pricing Forum. Medicines Law and Policy https://medicineslawandpolicy.org/2019/04/strong-call-for-transparency-on-medicine-prices-cost-of-rd-at-who-fair-pricing-forum/.

South Africa, where patents will only expire in 2033.[55] Brazil, as we will expose in more details, prices were also extremely high: unaffordable for patients and unsustainable for the public budget. It is further relevant to note that the basic patent of Trastuzumab has expired in many other countries, including the USA. In both USA and Europe, there are already biosimilar versions available in the markets, which contributes to reducing prices. In Brazil, due to the patent extension term for cases of backlog of patent applications (provided for by Article 40, sole paragraph, of the Industrial Property Law (Law 9279/1996) and currently pending constitutionality ruling at the Federal Supreme Court[56]), the patent will not expire until 16 June 2028.[57]

However, even the lack of patent is no guarantee of reduced prices *per se*. In India, where patent oppositions had been filed, Roche withdrew patent applications on Trastuzumab. Still, the company has relied on litigation against biosimilar producers through India's drug regulatory body, which effectively enables Roche to be the sole provider of the medicine in the country as well.[58] This has been taken to the Indian Competition Commission as a possible abusive conduct for stalling the approval of generic drugs.[59]

These facts are important evidence to highlight that high prices of Trastuzumab are not only caused by its uniqueness, as there are already biosimilar medicines available in international markets, and that the balancing between profits and health seem to be radically unaligned. The similarity of high prices around the world further denotes a tendency of monopoly pricing and abuse of patent.

The medicine was registered by the Brazilian regulatory agency ANVISA as early as 1999 and was incorporated as a treatment provided for by the public health

---

[55] See MSF Global day of action against Roche's inhumanity #RocheGreedKills. Press Release, 6 February 2017 https://msfaccess.org/global-day-action-against-roches-inhumanity-rochegreedkills.

[56] Direct Unconstitutionality Claim (ADIN 5529). The judgment is expected to scrutinize whether the mentioned Article 40, Sole Paragraph of the Industrial Property Law is constitutional or not. It provides an extension of patent terms due to patent backlog by establishing that a patent has a minimum term of 10 years of protection. Since the general term is 20 years, any patent application procedure that lasts longer than 10 years leads to an extension in the overall term of protection. However, the competition effects of such extensions are dramatic. The strongest interpretation of Brazilian constitutional legal system and the majority of commentators seems to note that such legal provision is unconstitutional—similar to provisions on pipeline patents, also not yet judged by the Brazilian STF. In this sense, it becomes clear how it is important to acknowledge how the lack of action by the court—in such cases by refraining from deciding—is a central piece in the understanding of their role in the implementation of patents in Brazil, and how they negatively affect the implementation of TRIPS flexibilities.

[57] According to the analysis by the Law and Poverty Research Group, University of São Paulo, the first known patent that refers to Trastuzumab was filed on 3 November 2008; its unionist priority dates back to 16 June 2008. See Grupo Direito e Pobreza (Law and Poverty Group) (2014), p. 6.

[58] See MSF Access Campaign Global day of action against Roche's inhumanity #RocheGreedKills (2017), https://msfaccess.org/global-day-action-against-roches-inhumanity-rochegreedkills.

[59] Competition Commission of India. Case No. 68 of 2016—Roche—Mylan Biocon CCI Order 68 of 2016.

system SUS in 2012. Cancer prevention, detection, treatment and control are all covered by the public health system. Nonetheless, diminishing prices was a condition for effective access to take place after its incorporation as a registered medicine paid by the SUS. During that occasion, and discounted taxes, prices of Trastuzumab were 62% higher than international price average and 115% of the lowest reported international price (surprisingly or not, in the United States). [60]

Public procurement bids were conducted by the Ministry of Health in order to generate economies of scale, later distributing to State Health Secretaries under Brazilian federalist system. After direct negotiations with Roche, prices were reduced from R$7.860,26 per dose, charged in 2007, to R$3.446,89 in 2012 (without taxes, prices in Brazilian Real). However, State Health Secretaries have also been obliged through individual health claims, to provide Trastuzumab. This is a consequence of Brazil's widespread "judicialization of health", which enables individuals to go to courts demanding specific medicines and treatments, also obliging public entities to provide them regardless of costs in the majority of cases. [61] In practice, this means that there were two main routes for access to Trastuzumab: via the general

[60] Grupo Direito e Pobreza (Law and Poverty Group) (2014).

[61] This is a direct translation from the Portuguese "judicialização da saúde", or "judicialización" in Spanish. Brazil's legal system is characterized by an ample recognition of the right to health, including universal health system, the SUS, which are both constitutionally protected (Articles 6 and 196, Federal Constitution of Brazil, 1988). This has been interpreted as a direct constitutional mandate which allows thousands of individual claims for medicines and treatments to reach courts, which have been in general granted in almost all cases, even experimental treatments and no matter the costs. The process has been also identified in other Latin American countries, particularly Colombia, Argentina and Costa Rica. In common, public budgets are overwhelmed by such claims, which are in certain cases a very large proportion of overall budgets. In 2019 and 2020, two landmark rulings by the Supreme Federal Court (STF), the country's highest judicial instance, drastically reduced such claims as to avoid an overburden for health systems, in light of the recognition that individual claims affected the social realization of health rights. For a critical overview, see Kapczynski (2019), available at: http://humanityjournal.org/issue10-1/the-right-to-medicines-in-an-age-of-neoliberalism/. She notes that "*The budgetary impact of the right to medicines cases has unsurprisingly been significant. According to government figures, from 2010–2016, the federal government spent 4.4 billion reais ($1.4 billion) to comply with judicial decisions, with most of this going to provide medicines.49 This sum has risen sharply over time, along with the number of cases.50 In 2016 alone, the federal government spent 1.2 billion reais ($400 million) to satisfy judicial mandates.51 The bulk of suits for access to medicines arises at the state level, where data are harder to come by. But analysis has found that states and municipalities may be spending anywhere from 3 to 10 per cent of their health budgets to satisfy right to health cases, and as much as 22 per cent of their medicines budgets to fulfill judgments mandating access to medicines.*". She further notes the impact of patents as one of the main causes for such high costs: "*Why are the medicines involved, or more accurately, some of the medicines involved, so profoundly expensive? It is common ground that the "exponential growth in costs" in Brazil "can be explained by a high concentration of cases demanding expensive patented drugs."81 Almost 80 per cent of the total sum spent by the federal government to satisfy judgments for medicines in 2011 was spent on just 20 medicines, for fewer than 0.05 per cent of litigants*". For a concern about the possibly deceptive and anti-distributive character of such claims, see Wang (2015), p. 617; for a defender of its counter-hegemonic potential as a grassroots instrument for the poor, despite its shortcomings, see Biehl et al. (2016).

Table 1 Unity prices of Trastuzumab before July 2012 (in Brazilian Real—BRL)

	Brazil			Lowest price		
Trastuzumab	CMED[a] PF[b] (with taxes)	CMED PF (without taxes)	CMED PF (without taxes and CAP[c])	USA	International Average	International Median
440 mg vial	R$ 9.417,81	R$ 7.640,60	R$ 5.969,60	R$ 3.555,67	R$ 4.728,98	R$ 4.832,21

[a]CMED is the acronym for "Câmara de Regulação do Mercado de Medicamentos" (Chamber of Regulation of Medicine Market), the Brazilian federal regulatory agency responsible for monitoring prices and establishing caps according to the prices of selected markets around the world, including the United States
[b]PF is "Preço de Fábrica" (Manufacturer's price)
[c]CAP is "Coeficiente de Aplicação de Preço" (Price Application Coefficient, in Portuguese) is a mandatory minimum discount applied for medicine purchases by public administration entities, such as the Ministry of Health
Recommendation Report by CONITEC/SUS—Trastuzumab for Treatment of Initiatial Stage Breast Cancer—July 2012, p. 16

universal public healthcare system and via individual court litigation. If this, on one hand, may pressurize public entities to provide better healthcare services and avoid individual claims, on the other hand, this dual system creates strong inequalities in terms of who may access medicines and when (often with "shortcuts"). An often-disregarded issue regarding this topic is how this system may also present an opportunity for abusive pricing conducts and patent abuses. In the specific case of Trastuzumab, Roche provided the medicine under a price agreed by the public bid, but refused to sell Trastuzumab for the same price in individual healthcare litigation cases, charging instead R$7.192,00—more than double the negotiated with the Ministry of Health. Further evidence shows that similar higher pricing occurred for all purchases not related to the centralized procurement, i.e., all individual litigations (Table 1).[62]

In light of this data, the Law and Poverty Research Group of the University of São Paulo (USP) produced a comprehensive report on the prices charged by Roche on Trastuzumab, reporting the figures above. It then filed in June 2014 a "representation" (i.e. a form of denunciation mechanism) for the Federal Public Ministry of Brazil, the authority mandated with the protection of collective rights in the country and general overseer of the public interest.[63]

The research group noted that the price differentiation between markets is a case of abuse of dominant position, a doctrine of competition law but applicable more broadly to this case also, and further noting a case of excessive pricing given the

[62] Grupo Direito e Pobreza (Law and Poverty Group) (2014).

[63] Grupo Direito e Pobreza (Law and Poverty Group) (2014).

existence of market power by Roche. The company in this case was apt to discriminate between consumers without justification, leading to an overprice.[64] According to the legal document, they are in violation of the constitutional economic order and of a conduct of arbitrary profits (Articles 170 and 173, §§4 and 5 of Brazilian Federal Constitution). In this sense, although some arguments are usually found only in competition/antitrust law, the case dealt with civil torts.

Finally, the average price charged in Brazil above the international average was utilized as grounds for another evidence of abusive conduct, according to Brazilian law. This takes into account precisely the monopolistic power of Roche in an international context, with discretion to charge higher prices in jurisdictions where, at least in theory, prices should be lower. With these elements, the research group's representation requested the launch of an investigation by the Federal Public Ministry, demanding damages in the benefit of the public, the compulsory licensing of Trastuzumab, the immediate parallel import of biosimilars and for all conditions for local manufacturing to be available.

Indeed, the Federal Public Ministry welcomed the document and later filed a collective claim ("Inquérito Civil n. 1.16.000.000699/2015-87", which proposed the civil public action) against Roche in 2016, replicating the arguments above and further considering that, while within the boundaries of the maximum regulated prices by CMED, they were still abusive due to the stark differentiation.[65] Notably, prices were much up to three times higher than those in the United States, and more than double of the international average. The decision to pursue a judicial litigation was rooted, among others, in the dissatisfaction with the laboratory's formal response. The Federal Public Ministry requested all purchases to be equated with the centralized public procurement price, and requested a compulsory licensing to be issued and the immediate authorization for parallel imports.

In August 2018, however, the Federal Court of the Federal District (Brasilia) responsible for the case agreed with Roche that there was no demonstration of price abuse nor illegal conduct, since Roche had brought justifications.[66] As a conclusion, the whole situation described above remained unchanged. While there was an appeal

---

[64] For a more thorough analysis of market power, and the use of the Lerner Index doctrine borrowed from competition law, see Salomão Filho (2013b), p. 152.

[65] The existence of a regulation on medicine prices does not remove it from the scope of potential abusive practices regarding prices, an argument that was inaccurately explored by Roche. In reality, the price regulation (not a direct price fixing) cannot be used to shield liability from abusive pricing. It means that the Judiciary should acknowledge that there is potential abusive conduct in charging excessive prices of medicines, even if they are regulated. Furthermore, CEMED's methodology is criticized for establishing excessively high price caps, which would also prove the point.

[66] Among the arguments of the defendant, Roche argued that logistics costs are much higher when destined to a specific litigation, unlike the larger public procurements. Indeed, the relatively more complex molecule (being a biological drug) and specific needs for storages do pose difficulties regarding its manufacturing and logistics. The weakness of the argument is demonstrated by the fact that Roche sells other drugs in different places in Brazil with no such regional differences—showing therefore that the difference in price is in effect due to market power and illegal price discrimination.

filed against such decision, taking the case to the Appeals' Federal Court and pending final decision, some members within the Federal Public Ministry (claimant) opposed the continuation of this litigation.

Meanwhile, Roche also joined a Partnership for Productive Development (PPD) with the Ministry of Health, securing transfer of technology for national laboratories Tecpar and Axis, while guaranteeing a market (following this agreement, 40% of all purchases by SUS would come from Roche). In theory, PPDs would lower prices, even if higher than direct competition. However, once again, prices went up, which led to another proceeding in August 2019, this time by the Union Audits Court ("Tribunal de Contas da União"), a quasi-judicial administrative court responsible for auditing public expenses, for abusive pricing. [67] This case is still pending at the conclusion of this paper.

From this description, a few preliminary comments can be made. In this particular case, the existence of patent protection over Trastuzumab was the defining feature that permitted Roche Brazil to charge monopolistic prices, putting the public health sector in an extremely unequal position (having one sole provider of a product with an extremely inelastic demand). If generics to Trastuzumab were available, individual litigations could also purchase from the alternative providers, and the bargaining power of Roche towards the Brazilian public sector would be much more limited. Moreover, it is possible to conceptualize this behavior in relation to public purchases and court rulings as an abuse of patent rights under Brazilian competition law: although often disregarded, the way market players may benefit economically from legal uncertainty, multiple case filings and lack of competitors should be under the scrutiny of competition and IP law alike, not only as background facts, but as evidences. All in all, this is equally an important call for the inclusion of responsibilities of companies in litigations of public interest such as those related to access to medicines.

What is the direct result of this federal judicial ruling? The maintenance of the status quo and an implicit legitimization of Roche's pricing practices. Also, while the new investigation at the Union Audits Court is unrelated to the previous one, it allows other reflections, including what is the relation between them and what are the possible legal impacts of one investigation in the other. The fact that this case has been framed as a "non-patent" issue or which has perceived the market monopoly power conferred by a patent as ancillary at best is the result of the limited understanding pointed out in the Introduction: failing to acknowledge the role of courts in individual litigations to enhancing the power stemming from a patent in this particular web of details, the ultimate result does not properly apply the public interest requirements of Brazilian IP and competition laws.

Finally, even though a preliminary analysis could possibly focus on the role of the individuals involved in the litigation, this description highlights in fact that the

[67] Junqueira (2019). Available at https://www1.folha.uol.com.br/cotidiano/2019/08/investigacao-do-tcu-aponta-sobrepreco-em-remedio-para-cancer-e-leva-a-desabastecimento.shtml.

functioning of the IP system is extremely reliant on the role of courts.[68] As stated before, this is less about individual biographies of adjudicators/attorneys/business-people and more about a judicial system based on silos and typically reluctant to commit to applying law in a more comprehensive manner, even in light of such socio-economic circumstances. This has been moreover a case where a hesitant and absent role of the Judiciary to address IP and access to medicines issues has directly impacted the possibility of implementing access to medicines policies, even if *at first glance* this seems to not be a case on patents or competition. Importantly, the argument of how price differentiation by Roche was only being possible due to the complex web of various litigations had indeed been brought to courts, but the decisions overall preferred to interpret the facts in a much more limited way.

5 The Sofosbuvir Case in Brazil

Sofosbuvir—sold under the brand name Sovaldi by pharmaceutical multinational company Gilead Sciences—is a key medicine for the treatment of Hepatitis C, for decades an incurable disease. It has been deemed a long-waited game changer for the treatment of the disease. The utilization of direct-acting antivirals (DAAs) such as Sofosbuvir, in combination with other drugs,[69] is able to provide a cure in a very high percentage of cases (over 95%), and also contains a drastic reduction of collateral effects in comparison with the most utilized treatment for decades until then, based on inter-venous use of Interferon. Since its launch, Sofosbuvir has been a major commercial success for Gilead around the world, with estimations of billions of dollars in profits, largely superseding its overall investments in R&D by any possible account.[70]

The major global concern on Sofosbuvir has been the fact that it is extremely costly in developed countries and in the majority of middle-income countries. It has been reported that the 12-week treatment has cost up to US$84.000 in the United States. In countries with generic offer, such as those coming from Egyptian generic company Pharco Pharmaceuticals, the same treatment can be provided for as low as US$300.[71] Importantly, Egypt did not grant the patent on Sofosbuvir, and Gilead

---

[68] See Sect. 2 for some inputs on this topic.

[69] Combinations include sofosbuvir with ledipasvir, velpatasvir, simeprevir and/or dataclasvir. Dataclasvir is patented by Bristol Meyer Squibb (BMS), while ledipasvir and velpatasvir have also been patented by Gilead. Other companies similarly have DAAs placed in markets and more are in the pipeline of new drugs.

[70] According to an estimation by Hep C Coalition, a patient's of hepatitis C advocacy group, in the period 2013–2018 the drug generated a profit of around US$25.8 billion. Nonetheless, access to Sofosbuvir globally was still extremely reduced due to pricing, patents and registration delays. See: https://hepcoalition.org/news/press-releases/article/hepatitis-c-cure-sofosbuvir-turns-5-years-old-the-vast-majority-of-people-still?lang=en#nb1.

[71] See: https://www.dndi.org/2018/media-centre/press-releases/new-affordable-hepatitis-c-combination-treatment-shows-97-cure-rate/.

has offered a much lower price of US$900 per treatment, since Pharco Pharmaceuticals was also able to produce it.[72] The real beneficiaries were consumers and the public health sector of Egypt, which could have access to a full treatment at substantially lower prices than the majority of countries in the world. Importantly, the fact that prices are so dramatically different around the world is another evidence that pricing is a process that is disentangled from innovation processes.[73]

Gilead established a large international scheme of voluntary licenses for certain Indian generic companies to produce and export Sofosbuvir at very low prices to least developed countries (LDCs).[74] However, middle-income countries (including Brazil) were not part of the scheme at all. Such agreements also prevent competition with non-licensee generic producers, and also impede exports to territories not covered by the licenses. Thus the majority of world population in need remained excluded from this beneficial scheme.[75] For those countries, the medicine remained an extremely pricy drug, and likely even more in countries with weaker health systems. This led Sofosbuvir to be at the central stage of global efforts for reduction of prices, campaigns for affordable and equitable access, and different attempts by governments to reduce prices, including the issuance of a compulsory license in Malaysia.[76] Patent oppositions have been filed in multiple countries, including Argentina, Brazil, Morocco, Egypt, Ukraine, Malaysia, India, China, Russia, the United States, Vietnam and in the European Patent Office (EPO),[77] some with successful outcomes to have a patent claim rejected or limited.

With millions of hepatitis C patients, Brazil incorporated DAAs as part of the universal public health system and opted in 2014 to negotiate prices of Sofosbuvir

[72] Correa and Velásquez (2018).

[73] While net prices do relate to numerous variables, including logistic costs, costs of APIs (active pharmaceutical ingredient), taxation, volume of purchases, reimbursement schemes, and others, these stark price differences between countries were mostly related to patents. The fact that Gilead Sciences as a transnational corporation group (despite separate legal entities) had the monopolistic power to discretionarily charge higher prices across jurisdictions shows this even more clearly. Medicine prices covered by patents are ultimately influenced by patents (therefore, by a monopoly), and not related to innovation. This is yet another caveat to the logic described in the previous section, to which a patent and its exercise, including the economic benefits arising from it, would be at least partly justifiable due to the innovation provided. What economic evidence shows, however, is that if prices and patents were really related to innovation, prices should be at least somewhat similar in the world, which does not happen at all. As such, this is a clear case of what antitrust law considers to be a monopoly pricing.

[74] Hill et al. (2016), pp. 28–31.

[75] Gilead. Chronic Hepatitis C Treatment Expansion – Generic Manufacturing for Developing Countries. Available at: https://www.gilead.com/-/media/files/pdfs/other/hcv-generic-agreement-fast-facts-11-15-17.pdf.

[76] Press Statement Minister of Health 20th September 2017 – Implementation of the Rights of Government for Sofosbuvir Tablet to Increase Access for Hepatitis C Treatment in Malaysia. Available at: https://kpkesihatan.com/2017/09/20/press-statement-minister-of-health-20th-september-2017-implementation-of-the-rights-of-government-for-sofosbuvir-tablet-to-increase-access-for-hepatitis-c-treatment-in-malaysia/.

[77] See https://www.patentoppositions.org/en/drugs/sofosbuvir.

with Gilead directly. While a positive initiative that prevented prices from being even higher, Sofosbuvir sold for the public health system through public procurement mechanisms was estimated to be up to 52 times more expensive than generic versions available in other countries, according to GTPI, a Brazilian civil society organization.[78] From the outset until the present moment, while lower than the maximum charged in the United States, prices in Brazil were substantially higher than countries with generic availability such as Egypt and Malaysia (following its compulsory license).

Multiple patent applications had been filed by Gilead at INPI, the Brazilian IP office. In February 2017, Fiocruz files a pre-grant opposition to the main patent application (PI0809654-6). MSF Brazil, GTPI/REBRIP, and other organizations would follow. From the very beginning, the patent applications were controversial: in March 2017, ANVISA denied the prior approval ("anuência prévia") to the patent.[79] In March, the National Council of Health ("Conselho Nacional de Saúde") issued a technical-political recommendation against the patent and called for attention to public health needs. However, in May 2017, a preliminary injunction questioned ANVISA's decision and it was therefore, according to the Brazilian legal system, legally bound to grant its prior approval—with the possibility of this decision to be upheld or overruled in later stages. In practice, the court ruled that the prior approval should be granted.

In its pre-grant opposition on the same patent application, GTPI/REBRIP, argued that it did not meet patentability criteria, but also further noted that the patent application in question referred to an essential drug, and therefore its granting would lead to violation of the right to health of Brazilian population. While this explicit public interest argument was not utilized, the INPI released on 19 April 2018 a preliminary technical examination report against the patent. While not legally binding, it signaled that the patent would not be granted. On 5 June 2018, ANVISA gave the regulatory approval for the generic drug to be produced locally by a Farmanguinhos-Fiocruz and Blanver (a generic company) partnership. It was largely expected that the patent would not be granted at this point. In June 2018, daclatasvir, dimeprevir and sofosbuvir were incorporated in the Brazilian SUS; they were expected to be distributed freely and universally by December 2018.

On 18 September 2018, in an unexpected decision, INPI granted the patent on one of the 126 substances filed, having denied 125 others and reversing its own

[78] Grupo de Trabalho da Propriedade Intelectual (GTPI). Brazil is excluded from license authorizing production of generic medicine for hepatitis C. Available at: http://deolhonaspatentes.org/media/file/GTPI_statement_Gilead_license_sofosbuvir.pdf.

[79] The prior approval was an innovation of the Brazilian Patent system whereby the regulatory agency ANVISA conducts an analysis of the patent application for pharmaceuticals, granting or not its "prior approval" before the INPI analysis. The interaction between the two agencies and the mandate of ANVISA have been hotly debated. In early times, ANVISA would conduct a full patentability criteria analysis and its decision was binding; this was later replaced to be an analysis of public health implications of the technology patent application, but no veto power per se is recognized as of now.

preliminary technical examination. The main compound was not patented, but still, the decision was met with outcry and major discontent by civil society and patient groups. Although in principle generics could be produced if they did not infringe this limited patent, any generics reaching markets, in this case, would be subject to costly and limiting litigation. This risk is substantially higher in Brazil for generic companies given the fact that damages for patent infringement are necessarily set at the highest possible amount, which hinders competition. [80] Subsequently, the generic medicine was legally and effectively blocked from entering the markets and Gilead enjoyed a *legal monopoly* due to its new patent.

Shortly thereafter, on 20 September 2018, Marina Silva, a former environment Minister and presidential candidate filed a federal lawsuit against the INPI decision in order to annul the patent, based on arguments of public health and on the precarity of the patent application, citing, among others, precedents in other countries. [81] The federal judge in Brasilia accepted the arguments and issued a preliminary injunction suspending the effects of the patent. [82] During this period, it can be said that there was a *competition* period, whereby patents were not a barrier to competition and the generic version was able to be commercialized and be part of public bids of Sofosbuvir-based treatments. The price reached an all-time low of R$64,84 (also see graphic below for the comparison).

In November 2018, combination medicines containing Sofosbuvir were procured at an emergency procedure by the Ministry of Health. Gilead filed a claim to impede its distribution due to patent infringement. In this context, a decision in favor of Gilead is taken but later overruled. [83] In December 2018, the preliminary ruling in Brasilia was overruled and the patent on Sofosbuvir is once again valid, leaving Gilead to wait for its patent letter to start enforcing it. It is noteworthy to mention that the decision by the Federal Court in Brasilia—1st Region was taken on procedural grounds and was therefore not based on substantive patentability requirements. [84]

Following the previous decision, a decision by a Rio de Janeiro Federal Court in December 2018 suspends, under request of Gilead, PDP between Blanver and

[80] See Articles 44, §1, 208 and 209 of the Brazilian Industrial Property Law. For an assessment of how this maximalist set of norms impacts competition by greatly increasing the risks for generic companies, see Gabriela et al. (2018), Fiocruz & Escola Nacional de Saúde Pública Sergio Arouca, pp. 122–139.

[81] Silva, Marina. Petição Inicial de Ação Popular (Statement of Claims of Popular Lawsuit).

[82] Ação Popular n. 1019631-97.2018.4.01.3400. Judgement on 23 September 2018. ("acknowledge that the INPI, by not facing explicitly the arguments that the patent application here questioned was not in tune with the social, technological and economic interest of the country (from the point of view of the Program to Combat Hepatitis C, maintained by the SUS), it disrespected its constitutional obligation to preventively oversee national sovereignty and public interest, in the exact extent of art. 5O, XXIX, Federal Constitution, and arts. 2 and 18, I, from Law n. 9.279/96"; free translation).

[83] See https://oglobo.globo.com/sociedade/em-nova-batalha-de-patentes-remedio-para-tratamento-da-hepatite-pode-ser-barateado-23584500.

[84] See https://www.jota.info/paywall?redirect_to=//www.jota.info/tributos-e-empresas/saude/juiz-revoga-liminar-que-quebrava-patente-de-remedio-contra-hepatite-c-21122018.

Fiocruz/Farmanguinhos for the production of generic Sofosbuvir until final decision on patent is taken. [85] This effectively suspended the generic in Brazil. Also in December 2018, Gilead commits to reducing prices in public procurement. [86] However, still much higher than the generic version. Gilead received its patent in mid-January 2019. In February 2019, Gilead won major public procurements of Sofosbuvir in Brazil.

This intricate description of events means temporally the occurrence of three main phases:

1. a *de facto* monopoly, when there was only a patent application and Gilead was the sole provider of Sofosbuvir; [87]
2. a short *competitive market* period where the recently granted patent was suspended due to a preliminary injunction based on public interest provisions, and the generic version was able to enter the market;
3. a *legal* monopoly phase after the patent was reinstated, with only Gilead again in the market. [88]

It should also be highlighted the number of legal actions taken by all parties, but in particular Gilead, which utilized various different legal tools, including infringement claims of its then suspended patent and attempts to nullify public procurement bids that would have competition. Furthermore, while indeed the patent granted to Sofosbuvir is not on its basic compound and some generics could theoretically still be produced, in practice, some of the public bids are only available to Gilead. In short, the current situation at the time of writing is of full legal and *de facto* monopoly for the patent holder (Table 2).

The most decisive feature of this case, however, deals with the prices charged after the patent was reinstated, as they were substantially higher than those from the competition phase, but also from the original *de facto* monopoly situation. According to another report by the Law and Poverty Research Group, there was a spike of up to 1421.55% between the competition market period in mid (prices as low as R$64,84 on average) and the later patented phase (R$986,57 on average),

[85] Case n. 05027709232018402510l, Federal Court of 2nd Region, Rio de Janeiro.

[86] See SBAC (2019) http://www.sbac.org.br/blog/2018/11/28/dona-de-patente-que-barra-generico-contra-hepatite-c-promete-desconto-a-governo/.

[87] As noted in footnote 80, in Brazil, patent applications provide a very strong market power in comparison to other countries. This is partly related to the legal provision that establishes damages for patent infringement (including patent applications) at the maximum possible level in favor of the patent holder (Articles 208 and 209, Industrial Property Law)—with retroactive effects (Article 44, §1 of the same Law), which greatly discourages competitors from entering markets. Brazilian legal doctrine in patent law has also similarly sustained a view that patent applications are deserving of an almost, if not equivalent, level of protection as granted patents. Due to this specificity, the possibility for Gilead to charge a monopolistic price even before the granting of a patent is much clearer than it would be in many other jurisdictions.

[88] See Grupo Direito e Pobreza (2019).

Table 2 (Extract from Law and Poverty Research Group report) Effect of Introduction of Generic Sofosbuvir (Blanver/Farmanguinhos) in National Market

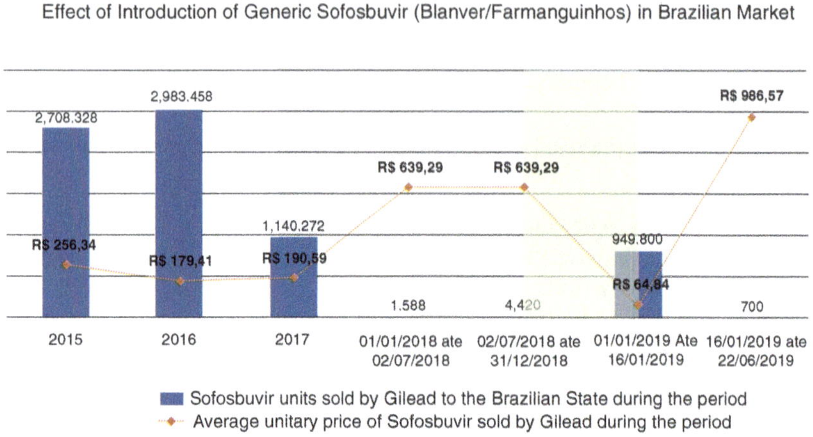

representing an overwhelming extra budget toll for the public sector.[89] Furthermore, between the legal monopoly phase in 2019 (patented market) and the *de facto* monopoly from 2015-2018, there is also a major difference in pricing. For instance, in 2016, where a large number of Sofosbuvir units were purchased, the average unit price was R$179,41, compared to R$986,57 charged in 2019 during the new patent monopoly.

This complex intertwinement in the case calls for antitrust scrutiny. In light of the situation, a group of nine different Brazilian civil society organizations, representing both patient, consumer and human rights groups, as well as the Public Defenders of Brazil, filed a joint formal notification to the competition authority (CADE[90]) in order to request the launch of an investigation for abusive anti-competitive practices (both excessive pricing as abuse of dominant position and abuse of patents) and asking for adequate remedies to be taken, including issuing a compulsory licensing

[89] Grupo Direito e Pobreza (2019). Importantly, Even though they refer to different public entities, as noted in the case of Trastuzumab, from a competition perspective, this is the same relevant market (public national health market, as essentially all procurements discussed here are made by the public sector, even if sometimes via different entities—e.g. Ministry of Health and Health Departments of States of Municipalities). The research also aggregated not only Sofosbuvir (Sovaldi), but also a combination of medicines: Harvoni (Sofosbuvir + ledipasvir) and Epclusa (sofosbuvir + velpatasvir).

[90] CADE—Conselho Administrativo de Defesa Econômica (Brazilian Administrative Council for Economic Defence).

for Sofosbuvir on the grounds of an anti-competitive conduct (Article 31k of TRIPS and Art. 38, IV, "a" of Brazilian Competition Law, Law 12.529/2011).

A preliminary administrative investigation was indeed launched by CADE, but the case remains open. It might reach the Administrative Tribunal Council, which decides upon antitrust cases in Brazil. At first impression, there seems to be more space for a competition authority to address the case than judicial courts.[91] However, the relatively more flexible administrative procedure under competition law and the stronger pressures on administrative bodies by government and interested private companies (patent holders) make the results uncertain. This is especially the case at a time in which pharmaceutical industries effectively threaten countries with possible delays in the supply of Covid-19 related medicines (Gilead's voluntary licensing of Remdesivir, which excludes middle-income countries—including Brazil—is an example[92]). Despite the yet inconclusive outcome of this preliminary investigation by CADE, the subsequent steps are largely dependent on how the institution decides to perform or not such role.

6 Theoretical Conclusions on the Role of Courts in IP Based on the Concrete Cases

The two cases reveal a number of issues on the interconnectedness between IP protection and the role of courts. A different kind of interpretation on the role of the Judiciary and other courts (including competition authorities' adjudication bodies and regulatory bodies, when applicable) with regards to patent protection may thus be enabled. This section aims at presenting some theoretical conclusions drawn partly from the cases discussed and examples presented.

a) *Courts can reshape markets (and are also influenced by them). As such, patents and patent use or abuse can be seen mainly as a legal phenomenon and their scope depends on the enforcement given to the monopoly in different jurisdictions.*

---

[91] For instance, given their broad mandate, their relative reduced number (if compared to judicial courts), and the transnational characteristics of most cases (which impact and deal with conducts/ structures in multiple jurisdictions), most competition authorities are equipped for joint international investigations, work through the sharing of information and to adopt a comparative approach in terms of arguments and remedies deployed. In this sense, they are more accustomed to use case law from other jurisdictions as direct and indirect basis for their own judgements. From an international economic law perspective, it is also true that there is also more policy space for competition authorities to pursue objectives than IP courts. Also, CADE has been one of the first authorities to particularly address an abusive conduct case pertaining to IP, which is the sham litigation case by pharmaceutical company Eli Lily (Administrative Proceeding N. 08012.011508/ 2007-91, from June 2015).

[92] Bermudez and Prabhala (2020). Gilead: o Brasil excluído no enfrentamento da pandemia. Available at: http://www.cee.fiocruz.br/?q=node/1176.

Firstly, courts affect competition. Instead of purely *arenas* where legal arguments meet in search of a ruling that clarifies the law, they are rather active *actors* that end up determining the behavior of the parties involved in an IP dispute, even when adjudicators refuse to recognize this role. In other words, judicial rulings and courts are a factor that influences the economic behavior of patent holders, competitors and governments.

As a consequence, they may in an intended or unintended manner expand the patent monopoly's effective scope. For instance, if companies are aware of the extreme success rates of individual health litigation cases, such as it was the case of Trastuzumab in Brazilian courts, and that there is no scrutiny for the prices charged to the public sector in order to enforce judicial orders, this means that the patent monopoly is enhanced exorbitantly. It becomes an implicit authorization to charge any price, even if likely anti-competitive. Similarly, if companies know that their litigation practices and their price discrimination (between different entities in a same jurisdiction and/or across different countries) are to be considered lawful from a competition law perspective, such as what has been argued in the ongoing Sofosbuvir case before the competition authority (CADE), they also see their patent monopoly reinforced, allowing them to pretty much shield themselves from antitrust suits. The monopoly legally granted by a patent is not supposed to be so overarching and comprehensive. However, it may become so due to courts. The conclusion is that access to drugs is directly restrained.

In general, it is not possible to disregard the impact of courts; the *absence* of the Judiciary decision is also often the main feature to expand patent monopolies. The absence of rulings from the Brazilian Constitutional Court (STF) on patent matters since the enactment of the 1988 Constitution and the 1996 Industrial Property Law until a May 2021 decision which ruled automatic patent term extensions unconstitutional is a present and dangerous example of this absenteeism. Therefore, in short, courts can reshape markets (and are also influenced by them). As such, patents and patent use or abuse can be seen mainly as a legal phenomenon and their scope depends on the enforcement given to patent rights and its flexibilities in different jurisdictions.

b) *"IP as crucial to innovation" wrongly becomes a legal argument, which hampers access*

Secondly, rhetorical and economic narratives have direct legal consequences when turned into arguments deployed or accepted by courts. By applying as a given fact that maximal IP protection will lead to more innovation (therefore, according to this view, IP protection *per se* is in the public interest), courts impede an evidence-based assessment of concrete cases, preferring to rely on a pre-set definition. Most laws themselves do not define the specific trade-off related to patents, access and innovation, and invariably will require robust interpretation by courts in practical terms.

This means that there will be no real balancing between, for instance, the effects for competition or the impacts on prices and consequential increase in medicine prices, and the protection of a certain patent claim. Furthermore, an analysis of even "technical" aspects, such as patentability criteria, will tend to be informed and biased by a tendency towards the granting of a patent—similarly to the notion adopted by some IP offices that patent applicants are "clients", and not public offices working for the public interest.

The economic narrative that equals IP with more innovation tends to overly expand the scope of protection of IP from a temporary monopoly granted by the State (quasi-public right, for some) to a naturalized and almost absolute right.[93] This, in a sense, is an effect of IP protection *on* the role of courts. This narrative has been implicitly seen in the two cases analyzed, especially through the arguments provided for by the law firms representing the pharmaceutical companies in Brazil. This is the main conventional stream of argumentation in pharmaceutical patent litigation and legislative debates around the world.[94]

c) *Anti-monopoly and IP law share public principles. As such, principles of competition/anti-monopoly law should be directly applicable to patents (neither as exemption nor complement)*

Thirdly, apart from an IP interpretation that is more sensitive to the socio-economic implications of IPRs, there is a case to be made about the applicability of principles of anti-monopoly laws to patents.[95] This should not be seen as an

[93] Oftentimes, the defense of TRIPS flexibilities mirrors the way the IP system is usually conceived: a tension between public and private interest, the public being the interest of society at large to benefit from more creations and inventions and access to them, and the private being the incentive/recognition of the inventor/author to benefit, particularly economically, from it. The access to medicines debate, in that sense, is normally portrayed as a defense of more public interest to the relative detriment of the private interest of the IP holder. When put under those terms, the IP debate is defined as a permanent imbalance and a constant pursue of the balance between public and private. However, this should not necessarily be the case. The disaggregated framing of the question allows for different considerations. An essential point often not referred to in the IP scholarship is the impact of TRIPS flexibilities to the protection of IP. The flexibilities are neither an annulment nor an attempt to impede the exercise of legitimate IPRs. When patents proliferate and are granted under lax patentability criteria, it is well-established that this leads to the granting of numerous patents to non-inventions (i.e. patent applications that do not fit the novelty or non-obviousness, inventive step and industrial application requirements). Conceptually speaking, they should not be granted in the first place. This means that, from the outset, patents are not synonyms of inventions. However, if the patents granted to non-inventions are never subject to legal scrutiny—for instance, through post-grant oppositions or through judicial rulings that invalidate patents—they will be legally enforced.

[94] Another good example of how this comes about is in the anxieties surrounding the likelihood of international investment arbitration panels based on the measures taken by States with regards to Covid-19 IP-protected technologies, which may cause hugely detrimental effects to certain countries, show how deeply engrained the "IP as innovation" approach is. Similarly, as noted by James Love, "*companies will be able to claim that anything that reduces the price reduces incentives to invest in more rapid development, and litigate that issue.*" See, Karlin-Smith (2020) https://www.politico.com/news/2020/03/05/coronavirus-drug-industry-prices-122412.

[95] See, for example, FTC v. Actavis US Supreme Court Case. In this case of a pay-for-delay agreement, the court acknowledged that competition law should be applied to patents. This is different from the previous US interpretation: before that, decision courts largely considered that a behavior that falls within the subject matter of the patent would be lawful, even if it had a negative

exception or as a complement to the legal discipline of patents and other IPRs, but as an *integral* part of the meaning of IP: there is no IP without competition, even if it may sound paradoxical at first.

In practice, in relation to the Trastuzumab civil federal case in Brazil, this would lead to the recognition that the stark price differentiation between the price of public procurement and the price charged resulting from a judicial ruling against the State is so high that it should have been considered illegal. To do so, an application of principles of competition law, in particular a discipline of abuse of dominant position, would have been in our view sufficient to prove the case. The doctrine of competition law abuse of dominant position should definitely be applicable to this case, even if it was being ruled by an instance outside of the Brazilian competition law system. This would be arguably also the case in other jurisdictions. Conversely, for the Sofosbuvir competition case, the differences in the historical series of prices, and between the *de facto* monopoly, the legal monopoly (patent protection) and the competition situations (with generic drugs available in the market), highlight another anti-competitive practice based on both excessive pricing (price demonstrated through price discrimination) and abuse of patent power.[96] As noted before, this case is still pending as of the conclusion of this paper.

While at first the difference in courts (federal judicial court and competition authority) would seem to lead to completely different legal reasonings and rationale of distinct bodies of law, in reality the similarity of cases denotes that the disciplines of IP and competition law—and also in tune with public interest provisions and fundamental rights—are or should be in fact in a path of merger. An IP court cannot dismiss competition law as much as a competition body should not ignore IP provisions; although they may have different organizing structures, and are usually seen as targeting different goals, they have increasingly similar objectives and intertwinements. Integrated principles and integrated disciplines does not mean conflating all norms, arguing that IP and competition law are the same (they are not), but it does mean passing from essentially private law spheres to a way of interpreting law that should be based on public principles, particularly in light of the demand that it should not reproduce socio-economic structures as natural entities, but instead seek to regulate them for their economic power, as we have argued before

effect on the market and could be considered anti-competitive. This highlights that even in a country so adamantly protective of patent rights, such as the United States, the possibility of applying patent law to competition law exists.

[96] There seems to be a proven argument in favor of an abuse of patent as an illicit anti-competitive conduct. This is a clear recognition under Brazilian law, but it is also a hypothesis clearly delineated by the TRIPS Agreement and therefore part of the national law of almost every jurisdiction around the world. Furthermore, even though the majority of pharmaceutical IP-related cases in antitrust bodies deals with "excessive pricing", such doctrine is neither the only nor the *sine qua non* legal argument to elicit the anti-competitive conduct. In other words, the illegality is not (only) in a price deemed excessive, but in the utilization of a legal monopoly position (the patent) in an abusive manner. Therefore the need to identify the two conducts.

in different occasions.[97] Both are informed by and conceptualized under public interest law more than bearers of private interests. This also means that the cases described above would have required a different kind of interpretation that adequately addresses competition impacts of IP protection both directly and indirectly—including the role of courts as such. As many have argued in terms of the evolution of both disciplines (IP and competition law), the trend towards a broader consideration of interests, consequences and stakeholders denotes a process of "publicization" of private law, rather than the opposite.[98]

d) *There is an emerging global (case) law of TRIPS flexibilities based on screening and transparency. The role of courts is not dissociated from, but rather based on, an interaction between academia, NGOs and other actors.*

Finally, a few notes should be made on how an emerging body of decisions taken by courts around the world has become a crucial feature for TRIPS flexibilities much beyond their own initial scope. Courts are increasingly required to navigate distinct "fields of law" and take into account other jurisdictions—both for the impact of their decisions and as sources of legal arguments.[99] There is also a "screening" process between courts.[100] Some national decisions have direct transnational repercussions, such as a ruling on the legality of parallel exports, which will impact countries which import or export medicines to that jurisdiction. An antitrust decision may deem illegal a conduct based on abusive exercise of IPRs, and may impose restrictions and sanctions that affect the outcomes of patent litigations in judicial courts.

---

[97] See Sect. 2.

[98] Salomão Filho (2015).

[99] While IP law seems to be tightly related to national jurisdictions and international treaties only, the increasing prominence of international licensing agreements in IP, the introduction of IP in investment arbitration panels and the interplay between different actors discussed in this paper as "pharmaceutical patent activism" highlight that courts need to navigate this much more complex landscape, both public and private, both national and transnational at the same time. This is at least partly applicable to this analysis. It also deals with other phenomena. For instance, in the field of constitutional law and international human rights law, some have referred to this as "courts' dialogue", whereby interpretation of certain rights and case law of regional human rights bodies such as the European Court of Human Rights and the American Court of Human Rights may influence each other, as well as national constitutional courts. Even if the expression may not be always accurate to describe constitutional practices, it does signal the possibility of cross-referencing based on sharing of experiences and case law. This does not compromise the sovereignty or the independence of courts, as evidently all such arguments and data needs to be assessed according to national laws and real cases. Instead, it provides more transparency and avenues for a better coordination between different societal actors, which may have the positive effect of increasing accountability.

[100] Positive screening is an expression most commonly found in the investment world of stock exchanges, whereby investors positively value companies with commitments such as environmentally-sound operations and human rights protection, among others. Here, the notion of "screening" is borrowed broadly from corporate governance in a critical way, where reputational costs and examples set by peers in a given market are an increasingly important form of informal governance.

But in other cases, there are indirect consequences, which cannot be underestimated either. Landmark rulings such as the USA Supreme Court Myriad Genetics Case [101] and the Indian Supreme Court Novartis Case [102] have been immensely discussed, read in law classrooms and utilized by courts around the world that in theory would not be bound anyhow by such decisions. Others have this emerging potential, such as the Kenyan High Court decision that, based on the right to health, struck down a law with a concept of "counterfeit" which ended up including safe and high-quality generic drugs. [103] In this sense, they are a real source of law for other courts.

Similarly, pharmaceutical patent applications also have a transnational dimension. Pharmaceutical companies file patents around the world, sometimes translating the content of application claims without proper adaption to national laws. [104] Civil society groups and generic competitors counter applications of key medicines through patent oppositions in one jurisdiction, such as India, which then become the basis for subsequent oppositions in other countries. This can be deemed a form of "patent activism". [105] The cases of Trastuzumab and Sofosbuvir, as previously noted in their respective descriptions, have both been subject to scrutiny and advocacy by patients' groups, and the dialogue between different actors and jurisdictions is a key feature for understanding the conducts and strategies deployed in Brazil.

---

[101] United States Supreme Court (2013), Assoc. for Molecular Pathology v. Myriad Genetics, Inc., 569 U.S. 576 (2013) (on patentability of an isolated gene).

[102] On constitutionality of Section 3(d) of the Indian Patent Act which establishes a robust inventive step requirement. For instance, Siva Tambisetty notes that "The decision in Novartis v UOI heralds a post-TRIPS coming of age for many jurisdictions like India, including Thailand, Brazil, Malaysia and Indonesia. There is an urgent need to build up legitimate legal standards, tests and principles around domestic patent legislation that do not replicate the predicament around patentability standards that several jurisdictions face". See Tambisetty, Siva. *Novartis v. Union of India* and the Person Skilled in the Art: A Missed Opportunity. LSE Law, Society and Economy Working Papers 2/2014. For Ahmed Abdel-Latif, the case was the first time a decision by a developing country court was so intensely scrutinized, and could bear consequences to other countries, see Abdel-Latif (2013), available at https://www.ip-watch.org/2013/04/15/the-novartis-decision-a-tale-of-developing-countries-ip-and-the-role-of-the-judiciary/. Similarly, see Bennett (2014), p. 535 and its possible impacts.

[103] For a comment, see Kapczynski (2019).

[104] As patents are territorial, patent applications also need to be filed in multiple jurisdictions. Multiple streamlined and/or joint systems do exist, such as the WIPO-administered Patent Cooperation Treaty (PCT) system and regional patent systems such as the ones enabled by the European Patent Office and the OAPI—Organisation Africaine de la Propriété Intellectuelle.

[105] See, for instance, the work of Médécins sans Frontières—Access Campaign, ITPC—International Treatment Patients Coalition, Third World Network (Malaysia), Lawyer's Collective (India), GTPI—Grupo de Trabalho da Propriedade Intelectual (Brazil, for only a few examples of organizations working specifically on this field. Furthermore, a database such as that of the Medicine Patent Pool's Medspal, the compilation of TRIPS flexibilities by the Medicines Law & Policy, or the compilation of compulsory licensing experiences such as that organized by the South Centre, are good examples that may be utilized by any courts around the world. For a comparison between India, Brazil and Nigeria (with a relative lack of "patent activism" in the latter), see Vanni (2020).

Theoretically, these and other cases may be understood as part of global and transnational law,[106] which may help to elucidate how specific courts are part of global economic governance, even as national decisions. As such, adjudicators are key actors in the consolidation of a global law of TRIPS flexibilities based on the sharing of positive experiences, transnational advocacy, international solidarity and in the benefit of developing countries.[107] It should include not only finalized cases, but also legal proceedings initiated but not prosecuted, injunctions granted or not, negotiations and settlements, and activists campaigns. Furthermore, developing countries have an ever-growing importance in IP jurisprudence.[108] The current Covid-19 pandemic and its multifaceted international reaction has a clear potential to accelerate and foster this process.

7 Concluding Remarks

This article sought to repurpose the relation between courts and the implementation of intellectual property. It argues for a shift from limited and uni-dimensional, i.e. "courts apply IP law neutrally", to broad and multi-dimensional, through which courts define the contours of IP law and are also mutually influenced by IP arguments, theories and stakeholders, all and each with specific socio-economic impacts. Access to medicines is a field where these considerations become more evident.

It proposed two main arguments. Firstly, that courts have an enormous impact on the implementation of TRIPS flexibilities. While they are and should not be the only variable in place, any efforts for advancing or curbing the flexibilities *involves* courts. In particular, tribunals shape markets, even when—and maybe particularly when—adjudicators decide to refrain from broader consideration of circumstances

[106] Again, as examples, refer to Muir-Watt, Horatia, 2013; Zumbansen, Peer, 2011. Sometimes, influences also come from non-state actors, such as arbitration panels, non-governmental entities such as ISO, ICANN and FIFA, and transnational private contracts. In private international law, notions of global law, transnational law and private ordering have been used to characterize a legal political economy—both from a descriptive and a normative point of view—that is not exclusively based on national and international law, but multiple normative setters.

[107] The theoretical framework of a decentralized and collective construction of a global/transnational law in IP means two things: on the normative side, that no single entity, no single individual and no single country should define the effective norms and policies of the whole world; on a descriptive point of view, that all players have an important role, and that this interplay between academia, civil society organizations, international organizations and judicial/administrative authorities is essential to construct a robust account of TRIPS flexibilities through example and mutual screening.

[108] Abbott, Drahos and Correa have argued that the world patent order was to be changed by the innovation and development of IP in developing countries, with a particular nod to the role of China, Brazil and India. This hypothesis can be now taken further to include the specific case law of these and other jurisdictions alike. Abbott et al. (2012).

and socio-economic impact of their own decisions. For this reason, the role of courts itself (e.g. a ruling or a lack thereof) has competition impacts and should be taken into account in legal interpretation.

Secondly, that a specific narrative which associates IP protection with fostering innovation is misleading, as it establishes an incorrect trade-off between access to health products and innovation. Since it is widely deployed by courts without further consideration, this narrative turned into legal argument is particularly problematic for over-expanding the effective protection of IP without a balance with the public interest. Thus, it should not be accepted as a juridical category or narrative.

The description of the cases of Trastuzumab and Sofosbuvir in Brazil serve as examples of how these different pieces come together, even if sometimes indirectly and not explicitly. Many other rulings can and should be described under those lenses. This article may present a framework for further analyses that include, rather than ignore, the specific role of courts and their respective arguments on TRIPS flexibilities.

A general conclusion is that this set of elements justifies a legal interpretation that is mindful of structures such as patents, including their effects on societies and the need for them to be reformed, rather than exclusively based on an allegedly formalist interpretation of laws. Such laws, as described above, already enable the restructuring of patent interpretation according to TRIPS flexibilities. This could be deemed a "neo-structuralist" approach to patent law. [109] These cases also lead to the recognition that IP and competition laws should be both interpreted jointly according to integrated public interest principles. [110]

Finally, the article posited that the increasing cross-referencing of courts and the transnational characteristics of IP and competition laws may be described—both descriptively and normatively—as an emerging global law of TRIPS flexibilities, based on screening and transparency. The reaction to the Covid-19 pandemic has the potential to accelerate this process. This is where other actors, including civil society and governments, through for instance patent oppositions, transparency of R&D costs and limitation of anti-competitive abuses, play a crucial role.

References

Abbott FM, Correa CM, Drahos P (2012) Emerging markets and the World Patent Order. Edward Elgar, Cheltenham

Abdel-Latif A (15 April 2013) The Novartis decision: a tale of developing countries, IP, and the role of the judiciary, intellectual property watch, Available at https://www.ip-watch.org/2013/04/15/the-novartis-decision-a-tale-of-developing-countries-ip-and-the-role-of-the-judiciary/

Ação Popular n. 1019631-97.2018.4.01.3400. Judgement on 23 September 2018

[109] Salomão Filho (2015).

[110] Salomão Filho (2015).

Amsden A (2001) The rise of the rest: challenges to the West from late industrializing economies. Oxford University Press, Oxford

Ascarelli T (1970) Teoria della concurrencia y de los bienes inmateriales. Bosch, Madrid, p 276

Baker D, Jayadev A, Stiglitz (July 2017) Innovation, intellectual property and development: a better set of approaches for the 21st century, Available at: http://ip-unit.org/wp-content/uploads/2017/07/IP-for-21st-Century-EN.pdf

Bennett WJ (2014) Indian pharmaceutical patent law and the effects of Novartis Ag v. Union of India. Wash Univ Global Stud Law Rev 13:535. and its possible impacts

Bently L (2011) Exclusions from patentability and exceptions to patentees' right: taking exceptions seriously. Curr Legal Prob 64:315–347

Bermudez J, Prabhala A (13 May 2020) Gilead: o Brasil excluído no enfrentamento da pandemia, Available at: http://www.cee.fiocruz.br/?q=node/1176

Biehl J, Socal MP, Amon JJ (2016) The judicialization of health and the quest for state accountability: evidence from 1,262 lawsuits for access to medicines in Southern Brazil. Health Human Rights J 18(1)

Boldrin M, Levine DK (2013) The case against patents. J Econ Perspect 27(1):3–22

Bonilla Maldonado D (2013) Constitutionalism of the Global South: the activist tribunals of India, South Africa, and Colombia. Cambridge University Press, Cambridge

Borowski SM (2009) Saving tomorrow from today: preserving innovation in the face of compulsory licensing. Fla St Univ Law Rev 36. http://ir.law.fsu.edu/lr/vol36/iss2/6

Burk D, Lemley M (2013) The patent crisis and how the courts can solve it. University of Chicago Press, Chicago

Case n. 05027709232018402510l, Federal Court of 2nd Region, Rio de Janeiro

Chang H-J (2002) Kicking away the ladder: development strategy in historical perspective. Anthem Press, London

Cimoli M, Dosi G, Maskus KE, Okediji RL, Reichman JH, Stiglitz JE (eds) (2014) Intellectual property rights: legal and economic challenges for development. Oxford University Press, Oxford

Competition Commission of India. Case No. 68 of 2016 – Roche – Mylan Biocon CCI Order 68 of 2016

Correa C (2016) Public health perspective on intellectual property and access to medicines, a compilation of studies prepared for WHO. South Centre, Geneva

Correa C, Velásquez G (2018) Acceso a Medicamentos: Experiencias com Licencias Obligatorias y Uso Gubernamental – el caso de la hepatitis C. Research Paper No. 85. South Centre, Geneva

Costa CG, Vieira MF, Renata R (2008) Access to medicines and intellectual property in Brazil: reflections and strategies of civil society. Revista Sur 8

Cueni T. Intellectual property is not a hindrance but a help to end Covid-19, Financial Times, available at: https://www.ft.com/content/e82dd07c-95c5-11ea-899a-f62a20d54625

Darling K, Perzanowski A (eds) (2017) Creativity without law: challenging the assumptions of intellectual property. NYU Press, New York

de Werra J (23 March 2016) Specialised intellectual property courts - issues and challenges. Published in: specialised intellectual property courts - issues and challenges, global perspectives for the intellectual property system, Issue Number 2: CEIPI-ICTSD. 2016, pp 15–41. Available at SSRN: https://ssrn.com/abstract=2761209

Deere C (2008) The implementation game: the TRIPS agreement and the global politics of intellectual property reform in developing countries. Oxford University Press, Oxford

Dezalay Y, Garth B (1996) Dealing in virtue: international commercial arbitration and the construction of a transnational legal order. University of Chicago Press, Chicago

DNDi (12 April 2018) New affordable hepatitis C combination treatment shows 97% cure rate. DNDi, https://www.dndi.org/2018/media-centre/press-releases/new-affordable-hepatitis-c-combination-treatment-shows-97-cure-rate/

Dreyfuss RC, Rodríguez-Gavarito C (2014) Balancing wealth and health: the battle over intellectual property and access to medicines in Latin America. Oxford University Press, Oxford

European Commission Press Release. "Coronavirus Global Response: €7.4 billion raised for universal access to vaccines". 4 May 2020, available at: https://ec.europa.eu/commission/presscorner/detail/en/ip_20_797

Fink C, Raffo J (2019) What role for intellectual property in industrial development. In: Correa C, Seuba X (eds) Intellectual property and development: understanding the interfaces. Springer, Berlin

Forbes (28 August 2019) Can Roche's blockbuster drug Herceptin's sales grow?, Available at: https://www.forbes.com/sites/greatspeculations/2019/08/28/can-roches-blockbuster-drug-herceptins-sales-grow/#62da696a42e5

Gabriela CC, Marcela V, da Costa Dorneles RF, Vianna MNS (2018) Medicamentos em situação de exclusividade financiados pelo Ministério da Saúde: Análise da Situação Patentária e das Compras Públicas. Fiocruz & Escola Nacional de Saúde Pública Sergio, Arouca, pp 122–139

Gawel CR (2016) Patent protection as a key driver for pharmaceutical innovation. Pharm Policy Law 18:45–53, in Valverde, J.L.; Pisani, Eduardo, The Globalisation of the Pharmaceutical Industry, 2016

Geiger C, Nard CA, Seuba X (2018) Intellectual property and the judiciary. Edward Elgar, Cheltenham

Gilead (November 2017) Chronic hepatitis C treatment expansion – generic manufacturing for developing countries, Available at: https://www.gilead.com/-/media/files/pdfs/other/hcv-generic-agreement-fast-facts-11-15-17.pdf

Grupo de Trabalho da Propriedade Intelectual (GTPI). Brazil is excluded from license authorizing production of generic medicine for hepatitis C. Available at: http://deolhonaspatentes.org/media/file/GTPI_statement_Gilead_license_sofosbuvir.pdf

Grupo Direito e Pobreza (2019) Abuso de Direito Patentário e Prática de Preços Abusivos no Caso Hepatite C e Sofosbuvir

Grupo Direito e Pobreza (Law and Poverty Group) (10 June 2014) University of São Paulo. Representation to the Federal Public Ministry of Brazil against Roche

Hailbronner M (2017) Transformative constitutionalism: not only in the global South. Am J Comp Law 65(3):527–565

Hein W, Moon S (2013) Informal norms in global governance: human rights, intellectual property rules and access to medicines. Routledge, Milton Park

Heller M (2010) Gridlock economy: how too much ownership wrecks markets, stops innovation, and costs lives, Michael Heller. Basic Books, New York

Heller, Michael & Eisenberg, Rebecca. Heller, M. A.; Eisenberg, R. (May 1998). Can patents deter innovation? The anticommons in biomedical research Science 280 (5364): 698–701

Hepatitis C cure (6 December 2018) Sofosbuvir, turns 5 years old: the vast majority of people still have not been treated, hepCoalition, https://hepcoalition.org/news/press-releases/article/hepatitis-c-cure-sofosbuvir-turns-5-years-old-the-vast-majority-of-people-still?lang=en#nb1

Hill A, Simmons B, Gotham D, Fortunak J (2016) Rapid reductions in prices for generic sofosbuvir and daclatasvir to treat hepatitis C. J Virus Erad 2(1):28–31

Hoen E (2019) Strong call for transparency on medicine prices, cost of R&D at WHO fair pricing forum. Medicines Law and Policy. https://medicineslawandpolicy.org/2019/04/strong-call-for-transparency-on-medicine-prices-cost-of-rd-at-who-fair-pricing-forum/

Hu Y, Eynikel D, Boulet P et al (2020) Supplementary protection certificates and their impact on access to medicines in Europe: case studies of sofosbuvir, trastuzumab and imatinib. J Pharmaceutical Policy Practice **13**:1

Inthira Y, Adun M, Sripen T, Chaisiri K, Yot T (2011) Government use licenses in Thailand: an assessment of the health and economic impacts. Global Health 7:28

Iyer V (2019) Constitution-making in Bhutan: a complex and Sui Generis experience. Chin J Comp Law 7(2):359–385

Juiz revoga liminar que quebrava patente de remédio contra hepatite C. https://www.jota.info/paywall?redirect_to=//www.jota.info/tributos-e-empresas/saude/juiz-revoga-liminar-que-quebrava-patente-de-remedio-contra-hepatite-c-21122018. LINK DOES NOT WORK

Junqueira D (17 August 2019) Investigação do TCU aponta sobrepreço em remédio para câncer e leva a desabastecimento. Folha de São Paulo, Available at https://www1.folha.uol.com.br/cotidiano/2019/08/investigacao-do-tcu-aponta-sobrepreco-em-remedio-para-cancer-e-leva-a-desabastecimento.shtml

Kang HY (2020) Patents as assets: intellectual property rights as market subjects and objects. In: Birch K, Muniesa F (eds) Turning things into assets: new lineaments in the study of technoscientific capitalism. MIT Press, Cambridge

Kapczynski A (2017) Order without intellectual property law: open science in influenza. Cornell Law Rev 102:1539. Available at: https://scholarship.law.cornell.edu/clr/vol102/iss6/3

Kapczynski A (26 April 2019) The right to medicines in an age of neoliberalism. Humanity Journal, available at: http://humanityjournal.org/issue10-1/the-right-to-medicines-in-an-age-of-neoliberalism/

Karlin-Smith S (2020) How the drug industry got its way on the coronavirus. Politico, https://www.politico.com/news/2020/03/05/coronavirus-drug-industry-prices-122412

Kennedy D (1997) A critique of adjudication (fin de siècle). Harvard University Press, Cambridge

Knowledge Ecology International (KEI). CPTech's 2003 reports for the RSA Competition Commission, in Hazel Tau et al. v GSK, Boehringer, et al. Available at: https://www.keionline.org/competition/2003-hazel-tau-tac

Lemos R, Castro O (2012) Tecnobrega. O Pará Reinventando o Negócio da Música (Tecnobrega. Pará reinventing the Music Business). Hunter Books, Nashville

Li X, Correa C (eds) (2009) Intellectual property enforcement – international perspectives. Edward Elgar & South Centre, Northampton

Matthews D (2011) Intellectual property, human rights and development, the role of NGOs and social movements. Edward Elgar, Cheltenham

Matthews D, Gurgula O (12 May 2016) Patent strategies and competition law in the pharmaceutical sector: implications for access to medicines. Queen Mary School of Law Legal Studies Research Paper No. 233/2016. Available at SSRN: https://ssrn.com/abstract=2779014

Mazzucato M (2013) The entrepreneurial state: debunking public vs. private sector myths. Anthem Press, London

Mazzucato M, Torreele E (27 April 2020) How to develop a COVID-19 vaccine for all. project syndicate, Available at: https://www.project-syndicate.org/commentary/universal-free-covid19-vaccine-by-mariana-mazzucato-and-els-torreele-2020-04

Mendes CH (2013) Constitutional courts and deliberative democracy, vol 1, 1st edn. Oxford University Press, Oxford, p 272

MSF Access Campaign Global day of action against Roche's inhumanity #RocheGreedKills (6 February 2017) Press release, https://msfaccess.org/global-day-action-against-roches-inhumanity-rochegreedkills

Muir-Watt H (2016) Private international law beyond the Schism. Transnational Legal Theory 2, 2011(3):347–428

Muir-Watt H, Arroyo D, Bíziková L, de Oliveira AB (2019) Adjudication without frontiers: the global turn in private international law. Edward Elgar, London

Open Covid Pledge: https://opencovidpledge.org/

Pankhuri A, Shamnad B (13 August 2018) The morality of sexual pleasure: patent office training? Spicy IP, Available at: https://spicyip.com/2018/08/the-morality-of-sexual-pleasure-patent-office-training.html

La Porta R, Lopez-de-Silanes F, Shleifer A, Vishny RW (1998) Law and finance. J Political Econ 106(6):1113–1155

Pottage A, Sherman B (2010) Figures of invention: a history of modern patent law. Oxford University Press, New York

Press Statement Minister of Health 20th September 2017 – Implementation of the Rights of Government for Sofosbuvir Tablet to Increase Access for Hepatitis C Treatment in Malaysia. Available at: https://kpkesihatan.com/2017/09/20/press-statement-minister-of-health-20th-

september-2017-implementation-of-the-rights-of-government-for-sofosbuvir-tablet-to-increase-access-for-hepatitis-c-treatment-in-malaysia/
Report of the United Nations Secretary-General High-Level Panel on Access to Medicines (2016)
Salomão Filho C (2007) Direito industrial, direito da concorrência e licenciamento compulsório. In: Basso M et al (eds) Direitos de Propriedade Intelectual & Saúde Pública. O acesso universal aos medicamentos anti-retrovirais no Brasil. IDCID, São Paulo, pp 160–161
Salomão Filho C (2013a) A legal theory of economic power – implications for social and economic development. Edward Elgar, Cheltenham
Salomão Filho C (2013b) Direito Concorrencial. Malheiros, São Paulo, p 152
Salomão Filho C (2015) Teoria Crítico-Estruturalista do Direito Comercial. Marcial Pons, São Paulo
Salomão Filho C, Ido VHP (2019) Global corruption and economic power. In: Horatia MW, Diego A, Lucia B, de Oliveira AB (eds) Adjudication without frontiers: the global turn in private international law. Edward Elgar, London
Sanghera B (6 November 2015) Unmasking Central Asia's neoliberal judges. Open democracy, Available at: https://www.opendemocracy.net/en/odr/unmasking-central-asias-neoliberal-judges/
SBAC (2019) Medicamento contra hepatite C terá descontó para o governo. http://www.sbac.org.br/blog/2018/11/28/dona-de-patente-que-barra-generico-contra-hepatite-c-promete-desconto-a-governo/
Schiff E (1971) Industrialization without National Patents: the Netherlands, 1869-1912; Switzerland, 1850–1907. Princeton University Press, Princeton
Sell SK (2003) Private power, public law: the globalization of intellectual property rights. Cambridge University Press, Cambridge
Shadlen K (2017) Coalitions and compliance: the political economy of pharmaceutical patents in Latin America. Oxford University Press, Oxford
Silva M. Petição Inicial de Ação Popular (Statement of Claims of Popular Lawsuit)
Stiglitz J (19 October 2017) Wealth before health? Why intellectual property laws are facing a counterattack. The Guardian, available at: https://www.theguardian.com/business/2017/oct/18/intellectual-property-laws-demand-a-21st-century-solution
Stiglitz J, Jayadev A (2010) Medicine for tomorrow: some alternative proposals to promote socially beneficial research and development in pharmaceuticals. J Generic Med 7(3):217–226
Syam N, Alas M, Ido VHP (2020) The 73rd World Health Assembly and resolution on COVID-19: quest of global solidarity for equitable access to health products. Policy Brief No. 78. South Centre, Geneva
Tambisetty S. Novartis v. Union of India and the Person Skilled in the Art: A Missed Opportunity. LSE Law, Society and Economy Working Papers 2/2014
United States Supreme Court (2013) Assoc. for Molecular Pathology v. Myriad Genetics, Inc., 569 U.S. 576 (on patentability of an isolated gene)
United States Trade Representative (USTR)'s Special 301 report of April 2020. Available at: https://ustr.gov/sites/default/files/2020_Special_301_Report.pdf
Uprimny R (2011) The recent transformation of constitutional law in Latin America: trends and challenges. Texas Law Rev 89(7):1587–1609
Vanni A (2020) Patent games in the Global South: pharmaceutical patent law-making in Brazil, India and Nigeria. Bloomsbury, London
Velásquez G (2020) Rethinking R&D for pharmaceutical products after the novel coronavirus COVID-19 shock. Policy Brief, No. 75. South Centre, Geneva
Velásquez G, Seuba X (2011) Rethinking global health: a binding convention for pharmaceutical products. Research Paper No. 42. South Centre, Geneva
Vieira M, Moon S (2019) Research synthesis: public funding of pharmaceutical R&D. Graduate Institute, Global Health Centre, Geneva, available at: https://www.knowledgeportalia.org/public-funding-of-r-d

Vieira M, Moon S (2020) Research synthesis: costs of pharmaceutical R&D. Graduate Institute, Global Health Centre, Geneva, available at https://www.knowledgeportalia.org/cost-of-r-d
Wang DWL (2015) Right to health litigation in Brazil: the problem and the institutional responses. Human Rights Law Rev 15:617
WHO COVID-19 Technology Access Pool (C-TAP): https://www.who.int/emergencies/diseases/novel-coronavirus-2019/global-research-on-novel-coronavirus-2019-ncov/covid-19-technology-access-pool
World Health Organization (2019) WHO model list of essential medicines, 21st List
Zumbansen P (2012) Transnational law, evolving. In: Smits J (ed) Encyclopedia of comparative law, 2nd edn. Edward Elgar, pp 899–925

Robust Patent Examination or Deep Harmonization? Cooperation and Work Sharing Between Patent Offices

Nirmalya Syam

Abstract Patent laws and regulations in many countries have utilized the flexibility available under the WTO TRIPS Agreement to apply nationally appropriate standards to define the patentability criteria of novelty, inventive step and industrial applicability, in order to ensure the grant of high-quality patents for genuine inventions. Robust search and examination are crucial for the application of this flexibility to ensure the grant of patents for genuine inventions, e.g., for secondary pharmaceutical patent applications which could lead to patent evergreening and adversely impact access to medicines by restraining generic competition. However, limited examination resources of patent offices have been stretched by the tremendous surge in the number of patent applications to be processed, leading to delays and backlogs. This has led patent offices to prioritize efficient and speedy processing of patent applications with their limited resources by using the search and examination work of other patent offices, sometimes to the extent of granting a patent on the basis of a corresponding grant by another patent office. This chapter discusses how work sharing has been driven by the major patent offices as part of a global patent harmonization agenda, both within the WIPO Patent Cooperation Treaty and through technical assistance and cooperation with other patent offices, and suggests how patent offices in developing countries could best harness the advantages of work sharing, particularly in a South-South cooperation framework, while safeguarding the ability to apply in practice the patentability requirements under their national laws through a robust search and examination of patent claims.

1 Introduction

Patent examination is one of the most critical tools available to a country to ensure that patents are granted for genuine inventions that satisfy the patentability requirements under the law of a country. Patent examination practices adopted by a patent

N. Syam (✉)
South Centre, Geneva, Switzerland
e-mail: syam@southcentre.int

C. M. Correa, R. M. Hilty (eds.), *Access to Medicines and Vaccines*,
https://doi.org/10.1007/978-3-030-83114-1_9

office plays a crucial role in the application of this important tool. Almost over the past four decades, patent offices all over the world have entered into collaborative relationships with each other that has effectively led to the creation of a global web of collaboration networks between patent offices. These networks have evolved in parallel to the pursuit of normative initiatives to harmonize substantive and procedural aspects of patent law in multilateral forums such as the World Intellectual Property Organization (WIPO) or in bilateral or regional trade agreements. While the normative patent harmonization agenda has been resisted, the administrative cooperation between patent offices has received relatively less attention. This chapter examines how the various kinds of cooperative work sharing arrangements that have evolved between patent offices can impact the ability of a patent office to conduct robust search and examination in accordance with their applicable national law and policy, and the opportunities and challenges that arise from the cooperation between patent offices.

2 Patent Examination: A Critical TRIPS Flexibility

Rigorous examination of patent applications to determine whether they satisfy the general patentability requirements of novelty, inventive step and industrial applicability is the core function of patent offices in most countries. The decision by a patent office to grant patents should be based on as thorough an examination of the patent application as possible to ensure that only claims that fully meet the patentability requirements under the national law are allowed. An erroneously granted patent would remain valid unless it is successfully challenged before a judicial authority or a tribunal.[1] Thus, the patent offices are expected to act as gatekeepers of the patent system and ensure that patents of questionable validity are not granted.[2]

Even while recognizing the possibility of grant of patents in all fields of technology as required under the TRIPS Agreement, countries can have different thresholds of novelty, inventive step and industrial applicability in relation to specific fields of technology, such as pharmaceuticals. Thus, the outcome of a patent application can vary from one country to another, depending on the standard of patentability thresholds that are applied. The provisions of the World Trade Organization's (WTO) Agreement on Trade Related Aspects of Intellectual Property Rights (TRIPS) provide the flexibility to WTO members to apply rigorous standards of

[1] Invalidation of a patent can take several years of litigation, during which period the patent can still be enforced, and involve investment of substantial technical and financial resources which may be difficult to access or afford, particularly in developing countries. Correa (2014a).

[2] Ibid, p. 2; the number of patent applications and grants have increased significantly in many countries without a corresponding genuine increase in innovation due to the application of low requirements of patentability.

patent examination to ensure that only genuine inventions that meet high thresholds of patentability criteria are granted a patent.[3]

Patent examination practices pursed by national or regional patent offices are often based on the application of legal fictions.[4] The adoption of some of these legal fictions by a patent office in its approach to the examination of a patent claim may be based on rules, regulations, bye-laws, guidelines or office practices. These may be also influenced by the adoption of treaty obligations for patent cooperation, technical assistance provided by influential patent offices, or administrative collaboration arrangements between patent offices based on memoranda of understanding (MOU) for such collaboration. Thus, even where the national law of a country lays down very strict requirements of patentability, its application can be significantly impacted by the practices followed by the patent office with regard to examination of patent applications.[5]

This situation demonstrates the need for not only establishing appropriate thresholds of patentability under the patent law, but also the important role that patent examiners play in applying the law. Patent offices in developing countries face challenges that impact the rigorous application of the patentability thresholds. These challenges include limited human resources for patent examination, high examiner attrition rates, surge in the number of patent applications in different technical fields, backlogs of pending applications,[6] and meeting expectations to increase efficiency through expedited disposal of patent applications while ensuring the robustness of the patents granted.[7] Patent offices in developing countries are thus required to make policy choices that essentially entail trade-offs between these challenges. Depending on the policy choice that is prioritised, these could adversely impact the ability of the patent offices to meet the other challenges.[8] In the face of

[3] Article 27.1 of the TRIPS Agreement requires patents to be granted in all fields of technology without discrimination as long as the patent applications satisfy the patentability criteria of novelty, inventive step and industrial applicability. However, WTO members can apply their own definitions of these criteria, and in doing so, can differentiate between fields of technology. *See* Correa (2012).

[4] The boundaries of patentability of claimed inventions have been stretched through the adoption of a number of legal fictions. For example, it is assumed that a fictional 'person skilled in the art' against whose level of knowledge the inventiveness or non-obviousness of a claim is to be determined, is a person of ordinary knowledge to whom even trivial developments would appear to be inventive. However, there is no obligation under any international agreement to apply such legal fictions. Correa (2014b).

[5] One study found that in spite of stricter thresholds of patentability established under the patent law in India, in some instances the Indian patent office has granted patent claims that had been rejected in the US and EU in spite of the application of liberal thresholds of patentability. Chaudhuri et al. (2010); a recent study found a 72% error rate in the grant of secondary pharmaceutical patent applications in India, in spite of the high threshold established under the Indian patent law (Ali et al. 2018).

[6] However, sometimes backlogs in processing patent applications could also lead to withdrawal of patent applications and save the resources of a patent office.

[7] Cruz and Olivos (2019).

[8] *See* Shadlen (2013), p. 87.

these conflicting policy priorities, patent offices often prioritise patent examination speed and use of limited human resources over ensuring the quality of granted patents.[9]

Patent offices can respond to these challenges by increasing human resources for patent examination,[10] use of automation technologies or by leveraging the search and examination capacity of other national or regional patent offices. Of these, automation and reliance on the work products of other patent offices can also drive, and in turn thrive, under a globally harmonized patent system. Reliance on automation and outsourcing of search and examination work to other patent offices, depending on the nature and extent of the use of automation and outsourcing, can have an impact on the outcome of the patent examination in terms of the examination standards and practices applied. In the context of pharmaceutical patent applications, if such reliance leads to the application of lower patentability requirements that liberally allow the grant of secondary patent claims, it can have a detrimental impact on access to medicines.[11]

3 Approaches to Patent Harmonisation

While patent laws are territorially limited in scope, the policy space for designing national patent law is circumscribed by the obligations of a State under applicable international IP treaties from the Paris Convention[12] to the TRIPS Agreement, as well as additional obligations incurred under bilateral or regional free trade agreements. Certain IP treaties like the Patent Law Treaty (PLT) and the Patent Cooperation Treaty (PCT) administered by WIPO also impose procedural obligations which must be followed by patent offices. These can apply to both the formality requirements in patent applications as well as to the timelines and other procedures to be followed. The scope of these treaties can also expand to shape the search and examination processes followed by national patent offices.

---

[9] Ibid, p. 88.

[10] It is reported that the Indian Patent Office has substantially reduced backlogs by hugely augmenting its human resources, alongside amendments of processing timelines and use of ICT tools to better leverage its internal examination capacities. The Brazilian Patent and Trademark Office has also substantially reduced backlogs through a increasing the number of patent examiners in parallel to accelerating examination of patent applications in specific sectors and utilizing prior art search conducted by other offices on corresponding applications. *See, e.g.*, Jayakumar (2017) and Nunes and Romano (2019).

[11] *See, e.g.*, European Commission (2009), pp. 385–390 (describing how strategic patenting is used by pharmaceutical companies to block the entry of generic competition).

[12] *See generally*, Dhavan (1990), p. 131 (tracing the historical evolution of the Paris Convention, its evolution towards greater protection for the patentee and less regulatory authority for member States, and the marked absence of any attempt to properly examine the public interest).

Besides the pursuit of a normative approach, collaboration between patent offices can also be used as a means of promoting harmonization. Such collaborations can be non-binding and persuasive in nature, in the form of technical assistance or work-sharing arrangements between patent offices. Patent office practices can acquire the force of a customary norm[13] over a long period of time.

3.1 Normative Approaches

Much of the focus on patent harmonisation has been on norm-setting processes that aim to advance harmonisation of substantive aspects of patent law. Soon after the establishment of WIPO in 1967 developing countries unsuccessfully moved proposals to reform the Paris Convention. These attempts were countered through attempts by the WIPO secretariat to advance proposals for a complementary treaty to the Paris Convention, some of the provisions of which were eventually transposed into the TRIPS Agreement in the WTO.[14] Some of the other provisions of this draft treaty were reflected in the text of the PLT that was negotiated in WIPO after the adoption of the WTO TRIPS Agreement, as well as in the Substantive Patent Law Treaty (SPLT) which was unsuccessfully negotiated in the WIPO Standing Committee on the Law of Patents (SCP) till 2005.[15]

The SPLT negotiations were part of an agenda being pursued in WIPO that regarded full and deep harmonisation of national laws relating to patentability as essential to the larger end "... to give national and regional patent authorities access to a common operational platform that permits them to cooperate, exchange information, share resources, and reduce duplication of their work."[16] This initiative, known as the WIPO Patent Agenda, also suggested exploration of other mechanisms in addition to deep substantive harmonisation, including "... not repeating work done elsewhere ..." to free up resources for the "... promotion of innovation, development of IP management skills, and other areas where active engagement may be required to realize the benefits of the patent system."[17] Rationalisation of resource use, with a major emphasis on reducing duplication by fully or partially relying on the work done by other offices either through formal treaty arrangements

[13] If States act in a certain consistent manner on a given subject matter over a period of time, it is assumed under the general principles of international law that they are acting in such a manner because they have a sense of a legal obligation, and hence such practice can be regarded as a rule of customary international law. If a majority of States believe that such a customary norm cannot be persistently objected to, it can acquire the status of a peremptory norm of international law, that would be binding on all States. Baker (2010), p. 173.

[14] Syam (2019), p. 18.

[15] Ibid.

[16] Assemblies of the member States of WIPO (2002).

[17] Ibid [10].

or through informal cooperation, was suggested as a matter of critical importance for both patent offices as well as patent applicants.[18]

This element of the WIPO patent agenda has continued to be pursued both within and outside of WIPO, even after the SPLT negotiations have been abandoned. Instead of treaty making, norm-setting on enabling reliance on the work of other patent offices is pursued through discussions on using soft law instruments such as amendment of the PCT Regulations and Administrative Instructions, or through the pursuit of exploratory discussions of patent office practices that draw from initiatives pursued in the form of cooperation between patent offices outside the framework of any WIPO treaty.

3.2 *Persuasive Approaches*

More than normative approaches, persuasive approaches have become the principal mode of promoting greater use of the work of other patent offices. The major mode of such persuasive approach has been the delivery of technical assistance and other forms of cooperation between patent offices, which have built confidence and reliance in the technical capacities, systems and work products of the patent offices from developed countries that provide such assistance and cooperation.[19] In some instances, patent offices that have received such assistance and cooperation have also agreed to fully recognise the patents granted by other patent offices without subjecting the same to further examination.[20]

3.2.1 Technical Assistance

Technical assistance is a very critical feature of cooperation between patent offices. The United States Patents and Trademarks Office (USPTO), the Japanese Patent Office (JPO) and the European Patent Office (EPO)—collectively known as the Trilateral Offices—act as the "...global hub of co-operation and convergence in patent administration."[21] Technical assistance to patent offices in developing countries has been a mode for the Trilateral Offices to introduce their technical systems for exchanging information and for search and examination of applications to the recipient offices. Indeed, such technical assistance has been delivered even before the adoption of the TRIPS Agreement.[22] The delivery of technical assistance to

---

[18] Ibid [12]–[32].

[19] Drahos (2008a), p. 151.

[20] Text to n 25.

[21] Drahos (2008a), p. 6.

[22] Ibid. For example, the 1995 annual report of the EPO which tacitly admits that its technical assistance to the ASEAN countries was driven by the objective of easing the process of prosecution

advance the economic interests of patent applicants from Europe still continues. The 2017 annual report of the EPO states that "Joint projects with our member states and patent offices from other regions are key to developing an efficient, quality-based international patent system. Tools and services developed by the EPO are often at the heart of these projects."[23]

One of the focus areas of cooperation for the EPO has been to enable recognition of European patents in foreign countries by concluding validation agreements with the EPO. The EPO has concluded validation agreements with the patent offices of Cambodia, Georgia, Moldova, Morocco, and Tunisia.[24] Pursuant to these validation agreements, a patent applicant may request that their patent applications filed or granted in the EPO be extended to these countries. Thus, where an applicant makes such a request to the EPO, the patent application filed in the EPO is recognised as a national patent application in the country with which a validation agreement has been concluded, and provisional protection is granted in that country. Subsequently, if the patent is granted in the EPO, it would have the same effect as a national patent in that country.[25] The validation requests in third countries can be made in respect of any application filed directly in the EPO as well as any international patent application filed under the PCT which subsequently entered the national phase in EPO region (European phase). The EPO is also negotiating similar validation agreements with some other countries and regional patent offices such as Brunei, Jordan, Lao PDR, the OAPI and Angola. According to the EPO, other countries in Asia have also "... signaled their interest in evaluating the possibility to enter into a validation agreement with the EPO."[26]

Countries concluding such validation agreements can, in effect, limit the flexibility that they have under the TRIPS Agreement to apply strict standards of patentability to limit or restrict frivolous patents on pharmaceutical products[27] granted by patent offices like the EPO, that apply patentability standards that are very liberal and allow some of the claims that could be rejected under a strict approach.[28] It should be noted that the examination processes do not allow patent offices to reach "definitive judgments on patentability" of a claim,[29] but rather weigh the balance of probability of a claim being patentable, without necessarily being absolutely certain.[30] If overly broad secondary pharmaceutical patents receive

of patent applications of European origin filed in those countries, through training of examiners, by incorporating search and examination results from other offices into the patent grant procedures of the patent offices that are given training, and automation of systems of patent administration.

[23] European Patent Office (2017).

[24] European Patent Office (n.d.)

[25] *See, e.g.*, European Patent Office (2016).

[26] European Patent Office (2017).

[27] 't Hoen (2020).

[28] Correa (n 4), pp. 13–16.

[29] Ibid, pp. 2–3.

[30] Ibid, p. 3.

validation outside the EPO pursuant to the validation agreements with EPO, such patents can have a negative impact on public health and access to medicines.

3.2.2 Quality of Patents

Cooperation arrangements between patent offices have been justified as a necessity in order to improve the quality of patents.[31] In this context, some national patent offices have focused on initiatives such as "... raising the threshold of inventive step, reducing the cost to examiners of rejecting an application, and reducing opportunities for applicants to manipulate the application process."[32] However, at the multilateral level, the discussion on quality of patents has largely focused on enhancing "productive efficiency"[33] in the examination process of patent offices rather than on strengthening the thresholds of patentability criteria applied in the examination process.

In the WIPO SCP developed countries have advanced several proposals for developing a work programme on "quality of patents" focusing on enhancing examination resources of patent offices through technical infrastructure development, improvement of patent office administrative processes, and exploring how patent offices can cooperate and collaborate in conducting search and examination work in order to improve patent granting processes.[34] The proposals essentially focus on using information technology solutions to build search and examination capacity, exchange information on the quality of patent office processes based on feedback given to patent offices by applicants, and identify ways in which search and examination processes can be improved.[35] Pursuant to this, the SCP has exchanged information and shared experiences on work-sharing programmes among patent offices and use of external information for search and examination.[36]

---

[31] *See,* Drahos (2008b).

[32] Ibid, p. 508. *See generally,* Correa (n 1), pp. 3–21 (describing legal and policy measures taken by various countries, including major developed countries, to reduce the proliferation of patents).

[33] Drahos (2008b), p. 508 (explaining how the backlog of patent applications beyond their search and examination capacity has driven the Trilateral offices to explore means to reduce pendency and ensure timely and expedited disposal of patent applications. Long-standing cooperation with the Trilateral Offices has also imbibed the quest for productive efficiency in the patent offices from developing countries).

[34] *See, e.g.,* WIPO (Standing Committee on the Law of Patents) (2011) and Proposal by the delegation of Denmark (2011).

[35] Ibid.

[36] *See, e.g.,* WIPO (Standing Committee on the Law of Patents) (2013a), Proposal by the delegations of the Republic of Korea, the United Kingdom and the United States of America regarding work sharing between offices in order to improve efficiencies of the patent system (2014), Proposal by the delegation of the United States of America on the study of worksharing (2015), and Proposal by the delegations of the Czech Republic, Kenya, Mexico, Singapore and the United Kingdom (2018).

In 2016, the twenty-fourth session of the SCP agreed to undertake a survey on how WIPO member States understood "quality of patents" and implementation of cooperation and collaboration between patent offices on search and examination of patent applications. The most frequently mentioned cooperation arrangements in responses to the survey[37] were the following: access to documents/databases/search systems of other offices; use of search and examination products from other offices; collaborative search and examination initiatives; carrying out search and examination for other offices; exchange of examiners with other patent offices; training on search and examination by other patent offices.

4 PCT Reforms

An important vehicle for promoting cooperation between patent offices all over the world is the PCT administered by WIPO. The PCT essentially allows the filing of an international patent application in the place of multiple national patent applications. The international patent application can designate countries where national phase entry of the application may be sought by the applicant after a preliminary review of the application (not an examination) by patent offices which are recognised as PCT International Search and Examination Authorities (International Authorities). This review is called the PCT international search and examination or the "international phase."[38] In the international phase, all PCT applications go through a mandatory international prior art search with the applicants having an option to also seek an international preliminary examination report after the international search report is produced. Upon national phase entry, the patent application filed under PCT is treated as a national patent application and examined as such by the relevant national patent office. The reports produced during the international phase are available to the national offices for reference, but it is not binding on them to rely on those reports in making their decision on a patent application.

[37] WIPO (Standing Committee on the Law of Patents) (2017) and Responses to the questionnaire on the term "Quality of Patents" and cooperation between patent offices in search and examination (part 2) (2017).

[38] The PCT international phase timelines allowed a patent applicant to delay the start of national processing of an international patent application. Under the Paris Convention, a patent must be filed in a country within 12 months from the date of first filing of the application in another country. Under PCT, while the international application must be filed within this 12-month period, the national phase entry can be delayed to 30 months from the priority date. This was done to enable an applicant to assess the viability of obtaining patent protection in a territory for a claimed invention before actually pursuing national search and examination. *See* Mossinghof (1999) (explaining that this was particularly important for pharmaceutical companies by enabling them to file a patent on a promising drug and then using the opportunity of delayed national examination in designated countries to assess the viability of pursing a national patent in a country based on factors as such clinical trial outcomes).

Though the reports produced in the PCT international phase are not binding upon national offices, this system also allows patent offices that produce the international search and examination report in their capacity as International Search and Examination Authority (ISEA) to influence the national examination of that application in a developing country.[39] As explained by the WIPO secretariat, one advantage of the PCT system is that "... the search and examination work of patent offices can be considerably reduced or *virtually eliminated* ... (emphasis added)."[40]

The accession of developing countries to the PCT has been made an obligation in various bilateral or regional free trade agreements.[41] However, while a large number of developing countries have acceded to the PCT, the system is predominantly used by applicants from a few countries.[42] Moreover, the international search and examination under the PCT system is conducted only by a few patent offices, and the majority of the international search and examination reports are produced by the EPO acting as an international search authority.[43] At the same time, many developing countries that have joined the PCT system lack capacity in conducting substantive examination, though they have witnessed significant increase in the number of patent applications filed in their countries through the PCT route.[44]

Developed countries have consistently pursued the objective of eliminating the need for search and examination of patent applications in the national phase in WIPO discussions on reforming the PCT system.[45] The PCT system that was established in 1970 has been significantly transformed today through incremental reforms

---

[39] Drahos (2008a).

[40] WIPO, 'Patent Cooperation Treaty ("PCT") (1970)' (wipo.int) <http://www.wipo.int/pct/en/treaty/about.html> accessed 9 May 2020.

[41] For example, article 18.7 of the Comprehensive and Progressive Trans-Pacific Partnership Agreement makes ratification or accession to the PCT a mandatory obligation for all countries that are party to the treaty. Government of Canada, 'Consolidated TPP Text – Chapter 18 – Intellectual Property' (international.gc.ca) https://www.international.gc.ca/trade-commerce/trade-agreements-accords-commerciaux/agr-acc/tpp-ptp/text-texte/18.aspx?lang=eng.

[42] May (2007), p. 49.

[43] According WIPO statistics, more than 70% of International Search Reports under PCT between 2000 to 2018 have been issued by EPO, USPTO and JPO. Though the number of International Search Reports from China and South Korea have significantly increased in recent years, the EPO, USPTO and JPO continue to produce more than 65% of these reports between 2015 to 2018. *See* World Intellectual Property Organization (n.d.).

[44] *See, e.g.*, Shashikant (2014), pp. 17–21 (pointing out that most patent applications in the African Regional Intellectual Property Office (ARIPO) are filed through the PCT route while the ARIPO has a capacity of 12 patent examiners, and that ARIPO relies heavily on the results of the PCT or foreign search and examination results and on the EPO guidelines).

[45] *See, e.g.*, WIPO (Committee on Reform of the Patent Cooperation Treaty) (2001) (proposal to make PCT search and examination binding on PCT Contracting Parties while simplifying PCT procedures for patent applicants); WIPO (Patent Cooperation Treaty (PCT) Working Group) (2018), (proposal by the WIPO secretariat to amend the PCT Regulations to enable national patent offices to delegate their national office functions to the office of any other PCT Contracting State or an intergovernmental organisation); *also see,* Rathod and Ali (2018).

introduced through amendments to the Rules, Regulations and Administrative Instructions through which the PCT system operates.

Several proposals have been advanced by developed countries to discourage duplication of international phase work under the PCT system in the national phase, encourage collaborative search and examination or work sharing between patent offices, or enable national search and examination to be dispensed with at the option of a PCT Contracting Party. The US had submitted a proposal at the PCT Union Assembly of WIPO in 2000 for reform of the PCT in two stages—first, simplifying certain procedures and aligning the PCT with the PLT, followed by a comprehensive overhaul of the PCT system.[46] This proposal had received broad support from most developed countries.

The US proposal was transmitted to the PCT Union Assembly by the WIPO secretariat with a recommendation to establish a special body that should consider the proposal along with other possible proposals and report to the PCT Union Assembly.[47] The PCT Union Assembly established an ad hoc Committee on Reform of the PCT. The committee met in two sessions from 2001 to 2002 and discussed a number of proposals from WIPO member States and observers.[48]

---

[46] WIPO (International Patent Cooperation Union (PCT Union) Assembly) (2000a), (the proposal pointed to the need to simplify PCT procedures and converge PCT and patent office practices to the extent possible to facilitate obtaining worldwide patent protection through simplified application, preferably in electronic format, and minimize the distinction between international and national processing of the patent applications. Eventually, the proposal envisaged adopting procedures that would enable substantive rights to be granted through the PCT. More specifically, the changes proposed to the PCT system in the first stage included the following: elimination of the concept of designation of PCT Contracting Parties in respect of which an international patent application is filed, thus making an international application applicable to all PCT Contracting Parties and relieving the applicant from paying the designation fees; eliminating residency and nationality requirements for filing international patent applications, thus enabling any person regardless of residence or nationality to file a PCT application in any patent office of a PCT Contracting Party; aligning PCT filing date requirements to the PLT; aligning PCT rules on filing of missing parts in an application to the rules in the PLT; enabling an applicant to request supplementary search and examination from multiple International Search Authorities; subjecting all PCT applications to a preliminary international examination following the international search report; enabling further delaying of national phase entry of an application at the option of the applicant; combining search and examination processes; and, facilitating electronic publication of the application and transmission of search and examination results. The comprehensive reforms envisaged were regional consolidation of international search and examination authorities; eliminating the distinction between national and international applications to avoid duplication of processing the application in the international and national phases; making positive examination results from certain PCT international search and examination authorities binding on Contracting States; and, allowing for further deferment of national phase entry of an international application at the option of the applicant).

[47] WIPO (International Patent Cooperation Union (PCT Union) Assembly) (2000b).

[48] *See,* WIPO (2001) (for the proposals made by the Austria, Australia, Canada, Cuba, the Czech Republic, Denmark, EPO, France, India, Israel, Japan, Republic of Korea, the Netherlands, Spain, Slovakia, Switzerland, Turkey, the UK and the USA).

4.1 Working Group on PCT Reforms

The Working Group on Reform of the Patent Cooperation Treaty was established by the PCT Union Assembly[49] pursuant to the recommendation of the ad hoc committee. In its first two sessions in 2001 and 2002, the working group discussed the issues that were identified for further examination by the committee. The WIPO secretariat prepared draft proposals[50] based on the recommendations of the working group and submitted the same to the committee at its second session in 2001. These proposals were broadly focused on three issues: improved coordination of international search and international preliminary examination under the PCT and the time limit for national phase entry; the concept and operation of the designation system; and changes related to the PLT.

4.1.1 Establishment of a Written Opinion on Patentability to Accompany the International Search Report

On the recommendation of the committee, the PCT Union Assembly amended the PCT Regulations to the effect that a patent office could act as an International Search Authority or an International Preliminary Examination Authority under the PCT if it also held an appointment in the other capacity.[51] This amendment effectively allowed the same patent office to act as both the search and the examining authority in the international phase. This also enabled the expansion of the role of the International Search Authority through another amendment to the PCT Regulations to require them to issue in addition to the International Search Report—that would identify prior art documents in their order of relevance in relation to the claims made in the international patent application—a Written Opinion on whether the claims satisfy the patentability requirements in the light of the prior art revealed in the international search. This fundamentally changed the international search phase in the PCT to include a written opinion in the nature of a first examination report (FER) on the patent application. If an international preliminary examination under chapter II of the PCT was not requested by the applicant, the International Bureau of WIPO was required to prepare an International Preliminary Report on Patentability (IPRP) based on the Written Opinion of the International Search Authority (WOISA).[52] Thus, even if the applicant does not exercise the option of seeking an international preliminary examination following the international search report and publication of the application, national offices today receive not just a search report but also an

[49] WIPO (International Patent Cooperation Union (PCT Union) Assembly) (2001).

[50] *See,* WIPO (Committee on Reform of the Patent Cooperation Treaty (PCT)) (2002) and WIPO International Patent Cooperation Union (2002a, b, c, d).

[51] WIPO (International Patent Cooperation Union (PCT Union) Assembly) (2002).

[52] WIPO (Committee on Reform of the PCT), PCT/R/2/7 (n 51) [10].

IPRP on whether the application *prima facie* meets the patentability criteria. Deeper harmonisation of patent examination procedures was thus set in motion.

4.1.2 Automatic Designation of all PCT Contracting Parties for National Phase Entry

The PCT Union Assembly also approved amendments to the PCT Regulations[53] to make the filing of a PCT application automatically applicable for national phase entry in all PCT Contracting Parties.[54] Thus, applicants are no longer required to designate national or regional patent offices for national phase entry and pay associated fees.

4.1.3 Establishment of an Optional Supplementary International Search

The committee recommended to continue future discussions on PCT reforms in the mode of the working group directly reporting to the PCT Union Assembly on the basis of the proposals submitted and future proposals. Several proposals relating to the reform of the PCT system were discussed in this working group in nine sessions held from 2001 to 2007.

The third session of the working group discussed the outstanding proposals relating to PCT reforms.[55] These included proposals relating to further improvement of the international search and examination system, for instance, to allow the applicants to opt for supplementary or top-up search.[56] The fourth session of the working group discussed an options paper on the future development of the international search and examination system, which suggested that the possibility of considering substantive revisions to the PCT for allowing search or examination by multiple authorities, introducing a supplementary search, a "top-up" search for new documents during the international examination, or even allowing a re-examination

[53] WIPO (International Patent Cooperation Union (PCT Union) Assembly), 'Report' (n 52).

[54] WIPO (Committee on Reform of the PCT), PCT/R/2/6 (n 51).

[55] WIPO (Working Group on Reform of the Patent Cooperation Treaty (PCT)) (2002a). The proposals were categorized into two groups based on whether the proposal would require an amendment of the treaty. Increasing reliance by national offices on the international search reports and IPERs, electronic transmission of search and examination results, establishment of regional patent offices as ISA, and technical assistance were among the issues that were deemed to not require any treaty amendment to be implemented. The working group also discussed whether the treaty itself should be revised, and the possible ways of undertaking its revision. It also recommended to the PCT Union Assembly to amend the PCT Regulations to allow the applicants to file for correction or addition of a priority claim in the international application within a stipulated time period.

[56] See, WIPO (Working Group on Reform of the Patent Cooperation Treaty (PCT)) (2002b).

by the International Authority after national phase entry of the application.[57] It was also suggested that the international examination report could also indicate whether the application included subject matter on which there is variance in national laws concerning their patentability.[58] It was assumed that this would facilitate non-duplication of search and examination at the national phase on subject matter regarding which the application of the patentability criteria was relatively harmonized in practice. It is pertinent to note here that such harmonisation was being pursued by the Trilateral Offices through their technical assistance and cooperation programmes with national and regional patent Offices of several countries.

The WIPO secretariat suggested that States that did not have their own search and examination systems, or wished to reduce duplication of search and examination done by other offices, or to have a system for validation of patents in certain cases, could consider adoption of an optional protocol to register patents based on national phase entry accompanied by the international search and examination report, or allow the applicant to amend the application in case of a negative international examination report so as to enter the national phase with a positive report on patentability, or seek a re-examination at the international phase even after national phase entry.[59] The working group requested the WIPO Director-General to undertake consultations on these options.[60]

At the sixth session of the working group, the WIPO secretariat submitted a proposal for amendments to certain rules under the PCT Regulations to allow the applicants to request for a supplementary international search by other International Search Authorities in order to obtain a more thorough search report, and also to request for an updated or "top-up" search during the international preliminary examination.[61] Following extended discussions over the next three sessions of the working group, consensus could not be reached. However, the 2007 PCT Union Assembly agreed to a proposal by France[62] and a related joint proposal by Japan and Spain[63] to amend the PCT Regulations to allow the applicants to make a request for a supplementary international search.[64]

[57] *See,* WIPO (Working Group on Reform of the Patent Cooperation Treaty (PCT)) (2003a).

[58] Ibid [18].

[59] WIPO (Working Group on Reform of the Patent Cooperation Treaty (PCT)) (2003b).

[60] WIPO (Working Group on Reform of the Patent Cooperation Treaty (PCT)) (2003c).

[61] WIPO (Working Group on Reform of the Patent Cooperation Treaty (PCT)) (2004).

[62] WIPO (International Patent Cooperation Union (PCT Union) Assembly) (2007a).

[63] WIPO (International Patent Cooperation Union (PCT Union) Assembly) (2007b).

[64] WIPO (International Patent Cooperation Union (PCT Union) Assembly) (2007c).

4.2 New PCT Working Group

The WIPO secretariat presented a report on the PCT reforms process to the 2007 PCT Union Assembly which noted that the working group had addressed all the issues on its agenda relating to the reform of the PCT and had reached agreement on amending the PCT Regulations on some of those issues.[65] However, it also noted that there would be an ongoing need for minor changes to the PCT Regulations in relation to certain proposals. It thus recommended the Assembly to formally declare the end of the mandate of the Committee on Reform of the PCT and the working group.[66] The Assembly agreed to a proposal by the WIPO secretariat to establish a new working group to do preparatory work on matters that would be considered by the Assembly in future.[67] This new working group—known as the PCT Working Group—has been meeting annually since 2008 with a broad mandate to discuss any matter which requires consideration of the PCT Union Assembly.

Discussions continued in the new PCT Working Group on promoting greater reliance on the International Search and Examination reports under the PCT system based on a preliminary discussion paper by the WIPO secretariat on enhancing the value of international search and preliminary examination under the PCT.[68] The discussion paper pointed to existing mechanisms within the PCT which can deliver similar benefits as work sharing mechanisms outside the PCT system, with the advantage of being more effective and being able to reach out to a larger audience. The paper raised certain questions for further consideration in order to improve the implementation or use of those mechanisms. The WIPO secretariat is of the view that any deficiency within the PCT system is primarily due to the way in which the system has been used sub-optimally by national offices, including International Authorities, and this could be addressed within the PCT system without engaging in any new PCT reform exercise.[69] At the request of the working group the WIPO secretariat produced another study on how to make the content of the international preliminary examination report more useful for the purpose of patentability assessment by national offices, and how to improve the international examination process itself.[70]

The second session of the working group also discussed a number of other proposals aimed at deeper reform of the PCT. These included a roadmap proposed by the WIPO secretariat on the work that could be undertaken to facilitate a greater use of the PCT system by national patent offices, including International Authorities, with a focus on reduction or elimination of unnecessary duplication of search and examination work undertaken in the international phase when the application enters

[65] WIPO (International Patent Cooperation Union (PCT Union) Assembly) (2007d).

[66] Ibid.

[67] WIPO (International Patent Cooperation Union (PCT Union) Assembly) (n.d.).

[68] WIPO (Patent Cooperation Treaty (PCT) Working Group) (2008).

[69] Ibid [3].

[70] WIPO (Patent Cooperation Treaty (PCT) Working Group) (2009a).

the national phase, greater use of work-sharing mechanisms developed outside the PCT system, and with the objective of ensuring high quality of granted patents while at the same time reducing the backlog of pending patent applications.[71] The working group also discussed other related proposals by the Republic of Korea for a three-track PCT system[72] and a proposal by the US for comprehensive PCT reform.[73]

The proposal by the WIPO secretariat on a roadmap for PCT reforms was discussed extensively through the session. The roadmap aimed to achieve a number of milestones[74] which included reaching agreement on establishing a second written opinion prior to the issuance of a negative international examination report so as to allow the applicant the opportunity to amend the claims, including a "top-up" search in the international examination phase for prior art that may not have been available at the time of the international search done earlier, and establishing a third party observation system in the international phase.

Some developing countries were particularly concerned that the proposals in the roadmap as well as the related proposals on work sharing and comprehensive PCT reform effectively promoted harmonization of national patent examination practices,

---

[71] WIPO (Patent Cooperation Treaty (PCT) Working Group) (2009b).

[72] WIPO (Patent Cooperation Treaty (PCT) Working Group) (2009c) (the Korean proposal sought to introduce amendments to the timelines in the PCT international search and examination phase to give the applicants the option to request for either accelerated examination, regular examination or deferred examination).

[73] WIPO (Patent Cooperation Treaty (PCT) Working Group) (2009d) (the US proposal suggested the establishment of a new PCT (PCT II) which would allow the applicant to submit prior art document along with the application, which would then be searched by two Authorities, and an international preliminary report on patentability would be established by a third International Authority, which would also receive third party observations. A positive international report on patentability would automatically form the basis for the grant of a national patent, unless a national office expressly rejects the report within a specified period).

[74] WIPO (Patent Cooperation Treaty (PCT) Working Group), PCT/WG/2/3 (n 71). The roadmap aimed to achieve the following milestones to improve the PCT system: (1) obtain a commitment from offices acting as International Search Authorities to not repeat the search done by them at the international phase when the application enters the national phase in the same office; (2) work towards elimination of reservations, notifications and declarations of incompatibility to the PCT, PCT Regulations and Administrative Instructions in order to ensure a consistent effect of the international patent applications in all Contracting States; (3) reaching an agreement that all International Authorities will issue at least one written opinion prior to the issuance of a negative international preliminary report on patentability, at least in cases where the applicant has provided a substantive response to the written opinion of the International Search Authority; (4) develop a system of third party observations on novelty and inventive step to be made available to the International Preliminary Examination Authorities and designated offices; (5) including a "top-up" search in international preliminary examination on patentability; (6) eliminating unnecessary processing of an application through both the national as well as the PCT route and exploring the reasons why applicants use different routes for filing the same application; (7) establish a pilot project on collaborative search and examination by testing models allowing examiners from at least 3 different offices to work on the same application to establish a common international search report or written opinion; and, (8) undertake discussion in the working group on measures that could be undertaken to ensure that procedures and fee structures are appropriate to encourage use of the PCT system in a manner which is efficient and beneficial for all applicants and offices.

which could limit the ability of national Offices to undertake search and examination of patent applications entering the national phase through the PCT route.[75] The working group agreed to undertake further discussion on the proposals based on an assessment of the need for any change in the PCT system in the light of existing problems and challenges facing the system, while ensuring that the freedom of Contracting States to prescribe, interpret and apply substantive conditions of patentability, and without seeking substantive harmonization or harmonization of national search and examination procedures.[76]

Thus, the third session of the PCT Working Group discussed a report[77] by the WIPO secretariat analysing the functioning of the PCT system and the problems and challenges it faced. The Working Group endorsed the recommendations made in the report related to backlogs and improving the quality of granted patents,[78] timeliness in the international phase,[79] the quality of international search and preliminary

[75] WIPO (Patent Cooperation Treaty (PCT) Working Group) (2009e).

[76] Ibid [94].

[77] WIPO (Patent Cooperation Treaty (PCT) Working Group) (2010a). The report advanced a number of recommendations to address the following challenges relating to the PCT system—assisting patent offices to address the problem of backlogs in processing patent applications and in improving the quality of granted patents; enhancing the actual and perceived quality of international search and examination in the PCT; creating incentives for the applicants to use the PCT system efficiently; addressing skills and manpower shortage in patent offices; addressing the need for access to effective search systems for national offices; addressing cost and accessibility of the PCT system for applicants; addressing the consistency and availability of safeguards in the form of reservations, notifications or declarations of incompatibility to the PCT, the regulations and administrative instructions; provision of technical assistance; and use of PCT information for technology transfer.

[78] Ibid [143], [146], [149]. These recommendations are the following: (1) Offices which act as International Authorities should take steps to improve the actual and perceived quality of the reports they establish under the PCT system to ensure that they provide content that designated and elected offices wish to take into account; (2) designated and elected offices should review the content of ISRs and IPRPs and make recommendations for their improvement; (3) the International Bureau of WIPO and the International Authorities should review the proposals for changes in the content of ISRs and IPRPs and report back to the next session of the Working Group; (4) the exercise should in no way affect the right of designated and elected offices to use the ISRs and IPRPs as they see fit in accordance with their national laws and policies; (5) national offices which conduct search and examination in the national phase should consult with the International Bureau of WIPO on ways of making their national reports available to other national Offices and the International Bureau should ensure making these reports available through WIPO's PATENTSCOPE database; (6) the International Bureau of WIPO should make available a system of allowing third party observations on published international applications. The Working Group also recommended that the Chief Economist of WIPO should undertake a study to analyse the root causes behind the surge in patent applications and the consequent heavy load on the international patent system.

[79] Ibid [152]. One of these recommendations required International Authorities to ensure they have adequate resources to conduct the expected number of international search and preliminary examination in addition to their national work and give appropriate priority to international work in case of backlogs to ensure timely availability of the results to the other national offices.

examination,[80] incentives for applicants to effectively use the system,[81] skills and manpower shortages,[82] access to effective search systems,[83] cost and other accessibility issues,[84] consistency and availability of safeguards,[85] technical assistance, PCT information and technology transfer.[86] The Working Group also discussed a

---

[80]Ibid [165], [170]. These recommendations were the following: (1) International Authorities should develop internal quality management systems in accordance with the quality framework under the International Search and Preliminary Examination Guidelines, with the objective of developing high quality ISRs and IPRPs; (2) International Authorities should seek ways to effectively search documentation in other languages; (3) national offices whose national patent collections are not readily available in electronic form should consider digitizing them; (4) the international Bureau should coordinate the development of a centralized system for designated offices to give feedback to International Authorities; (5) International Authorities should recognise the quality of their own work and not routinely conduct more than a "top-up" search for the same application in the national phase; (6) International Authorities should seek to make more information available relating to search strategies so that designated offices can easily assess the scope of the international search conducted; (7) International Authorities should seek to cite documents from a wide range of sources where possible; (8) International Authorities should encourage examiners to give good explanation of the relevance of cited documents, especially where the examiner considers there is lack of inventive step.

[81]Ibid [176]. These recommendations were the following: (1) the International Bureau and national offices should recommend applicants to prepare their applications in good time and conduct their own prior art search before drafting their claims; (2) International Authorities should offer applicants a good opportunity for dialogue with the examiner during the international preliminary examination, including at least one written opinion before establishing a negative IPRP; (3) Contracting States should consider possible incentives which could be introduced at the international or national level to encourage applicants to file higher quality applications and have defects corrected in the international phase.

[82]Ibid [181]. National offices which are able to offer training in search and substantive examination were encouraged to coordinate their activities in order to provide complementary training.

[83]Ibid [185]. The International Bureau and Contracting States were encouraged to seek practical and affordable ways for national offices to develop online searching capabilities.

[84]Ibid [193]. The International Bureau and Contracting States were recommended to consider ways in which procedures could be simplified for applicants without needing to change national laws; review the level of fees for different types of applicants; review the PCT Applicant's Guide to ensure that it is updated and provides information that is useful and easy to understand; ensure while updating the PCT online systems that the language, interfaces and associated help reduce the need to consult the PCT Regulations by the users.

[85]Ibid [198]. Contracting States were recommended to review their notifications of incompatibility with the PCT Regulations and Administrative instructions and seek to determine whether they can withdraw the notifications of incompatibility.

[86]Ibid. The following recommendations were adopted: (1) when requesting technical assistance in the context of the PCT offices and Contracting States should ensure that the purpose of the request is clear and that the International Bureau is aware of the related national policies and ensure that the advice, training and systems which are delivered take the needs and national policies properly into account; (2) a study be conducted by the International Bureau to look into the issue of coordination of technical assistance for developing countries under Article 51 of the PCT; (3) that the international Bureau work with national offices to deliver effective patent status information; (4) a system of promoting licensing of patented technologies should be established enabling patentees to indicate their willingness to out license their patented technologies; (5) that the International Bureau

proposal by the WIPO secretariat for establishing a third-party observation system in the PCT and recommended that the WIPO secretariat should begin the development of such a system[87] which has been operational since July 2012.

In the following sessions of the working group, some of PCT International Authorities reported on implementation of pilot projects between them on collaborative search and examination[88] as well as integration of existing work sharing mechanisms outside the PCT system with the PCT. The PCT Regulations and Administrative instructions were also further amended to require International Preliminary Examination Authorities to conduct a mandatory "top-up" search for additional prior art that may not have been available at the time of conducting the international search.[89] Subsequent sessions of the PCT have continued to discuss proposals on work sharing within the PCT system and share experiences of work sharing arrangements between national offices as well as pilot projects within the PCT system.

5 Work Sharing Arrangements Between Patent Offices

Since the 1980s, the Trilateral Offices have entered into MOUs which have effectively made them "... the global hub of co-operation and convergence in patent administration."[90] An integral part of this cooperation between the Trilateral Offices, which have been gradually extended to include other patent offices, has been the exploration of various work sharing arrangements relating to different aspects of the work of a patent office, involving two or more patent offices. The possibility of integration of such work sharing arrangements inside the PCT system is also being discussed in the PCT Working Group of WIPO. The WIPO SCP discussions on quality of patents have also focused on sharing experiences of such work sharing arrangements.

Work sharing arrangements have typically evolved through cooperation between patent offices over time through an incremental approach, led by the few major patent offices that process the bulk of the world's patent applications. Such cooperation leverages the use of information and communications technologies (ICT) through digitization of patent documents, machine translation, electronic exchange of priority documents as well as search and examination reports. From mere exchange of information and reports, the work sharing arrangements can develop

undertake a follow up study on how effectively the PCT system has functioned in terms of disseminating technical information and facilitating access to technology and technical assistance to developing countries.

[87] WIPO (Patent Cooperation Treaty (PCT) Working Group) (2010b).

[88] WIPO (Patent Cooperation Treaty (PCT) Working Group) (2012).

[89] WIPO (Patent Cooperation Treaty (PCT) Working Group) (2013).

[90] Drahos (2008a).

further to include greater cooperation wherein offices agree to make use, sometimes to the best possible extent, the work products of other offices. The emphasis, as discussed previously, is on increasing productive efficiency through speeding up the search and examination process.

5.1 Trilateral Cooperation

The EPO, JPO and the USPTO have implemented a number of work sharing arrangements between them under the Trilateral Cooperation that was launched in 1983 in order to deal with the dramatic increase in the number of patent application filings impacting the Trilateral Offices.[91] The initial area of cooperation was focused on digitization of all patent documents issued after 1920 and creating a common database of such documents. This was further expanded in subsequent years by the Trilateral Offices to develop a network for exchanging priority documents, an electronic exchange format for priority documents and a common patent application format.[92]

Digitization, creation of technology specialized databases, and creation of a common ICT architecture facilitated electronic filing of applications and the conduct of paperless electronic search. However, the Trilateral Cooperation was not limited to facilitating exchange of documents. A number of comparative studies conducted by the Trilateral Offices on examination practices and the application of patentability criteria resulted in the harmonization of patent examination practices in various emerging technology fields, and also led to efforts to revise the PCT international search and examination guidelines.[93]

The Trilateral Offices have also explored a number of projects for collaborative search and examination on a common patent application. In 2007 the USPTO and JPO launched a pilot project called "New Route" under which a national or regional patent application filed in either of the offices is deemed to be an application in the other office, and the search and examination results produced by the office of first filing can be used by the office of second filing in their own search and examination of the application. The applicant is also provided additional time, similar to that available under the PCT, to decide on whether to pursue the application in the other office, based on the search and examination results in the office of first filing.[94] The Trilateral Offices also agreed to undertake a pilot project known as the "Triway Pilot Programme" from 2008 to 2009, wherein all three offices agreed to conduct their own prior art search on a corresponding national application filed in all three offices

---

[91] Trilateral (n.d.-a).

[92] Trilateral (n.d.-b).

[93] *See* Trilateral (n.d.-c).

[94] *See,* Trilateral, 'New Route' (trilateral.net) https://www.trilateral.net/projects/worksharing/new-route/new-route_index.

and share the search results with each other in a timely manner.[95] In 2008, the Trilateral Offices also launched a pilot project on Strategic Handling of Applications for Rapid Examination (SHARE) under which each office agreed to give procedural priority to examining applications for which it is the office of first filing, with the understanding that the office of second filing would use the search and examination results of the office of first filing to the maximum extent practicable.[96]

5.2 *IP5 Cooperation*

With the emergence of the patent offices of China (CNIPA) and South Korea (KIPO) among the leading patent offices in the world alongside the EPO, JPO and the USPTO, a similar framework of cooperation as among the Trilateral Offices has been established to include the CNIPA and KIPO.[97] This group is known as the IP5. The IP5 cooperation is particularly significant because almost 80% of the total patent applications in the world and almost 95% of the international patent applications under the PCT are processed by the IP5 offices.[98] The IP5 was launched in 2007 as a forum for cooperation among the leading five patent offices with a focus on "the elimination of unnecessary duplication of work among the offices, enhancement of patent examination efficiency and quality, and guarantee of the stability of patent right."[99] In 2017, the IP5 expanded their vision to cooperate on "Patent harmonization of practices and procedures, enhanced work-sharing, high-quality and timely search and examination results, and seamless access to patent information to promote an efficient, cost-effective and user-friendly international patent landscape."[100]

It should be noted, as discussed in the previous section, that around the same time as the IP5 was launched, similar initiatives focused on promoting work sharing with a focus on elimination of "unnecessary duplication" was also being pursued in the WIPO discussions on PCT reforms. This means that when the proposals for reforms in the PCT international phase were advanced in the PCT working group discussions, the patent offices that handled almost the entire workload of the PCT international phase work were largely aligned to the proposed reforms. Reform of the PCT system is an integral part of the work of the IP5 which has also initiated a pilot project on collaborative search and examination of international applications under the PCT. The IP5 group's perspectives and initiatives on quality management systems and work sharing arrangements are also discussed for possible integration in the PCT system.

[95] Hu (2017).

[96] Neppel (2012).

[97] Ibid.

[98] fiveIPoffices (n.d.).

[99] Ibid.

[100] Ibid.

One of the areas of cooperation among the IP5 offices is harmonization of patent classification systems among the IP5 offices as well as revision of the International Patent Classification (IPC) system administered by WIPO, to align the same to the Cooperative Patent Classification (CPC) system of the IP5 and to introduce new classifications in fast moving emerging technology areas.[101] Such cooperation is also part of the Trilateral Cooperation discussed above.

Another major area of focus for the IP5 has been the "Global Dossier" project which seeks to offer, in a single portal, free and secure access to the dossier information on all applications in the same patent family that have been filed in the IP5 offices. The Global Dossier information has been expanded and linked with the WIPO Centralized Access to Search and Examination (CASE) system to include dossier information on patent applications under the same family filed in other patent offices outside the IP5 group.[102]

Beyond the creation and expansion of systems to facilitate sharing of dossier information and conducting collaborative search and examination, the IP5 have also been exploring harmonisation of patent office practices within the IP5 in respect of patent application and grant procedures. It is possible that as the office practices are harmonised within the IP5, these could be extended through bilateral cooperation arrangements by the any of the IP5 offices to other patent offices across the world.

5.3 The Vancouver Group

In 2008, the IP offices of Australia, Canada and the United Kingdom (UK) formed a collaboration arrangement between them known as the Vancouver Group, with a similar focus as the IP5 and parallel discussions in WIPO on elimination of unnecessary duplication and ensuring more effective work sharing. Mutual exploitation of the work of each office with regard to patent search and examination has been a priority area of the collaboration between the Vancouver Group offices. Thus, the Vancouver Group has agreed on a set of principles on the basis of which mutual exploitation can be undertaken. These include relying on the grant of patent or the search and examination report of another Vancouver group office where possible, taking self-initiative for such work sharing without requiring the applicant to make a request, and utilizing the WIPO CASE system for the same.[103]

[101] fiveIPoffices, 'Classification (Working Group 1)' (fiveipoffices.org) https://www.fiveipoffices.org/activities/class.

[102] WIPO (n.d.-a).

[103] *See*, Vancouver Group (n.d.).

5.4 PROSUR

PROSUR is a regional collaboration initiative launched in 2010 between IP offices of 13 Latin American countries.[104] The PROPSUR initiative seeks to enhance efficiency and quality in the search, examination and decision-making processes of the participating IP offices through the exchange of data and information systems. The primary focus of the PROSUR countries is on exchange of information and opinions on patent applications, which can be available as a reference for the other participating offices in the conduct of their own search and examination.[105] The information is shared among the PROSUR countries using ICT such as WIPO CASE and the electronic platform for collaborative examination (e-PEC) created by the patent offices of Argentina and Brazil.

5.5 ASPEC

In 2009 the nine member States of the Association of South-East Asian Nations (ASEAN) launched a regional patent work sharing programme called the ASEAN Patent Examination Cooperation (ASPEC).[106] Similar to PROSUR, ASPEC allows IP offices from ASEAN Member States to utilise search and examination results on a corresponding application in other ASEAN Member States. In 2019, applicants were also given the possibility of requesting utilizing the ASPEC mechanism to use international search and examination reports produced under the PCT in relation to a corresponding application by an International Authority within the ASPEC participating countries.

5.6 IP BRICS

The IP offices of Brazil, Russia, India, China and South Africa (BRICS) launched a cooperation among the BRICS IP offices in 2012. In 2013 the IP BRICS agreed to a roadmap for cooperation.[107] The areas of cooperation agreed upon in this forum include exchange of IP office staff and examiner trainings, exchange of examination related patent information data and IP documentation exchange and sharing, and

---

[104] The countries that are represented in PROSUR are Argentina, Brazil, Chile, Colombia, Costa Rica, the Dominican Republic, Ecuador, El Salvador, Nicaragua, Panama, Paraguay, Peru, and Uruguay. *See*, PROSUR (n.d.).

[105] Castillo (2012).

[106] ASEAN Intellectual Property Portal (n.d.).

[107] IP BRICS (2013).

patent processes and procedures.[108] As part of this cooperation, annual meetings of the heads of the BRICS IP offices have been held since 2013, and 2 patent examiner trainings have been organized till date.[109] Studies to explore examination practices and procedures relating to specific kinds of patent claims, such as Markush claims[110] relating to pharmaceutical patents, have also been proposed.[111]

5.7 *Patent Prosecution Highway*

The Patent Prosecution Highway (PPH) is the most extensive work sharing arrangement outside the PCT system. The PPH is a collaboration framework between participating patent offices in which an applicant receiving a positive determination on the patentability of a claim can make a request for accelerated examination of the corresponding claim in another participating patent office by using the search and examination results from the first office. According to the USPTO, an examiner will generally examine the application within 2–3 months of the PPH examination request being granted,[112] though there is no maximum time-period within which the examination should be done by the office conducting the accelerated processing. The processing time would obviously vary from one patent office to another relative to the number of applications they have to examine, with offices with a lower number of applications processing PPH accelerated search and examination faster than offices with higher number of applications.[113]

The PPH began in 2006 as a pilot project between the USPTO and the JPO within the framework of the Trilateral Cooperation. Within a decade, the PPH has expanded to include a large number of national and regional patent offices, including from developing countries, into some form of a PPH agreement. The PPH agreements are

[108] IP BRICS (n.d.-a).

[109] IP BRICS (n.d.-b).

[110] Markush claims are patent claims on a general chemical formula that includes a wide range of possible alternative chemical compounds. Drafting a Markush claim enables a patent applicant to claim through a single application a patent covering several alternative compounds that could be used. However, applications with Markush formulas only provide a few examples of possible alternative compounds while claiming a much broader range of such possible compounds without actually disclosing those compounds in the application. Thus, patents granted on Markush formulas "... allow the patentee to control a large number of compounds that have not been actually obtained..., but only theoretically inferred from their possible equivalence with other compounds covered by the general formula." Correa (n 4), pp. 16–17.

[111] IP BRICS, 'Patent Processes and Procedure – Procedures for patent examination involving Markush claims', http://www.ipbrics.org/secondpage/project/d004.html.

[112] USPTO (n.d.-a).

[113] For instance, in 2019 the average pendency from a PPH request by the applicant to the final decision in the second office was 1.3 months in Australia and 18.4 months in the U.S. *See*, Patent Prosecution Highway Portal Site, 'Statistics'(jpo.go.) https://www.jpo.go.jp/e/toppage/pph-portal/statistics.html.

in the nature of memorandum of understanding or collaboration agreements between patent offices and not legal treaties. Hence, implementation of the PPH mechanism does not require amendment of the national law and can be done merely through administrative regulations or bye laws that patent offices are allowed to adopt within the framework of the national patent law.

The PPH became a permanent mechanism between the USPTO and JPO at the end of the pilot period and was extended as a pilot project in 2008 between the USPTO and the EPO. In 2009, the EPO agreed to undertake a pilot PPH project with the JPO. Thus, the PPH was seeded and began to develop several shoots of bilateral PPH collaboration within the Trilateral Offices. The USPTO[114] and the JPO have also concluded several bilateral PPH agreements with other IP offices outside the Trilateral. In 2014, the pilot project on a PPH mechanism between the IP5 offices was launched by attempting leverage fast track patent examination procedures already in place at the IP5, marking further expansion of the PPH. Existing bilateral PPH arrangements that had been established between the offices within the Trilateral and the IP5 group were integrated under this IP5 PPH project.[115] In the same year, three offices from the IP5—JPO, KIPO and the USPTO—launched a "Global PPH" (GPPH) pilot project along with 23 other national and regional patent offices—Australia, Canada, UK (the Vancouver Group), Austria, Colombia, Denmark, Estonia, Finland, Germany, Hungary, Iceland, Israel, New Zealand, Norway, the Nordic Patent Institute, Peru, Poland, Portugal, the Russian Federation, Singapore, Spain, Sweden, the Visegrad Patent Institute.[116] Both the IP5 PPH and the GPPH allow participating offices to use all the search and examination work products of the office of first filing or examination among the participating patent offices, including search and examination reports and written opinions produced by them as International Authorities under the PCT. In parallel with these initiatives, more countries are increasingly being brought within the ambit of the PPH through bilateral PPH agreements. Currently, more than 50 national or regional patent offices are part of the PPH network through a slew of bilateral or global PPH agreements.

Even where a patent office is a party to the PPH network through some form of PPH agreement, the extent to which offices use the PPH system can vary, with some offices using the PPH more widely than others. For example, under bilateral PPH agreements, the PPH route is only available to the patent applicants from the respective parties, and there can be a maximum limit on the number of applicants who can make use of this route. The PPH agreement could be limited to certain specific technology sectors while excluding other sectors with sensitive public

[114]The USPTO has bilateral PPH agreements with the IP offices of Brazil, Chile, the Czech Republic, the Eurasian Patent Office, Mexico, Nicaragua, the Philippines, Nicaragua, Saudi Arabia, and the Taiwan Intellectual Property Office. USPTO (n.d.-b).

[115]WIPO (Standing Committee on the Law of Patents) (2013b).

[116]Ibid.

interest concerns, such as pharmaceuticals.[117] However, like most work sharing schemes, the PPH has also expanded through a gradual and incremental approach. Therefore, the extension of existing PPH arrangements that are limited to specific technology sectors could be extended to incrementally include processing of patent applications in other technology sectors.

6 Opportunities and Challenges

Patent cooperation and work sharing between patent offices presents both opportunities and challenges for patent offices. For resource constrained national patent offices, work sharing can be an attractive mechanism to ensure timely processing of patent applications. Use of ICT, digitization, automation, machine translation, etc. have made work sharing an attractive and realistic proposition. At the same time, work sharing could present the risk of trade-offs being made by patent offices in favour of efficient, accelerated and timely completion of search and examination work, over ensuring robustness of the search and examination itself. The risk of such trade-off is much more where work sharing arrangements apply to fields of technology, such as pharmaceuticals, where there can be significant variance between the patentability thresholds under the applicable national law.

6.1 South-South Cooperation

While a number of patent offices in developing countries have bilateral MOUs on cooperation with patent offices in developed countries, cooperation between patent offices of developing countries has been very limited. Exploring work sharing or collaboration between patent offices among developing countries on the basis of South-South cooperation could be explored further. Work sharing arrangements like PROSUR and ASPEC enable patent offices in Latin America and the ASEAN to utilise their search and examination results on corresponding patent applications in their respective offices. Beyond formal work sharing agreements, patent offices in developing countries could also cooperate to undertake examiner exchange programmes, sharing of sector specific guidelines on patent examination, sharing of search and examination reports, objections or questions raised in first examination reports (FER), results of pre-grant opposition proceedings, and information on post-grant revocation or grant of any compulsory license on a patent. For instance, initiatives similar to the project proposed by INPI of Brazil under the IP BRICS

[117] *E.g.*, Intellectual Property India (n.d.) (limiting PPH requests to 100 applications per year and excluding pharmaceutical patent applications from the scope of PPH under the bilateral PPH between the Indian Patent Office and the Japanese Patent Office).

cooperation to undertake a study on examination procedures on patent applications containing Markush formulas with the objective of standardizing examination guidelines relating to such claims, could be further explored by other developing country patent offices and also be extended to include other forms of secondary patent claims made in the pharmaceutical sector.

It is critical that patent offices in developing countries engage in cooperation among them within a South-South framework not only in form but also in terms of policy orientation. The focus of South-South patent cooperation should be on harnessing the resources of their national and regional patent offices to ensure that those resources could be deployed efficiently to ensure robust examination of patent applications. To persuade the patent offices to collaborate with this orientation, it would be necessary to utilise existing forums of South-South cooperation such as IBSA,[118] MERCOSUR,[119] UNASUR, the regional economic communities (REC) in Africa,[120] as well as regional cooperation forums in Asia to provide guidance to the respective national and regional patent offices of their member States, to cooperate in pursuit of this objective.

A priority area of focus in this regard should be on the examination of pharmaceutical patent applications with the objective of enabling patent offices to fully utilise the flexibilities available under the TRIPS Agreement with regard to the differential application of the patentability criteria of novelty, inventive step and industrial applicability by taking into account the specificities of the technological sector. Thus, patent offices from developing countries can collaborate to share experience and knowledge and develop tools such as patent examination guidelines to enable the conduct of search and examination of pharmaceutical patent applications by applying rigorous standards. Objections or clarificatory questions raised in FERs by applying such rigorous standards could be shared through appropriate ICT tools with other patent offices for their reference. Other offices could consider whether similar questions could be raised in the context of the requirements under their national law or regulations. High quality FER objections can result in the withdrawal or abandonment of frivolous applications.

[118] *See, e.g.*, India-Brazil-South Africa Dialogue Forum (Second Summit of Heads of State/Government) (2007) (agreeing to work towards a trilateral initiative on cooperation in the field of IP including capacity building and human resource development).

[119] *See*, Velásquez (2015) (referring to the MERCOSUR health ministers' declaration of 2 December 2009 calling for development and application of patentability criteria in view of proliferation of low quality patents and particularly to adopt criteria to protect public health through patentability guidelines).

[120] *See, e.g.*, East African Community (2013); *see generally*, Vawda and Shozi (2020).

6.2 Safeguarding and Utilising TRIPS Flexibilities

While South-South cooperation could be explored in the area of patent search and examination as a means of strengthening the implementation of robust patent examination standards, a critical challenge for patent offices from developing countries in respect of patent cooperation or work sharing arrangements with the major patent offices such as the Trilateral or IP5 offices will be to effectively retain and safeguard the capacity to conduct such robust search and examination. Technical assistance programmes, examiner exchanges can expose and orient patent examiners from developing countries not only to the search tools, systems and techniques, but also to certain perspectives through which patent claims could be deemed to satisfy the criteria of patentability in a flexible way. For example, though under a strict interpretation a selection patent claim could be considered to be not novel as it is previously disclosed in an earlier application, patent examiners receiving technical assistance from the EPO could consider such claims to be permissible.[121] Therefore, developing countries must ensure that patent examiners are exposed to trainings that offer different perspectives, and expose them to the development and public policy implications of the possible approaches that could be taken to interpret the patentability of a claim.

With regard to work sharing collaborations such as the PPH that go beyond merely offering access to search and examination results of one office to another but encourage reliance on the reports produced by an office of first filing or examination, developing countries should exercise caution. A prudent approach in this respect, which some developing countries have taken,[122] is to limit such work sharing arrangements to exclude particularly sensitive fields of technology such as pharmaceuticals, and limit the number of applications to be processed under such arrangements.

6.3 Use of Technology

Digitization, ICT, machine translation, etc. have immensely aided patent offices to stay connected and share information rapidly and securely. While continuing to expand the use of such technologies to enable access to more information to conduct

[121] A selection patent claim is a secondary patent claim on a specific compound that is selected from the broad range of compounds that have been claimed earlier through a Markush formula, on the basis of a legal fiction that is followed by some patent offices influenced by the EPO, that the compound being claimed as selected from the range under a Markush formula, was not specifically disclosed under the earlier patent claim based on the Markush formula. In this way, selection patent claims have been a major route for effectively extending the term of a patent by claiming a specific selection of a compound as the term of the original patent claim nears its expiry. *See* Correa (n 4), p. 17.

[122] *E.g.*, Intellectual Property India (n.d.).

more comprehensive search and examination, facilitate electronic filing of patent applications, communication between the patent office and the applicants during the search and examination, as well as receiving oppositions or third party observations, there is need for caution with regard to use technologies to the decision-making itself. A number of patent offices have undertaken projects to use artificial intelligence (AI) and machine learning for patent classification as well as patent search. However, AI and machine learning tools can be used to even conducting the patent examination itself.[123] Therein lies the risk for developing countries, particularly those which fully rely on the decisions of foreign patent offices, such as under the validation agreements with the EPO.

6.4 Administrative Law Oversight

The global network of patent offices is a reality. If utilized appropriately, collaboration between patent offices can certainly provide efficiency gains for the conduct of the business of patent offices. At the same time, patent offices also have a regulatory role to play in the public interest by ensuring as far as possible that patents of questionable validity are not granted. The patent cooperation and work sharing arrangements that patent offices engage in with their counterparts from other countries obviously have a bearing on this function. However, these arrangements are often implemented as pilot projects, as cooperation activities under MOUs. At most, implementation of these activities would involve a revision of the regulations, rules or guidelines developed by the patent office as subordinate rules under the framework of the patent law enacted by the legislature. Thus, implementation of principles of administrative law can be crucial to ensure that the functions of the patent office as a sentinel of the public interest through the conduct of robust search and examination to decide on the grant of a patent in accordance with the national law is safeguarded, while attempting to secure speed and efficiency in disposal of the workload of patent offices through mutual collaboration. Thus, patent offices should be required to undertake sufficient public consultations prior to engaging in collaborative work sharing arrangements, as well as when considering expansion of the scope of such collaborations. Legislative oversight should also be exercised to ensure that collaborations between patent offices are effectively enabling, and not limiting, the implementation of the substantive patentability criteria under the national law.

[123] EPO is developing business solutions using Machine Learning and AI to manage patent files at various degrees of implementation: Automatic annotation of patent literature; Automatic detection of problem/solution in patent document; Automatic detection of exclusion from patentability. *See generally*, WIPO (n.d.-b).

7 Conclusion

Rigorous examination of a patent application to determine whether a patent claim satisfies the requirements of novelty, inventive step and industrial applicability, and sufficiently discloses the best enabling mode of working the claimed invention, is the most important role of a patent office. This makes it critical that patent offices are able to perform this role well by ensuring that the patentability thresholds as defined under the national law and the public policy objectives that inform the law, are given effect to in the process of interpretation of the patentability of a technical patent claim. Thus, how a patent examiner views a claim matters. The perspective of the examiner can be influenced by technical assistance or administrative collaboration arrangements between patent offices. Patent offices in developing countries also face challenges, such as limited human resources for patent examination, surge in the number of patent applications in different technical fields, associated backlogs, and the pressure to speedily dispose the applications. These challenges can impact the rigorous application of the patentability thresholds as patent offices have to make a choice of prioritizing between speed and efficiency in completing the search and examination work and robustness of the examination. Increasing human resources for search and examination, use of automation technologies and leveraging the search and examination capacity and work products of other patent offices are possible approaches being deployed by patent offices to address this challenge.

Digitization and use of ICT systems has enabled offices to collaborate in conducting search and examination work more easily. However, this has also enabled the major patent offices such as the Trilateral Offices and the IP5 to play an influential role in influencing the work of other patent offices. Indeed, work sharing has been explicitly recognized as part of an agenda of achieving a harmonized global patent system. While the negotiations for a Substantive Patent Law Treaty was unsuccessful in WIPO, soft law reforms of the PCT system has been undertaken through an incremental approach, and work sharing arrangements developed by the major patent offices outside the PCT system are also being promoted both in terms of their integration to the PCT through pilot projects (such as the PCT-PPH pilot project by EPO) as well as experience and best practices sharing sessions on "quality of patents" in the WIPO SCP discussions.

The nature of collaborations between patent offices vary. While some patent offices have entered into agreements to outsource search and examination work to the more resourceful patent offices or recognise within their territories the patents granted by another office (such as under the EPO validation agreements), other offices may collaborate merely to share information and documents relating to prior art, and search and examination results. Many patent offices have also agreed to engage in projects such as the PPH with one or more countries wherein they agree to not only share the search and examination results, but to use the search and examination results on a claim by one office to accelerate the examination of the claim in the other office. While engaging in such arrangements, patent offices in developing countries should ensure that the flexibility available to them under the

TRIPS Agreement to apply the patentability criteria as defined under the national law and policy is effectively safeguarded. Some patent offices have excluded sensitive sectors such as pharmaceuticals from their PPH agreements and have limited the number of applications to. Which the accelerated procedure could apply. However, it is possible that over time the PPH agreements could be expanded to include technology sectors that are currently excluded and could also be extended to patent applications from more countries. Patent offices in developing countries should also ensure that patent examiners are exposed to trainings that offer different perspectives on how patent claim could be interpreted differently by application of the patentability criteria under a strict or relaxed standard.

Patent cooperation and work sharing presents both opportunities and challenges for patent offices. Patent offices in developing countries could engage in cooperation with each other in a South-South framework to undertake examiner exchange programmes, sharing of sector specific guidelines on patent examination, sharing of search and examination reports, objections or questions raised in first examination reports (FER), results of pre-grant opposition proceedings, and information on post-grant revocation or grant of any compulsory license on a patent. South-South cooperation should be undertaken with a focus on enabling patent offices to utilise their resources for ensuring robust examination of patent applications. A priority area of focus in this regard should be on the examination of pharmaceutical patent applications.

Finally, cooperation between patent offices typically take place in the form of projects implemented under MOUs, which are undertaken in exercise of the administrative discretion that patent offices have. While exercising such discretion, it would be pertinent for patent offices to also assess the implications of such cooperation on their regulatory function of ensuring grant of robust patents in the public interest. It would this be pertinent to undertake public consultations and also exercise legislative oversight by application of the principles of administrative law, to ensure that cooperation that patent offices enter into in exercise of their discretionary powers, are exercised in the public interest and do not impede the attainment of the public policy objectives that inform the patent law.

References

Ali F, Rajagopal S, Raman VS, John R (2018) Pharmaceutical patent grants in India: how our safeguards against evergreening failed, and why the system must be reformed. accessibsa.org, 2018. https://accessibsa.org/media/2018/04/Pharmaceutical-Patent-Grants-in-India.pdf. Accessed 24 Feb 2021

ASEAN Intellectual Property Portal (n.d.) What is ASPEC? https://www.aseanip.org/Services/ASEAN-Patent-Examination-Co-operation-ASPEC/What-is-ASPEC. Accessed 24 Feb 2021

Assemblies of the Member States of WIPO (2002) WIPO patent agenda: options for development of the international patent system, 19 August 2002, A/37/6 [9]. https://www.wipo.int/edocs/mdocs/govbody/en/a_37/a_37_6.pdf. Accessed 24 Feb 2021

Baker R(R)B (2010) Customary international law in the 21st century: old challenges and new debates. Eur J Int Law 21(1):173. https://doi.org/10.1093/ejil/chq015. Accessed 24 Feb 2021
Castillo S (2012) The PROSUR approach to patents: shared information, independent decisions. American University Intellectual Property Brief. http://www.ipbrief.net/2012/07/28/the-prosur-approach-to-patents-shared-information-independent-decisions/. Accessed 24 Feb 2021
Chaudhuri S, Park C, Gopakumar KM (2010) Five years into the product patent regime: India's response. United Nations Development Programme, 2010. https://www.undp.org/content/dam/aplaws/publication/en/publications/hiv-aids/five-years-into-the-product-patient-regime-indias-response/Five%20years%20into%20the%20product%20patent%20regime-India%20Response.pdf. Accessed 24 Feb 2021
Correa CM (ed) (2012) A guide to pharmaceutical patents. South Centre, Geneva. https://www.southcentre.int/wp-content/uploads/2016/05/Bk_2012_A-Guide-to-Pharmaceutical-Patents_EN.pdf. Accessed 24 Feb 2021
Correa CM (2014a) Tackling the proliferation of patents: how to avoid undue limitations to competition and the public domain. Research Paper No. 52, South Centre, Geneva, 9. https://www.southcentre.int/wp-content/uploads/2014/09/RP52_Tackling-the-Proliferation-of-Patents-rev_EN.pdf. Accessed 24 Feb 2021
Correa CM (2014b) Patent examination and legal fictions: how rights are created on feet of clay. Research Paper No. 58 South Centre, Geneva. https://www.southcentre.int/wp-content/uploads/2014/12/RP58_Patent-Examination-Legal-Fictions-rev2_EN.pdf. Accessed 24 Feb 2021
Cruz MS, Olivos C (2019) The twenty-first century intellectual property office. In: Correa C, Seuba X (eds) Intellectual property and development: understanding the interfaces – Liber amicorum Pedro Roffe. Springer, Heidelberg
Dhavan R (1990) Lindsay Harris and Gopal Jain, 'Conquest by Patent: The Paris Convention Revisited'. J Indian Law Inst 32(2):131
Drahos P (2008a) "Trust Me": patent offices in developing countries. Am J Law Med 34(2–3):151. https://doi.org/10.1177/009885880803400205. Accessed 24 Feb 2021
Drahos P (2008b) Regulating patent offices: countering pharmaceutical hegemony. SCRIPTed 5 501. https://script-ed.org/wp-content/uploads/2016/07/5-3-Drahos.pdf. Accessed 24 Feb 2021
East African Community (2013) EAC regional intellectual property policy on the utilisation of public health-related WTO-TRIPS flexibilities and the approximation of National Intellectual Property Legislation. https://ipaccessmeds.southcentre.int/wp-content/uploads/2019/12/EACTRIPSPolicy.pdf. Accessed 24 Feb 2021
European Commission (2009) Pharmaceutical sector inquiry: final report (8 July 2009), pp 385–390. https://ec.europa.eu/competition/sectors/pharmaceuticals/inquiry/staff_working_paper_part1.pdf. Accessed 24 Feb 2021
European Patent Office (2016) Validation of European patents in Morocco (MA). Official Journal EPO, 29 January 2016. https://www.epo.org/law-practice/legal-texts/official-journal/2016/01/a5.html. Accessed 24 Feb 2021
European Patent Office (2017) Working with our partners worldwide. https://www.epo.org/about-us/annual-reports-statistics/annual-report/2017/highlights/worldwide-influence.html. Accessed 24 Feb 2021
European Patent Office (n.d.) Validation states (EPO). https://www.epo.org/about-us/foundation/validation-states.html. Accessed 24 Feb 2021
fiveIPoffices (n.d.) About IP5 co-operation. https://www.fiveipoffices.org/about. Accessed 24 Feb 2021
Hu W (2017) International patent rights harmonisation: the case of China. Routledge
India-Brazil-South Africa Dialogue Forum (Second Summit of Heads of State/Government) (2007) Tshwane Declaration, Tshwane 17 October 2007. http://www.ibsa-trilateral.org/images/2nd_IBSA_Summit_Declaration_-_Tshwane_2007.pdf. Accessed 24 Feb 2021
Intellectual Property India (n.d.) Procedure guidelines for Patent Prosecution Highway (PPH). http://www.ipindia.nic.in/writereaddata/Portal/News/591_1_PPH_Procedure_Guideline_combined_20191128_final.pdf. Accessed 24 Feb 2021

IP BRICS (2013) BRICS Intellectual Property Offices Cooperation Roadmap. http://www.ipbrics.org/secondpage/aboutus/2013Roadmap%20final%20version%20signed%20IP-BRICS_2013.pdf. Accessed 24 Feb 2021

IP BRICS (n.d.-a) Projects. http://www.ipbrics.org/secondpage/project.html. Accessed 24 Feb 2021

IP BRICS (n.d.-b) Meetings. http://www.ipbrics.org/secondpage/meeting.html. Accessed 24 Feb 2021

Jayakumar PB (2017) We can clear the patent backlog within next two years. Business Today, 23 April 2017, Delhi. https://www.businesstoday.in/magazine/features/we-can-clear-the-patent-backlog-within-next-two-years/story/249173.html. Accessed 24 Feb 2021

May C (2007) The World intellectual Property Organization: resurgence and the development agenda. Routledge, p 49

Mossinghof GJ (1999) LECTURE: World Patent System Circa 20XX A.D. Yale J Law Technol 1 (1):2. https://digitalcommons.law.yale.edu/cgi/viewcontent.cgi?referer=https://www.google.com/&httpsredir=1&article=1071&context=yjolt. Accessed 24 Feb 2021

Neppel C, Rutz B, Carmichael G, Karachalios K, Elahi S, McGinley C (2012) The future of IP in Europe. In: Shimanami R (ed) The future of the patent system. Edward Elgar, Cheltenham

Nunes RD, Romano RS (2019) Brazil's patent backlog days are numbered. Managing IP, 23 September 2019. https://www.managingip.com/article/b1kbm141jmzzwm/brazils-patent-backlog-days-are-numbered. Accessed 24 Feb 2021

Proposal by the delegation of Denmark (20 October 2011) SCP/17/7 https://www.wipo.int/edocs/mdocs/scp/en/scp_17/scp_17_7.pdf. Accessed 24 Feb 2021

Proposal by the delegation of the United States of America on the study of worksharing, 20 November 2015, SCP/23/4. https://www.wipo.int/edocs/mdocs/scp/en/scp_23/scp_23_4.pdf. Accessed 24 Feb 2021

Proposal by the delegations of the Czech Republic, Kenya, Mexico, Singapore and the United Kingdom, 18 June 2018, SCP/28/8. https://www.wipo.int/edocs/mdocs/scp/en/scp_28/scp_28_8.pdf. Accessed 24 Feb 2021

Proposal by the delegations of the Republic of Korea, the United Kingdom and the United States of America regarding work sharing between offices in order to improve efficiencies of the patent system, 22 January 2014, SCP/20/11 Rev. https://www.wipo.int/edocs/mdocs/scp/en/scp_20/scp_20_11_rev.pdf. Accessed 24 Feb 2021

PROSUR (n.d.) About us. http://prosur.org/quienes-somos/. Accessed 24 Feb 2021

Rathod SK, Ali F (2018) Inside views: deference, not delegation! - WIPO PCT negotiations. Intellectual Property Watch, 17 June 2018. http://www.ip-watch.org/2018/06/17/deference-not-delegation-wipo-pct-negotiations/#_ftn1. Accessed 24 Feb 2021

Responses to the questionnaire on the term "Quality of Patents" and cooperation between patent offices in search and examination (part 2), 2 June 2017, SCP/26/4. https://www.wipo.int/edocs/mdocs/scp/en/scp_26/scp_26_4.pdf. Accessed 24 Feb 2021

Shadlen KC (2013) The patent policy trilemma. Journal fur Entwicklungspolitik 29(2):87

Shashikant S (2014) The African Regional Intellectual Property Organization (ARIPO) Protocol on Patents: implications for access to medicines. Research Paper No. 56, South Centre, 17–21. https://www.southcentre.int/wp-content/uploads/2014/11/RP56_The-ARIPO-Protocol-on-Patents_ENl.pdf. Accessed 24 Feb 2021

Syam N (2019) Mainstreaming or dilution? Intellectual property and development in WIPO. Research paper no. 95, South Centre, Geneva, p 18. https://doi.org/10.2139/ssrn.3559643

't Hoen E (2020) The expanding reach of the European Patent Office. Good for health? Medicines Law & Policy, 18 March 2020. https://medicineslawandpolicy.org/2020/03/the-expanding-reach-of-the-european-patent-office-good-for-health/. Accessed 24 Feb 2021

Trilateral (n.d.-a) About us. https://www.trilateral.net/about. Accessed 24 Feb 2021

Trilateral (n.d.-b) Significant achievements. https://www.trilateral.net/about/achievements. Accessed 24 Feb 2021

Trilateral (n.d.-c) The 30th anniversary: a brief history of the trilateral cooperation. https://www.jpo.go.jp/news/kokusai/nichibeiou/document/nitibeiou_meeting_30/pamphlet.pdf. Accessed 24 Feb 2021

USPTO (n.d.-a) Patent Prosecution Highway: frequently asked questions. https://www.uspto.gov/sites/default/files/documents/FAQ%20for%20PPH%20final-%2004192018.pdf. Accessed 24 Feb 2021

USPTO (n.d.-b) Patent Prosecution Highway (PPH) – fast track examination of applications, uspto.gov. https://www.uspto.gov/patents-getting-started/international-protection/patent-prosecution-highway-pph-fast-track. Accessed 24 Feb 2021

Vancouver Group (n.d.) Technical infrastructure for improved international collaboration on search and examination. https://www.wipo.int/export/sites/www/patents/en/topics/worksharing/pdf/vancouver_group.pdf. Accessed 24 Feb 2021

Vawda YA, Shozi B (2020) Eighteen years after Doha: an analysis of the use of public health TRIPS flexibilities in Africa. Research paper no. 103, South Centre, Geneva. https://www.southcentre.int/wp-content/uploads/2020/02/RP103_Eighteen-Years-After-Doha-An-Analysis-of-the-Use-of-Public-HealthTRIPS-Flexibilities-in-Africa_EN.pdf. Accessed 24 Feb 2021

Velásquez G (2015) Guidelines on patentability and access to medicines. Research paper no. 61, South Centre, Geneva, p 30. https://www.southcentre.int/wp-content/uploads/2015/03/RP61_Guidelines-on-Patentability-and-A2M_EN.pdf. Accessed 24 Feb 2021

WIPO (2001) PCT Union – Committee on Reform of the Patent Cooperation Treaty (PCT). wipo.int, 21–25 May 2001. https://www.wipo.int/meetings/en/details.jsp?meeting_id=4306. Accessed 24 Feb 2021

WIPO (n.d.-a) WIPO CASE – Centralized Access to Search and Examination, wipo.int. https://www.wipo.int/case/en/. Accessed 24 Feb 2021

WIPO (n.d.-b) Index of AI initiatives in IP offices. https://www.wipo.int/about-ip/en/artificial_intelligence/search.jsp. Accessed 24 Feb 2021

WIPO (Committee on Reform of the Patent Cooperation Treaty (PCT)) (2002) Language of the international application and translations, 31 May 2002, PCT/R/2/3. https://www.wipo.int/edocs/mdocs/pct/en/pct_r_2/pct_r_2_3.pdf. Accessed 24 Feb 2021

WIPO (Committee on Reform of the Patent Cooperation Treaty) (2001) Reform of the PCT: proposals by the United States of America, 23 March 2001, PCT/R/1/2. http://www.wipo.int/edocs/mdocs/pct/en/pct_r_1/pct_r_1_2.pdf. Accessed 24 Feb 2021

WIPO (International Patent Cooperation Union (PCT Union) Assembly) (2000a) Reform of the Patent Cooperation Treaty, 18 August 2000, PCT/A/29/3. https://www.wipo.int/edocs/mdocs/govbody/en/pct_a_29/pct_a_29_3.pdf. Accessed 24 Feb 2021

WIPO (International Patent Cooperation Union (PCT Union) Assembly) (2000b) Report, 3 October 2000, PCT/A/29/4. https://www.wipo.int/edocs/mdocs/govbody/en/pct_a_29/pct_a_29_4-main1.pdf. Accessed 24 Feb 2021

WIPO (International Patent Cooperation Union (PCT Union) Assembly) (2001) Report, 3 October 2001, PCT/A/30/7. https://www.wipo.int/edocs/mdocs/govbody/en/pct_a_30/pct_a_30_7.pdf. Accessed 24 Feb 2021

WIPO (International Patent Cooperation Union (PCT Union) Assembly) (2002) Report, 1 October 2002, PCT/A/31/10. https://www.wipo.int/edocs/mdocs/govbody/en/pct_a_31/pct_a_31_10.pdf. Accessed 24 Feb 2021

WIPO (International Patent Cooperation Union (PCT Union) Assembly) (2007a) Supplementary international search: proposed amendments of the PCT regulations, 17 August 2007, PCT/A/36/7. https://www.wipo.int/edocs/mdocs/govbody/en/pct_a_36/pct_a_36_7.pdf. Accessed 24 Feb 2021

WIPO (International Patent Cooperation Union (PCT Union) Assembly) (2007b) Supplementary international search: proposed amendments of the PCT regulations, 19 September 2007, PCT/A/36/7Add. https://www.wipo.int/edocs/mdocs/govbody/en/pct_a_36/pct_a_36_7_add.pdf. Accessed 24 Feb 2021

WIPO (International Patent Cooperation Union (PCT Union) Assembly) (2007c) Report, 12 November 2007, PCT/A/36/13 [153]. https://www.wipo.int/edocs/mdocs/govbody/en/pct_a_36/pct_a_36_13.pdf. Accessed 24 Feb 2021
WIPO (International Patent Cooperation Union (PCT Union) Assembly) (2007d) Reform of the PCT, 23 July 2007, PCT/A/36/1. https://www.wipo.int/pct/en/texts/articles/a36.html. Accessed 24 Feb 2021
WIPO (International Patent Cooperation Union (PCT Union) Assembly) (n.d.) PCT/A/36/13 (n 64) [134]
WIPO (Patent Cooperation Treaty (PCT) Working Group) (2008) Enhancing the value of international search and preliminary examination under the PCT, 21 April 2008, PCT/WG/1/3. https://www.wipo.int/edocs/mdocs/pct/en/pct_wg_1/pct_wg_1_3.pdf. Accessed 24 Feb 2021
WIPO (Patent Cooperation Treaty (PCT) Working Group) (2009a) Enhancing the value of international search and preliminary examination under the PCT: making international preliminary examination more useful, 14 April 2009, PCT/WG/2/6. https://www.wipo.int/edocs/mdocs/pct/en/pct_wg_2/pct_wg_2_6.pdf. Accessed 24 Feb 2021
WIPO (Patent Cooperation Treaty (PCT) Working Group) (2009b) The future of the PCT, 3 April 2009, PCT/WG/2/3. https://www.wipo.int/edocs/mdocs/pct/en/pct_wg_2/pct_wg_2_3.pdf. Accessed 24 Feb 2021
WIPO (Patent Cooperation Treaty (PCT) Working Group) (2009c) Three track PCT system, 24 April 2009, PCT/WG/2/11. https://www.wipo.int/edocs/mdocs/pct/en/pct_wg_2/pct_wg_2_11.doc. Accessed 24 Feb 2021
WIPO (Patent Cooperation Treaty (PCT) Working Group) (2009d) Comprehensive proposal for PCT reform, 24 April 2009, PCT/WG/2/12. https://www.wipo.int/edocs/mdocs/pct/en/pct_wg_2/pct_wg_2_12.pdf. Accessed 24 Feb 2021
WIPO (Patent Cooperation Treaty (PCT) Working Group) (2009e) Report, 24 July 2009, PCT/WG/2/14 [24]. https://www.wipo.int/edocs/mdocs/pct/en/pct_wg_2/pct_wg_2_14.pdf. Accessed 24 Feb 2021
WIPO (Patent Cooperation Treaty (PCT) Working Group) (2010a) The need for improving the functioning of the PCT system, 5 May 2010, PCT/WG/3/2. https://www.wipo.int/edocs/mdocs/pct/en/pct_wg_3/pct_wg_3_2.pdf. Accessed 24 Feb 2021
WIPO (Patent Cooperation Treaty (PCT) Working Group) (2010b) Report, 18 June 2010, PCT/WG/3/14 Rev. [139]. https://www.wipo.int/edocs/mdocs/pct/en/pct_wg_3/pct_wg_3_14_rev.pdf. Accessed 24 Feb 2021
WIPO (Patent Cooperation Treaty (PCT) Working Group). Progress report on the Collaborative Search and Examination (CS&E) Second Pilot Project, 14 May 2012, PCT/WG/5/9. https://www.wipo.int/edocs/mdocs/pct/en/pct_wg_5/pct_wg_5_9.pdf. Accessed 24 Feb 2021
WIPO (Patent Cooperation Treaty (PCT) Working Group). Summary by the Chair, 24 May 2013, PCT/WG/6/23. https://www.wipo.int/edocs/mdocs/pct/en/pct_wg_6/pct_wg_6_23.pdf. Accessed 24 Feb 2021
WIPO (Patent Cooperation Treaty (PCT) Working Group) (2018) Delegation of designated or elected office functions, 11 April 2018, PCT/WG/11/7. https://www.wipo.int/edocs/mdocs/pct/en/pct_wg_11/pct_wg_11_7.pdf. Accessed 24 Feb 2021
WIPO (Standing Committee on the Law of Patents) (2011) Revised proposals from the delegations of Canada and the United Kingdom, 19 October 2011, SCP/17/8. https://www.wipo.int/edocs/mdocs/scp/en/scp_18/scp_18_ref_scp_17_8.pdf. Accessed 24 Feb 2021
WIPO (Standing Committee on the Law of Patents) (2013a) Work sharing programs between patent offices and use of external information in search and examination, 4 December 2013, SCP/20/8. https://www.wipo.int/edocs/mdocs/patent_policy/en/scp_20/scp_20_8.pdf. Accessed 24 Feb 2021
WIPO (Standing Committee on the Law of Patents) (2013b) Work-sharing programs among patent offices and use of external information for search and examination, 4 December 2013, SCP/20/8. https://www.wipo.int/edocs/mdocs/patent_policy/en/scp_20/scp_20_8.pdf. Accessed 24 Feb 2021
WIPO (Standing Committee on the Law of Patents) (2017) Responses to the questionnaire on the term "Quality of Patents" and cooperation between patent offices in search and examination

(Part 1), 2 June 2017, SCP/26/3. https://www.wipo.int/edocs/mdocs/scp/en/scp_26/scp_26_3.pdf. Accessed 24 Feb 2021
WIPO (Working Group on Reform of the Patent Cooperation Treaty (PCT)) (2002a) Outstanding proposals for reform of the Patent Cooperation Treaty (PCT), 18 October 2002, PCT/R/WG/3/1. https://www.wipo.int/edocs/mdocs/pct/en/pct_r_wg_3/pct_r_wg_3_1.pdf. Accessed 24 Feb 2021
WIPO (Working Group on Reform of the Patent Cooperation Treaty (PCT)) (2002b) Summary of the session, 22 November 2002, PCT/R/WG/3/5. https://www.wipo.int/edocs/mdocs/pct/en/pct_r_wg_3/pct_r_wg_3_5.pdf. Accessed 24 Feb 2021
WIPO (Working Group on Reform of the Patent Cooperation Treaty (PCT)) (2003a) Options for future development of international search and examination, 21 March 2003, PCT/R/WG/4/7. https://www.wipo.int/edocs/mdocs/pct/en/pct_r_wg_4/pct_r_wg_4_7.pdf. Accessed 24 Feb 2021
WIPO (Working Group on Reform of the Patent Cooperation Treaty (PCT)) (2003b) Options for future development of international search and examination: making greater use of international reports, 19 September 2003, PCT/R/WG/5/9. https://www.wipo.int/edocs/mdocs/pct/en/pct_r_wg_5/pct_r_wg_5_9.pdf. Accessed 24 Feb 2021
WIPO (Working Group on Reform of the Patent Cooperation Treaty (PCT)) (2003c) Summary of the session, 21 November 2003, PCT/R/WG/5/13 [127]. https://www.wipo.int/edocs/mdocs/pct/en/pct_r_wg_5/pct_r_wg_5_13.pdf. Accessed 24 Feb 2021
WIPO (Working Group on Reform of the Patent Cooperation Treaty (PCT)) (2004) Improving the quality of international searches, 6 April 2004, PCT/R/WG/6/9. https://www.wipo.int/edocs/mdocs/pct/en/pct_r_wg_6/pct_r_wg_6_9.pdf. Accessed 24 Feb 2021
WIPO International Patent Cooperation Union (2002a) Missed time limit for entering the national phase, 31 May 2002. https://www.wipo.int/edocs/mdocs/pct/en/pct_r_2/pct_r_2_4.pdf. Accessed 24 Feb 2021
WIPO International Patent Cooperation Union (2002b) Right of priority and priority claims, 5 June 2002, PCT/R/2/5. https://www.wipo.int/edocs/mdocs/pct/en/pct_r_2/pct_r_2_5.pdf. Accessed 24 Feb 2021
WIPO International Patent Cooperation Union (2002c) Automatic indication of all designations possible under the PCT; related proposals: elections; international filing fee; "communication on request" system, 7 June 2002, PCT/R/2/6. https://www.wipo.int/edocs/mdocs/pct/en/pct_r_2/pct_r_2_6.pdf. Accessed 24 Feb 2021
WIPO International Patent Cooperation Union (2002d) Enhanced international search and preliminary examination system, 7 June 2002, PCT/R/2/7. https://www.wipo.int/edocs/mdocs/pct/en/pct_r_2/pct_r_2_7.pdf. Accessed 24 Feb 2021
World Intellectual Property Organization (n.d.) IP Statistics Data Center (WIPO). https://www3.wipo.int/ipstats/index.htm. Accessed 24 Feb 2021

Intellectual Property Rights (IPRs), Competition Law and Excessive Pricing of Medicines

Mor Bakhoum

1 Introduction

This chapter wrestles with the interface between Intellectual Property Rights (IPRs), competition law and access to medicines. It emphasizes the important role that competition law may play, in addition to the internal IP flexibilities, in order to foster access and dissemination of medical products. Of course, competition law could also be considered as a flexibility within the TRIPS agreement. In our analysis, we consider competition law separately given its role in creating competitive markets within which IP products are commercialized. Relying on the recent case law in the EU, in Italy and in South Africa on the application of competition law in the pharmaceutical sector, with a focus on the prohibition of excessive pricing of pharmaceuticals, this paper argues that TRIPS flexibilities are an important regulatory tool to control prices and to foster access to medicines. However, in certain circumstances, IP flexibilities are operational only within a competitive market that is guaranteed by a functioning competition law.

Section 2 of the paper, which sets the stage, discusses the interface between TRIPS and Competition Policy and the enforcement orientation of competition law in the pharmaceutical sector since the entry into force of the TRIPS Agreement. This section presents the TRIPS competition-related provisions and their approach as a flexibility instrument. In addition to serving as a technology transfer instrument,[1] TRIPS competition-related provisions may also be used in order to foster access to medicines. In this regard, this section emphasises the IP-related restrictions of

[1] See for discussion, Ullrich (2005), pp. 727–756.

M. Bakhoum (✉)
UVS Doctoral School, Université Virtuelle du Sénégal (UVS), Dakar, Senegal

Max Planck Institute for Innovation and Competition, Munich, Germany
e-mail: mor.bakhoum@uvs.edu.sn

C. M. Correa, R. M. Hilty (eds.), *Access to Medicines and Vaccines*,
https://doi.org/10.1007/978-3-030-83114-1_10

competition in the pharmaceutical sector that can affect access to medicines. The discussion is informed by both the findings of the 2009 and 107 EU reports on the pharmaceutical sector and the case law on reverse payment settlements in the EU and the US.

Section 3 of the paper focuses on the recent trends of competition law enforcement in the pharmaceutical sector with the emerging case law on excessive (high) pricing of pharmaceuticals. The discussion is informed by the Aspen Case on excessive pricing decided by the Italian competition authority and the ongoing investigations against Aspen in the EU and in South Africa.

Section 4 deals with excessive pricing of pharmaceuticals in relations to IP flexibilities. It showcases that creating competitive pharmaceuticals markets by dealing with IP related restrictions of competition is in most cases important for TRIPS flexibilities to be operational. In addition to emphasizing the role of competition law enforcement as a complement to the TRIPS flexibilities, the section outlines situations where competition law enforcement is warranted.

Section 5 concludes with policy recommendation on how to align IP flexibilities and competition law enforcement in order to foster access to pharmaceuticals.

2 TRIPS and Competition Policy: Orientations and Enforcement Trends in the Pharmaceutical Sector

This section discusses three aspects: first, from a conceptual point of view, the interface between IP and Competition Law, second, TRIPS and Competition Policy with a reminder of TRIPS' approach to competition law and, third, the enforcement trends of competition law in the pharmaceutical sector since the entry into force of the TRIPS Agreement.

2.1 The Interface Between IPRs and Competition Law

The interplay between IP and competition law is dynamic. The IP system provides, in theory incentives for innovation and the development of cultural markets. However, IPRs do not operate in a vacuum. IPRs are exercised and commercialized in markets that are mostly regulated. As a market regulatory tool, competition law determines the framework within which IPRs are commercialized. However, the potential of competition law to serve as a market regulatory tool differs from country to country. Hence, competition law is still not implemented everywhere and in developing countries, strong enforcement is lacking. Competition law used to be approached as a regulatory instrument that limits the exercise of IPRs. This "conventional" and conflicting approach of the interface between IPRs and competition law is exemplified by the TRIPS competition-related provisions[2] which are designed as a limit to the exercise of IPRs. This approach of the interface between IPRs and competition law is not in line with the approach of the relationship between IP and competition law as being complementary.[3]

The protection granted by the IP system to the right holders is not a reward as such. IP protection provides only to the right holder an opportunity to extract a reward from the market[4] by commercializing its invention. The development and successful commercialisation of new technologies and products is closely related to the competitiveness of the markets within which they are commercialized. Hence, in most cases, the markets conditions determine whether a new technology is successful or not. With regards to the flexibilities within the IP system, building competitive markets is also a precondition for their operability. Of course, in complement to using competition law as a regulatory tool, using IP flexibilities participate to building competitive markets. Hence, as we shall see in this chapter, anticompetitive behaviours may hinder the build-in flexibilities of the IP system. With regards to access to pharmaceuticals, which is the focus of this paper, a number of anticompetitive behaviours (limitation of compulsory licensing, limitation of parallel import, or extension of the duration of the patent-reverse payment settlements) that affect the competitiveness of the pharmaceutical markets, and may affect the IP flexibilities that are crucial to access to pharmaceuticals.

2.2 *TRIPS and Competition Law: Competition Law as Flexibility Tool*

TRIPS is the first international instrument that recognizes the possibility to police the exercise of IPRS. TRIPS prohibits IPR-related restrictions of competition. Articles 8, 31 (k) and 40 of TRIPS, which are usually referred to as the TRIPS competition-related provisions, are largely conceived as legal tools to monitor the exercise of IPR (s) based on competition considerations.[5] Competition law is part of the flexibility tools of the IP system. Competition related provisions within TRIPS are part of the general architecture of the Agreement and they provide a necessary balance to potential abusive exercise of IPRS. They should be read as part of the rights recognized to IP owner, and, also, their limits.

The competition-related provisions in the TRIPS were a result of a compromise between developed and developing countries during the negotiation of the TRIPS agreement.[6] Developing countries which feared a monopolistic exercise of IPRs

[2] Which focus on technology transfer. See for discussion, Ullrich (2005), pp. 727–756.

[3] Bakhoum and Gallego (2016), p. 9, see specially reference in fn. 33.

[4] See Ullrich and Heinemann (2007), p. 146.

[5] Bakhoum and Gallego (2016).

[6] Ullrich (2005), pp. 727–756.

managed to have provisions on competition law included in order to mitigate potential abuses in the exercise of IPRs.

Initially, competition law in TRIPS was associated with technology transfer.[7] In licensing agreements, competition law was considered as an instrument that protects the weaker licensee party against potential abuses of the IP right holder. As a consequence, TRIPS provides a detailed treatment of anticompetitive practises in licensing agreements.[8]

The reach of TRIPS competition related provisions is, however, not only limited to technology transfer. In additional to facilitating technology transfer, TRIPS competition related provisions can be read as an innovation policy tool.[9]

With regards to access to pharmaceuticals/medical products, TRIPS competition-related provisions may also be used as an access to medicines tool. This approach is proven by the increased reliance on competition law in the pharmaceutical industry since the entry into force of the TRIPS agreement.[10] Competition enforcement is a complement to the IP flexibilities[11] *stricto sensu*.

TRIPS does not create a binding international framework that obliges signatory members to apply competition law to IP-related restrictions of competition. The effectiveness of using competition law as a flexibility tool in the pharmaceutical sector depends on the institutional framework of each country. Unlike in IP law, there is no binding multilateral instrument that regulates competition law.[12] The use of competition law as a flexibility tool is optional. Member States are given leeway to define their own policies when it comes to applying their competition law to IP-related restrictions.

This situation creates an imbalance from an international perspective. On the one hand, there is a harmonization, from the top, of the protection of IPRs. On the other hand, the use of competition law is 'deregulated' and left to the choice of each member to define its own policy. This "deregulation" of competition law enforcement has consequences, especially for developing countries, when applying competition law in the pharmaceutical sector.

---

[7] Ullrich (2005), pp. 727–756.

[8] Article 40 TRIPS reads: "1. Members agree that some licensing practices or conditions pertaining to intellectual property rights which restrain competition may have adverse effects on trade and may impede the transfer and dissemination of technology.

2. Nothing in this Agreement shall prevent Members from specifying in their legislation licensing practices or conditions that may in particular cases constitute an abuse of intellectual property rights having an adverse effect on competition in the relevant market. As provided above, a Member may adopt, consistently with the other provisions of this Agreement, appropriate measures to prevent or control such practices, which may include for example exclusive grantback conditions, conditions preventing challenges to validity and coercive package licensing, in the light of the relevant laws and regulations of that Member".

[9] Bakhoum and Gallego (2016).

[10] See infra, enforcement trends in the pharmaceuticals sector. See also, European Commission (2009–2017) https://ec.europa.eu/competition/sectors/pharmaceuticals/report2019/report_en.pdf.

[11] See, Berger (2006), p. 182.

[12] Drexl (2004), pp. 419–457.

2.3 *Enforcement Trends of Competition Law in the Pharmaceutical Sector*

IPRs have expanded both in quantity and quality since the entry into force of the TRIPS agreement. New types of technologies, works and trademarks have been found eligible for protection;[13] rights holders have been granted new exclusive prerogatives;[14] the terms of protection for certain subject matter have been extended;[15] and enforcement mechanisms and remedies have been strengthened and taken on an increasingly punitive character.[16]

From an international perspective, we notice a proliferation of the so-called TRIPS-Plus agreements through bilateral and regional trade agreements. As a result, standards of IPR protection of developed countries have been transferred to developing countries without due regard for the socio-economic, political and social context of the latter.[17] This development reduces the policy space of developing countries to use TRIPS flexibilities, including in order to foster access to pharmaceuticals.

In reaction to the enhanced protection of IPRs through the TRIPS-Plus agreements there is a parallel push on how to best use the flexibilities embodied within TRIPS. The development in the framework of Doha with the Doha Declaration on IP and public health and subsequent article 31*bis*, which took over a decade to be implemented, to allow WTO members to issue compulsory licenses for export are prime examples of this development.[18] Parallel to harnessing the use of TRIPS flexibilities, competition law enforcement is increasingly taking place in developed countries with mature competition law system and in some developing countries South Africa is an example of a developing countries pushing for a proactive enforcement of competition law in the pharmaceutical sector.

Anticompetitive behaviours in the pharmaceutical sector may affect both innovation and access to medicines. The 2009 Pharmaceutical Sector Inquiry Report of the European Commission and the subsequent enforcement report of 2017 have

[13] See e.g. Directive 96/9/EC of the European Parliament and of the Council of 11 March 1996 on the legal protection of databases, OJ L 77, 27 March 1996, pp. 20–28.

[14] In the copyright field, for example, new forms of digital infringement related to the protection of technological protection measures have been created; see e.g. Directive 2001/29/EC of the European Parliament and of the Council of 22 May 2001 on the harmonization of certain aspects of copyright and related rights in the information society, OJ L 167, pp. 10–19.

[15] See e.g. Directive of the European Parliament and of the Council of 27 September 2011 amending Directive 2006/116/EC on the term of protection of copyright and certain related rights, OJ L 265, 11 October 2011, pp. 1–5; Sonny Bono Copyright Term Extension Act, Pub. L. No.105-298, 112 Stat. 2827 (1998).

[16] See e.g. Directive 2004/48/EC of the European Parliament and of the Council of 29 April 2004 on the enforcement of intellectual property rights, OJ L 195, 2 June 2004, pp. 16–25.

[17] For an overview and analysis of the most significant free trade agreements (FTAs) see Roffe (2014), pp. 17–40.

[18] Bakhoum and Gallego (2016).

identified patenting strategies that block the development of competing medicines by reducing the incentives of other originator companies to continue their own R&D efforts.[19] With regards to access, patenting strategies may also delay competition by generics.[20] In 2007, the European Commission started an investigation against Boehringer Ingelheim after a competing pharmaceutical company had raised concerns that Boehringer's patent applications would have the potential of blocking its competing medicines. The case was settled between the companies.[21]

Since the entry into force of the TRIPS agreement, there is an increased scrutiny by competition authorities of behaviours in the pharmaceutical sector that negatively impact the timely entry of generics.[22] In the EU, since the publication of the sector inquiry report on the pharmaceutical sector in 2009 there is an increased scrutiny of these practises.[23]

With regard to the interface between IP and Competition law, three different types of conducts may be identified: Category one concerns practices that are within the ambit of the patent system (*Italian Pfizer, AstraZeneca*) and involve the misuse of the patent and regulatory system which may impact innovation and access. Category two concerns behaviors that are outside of the boundaries of the patent system (such as ever-greening) while category 3 comprises practices half-way between the other two categories (*pay for delay cases, FTC v Actavis, Lundbeck*).[24]

---

[19] European Commission (2009), pp. 16 and 19. http://ec.europa.eu/competition/sectors/pharmaceuticals/inquiry/staff_working_paper_part1.pdf.

Generally, the Sector Inquiry Report is concerned with two different sets of strategic patenting practices: on the one hand, those which aim at extending the exclusivity period to delay market entry of generics, and on the other hand, those whose objective is to block substitutive innovations by competitors. Regarding the later, blocking patents can be applied for either to broaden the applicant's own field of activity (defensive blocking patents) or to limit the scope of action of competitors (aggressive blocking patents); see Ullrich (2013), pp. 244 and 248.

[20] The Commission and the two European courts have confirmed the application of Article 102 of the Treaty on the Functioning of the European Union (TFEU) to a strategic use of patent procedures aimed at delaying generic entry in the Astra Zeneca case; see Commission Decision of 15 June 2005 relating to a proceeding under Article 82 of the EC Treaty and Article 54 of the EEA Agreement, Case COMP/A.37.507/F3 – *Astra Zeneca*, http://ec.europa.eu/competition/antitrust/cases/dec_docs/37507/37507_193_6.pdf (accessed 23 October 2014); GC, Case T-321/05, Astra Zeneca v. Commission, [2010] ECR 2010 II-2805; CJ, Case C-457/10 P, Astra Zeneca v. Commission, [2012] ECR I-770. On the relevance of the Astra Zeneca rulings for the assessment of blocking patents see Drexl (2013), pp. 312 et seq.

[21] See European Commission, Press Release of 6 July 2011, IP/11/842. http://europa.eu/rapid/press-release_IP-11-842_en.htm.

[22] See the different cases discussed in this paper: See Case T-472/13, *Lundbeck v. Commission*, infra, box n° 1; Case C-142/18, J&J et al. vs. Commission ("Fentanyl"), infra, box n° 2; Case U.S. Supreme Court No. 12-416, *FTC v. Actavis, infra, box 3;* Case T-691/14, *Servier and others v. Commission* (still pending).

[23] See Contribution by the European Commission, UNCTAD Roundtable on The Role of Competition in the Pharmaceutical Sector and its Benefits for Consumers. https://unctad.org/system/files/non-official-document/CCPB_7RC2015_RTPharma_EC_en.pdf.

[24] Such distinction was made by Gallasch (2015). http://unctad.org/meetings/en/Presentation/CCPB_7RC2015_PRES_RTPharma_Gallasch_en.pdf.

In addition to "traditional" types of anticompetitive behaviours that affect pharmaceutical markets (cartels, bid rigging, and boycotts are conventional behaviours that aim to fix prices and earn monopoly profits), a particular type of anticompetitive agreement in the pharmaceutical industry has drawn the attention of competition law enforcers in recent years: the practice commonly known as a "pay for delay" agreement or, since it often involves a payment from the patentee to the alleged infringer, a "reverse payment" settlement agreement. Basically, it concerns situations where a brand-name pharmaceutical company, as patent holder, and a generic producer, agree to settle either a patent infringement suit or a dispute concerning the validity of the patent under terms that require, firstly, the generic manufacturer not to produce and/or to distribute the patented product until the expiration of the patent, and secondly, the patent holder to "compensate" the generic company for staying out of the market.

Both in the United States and in Europe, the competition agencies and national/regional courts have perceived such arrangements as an attempt to allocate markets and preserve monopolistic conditions[25] and have condemned them as clear violations of competition law.[26] In the United States the Supreme Court has already had the opportunity to pronounce on the legal assessment of this kind of patent settlements.[27]

In July 2013, the European Commission fined Lundbeck and several producers of generic medicines for delaying generic market entry of Citalopram.[28] In December

[25] Announcing the Commission's decision on the *Servier* case, then Competition Commissioner Joaquín Almunia stated "Servier had a strategy to systematically buy out any competitive threats to make sure that they stayed out of the market. Such behavior is clearly anti-competitive and abusive. Competitors cannot agree to share markets or market rents instead of competing, even when these agreements are in the form of patent settlements. Such practices directly harm patients, national health systems and taxpayers". See European Commission, Press Release of 9 July 2014, IP/14/799. http://europa.eu/rapid/press-release_IP-14-799_en.htm.

[26] In Europe, see European Commission, Press Release of 19 June 2013, IP/13/563 (Antitrust: Commission fines Lundbeck and other pharma companies for delaying market entry of generic medicines). http://europa.eu/rapid/press-release_IP-13-563_en.htm?locale=en; Press Release of 10 December 2013, IP/13/1233 (Antitrust: Commission fines Johnson & Johnson and Novartis € 16 million for delaying market entry of generic pain-killer fentanyl). http://europa.eu/rapid/press-release_IP-13-1233_en.htm; Press Release of 9 July 2014, IP/14/799 (Antitrust: Commission fines Servier and five generic companies for curbing entry of cheaper versions of cardiovascular medicine). http://europa.eu/rapid/press-release_IP-14-799_en.htm. All press releases accessed 23 October 2014. At the time of writing this contribution, no public version of these decisions was yet available. For an overview of the FTC's practice see Cook (2001), pp. 437 et seq. (commenting particularly on *In re Schering-Plough Corp.*, 136 F.T.C. 956 (2003); *FTC v. Watson Pharm., Inc.*, 611 F. Supp. 2d 1081 (C.D. Cal. 2009) and *FTC v. Cephalon, Inc.*, 551 F. Supp 2d 21 (D.D.C. 2008)).

[27] See *Actavis* decision.

[28] Press release Commission: http://europa.eu/rapid/press-release_IP-13-563_en.htm?locale=en Information of General Court upon time of completion not available (July 2015).

2013, the Commission fined Novartis and J&J[29] which concluded an agreement whose aim was to delay the market entry of cheaper generic version of Fentanyl, a painkiller. This was a straightforward pay-for-delay case as it did not involve any patent dispute or litigation.

In the US, the *Actavis* decision of the Supreme Court[30] sets the legal standard for the appreciation of pay-for-delay cases. After a discrepancy of decisions from lower courts, the Supreme Court concluded that the rule of reason should be applied to reverse payment settlements.

3 Excessive Pricing of Pharmaceuticals: An Emerging Enforcement Trend

Three aspects are discussed in this section: first, pricing of pharmaceuticals and IPRs, second, the case law on excessive pricing, third, the competition related issues raised by the case law on excessive pricing.

3.1 Pricing of Pharmaceuticals and IPRs

IPRs affect the pricing of pharmaceuticals. The IP system has two dimensions: On the one hand, it regulates the conditions of acquisition of IPRs. On the other hand, it allows the right holder to exercise the exclusivity of the right conferred, by, for instance setting a given price for IP embodied products such as pharmaceuticals. Hence, an important right of IPRs holders is the freedom of pricing of IP embodied products. Freedom of pricing of pharmaceuticals is part of the exclusivity the IPRs holder enjoys. However, freedom of pricing pharmaceutical, as a right, is not absolute. It should be exercised in accordance with the principles of the market. Hence, pricing of pharmaceuticals should not be anticompetitive.

From a competition law perspective, a core principle of the market economy and competition is the freedom of the pharmaceutical companies to set the prices of their products. Freedom of pricing pharmaceuticals is an expression of the general freedom of contract (freedom to enter into business dealings) which also is a tenet of the market economy.[31] When an IPR is involved, contractual freedom may be exercised through licensing agreements. Sometimes, as part of the general IP policy

[29] See press release of Commission: http://europa.eu/rapid/press-release_IP-13-1233_en.htm; full text of judgment available at http://ec.europa.eu/competition/antitrust/cases/dec_docs/39685/39685_1976_7.pdf.

[30] 570 ***U.S.*** 133 S. Ct. 2233 (2013). Judgment of the US Supreme Court available at: http://www.supremecourt.gov/opinions/12pdf/12-416_m5n0.pdf.

[31] For discussion on freedom of contract and competition law, see, Bakhoum (2018), pp. 157–186.

and the need to prevent potential abuse exercise of IPRs, freedom of contract, and of pricing, may be limited in order to protect the competitiveness of the markets and consumers. Contractual freedom and the freedom to set prices should not lead to anticompetitive practices that could take a form of high pricing of pharmaceuticals. High pricing is considered, in some competition law, as a form of abuse of dominant position.

3.2 Overview of the Case Law on Excessive Pricing of Pharmaceuticals

Excessive pricing is considered a type of abuse of dominant position in number of jurisdictions. This is the case in the EU and some of its Member States. In South Africa also high pricing is considered an abuse of dominant position. If in principle, this form of prohibition is recognized, in practice, competition authorities have been very reluctant in dealing with excessive pricing cases.

Recently, however, high pricing of pharmaceuticals has attracted the attention of competition authorities with a number of cases in the UK, the EU and in South Africa. In the EU, the Aspen case on excessive pricing decided by the Italian Competition Authority has attracted significant attention. Ongoing investigations both in the EU and in South Africa illustrate what could be considered as an emerging enforcement trend on the application of competition law in the pharmaceutical sector.

The Italian Aspen case illustrates how important it is to have competitive markets in order to make TRIPS flexibilities operational. In this case, the Italian Competition Authority fined Aspen for infringing Article 102 (a) of the TFEU. The Italian Competition Authority considered that Aspen "had fixed unfair prices with increases up to 1500%".[32] It results from the facts that Aspen had acquired an off-patent cancer drug package from GlaxoSmithKline. The antitumor drugs are considered life-saving and irreplaceable especially in the treatment of children and elderly patients.

After acquiring the rights on the drugs, Aspen initiated "negotiations with the Italian Medicines Agency (*Agenzia Italiana del Farmaco - AIFA*) with the sole aim to obtain a high increase in prices, even in the absence of any necessary economic justifications".[33] An important factual element in the Aspen case is that there was a public procurement with the authorities purchasing directly the drugs from Aspen. Aspen used aggressive negotiation strategy with the Italian Medicines Agency and

[32] See Press release on the Aspen case, 14/10/2016, available at: http://www.agcm.it/en/newsroom/press-releases/2339-a480-price-increases-for-cancer-drugs-up-to-1500-the-ica-imposes-a-5-million-euro-fine-on-the-multinational-aspen.html. For discussion of the case, see also, Lanza and Sfasciotti (2018), pp. 382–388.

[33] See Press release on the Aspen case, op. cit.

threaten to interrupt supply to the Italian market.[34] As a consequence of its negotiation strategy Aspen obtained extremely high prices ranging between 300% and 1500% of the initial levels.[35]

Two aspects were considered by the Italian Competition Authority when assessing the excessiveness of the prices charged by Aspen. It first considered the disproportion between price and cost. Second, it considered additional aspects such as the "specific context and behavioural factors, such as: the inter-temporal comparison of prices, the absence of economic justifications for the increase, the absence of any extra-economic benefits for patients, the nature of Comos's drugs, the characteristics of the Aspen group, and the damage caused to the National Health System (Sistema Sanitario Nazionale – SSN)".[36]

Similar investigations on excessive pricing have been opened by other competition authorities. In 2017 the EU Commission opened its first formal investigation on excessive pricing against Aspen for life saving cancer medicines.[37] The facts of the ongoing case are the same as the facts in the Aspen Italian case. The medicines in question were off-patent and Aspen acquired them after their patents had expired. As in the Italian case, "Aspen has imposed very significant and unjustified prices increases of up to several hundred percent (. . .)".[38] Moreover, "Aspen has threatened to withdraw the medicines in question in some Member States and has actually done so in certain cases".[39]

In the UK, the Competition and Markets Authority (CMA) in 2016 fined Pfizer, Inc. (**Pfizer**) and Flynn Pharma Limited (**Flynn**) for charging excessive price for an anti-seizure drug. The CMA found that both Pfizer and Flynn were dominant in their respective markets of manufacturing and distribution of Epanutin and had significantly improved their cost-profit margins by increasing the sale price by 2600%.

In South Africa, the South African Competition Authority had opened investigations against Roche, Pfizer and Aspen on high pricing.[40] The Commission mentioned that Roche has and *"continue[s] to engage in excessive pricing, price discrimination and/or exclusionary conduct in the provision of breast cancer medicine in South Africa"*.[41] The Commission added that *"as a result of exorbitant*

---

[34] See Press release on the Aspen case, op. cit.

[35] See Press release on the Aspen case, op. cit.

[36] See Press release on the Aspen case, op. cit.

[37] European Commission, Press Release, Antitrust: Commission opens formal investigation into Aspen Pharma's pricing practices for cancer medicines, May 15, 2017, http://europa.eu/rapid/press-release_IP-17-1323_en.htm.

[38] May 2017 European Commission, Press Release, Antitrust: Commission opens formal investigation into Aspen Pharma's pricing practices for cancer medicines, May 15, 2017.

[39] May 2017 European Commission, Press Release, Antitrust: Commission opens formal investigation into Aspen Pharma's pricing practices for cancer medicines, May 15, 2017.

[40] Media release, South African Competition Commission, 13 June 2017, available at: http://www.compcom.co.za/wp-content/uploads/2017/01/International-pharmaceutical-companies-investigated-for-cancer-medicine-prices.pdf.

[41] Media release, South African Competition Commission, 13 June 2017, op. cit.

prices, most breast cancer patients in both the private and the public sectors are unable to get treatment".[42] The investigation against Pfizer relates also to *excessive pricing* of lung cancer medication. According to the Commission, *"Pfizer is the only provider of lung cancer treatment medication known as xalkori crizotinib in South Africa"*.[43] The investigation seems to be based on the fact that *lung cancer treatment is unaffordable in South Africa* given the high prices that the consumers are unable to afford. A Parallel investigation to the ongoing investigation in the EU is open against Aspen. The Investigation is based on a *"reasonable suspicion that Aspen has and continues to engage in excessive pricing in the provision of certain cancer medicines (...)"*.[44]

In the context of South Africa, the open investigations are in line with the earlier trend of the Commission to investigate anticompetitive practices in the pharmaceutical sector. A complaint was lodged before the South African Competition Commission against *GlaxoSmithKline South Africa (Pty) Ltd ("GSK") & Boehringer Ingelheim (Pty) ("BI")*,[45] (hereinafter *GSK/BI* case), initially for high pricing, but then the Commission extended the investigation to include an alleged violation of Section 8(b) and (c) of the Competition Act, which deals respectively with the essential facilities doctrine and exclusionary conduct.[46] The Competition Commission concluded its investigation with a finding that GSK and BI abused their dominant position by *charging excessive prices, refusing to grant access to essential facilities to a competitor* and *engaging in exclusionary conduct*. The matter did not come before the Competition Tribunal, as GSK and BI accepted a settlement, which resulted in a drastic reduction in the prices of the pharmaceuticals in South Africa.

What can be learned from the Aspen Italian case and the ongoing investigations on excessive pricing of pharmaceuticals?

3.3 Competition and IP Issues Raised by the Case Law on Excessing Pricing of Pharmaceuticals

A number of lessons can be learned from the case law on excessive pricing of pharmaceuticals. There is an IP dimension and a competition law dimension in the analysis.

---

[42] Media release, South African Competition Commission, 13 June 2017, op. cit.

[43] Media release, South African Competition Commission, 13 June 2017, op. cit.

[44] Media release, South African Competition Commission, 13 June 2017, op. cit.

[45] The case was settled. For discussion of the background of the case, see, Berger (2004), pp. 197–201. The Commission's comments on the case at: South African Competition Commission Newsletter, edition.15, pp. 1–2. http://www.compcom.co.za/assets/Uploads/AttachedFiles/MyDocuments/March-04-Newsletter.pdf.

[46] For a discussion of the case, see Ngobese and Mncube (2011).

3.3.1 IP, Patent Term and Excessive Pricing of Pharmaceuticals

The case law on excessive pricing raises a number of issues that question the rationale of the IP system regarding access to pharmaceuticals.

The Italian Aspen case is not about IPRs and an abuse of a monopoly by a right holder during the protection term. It is true that pharmaceuticals are involved in the case. However, the pharmaceuticals patents for the cancer drugs had already expired when Aspen acquired them. As a consequence, IPRs cannot be invoked in order to justify the high prices charged by Aspen. The rationale of the IP system according to which the right holder has the exclusivity to commercialize its products at "monopoly price" is not applicable in this case. Aspen had acquired the pharmaceuticals at the end of the protection period. At the end of the exclusivity term, Aspen could still charge prices that are even higher than the prices of the pharmaceuticals when the patents were into force. The behavior of Aspen contradicts the very rationale of the IP system according to which price competition by generics should, in principle, drive the prices of pharmaceuticals down. Hence, at the end of the patent term, the rationale of the IP system that generic competition should take place and drive the prices down is not operational in this case. This is an important aspect of the Aspen Italian case. In Fact, the prices of the pharmaceuticals when the patents were in force were lower than the prices charged by Aspen when the drugs were off-patent.

Price competition by generics does not necessarily follow the end of the exclusivity period. For price competition by generics to take place the market conditions have to be attractive enough for generic companies to enter the market at the end of the patent term. If there is not price competition at the end of the exclusivity period, the patent holder still can charge high prices.

Another important element of the analysis is that the drugs had not been developed by Aspen. The usual justification of the recognition of the right of the IP holder to charge high prices is the investment made for the development of the IP embodied product. In this case, this rationale does not justify the high prices charged post-patent term. In fact, in the Italian Aspen case, the cancer drugs are produced by third party companies without any mobilization of resources by Aspen. To the contrary, the production costs of the medicines have considerably decreased over time.[47] The increase of prices could not be justified by any costs since Aspen did not make any additional investment nor did it face any increase of production costs. Aspen did not make any improvement on the medicines and their related services.[48]

[47] See Lanza and Sfasciotti (2018), p. 386.

[48] Ibid.

3.3.2 Competition Law and Excessive Pricing of Pharmaceuticals: Market Conditions and Pricing

Market Power, Size of the Market and High Pricing

The structure of a given market and its competitive conditions influence prices. If a market is open with low entry barriers and substitute products or services are available, there is a likelihood that the prices become competitive. If to the contrary, a market is very small, only one undertaking offers a service or product, and there is no substitute, there is a likelihood to have dominance and market power which allow the undertaking to charge high prices. In pharmaceuticals markets, this may happen even for off-patent drugs. In the Aspen case, for example, the small size of the market of the pharmaceuticals involved afforded Aspen market power and allowed it to charge high prices. Blood cancer drugs in the case "has a small incidence on the population and the specific categories of patients treated with Aspen's drugs further restrict the market size".[49] The small size of the market for blood cancer drug afforded Aspen sufficient power to bargain for high prices with the Italian Medicines Agency. Aspen's market power allowed it to charge high prices without fear of losing market shares. Compared to the prices of the pharmaceuticals when the patents were in force, the prices increased from 300% to 1500%. The prices of the patented medicine were more affordable than the prices of the same medicine off-patent. This price increase was only possible because the market was not competitive and Aspen did not face any competition constraints that obliged it to reduce its prices.

Market power allows an undertaking to behave into the market without taking into account actual or potential competition. It allows, for instance, an undertaking to set prices without fear of losing market share. The negotiation strategy adopted by Aspen confirms its market power. Using its market power, Aspen adopted an aggressive negotiation strategy and threatened to interrupt the supply of the Italian market.[50] Aspen was able to use its superior bargaining power since it has market power and did not face any competition. As pointed out, "the absence of any medical alternative for the cure of the weakest fringe of patients made them non-substitutable (essential) for the NHS, thereby depressing AIFA's bargaining power in the negotiation with the company".[51]

Absence of Substitutability and High Pricing of Pharmaceuticals

The concept of substitutability is used in competition law analysis in order to determine whether two products or services belong to the same market. It allows

[49] Ibid.

[50] Ibid.

[51] Lanza and Sfasciotti (2018), p. 386.

the competition authorities to define the relevant market and thereby determine whether a given undertaking enjoys a dominant position. If a market is small and there is no substitute for a given product, there is a strong likelihood that the undertaking offering the product will be found dominant. However, as a reminder, the simple fact of being dominant is not prohibited. Only abusive behavior resulting from a dominant position, such as charging excessive prices, is prohibited.

In the Aspen Italian case, Aspen's market power was reinforced by the absence of alternative medicines in the market. Hence, no substitutable drugs existed in the market for the category of patients in Aspen's market. This absence of substitutability of Aspen's pharmaceuticals limit the ability of the consumers to turn to substitute products when prices become high. No substitute existed for the pharmaceuticals involved in the case which are used to treat severe oncological diseases for children and elderly people. In other words, consumers could not shift to alternative pharmaceuticals that have similar therapeutic virtues when the prices become high. Given the absence of substitute pharmaceuticals, the Italian Medical Agency did not have a choice but to accept the prices charged by Aspen.

Consumer Choice/Behavior (Rationality) and the Specificity of Pharmaceuticals

What has been termed as "consumer rationality"[52] is also an element to be considered when pharmaceuticals are involved in a given case. Hence, if life saving drugs are involved, consumer behavior may be different. For life saving pharmaceuticals, in the absence of alternative drugs, consumers have a strong willingness to pay, no matter how high the prices are. Consumer rationality that commands consumers to seek alternative, more affordable, sources of supply when prices become high is not strong in the case of pharmaceuticals. If life saving drugs are involved, and there is no substitute, consumer rationality becomes absent.

From a contract law perspective, an argument can be made that since consumers are willing to pay competition authorities should not intervene in the contract relationships. However, the absence of substitute medicines and the uneven bargaining powers[53] between consumers and Aspen, which has market power, should limit the freedom of contract.

The combined factors which are Aspen's market power, the lack of alternative products (substitute) and the absence of consumer rationality allowed Aspen to impose high prices on consumers.

---

[52] Ibid.

[53] For discussion on freedom of contract and competition law, see, Bakhoum (2018).

The Issue of the Determination of an Excessive Price

Competition authorities have been very reluctant to deal with excessive pricing given the issues raised by the assessment of high pricing. What amounts to an excessive price is a first hurdle that makes competition law intervention difficult. Whether dealing with excessive pricing is a form of regulation by competition authorities is another issue. By dealing with excessive pricing, competition authorities can be seen as price regulators. Regulating prices is not in principle the role of competition authorities. If from a theoretical point of view dealing with excessive pricing raises a number of issues, a number of competition laws still consider high pricing as a form of abuse of dominant position. A firm with a dominant position may charge excessive prices without the risk of market entry of competitors and thus without the risk of competition. How to determine high prices? What is the relation between the economic value of a product or service and high prices?

Excessive pricing may be assessed in relation to costs. In the Aspen case, the Italian Competition Authority applied the following method:

- An estimation of excessiveness based on "percentage gross margin"
- A profitability analysis—based on an approximation of the economic value of the drugs which takes into account all overall costs of making and commercializing the drug—compared to actual prices charged.[54]

The cost price analysis was the main approach of the Italian Competition Authority in determining excessive pricing: As pointed out, *"ICA's investigation on the unfair practice was carried out through a two-phase test that measured the disproportion between prices and costs. The unreasonableness of the mentioned disproportion resulted indicative of unfair prices also in the light of specific context and behavioural factors, such as: the inter-temporal comparison of prices, the absence of economic justifications for the increase, the absence of any extra economic benefits for patients, the nature of Comos's drugs, the characteristics of the group Aspen and the damage caused to the National Health System (Sistema Sanitario Nazionale – SSN)".*[55]

Although Aspen did not incur any additional costs, it has substantially increased the prices. As indicated, there was "no investment to be recovered, no risk assumption by Aspen, no dry hole; no owned production facility, no freeze of financial resources by Aspen; no need to promote the drugs, no promotional costs to be recovered; no actual competitor, due to the absence of substitutability".[56] From a cost perspective, Aspen did not bring forth additional arguments that justify the increase of prices.

---

[54] See, Lanza and Sfasciotti (2018), p. 385.

[55] See Press release on the Aspen case, op. cit.

[56] See, Lanza and Sfasciotti (2018).

4 Excessive Pricing of Pharmaceuticals and TRIPS Flexibilities: Lessons from the Excessive Prices Cases

A number of lessons can be learned from the case law on excessive pricing, especially the Italian Aspen case in relation to the rationale of the IP system and Competition law as a flexibility tool.

Although pharmaceuticals were involved in the Aspen case, one can argue that the case raised only competition law issues. Since the patents of the cancer drugs involved in the Aspen case had already entered the public domain when Aspen acquired them, the behavior of Aspen could not be considered as an abuse of IPRs. The exclusivity afforded to the right holder of the pharmaceuticals ended with the patent term. The subsequent price increase at the end of the patent period could not, in principle, be considered an abuse of IPRs since the patented pharmaceutical has entered the public domain. However, in practice, the right holder of the off-patent pharmaceuticals continued to enjoy a *de facto* exclusivity and was able to charge high prices. Hence, although the pharmaceuticals involved in the Aspen case were no longer patented, the prices were not reduced. Such situation is not in line with the very rationale of the IP system according to which at the end of the patent term generic competition should kick in and drive the prices down. Similar to the reverse payment settlement cases that delay the entry in the market of generics, an abuse of dominant position post patent term may also slow the competition by generics.

Price reduction of pharmaceuticals is not automatic at the end of the patent term. There is a close link between the competitiveness of the market post patent and the reduction of prices at the end of the patent term. Whether prices of pharmaceuticals would be reduced at the end of the exclusivity period depends on the competitiveness of the market. If the market is open and competitive at the end of the exclusivity period with a possibility of entry of generics, prices may be reduced. However, generic entry is not automatic either. Generic entry takes place only if the market is attractive and that there is a strong likelihood to have return on investment. In the Italian Aspen case, there was no competition by generics despite the absence of patents attached to the drugs. Absent generic competition, the right holder continues to enjoy a *de facto* exclusivity and to be able to charge high prices. If a given market is small enough so that a pharmaceutical company enjoys a monopoly position, it can continue to charge excessive prices even at the end of the exclusivity period.

Substitutability and consumer choice are important for price reduction of pharmaceuticals to take place. Absence of substitute and consumer choice, a patent owner may continue to have market power and to charge high prices at the end of the patent protection. This is a de facto extension of the exclusivity rights. Patent protection does not necessarily create market dominance. However, market dominance may exist after the expiration of the exclusivity period if there is no competition in the market. Under certain market conditions at the expiration of the exclusivity period (market power, absence of substitute, no generic competition, price inelasticity, strong willingness of consumers to pay) the IP owner may still charge monopoly prices without fear of losing market shares.

The Aspen case showcases how important it is to create competitive markets and to protect/promote competition in pharmaceuticals markets through a strong competition law enforcement. When IP flexibilities and the very rationale of the IP system are not operational at the end of the exclusivity period, competition law can be used as a tool to correct the anticompetitive behavior and to complement the IP system. As already pointed out, the design of TRIPS which have a competition law dimension as a flexibility tool gives to Member States the possibility to create strong competition law institutions in complement to the IP related flexibilities *stricto sensu*.

It also results from the Aspen case that under certain circumstances, access is more guaranteed (and prices are lower) during the exclusivity period, when the patent is still into force. This is the case when the flexibilities are fully applicable during the exclusivity period. It is possible during the patent term to use the flexibilities of the IP system such as issuing compulsory licenses. This possibility does not exist at the end of the exclusivity period.

There is a close link between the operability of the rationale of the IP system and its flexibilities and the market conditions. As highlighted in the discussion in this paper, having competitive markets participate to the operability of the core principles of the IP system and its flexibilities.

5 Conclusions

Competition law enforcement is a complement of the IP system and its flexibilities. IP and competition law are two regulatory instruments that both have their potential and limits. IP affords rights. Competition law defines the framework for the commercialization. The freedom of IP owners to determine the price of pharmaceuticals should be exercised while respecting the market (competition) rules.

The IP system and its flexibilities of the IP system have intrinsic limitations that affect their operability. They may not, in some situations, have the expected effect on access to pharmaceuticals. The Doha declaration and article 31*bis* of the TRIPS agreements illustrate the difficulties to use the IP system in order to foster access to pharmaceuticals. There exist also some limits related to the scope of the IP system and its flexibilities. The IP system does not address the behavior of right holders that may affect prices of pharmaceuticals after the expiration of the patent term. Post patent term abusive behavior are beyond the reach of the IP system. In such situations, as illustrated by the Aspen case, only competition law may help reinstate the balance of the IP system.

The scope of application of competition law is more extended than the application of the IP flexibilities. Competition law polices the behaviors of market participants. It addresses practices when IPRs are into force and at the end of the protection term. Competition law is applicable when patented and off-patent products are involved such as in the Aspen case. Competition authorities are required to evidence a clear breach of the rules of the markets (e.g. cartels, abuse of dominance) and a clear framework of analysis is provided by the law. The evolution of competition enforcement in the pharmaceuticals sector since the entry into force of the TRIPS agreement has illustrated an evolutive approach that could have a positive impact of competition law enforcement on access to pharmaceuticals. The cases discussed in the UE, in Italy and in South Africa illustrate this trend to use a proactive role of competition law as an access to pharmaceuticals tools.

But competition law application in the pharmaceuticals sector is not without its issues: enforcement of competition law to IP related restrictions may be problematic. Hence, an argument can be made that strong enforcement may chill investment in R&D and innovation. However, in addition to access, competition law takes into account the innovation parameters when applied to IP related restrictions. With regards to pharmaceuticals patents, the question of the balance between access and innovation raises issues. Can lower prices of pharmaceuticals (access) and innovation (bringing new pharmaceuticals into the market) be aligned? Does one want lower prices of pharmaceuticals or is innovation more important?

In cases involving charging high prices post patent term, as it was the case in Aspen, the innovation argument cannot be strongly supported. One could argue that in post patent term cases, after the expiration of the patent, the incentives to innovate argument should not be considered since the exclusivity rights have expired. The patent holder has already reaped the benefits and rewards of the invention. However, one also should take account of the argument that even after the expiration of the patent, strong enforcement of competition law and regulation of prices may affect R&D incentives.

Four different situations can be contemplated:

- If the flexibilities within the IP system work and may be used in order to enable the reduction of prices, one could consider that there may not be an access problem even if IP protection exists.
- IP flexibilities may work but anticompetitive conduct restricts their positive impact on prices and access. If for instance IP flexibilities are not operational because of anticompetitive practices, one could argue that there is a case for competition law intervention.
- If IP flexibilities do not work the question arises as to whether there is a case for competition law to correct the shortcomings.
- No IP flexibilities because IP protection expired: one could argue that there is a case also for competition law intervention as illustrated by the Aspen case. IPRs could no longer be an obstacle to competition law intervention.

The discussions of the paper is largely based on the case law in developed jurisdictions. However, developing and LDC countries can learn a lot from the approach of developed countries of using competition law as an external flexibility in order to foster access to medicine during the patent term and after the expiration of the patent. South Africa is making efforts in that direction. Developing countries with limited competition culture and resources still face the challenge of enforcing their competition law to restrictions of competition affecting access to medicines. Though the lack of challenges is an issue, it is crucial for policy makers and enforcer to encourage the application of competition law in the pharmaceutical sector in combination to the TRIPS flexibilities.

References

570 ***U.S.*** 133 S. Ct. 2233 (2013). Judgment of the US Supreme Court available at: http://www.supremecourt.gov/opinions/12pdf/12-416_m5n0.pdf. Accessed 24 Feb 2021

Bakhoum M (2018) Abuse without dominance in competition law: abuse of economic dependence and its interface with abuse of dominance. In: Di Porto F, Podszun R (eds) Abusive practices in competition law (ASCOLA Competition Law series). Edward Elgar Publishing, Cheltenham, UK; Northampton, MA, USA, pp 157–186

Bakhoum M, Gallego BC (2016) TRIPS and competition rules: from transfer of technology to innovation policy. In: Ullrich H, Hilty RM, Lamping M, Drexl J (eds) TRIPS plus 20 – from trade rules to market principles, p 9

Berger J (2004) Advancing public health by other means: using competition policy, pp 197–201

Berger J (2006) Advancing public health by other means: using competition policy. In: Roffe P, Tansey G, Vivas-Eugui D (eds) Negotiating health: intellectual property and access to medicine. Earthscan, London, p 182

Case T-472/13, Lundbeck v. Commission, infra, box n° 1; Case C-142/18, J&J et al. vs. Commission ("Fentanyl"), infra, box n° 2; Case U.S. Supreme Court No. 12-416, FTC v. Actavis, infra, box 3

Case T-691/14, Servier and others v. Commission (still pending)

Cook A (2001) Pharmaceutical patent litigation settlements: balancing patent & antitrust policy through institutional choice. Mich Telecommun Technol Law Rev 17(2):417–458

Directive 2001/29/EC of the European Parliament and of the Council of 22 May 2001 on the harmonization of certain aspects of copyright and related rights in the information society, OJ L 167, pp 10–19

Directive 2004/48/EC of the European Parliament and of the Council of 29 April 2004 on the enforcement of intellectual property rights, OJ L 195, 2 June 2004, pp 16–25

Directive 96/9/EC of the European Parliament and of the Council of 11 March 1996 on the legal protection of databases, OJ L 77, 27 March 1996, pp 20–28

Directive of the European Parliament and of the Council of 27 September 2011 amending Directive 2006/116/EC on the term of protection of copyright and certain related rights, OJ L 265, 11 October 2011, pp. 1–5; Sonny Bono Copyright Term Extension Act, Pub. L. No.105–298, 112 Stat. 2827 (1998)

Drexl J (2004) International competition policy after Cancún: placing a Singapore issue on the WTO development agenda. World Compet 27(3):419–457

Drexl J (2013) Astra Zeneca and the EU sector inquiry: when do filings violate competition law? In: Drexl J, Lee N (eds) Pharmaceutical innovation, competition and patent law – a trilateral perspective. Edward Elgar, Cheltenham, pp 290–322

European Commission (2009) Pharmaceutical Sector Inquiry – Final Report. http://ec.europa.eu/competition/sectors/pharmaceuticals/inquiry/staff_working_paper_part1.pdf. Accessed 24 Feb 2021, pp 16 and 19

European Commission, Competition enforcement in the pharmaceutical sector (2009–2017), available at: https://ec.europa.eu/competition/sectors/pharmaceuticals/report2019/report_en.pdf

European Commission, Antitrust: Commission welcomes improved market entry for lung disease treatments. Press Release of 6 July 2011, IP/11/842. http://europa.eu/rapid/press-release_IP-11-842_en.htm. Accessed 24 Feb 2021

European Commission, Press Release, Antitrust: Commission opens formal investigation into Aspen Pharma's pricing practices for cancer medicines, 15 May 2017. http://europa.eu/rapid/press-release_IP-17-1323_en.htm. Accessed 24 Feb 2021

European Commission, Press Release of 10 December 2013, IP/13/1233 (Antitrust: Commission fines Johnson & Johnson and Novartis € 16 million for delaying market entry of generic pain-killer fentanyl). http://europa.eu/rapid/press-release_IP-13-1233_en.htm. Accessed 24 Feb 2021
European Commission, Press Release of 19 June 2013, IP/13/563 (Antitrust: Commission fines Lundbeck and other pharma companies for delaying market entry of generic medicines). http://europa.eu/rapid/press-release_IP-13-563_en.htm?locale=en. Accessed 24 Feb 2021
European Commission, Press Release of 9 July 2014, IP/14/799 (Antitrust: Commission fines Servier and five generic companies for curbing entry of cheaper versions of cardiovascular medicine). http://europa.eu/rapid/press-release_IP-14-799_en.htm. Accessed 24 Feb 2021
Gallasch S (2015) Pharmaceutical antitrust: use but with caution, contribution Keynote Speech at UNCTAD Roundtable on The Role of Competition in the Pharmaceutical Sector and its Benefits for Consumers, 8 July 2015 http://unctad.org/meetings/en/Presentation/CCPB_7RC2015_PRES_RTPharma_Gallasch_en.pdf. Accessed 24 Feb 2021
Lanza EM, Sfasciotti PR (2018) Excessive price abuses: the Italian Aspen case. J Eur Compet Law Pract 9(6):382–388
Media release, South African Competition Commission, 13 June 2017., available at: http://www.compcom.co.za/wp-content/uploads/2017/01/International-pharmaceutical-companies-investigated-for-cancer-medicine-prices.pdf
Ngobese M, Mncube L (2011) Competition policy in South Africa's pharmaceutical sector: balancing competition and innovation (unpublished)
Press release on the Aspen case, 14/10/2016. http://www.agcm.it/en/newsroom/press-releases/2339-a480-price-increases-for-cancer-drugs-up-to-1500-the-ica-imposes-a-5-million-euro-fine-on-the-multinational-aspen.html
Roffe P (2014) Intellectual property chapters in free trade agreements: their significance and systemic implications. In: Drexl J, Grosse Ruse-Khan H, Nadde-Phlix S (eds) EU bilateral trade agreements and intellectual property: for better or worse? Springer, Berlin, p 17 et seq
Ullrich H (2005) Expansionist intellectual property protection and reductionist competition rules: a TRIPS perspective. In: Maskus KE, Reichman JH (eds) International public goods and transfer of technology under a globalized intellectual property regime, pp 727–756
Ullrich H (2013) Strategic patenting by the pharmaceutical industry: towards a concept of abusive practices of protection. In: Drexl J, Lee N (eds) Pharmaceutical innovation, competition and patent law – a trilateral perspective. Edward Elgar, Cheltenham, pp 241–272
Ullrich H, Heinemann A (2007) Die Anwendung der Wettbewerbsregel auf die Verwertung von Schutzrechten und sonst geschützten Kenntnissen. In: Immenga U, Mestmäcker E-J (eds) Wettbewerbsrecht, Band I. EG/Teil 2, Kommentar zum Europäischen Kartellrecht, p 146
UNCTAD Roundtable on The Role of Competition in the Pharmaceutical Sector and its Benefits for Consumers, Geneva, 6-10 July 2015. https://unctad.org/system/files/non-official-document/CCPB_7RC2015_RTPharma_EC_en.pdf

The Impact of 'TRIPS-Plus' Rules on the Use of TRIPS Flexibilities: Dealing with the Implementation Challenges

Mohammed El Said

Abstract Improving the health and well-being of society is a priority to many governments. One essential element within this debate focuses on the accessibility and affordability of medicines for patients. Although interest in this area has persisted for decades, the recent shift in this field is manifested by this now being treated as a global concern, rather than as a regional or a national one. Patients in both developed and developing countries alike are facing the same challenges and are under an increased pressure to access and afford treatment. The recently published UN High Level Panel for Access to Medicines Report explicitly stated its view of 'access to medicines, vaccines, diagnostics and related health technologies as a serious, multidimensional global problem, with challenges that affect all people and all countries.. . .the High-Level Panel recognizes that the costs of health technologies are rising globally and are being felt by individuals and by public and private insurance schemes in both wealthy and resource-constrained countries alike' (UN Secretary General High Level Panel, 'The United Nations Secretary-General High-Level Panel on Access to Medicines Report: Promoting Innovation and Access to Health Technologies', (September 2016), 12. https://apps.who.int/medicinedocs/documents/s23068en/s23068en.pdf.). This thinking represents a fundamental departure from the previous approach which classified the problem related to access to medicines as one mainly attributed to developing and least developed nations. It is within this debate that the role of intellectual property protection in general and by way of the rise of TRIPS-Plus agreements and their impact on accessibility and affordability of medicines takes centre stage.

The author would like to thank Professor Graham Dutfield for his valuable feedback and insights on this chapter. The usual disclaimer applies.

M. El Said (✉)
School of Justice, UCLAN, Preston, UK
e-mail: mel-said@uclan.ac.uk

C. M. Correa, R. M. Hilty (eds.), *Access to Medicines and Vaccines*,
https://doi.org/10.1007/978-3-030-83114-1_11

1 Introduction

There are many factors which impacts the access to medicines debate. Government policy, industrial development, demography, manufacturing capabilities, market conditions and procurement and tax regimes are some factors. However, for some time, the role of intellectual property monopolies especially patents granted to innovator drug companies to protect their research and development (R&D) investments and provide market exclusivity by restricting competition became an integral part of this debate.[1] This chapter will look at various factors affecting the accessibility and affordability debate and will focus on the role of intellectual property protection in that process. It will provide useful examples of the positive impact arising from the use of the TRIPS flexibilities and on the other hand will explain the dangers affiliated with adopting TRIPS-Plus regimes in this regard. It will also provide examples of practises and strategies which would limit the impact of TRIPS-Plus commitments under national laws.

2 Expensive Medicines: National Implications and Global Challenges

The price of medicines has been on a steady increase for some years. In the US, prices for branded prescription drugs doubled in five years between the period of 2011–2016.[2] Further, it was projected that the prices of medicines in the US will increase on average 5.8% in 2020.[3] More than 13% of Americans—about 34 million people—say a friend or family member recently passed away in the last five years after being unable to afford treatment for a condition while 58 million adults report inability to pay for needed drugs in the past year, according to a new poll from Gallup and West Health.[4] A recent study in the UK found that total National Health Service (NHS) spending on medicines in England has grown from £13 billion in 2010/11 to £17.4 billion in 2016/17—an average growth of around 5% a year. The

[1] It should be highlighted that there are also other regulatory regimes and intellectual property exclusivities—apart from patents—aimed towards extending protection including those protecting use of test data, various regulatory linkages, and also trademarks covering not just names but also shapes and colours.

[2] MSF (2016). http://apps.who.int/medicinedocs/documents/s23020en/s23020en.pdf.

[3] In 2019 more than 50 companies raised the prices on hundreds of drugs in the US by an average of more than 6%, according to the analysis. Hopkins explains that the price of rheumatoid arthritis treatment Humira, the world's top-selling drug, was raised by 7.4%. Similarly, heparin products—which are generic blood thinners typically administered in hospitals—prices rose by 15%. For more see Hopkins (2020) <https://www.marketwatch.com/story/drug-prices-rise-58-on-average-in-2020-2020-01-02>.

[4] Gallup and West Health (2019). https://news.gallup.com/poll/268094/millions-lost-someone-couldn-afford-treatment.aspx?version=print.

same study concludes, 'These figures are uncertain due to gaps in data, but the rate of increase is substantially faster than for the total NHS budget over the same period'.[5] With the prevalance of the COVID 19 pandamic, pressure on national health providers have reached unprecedented levels.

The year 2019 was phenomenal in terms of setting new high records in medicines prices. In March 2019, the United States Food and Drug Administration (USFDA) approved the most expensive medicine in history up to date called Zolgensma (priced at $2.125 million), a medicine used for a rare disorder that destroys a baby's muscle control and kills nearly all of those with the most common type of the disease within a couple of years. Other more commonly used medicines' prices have also been notably high. For example, a 2018 WHO report on cancer medicines concluded that 'in the absence of insurance coverage, cancer treatment is unaffordable for many patients. A course of standard treatment for early stage HER2 positive breast cancer (doxorubicin, cyclophosphamide, docetaxel, trastuzumab) would cost about 10 years of average annual wages in India and South Africa and 1.7 years in the United States of America. The costs associated with other medical care and interventions (such as surgical interventions and radio-therapy) and supportive care (such as anti-emetics and haematopoietic growth factors) would make overall care even more unaffordable. Even with insurance coverage, patients living with cancer in many countries have reported financial stress, to the extent that they may lower the treatment dose, partially fill prescriptions or even forego treatment altogether'.[6] In France, in December 2015, the Ligue contre le cancer—which spends around €38 million ($43 million) a year on cancer research, making it the largest French non-governmental funder of cancer R&D—condemned cancer drug prices as 'exorbitant, unfair and unbearable' and warned that if unabated, price inflation for new drugs posed a direct threat to the French medical system[7] while others have expressed that "economic considerations significantly influence and, in some instances, take precedence over the scientific evidence" with relation to French Guidelines on antiretroviral therapy treatment.[8]

Newly developed hepatitis C drugs' prices have also raised eyebrows. The efficient drug Sovaldi was launched at a list price of $84,000 for a standard twelve-week treatment course, or about $1000 a pill. At the most recent average net price of $45,000 per patient for all sofosbuvir-based products in the US, it would cost $135 billion dollars to treat the estimated three million people with chronic hepatitis C in the US—over one third of total annual spending on all prescription drugs in the US.[9] In the UK, the list price for a 12-week course of sofosbuvir was

[5] The King's Fund (2018) https://www.kingsfund.org.uk/sites/default/files/2018-04/Rising-cost-of-medicines.pdf.

[6] WHO (2018), p. xi https://apps.who.int/iris/bitstream/handle/10665/277190/9789241515115-eng.pdf?sequence=1&isAllowed=y.

[7] Sciences Avenir with AFP (2015). http://www.sciencesetavenir.fr/sante/cancer/20151216.OBS1499/la-ligue-contre-le-cancer-denonce-les-prixexorbitants-des-medicaments-innovants.html.

[8] Raffi and Reynes (2014), p. 1158.

[9] I-MAK (2017).

nearly £35,000 (excluding VAT) and double that for a 24-week course.[10] Notwithstanding the high price, in early 2015 sofosbuvir was recommended for funding based on its cost effectiveness. However, because of the budget impact of the treatment, in the following months the NHS England delayed consistent provision of sofosbuvir, instead phasing introduction through the use of quotas and prioritising patients with the most severe need.[11] From 2012 to 2019, the average price of AbbVie's rheumatoid-arthritis drug Humira climbed from $19,000 a year to $60,000 a year.[12]

The effects of this are felt in both developed and developing countries. Greater number of patients are now unable to afford medicines while governmental health budgets are struggling to cater for the needs of its citizens, a situation made worse during the COVID 19 pandamic. Henceforth, patients in the developing countries are lacking essential medicines and lifesaving treatments, diabetics have died in the US due to high price of insulin while the Dutch government has had to suspend its acquisition of the immune-oncology drug Keytruda (despite the fact that it helped in its development) because it was too expensive.[13] The NHS in the UK—a wealthy country which, unlike the United States, has a publicly funded and all-inclusive health service with considerable bargaining power—is having to ration the supply of cancer drugs due to financial restrictions on treatment[14] while waiting times for those actually offered the treatment are far too lengthy.[15]

3 Unequal Investment and More Monopoly

The problem which high prices of medicines poses should not be viewed in isolation of other contributing factors engulfing this debate. One issue which ranks high within this context is the challenge of inadequate funding for diseases primarily affecting the financially underprivileged or for which the opportunities to make large and long-term profits are considered by the industry to be limited.

Growing criticism has been made regarding the deficiency of the global regime in finding solutions to long standing diseases (or as some refer to as neglected

[10] Boseley (2015) https://www.theguardian.com/society/2015/jan/16/sofosbuvir-hepatitis-c-drug-nhs.

[11] Gornall et al. (2016), p. 4117.

[12] Entis (2019).

[13] The Economist (2019).

[14] Donnelly (2015). The article further identifies that in total, 17 cancer drugs for 25 different indications will no longer be paid for in future in the UK.

[15] According to January 2019 NHS England data, almost 25% of cancer patients didn't start treatment on time despite an urgent referral by their primary care doctor. This represents the worst performance since records began in 2009. For more see Pipes (2019). https://www.forbes.com/sites/sallypipes/2019/04/01/britains-version-of-medicare-for-all-is-collapsing/#4c6ebeb736b8.

diseases) or the unequal distrbution of COVID 19 vaccines as an example. One visible area of concern is that related to the development of new antibiotics, an issue the WHO have classified as a global challenge in recent years. According to WHO, "No major new class of antibiotics has been discovered since 1987 and too few antibacterial agents are in development to meet the challenge of multidrug resistance."[16] One of the main issues related to lack of investment and R&D in this field is attributed to the industry's fear that resistance to these drugs would develop eventually hence eliminate the usefulness of the drug rapidly which may explain why most major pharmaceutical companies have stopped research in this area, a situation that has been described as a "serious market failure" and "a particular cause for concern".[17]

In a recently published two reports, the WHO warned about the adverse effects of the declining private investment and lack of innovation in the development of new antibiotics. The WHO further highlighted how this is also undermining efforts to combat drug-resistant infections and diseases. The WHO reports found that the 60 products currently in development (50 antibiotics and 10 biologics) bring little benefit over existing treatments and very few target the most critical resistant bacteria (Gram-negative bacteria).[18] The Chairman of the UK Review on Antimicrobial Resistance warned recently that, if left unaddressed, drug-resistant infections could be responsible for the deaths of some ten million people a year by 2050, and $100 trillion in economic damage.[19]

Other neglected diseases also share similar challenges and evident lack of investment and innovation. For example, a 2002 analysis of new chemical entities developed between 1975 and 1999 found that only 1.1% were actually treatments devoted to tuberculosis (TB) and tropical diseases, despite them causing 11.4% of the global disease burden.[20] Although the years between 2000 and 2011 witnessed some improvement whereby of the 850 new therapeutic products registered, 4.4% were for neglected diseases.[21] However, according to the same study, only 4 of the 336 new chemical entities brought to the market during the same period were for neglected diseases (including malaria)—just 1.2% of the total.

[16] WHO (2015), p. 5 http://apps.who.int/iris/bitstream/10665/193736/1/9789241509763_eng.pdf. However, it was announced in late 2019 that a new antibiotic for drug-resistant tuberculosis—pretomanid was finally approved by the FDA. Interestingly, the drug was developed by the non-profit TB Alliance rather than the industry. For more see Dearment (2019) https://medcitynews.com/2019/08/new-antibiotic-for-drug-resistant-tuberculosis-scores-fda-approval/.

[17] Ibid, 11.

[18] The two WHO reports cited below also found that research and development for antibiotics is primarily driven by small- or medium-sized enterprises with large pharmaceutical companies continuing to exit the field. For more see WHO (2017) https://apps.who.int/iris/bitstream/handle/10665/258965/WHO-EMP-IAU-2017.11-eng.pdf?sequence=1, and WHO (2019) https://apps.who.int/iris/bitstream/handle/10665/330290/WHO-EMP-IAU-2019.12-eng.pdf.

[19] O'Neill (2015).

[20] Trouiller et al. (2002), p. 2188.

[21] Pedrique et al. (2013), p. 371.

TB which is the biggest infectious disease killer in the world today is another case in point, whereby the death toll alone in 2014 was 1.5 million lives. Until very recently, no new drug was introduced for nearly 50 years.[22] Furthermore, the last treatment—largely inadequate due to its side effects—developed for Chagas disease (leading cause of infectious heart disease in Latin America) was over 40 years ago.

Ebola also placed the global treatment regime under security. Médecins Sans Frontières (MSF) who often operates within the disease-stricken countries further states that the 'fact that MSF frontline health workers lacked a treatment or a vaccine for Ebola virus as the outbreak engulfed Guinea, Sierra Leone and Liberia in 2014 is a poignant illustration of this problem. But the problem of inadequate or non-existent treatments and vaccines was a challenge for MSF long before 2014'.[23] Notably, it was only in late 2019, it was announced that a new vaccine was approved in the US and EU for Ebola.[24]

4 The Double Taxation of Society

One of the strongest criticisms against pharmaceutical companies is the way they engage in business activities and R&D operations. It is vital to acknowledge that innovator pharmaceutical companies need incentives to protect their investments. Yet to what extent that should be sought at the expense of public health policy concerns is questionable. The high prices of medicines does not only have a negative effect regarding accessibility, but have also attracted criticism due to the fact that a vast number of medicine discoveries and some of the subsequent drug development, or indeed much of it in some cases, was funded by tax payers. The situation is made worse by anticompetitive behaviour of some of these companies.

It is no secret that the governmental levels of financial and technical support for biomedical innovations are considerable. The public sector makes substantial contributions to research and development upfront, through grants, subsidies and tax credits. In fact, some studies suggest that 30% of the estimated $240 billion yearly total global investment across all health R&D comes from the public sector.[25]

Several cases illustrate this, including Truvada. The drug was initially developed and patented by the US government after the Centers for Disease Control and Prevention (CDC) received $50 million in federal grants in addition to $7 million from the Bill and Melinda Gates Foundation in 2015. However, the government did not receive any income and no improvement in terms of accessibility rates was observed (it is believed that less than 10 percent of the 1.1 million people who should be on treatment are receiving it) despite the fact that Gilead Sciences the maker of the

[22] See MSF (2016).

[23] See MSF (2016), p. 8.

[24] For more see Herder et al. (2020), pp. 1–14.

[25] Røttingen et al. (2013), p. 1286, also see MSF (2016).

drug earned $3 billion in sales in 2018 prompting the US government to initiate legal action against Gilead.[26]

Moreover, a study found that during the past four decades, 153 new FDA-approved drugs, vaccines, or new indications for existing drugs were discovered through research carried out in public sector research institutions (PSRIs). It was reported that these drugs included 93 small-molecule drugs, 36 biologic agents, 15 vaccines, 8 in vivo diagnostic materials, and 1 over-the-counter drug. More than half of these drugs have been used in the treatment or prevention of cancer or infectious diseases.[27]

Similar trends are observed elsewhere outside the US. In 2017, campaigners in the UK claimed that the NHS spent more than £1 billion on drugs developed from publicly funded research in 2016. A report published by campaign groups Global Justice Now and Stop Aids claimed that UK tax payers and patients worldwide are being denied the medicines they need, despite the public sector playing a pivotal role in the discovery of new medicines. It concluded that 'In many cases, the UK taxpayer effectively pays twice for medicines: first through investing in R&D, and then by paying high prices for the resulting medicine once ownership has been transferred to a private company.'[28] The report cites several examples of drugs which received public funding but now are out of the reach of majority of patients. For example, the report explains how Alemtuzumab was originally developed at Cambridge University and first approved for the treatment of B-cell chronic lymphocytic leukaemia (B-CLL). Cambridge scientists then led further investigations of its usefulness, at a smaller dosage, in treating multiple sclerosis (MS). Sanofi Genzyme, who had acquired the rights to the drug, removed it from the market as a B-CLL medicine and re-launched it as a medicine for MS. The Report verifies that 'At the time of withdrawal there was speculation that the exercise was motivated by commercial reasons. When it was used off-label (i.e. used for a non-licenced purpose) for MS prior to being withdrawn from the market, the pricc in the UK was around £2,500 per MS treatment course in 2012'. In 2017, it costs was £56,000 per treatment course—a 22-fold increase.[29]

On the other hand, several anticompetitive practises have had a far-reaching impact on prices. Even when there are opportunities to reduce prices, we find that this is not taken advantage of (and even intentionally delayed). A recent study found that of the more than 1600 generic drugs approved by the FDA since January 2017, more than 700—or 43 per cent—are not for sale in the US.[30]

---

[26] Rowland (2019).

[27] Stevens et al. (2011), p. 535.

[28] Global Justice Now and Stop AIDS (2017), p. 7. https://www.globaljustice.org.uk/sites/default/files/files/resources/pills-and-profits-report-web.pdf.

[29] Ibid at 10.

[30] Mole (2019) https://arstechnica.com/science/2019/02/drug-companies-are-sitting-on-generics-43-of-recently-approved-arent-for-sale/.

Delaying tactics have also incurred huge costs on society. One study estimates that the American health system is poised to incur $55 billion during the next 15 years on three drugs (related cancer and hepatitis C treatment) alone due to patents blocking and delaying the entry of generic competition on these drugs only. Product lifecycle management, whereby branded companies obtain unmerited patents to delay competition,[31] is the primary strategy identified and evaluated by this study. The study also highlights that another related strategy is "pay-for-delay" whereby branded companies pay generics to stay off the market for some time.[32]

5 More Pharmaceutical Patents, Weaker Innovation

An equally troubling development which has contributed to the increase in medicines prices and extended monopoly patent terms in recent years is the increase in the number of drug patents granted, particularly those 'inventions' which are of a low and inferior quality, or as may be referred to as frivolous/trivial patents. This process is leading to what is referred to as the 'evergreening' of drugs.[33]

This development may be explained by looking at some national statistics in this regard. For example, it was found that between the years 2006 and 2016, the number of drug patents granted in the US doubled. The granted patents were mainly dedicated to accumulating patents not for new medicines but rather for small changes to existing ones, which allows them to build and extend monopolies, block

[31] It should be noted that the product lifecycle management starts at the development and regulatory approval stages and extends beyond the expiry of the granted patent. Notably, drug manufacturers do not only rely on patent protection when devising their lifecycle strategies. For example, reliance on trademark protection and branding is also vital in providing effective means to secure and maintain a strong market position. For more on this see Dutfield (2020). file:///C:/Users/melsaid/Downloads/Not_Just_Patents_and_Data_Exclusivity_Th.pdf.

[32] I-MAK identifies the following three multi-billion-dollar drugs as having questionable patents that are providing excess exclusivity periods:

- Revlimid® (lenalidomide): Unmerited patents enable a minimum exclusivity period from 2019 through 2028. Payers are projected to spend $45 billion in excess costs for the drug within this period, prior to the first generic product entering the market.
- Sovaldi® (sofosbuvir): Unmerited patents will prevent competition from now through 2034, when final patents held by Gilead Sciences expire on the drug. Payers are projected to incur $10 billion in excess costs.
- Gleevec® (imatinib): In the one-year period from 2015–16, approximately $700 million dollars in excess costs were passed onto payers as a result of a pay-for-delay deal cut by Novartis to a generic company in exchange for delaying the entry of generic imatinib.

For more see I-MAK (2017).

[33] The majority of these patents focuses on developing so-called 'me-too' drugs—medicines which have only small clinical advantages over existing drugs, but which can be patented and bring substantial profits. The effects of evergreening vary but the primary impact would be to extend the monopoly term granted to patents. For more see Kesselheim et al. (2006), p. 1637.

competition and drive prices up.[34] Moreover, on the 12 best-selling drugs in the US, drug makers have filed an average of 125 patent applications and have been granted an average of 71 patents for each.[35] Another study found that 74 applications have been filed on Lantus (it is a man-made form of a hormone (insulin) that is produced in the body which works by lowering levels of glucose (sugar) in the blood) only in the US, which have the potential to delay competition for 37 years.[36] This kind of "over patenting" blocks competition and enables pharmaceutical companies more freedom to regulate the pricing market of medicines.[37]

Elsewhere the findings are similar. A study in Australia found an average of 49 secondary patents granted for each of the 15 highest-cost drugs over a 20-year period. One-quarter of these secondary patents were believed to be evergreening patents.[38] The Office of Patented Medicines and Liaison at the Therapeutic Products Directorate of Health Canada estimates that 44% of the 419 medicines on the Patent Register are covered by more than one patent.[39]

Moreover, an EU investigation concluded in 2008 that out of the 219 molecules in the sample under the investigation, originator and generic companies identified at least 1300 patent-related out of court contacts and disputes concerning the launch of generic products in the period 2000 to 2007. The vast majority of disputes were initiated by the originator companies, which most often invoked their primary patents, e.g. by sending warning letters. In this respect the inquiry finds that individual medicines are protected by up to nearly 100 product-specific patent families, which can lead to up to 1300 patents and/or pending patent applications across the Member States. Despite the lower number of underlying patent families based on European Patent Office (EPO) applications, looking from a commercial perspective, 'a challenger may, in the absence of a European Community patent, need to analyse and possibly confront the sum of all existing patents and pending patent applications in those Member States in which the generic company wishes to enter'.[40]

---

[34] Amin and Kesselheim (2012), p. 2286.

[35] I-MAK (2018a) http://www.i-mak.org/wp-content/uploads/2018/08/I-MAK-Overpatented-Overpriced-Report.pdf.

[36] I-MAK (2018b). http://www.i-mak.org/wp-content/uploads/2018/10/I-MAK-Lantus-Report-2018-10-30F.pdf.

[37] Amin and Kesselheim examined patents granted for two HIV drugs (ritonavir and lopinavir/ritonavir) and found that Abbott owned 82 secondary patents and had a further 26 pending applications in the US, all of which involved small variations on the original patents for these drugs. They found that these evergreening patents could delay generic competition for 19 years beyond the date from which generic entry would have been anticipated. For more see Amin and Kesselheim (2012).

[38] Christie et al. (2013), p. e60812.

[39] Office of Patented Medicines and Liaison (2005).

[40] EU Commission (2008), p. 10. https://ec.europa.eu/competition/sectors/pharmaceuticals/inquiry/communication_en.pdf.

Elsewhere, another analysis found of the 1015 new drugs and indications approved in France between 2004 and 2013, only 6.3% offered a clear therapeutic advantage, almost none were considered breakthroughs, and the majority (69.3%) offered no clear therapeutic benefit or were prematurely approved even though their clinical evaluation showed them to be more harmful than beneficial.[41] A second analysis found that 85 to 90% of new products approved over the last four decades have provided only limited benefits.[42] A third study that looked not just at registered products, but specifically at new chemical entities and new biologics, found that the majority of those launched in the UK between 2001 and 2012 were only "slightly innovative" and only a quarter (26%) were believed to be "highly innovative".[43]

Rather than using the patent regime as an incentive to innovate and recoup investment for worthy inventions, 'evergreening' tactics and practises are in fact blocking accessibility and weakening innovation capabilities by undermining the true foundations of the patent regime and turning it into monopoly creator with no positive contribution to society's needs.[44]

6 Increased IP Standards: From TRIPS-Minus to TRIPS-Plus

The global regulation of intellectual property rights is a relatively modern concept. Prior to the creation of the World Trade Organization (WTO) in 1996, countries had considerable policy space and full discretion in designing their national intellectual property legal regimes in accordance with their development stage and national priorities.[45] As such, a large number of countries did not award legal protection to patents related to drugs and pharmaceutical products.[46]

This was no longer the case with the creation of the WTO. The Agreement on Trade Related Aspects of Intellectual Property Rights (the TRIPS Agreement)[47] obligated member states to provide legal protection for inventions in all technological fields including pharmaceutical products. This was an important development whereby for the first time in history, countries lost the ability to regulate their

---

[41] Prescrire International (2005), pp. 68, 71.

[42] Light and Warburton (2016), p. 34.

[43] Ward et al. (2014), p. 6235.

[44] Drahos (2010).

[45] See generally Machlup and Penrose (1950), p. 1.

[46] See El Said (2010).

[47] See the Agreement on Trade-Related Aspects of Intellectual Property Rights, Apr. 15, 1994, Marrakesh Agreement Establish the World Trade Organization, Annex 1C, 1869 U.N.T.S. 299 [hereinafter TRIPS Agreement] (listing the limitations on use of intellectual property by third parties authorized by the government).

national intellectual property regimes freely and in accordance with their national development plans.

Reaching consensus regarding the TRIPS agreement was not a simple act. The intellectual property negotiations during the Uruguay Round of Trade Negotiations were amongst the most contentious and complex. As such and in order to strike a balance between the rights of users and intellectual property holders on the one hand, and the society on the other, several 'flexibilities' were introduced within TRIPS in order to curtail the negative impact which may arise from excessive intellectual property protection and at the same time to enable countries to deal with their public health challenges and emergencies.

6.1 The Flexibilities Explained

The TRIPS 'flexibilities' may best be explained as options available to member states allowing them to comply with the TRIPS Agreement requirements and at the same time maximise the implementation space available to them in accordance with their priorities.[48] Following are some examples of the health-related flexibilities available under the agreement to member states:

- ***Transitional periods.*** According to the WTO, least developed countries (LDCs) are given an extended transition period to protect intellectual property under the WTO's TRIPS Agreement. This is in recognition of their special requirements and status, their economic, financial and administrative constraints, and the need for flexibility so that they can create a viable technological base. Several extensions of the transition period were provided by the TRIPS Council. The last 6th of November 2016 Council decision extends until January 2033 the period during which key provisions of the WTO's intellectual property agreement, the TRIPS Agreement, do not apply to pharmaceutical products in LDCs.[49] This means LDCs can choose whether or not to protect pharmaceutical patents and clinical trial data before 2033. The decision also keeps open the option for further extensions beyond that date.[50]

[48] There is a general differentiation in the literature between expressly provided safeguards, limitations/exceptions and countervailing legal principles and objectives on the one hand, and vague terminology on the other hand where there are provisions and omissions whose scope is subject to a wide range of interpretations in accordance with national and international legal regimes. For more see El Said (2010).

[49] See the Council for Trade-Related Aspects of Intellectual Property Rights, Extension of the Transition Period under Article 66.1 of the TRIPS Agreement for Least Developed Country Members for Certain Obligations with Respect to Pharmaceutical Products, Decision of the Council for TRIPS of 6 November 2015.

[50] In 2019, Uganda notified the African Regional Intellectual Property Organisation (ARIPO) that it is exercising its right as a least-developed country by stating that pharmaceutical inventions are not

- ***Compulsory licensing.*** A tool through which the state authorizes a third party to exploit patented inventions, generally against a specified royalty paid to the patent holder provided that several conditions set under the TRIPS Agreement (Article 31) are complied with. The objective behind this is to curtail anti-competitive behaviour and ensure the transfer of technology and dissemination of knowledge.[51]
- ***Government use exceptions.*** A tool which grants the state the right to use the patent without obtaining the consent of the patent holder for the purpose of public interest, including public health necessities. Although government use conditions are similar to compulsory licensing, government use exceptions provide an added advantage by fast-tracking the process, through granting the government the right to use the pharmaceutical patent without the need for prior negotiations with the owner.
- ***Parallel importation.*** This tool gives the option to member states to obtain patented products when they are lawfully available in a foreign market at a lower price, thus enabling countries to shop for cheaper patented products. This requires as a prerequisite that a country adopt an exhaustion regime suitable to its needs and priorities.[52]
- ***Exceptions to patents rights.*** Article 30 of TRIPS provides that members "may provide limited exceptions to the exclusive rights conferred by a patent, provided that such exceptions do not unreasonably conflict with a normal exploitation of the patent and do not unreasonably prejudice the legitimate interests of the patent owner, taking account of the legitimate interests of third parties."[53] However, the above provision does not define the scope of the permissible exceptions thus awarding member countries some considerable discretion to operate. Examples of these exceptions include the Bolar exception[54] and the research and experimental use exception.
- ***Standards of patentability.*** Under TRIPS, patent protection must be granted for products and processes which are *new*, involve an *inventive step* and are *industrially applicable*.[55] However, each of these are not defined and can be interpreted

---

eligible for patent protection in the country. See 't Hoen (2019). https://medicineslawandpolicy.org/2019/10/uganda-tells-aripo-no-more-patents-for-pharmaceuticals/.

[51] The special compulsory licensing system in the amended TRIPS Agreement, and the earlier 2003 waiver decision, (sometimes called the "Paragraph 6 System" because it refers to paragraph 6 of the Doha Declaration) only deals with compulsory licences to produce medicines expressly for export purposes.

[52] See TRIPS Agreement, Article 6.

[53] See TRIPS Agreement, Art. 30.

[54] This important exception facilitates the production and introduction of generic medicines into the market on the date of patent expiry. Accordingly, this exception permits the use of an invention for the purpose of obtaining approval of a generic product before the patent actually expires and without having to obtain the patentee's approval. The WTO ruled that the use of this exception is TRIPS-compliant. For more see the WTO (2000).

[55] See TRIPS Agreement, Art. 27.

and applied by member states in accordance with their national priorities and objectives. For example, TRIPS do not specify the patenting of new uses of known products, including pharmaceutical drugs, thus allowing member countries the possibility of rejecting these new uses for lack of novelty, inventive step or industrial applicability.
- ***Other procedural flexibilities.*** Another identified policy tool that may be used to improve the quality of granted patents and limits "evergreening" is pre-grant and post-grant patent oppositions, in addition to patent revocation proceedings. These methods have been used at different times in a wide range of developed and developing countries. Such proceedings enable interested parties to bring claims before the patent office on the basis that a particular patent does not meet local requirements.

6.2 *Putting the Flexibilities into Use*

We now have a considerable body of literature and empirical research dedicated to the benefits of utilising the TRIPS Agreement's flexibilities under national laws. Despite this, some would still argue that the use 'of the TRIPS flexibilities has been sporadic and limited'[56] and that more could still be achieved in this regard.[57]

A much widely affiliated issue with the use of the flexibilities is the issue related to the impact of generic drugs entry into the market and the savings achieved as a result. In many cases, this is enabled by the flexibilities effect in curtailing 'evergreening' and in opposing low quality patents. As such, it is common to see medicine prices dropping substantially (ranging between 30–90 percent in some cases) when generic medicines enter a market following the expiry of a patent.[58]

Compulsory licensing is the most used flexibility in this regard.[59] There is no scarcity of evidence with relation to the positive impact compulsory licensing has had upon improving access to medicines. Malaysia was one of the latest countries to issue a "government use" compulsory license to obtain much cheaper version of a generic version of the famously known hepatitis C medicine Sofosbuvir in September 2017. It is believed that compulsory license issuance have enabled treatment cost at RM1000 to RM1200 ($240–$285) for 12 weeks course, compared to RM300,000 (approx. $72,000) which was the cost of treatment with the patented

[56] 't Hoen et al. (2018), pp. 185–193.

[57] For more see El Said (2014), p. 60.

[58] See El Said (2010).

[59] See number of compulsory licenses issued in 't Hoen et al. (2018), p. 188. However, it should be kept in mind that the ability to use compulsory licensing is not an available option to all countries equally but is rather more relevant to those which possess manufacturing capabilities.

version and prior to issuance of the license.[60] Moreover, it was reported that between 2013 and 2017, the Ecuadorian Institute of Intellectual Property (IEPI) issued ten compulsory licences for various medications including antiretroviral drugs.[61] According to health officials in Ecuador, the compulsory licenses granted between 2013 and 2014, generated the potential for savings of 23 per cent to 99 per cent.[62] Similar findings may also be found in the case of other compulsory licenses issued by Thailand, India, Indonesia, Brazil and Columbia.[63]

One of the other important flexibilities available to countries is related to the issue of patentability standards. As highlighted, member countries have a wide discretion and freedom to apply and define the patentability criteria of an invention under their national regime. As such, India has applied a strict patentability criteria aimed towards limiting the number of frivolous or secondary pharmaceutical patents granted.[64] Although we cannot measures the direct price impact this will have on medicines nevertheless it is believed that the utilisation of this flexibility have a substantial impact in preventing patent abuses and the granting of low quality patents (anti-evergreening strategy).[65] Other countries such as China and Philippines are following a similar approach to the Indian one in this regard.[66]

Egypt provides an interesting case as well. The country is home to the highest rate of HCV infections in the world. The Egyptian's Patent Office practise won praise couple of year ago when it rejected one of Sofosbuvir patent applications through its application of a strict patentability criteria. This allowed a local generic producer to produce the drug for less than $200 per 12-week treatment.[67]

---

[60] For more see Ling (2019). http://english.astroawani.com/malaysia-news/using-compulsory-licence-affordable-medicines-200558.

[61] The issued compulsory license were for three ARV medicines namely Ritonavir+Lopinavir and Lamivudine+Abacavir, for Etoricoxib (Arcoxia® for the treatment of diseases with acute pains); Mycophenolate Sodium (MYFORTIC) used in the treatment of reception of kidney transplants; sunitinib, an anticancer drug used for the treatment of carcinoma renal cells (CRC) and gastrointestinal stromal tumours (GISTs); and finally Certolizumab, used to counteract rheumatoid arthritis. See Correa and Velásquez (2019), p. 16. https://www.southcentre.int/wp-content/uploads/2019/04/RP85_Access-to-Medicines-Experiences-with-Compulsory-Licenses-and-Government-Use-The-Case-of-Hepatitis-C_EN-1.pdf.

[62] Ibid, 18.

[63] For more see El Said (2016), p. 374.

[64] See Chatterjee (2013). https://www.ip-watch.org/2013/04/01/novartis-loses-patent-bid-lessons-from-indias-3d-experience/.

[65] See Sampat and Shadlen (2017), p. 693.

[66] Other countries are increasingly following India's patentability path. The Philippines patent law, as amended in 2008, introduced a section similar to the Indian 3(d) section (although less stringent than India's Patent Act).177

China has reformed its Patent Act in 2008 and 178. See Patent Law (promulgated by the Standing Comm. Nat'l People's Cong., Mar. 12, 1984, rev'd Dec. 27, 2008), art. 22. For more see El Said (2016).

[67] Velasquez (2019), p. 108.

Parallel importation is another flexibility already used by several countries with positive results. For example, six African countries (Ghana, Kenya, Mauritius, Namibia, South Africa and Zimbabwe) have incorporated an international exhaustion regime in their laws, allowing parallel imports from anywhere in the world. More specifically, Kenya has actively and effectively used parallel importation to improve access to antiretroviral medications.[68]

Opposition procedures have been applied usefully and efficiently in several countries. This issue is posed to gain more importance due to the increased volume of pharmaceutical patents granted worldwide. To give a glimpse, it is believed that current estimates suggests that at least 27% of current patents would be found invalid by US courts due to low quality.[69]

There are many more examples of the use of the flexibilities by both developed and developing countries which this chapter will not delve into. However, a number of observations could be made about the efficient and successful use and implementation of these flexibilities under national regimes. First, the need for a proactive national legislature is fundamental for the success of this process. Although these flexibilities are available under the international intellectual property regime, their implementation would not take place directly without legislating—in details—them under national laws and regulations. Second, awareness about the existence of these flexibilities is vital for their utilisation. Thirdly, the need for an engaged public, national entities and active civil society is essential for the success of this process as demonstrated by many thus far. Lastly, independent and highly trained judiciary is vital in the process of implementation and interpretation of these flexibilities under national legal frameworks.

6.3 The Shift Towards TRIPS-Plus

The TRIPS Agreement was subsequently used as a platform for further regulation of intellectual property rights globally. Although the initial understanding of developing countries was that TRIPS would put an end to unilateralism and coercion in the regulation and enforcement of intellectual property by developed countries particularly the United States, that vision turned out to be misguided. Within a short period of time following the creation of the TRIPS Agreement, a new generation of bilateral and regional Free Trade Agreements (FTAs) started to emerge, with a far-reaching WTO-Plus agenda.

With relation to intellectual property, FTAs often contained dedicated chapters incorporating extensive intellectual property provisions which often include TRIPS-Plus obligations going beyond those required by the TRIPS Agreement. These

[68]UNAIDS (2011), p. 15. https://www.unaids.org/sites/default/files/media_asset/JC2260_DOHA%2B10TRIPS_en_0.pdf.

[69]Miller (2012). https://papers.ssrn.com/sol3/papers.cfm?abstract_id=2029263.

TRIPS-Plus obligations restricted the available policy space of member states and gradually eliminated the options and flexibilities available to them under the TRIPS Agreement.[70] Although the full impact of these TRIPS-Plus agreements is yet to materialise, we already have a considerable and rather frightening understanding—as will be explained in the next part of this chapter—about the negative impact these agreements have on affordability and accessibility to medicines.

6.4 *Impact and Examples of TRIPS-Plus Obligations*

Before looking into the negative impact of TRIPS-Plus, it would be helpful to understand how do FTAs increase intellectual property protection levels beyond the TRIPS standards? An important objective of TRIPS-Plus obligations is to limit the use of the flexibilities available under the international intellectual property regime thus making it more difficult to utilise such flexibilities. There are a number of areas where this may take place with relevance to patents and public health. These include the following examples:

- **Expanding the scope of pharmaceutical patents and creating new drug monopolies:** this is achieved through a number of ways such as:
  - lowering the patentability standards,
  - requiring patents be available for surgical and treatment methods,
  - minor variations on old medicines, new and second uses, and[71]
  - Further extension of protection to biological products which include vaccines, blood and blood components, and gene therapies in addition to other forms of protection.
- **Extension of monopolies** by extending patent terms if review at the patent office or regulatory authority failed completion within a certain period of time.
- **Risk facilitating patent abuse** by requiring countries to condition marketing approval on patent status (patent linkage).
- **Protection and Extension of "data exclusivity":** by providing at least 5 years exclusivity for information related to new products and 3 more in cases of new uses for old medicines—even when that information is disclosed and available in the public domain. More recent FTAs have also provided 10 years of "effective market protection" for biologics.[72]
- **Prohibition/restriction pre-grant oppositions**—forbid challenges to weak or invalid patents until after they have been granted.

[70] See Drahos (2001), p. 791 and El Said (2005), pp. 53–66.

[71] For more on this from an EU perspective please see Dutfield (2017), p. 453.

[72] Ney (2019). https://www.centerforbiosimilars.com/contributor/joshua-ney/2019/08/exclusivity-for-biologic-products-under-the-usmca-what-is-changing-and-what-happens-next.

- **Regulate the decisions to reimburse new drugs:** this gives drug companies new rights to challenge decisions on reimbursements if not favourable as currently proposed under the Transatlantic Trade and Investment Partnership (TTIP).
- **Require new forms of intellectual property enforcement–grant:** customs authorities detaining shipments, including in-transit shipments, suspected of non-criminal trademark/copyright/patent infringements; require mandatory injunctions for alleged intellectual property infringements; raise damages amounts, etc.
- **Introducing Investor-State Dispute Settlement (ISDS) procedures:** this leads to bypassing the WTO's multilateral dispute settlement procedure and opting for a more pro-investment one. This development has been highly controversial as this grant private investors considerable power, especially big multinational corporations, to claim high amounts of money of compensation from investor sympathetic tribunals. Indirectly, this questions the impact of these claims on states' power to regulate in the public interest, in order to safeguard public health priorities. Other flaws of the ISDS system include the lack of consistency in decision making and the huge costs incurred. There is now growing evidence that the threat of using these ISDS procedure is enough to obligate countries to change their policies.[73]

The undisputed recommendation in this regard from a public health perspective remains that countries should avoid entering into arrangements which obligates them to apply TRIPS-Plus standards under national law. As states by UNDP and UNAIDS:[74]

> Countries at minimum should avoid entering into FTAs that contain TRIPS-plus obligations that can impact on pharmaceuticals price or availability. Where countries have undertaken TRIPS-plus commitments, all efforts should be made to mitigate the negative impact of these commitments on access to treatment by using to the fullest extent possible, remaining public health related flexibilities available.

The thus far realised impact of TRIPS-Plus obligations on public health and access to medicines is frightening upon both developed and developing nations.[75] In one of the first studies ever conducted on the impact of TRIPS-Plus obligations, a 2007 Oxfam study on the effect of the US-Jordan FTA found that since 2001 (which is the year the FTA was signed with the US), the prices of medicines in Jordan have increased by 20% (this led to price increases between two and ten-fold for key medicines to treat cardiovascular disease and cancer), and data protection provisions has resulted in delaying generic drugs entry for 79% of medicines newly launched between the years 2002 and 2006.[76] The study estimates that the availability of

---

[73] For instance, in 2016; and Ukraine de-registered a generic hepatitis C medicine after Gilead indicated that it would pursue arbitration. For more see Gleeson et al. (2019), p. 78.

[74] UNDP and UNAIDS (2012) https://www.unaids.org/sites/default/files/media_asset/JC2349_Issue_Brief_Free-TradeAgreements_en_0.pdf.

[75] See El Said (2010).

[76] Oxfam (2007), p. 5 https://oxfamilibrary.openrepository.com/bitstream/handle/10546/114080/bp102-all-costs-no-benefits-trips-210307-en.pdf%3Bjsessionid%3D089750820CF675173F0C3204C369D63F%3Fsequence%3D1. Also see El Said (2006), p. 501.

generic equivalents would have reduced Jordan's expenditure on medicines by $6.3 and $22 million between mid-2002 and 2006.[77] The study also shows that no real know-how transfer has occurred in the country despite the rhetoric that FTAs would in fact encourage the flow of know-how and Foreign Direct Investment (FDI).

Although the 2007 Oxfam study was conducted under less than 5 years of the FTA implementation, we came a long way since then in terms of assessing and understanding the impact of FTAs on accessibility and affordability of medicines. More and more studies are affirming and exposing the negative impact of these obligations on public health and access to medicines.

Amin and Keselheim conducted a study on the impact of 'evergreening' resulting from the granting of secondary patents. The authors concluded that secondary patents could extend market exclusivity and thus delay generic competition from entering the market for many years. The study identified 108 patents related to two HIV medicines (ritonavir (Norvir) and lopinavir/ritonavir (Kaletra)) which impact could delay generic competition until at least 2028. This is a twelve years additional period after the expiration of the patents on the drugs' base compounds and thirty-nine years after the first patents on ritonavir were filed.[78]

For instance, research by Lexchin concluded that extension of legal protection in data protection for biologics have resulted in increase in spending in drug expenditure in Canada. He estimated the lost savings from data protection extension to range from $0 to $305.8 million.[79] Another study in Australia found:[80]

> At the time that the EOT [extension of the term] was introduced, the annual cost to the Pharmaceutical Benefit Scheme (PBS) was estimated to grow from $6 million in 2001-02 to $160 million in 2005-06. This cost arises because there is a delayed entry to the PBS of cheaper generic drugs. The estimate for 2012-13 is around $240 million in the medium term and, in today's dollars, around $480 million in the longer term. The total cost of the EOT to Australia is actually about 20 per cent more than this, because the PBS is only one source of revenue for the industry.

Another study conducted by the Australian Generic Medicines Industry Association analysed the costs to the health system for 39 PBS-listed medicines for which generic competition was delayed after the patent on the active pharmaceutical ingredient expired, as a result of secondary patenting found that in the 12 months to November 2012, the cost of delayed generic launch was calculated at $37.8–$48.4 million.[81] This estimate does not include subsequent price reductions due to price

---

[77] Oxfam, Ibid.

[78] See Amin and Kesselheim (2012).

[79] Lexchin (2019), p. 10.

[80] Harris et al. (2013), p. vi https://www.ipaustralia.gov.au/sites/default/files/2013-05-27_ppr_final_report.pdf?acsf_files_redirect. The Report found that about 58% of new molecules listed on the PBS from 2003 to 2010 received extensions of term. Of the term extensions granted since 1999, 47% received the full 5 years.18 The cost of these extensions to the PBS in 2012–13 was estimated at about $240 million in the medium term and about $480 million in the longer term.

[81] Gleeson et al. (2015), p. 306.

disclosure. Another study estimated the costs of patent extensions to the PBS in 2012–13 at about $240 million in the medium term and about $480 million in the longer term.[82] It was also found that data protection had no impact on the levels of pharmaceutical investment in the country as highlighted with the case of the US FTA with Jordan.

There has been much more work conducted recently in terms of alerting to the negative impact of the highly controversial Trans-Pacific Partnership Agreement (TPPA) agreement in this regard.[83] The TPPA which is widely promoted as a "model for 21st century trade agreements" is a comprehensive trade and investment deal covering many areas including trade, investment, labour and intellectual property rights in in addition to its investor-state dispute settlement procedure.[84] Brook concludes that 'Provisions in the Intellectual Property (IP) Chapter of TPP lengthen, broaden, and strengthen patent-related monopolies on medicine and erect new monopoly protections on regulatory data as well. IP Chapter enforcement provisions also mandate injunctions preventing medicines sales, increase damage awards, and expand confiscation of medicines at the border'.[85]

In comparing the TPPA with similar agreements, a study found that the US-Mexico-Canada Agreement's (USMCA) intellectual property chapter is closely based on the corresponding chapter of the TPPA, but includes 10 years of "effective market protection" for biologics in addition to including a broader definition of biologics, potentially expanding the array of drugs which will be eligible for this longer period of exclusivity, longer than the period negotiated in the TPPA.[86] For Canada, this will increase the period of market protection for biologics by 2 years; two studies of the potential impact on pharmaceutical expenditure (using different methods and based on different assumptions) have estimated the savings foregone at between CDN$0 and $305.8 and up to CDN$169 by 2029.[87]

7 What Could Be Done and What Is Done?

As explained, we have a considerable wealth of empirical research about the positive impact of TRIPS flexibilities use and the negative impact of TRIPS-Plus obligations on the health care and access to medicines regimes in several developed and developing countries. However, it has been more difficult to observe how countries

---

[82] Harris et al. (2013).

[83] The Office of the U.S. Trade Representative (USTR) issued a letter in 2019 to signatories of the Trans-Pacific Partnership Agreement that the United States has formally withdrawn from the agreement.

[84] The TPP is the first trade agreement to include provisions on pharmaceuticals that are, or contain, biologics, compounds produced through biological processes and which are used primarily for treating cancer and immune conditions.

[85] Baker (2016), p. e1001970.

[86] Swanson (2019). https://www.nytimes.com/2019/03/21/us/politics/nafta-drug-prices.html.

[87] Gleeson et al. (2015).

with TRIPS-Plus regimes have in fact attempted to utilise the remaining policy space available to them in order to mitigate the negative impact these TRIPS-Plus rules have on their national health care regimes. This is so primarily due to the difficulty in observing national practises and the lack of international jurisprudence arising from disputes about the implementation of these obligations (or rather about if such an implementation was in line with international norms or otherwise) under national frameworks.

In addition, it should be realised from the outset that the effect of TRIPS-Plus commitments will vary from each country and will depend on many factors, including market side, pharmaceutical protection capacity, development of legal regime, judiciary and so forth.

Nevertheless, and despite the above-mentioned difficulties, by looking into several cases, we have been able to observe some important contributions in this regard. The important aspect in this case is to continue applying and implementing a nationally creative thinking and interpretive policy aimed towards limiting the negative impact of the committed TRIPS-Plus rules. Following are examples of a number of national experiences of how countries attempted to limit the negative impact arising from TRIPS-Plus obligations.

7.1 Australia

One of the countries which have taken several serious steps in this field is Australia. This is because the country has agreed to a TRIPS-Plus obligations regime arising from the US-Australia FTA[88] which had a huge cost on the national health budget and the accessibility and affordability of medicines. Accordingly, in 2013,[89] the Australian legislator (following national consultation) introduced a number of reforms aimed towards mitigating the effects of the 'evergreening' of patents starting with applying a stricter patentability criteria by removing any geographical limitation upon the common general knowledge and by removing the requirement for a prior art document to be "ascertained".[90] The effect of this is to require a higher and more consistent inventive step standard for Australian patents granted in the country.

Another area tackled by the Australian legislator is the issue of patent term extension granted in order to compensate for the delays during marketing approval as dictated under the FTA with the US.[91] To start with, the 2013 Patent Law reform

---

[88] The US-Australia Free Trade Agreement (US-AUS FTA) signed in 2004.

[89] Intellectual Property Laws Amendment (Raising the Bar) Act 2012 No. 35, 2012 as amended. Start date15 April 2013, hereafter the 2013 Patent Law.

[90] Dixon (2017).

[91] See US-AUS FTA, Art.17.9.8(b) states:

> [E]ach Party shall make available an adjustment of the patent term to compensate the patent owner for unreasonable curtailment of the effective patent term as a result of the marketing approval process.

attempted to limit the possibilities of allowing patent term extension by further confining such type of extensions to certain and specific categories of products related to patents claiming new active ingredients or formulations only.[92]

Moreover, the Australian 2013 Patent Law reform imposes additional substantive conditions specifically applicable for the extension of patent duration for "pharmaceutical substances." Based on this, the extension of the term is possible only if either or both of the following conditions are satisfied:[93]

(a) one or more pharmaceutical substances per se must in substance be disclosed in the complete specification of the patent and in substance fall within the scope of the claim or claims of that specification;
(b) one or more pharmaceutical substances when produced by a process that involves the use of recombinant DNA technology, must in substance be disclosed in the complete specification of the patent and in substance fall within the scope of the claim or claims of that specification.

In addition, both of the following conditions must be satisfied in relation to at least one of those pharmaceutical substances:

(a) goods containing, or consisting of, the substance must be included in the Australian Register of Therapeutic Goods;
(b) the period beginning on the date of the patent and ending on the first regulatory approval date for the substance must be at least 5 years.

(4) The term of the patent must not have been previously extended under this Part. Meaning of first regulatory approval date.

More reforms were introduced with relation to opposition procedures as well. As such, detailed and expansive opposition grounds against patent term extension procedures were included under the 2013 Patent Law reform. Accordingly, Article 78 of the Patent Law states:

If the Commissioner grants an extension of the term of a standard patent, the exclusive rights of the patentee during the term of the extension are not infringed:

(a) by a person exploiting:
    (i) a pharmaceutical substance *per se* that is in substance disclosed in the complete specification of the patent and in substance falls within the scope of the claim or claims of that specification; or
    (ii) a pharmaceutical substance when produced by a process that involves the use of recombinant DNA technology, that is in substance disclosed in the complete specification of the patent and in substance falls within the scope

[92] See El Said (2016).

[93] See Patents Act 1990 (Cth) ch 6 pt 3 s 70 sub-divs (2)-(3) (Austl).

of the claim or claims of that specification; for a purpose other than therapeutic use; or

(b) by a person exploiting any form of the invention other than:

 (i) a pharmaceutical substance *per se* that is in substance disclosed in the complete specification of the patent and in substance falls within the scope of the claim or claims of that specification; or
 (ii) a pharmaceutical substance when produced by a process that involves the use of recombinant DNA technology, that is in substance disclosed in the complete specification of the patent and in substance falls within the scope of the claim or claims of that specification.

Patent linkage is another TRIPS-Plus issue whereby Australia's approach may provide some valuable lessons for others. Article 17.10.4 (in the Intellectual Property chapter) of the US-AUS FTA provides for an attenuated or 'weak' form of patent linkage with relation to two aspects as explained by Son et al:[94]

(a) measures in the marketing approval process to prevent a third party from marketing a product during the term of a patent without the consent of the patent owner; and
(b) no provision for the owner to be notified of a marketing approval request made during the term of a patent. This wording provided scope for Australia to implement a patent linkage mechanism in a very different way to the United States.

In addition, the Australian regime excludes from protection patents covering (1) the drug substance, (2) the drug product including composition and formulation, and (3) the approved use from the patent linkage mechanism.[95] Penalties for providing false or misleading information, however, are disproportionately higher for a patent holder certificate than for a generic producer certificate. Moreover, Australia's Pharmaceutical Benefit Scheme (PBS) imposes automatic and irreversible price cuts on medicines as soon as competing versions enter the market, this often incentivise generic companies to launch faster at risk, and innovator companies must pursue preliminary injunctions in order to resolve patent disputes.[96] At the same time, since 2012, Australia's Department of Health has pursued market-sized pecuniary damages (on top of those sought by the generic company) aimed at compensating for a delay in the PBS price reduction that would have been applied to a patented medicine during the period of a provisional enforcement measure.[97] However, there is no corresponding mechanism for the government to compensate

---

[94] Son et al. (2018), p. 101.

[95] Son et al. (2018), p. 101.

[96] GIPC (2019). https://www.theglobalipcenter.com/wp-content/uploads/2019/09/GIPC-Linkage-Zoom-In-Report.pdf.

[97] Australian Government Department of Health (2016). http://www.pbs.gov.au/industry/pricing/price-disclosure-spd/price-disclosure-operational-guidelines-06-2016.pdf.

innovators for the aforementioned losses if an infringing product is launched prematurely.[98]

Although such reforms are vital, they should not be viewed as the only solutions to the accessibility of medicines challange and therefore the intellectual property regime should be viewed as one of several components and government strategies—one element of an eco-system—in this regard which would improve accessibility and affordability of medicines. For an example, in February 2019, the Australian government signed a five-year deal with pharmaceutical companies, involving a lump sum payment of about $ 766 million for an unlimited five-year supply of the most advanced Hepatitis C (HCV) drugs.[99] This innovative approach which has been called the "subscription" or "Netflix" model, have reduced the per-patient costs of these cutting-edge treatments by roughly 85% in the country.[100]

7.2 Chile

Chile also proved an interesting case of a developing country which adopted a TRIPS-Plus regime as a result of signing an FTA with the US in 2006 (the US-Chile FTA). Following a rigorous national debate with relation to the negative effect of data exclusivity and patent linkage included under the FTA, the Chilean government amended the patent law by limiting the availability of data protection under its national law to those pharmaceutical products that have been marketed in the national territory in the year after the grant of marketing approval and therefore if the drug was not marketed within a year, the test data submitted for approval purposes will not be protected.[101] The rationale behind such a requirement is to encourage early registration of drugs after first registration abroad, so that the period of protection for the pharmaceutical test data starts early.

In addition, the law excluded several elements from the scope of protection. Accordingly, article 91 of the Chilean law states:

The protection of this Paragraph shall not apply when:

[98] GIPC (2019).

[99] The government also announced an investment of more than 1 Billion USD to enable universal access to HVC treatment. See Velásquez (2017). https://www.southcentre.int/wp-content/uploads/2017/05/RP77_Access-to-Hepatitis-C-Treatment-A-Global-Problem_EN-2.pdf.

[100] Moon and Erickson (2019), p. 607. Furthermore, the State of Louisiana announced in January 2019 that it was pursuing a similar approach for HCV. For more see Crisp (2019) https://www.theadvocate.com/baton_rouge/news/politics/article_614e4f42-1523-11e9-8c90-4fcb305d17e8.html.

[101] Law No. 19,039 art. 90, September 30, 1991 (modified on December 1, 2005 by Law 19,996, which classifies active ingredients as new chemical entities if they have not been marketed in the country prior to the health registration or authorization application). See also Biadgleng and Maur (2011), p. 20.

(a) The owner of the test data referred to in Article 89 has engaged in forms of conduct or practices declared as contrary to free competition in direct relation to the use or exploitation of that information, according to the final decision of the free competition court.
(b) For reasons of public health, national security, non-commercial public use, national emergency or other circumstances of extreme urgency declared by the competent authority, ending the protection referred to in Article 89 shall be justified.
(c) The pharmaceutical or chemical-agricultural product is the subject of a compulsory license, according to what is established in this Law.
(d) The pharmaceutical or chemical-agricultural product has not been marketed in the national territory after 12 months from the health certificate or clearance granted in Chile.
(e) The pharmaceutical or chemical-agricultural product has a health certificate

Furthermore, Chile implemented the linkage obligation established by the US-Chile FTA through the provision of information to the patent owner about a third party intending to commercialize a product with similar characteristics to one that is already patented.[102]

The aim of these measures is to explore whatever policy space remains available to the country in order to restrict the application of data exclusivity.

7.3 *What Others Are Doing and How They Are Doing It?*

There are many examples of interpretations and flexibility use taking place regularly in different parts of the globe.[103] These developments are either legislative, administrative or judicial in nature. Calls are made for countries to take advantage of the remaining policy space in this regard and share their experiences with others. Following are some non-exhaustive recommendations.

Several recommendations were made more with connection to data exclusivity obligations. As a result, it is advisable for those regimes' committing to TRIPS-Plus data exclusivity provisions not to grant protection unless a specific application is made (within a specific period—no more than 6 months—of time after the first approval in the world of a medicine) and where certain conditions are met. Countries

[102]Correa remarks that on September 2nd, 2002 the Quinta Sala from the I Corte de Apelaciones (I Court of Appeals, Fifth Chamber) of Chile ruled that the Instituto de Salud Publica, which issues sanitary registries, 'had no power whatsoever to either deny a marketing approval or to acknowledge rights derived from a patent'. See Correa (2017). https://www.southcentre.int/wp-content/uploads/2017/02/RP74_Mitigating-the-Regulatory-Constraints-Imposed-by-Intellectual-Property-Rules-under-Free-Trade-Agreements_EN-1.pdf. See also Chandler (2010), https://papers.ssrn.com/sol3/papers.cfm?abstract_id=1602883.
[103]See Correa (2017).

may also charge for these applications and require annual maintenance fee (such as those applicable to trademarks). In addition, detailing when protection will terminate is recommended. Correa suggests the following situations as examples:[104]

- When the right-holder or a person authorised by him does not commercialise the approved product in a manner sufficient to supply the demand within a period (e.g. twelve months) from the date of approval for commercialisation or when the commercialisation is interrupted, for more than x consecutive months (e.g. six months), except in cases of force majeure or government's acts that prevent such commercialisation.
- For public interest reasons such as national security, emergency or circumstances of extreme urgency that justify the termination of the period of exclusivity.
- When, as a result of administrative or judicial procedures, it is determined that the right-holder has abused his rights, for example, through practices declared as anticompetitive.

Keeping health out of the FTA agenda is one right step in this regard. We can observe some positive steps taken in this area. The recently concluded FTA between Australia and Peru have explicitly excluded public health measures and/or specific health programs from its scope. Article 8. 16 of the FTA states:[105]

> Nothing in this Chapter shall be construed to prevent a Party from adopting, maintaining or enforcing any measure otherwise consistent with this Chapter that it considers appropriate to ensure that investment activity in its territory is undertaken in a manner sensitive to environmental, health or other regulatory objectives.

Compulsory licensing in TRIPS agreements is stated with ambiguous wording such as 'national emergency', 'other circumstances of extreme urgency', and 'public non-commercial use'. To deal with this ambiguity, active interpretations of these terms should be persued. In this context, the Thai experience is noteworthy. The legislator there defined public non-commercial use as 'nutrition and public health service' and 'protection of natural resources and environment'. Also, the legislater interpreted the non-use of a patent as 'insufficient use of a patent due to the high price' and 'severe shortage of food and drugs'.[106]

It is worth noting that the above referred to examples should not emanate from separate national initiatives but rather as a part of a more comprehensive approach dealing with public health challenges within these countries. As seen, several developed countries acknowledge today the negative consequences to TRIPS-Plus rules on public health and have taken steps to rectify the situation. Developing countries should follow suit and take serious notice of such implications.

---

[104] Correa (2017).

[105] See the Australian Government Department of Foreign Affairs and Trade. Chapter 8: Investment. Peru-Australia Free Trade Agreement. https://www.dfat.gov.au/trade/agreements/in-force/pafta/Pages/peru-australia-fta.aspx.

[106] Kuanpoth (2006), p. 149.

8 Final Thoughts

The world is at a crossroads. At the time of completion of this chapter, the world was struggling in confronting the outbreak pandemic of the Corona virus (Covid-19). Although several vaccines are available today, the daily loss of life is having grave ramifications for the global economic and public health regimes. These outbreaks are not new, however how we deal with them will depend on our ability to access and grant funding for those working around the clock to find a cure. The intellectual property regime needs reorientation to become truly an incentive rather than an impediment to accessibility and treatment.

Some final thoughts could be made here with relation to supressing the impact of TRIPS-Plus conditions on access to medicines within the framework of trade and investment agreements. First, comprehensive assessment of the health impact of FTAs and TRIPS-Plus commitments should be undertaken by policy makers and negotiators. This should take place before an agreement is entered into. Second, public and stakeholder engagement and collaboration is needed and should be a priority. A national intellectual property committee with authorities and mandates should be tasked with implementing a balanced national intellectual property Agenda. Alternative and new business models for research and development are needed to achieve better pricing of medicines. Push, pull and pooling strategies should be given more thought and experimented with in this regard.[107] Finally, transparency in drug pricing is pivotal to ensure that (i fair compensation is granted to those who invest in finding medical solutions to diseases, and (ii affordable drug prices are applied so that patients can afford them. The 2019 World Health Assembly's resolution supporting greater public disclosure of prices for medicines and other health products is a step in the right direction.[108]

The legal recommendation stands today the same as before; governments should resist accepting and introducing TRIPS-Plus obligations even if others do so. At the same time, those who committed to such obligations should undertake a thorough review in order to identify areas where they can still utilise the TRIPS Flexibilities. We may not be able to stop the spread of TRIPS-Plus commitments around the globe; however, we should try and do our best to slow down the process of eroding the remaining policy space.

---

[107] See Suleman et al. (2020), p. 368. See also more generally the UN Secretary General High-Level Panel (n 1).

[108] Fletcher (2019). https://www.healthpolicy-watch.org/world-health-assembly-approves-milestone-resolution-on-price-transparency/.

References

Agreement on Trade-Related Aspects of Intellectual Property Rights, Apr. 15, 1994, Marrakesh Agreement Establish the World Trade Organization, Annex 1C, 1869 U.N.T.S. 299

Amin T, Kesselheim A (2012) Secondary patenting of branded pharmaceuticals: a case study of how patents on two HIV drugs could be extended for decades. Health Aff 31(10):2286

Australian Government Department of Foreign Affairs and Trade. Chapter 8: Investment. Peru-Australia Free Trade Agreement. https://www.dfat.gov.au/trade/agreements/in-force/pafta/Pages/peru-australia-fta.aspx. Accessed 3 Mar 2021

Australian Government Department of Health (2016) Pharmaceutical benefits scheme price disclosure arrangements: procedural and operational guidelines. http://www.pbs.gov.au/industry/pricing/price-disclosure-spd/price-disclosure-operational-guidelines-06-2016.pdf. Accessed 3 Mar 2021

Baker B (2016) Trans-pacific partnership provisions in intellectual property, transparency, and investment chapters threaten access to medicines in the US and elsewhere. PLoS Med 13(3): e1001970

Biadgleng ET, Maur J-C (2011) The influence of preferential trade agreements on the implementation of intellectual property rights in developing countries: a first look. International Centre for Trade and Sustainable Development, Issue Paper No. 33, vol 21, p 20

Boseley S (2015) Hepatitis C drug delayed by NHS due to high cost. The Guardian (London, 16 January 2015). https://www.theguardian.com/society/2015/jan/16/sofosbuvir-hepatitis-c-drug-nhs. Accessed 3 Mar 2021

Chandler D (2010) Pharmaceutical patents and marketing approvals within the U.S. – Chile Free Trade Agreement Context: a brief analysis. IPR University Center 201. https://papers.ssrn.com/sol3/papers.cfm?abstract_id=1602883. Accessed 3 Mar 2021

Chatterjee P (2013) Novartis loses patent bid: lessons from India's 3(d) experience. Intellectual Property Watch (4 Jan. 2013). https://www.ip-watch.org/2013/04/01/novartis-loses-patent-bid-lessons-from-indias-3d-experience/. Accessed 3 Mar 2021

Christie AF, Dent C, McIntyre P (2013) Patents associated with high-cost drugs in Australia. PLOS One 8:e60812

Correa C (2017) Mitigating the regulatory constraints imposed by intellectual property rule under free trade agreements. Research Paper No. 74, South Centre, Geneva. https://www.southcentre.int/wp-content/uploads/2017/02/RP74_Mitigating-the-Regulatory-Constraints-Imposed-by-Intellectual-Property-Rules-under-Free-Trade-Agreements_EN-1.pdf. Accessed 3 Mar 2021

Correa C, Velásquez G (2019) Access to medicines: experiences with compulsory licenses and government use – the case of hepatitis C. Research Paper No. 85, South Centre, Geneva, p 16. https://www.southcentre.int/wp-content/uploads/2019/04/RP85_Access-to-Medicines-Experiences-with-Compulsory-Licenses-and-Government-Use-The-Case-of-Hepatitis-C_EN-1.pdf. Accessed 3 Mar 2021

Council for Trade-Related Aspects of Intellectual Property Rights, Extension of the Transition Period under Article 66.1 of the TRIPS Agreement for Least Developed Country Members for Certain Obligations with Respect to Pharmaceutical Products, Decision of the Council for TRIPS of 6 November 2015

Crisp E (2019) Louisiana moves ahead with subscription model to pay for hepatitis C drugs for thousands. The Advocate (10 January 2019). https://www.theadvocate.com/baton_rouge/news/politics/article_614e4f42-1523-11e9-8c90-4fcb305d17e8.html. Accessed 3 Mar 2021

Dearment A (2019) New antibiotic for drug resistant tuberculosis scores FDA approval. MedCity News (15 August 2019). https://medcitynews.com/2019/08/new-antibiotic-for-drug-resistant-tuberculosis-scores-fda-approval/. Accessed 3 Mar 2021

Dixon G (2017) Has "Raising the Bar" actually raised the bar on inventive step? Shelston (2 March 2017). https://shelstonip.com/insights/publications/has-raising-the-bar-actually-raised-the-bar-on-inventive-step/. Accessed 3 Mar 2021

Donnelly L (2015) Thousands of cancer patients to be denied treatment. common drugs for breast, bowel, prostate, pancreatic and blood cancer will no longer be funded by the NHS following sweeping cutbacks. The Telegraph (4 September 2015)

Drahos P (2001) BITS and BIPS: bilateralism in intellectual property. J World Intellect Prop 4:791

Drahos P (2010) The global governance of knowledge: patent offices and their clients. Cambridge University Press

Dutfield G (2017) Healthcare innovation and patent law's pharmaceutical privilege: is there a pharmaceutical privilege? And if so, should we remove it? Health Econ Policy Law 12(4):453

Dutfield G (2020) Not just patents and data exclusivity: the role of trademarks in pharmaceutical life cycle management strategy – where lies the public interest? (Forthcoming 2020), To be published in Intellectual Property Law and the Right to Health: A History of TRIPS and Access to Medicine (Srividhya Ragavan and Amaka Vanni eds., 2020 Forthcoming). https://www.academia.edu/43144830/Not_Just_Patents_and_Data_Exclusivity_The_Role_of_Trademarks_in_Pharmaceutical_Life_Cycle_Management_Strategy_Where_Lies_the_Public_Interest. Accessed 3 Mar 2021

El Said M (2005) The road from TRIPS-Minus to TRIPS to TRIPS-Plus: implications of IPRs for the Arab world. J World Intellect Prop 8(1):53–66

El Said M (2006) The evolution of the Jordanian TRIPS-Plus model: multilateralism vs bilateralism and the implications for the Jordanian IPRs regime. Int Rev Intellect Prop Compet Law 37 (5):501

El Said M (2010) Public health related TRIPS-PLUS provisions in bilateral trade agreements, a policy guide for negotiators and implementers in the WHO Eastern Mediterranean Region. WHO-EMRO

El Said M (2014) The accession of Arab countries to the TRIPS agreement: the past, the present and the future. Manchester J Int Econ Law 11(1):60

El Said M (2016) TRIPS-Plus, public health and performance-based rewards schemes options and supplements for policy formation in developing and least developed countries. Am Univ Int Law Rev 31(3):374

Entis L (2019) Why does medicine cost so much? Here's how drug prices are set. TIME (19 April 2019)

EU Commission (2008) Executive Summary of the Pharmaceutical Sector Inquiry Report (Report, 2008). https://ec.europa.eu/competition/sectors/pharmaceuticals/inquiry/communication_en.pdf. Accessed 3 Mar 2021, p 10

Fletcher E (2019) World health assembly approves milestone resolution on price transparency. Health Policy Watch (25 May 2019). https://www.healthpolicy-watch.org/world-health-assembly-approves-milestone-resolution-on-price-transparency/. Accessed 3 Mar 2021

Gallup and West Health (2019) Millions in U.S. lost someone who couldn't afford treatment. Gallup (13 November 2019). https://news.gallup.com/poll/268094/millions-lost-someone-couldn-afford-treatment.aspx?version=print

GIPC (2019) Providing certainty and predictability: how patent linkage mechanisms help innovators, follow-on manufacturers and patients. GIPC. https://www.theglobalipcenter.com/wp-content/uploads/2019/09/GIPC-Linkage-Zoom-In-Report.pdf. Accessed 3 Mar 2021

Gleeson D, Moir H, Lopert R (2015) Costs to Australian taxpayers of pharmaceutical monopolies and proposals to extend them in the Trans-Pacific Partnership Agreement. Med J Aust 202 (6):306 citing Generic Medicines Industry Association. Public response to the 2013 Pharmaceutical Patents Review, Sydney: GMiA, 2013: 11

Gleeson D, Lexchin J, Labonté R, Townsend B, Gagnon M-A, Kohler J, Forman L, Shadlen K (2019) Analysing the impact of trade and investment agreements on pharmaceutical policy: provisions, pathways and potential impacts. Glob Health 15(1):78

Global Justice Now and Stop AIDS (2017) Pills and profits how drug companies make a killing out of public research (Report, October 2017). https://www.globaljustice.org.uk/sites/default/files/files/resources/pills-and-profits-report-web.pdf. Accessed 3 Mar 2021, p 7

Gornall J, Hoey A, Ozieranski P (2016) A pill too hard to swallow: how the NHS is limiting access to high priced drugs. Br Med J 354:4117
Harris T, Nicol D, Gruen N (2013) Pharmaceutical Patents Review Report. Commonwealth of Australia, Canberra, p vi. https://www.ipaustralia.gov.au/sites/default/files/2013-05-27_ppr_final_report.pdf?acsf_files_redirect. Accessed 3 Mar 2021
Herder M, Graham J, Gold R (2020) From discovery to delivery: public sector development of the rVSV-ZEBOV Ebola vaccine. J Law Biosci:1–14
't Hoen E (2019) Uganda tells ARIPO: no more patents for pharmaceuticals. Medicine Law and Policy (8 October 2019). https://medicineslawandpolicy.org/2019/10/uganda-tells-aripo-no-more-patents-for-pharmaceuticals/. Accessed 3 Mar 2021
't Hoen E, Veraldi J, Toebes B, Hogerzeil H (2018) Medicine procurement and the and the use of the flexibilities in the agreement on trade-related aspects of intellectual property rights, 2001-2016. Bull World Health Organ 96(3):185–193
Hopkins JS (2020) Drug prices rise 5.8% on average in 2020. Market Watch (2 January 2020) https://www.marketwatch.com/story/drug-prices-rise-58-on-average-in-2020-2020-01-02
I-MAK (2017) America's overspend: how the pharmaceutical patent problem is fuelling high drug prices (Report, October 2017). https://www.i-mak.org/americas-overspend/. Accessed 3 Mar 2021
I-MAK (2018a) Over-patented, overpriced: how excessive pharmaceutical patenting is extending monopolies and driving up drug prices (Report, August 2018). http://www.i-mak.org/wp-content/uploads/2018/08/I-MAK-Overpatented-Overpriced-Report.pdf. Accessed 3 Mar 2021
I-MAK (2018b) Lantus (Insulin Glargine) (Report, 2018). http://www.i-mak.org/wp-content/uploads/2018/10/I-MAK-Lantus-Report-2018-10-30F.pdf. Accessed 3 Mar 2021
Kesselheim A, Fischer M, Avorn J (2006) Extensions of intellectual property rights and delayed adoption of generic drugs: effects on Medicaid spending: what are the cost implications of generic substitution for three commonly prescribed drugs? Health Aff 25(6):1637
Kuanpoth J (2006) Patents and access to medicines in Thailand: the DDL case and beyond. Intellect Prop Q 2:149
Lexchin J (2019) Increase in drug spending in Canada due to extension of data protection for biologics: a descriptive study. Health Policy 14(3):10
Light D, Warburton R (2016) Demythologizing the high costs of pharmaceutical research. BioSocieties 6(1):34
Ling CY (2019) Using compulsory licence for affordable medicines. Astro Awani (9 March, 2019). http://english.astroawani.com/malaysia-news/using-compulsory-licence-affordable-medicines-200558. Accessed 3 Mar 2021
Machlup F, Penrose E (1950) The patent controversy in the nineteenth century. J Econ Hist 10(1):1
Miller S (2012) Where's the innovation?: An analysis of the quantity and qualities of anticipated and obvious patents, 2 (10 February 2012). https://papers.ssrn.com/sol3/papers.cfm?abstract_id=2029263. Accessed 3 Mar 2021
Mole B (2019) MIA drugs — drug companies are sitting on generics—43% of recently approved aren't for sale. ars Technica (2 September 2019). https://arstechnica.com/science/2019/02/drug-companies-are-sitting-on-generics-43-of-recently-approved-arent-for-sale/. Accessed 3 Mar 2021
Moon S, Erickson E (2019) Universal medicine access through lump-sum remuneration — Australia's approach to hepatitis C. North Engl J Med 380:607
MSF (2016) Lives on the edge: time to align medical research and development with people's health needs (May 2016)
Ney J (2019) Exclusivity for biologic products under the USMCA: what is changing, and what happens next? Biosimilars (14 October 2019). https://www.centerforbiosimilars.com/contributor/joshua-ney/2019/08/exclusivity-for-biologic-products-under-the-usmca-what-is-changing-and-what-happens-next. Accessed 3 Mar 2021
O'Neill J (2015) Buy back or pay forward? Project Syndicate (6 May 2015)

Office of Patented Medicines and Liaison (2005) Therapeutic products directorate statistical report 2004: patented medicines (notice of compliance) regulations (2005, Health Canada)
Oxfam (2007) All costs, no benefits: how TRIPS-Plus intellectual property rules in the US-Jordan FTA Affect Access to Medicines 7 (Oxfam Int'l, Briefing Paper No. 102, 2007). https://oxfamilibrary.openrepository.com/bitstream/handle/10546/114080/bp102-all-costs-no-benefits-trips-210307-en.pdf%3Bjsessionid%3D089750820CF675173F0C3204C369D63F%3Fsequence%3D1. Accessed 3 Mar 2021, p 5
Patent Law (promulgated by the Standing Comm. Nat'l People's Cong., Mar. 12, 1984, rev'd Dec. 27, 2008), art. 22
Pedrique B, Strub-Wourgaft N, Some C, Olliaro P, Trouiller P, Ford N (2013) The drug and vaccine landscape for neglected diseases (2000-11): a systematic assessment. Lancet Global Health 6 (1):371
Pipes S (2019) Britain's version of 'Medicare for all' is struggling with long waits for care. Forbes (1 April 2019). https://www.forbes.com/sites/sallypipes/2019/04/01/britains-version-of-medicare-for-all-is-collapsing/#4c6ebeb736b8. Accessed 3 Mar 2021
Prescrire International (2005) A review of new drugs in 2004: floundering innovation and increased risk-taking. Prescrire International 14:68, 71
Raffi F, Reynes J (2014) Antiretroviral Treatment French Guidelines 2013: economics influencing science. J Antimicrob Chemother 69:1158
Røttingen J, Regmi S, Eide M, Young A, Viergever R, Årdal C (2013) Mapping of available health research and development data: what's there, what's missing, and what role is there for a global observatory? Lancet 382:1286
Rowland C (2019) An HIV treatment cost taxpayers millions, the government patented it, but a pharma giant is making billions. Washington Post (27 March 2019)
Sampat B, Shadlen K (2017) Secondary pharmaceutical patenting: a global perspective. Res Policy 46(3):693
Sciences Avenir with AFP (2015) The league against cancer denounced the "exorbitant" prices for innovative medicines (16 December 2015). http://www.sciencesetavenir.fr/sante/cancer/20151216.OBS1499/la-ligue-contre-le-cancer-denonce-les-prixexorbitants-des-medicaments-innovants.html
Son K-B, Lopert R, Gleeson D, Lee T-J (2018) Moderating the impact of patent linkage on access to medicines: lessons from variations in South Korea, Australia, Canada, and the United States. Glob Health 14(6):101
Stevens A, Jensen J, Wyller K, Kilgore P, Chatterjee S, Rohrbaugh M (2011) The role of public-sector research in the discovery of drugs and vaccines. N Engl J Med 364:535
Suleman F, Low M, Moon S, Morgan S (2020) New business models for research and development with affordability requirements are needed to achieve fair pricing of medicines. BMJ:368
Swanson A (2019) Drug company protection are latest stumbling block for NAFTA rewrite. New York Times (New York, 21 March 2019). https://www.nytimes.com/2019/03/21/us/politics/nafta-drug-prices.html. Accessed 3 Mar 2021
The Economist (2019) The global battle over high drug prices: western countries, as well as poor ones, are demanding transparency in the cost of drugs. The Economist (21 May 2019)
The King's Fund (2018) The rising cost of medicines to the NHS: what's the story? (Briefing, April 2018). https://www.kingsfund.org.uk/sites/default/files/2018-04/Rising-cost-of-medicines.pdf
Trouiller O, Olliaro P, Torreele E, Orbinski J, Laing R, Ford N (2002) Drug development for neglected diseases: a deficient market and a public-health policy failure. Lancet 359:2188
UN Secretary General High Level Panel (2016) The United Nations Secretary-General High-Level Panel on Access to Medicines Report: Promoting Innovation and Access to Health Technologies (September 2016), p 12. http://www.unsgaccessmeds.org/final-report. Accessed 3 Mar 2021
UNAIDS (2011) DOHA+10 TRIPS flexibilities and access to antiretroviral therapy: lessons from the past, opportunities for the future, p 15. https://www.unaids.org/sites/default/files/media_asset/JC2260_DOHA%2B10TRIPS_en_0.pdf. Accessed 3 Mar 2021

UNDP and UNAIDS (2012) The potential impact of free trade agreements on public health. https://www.unaids.org/sites/default/files/media_asset/JC2349_Issue_Brief_Free-TradeAgreements_en_0.pdf. Accessed 3 Mar 2021, p 5

Velásquez G (2017) Access to hepatitis C treatment: a global problem. Research Paper No. 77, South Centre, Geneva. https://www.southcentre.int/wp-content/uploads/2017/05/RP77_Access-to-Hepatitis-C-Treatment-A-Global-Problem_EN-2.pdf. Accessed 3 Mar 2021

Velasquez G (2019) Seeking remedies for access to medicines and intellectual property: recent developments. South Centre, Geneva, p 108. https://www.southcentre.int/wp-content/uploads/2019/11/Bk_2019_Seeking-Remedies-for-Access-to-Medicines-and-Intellectual-Property_EN.pdf

Ward D, Slade A, Genus T, Martino O, Stevens A (2014) How innovative are new drugs launched in the UK? A retrospective study of new drugs listed in the British National Formulary (BNF) 2001-2012. BMJ 4(10):6235

WHO (2015) Global action plan on antimicrobial resistance, p 5. http://apps.who.int/iris/bitstream/10665/193736/1/9789241509763_eng.pdf. Accessed 3 Mar 2021

WHO (2017) Antibacterial agents in clinical development: an analysis of the antibacterial clinical development pipeline, including tuberculosis (Report, Geneva, 2017). https://apps.who.int/iris/bitstream/handle/10665/258965/WHO-EMP-IAU-2017.11-eng.pdf?sequence=1. Accessed 3 Mar 2021

WHO (2018) Pricing of cancer medicines and its impacts: a comprehensive technical report for the World Health Assembly Resolution 70.12 (Technical Report, 2018), p xi. https://apps.who.int/iris/bitstream/handle/10665/277190/9789241515115-eng.pdf?sequence=1&isAllowed=y

WHO (2019) Antibacterial agents in preclinical development: an open access database (WHO, Geneva). https://apps.who.int/iris/bitstream/handle/10665/330290/WHO-EMP-IAU-2019.12-eng.pdf. Accessed 3 Mar 2021

WTO (2000) Canada—patent protection of pharmaceutical products. Geneva, WTO Dispute Panel Report, WT/DS114/1

Patent Linkages and Its Impact on Access to Medicines: Challenges, Opportunities for Developing Countries

K. D. Raju

Abstract Linking patent protection to generics' regulatory approvals is a heated topic of discussions and a friction point among countries proposing higher protection for patented drugs. Patent linkage has been pushed through bilateral and regional agreements outside of the WTO system. It is widely understood that patent linkage is implemented to delay the market entry of generic medicines. It is argued here that developing countries are not obliged to take up TRIPs plus patent-linkage obligations.

A list of approved drugs and their therapeutic equivalence can be published by every country. The patent information can also be published to be made known to everybody. Regulatory mechanisms and patent protection should be kept in separate parallel tracks. Any attempt to link the two streams to prevent the registration of generics based solely on alleged patent infringement would negatively affect access to medicines worldwide.

Patent linkage provisions are TRIPS-plus commitments, as there is no such obligation under the WTO TRIPS Agreement. The analysis of 16 countries which provide for patent linkage shows that it is, in most cases, a resulting commitment from regional trade agreements or bilateral agreements. Patent linkage provisions are not acceptable to the developing world, and any attempt to introduce these will affect the accessibility and affordability of generic medicines in the developing world.

K. D. Raju (✉)
Rajiv Gandhi School of Intellectual Property Law, Indian Institute of Technology, Kharagpur, Kharagpur, West Bengal, India
e-mail: kdraju@rgsoipl.iitkgp.ac.in

C. M. Correa, R. M. Hilty (eds.), *Access to Medicines and Vaccines*,
https://doi.org/10.1007/978-3-030-83114-1_12

1 Introduction

Access to essential medicines is a developmental challenge to developing countries under the WTO Agreement on Trade-Related Aspects of Intellectual Property Rights (TRIPs).[1] Accessibility, affordability, and availability of medicines (medicines and drugs are interchangeably used in this paper hereinafter) are the prime objectives of any developing country's public health policy.[2] Access to drugs is vital in the background that, after food, the second-largest household expenditure is on medication, and this is paid out of pocket in these countries due to a lack of sufficient public health programs. Many countries drafted their medicines policies keeping this issue in mind. The challenging problem is that pandemics' growing burden in developing and least developed countries raised a high demand for cost-effective medicines. Countries like India have previously met this increased demand by providing low-cost generic drugs to the world and helping them fight pandemics.[3]

Developing and developed countries alike have realized the importance of generic drugs in healthcare.[4] The European Generics Medicines Association (EGA) formed "Medicines for Europe" in the year 2000 to support the generic and biosimilar industry, which supplies 67% of all medicines in Europe.[5]

Developing countries face challenges in the form of TRIPs-plus obligations imposed on them through various means, mainly bilateral and regional trade agreements. The availability and accessibility of medicines will be affected by policy choices, such as adopting a patent linkage. Patent linkage refers to the system or process by which a country links drug-marketing approval to the status of the patent (s) corresponding to the originator's patented product.[6]

---

[1] WHO (2011–2016), available at https://apps.who.int/iris/bitstream/handle/10665/207519/9789290615705_eng.pdf.

[2] Ravikant et al. (2013), pp. 316–322.

[3] India recently sent an anti-malarial drug, Hydroxychroloquine, to 55 countries hit with Coronavirus. This drug is identified by the US Food and Drug Administration as a possible drug to treat Covid-19 disease, though its safety and efficacy are not yet established. See India Today, New Delhi, April 17, 2020, https://www.indiatoday.in/india/story/india-sending-hydroxychloroquine-55-coronavirus-hit-countries-1667786-2020-04-17. Later the accepted the Solidarity Trial's International Steering Committee recommendation to discontinue the trial's hydroxychloroquine and lopinavir from the treatment of COVID-19 patients. See WHO (2020). https://www.who.int/emergencies/diseases/novel-coronavirus-2019/advice-for-public/myth-busters?gclid=EAIaIQobChMIjoGlirH06wIVhzMqCh3ISAVnEAAYASABEgKMz_D_BwE.

[4] European Generic Medicines Association (2009). https://www.medicinesforeurope.com/wp-content/uploads/2016/03/Market_Barriers_Report_FINAL_update_How_to_Increase_Patient_Access_to_Generic_Medicines.pdf.

[5] Medicines for Europe, https://www.medicinesforeurope.com/medicines-for-europe/.

[6] https://www.wipo.int/export/sites/www/meetings/en/2007/lifesciences/sym_regulation/lss3_ge_07_ferrite.pdf.

The present IP regime in 164 countries are under the WTO's[7] TRIPs Agreement concluded in 1995. Every WTO member country has to implement minimum standard of intellectual property at the domestic level according to TRIPs provisions. Article 1 of the Agreement stipulates, "Members may, but shall not be obliged to, implement in their law more extensive protection than is required by this Agreement."[8] Hence, it is clear that members are not obliged to implement higher standards than prescribed in the TRIPs agreement.[9]

The basic concept of patent protection is that once the patent term is over (presently 20 years under the TRIPS agreement), the product would be in the public domain and freely used, including for commercial purposes.[10] This eclipse of patent protection is supposed to increase consumer welfare, and society would be better off from evergreening protection. Pharmaceutical regulatory approval is entirely different from patent protection. Moreover, it differs from country to country based on domestic legislation. Linking such regulatory and marketing approval to the originator's patent status would affect the generic drug industry at large and accessibility and affordability.

Patent linkage involves linking the marketing approval of generic drugs with the originator drug's patent status and refusing to allow marketing approval until the patent is expired.[11] The United States (US) first introduced the concept through the Hatch Waxman Act, 1984.[12] This law provides for protecting the interest of patent holders through linking patent status of originators' drugs and their regulatory approval in the "Orange Book."[13] Thus, a generic drug would not get marketing approval if it would potentially infringe one or more patents listed in the Orange Book. The US patent linkage system can be seen as a ploy by the patent holder to delay the entry of generic drugs in the market.[14] However, the originator industry argues that this will help them prevent anticipated patent infringement and promote innovation and investment by giving inventors more certainty over their patent rights.[15] However, generic manufacturers argue that TRIPs plus commitment undermines the rapid approval of generic medicines. Besides, most countries' drug regulatory authorities need not inform the inventors about the application for marketing approval or the actual approval of a generic version of patented drugs. Early working allows immediate marketing at the end of the patent period, equips the

[7] Presently, the World Trade Organization has 164 member countries, which constitute 99 percent of the world trade.

[8] Article 1 of the TRIPS Agreement. https://www.wto.org/english/docs_e/legal_e/27-trips.pdf.

[9] Ibid.

[10] Correa (2016).

[11] Mirandah (2012), p. 50.

[12] https://www.congress.gov/bill/98th-congress/senate-bill/01538.

[13] Orange Book: Approved Drug Products with Therapeutic Equivalence Evaluations. https://www.accessdata.fda.gov/scripts/cder/ob/index.cfm.

[14] Son et al. (2018), p. 101. https://www.ncbi.nlm.nih.gov/pmc/articles/PMC6201583/.

[15] Ellis (2019). https://geneva-network.com/article/patent-linkage/.

generic companies to provide cheap drugs in developing countries without delay.[16] This early working limited exception under Article 30 of the TRIPs Agreement does not infringe patented drug owners' rights. Nonetheless, there is a concerted effort to introduce a link between the patent status of drugs and the regulatory approval of generic medicines in the recent past through regional and bilateral trade agreements.

This paper argues that linking a generic drug's market approval to its branded equivalent's patent status is detrimental to access to medicines in developing countries and least developed countries. It is argued that India and other developing countries should not statutorily link patent protection with marketing approvals of generic drugs, which is well beyond the TRIPs obligations. The backdoor entry of these provisions through regional trade agreements should be prevented to allow the production of cheap drugs for the developing world.

This paper analyses the legal regimes adopted to implement drug-related patent-linkage provisions, enforcement, and standard practices of 21 jurisdictions.[17] The legal system of patent linkage countries (15 in number) and non-patent linkage countries (6 countries) is analyzed mainly in South-east Asian countries to understand these countries' legal obligations and its implications in access to medicines. The Indian experience is examined carefully, along with compulsory licensing practice. Important judicial decisions are also analyzed to understand its effect on access to drugs. The paper concludes that linking patent rights with marketing approvals for generic medicines has far-reaching adverse consequences in developing countries' access to drugs. Patent linkage has an incentive for extending monopoly rights beyond 20 years of the patent term and will negatively affect generic drugs' entry after the expiry of patent rights. It is relevant to note that only 15 countries implemented patent linkage directly among the WTO Members,[18] but regional trade agreements have patent linkage provisions, and their adoption will increase the number.[19] All the countries with direct patent linkage provisions are included for a better understanding of the provisions.

[16]See Chapter 5.

[17]This include the US, EU, Canada, Australia, Japan, South Korea, China, Taiwan, Russia, Ukraine, Thailand, Philippines, Singapore, Malaysia, Indonesia, Vietnam, Thailand, Jordan, UAE, Peru and India.

[18]US, Canada, Japan, Australia, South Korea, China, Taiwan, Russia, Ukraine, Philippines, Singapore, Jordan, Mexico, UAE and Peru.

[19]Townsend et al. https://www.bilaterals.org/IMG/pdf/ssrn-id2850294.pdf.

2 Perspectives on Patent Linkage

2.1 US

In the US, patent linkage is included in the Drug Price Competition and Patent Term Restoration Act, 1984 (Hatch Waxman Act) to regulate the generic industry. Patent extensions are also allowed in the US for up to five years for qualifying patents.[20] The patented drug must not have been infringed until expired or held invalid. However, the legislation also provides some benefits for the generic industry.[21]

The Act has passed with an objective of hassle-free approvals to generic drugs and unnecessary disputes with branded and patented drugs. Unfortunately, the multinational drug companies exploit the loopholes in the Act in favor of them to extend the patent protection.

In the US, the generic drug approval is linked to pioneer drug patents under the Hatch Waxman Act, 1984 through Orange Book, certification process, and a limited 180-day generic market exclusivity period for first generic applicants who challenge the validity of the patent or claim it would not be infringed under the Act's Paragraph IV certificate system. Under the "patent linkage" provisions, the new drug application should include patent details, and the FDA reflects the existence of patents as part of the approval process for specific drug applications. If a valid patent exists, marketing approval will not be granted to a generic drug until the patent has expired or declared invalid by competent authorities. This generic marketing approval is "linked" to the expiration of the patented drug. Such patent information can be published in "Orange Book." This Book lists approved drugs, discontinued drugs, and patent and exclusivity information. It is argued that the patent linkage system

[20] West and Allison Hoppert. https://www.oblon.com/A11960/assets/files/News/125.pdf.

[21] They can be summarized as follows:

- Generic drugs need not prove their safety and efficacy but must demonstrate the product's bioequivalence to the original patented drug. This will reduce the cost and delay of clinical trials of generic medicines.
- Generic drugs are granted 180 days of exclusivity limited to the first generic entrant who files a paragraph IV certification and thereby challenges the patent's validity or claims that it will not be infringed.
- Abbreviated New Drug Application (ANDA) applicant is not required to produce independent evidence of the generic drug's safety and effectiveness. He has to prove also that the generic drug is bio-equivalent to reference listed drug (RLD).
- If the applicant submits a paragraph I or II certification, the patent in question will not delay ANDA approval.
- If the applicant submits a paragraph III certification, the applicant agrees to wait until the relevant patent has expired before seeking the ANDA's final approval.
- Paragraph IV certification does not survive the expiry of a listed patent. In making paragraph IV certification, the generic drug maker says he believes that the patented drug is invalid, not infringed, or unenforceable.
- If the NDA holder brings a suit for infringement, the FDA can't approve it for 30 months or whenever the court determines the issue.

increased the efficiency and productivity of the research and development sector of a generic company and patent holder company. However, generic drug approvals are vital for developing countries in curing pandemics.

Studies have revealed that generic drug approval applications were late by 30 months due to patent linkage provisions and the infringement litigation.[22] These infringement cases increase the cost of drugs, and the generics lost the right to enter the market during the stay period. S.156 provides for patent term extension up to five years if certain conditions are met like any patent term adjustment granted under section 154(b).[23]

The Act's misuse includes "reverse payments" from originator companies to generic companies during the 180 days exclusive period not to enter the market. This is popularly known as the "pay-for-delay" program adopted by the originator companies. The FTC has taken a strong exception to this anti-competitive practice and believes that such practices are per-se illegal. To stop this practice, Congress passed the Medicare Prescription Drug Improvement Modernization Act, 2003. This Act stipulates that within ten days of reverse settlements, companies to register such settlements with FTC.[24] As per the FTC estimate, consumers lost $3.5billion higher drug cost every year due to this "pay-for-delay" tactics of the originator companies.[25] But in some cases like in *In re Tamoxifen Citrate Antitrust Litig.*,[26] the Second Circuit rejected the *per se* rule and held that reverse payment settlements do not violate anti-trust laws if they fall within the exclusionary zone of the patent. But the US Supreme Court, in a landmark judgment, *FTC v. Actavis*,[27] held that the pay-for-delay practice of originator companies for settling patent disputes with generics and delay in entering the market could have significant anti-competitive effects and violate anti-trust laws.[28]

Patent linkage is similar to that of the branded drug companies' pay-for-delay program to delay the entry of generics into the market. Thus access to cheaper medicines is denied in developed and developing countries if patent linkage or similar provisions are implemented.

Other tactics used by the originator companies, including asking the FDA to take action on any ANDA application under "Citizen Petition" provision, will likely delay the generic version of drugs. FDA has to take a decision not longer than 150 days. Again, this will delay the generic entry for another 150 days, and

---

[22] Winkler et al. (2018). https://www.finnegan.com/en/insights/requirements-benefits-and-possible-consequences-of-listing-patents-in-fdas-orange-book.html.

[23] *Merc & Co.Inc v. High Tech Pharmaceuticals Inc*,, US Court of Appeals No. 2006-1401, decided on March 29, 2007.

[24] Meagher (2017), p. 589. Available at: https://brooklynworks.brooklaw.edu/bjcfcl/vol11/iss2/12.

[25] Pay for Delay, Federal Trade Commission. https://www.ftc.gov/news-events/media-resources/mergers-competition/pay-delay.

[26] 466 F.3d 187, 228 (2d Cir. 2006).

[27] 570 US. 136, 2013.

[28] Decided on June 17, 2013, https://www.supremecourt.gov/opinions/12pdf/12-416_m5n0.pdf.

originators can file multiple, successive petitions. Another methodology adopted by the branded companies is "product hopping" or "forced Switch schemes." These are branded companies' strategies to come up with alternative versions of the medicine shortly before the patent expiry with the effect of withdrawing the existing product registration, which might be thwarted registration of the generic equivalent. A patient who is using a particular branded medicine has the least possibility of switching to a new generic drug; instead, continue with the altered version of the branded drug. Thus, they were compelled to use essentially the same medicine with the same company for a higher price; this maintains the originator company's monopoly for a more extended period than prescribed. Since the decision in *Actavis* by the US Supreme Court, the number of pay-for-delay cases has been decreased.[29]

2.2 EU

The EU does not follow the patent linkage system. But at any time, the patent holder can get an injunction against any infringement throughout Europe. EU believes that any tinkering with the bolar provision through patent linkage will delay the entry of generic drugs into the European market.[30] EU directives do not prohibit experimenting with any patented drug during the patent term and generating test data, which can be submitted to the regulatory authorities for marketing approval.[31] EU's Pharmaceutical Sector Inquiry preliminary report of November 28, 2008, accounts that 700 patent litigations were filed to prevent or delay the entry of registered generic drugs into the market.[32]

The European Medicines Agency is responsible for the marketing approvals of a generic drug in the EU.[33] Article 81, Regulation No.EC726/2004[34] and Article 126 of Directive EC 2001/83 laying down community procedures for authorization of medicinal products.[35] EU believes that patent linkage provisions are beyond the TRIPs obligations and not desirable in the EU. The bolar rule is strictly implemented

[29] Michael Carrier FTC v. Actavis: Where We Stand After 5 Years, 18 June 2018.

[30] Article 10.6. of Directive 2001/83/EC as amended).

[31] Data Exclusivity/Patent Linkage in the Context of EU Generic and Biosimilar Applications. Presentation by Suzette Kox at the WIPO Life Sciences Symposium: Intellectual Property and Life Sciences Regulation, 16 November 2017. https://www.wipo.int/export/sites/www/meetings/en/2007/lifesciences/sym_regulation/lss3_ge_07_kox.pdf.

[32] European Commission (2008). https://ec.europa.eu/competition/sectors/pharmaceuticals/inquiry/preliminary_report.pdf.

[33] European Medicines Agency Generic and Hybrid Medicines. https://www.ema.europa.eu/en/human-regulatory/marketing-authorisation/generic-hybrid-medicines.

[34] https://ec.europa.eu/competition/sectors/pharmaceuticals/archive/4_Regulator_framework.pdf.

[35] https://ec.europa.eu/health/sites/health/files/files/eudralex/vol-1/reg_2004_726/reg_2004_726_en.pdf.

in the EU through Article 10.6 of Directive 2001/83/EC as amended.[36] Generic companies are applying for marketing approval to demonstrate that it is bioequivalent to the originator product. For that, the generic companies can refer to the test data submitted by the originator companies. The test data provided by the originator firms will get data exclusivity period for eight years, but during the additional two-year market exclusivity provision, generic producers can early work and apply for marketing approval.[37] Moreover, the EU practices a maximum of five years of extension based on the Supplementary Protection Certificate (SPC). Submission of generic biosimilar applications only possible after the data exclusivity period.[38]

In 2012, the European Commission[39] formally asked Italy to remove patent linkage provisions outlined in Law No 30 of 2005 (the IP Code), namely paragraph 1-bis of Article 68 containing a clear patent linkage., which harm and delay the entry of generic medicines in the market.[40] The provision allows generic drug manufacturers to start the drug registration process only during the "last year" of the patent or supplementary protection certificate's validity. The Italian provision violated Article 10 of Directive 2001/83/EC in the community code relating to medicinal products. In 2012, Law No. 27/2012 made the Italian law in compliance with the EU Regulation. Now the marketing authorization application for a generic drug can be filed more than one year before the patent or supplementary protection certificate expiry. But manufacture, import, or sale of the drug would be considered as an infringement. But Law No. 189/2012 excluded generic drugs from the National Health Care Service. It means that generic drugs cannot be listed for reimbursement until the patent is expired. But in the name of secondary patents, the generics have to wait until its expiry as well.[41]

On 1 July 2019, Regulation UE 2019/933 introduced some amendments to the previous Regulation (EC) 469/2009 concerning the SPC, setting forth a waiver

---

[36] https://ec.europa.eu/health/sites/health/files/files/eudralex/vol-1/dir_2001_83_consol_2012/dir_2001_83_cons_2012_en.pdf.

[37] Medicines and Law Policy (2019). https://medicineslawandpolicy.org/wp-content/uploads/2019/06/European-Union-Review-of-Pharma-Incentives-Data-Exclusivity.pdf.

[38] Data Exclusivity/Patent Linkage in the Context of EU Generic and Biosimilar Applications. Presentation by Suzette Kox at the WIPO Life Sciences Symposium: Intellectual Property and Life Sciences Regulation, 16 November 2017. https://www.wipo.int/export/sites/www/meetings/en/2007/lifesciences/sym_regulation/lss3_ge_07_kox.pdf.

[39] Daniela Ampollini (Trevisan & Cuonzo) (2011). http://patentblog.kluweriplaw.com/2011/04/08/patent-linkage-infringement-proceedings-by-the-european-commission-against-italy/.

[40] Intellectual Property Watch (2012). https://www.ip-watch.org/2012/01/31/european-commission-orders-italy-to-drop-patent-linkage-delaying-generics/.

[41] Decision of the Regional Administrative Court of Rome on January 2018 (T.A.R. Lazio, sez. III, - Roma, 19 January 2018, No 662).

under certain conditions to export such manufactured drugs outside the EU jurisdictions.[42]

Other EU countries like Hungary, Portugal, and Czech are trying to establish different kinds of linkages with patents.[43] Italy and Belgium have restrictions on the reimbursement by National Health Service on drugs that infringe third-party patents. In Hungary and Egypt, declarations of non-infringement are sought by applicants at the time of filing.

The introduction of patent linkage would increase litigation frequency in patent enforcement and delay generics' entry in the EU market.[44] The EU Council of Ministers expressed concern over very high, unsustainable drug prices in the EU.[45] The FDA style patent linkage cannot be implemented in the EU because there is no single patent in the entire EU jurisdiction. Instead, it is a bundle of patents filed in the European Patent Office (EPO). However, in the Italy case, the European Commission made it clear that patent linkage delays the entry of generic medicines and a clear abuse of the EU regulatory system.[46] Patent linkage is considered illegal in the EU under Regulation (EC) No 726/2004 and Directive (EC) No 2001/83).[47]

2.3 *Canada*

In 1993 Canada first adopted a patent linkage system closely patterned on US law. These regulations were adopted to ensure that the early exception is not abused by generic drug applicants seeking to sell their products during the patent term. Notice of compliance provisions is similar to that of the Hatch – Waxman Act. Canada also keeps a Patent Book like Orange Book. Notice of allegation (NOA) and notice under Paragraph IV of the HW Act are similar. The statutory stay of approval in Canada is 24 months, and it is 30 months in the US. In 2017, significant amendments were made to the Patented Medicines (Notice of Compliance) Regulations1993 (PM-NOC-amended) to align with Canada's obligations under the

[42] https://practiceguides.chambers.com/practice-guides/patent-litigation-2020/italy/trends-and-developments#:~:text=The%20European%20Union%20does%20not,advance%20of%20the%20patent%20expiration.

[43] Research Report on Establishing System of Linking New Drug Application and Patent Protection, BIPI Research (2016) No. 002. http://www.theglobalipcenter.com/wp-content/uploads/2017/03/full-report-E.pdf.

[44] European Generic Medicines Association (2008).

[45] Catherine Drew (2017). https://www.pinsentmasons.com/out-law/analysis/eu-unlikely-to-follow-us-with-patent-linkage-system-says-expert.

[46] Intellectual Property Watch (2012).

[47] Pharmaceutical Sector Inquiry – Preliminary Report, Fact Sheet "Regulatory Framework". https://ec.europa.eu/competition/sectors/pharmaceuticals/archive/4_Regulator_framework.pdf.

Canada-European Union Comprehensive Economic and Trade Agreement (CETA).[48] The changes in the amendments can be summarized below:

1. The Minister of Health was given the power to maintain the Patent Register.
2. Generic or bio-similar manufacturers are required to serve a notice of allegation (NOA).
3. All NOAs need to include a searchable electronic copy of the second person's drug submissions and copies of documents to be submitted.
4. First-person cannot seek a prohibition order against the Minister of Health.
5. First-person, who brings an action under the law, will be able to renounce the 24-month stay.
6. An un-successful action for patent infringement under the law, the second person will be able to sue all the plaintiffs for section 8 damages.[49]

It is worth noting that Canada introduced a Bolar exception provision in 1991.[50] Section 55.2 of the Act provides for two exceptions to patent infringement. These are "early working" and "stockpiling" exceptions. EU filed a case in the WTO dispute settlement against this provision. In the year 2000, the Panel held that the early working provision did not violate the TRIPs agreement.[51] However, the Panel held that the manufacturing and stockpiling of drugs in the last six months of the patent expiry term violate the Agreement. Later on, the stockpiling provision was repealed.

2.4 *Australia*

Australia effectively implemented patent linkage through Section 26B of the Therapeutic Goods Act 1989 and AUSFTA and consequent legislation, the US Free Trade Agreement Act, 2004. The generic companies seeking marketing approval must provide a patent certificate stating that the generic did not infringe any originator drug patents and notice the patentee.

If the generic drug infringes, no marketing approval will be granted. Moreover, an injunction will be issued, which will delay generic entry for another three years.[52] The Australian courts are generally in favor of patentees, and permanent injunctions are usually granted to the originators.[53]

---

[48] https://laws-lois.justice.gc.ca/eng/regulations/sor-93-133/index.html.

[49] White et al. (2017). https://www.osler.com/en/resources/regulations/2017/canada-s-patent-linkage-regulations-get-long-await.

[50] Correa (2016).

[51] WT/DS114/R.

[52] Palombi (2014). http://theconversation.com/its-time-to-fix-the-free-trade-bungle-on-the-cost-of-medicines-32574.

[53] Managing IP (2019). https://www.managingip.com/Article/3865388/Australia-Protecting-pharmaceutical-market-share-in-Australia.html.

The patent linkage provision is included under Section 26B of the Therapeutic Goods Act 1989.[54] An applicant seeking marketing approval of a generic or biosimilar medicine must certify either that:

(i) it will not market the drug in a manner that would infringe a valid patent *or*;
(ii) It has notified the rights holder of their intention to market the drug before the patent term expiry.[55]

However, Australia claims that there is no administrative patent linkage in the country—after the potentially infringing applicant's notice, the patent holder must sue to protect its rights.[56] Permanent injunctions are an effective way for originators to prevent generics from entering the market. The Australian High Court considered the question in *Aktiebolaget Hassle v. Alphapharm Pty. Ltd.*[57] Evergreening and linkage of the patent were discussed by the Court in this case and discussed how the patent owners use a regulatory process to extend their blockbuster drugs patent term for rent-seeking. The linkage-form of evergreening is the new method developed by the drug companies following the US Hatch – Waxman legislation. The companies try their luck in other jurisdictions even though there are no patent linkage provisions in Australia.[58] The Astra group filed a patent infringement case against a generic drug manufacturer, Alphapharm, who started importing the drug to the Australian market at the end of the patent term. Justice Kirby, in his judgment, observed the tactics of the originators to delay the generic entry even after the patent term, in its most persuasive words:

> The strategies that large pharmaceutical manufacturers have employed to avoid such generic competition, which include the use of intellectual property law, have been detailed elsewhere. They are attracted to the attention and response of the Federal Trade Commission in the United States. Such battles have had their counterparts in many other countries. They present serious issues for the developing world. . .in its interpretation of the legislation, and in identifying the proper approach to the ultimate factual determination of obviousness called for by that statute, this Court should avoid creating fail-safe opportunities for unwarranted extensions of monopoly protection that are not sustained by law.[59]

AUSFTA, Article 17.10.04, provides that the branded drug manufacturer would be informed of an anticipated product.[60] The regulatory process and marketing approval for generic pharmaceuticals would be connected with patent infringement status through this provision. It is also required to notify the patent holder of any

[54] Australian Government, About the Australian therapeutic goods legislation. https://www.tga.gov.au/about-australian-therapeutic-goods-legislation.

[55] Son et al. (2018).

[56] DrugPatentWatch Patent linkage: Balancing patent protection and generic entry https://www.drugpatentwatch.com/blog/patent-linkage-resolving-infringement/.

[57] (2062) HCA 59, 12 December 2002.

[58] Faunce and Lexchin (2007). https://anzhealthpolicy.biomedcentral.com/articles/10.1186/1743-8462-4-8.

[59] *Aktiebolaget Hassle v. Alphapharm Pty Ltd*, 212 CLR 411, para 101 2002.

[60] Faunce and Lexchin (2007).

generic marketing approval application.[61] Originators have used the preliminary injunction route for successfully stalling the entry of generics in the market. The high degree of proof is with the generic industry to prove that they are not violating any patents. Besides, AUSFTA provision 17.10.4(b) required that the patent holder be notified of a generic marketing approval application. This provision is criticized as an attempt to delay the entry of generic medicines in the Australian market.[62]

2.5 *Japan*

Even though Japan directly did not implement the patent linkage system, the de-facto patent linkage system was implemented through a government regulation to approve generic drugs.[63] During the active patent validity period, no generic approval will be granted.[64] The patent linkages are secured in two stages of regulatory approval and drug price listing.[65] If there is a delay in getting marketing approval of the patented drug, the duration can be stretched for a period of up to five years.[66]

After an amendment to the Patent Act in 2018, the patentee can claim patent extension if it is granted after five years of application. The patent extension term will mostly depend upon the period in which the originator is unable to use the patented drug during a marketing approval process. Japan also keeps a US-style Orange Book[67] and patent linkage.[68] The Minister will not approve any generic drug when a patent right prevents the generic drug from being marketed.[69] However, under the price regulation system, the drug prices in Japan are determined by the state.

Any dispute between originator drug manufacturers and generic manufacturers must be reported to the Ministry of Health, Labor and Welfare.

---

[61] AUSFTA Article 17.10.4(b).

[62] Faunce and Lexchin (2007).

[63] IP Litigation in Life Sciences – Costs, Duration and Enforceability in Japan. Presentation by Yoichi Okumura, Global Head of IP, Takeda Pharmaceutical Company Limited. WIPO Conference on IP Dispute Resolution in Life Science, 22 May 2015. https://www.wipo.int/export/sites/www/amc/en/docs/basel2015_okumura.pdf.

[64] Abe (2019). https://www.managingip.com/Article/3888280/Japan-What-impact-do-generic-drugs-have-on-the-Japanese-market.html.

[65] https://system.jpaa.or.jp/patent/viewPdf/3066.

[66] Law No. 145 of 1960.

[67] Approved Drug Products with Therapeutic Equivalence Evaluations.

[68] Notification No. 0605001 of the Economic Affairs Division, Health Policy Bureau of 2009 and Notification No. 0605014 of the Evaluation and Licensing Division, Pharmaceutical and Food Safety Bureau of the Ministry of Health, Welfare and Labour of 2009.

[69] Koizumi et al. (2011). https://www.amt-law.com/asset/res/news_2011en_pdf/110225_2055.pdf.

Japan allows experimentation exemption under the Patent Act 2006 (Amended).[70] Tests conducted during the patent term for submission to the regulatory approval is not an infringement under the Japan patent law.[71]

Price competition between originator drug and generic drug is significantly less in Japan due to state price control. Reverse payments are considered as an anti-competitive activity in Japan. Unlike the US, the ANDA 180-day exclusivity to the first filer is not available in Japan. All these measures show that patent linkage is not so intense that compared to the US. Nevertheless, Japan is a party to the RCEP Agreement and may be forced entirely to implement patent linkages if these are included in the final agreement.

2.6 South Korea

South Korea is another country that implemented the patent linkage system, in line with the US Hatch-Waxman Act of 1984. This was done through a back door of the US – Korea Bilateral Free Trade Agreement signed in 2007,[72] entered into force in 2012 (Article 18.9.5 – IP Chapter).[73] The amendment introduced the patent list and the notification system. In addition to that, the government implemented a nine-month stay on marketing approval and nine-month first generic exclusivity in 2015. It was reported that the amendment increased the number of patent challenges as well as marketing approvals related litigations.[74] According to the Agreement, Korea agreed to the following additional commitments over and above the TRIPs agreement:

- Extended patent term to compensate for the patent prosecution delays from the Korean Intellectual Property Office and other regulatory review delays.
- Data exclusivity should be granted for efficacy information submitted to support a prior approved drug (three years) or newly approved drug (five years).
- Patent linkage provision informing patentees of an applicant's identity before granting marketing approval of a generic drug.
- Marketing approval will not be granted for a generic drug without the original patent owner's consent during the valid patent period.

The South Korean Pharmaceutical Affairs Act permits clinical test data submitted by originators to be used by generic drug manufactures seeking marketing approval. Korean patent listing is also strictly policed by MFDS, and it allows Korean generic

[70] www.japaneselawtranslation.go.jp.

[71] *Ono Pharmaceuticals Co., Ltd. v. Kyoto Pharmaceuticals Industries, Ltd.* Judgment dated 16 April 1999.

[72] Son et al. (2019).

[73] See Raley (2019a), pp. 459–492.

[74] Son and Lee (2017), pp. 1169–1178.

manufacturers to institute administrative hearings before the patent hearing. The branded companies must petition MFDS for the stay of generic drug sales, and the stay lasts for nine months, but the branded manufacturers to obtain a stay of generic drug FDA approval for up to 30 months like in the US.[75] South Korea also provides patent term extension up to five years for pharmaceuticals and agrochemicals. South Korea is a part of RCEP negotiations. The leaked Korean RCEP draft on IP provides for patent term extension for unreasonable delays in granting patents. Unreasonable delay is defined as the delay for more than four years from the date of filing of the application or three years after the request for examination of the application, whichever is later [Article X.D.1.4(a)].[76]

2.7 China

The Administrative Measures for Drug Registration 2002 provides for the protection of patent rights related to drugs. The applicant has to prove the patent status and declare that it did not infringe on any patents. Attempts were made in 2005 and 2007 to include patent linkage provisions but are never happened until 2017.

In 2017, the Chinese Communist Party proposed reforms in the medical device approval system and issued Reform Opinion (Order No. 55) to implement the US model patent linkage system in drug regulation.[77] China implemented "bolar exemption" provisions through patent amendments laws in 2008, known as the "Naked Bolar Exemption."[78] Article 16 of "Opinion on Deepening Approval and Review System Reform and Encouraging Innovation of Drug and Medical Apparatus" of 2017 describes the patent linkage system in China. It includes notifying the relevant patentee of the generic drug and patent term adjustment system's marketing approval process. The long term review process and delays will be compensated through a reasonable extension of the patent period. However, the Chinese new Drug Administration Law, 2019, took effect from December 1, has a patent linkage provision.[79] The new law provides for a nationwide drug marketing authorization holder system.[80] The Chinese model of Orange book now has more than 131 drugs as well.[81]

Order 55 provides for the following:

---

[75] Raley (2019b).

[76] Townsend et al. https://www.bilaterals.org/IMG/pdf/ssrn-id2850294.pdf.

[77] Chen and Shi (2017), pp. 1484–1487.

[78] Article 69.

[79] China IPR (2021). https://chinaipr.com/category/patent-linkage/.

[80] Global Legal Monitor (2019). https://www.loc.gov/law/foreign-news/article/china-drug-administration-law-revised/.

[81] Zhang et al. (2018). http://patentblog.kluweriplaw.com/2018/04/03/china-establish-patent-linkage/.

1. A generic drug applicant shall notify the known patents at the time of drug filing.
2. If the drug applicant challenges a patent, it should declare that his drug does not infringe on any patent.
3. The patent owner should start patent infringement proceeding within 20 days after the drug filing.
4. The CFDA has the discretion to make the application pending for 24 months before drug approval.
5. If there is no judicial remedy within the waiting period of 24 months, CFSA can approve the generic drug.
6. If there is any infringement suit after the generic drug's approval, it will be subject to the judicial decision's outcome.

On 15th January 2020, China and the US signed an Economic and Trade Agreement to ease trade between the countries required to build a patent linkage and patent term restoration system in China.[82] Article 1.12 of the agreement provides for patent extensions in case of unreasonable delays while examining the patent application and delays in marketing approvals. The excessive delay means more than four years from filing or three years from requesting examination. The patent validity can be extended by a maximum of five years in case of marketing approval delays.[83] China was an active participant in the RCEP negotiations on patent linkage.[84]

2.8 *Taiwan*

Taiwan has implemented a patent linkage system from 20 August 2019 following the amended Pharmaceutical Affairs Act. A new chapter of "Patent Linkage of Western Pharmaceuticals" was added to the law.[85] The new generic drug manufacturers seeking marketing approval of generic drugs has to submit a declaration that the new drug is not patented, or the patent has expired, or the approval must be given after the expiry of the patent, or the patent on the new drug is not valid or not infringed by the generic drug. Patent listing has to be made through online systems under the Taiwan Food and Drug Administration (TFDA). Patentees to upload information about originator drugs within 45 days form the approval of the TFDA.

[82] BRIEF—China progressing drug-related patent laws, The Pharma Letter, 22 April 2020. https://www.thepharmaletter.com/in-brief/brief-china-progressing-drug-related-patent-laws.

[83] Reddie & Grose LLP (2020) https://www.reddie.co.uk/2020/01/23/what-does-the-us-china-trade-deal-mean-for-pharmaceutical-patent-holders/.

[84] Li and Tong (2018), pp. 270–280. See also https://www.bilaterals.org/IMG/pdf/ssrn-id2850294.pdf.

[85] Reddie & Grose LLP (2020) https://www.reddie.co.uk/2020/01/23/what-does-the-us-china-trade-deal-mean-for-pharmaceutical-patent-holders/.

The originator can file infringement suits within this period and delay a generic drug's approval for up to 12 months.[86]

2.9 *Russia*

Presently there is a positive trend towards the implementation of linkage in Russia. The Russian Civil Code provides a patent owner to file a claim to cease any activities that infringe the patent, including marketing approvals for the generics. Infringing activities include offering to sale, producing, storing, or distributing a general medicine. Threatening of infringement, obtaining marketing approvals, and registering maximum sales price provided that the relevant patent is used to manufacture the generic. The marketing authorization will be canceled if the generic is not presented in the Russian market for three or more years. If the generic drug is already in the market, the originators try to get a judgment from the court in their favor and refer the matter to the Ministry of Healthcare for canceling the marketing approval.

Russia is a member of the Eurasian Economic Union (EAEU) rules, which entered into force in 2017. The EAEU rules stipulate that the application for generic marketing approval must include information on patents covered and a statement to the effect that the medicine does not infringe on any parties' intellectual property rights. Submission of inaccurate information is a ground for revocation of marketing approval of the generics. From the year 2021, national legislation has to include all obligations under EAEU rules, including patent linkage. In April 2019, Russia launched state registration of drugs and pending applications before MoH.[87]

In a 2018 Judgement by the Russian Intellectual Property Court dated 24 April 2018, it was held that preparations to launch a generic drug three years before the expiry of the patent constitutes a threat of patent infringement.[88] This decision overrules an earlier position that Russian law does not recognize generic drugs' registration during the patent validity term as an act of infringement (Art. 1359 (2) of the Russian Civil Code.[89]

The MoH has prepared an amendment to the Law on Drugs, which states that "any company seeking to register a new drug (original or generic) shall indicate all patents and trademarks relevant for this new drug. Another obligation is to warrant that registration of this new drug would not infringe any third party's intellectual rights, under the risk of penalties."[90]

[86] Celebrating the Start of Patent Linkage, Taiwan Business TOPICS, 9 September 2019. https://topics.amcham.com.tw/2019/09/celebrating-patent-linkage/.

[87] https://grls.rosminzdrav.ru/StatementRUInfo.aspx.

[88] Case No. A41-85807/2016. http://www.lidings.com/eng/legalupdates2?id=388.

[89] Decision of the Supreme Commercial Court in case No. A40-65668/2008, dated 06.16.2009.

[90] Malakhov (2019).

2.10 Ukraine

In Ukraine, Article 9 of the Ukrainian Law on Medicines and Drugs, 1996[91] provides that marketing approval of a generic drug before the expiration of the originator's drug patent may be considered a violation of the patent owner's rights. Medicinal products shall be allowed only after registration with the Ministry of Health (MoH).[92] A generic applicant has to file a guarantee that the generic drug is not infringing any patented drugs. Patent infringement is a ground for the cancellation of marketing approval of generic drugs.

Article 34 of the Ukrainian Law on the Protection of Rights to Inventions[93] provides that the manufacturing and selling of generic drugs before the expiration of the originator drug's patent may be considered patent infringement. But it is not clear whether an application for marketing approval itself violates a patent or is regarded as an infringement. However, at the same time, a valid patent is not a guarantee for refusing a marketing approval for a generic drug by the MoH. As the patent linkage is not fully implemented in Ukraine, the originator patent owners have to monitor the marketing approvals and subsequently file patent infringement suits against generic drug applicants and cancel the marketing approval and issuance of an injunction.[94] It is also to note that in Ukraine, there is no bolar provision available in any legislation for the early production of the generic drug before the expiry of the patent term.

Ukrainian law provides that the applicant for marketing approval must submit a sample of medicine to state regulatory bodies as part of the marketing authorization procedure. Production of such a sample of the drug itself will also be considered as patent infringement without any difference, whether it was just a non-commercial medicine production or not.[95]

The Ukrainian Supreme Court made vital observations on disputes between originator and generic drug manufacturers in *Merck Sharp & Dohme Corp v. Aurobindo Pharma Limited.*, and granted injunctions against the generic manufacturers.[96] The court of appeal clarified that state registration of the pharmaceutical, as well as any preparatory actions without the actual placing of the product on the market, are not included in the concept of "use" of a patented invention within the

---

[91] No. 123/96BP, 4 April 1996.

[92] https://www.wto.org/english/thewto_e/acc_e/ukr_e/WTACCUKR139_LEG_8.pdf.

[93] LAW OF UKRAINE on the Protection of Rights to Inventions and Utility Models https://ukrpatent.org/i_upload/file/law-special-1.pdf.

[94] *H.Lundbeck A/S v.Farmak JSC*, http://reyestr.court.gov.ua/Review/3683167. In this case the patent holder, Lundbeck, brought a claim because Farmak started the procedure to prepare the launch of a generic medicine while the patent was still in force. The court issued an injunction against, inter alia, the production, sale and offering for sale and the launch of the marketing authorization process.

[95] *H. Lundbeck A/S v Chemo Iberica, S.A.*, http://www.reyestr.court.gov.ua/Review/10026637.

[96] Ukraine: Interim injunctions in pharma cases, Vasil Kisil & Partners. Lexology https://www.lexology.com/library/detail.aspx?g=0eb0c844-233d-4988-9774-efffe9ebcabd.

meaning of Article 28(2) of the Law of Ukrainian Law, "On Protection of Rights to Inventions and Utility Models." The Supreme Court dismissed the Court of Appeal's order and upheld the ruling of the court of the first instance that refused to prohibit Aurobindo pharma from placing the drug on Ukraine's market.[97] Mostly the courts are in granting injunctions against marketing approval of generic medicines and favor originator companies.[98]

2.11 *Thailand*

Presently there are no patent linkage laws applicable in Thailand. However, in 2017, Thailand constituted a committee to monitor various agencies, including the Food and Drug Administration (FDA) and 15 other governmental agencies. It establishes a clear linkage between agencies involved in the enforcement of IP, especially the Department of Intellectual Property (DIP) and FDA, indirectly.[99]

The FDA imposed a condition that all applicants of a new drug must fill a form listing all existing patents. Section 80 is included in the draft 2018 amendment to the Drug Act 1967.[100] This is a mandatory requirement from generic drug manufacturers to find out possible infringement.[101] Thailand wants to be part of the 11 member TPP agreement, but the discussions stalled due to the COVID-19 pandemic.[102] The Pharmaceutical Affairs Act was amended and taken effect from 13 October 2019.[103] Amendment to Section 80 provides for a "new drug or a new traditional drug applicant would be required to include documents showing patent/petty patent rights (Patent Information) or rights related to traditional Thai medicinal wisdom for regulatory approval of a drug."[104] This will formalize a system since 2008; the FDA has required that all applicants for a new drug fill out a form listing all of their

---

[97] Judgment dated 14 August 2018. (http://reyestr.court.gov.ua/Review/75896089).

[98] Polikarpov (2015). http://patentblog.kluweriplaw.com/2015/02/19/bolar-provision-in-ukraine-fiction-or-reality/.

[99] https://www.tilleke.com/resources/ip-linkage-thai-government%E2%80%99s-efforts-connect-agencies.

[100] Baker McKenzie, Thailand: Proposed Addition to Drug Act - Move Towards Patent Linkage Concept. https://www.lexology.com/library/detail.aspx?g=f19da913-6e8d-4498-8d4e-8b5f53da695e.

[101] Bangkok Post (2017). https://www.tilleke.com/resources/ip-linkage-thai-government%E2%80%99s-efforts-connect-agencies.

[102] Bangkok Post, February 17, 2020. https://www.bangkokpost.com/business/1859454/thailand-to-decide-on-trade-pact-around-april-japan-minister.

[103] Drug Act (No. 6), B.E. 2562 (AD 2019). https://www.lexology.com/library/detail.aspx?g=8f66805c-64eb-49e1-87cc-25f6c716feb0.

[104] Baker McKenzie, Thailand: Proposed Addition to Drug Act.

existing patents.[105] The Patent Act allows the patent owner to take criminal and civil actions against infringers. The penalty for infringement is not more than two years imprisonment or a fine up to THB 400,000.[106]

2.12 Philippines

The Philippines removed the patent linkage system in 2006. The Government Order permits acceptance of product registration without verifying whether there is a relevant patent. However, the FDA shall comply with any court order. An originator cannot prevent a generic drug manufacturer from getting a Certificate of Product Registration (CPR). The innovator must file a civil, criminal, or administrative case and get an injunction against CPR issuance. The Intellectual Property Code provides provisions for patent infringement. Criminal action is available only for repeated infringers. Philippines will be affected by the RCEP agreement, which is pending for approval from India. Then patent linkage will be implemented throughout these countries.[107]

2.13 Singapore

After entering a free trade agreement with the US and both countries, Singapore introduced a patent linkage system, and both countries implemented it from January 1, 2004.[108] The system allows the patent owners to monitor the generic drug marketing application and imposes mandatory disclosures.[109] Patent linkage provisions are incorporated in Regulation 23(2) of the Health Products (Therapeutic Products) Regulations 2016 ('TPR'). The Health Science Authority (HAS) of Singapore administers regulation on drug approval. Registration of any therapeutic product needs a declaration to the effect that no patent is infringed. The applicant must also declare that (1) the patent owner has given consent to the launch of the generic version; (2) the patent is invalid; or (3) the patent will not be infringed by acts relating to the therapeutic product.

[105] https://www.tilleke.com/sites/default/files/2017_Apr14_IP%20Linkage_The%20Thai%20Government%E2%80%99s%20Efforts%20to%20Connect%20Agencies.pdf.

[106] McKenzie (2019). https://www.bakermckenzie.com/en/insight/publications/guides/global-guide-to-patent-linkage.

[107] Mirandah (2012), p. 50. https://www.lexology.com/library/detail.aspx?g=73ee9ee5-1873-457e-b24f-8af6e96721ff.

[108] United States – Singapore Free Trade Agreement. https://wits.worldbank.org/GPTAD/PDF/archive/US-Singapore.pdf.

[109] https://www.tilleke.com/resources/ip-linkage-thai-government%E2%80%99s-efforts-connect-agencies.

Filing of the false information is an offense with a fine and imprisonment of up to 12 months. If a generic company applies for marketing approval in the last 18 months of the patent's life, to be granted after the patent period's expiry, the marketing approval process will continue. Upon notice to the patentee, the marketing approval can be stalled for 45 days (notice period). The HAS may register the therapeutic product without further notice to the patent's proprietor if no Order or Declaration has been made at the end of 30 months after the date of the application for the Order or Declaration. The patent holders get a 30-month stay of approval of any product license upon applying for the necessary Order or Declaration. This prolonged delay of up to 31.5 months in total leads to uncertainty among generic manufacturing seeking marketing approval and the patentee.[110] A person who made a false declaration shall be liable for conviction to a fine of $\leq$SGD 20,000 and/or imprisonment for a term $\leq$12 months. The result of marketing approval in such cases will depend upon the court decision.

In *AstraZeneca AB (SE) v. Sanofi-Aventis Singapore Pte. Ltd*, the High Court discussed delaying originator drug makers' tactics.[111] This case was examined under the Medicines Act, which was replaced by the TPR, 2016. Sanofi has applied for marketing approval for film-coated tablets comprising rosuvastatin and a stabilizer. Sanofi declared that the product would not infringe AstraZeneca's Singapore Patent No.SG89993 (993), because of a different combination. AstraZeneca argued that its patents are infringed, and hence, a 30-month stay in the application process is applicable. Sanofi was forced to disclose its composition of their product under the court order. High Court observed that the 30 months' objective is to settle the dispute before the product enters the market. However, this provision may be misused for delaying the entry of drugs by the originators and, therefore, have the effect of delaying public access to competitors' products. The Court concluded that "By way of a parenthetical concluding observation, where a claim has serious consequences to the public and a defendant's legitimate business, as a matter of good practice, the plaintiff should be required to give proper particulars of its claim" to save a considerable amount of time, energy and expense.[112]

What kind of information could be disclosed to the patentee during marketing approval is also under discussion in *Millaneium Pharmaceuticals, Inc. v. Drug Houses of Australia Pte Ltd.*[113] Millennium Pharmaceuticals owns two patents in Singapore nos. SG 151322 and SG 182998, which are the process for manufacturing bortezomib. Drug Houses of Australia (DHA) obtained marketing approval of bortezomib, an anti-cancer drug in Singapore. The declaration filed as a part of the marketing approval process was never made available, and Millenium was not

[110] 30 months stay period and 45 days notice period.

[111] [2013] SGHCR 7.

[112] AstraZeneca AB (SE) v Sanofi-Aventis Singapore Pte Ltd [2013] SGHCR 7 https://www.supremecourt.gov.sg/docs/default-source/module-document/judgement/2013-sghcr-7.pdf.

[113] (2018) SGHC 149 (First Instance); Appeal (2019) SGCA 31.

served notice about the application and thus prevented from commencing litigation under the TPR.

Millennium argued before the High Court that failing to declare the patents and lack notice is in violation of laws, and the patents are infringed and a consequent injunction restraining DHA from infringing patents. The court held that generic companies must declare all patents which could be considered relevant to the product in question. The High Court sided with Millenium and confirmed that the defendant had made a misleading statement. In this case, generic companies would be compelled to disclose process patents formulation patents related to the generic to be granted marketing approval.[114]

Singapore provides data-exclusivity for five years from the dare of the original marketing approval. HAS will not grant authorization for a generic drug based on the actual test data without the originator company's approval. Patent term extensions and adjustments are available in Singapore, similar to that of the US. Patent term adjustments are possible only due to a delay in prosecution by the Singapore Patent Office.

The patent linkage regime in Singapore is in favor of originator companies. The generic drug manufacturers have to inform the innovator of any possibility of infringing the patent, and consequent litigation prolongs the entry of generics in the market. Failure to inform about the possible patent infringement will lead to the cancellation of the marketing approval and even criminal sanctions.[115]

2.14 *Malaysia*

Presently, there is no patent linkage in Malaysia. The exclusive use of the patentee is protected under section 36 of the Patent Act 1983. The drug regulatory body has no power to contravene the rights of the patentee. The generic marketing approval cannot be considered as an excuse for infringement.

In March 2018, Malaysia signed the Comprehensive and Progressive Agreement for Trans-Pacific Partnership (CPTPP), and the agreement is entered into force on 30 December 2018. Chapter 18 of the CPTPP provides a patent linkage system. However, the CPTPP has not yet been ratified by Malaysia,[116] and technically there is no patent linkage in Malaysia. However, the Drug Control Authority (DCA) monitors newly approved drugs when patent holders commence infringement

[114]Khoo and Lucas (2020). https://www.mondaq.com/patent/927960/patent-linkage-in-singapore-better-to-be-safe-than-sorry.

[115]Lexology (2020). https://www.lexology.com/library/detail.aspx?g=3f5760db-39a8-47fd-8d86-95de83072e36.

[116]Trans-Pacific Partnership Agreement (TPP) & Comprehensive and Progressive Agreement for Trans-Pacific Partnership (CPTPP) https://fta.miti.gov.my/index.php/pages/view/71#:~:text=Malaysia%20is%20still%20evaluating%20the,Prime%20Minister%20and%20his%20Cabinet.

proceedings against marketers and manufacturers of generic medicines. However, according to Section 37(1A) of the Patent Act 1983, no action can be taken against the generic companies registering the drug, and no commercial activities in Malaysia before the patent expiry. Nevertheless, if the generic manufacturers manufacture the drug and stockpile, advertise, originators can file an "imminent infringement" suit against the company under Section 59(2) of the Patent Act. This provision is similar to that of the US, and the originators can sue the generic manufacturer before the expiry of the patent.

The originator companies can monitor the notifications published by the National Pharmaceutical Regulatory Agency (NPRA) related to a new drug product that has been approved. The legal proceeding can be commenced against the generic drug manufacturers those who infringe any patents. The generic companies can register their products during the validity of the patent. However, other than registration, no commercial activity is allowed. Evidence of patent infringement can be obtained through an Anton Piller Order.[117] The court will issue such an order only when the originator producer *prima facie* case against the infringer.

There is no criminal punishment for infringements; only civil action can be initiated before the "IP High Court" bench. The remedies available are permanent injunction, impounding of the infringed products (Discovery Order), and compensation by way of damages.

In *Ranbaxy (M) Sdn. Bhd. v. EI Du Pont Nemours and Co.*,[118] the Court of Appeal of Malaysia upheld a decision of the High Court of Malaysia relating to patent infringement. The Generic manufacturer Ranbaxy argued that the regulatory approval granted by the National Pharmaceutical Control Board (NPCB) means that the manufacturing and sale of a patented pharmaceutical product are valid and not an infringement. The plaintiff obtained regulatory approval in Malaysia to manufacture and market a pharmaceutical drug known as COVANCE containing potassium losartan. The defendant alleged infringement of one of the claims. The court further held that the patent claim's description sufficiently and adequately described or taught the invention and supported the invention, and there is sufficient disclosure to understand the patent. The Court of Appeal found that the appellant to have infringed the patent.[119] The court rejected the argument of linking regulatory approval with the patent rights of originators in this case.[120] A study on the impact

---

[117] An Anton Piller Order is a form of civil search warrant which allows the plaintiff to enter the defendant's premises and conduct a search. It takes the name from the famous case of *Anton Piller KG v. Manufacturing Processes Ltd.*, [1976] 1 All. E.R. 779, [1976] Ch. 55, [1976] 2 W.L.R. 162, [1975] EWCA Civ 12.

[118] 2011, 1 AMCR 857.

[119] Court of Appeal upholds a drug-related patent infringement claim, International Law Office, 12 November 2012 https://www.internationallawoffice.com/Newsletters/Intellectual-Property/Malaysia/Shook-Lin-Bok-Kuala-Lumpur/Court-of-Appeal-upholds-a-drug-related-patent-infringement-claim.

[120] Pharmaceutical Association of Malaysia www.phama.org.my.

of patent linkage on Malaysia by Rafiq Idris reveals that patent linkage will increase Malaysia's drug cost.[121]

2.15 Vietnam

In Vietnam, also, there are no declared patent linkage provisions. Even though the Drug Administration of Vietnam (DAV) is notified about the potential infringement, a generic drug's marketing approval will not be stopped. The marketing approval will be withdrawn after a suit for infringement is successful. Usually, preliminary injunctions have not been granted in infringement cases.[122] Article 126 of the Vietnam Intellectual Property Law, 2005 amended in 2009 and 2019. Using the patent for personal, non-commercial purposes, for research, evaluation, analysis, and testing, is not considered patent infringement under Article 125(2) of the IP Act. Article 13.4 of Circular 44/2014/TT-BYT, the DAV, is obligated to revoke the marketing approvals in case of any patent infringement. Drugs can be imported without any license or marketing approvals under "special import quota." A patentee can seek revocation of such quota on the strength of a conclusion of infringement from a competent body.

In 2015, the Ministry of Science and Technology (MOST) conducted a raid in a generic manufacturers facility in South Vietnam, on a complaint from an American patentee. The patentee was aware of the generic drug's entry in 2014 for treating diabetes and filed a possible patent infringement against the manufacturer who got a marketing approval. MOST ceased hundreds of finished tablets and raw materials. A cease and desist order was also passed against the manufacturer, along with revoking marketing approvals. This case shows an effective administrative action from originator drug manufacturers during a valid patent period.[123]

2.16 Indonesia

Presently there is no patent linkage system in Indonesia. In Indonesia, BPOM Regulation No. 3/2011 deals with the registration of drugs. It allows registration of generic drugs and issues distribution licenses, which will take effect only after the patent period expires. Criminal actions can be taken against the infringers, including search, seizure, and closing infringers' business. Infringement is punishable with

[121] Idris (2016), pp. 1672–1676.

[122] Managing IP (2017). https://www.managingip.com/article/b1kbpj5jsl30y6/vietnam-improving-pharmaceutical-ip-protection.

[123] Le and Mai (2015), pp. 57–58. https://www.tilleke.com/sites/default/files/2015_Apr_Pharma_Maze_Patent_Enforcement_Vietnam.pdf.

four years of imprisonment and a fine up to IDR 1 billion. The patent holder may file civil proceedings as well for damages.

2.17 Jordan

Marketing approval is not provided for pharmaceutical products during the period of patent validity. Since the WTO accession in 1999 was amended in 2001,[124] Jordan maintained a patent linkage system and prevented generics' registration corresponding to a patent. Before enacting the patent law in 1999, consistent with the TRIPs agreement, Jordan was a heaven of copycat drugs infringing patents.[125] In 2002, the Minister of Health clarified that there would be no acceptance of dossiers for generics' marketing approval during the patent period. An application for a new drug marketing approval will be accepted by the Ministry only if the new drug produced by the domestic manufacturer is "similar but not the same as a patented one."[126]

2.18 Mexico

In Mexico, the Mexican Institute of Industrial Property (IMPI)[127] and the Federal Commission for Protection against Health Risks (COFEPRIS)[128] work together to avoid granting marketing approvals for allopathic drugs which may infringe a patent in force. IMPI established a system of publication of patents through special Gazette listing patents and their non-proprietary names (INN). The linkage system is established under Article 167 bis of the Health Supplies Regulation and Article 47 bis of the Industrial Property Regulations in 2003. An application for marketing approval to COFEPRIS relating to "substances or active ingredients" are obligated to indicate whether they are the patent holder or licensee of the existing patent.[129] If the applicant is not the patentee or the licensee, they must provide a declaration, under oath, that the application for marketing approval does not infringe the patent holder's rights. The COFEPRIS works with IMPI for ten days to determine the product's

[124] Jordan, Patents of Invention Law, Law No. 32 for the Year 19991 (and its amendment by: Temporary Law No. 71 for the Year 2001). https://www.sabaip.com/wp-content/uploads/2018/04/Jordan-Patent-Law.pdf.

[125] Armouti and Nsour (2018). http://www.hjil.org/wp-content/uploads/Nsour-FINAL.pdf.

[126] report.nat.gov.tw.

[127] https://www.gob.mx/impi/, accessed on September 30, 2020.

[128] https://www.gob.mx/cofepris/, accessed on September 30, 2020.

[129] By Jorge (2019). https://www.southcentre.int/wp-content/uploads/2019/07/PB64_The-USMCA-must-be-amended-to-ensure-access-to-affordable-drugs-in-Mexico_EN-1.pdf.

patent status for a pending marketing application. If a patent is listed in the Gazette, the Ministry of Health has not provided marketing approval for a new product that would infringe the patent.[130]

2.19 United Arab Emirates (UAE)

In UAE, Pharmaceutical patent registration is governed by Federal Law No. 17 of 2002 (as amended by Federal Law No. 31 of 2006) (Patent Law) and Ministry of Health Decree No. 404 of 2000 (Patent Resolution). The Drug Control Department (DCD) of the Ministry of Health (MOH) reviews applications for pharmaceuticals' marketing exclusivity under the Patent Resolution.[131]

Applications for generic drugs will be accepted 12 months before the expiry of UAE patent protection provided that the application does not contain any information relating to the patentee, which is protected under Article 36 of the TRIPS agreement.[132]

The UAE Ministry of Health[133] Resolution provides that the Ministry deny marketing approval for a product that would infringe an existing patent in UAE or the country of import of that drug. The Ministry will either reject the application or keep abeyance of the application until the patent term expires. This system provided patent infringements by generic drugs infringing patents.[134]

3 Patent Linkage Provisions in Regional and Bilateral Trade Agreements

3.1 CPTPP

The Trans-Pacific Partnership (TPP) agreement was dropped after the US refused to participate in the negotiations in 2017. TPP minus the US lead to the Comprehensive and Progressive Agreement for Trans-Pacific Agreement (CPTPP) agreement, a free trade agreement between 11 countries in the Asia-Pacific Region. The countries involved are New Zealand, Australia, Brunei Darussalam, Canada, Chile, Japan,

---

[130] Moeller IP, Patent Linkage in Mexico. https://www.moellerip.com/patent-linkage-in-mexico/.

[131] https://www.firstconsulting.com.

[132] Aljurf and Murray (2018). https://content.next.westlaw.com/Document/I81997321b69811e698dc8b09b4f043e0/View/FullText.html?contextData=(sc.Default)&transitionType=Default.

[133] United Arab Emirates Ministry of Health and Prevention, Health Legislation. https://www.mohap.gov.ae/en/Aboutus/Pages/PublicHealthPolicies.aspx.

[134] http://www.theglobalipcenter.com/wp-content/uploads/2018/02/United_Arab_Emirates.pdf.

Malaysia, Mexico, Peru, Singapore, and Viet Nam. Article 18.53 requires that the generic manufacturer notify the patent holder about the marketing of such a pharmaceutical product. The provision allows patent owners to intervene to prevent the marketing approval issuing and avoids the chance of infringing their patents.[135] CPTPP came into force for the first six countries, Canada, New Zealand, Australia, Japan, Mexico, and Singapore, on December 30, 2018. On January 14, 2019, it came to force for Viet Nam.[136] Canada, Australia, Japan, and Singapore have patent linkage provisions; others have to include provisions once they ratify the agreement. Peru signed the CPTPP in 2018 and agreed to implement the patent linkage provisions.

3.2 US – Peru FTA

The US-Peru Free Trade Agreement, which entered into force in 2009, Article 16.10.4, provides patent linkage. The generic drug will undergo a bioequivalence test before getting marketing approval. Notice to the patent holder is mandatory for getting marketing approval for the generic drug. The marketing approval will be deferred until the patent has expired, or sufficient time has to be given for adjudicating the dispute on the status of the patent. Un-authorized marketing of the product is prohibited before the expiry of the patent. Legislative decree of Peru 1075 imposed penalties and sanctions on a party deliberately provide false information to the regulatory authorities.[137]

3.3 AUSFTA

The Australia-US Free Trade Agreement (AUSFTA) 2005 provides for patent linkage (Article 17.10.4 – IP Chapter). There are measures in the marketing approval process to prevent others from marketing a product during the patent term without the patent owner's consent. The owner will be informed of a marketing approval application.[138] In Aktiebolaget Hassle v. *Alphapharm Pty Limited.,* the High Court

---

[135] https://www.mfat.govt.nz/assets/Trans-Pacific-Partnership/Text/18.-Intellectual-Property-Chapter.pdf.

[136] https://www.international.gc.ca/trade-commerce/trade-agreements-accords-commerciaux/agr-acc/cptpp-ptpgp/index.aspx?lang=eng.

[137] Kiliç and Maybarduk (2011). https://www.citizen.org/wp-content/uploads/comparative_analysis_of_the_u.s._intellectual_property_proposal_and_peruvian_law.pdf.

[138] Australian Government, Australia–United States Free Trade Agreement, Chapter Seventeen – Intellectual Property Rights.
https://www.dfat.gov.au/about-us/publications/trade-investment/australia-united-states-free-trade-agreement/Pages/chapter-seventeen-intellectual-property-rights.

of Australia observed that pharmaceutical manufacturers had employed many ways to delay the generic competition. It held that "the court should avoid creating fail-safe opportunities for unwarranted extensions of monopoly protection that are not sustained by law."[139]

3.4 RCEP

Negotiations for a Regional Comprehensive Economic Partnership (RCEP), as launched in 2013, involved ASEAN member states and six of its trading partners, including; China, India, Japan, Australia, New Zealand, and South Korea. In November 2019, India decided to pull out of the negotiations citing its internal economic concerns, mainly the trade deficit with China. The RCEP was signed in November 2020. The IP chapter does not provide for patent linkage. An earlier leaked draft of the RCEP agreement[140] had patent linkage provisions for "prevention of marketing pharmaceutical products infringing effective patent."[141] This provision sought to tie the marketing approval process to the patent validity, originators extension of the patent, and delay in the entry of generics. It would create a burden on the regulatory authorities to look into the validity of the patent. Presently, most of the countries do not have patent term extension provisions. But the draft included a patent extension provision both in Japan and South Korea's drafts.[142]

3.5 KOREA - US FTA

The U.S.-Korea Free Trade Agreement (KORUS FTA) entered into force on March 15, 2012.[143] Under Article 18.9.5 of the agreement provides that when a non-originator of a pharmaceutical product applies for marketing approval, the patent owner must be notified of the identity of the person making such a request. The government must make administrative arrangements to see that no marketing approvals will be granted without the patent owner's consent. Patent linkage for biologics and generics was included in the Korean Pharmaceutical Affairs Act, amended in 2015 following obligations under the KORUS FTA. It is similar to that of the US provisions, provides for notice to the patent owner not less than

[139] *Aktiebolaget Hassle v Alphapharm Pty Ltd.*, 212 CLR 411, para 101. 2002.

[140] Weatherall (2016).

[141] https://www.bilaterals.org/IMG/pdf/ssrn-id2850294.pdf.

[142] Bouchard et al. (2010), pp. 174–227.

[143] U.S. - Korea Free Trade Agreement. https://ustr.gov/trade-agreements/free-trade-agreements/korus-fta.

180 days before the first marketing date of the bio-similar. Korea followed the US system as it is and is severely criticized in Korea.[144]

4 Indian Scenario

India does not presently provide for patent linkage under its patent law. The Indian drug industry is one of the largest in the world, with 20 percent (value)[145] in all generics and accounts for 75 percent of the Indian market share.[146] The US is the prime destination of Indian generic exports. In 2008, the Department of Pharmaceuticals started a program in the name of "Jan Aushadhi" (medicine for people) shops to made available unbranded generic drugs available to the poor people in the country at a reasonable and affordable price. Until June 30, 2019, 5300+ "Pradhan Mantri Bhartiya Janaushadhi Kendras" are functional spread over 35 States/UTs of our country.[147] Under the umbrella of "Bureau of Pharma PSUs of India," more than 900 drugs and 154 surgical & consumables covering almost all major therapeutic groups have been supplying.

The prime objective of Draft Pharmaceutical Policy, 2017[148] of India, declares, "making essential drugs accessible at affordable prices to the common masses." To fulfill the policy objective, the Government has come out with a price regulation mechanism through the National List of Essential Medicines. The National Health Policy, 2017 also emphasizes affordability as one of the fundamental principles.[149] The policy's goal is to "achieve the highest possible level of good health and well-being for all Indians through a preventive and promotive healthcare orientation in all developmental policies." These policy objectives cannot be achieved without a vibrant generic drug industry.

The Government of India's Pharma Vision 2020[150] aims to make India a global leader in end-to-end- drug manufacturing. The export of pharma products is expected to reach $20 billion by 2020 and the total market to the tune of USD$55 billion.[151] India supplies 20 percent of the global generic drug demand.[152] It is more

[144]Laurenza (2015), pp. 439–442.

[145]http://www.uniindia.com/generic-drugs-holds-70-pc-market-share-in-pharmaceutical-sector-in-india/south/news/1512004.html.

[146]Indian Generic Drug Market Outlook 2020, September 2015. https://www.rncos.com/Market-Analysis-Reports/Indian-Generic-Drug-Market-Outlook-2020-IM779.htm.

[147]http://janaushadhi.gov.in/mesgceo.aspx.

[148]http://www.indiaenvironmentportal.org.in/files/file/draft%20pharmaceutical%20policy%202017.pdf.

[149]https://mohfw.gov.in/sites/default/files/9147562941489753121.pdf.

[150]India Pharma 2020: Propelling access and acceptance, realising true potential https://online.wsj.com/public/resources/documents/McKinseyPharma2020ExecutiveSummary.pdf.

[151]Ibid.

[152]Press Information Bureau (2018). https://pib.gov.in/newsite/PrintRelease.aspx?relid=186696.

important to note that Indian pharmaceutical firms supply over 80 percent of the antiretroviral drugs used internationally to combat AIDS (Acquired Immune Deficiency Syndrome). The Indian industry provides even 30 percent of the US generic drug market.[153] Any changes in the global and regional policies will severely affect the Indian generic industry. There is a direct correlation between generic drugs and price affordability. However, there is a conflict of interest between patented drug manufacturers and the generic drug industry, and allegation of patent infringements are common in many cases. It is alleged that the originator drug industry is charging exorbitant prices on their patented drugs, which is no match to their investments. In India, the Madras High Court in the famous *Novartis* case discussed this issue.[154]

4.1 Drugs and Cosmetics Act, 1940

Rule 122E (Drugs & Cosmetics Rules) 1945 defines "new drug". A generic drug has not been defined in the Act nor Rules. The Central Drugs Standards Control Organization (CDSCO) under the Directorate General of Health Services is responsible for the approval of drugs in India. The objective of the Act is to examine the safety and security of drugs that are manufactured and imported. There is no interlinkage between the Drugs and Cosmetics Act and Patent Act 2005. Grant of a patent by the Patent Controller General of India has no impact on whether or not marketing approval should be granted. Patents can be opposed by pre-grant [section 25(1)], and post-grant [section 25(1) (t)] opportunities, or even it can be canceled (Section 64). The Drugs Controller of India (DCGI) under the Drugs and Cosmetics Act, 1940, is the statutory authority to grant manufacturing and marketing approval. However, none of the legislations in India neither permits nor intends to provide patent linkage.

4.2 Bristol Myers Squibb v. Hetero Drugs Ltd. – 2008

The petitioner successfully got an ex-party injunction against the Hyderabad-based Hetero Drugs, which effectively linked patent status with marketing approval of the generic version of the originator drug, in this case, Dasatinib, a cancer drug. The Delhi High Court granted an injunction against the defendant and restrained generic company from "manufacturing, selling, distributing advertising, exporting, offering for sale or in any manner dealing directly or indirectly in any product infringing the plaintiff's patent..." The court also observed that the DCGI must see that such approvals are not infringing any patent. The court held that "It is expected that the

[153]https://www.ibef.org/industry/pharmaceutical-india.aspx.

[154]Raju (2009), pp. 7–32.

Drugs Controller while performing statutory functions will not allow any party to infringe any laws and if the drug for which the defendants have sought approval is in breach of the patent of the plaintiffs, the approval ought not to be granted to the defendant." This judgment created unrest and concerns in the generic industry. Unfortunately, this is far beyond the court's jurisdiction without adequately examining the Drugs and Cosmetics Act's provisions about the mandate of the DCGI. It is not the duty of the DCGI to enforce the patent rights in India. Its mandate is to ensure the safety and quality of the drugs sold or imported into India. This will automatically stall India's generics' approval process during the patent term, which is a derogation from the bolar provision contained in Section 107A of the Patent Act.

There is no linkage in India, and neither the Patent Act nor the Drugs and Cosmetics Act has provisions for connecting this. The court tried to implement patent linkage, which is not envisaged, nor the legislature intended to include in the concerned laws during its drafting. The court has attempted to fill the gap, which is never existed. The costly originator medicines are a severe threat to needy patients in India. On one side, the foreign companies argue for patent linkage, and on the other hand, the generic companies and non-governmental organizations working in access to medicines are objecting to the patent linkage. This decision caused unrest in the well established generic industry in India. The court had delivered this judgment when the DCGI was not even a party to the dispute. Effectively this judgment made patent policing by the court without any legislative sanctions.

4.3 Bayer - Cipla Case

In *Bayer v. Cipla, Union of India and Others*, 2009,[155] the Supreme Court held that submission of clinical data for getting marketing approval is not an infringement of the originator. Bayer has filed a case against Cipla, an Indian generic manufacturer in the High Court of Delhi, alleging that "sorafenib," is a spurious drug, which is an imitation of the originator patented drug "Sorafenib tosylate." A single Judge of the court dismissed the petition in August 2009, rejecting Bayer's argument that inferring drug agencies' role in patent policing or enforcement is unacceptable. Bayer appealed before the Division Bench of the High Court, and the judgment was delivered by the court in February 2010,[156] upholding the position of the single judge in this case and refused to issue a restraint order against the grant of marketing approval to Cipla for its generic drug "Soranib." Bayer filed a Special Leave Petition (SLP)[157] before the Supreme Court, which decides the case in December 2010, upholding the decision of the Delhi High Court.

[155]WP(C) No. 7833/2008.

[156]LPA 443/2009-9 February 2010.

[157]Special Leave to Appeal (CIVIL) No. 6540/2010.

It is interesting to know that Bayer argued that S.2 of the Drugs and Cosmetics Act (DCA) read with S.48 of the Patent Act provides for inbuilt provision for "patent linkage." The marketing approval granted under S.2 shall not derogate any other legislation, i.e., Patent law S.48, patentee's rights. Bayer argued that patent linkage could be inferred from the joint reading of Section 2 of the Drugs and Cosmetic Act and Section 48 of the Patent Act. On the other hand, Cipla clearly said that submitting information to the drug regulatory is not an infringement of the patent. The Drugs Controller, given the regulatory approval to Cipla based on the drug, was safe, effective, and not an act of "making, using, offering for sale, selling or importing" the petitioner's patented product.[158] Section 107A(a) is known as the Indian "Bolar" provision, permits any drug manufacturer to experiment with any patented drug to generate data that could then be submitted to a drug control authority. The aim of the rule is that ensuring the immediate entry of generic drugs on patent expiration. "Spurious drug" is defined under section 17B of the Drugs Act, which does not include a generic version of any medicines. The court rejected Bayer's argument that Rule 122B(1)(b) of the Drugs Rules, read with Form 44, and the data required (Appendix 1 to Schedule Y) intends patent linkage.

To suggest that patent linkage is established only because an entry in Form 44 asks the applicant to indicate the drug's patent status is to misconstrue the provisions as they stand. A form in an appendix to a statutory rule (in this case, the DCR) cannot be understood contrary to the statute's scheme. Court agreed with the respondent's contention that the Drug Controller General of India's (DCGI) office is not equipped to deal with patents' validity. The office and functions of DCGI are governed under the Drugs and Cosmetics Act (DCA) and not under the Patents Act. The court observed that "spurious drugs" and "generic drugs" are two different concepts. The court found that patent linkage is a "TRIPs plus" obligation, and TRIPs do not deal with the concept of patent linkage.

The court concluded that patent linkage could not be read into the provisions of the Drugs and Cosmetics Act and Patent Act, and such systems are undesirable for the Indian context. Some of the other observations are very pertinent, as follows:

- Policing of patent rights is not the duty of the regulators.
- Patent rights are private rights, and they cannot be mix with public rights.
- Patent linkage will undermine the "Bolar" provision.
- Article 27 of the TRIPs Agreement requires that patents are made available without discrimination by the field of technology, patent linkage only specific to the pharmaceutical industry alone.

The Court elaborately discussed the objectives of the two legislations. Delhi High Court when dismissing the petition and imposed a cost of Rs. 6,75,000/- payable in equal shares to the Union of India and Cipla for vexatious and luxury litigation. The Supreme Court held that there is no room for patent linkage in India, and no such system could be encompassed into the existing Indian laws. Some scholars argue

[158] Mittal (2010), pp. 187–196.

that denial of patent linkage in India is a negative development, and the availability of life-saving drugs must be ensured through compulsory licenses, not through giving parallel approval to generic drug manufacturing by DCGI.

Access to life-saving drugs in developing countries is essential and an essential public interest topic in India. Adopting patent linkage, either legislatively or judicially, would severely affect the generic drug industry in India.

5 Conclusions

The objective of patent rights is to give incentives to the innovator for further research and development. This protection is for a limited period, 20 years, as fixed under the TRIPs agreement. Presently, 164 WTO members are subscribed to this agreement and obliged to implement at the domestic level since 1995. The protection of patent rights is inevitable to promote innovation in the pharmaceutical sector. At the same time, generic medicines also play a crucial role in pharmaceutical innovation, especially affordability and accessibility in developing and developed countries. But an inappropriate extension of the monopoly rights beyond the permitted period of 20 years must be considered an abuse of the patent system. Patent linkage is how the country allows linking marketing approval of the generic drug with the originator drug's patent status. The practice requires that generic companies applying for marketing approval must prove that they are not violating any valid patent. Under the arrangement, national regulatory authorities should prevent the registration and marketing of generic pharmaceuticals.

Originally, patent linkage introduced through the Hatch-Waxman Act 1984 in the US intended to encourage the manufacture of generic drugs without infringing any patents and to promote innovation in the pharmaceutical industry. However, there were no many takers of patent linkage provisions in other countries. The declared objective of the law is to facilitate the entry of generic drugs in the US market. But it is turned out to be a barrier for the generic companies to get regulatory approvals by filing an ANDA.

For the last 36 years, since the introduction of the patent linkage in the US, approximately 15 countries have adopted patent linkage provisions. Precisely, these provisions are pushed through regional or bilateral trade agreements by the US. There is no obligation under the TRIPs agreement to implement patent linkage. Originator companies argue that patent linkage is a rational means of ensuring patent rights and regulatory agencies not helping patent infringement. However, the objective of patent law and regulatory approvals are different, and their functions are dissimilar. Patent linkage is not mentioned in the TRIPS agreement at all. The US has made the patent linkage provision to create a second tier of protection for a patent monopoly. Patent rights are private rights and have to be enforced privately, and it cannot be implemented through government regulatory authorities.

The passive approach to free trade agreements and IP standard setting is evident. Most of the bilateral trade agreements include IP chapters. The TRIPs flexibilities are breathing space for many developing and least developed countries, including India. Eroding these flexibilities will kill the golden goose who produces a significant chunk of the generic medicines for the developing world. Patent law requires enforcement of patent rights, but linkage inappropriately uses regulatory authorities to prevent infringement. These authorities may not be competent enough to determine patents' validity, and their mandates are different. Marketing regulatory procedures should not be subject to patent law. Only the courts can decide if the patent is infringed or not after adducing sufficient evidence, and it is not the duty nor expertise of the regulators to do it.

EU does not support the idea of patent linkage because it will adversely affect the implementation of the bolar provision to manufacture generics and biosimilars in advance of patent expiry. However, Patent term extension is already granted in the EU in the form of supplementary protection certificates (SPC) on a national basis. It is alleged that patent linkage's main objective is to extend the patent term by delaying generic medicines' entry. A centralized "Orange book" also is missing in the EU. In the *Italian* patent linkage provision case, the European Commission made it clear that patent linkage delays generic medicines' entry and a clear abuse of the EU regulatory system. It is also noticed that the originators are misusing the system by filing frivolous litigations against the generic industry. In 2007, 20 such cases were filed by the originators against generics and regulators in Portugal.[159]

Canada amended the Patent Act in 2017 and introduced patent linkage provisions. The patent register is available similar to that of the "orange book" in the US. However, 180 days exclusivity period is absent for the generic manufacturers to challenge the patent. The statutory stay of generic is for 24 months less than the US period of 30 months.

Japan also implemented patent linkage in the country. The patent linkages are secured in two stages of regulatory approval and drug price listing. During the active patent period, no generic approvals will be granted. Patent extension up to five years is available.

Australia implemented a patent linkage through AUSFTA and consequent domestic legislation. South Korea also implemented patent linkage through the US – Korea Bilateral Free Trade Agreement. China effectively implemented linkage through the Chinese new Drug Administration Law in 2019. On 15th January 2020, China and the US signed an Economic and Trade Agreement to effectively implement patent linkage provisions. These provisions are similar to that of the US provisions under 35 U.S.C.§.154(b). Chinese Taipei (Taiwan) also added patent linkage provisions to the Pharmaceutical Affairs Act in 2019. The linkage provisions have close similarities with Chinese provisions.

Thailand effectively implemented patent linkage through "Drug Patent Approval Linkage" in 2019. Brunei, Singapore, New Zealand, and Chile signed the Trans-Pacific Partnership (TPP) in 2006, and patent linkage is introduced through this

[159] https://www.medicinesforeurope.com/wp-content/uploads/2009/06/EGA-IP_Barriers_web.pdf.

agreement. Singapore's judicial decisions made it clear that the courts favor more excellent protection to the patentees and already implemented patent linkage.

Even though Malaysia claims there is no patent linkage system, but it effectively implemented the CPTPP. The High Court and Court of Appeal of Malaysia held that the regulatory approval is nothing to do with any authorization to work on the patent. It means that in Malaysia, there is still room for the generic industry to get marketing approval.

It is interesting to note that regional trade agreements are taking the main stage in implementing the patent linkage provisions. AUSFTA and US-Peru FTA also have patent linkage provisions. Patent linkage provisions were also proposed in RCEP. These TRIPs-plus provisions could substantially increase generic medicines' costs in the countries and threaten access to essential drugs in most states.

There is no patent linkage in India so far, and the courts are made it clear that these two systems cannot be connected. Indian courts actively prevented patent linkage successfully. The Satwant Reddy Committee Report in 2006 suggested the gradual adoption of patent linkage in India. However, the Indian scenario is unique, and it is the warehouse of generic medicines. Nevertheless, the jurisprudence from India gives mixed feelings. In the *Bristol Myers Squibb* dispute, Delhi High Court held that the Drug Controller General, when granting marketing approval to the generic drug, must see that no valid patent is infringed.

On the other hand, in *Bayer v. Cipla,* the same Delhi High Court (another bench) held that patent rights are private rights, and patent rights policing is not the regulators' duty. Court also observed that linkage would undermine the bolar exemption granted under the TRIPs agreement. The dispute has gone to the Division Bench of the High Court and Supreme Court of India but confirmed the first ruling in favor of generic drugs in India.

However, the story in *Roche Ltd. & Anr. v. Cipla* is protracted litigation for almost a decade. Initially, the case was in favor of Cipla and lost the dispute up to the Supreme Court. Nevertheless, the second phase of the dispute was absolutely in favor of Roche. The case reached the Supreme Court in 2017 again and finally settled out of court.

Later, Roche filed a series of suits against Indian generic pharmaceutical companies like Glenmark Pharma, Reddy's Lab, Natco Pharma, Innova Pharma, Cipla, Aureate Healthcare, BDR Pharma, Oncare Lifesciences, Accuracare Pharmaceuticals, and Metrix. This shows the ill intentions of the originator companies for using litigation as a coercive measure in India.

Linking patent rights with regulatory and marketing approvals will have undesirable results in developing countries and have a negative effect on access to medicines in developing and least developed countries. Patent linkage introduces a significant obstacle to the timely availability of generic medicines. With this analysis of many countries' linkage provisions, it is clear that while some developed countries adopt these provisions, many do not, and imposing this in the developing countries like SAARC has an everlasting negative impact on the availability and accessibility of generic drugs. The comparative analysis of the patent regimes of different jurisdictions reveals no unanimity about patent linkage's importance or utility. Enforcement of regional trade agreements with patent linkage provisions will change this scenario. Patent linkage provisions will be used as a restrictive measure upon drug development in the developing nations. This provision favors multinational pharmaceutical companies those who want to extend their patent term for maximum exploitation.

5.1 Suggestions

- TRIPS-plus obligations such as patent linkage should not be imposed on developing countries.
- Pre-emptive patent infringement suits only delay the entry of generic drugs, and such infringement suits may not be entertained by courts when public interest is involved.
- The role of licensing or regulatory authority and patent granting authority has to be separated. Regulatory officers cannot make an informed decision about the applicability of the patented drug and generic drugs. It must leave it to the court to decide the status.
- TRIPs plus patent linkage obligations should not be imposed on developing countries through regional trade agreements.
- Originator companies can very well file patent infringement suits even without patent linkage provisions and seek to enforce their private rights through courts.
- Patent infringement suits must be based on good faith. Hefty fines should be imposed on companies who file frivolous litigations to delay marketing approvals of generics.
- Administrative procedures may be simplified, transparent, and a national registry should list all new drug applications.
- Declaration of non-infringement can be taken for generic approvals to avoid unnecessary litigations.
- The originator company should disclose all its patent registrations for products/ process while filing the regulatory approval.
- The patent application status should not be a ground for refusal, suspension, or prevention of marketing approvals.
- Patent linkage is an administrative procedure and nothing to do with the concept of patent protection. But some of the countries like Hungary made a provision for declaring the patent status when applying for marketing approval of the generic.
- Reject all efforts to introduce patent linkage in any form in developing countries.

References

Abe T (2019) Japan: what impact do generic drugs have on the Japanese market? Managing IP Asia Pacific https://www.managingip.com/Article/3888280/Japan-What-impact-do-generic-drugs-have-on-the-Japanese-market.html. Accessed 8 Mar 2021

Aktiebolaget Hassle v. Alphapharm Pty Ltd, 212 CLR 411, para 101 2002

Aljurf S, Murray M (2018) Pharmaceutical IP and competition law in the United Arab Emirates: overview. https://content.next.westlaw.com/Document/I81997321b69811e698dc8b09b4f043e0/View/FullText.html?contextData=(sc.Default)&transitionType=Default. Accessed 8 Mar 2021

Anton Piller KG v. Manufacturing Processes Ltd., [1976] 1 All. E.R. 779, [1976] Ch. 55, [1976] 2 W.L.R. 162, [1975] EWCA Civ 12

Armouti W, Nsour M (2018) Data exclusivity for pharmaceuticals in free trade agreements: models in selected United States free trade agreements. http://www.hjil.org/wp-content/uploads/Nsour-FINAL.pdf. Accessed 8 Mar 2021

Article 1 of the TRIPs Agreement. https://www.wto.org/english/docs_e/legal_e/27-trips.pdf. Accessed 5 Mar 2021

AstraZeneca AB (SE) v Sanofi-Aventis Singapore Pte Ltd [2013] SGHCR 7. https://www.supremecourt.gov.sg/docs/default-source/module-document/judgement/2013-sghcr-7.pdf. Accessed 8 Mar 2021

Australian Government, Australia–United States Free Trade Agreement, Chapter Seventeen – Intellectual Property Rights. https://www.dfat.gov.au/about-us/publications/trade-investment/australia-united-states-free-trade-agreement/Pages/chapter-seventeen-intellectual-property-rights. Accessed 8 Mar 2021

Australian Government, About the Australian therapeutic goods legislation. https://www.tga.gov.au/about-australian-therapeutic-goods-legislation. Accessed 5 Mar 2021

Bangkok Post, 2017. https://www.tilleke.com/resources/ip-linkage-thai-government%E2%80%99s-efforts-connect-agencies

Bangkok Post, February 17, 2020. https://www.bangkokpost.com/business/1859454/thailand-to-decide-on-trade-pact-around-april-japan-minister

Bouchard RA, Hawkins RW, Clark R, Hagtvedt R, Sawani J (2010) Empirical analysis of drug approval-drug patenting linkage for high value pharmaceuticals. Northwest J Technol Intellect Prop 8(2):174–227

BRIEF—China progressing drug-related patent laws, The Pharma Letter, 22 April 2020. https://www.thepharmaletter.com/in-brief/brief-china-progressing-drug-related-patent-laws. Accessed 8 Mar 2021

Bureau of Pharma PSUs of India (BPPI). http://janaushadhi.gov.in/mesgceo.aspx. Accessed 8 Mar 2021

Case No. A41-85807/2016. http://www.lidings.com/eng/legalupdates2?id=388. Accessed 8 Mar 2021

Catherine Drew (2017) EU unlikely to follow US with 'patent linkage' system, says expert, Out-Law Analysis. https://www.pinsentmasons.com/out-law/analysis/eu-unlikely-to-follow-us-with-patent-linkage-system-says-expert. Accessed 5 Mar 2021

Celebrating the Start of Patent Linkage, Taiwan Business TOPICS, 9 September 2019. https://topics.amcham.com.tw/2019/09/celebrating-patent-linkage/. Accessed 8 Mar 2021

Chen J, Shi L-W (2017) Research on pharmaceutical patents listing rules as a part of patent linkage system in United States. Chin J New Drugs 26:1484–1487

China IPR (2021) Patent litigation, IP monetization and technology decoupling: lessons for the future. https://chinaipr.com/category/patent-linkage/. Accessed 8 Mar 2021

Correa CM (2016) The Bolar Exception: legislative models and drafting options, Research Paper No. 66. South Centre, Geneva. https://www.southcentre.int/research-paper-66-march-2016/

Court of Appeal upholds a drug-related patent infringement claim, International Law Office, 12 November 2012. https://www.internationallawoffice.com/Newsletters/Intellectual-Property/

Malaysia/Shook-Lin-Bok-Kuala-Lumpur/Court-of-Appeal-upholds-a-drug-related-patent-infringement-claim. Accessed 8 Mar 2021

Daniela Ampollini (Trevisan & Cuonzo) (2011) Patent linkage? Infringement proceedings by the European Commission against Italy, Kluwer Patent Blog. http://patentblog.kluweriplaw.com/2011/04/08/patent-linkage-infringement-proceedings-by-the-european-commission-against-italy/. Accessed 5 Mar 2021

Data Exclusivity/Patent Linkage in the Context of EU Generic and Biosimilar Applications. Presentation by Suzette Kox at the WIPO Life Sciences Symposium: Intellectual Property and Life Sciences Regulation, 16 November 2017. https://www.wipo.int/export/sites/www/meetings/en/2007/lifesciences/sym_regulation/lss3_ge_07_kox.pdf. Accessed 5 Mar 2021

Decided on June 17, 2013., https://www.supremecourt.gov/opinions/12pdf/12-416_m5n0.pdf. Accessed 5 Mar 2021

Decision of the Regional Administrative Court of Rome on January 2018 (T.A.R. Lazio, sez. III, - Roma, 19 January 2018, No 662)

Decision of the Supreme Commercial Court in case No. A40-65668/2008, dated 06.16.2009

Draft Pharmaceutical Policy – 2017. http://www.indiaenvironmentportal.org.in/files/file/draft%20pharmaceutical%20policy%202017.pdf. Accessed 8 Mar 2021

Drug Act (No. 6), B.E. 2562 (AD 2019). https://www.lexology.com/library/detail.aspx?g=8f66805c-64eb-49e1-87cc-25f6c716feb0. Accessed 8 Mar 2021

DrugPatentWatch Patent linkage: Balancing patent protection and generic entry https://www.drugpatentwatch.com/blog/patent-linkage-resolving-infringement/. Accessed 5 Mar 2021

Ellis J (2019) The promise of patent linkage. https://geneva-network.com/article/patent-linkage/. Accessed 5 Mar 2021

European Commission (2008) Pharmaceutical Sector Inquiry, Preliminary Report. https://ec.europa.eu/competition/sectors/pharmaceuticals/inquiry/preliminary_report.pdf. Accessed 5 Mar 2021

European Generic Medicines Association (2008) Patent-related barriers to market entry for generic medicines in the European Union. http://www.ieis.org.tr/ieis/assets/media/EGA%20-%20IP_Barriers_web.pdf. Accessed 5 Mar 2021

European Generic Medicines Association (2009) A Report by the EGA Economics Committee, 2009. https://www.medicinesforeurope.com/wp-content/uploads/2016/03/Market_Barriers_Report_FINAL_update_How_to_Increase_Patient_Access_to_Generic_Medicines.pdf. Accessed 5 Mar 2021

European Medicines Agency Generic and Hybrid Medicines. https://www.ema.europa.eu/en/human-regulatory/marketing-authorisation/generic-hybrid-medicines. Accessed 5 Mar 2021

Faunce TA, Lexchin J (2007) "Linkage" pharmaceutical evergreening in Canada and Australia. Aust N Z Health Policy 4(8). https://anzhealthpolicy.biomedcentral.com/articles/10.1186/1743-8462-4-8. Accessed 8 Mar 2021

Global Legal Monitor (2019) China: Drug Administration Law Revised. https://www.loc.gov/law/foreign-news/article/china-drug-administration-law-revised/. Accessed 8 Mar 2021

Government of Canada, Comprehensive and Progressive Agreement for Trans-Pacific Partnership (CPTPP). https://www.international.gc.ca/trade-commerce/trade-agreements-accords-commerciaux/agr-acc/cptpp-ptpgp/index.aspx?lang=eng. Accessed 8 Mar 2021

H. Lundbeck A/S v Chemo Iberica, S.A., http://www.reyestr.court.gov.ua/Review/10026637. Accessed 8 Mar 2021

H. Lundbeck A/S v. Farmak JSC., http://reyestr.court.gov.ua/Review/3683167. Accessed 8 Mar 2021

https://ec.europa.eu/health/sites/health/files/files/eudralex/vol-1/dir_2001_83_consol_2012/dir_2001_83_cons_2012_en.pdf. Accessed 5 Mar 2021

https://ec.europa.eu/health/sites/health/files/files/eudralex/vol-1/reg_2004_726/reg_2004_726_en.pdf. Accessed 5 Mar 2021

https://grls.rosminzdrav.ru/StatementRUInfo.aspx. Text in Russian?

https://mohfw.gov.in/sites/default/files/9147562941489753121.pdf

https://practiceguides.chambers.com/practice-guides/patent-litigation-2020/italy/trends-and-developments#:~:text=The%20European%20Union%20does%20not,advance%20of%20the%20patent%20expiration
https://system.jpaa.or.jp/patent/viewPdf/3066. Text in Foreign Language
https://www.congress.gov/bill/98th-congress/senate-bill/01538. Accessed 5 Mar 2021
https://www.mfat.govt.nz/assets/Trans-Pacific-Partnership/Text/18.-Intellectual-Property-Chapter.pdf
https://www.tilleke.com/resources/ip-linkage-thai-government%E2%80%99s-efforts-connect-agencies
https://www.tilleke.com/sites/default/files/2017_Apr14_IP%20Linkage_The%20Thai%20Government%E2%80%99s%20Efforts%20to%20Connect%20Agencies.pdf
https://www.wipo.int/export/sites/www/meetings/en/2007/lifesciences/sym_regulation/lss3_ge_07_ferrite.pdf
https://www.wto.org/english/thewto_e/acc_e/ukr_e/WTACCUKR139_LEG_8.pdf
Idris R (2016) Patent linkage: possible impact on Malaysia's access to medicines. Scholars J Appl Med Sci 4(5C):1672–1676
India Brand Equity Foundation (IBEF). https://www.ibef.org/industry/pharmaceutical-india.aspx. Accessed 8 Mar 2021
India Pharma 2020: Propelling access and acceptance, realising true potential. https://online.wsj.com/public/resources/documents/McKinseyPharma2020ExecutiveSummary.pdf. Accessed 8 Mar 2021
India Today, New Delhi, April 17, 2020. https://www.indiatoday.in/india/story/india-sending-hydroxychloroquine-55-coronavirus-hit-countries-1667786-2020-04-17
Indian Generic Drug Market Outlook 2020, September 2015. https://www.rncos.com/Market-Analysis-Reports/Indian-Generic-Drug-Market-Outlook-2020-IM779.htm. Accessed 8 Mar 2021
Intellectual Property Watch (2012) European Commission orders Italy to drop patent linkage delaying generics. https://www.ip-watch.org/2012/01/31/european-commission-orders-italy-to-drop-patent-linkage-delaying-generics/. Accessed 5 Mar 2021
IP Litigation in Life Sciences – Costs, Duration and Enforceability in Japan. Presentation by Yoichi Okumura, Global Head of IP, Takeda Pharmaceutical Company Limited. WIPO Conference on IP Dispute Resolution in Life Science, 22 May 2015. https://www.wipo.int/export/sites/www/amc/en/docs/basel2015_okumura.pdf. Accessed 8 Mar 2021
Japanese law Translation. www.japaneselawtranslation.go.jp. Accessed 8 Mar 2021
Jordan, Patents of Invention Law, Law No. 32 for the Year 19991 (and its amendment by: Temporary Law No. 71 for the Year 2001). https://www.sabaip.com/wp-content/uploads/2018/04/Jordan-Patent-Law.pdf. Accessed 8 Mar 2021
Jorge MF (2019) The USMCA must be amended to ensure access to affordable drugs in Mexico. Policy Brief No. 64, South Centre. https://www.southcentre.int/wp-content/uploads/2019/07/PB64_The-USMCA-must-be-amended-to-ensure-access-to-affordable-drugs-in-Mexico_EN-1.pdf. Accessed 8 Mar 2021
Khoo KH, Lucas M (2020) Singapore: patent linkage in Singapore – better to be safe than sorry, Mondaq. https://www.mondaq.com/patent/927960/patent-linkage-in-singapore-better-to-be-safe-than-sorry. Accessed 8 Mar 2021
Kiliç B, Maybarduk P (2011) Comparative analysis of the United States' TPPA Intellectual Property Proposal and Peruvian Law, Public Citizen, October 2011. https://www.citizen.org/wp-content/uploads/comparative_analysis_of_the_u.s._intellectual_property_proposal_and_peruvian_law.pdf. Accessed 8 Mar 2021
Koizumi S, Yamanouchi M, Eagan JA (2011) Recent changes concerning regulatory protections for pharmaceutical companies in Japan. https://www.amt-law.com/asset/res/news_2011en_pdf/110225_2055.pdf. Accessed 8 Mar 2021
Laurenza EC (2015) The scope of 'patent linkage' in the US-South Korea Free Trade Agreement and the potential effects on international trade agreements. Eur J Risk Regul 6(3):439–442

LAW OF UKRAINE on the Protection of Rights to Inventions and Utility Models. https://ukrpatent.org/i_upload/file/law-special-1.pdf. Accessed 8 Mar 2021
Le LX, Mai LD (2015) The pharma maze: patent enforcement in Vietnam. Intellect Prop Mag:57–58. https://www.tilleke.com/sites/default/files/2015_Apr_Pharma_Maze_Patent_Enforcement_Vietnam.pdf. Accessed 8 Mar 2021
Lexology (2020) Singapore's patent linkage scheme and its effects on marketing approval for generic drugs. https://www.lexology.com/library/detail.aspx?g=3f5760db-39a8-47fd-8d86-95de83072e36. Accessed 8 Mar 2021
Li W, Tong T (2018) Studies of legal issues related to the implementation of the patent linkage system in China. Biotechnol Law Rep 37:270–280. https://doi.org/10.1089/blr.2018.29090.wl
Malakhov B (2019) Russia: on a slow boat to patent linkage? Kluwer Patent Blog. http://patentblog.kluweriplaw.com/2019/05/22/russia-on-a-slow-boat-to-patent-linkage/. Accessed 8 Mar 2021
Managing IP (2017) Vietnam: improving pharmaceutical IP protection. https://www.managingip.com/article/b1kbpj5jsl30y6/vietnam-improving-pharmaceutical-ip-protection. Accessed 8 Mar 2021
Managing IP (2019) Australia: protecting pharmaceutical market share in Australia. https://www.managingip.com/Article/3865388/Australia-Protecting-pharmaceutical-market-share-in-Australia.html. Accessed 5 Mar 2021
McKenzie B (2019) Global guide to patent linkage. https://www.bakermckenzie.com/en/insight/publications/guides/global-guide-to-patent-linkage. Accessed 8 Mar 2021
McKenzie B, Thailand: proposed addition to drug act - move towards patent linkage concept. https://www.lexology.com/library/detail.aspx?g=f19da913-6e8d-4498-8d4e-8b5f53da695e. Accessed 8 Mar 2021
Meagher K (2017) Abuse of the Hatch Waxman Act: Mylan's ability to monopolize reflects weakness. Brookline J Corp Financ Commer Law 11(2):589. Available at: https://brooklynworks.brooklaw.edu/bjcfcl/vol11/iss2/12. Accessed 5 Mar 2021
Medicines and Law Policy (2019) Data exclusivity in the EU: briefing document. https://medicineslawandpolicy.org/wp-content/uploads/2019/06/European-Union-Review-of-Pharma-Incentives-Data-Exclusivity.pdf. Accessed 5 Mar 2021
Medicines for Europe., https://www.medicinesforeurope.com/. Accessed 5 Mar 2021
Merc & Co.Inc v. High Tech Pharmaceuticals Inc,, US Court of Appeals No. 2006-1401, decided on March 29, 2007
Michael Carrier FTC v. Actavis: Where We Stand After 5 Years, 18 June 2018. https://www.ipwatchdog.com/2018/06/18/ftc-v-actavis-stand-5-years/id=98536/. Accessed 5 Mar 2021
Mirandah A (2012) Patent linkage in Asian countries compared to the US. Asia IP Mag 4(4):50. https://www.lexology.com/library/detail.aspx?g=73ee9ee5-1873-457e-b24f-8af6e96721ff. Accessed 8 Mar 2021
Mittal A (2010) Patent linkage in India: current scenario and need for deliberation. J Intellect Prop Rights 15:187–196
Moeller IP, Patent linkage in Mexico. https://www.moellerip.com/patent-linkage-in-mexico/. Accessed 8 Mar 2021
Ono Pharmaceuticals Co., Ltd. v. Kyoto Pharmaceuticals Industries, Ltd. Judgment dated 16 April 1999
Orange Book: Approved drug products with therapeutic equivalence evaluations. https://www.accessdata.fda.gov/scripts/cder/ob/index.cfm. Accessed 5 Mar 2021
Palombi L (2014) It's time to fix the free trade bungle on the cost of medicines, The Conversation. http://theconversation.com/its-time-to-fix-the-free-trade-bungle-on-the-cost-of-medicines-32574. Accessed 5 Mar 2021
Patented Medicines (Notice of Compliance) Regulations. https://laws-lois.justice.gc.ca/eng/regulations/sor-93-133/index.html. Accessed 5 Mar 2021
Pay for Delay, Federal Trade Commission. https://www.ftc.gov/news-events/media-resources/mergers-competition/pay-delay
Pharmaceutical Association of Malaysia www.phama.org.my

Pharmaceutical Sector Inquiry – Preliminary Report, Fact Sheet "Regulatory Framework". https://ec.europa.eu/competition/sectors/pharmaceuticals/archive/4_Regulator_framework.pdf

Polikarpov A (2015) "Bolar provision" in Ukraine: fiction or reality? Kluwer Patent Blog. http://patentblog.kluweriplaw.com/2015/02/19/bolar-provision-in-ukraine-fiction-or-reality/. Accessed 8 Mar 2021

Press Information Bureau (2018) Government of India Make India the international capital for Generic Medicines: Vice President, 21 December 2018. https://pib.gov.in/newsite/PrintRelease.aspx?relid=186696. Accessed 8 Mar 2021

Raju KD (2009) Interpretation of Section 3(d) in the Indian Patent Act 2005: a case study of Novartis. Indian J Intellect Prop Law 2:7–32

Raley KT (2019a) The South Korean patent linkage system: a model for reforming the United States Hatch–Waxman Act. Emory Int Law Rev 33:459–492

Raley KT (2019b) The South Korean patent linkage system: a model for reforming the United States Hatch–Waxman Act. Emory Int Law Rev 33(3). https://law.emory.edu/eilr/content/volume-33/issue-3/comments/south-korean-patent-linkage-reforming-hatch-waxman-act.html. Accessed 8 Mar 2021

Ravikant, Raju, Padmavati (2013) The impact of patent linkage on marketing of generic drugs. J Intellect Prop Rights 18:316–322

Reddie & Grose LLP (2020) What does the US-China trade deal mean for pharmaceutical patent holders? https://www.reddie.co.uk/2020/01/23/what-does-the-us-china-trade-deal-mean-for-pharmaceutical-patent-holders/. Accessed 8 Mar 2021

Research Report on Establishing System of Linking New Drug Application and Patent Protection, BIPI Research (2016) No. 002. http://www.theglobalipcenter.com/wp-content/uploads/2017/03/full-report-E.pdf. Accessed 5 Mar 2021

Son K-B, Lee T-J (2017) The trends and constructive ambiguity in international agreements on intellectual property and pharmaceutical affairs. Global Public Health 13:1169–1178

Son K-B et al (2018) Moderating the impact of patent linkage on access to medicines: lessons from variations in South Korea, Australia, Canada and the United States. Global Health 14:101. https://www.ncbi.nlm.nih.gov/pmc/articles/PMC6201583/. Accessed 5 Mar 2021

Son K-B et al (2019) Does the patent linkage system prolong effective market exclusivity? Recent evidence from the Korea-U.S. Free Trade Agreement in Korea. Int J Health Serv 49(2). https://doi.org/10.1177/0020731418822237. Accessed 8 Mar 2021

Taiwan International Patent and Law Office (2019) Taiwan FDA completes draft of enforcement rules for Western pharmaceuticals patent linkage. https://www.tiplo.com.tw/en/tn_in.aspx?mnuid=1284&nid=46776. Accessed 8 Mar 2021

Townsend B, Gleeson D, Lopert R. The regional comprehensive economic partnership, intellectual property protection and access to medicines. https://www.bilaterals.org/IMG/pdf/ssrn-id2850294.pdf. Accessed 5 Mar 2021

Trans-Pacific Partnership Agreement (TPP) & Comprehensive and Progressive Agreement for Trans-Pacific Partnership (CPTPP) https://fta.miti.gov.my/index.php/pages/view/71#:~:text=Malaysia%20is%20still%20evaluating%20the,Prime%20Minister%20and%20his%20Cabinet. Accessed 8 Mar 2021

U.S. - Korea Free Trade Agreement. https://ustr.gov/trade-agreements/free-trade-agreements/korus-fta. Accessed 8 Mar 2021

Ukraine: Interim injunctions in pharma cases, Vasil Kisil & Partners. Lexology. https://www.lexology.com/library/detail.aspx?g=0eb0c844-233d-4988-9774-efffe9ebcabd. Accessed 8 Mar 2021

United Arab Emirates Ministry of Health and Prevention, Health Legislation. https://www.mohap.gov.ae/en/Aboutus/Pages/PublicHealthPolicies.aspx. Accessed 8 Mar 2021

United News of India (2019) Generic drugs holds 70 pc market share in pharmaceutical sector in India. http://www.uniindia.com/generic-drugs-holds-70-pc-market-share-in-pharmaceutical-sector-in-india/south/news/1512004.html. Accessed 8 Mar 2021

United States – Singapore Free Trade Agreement. https://wits.worldbank.org/GPTAD/PDF/archive/US-Singapore.pdf. Accessed 8 Mar 2021

Weatherall K (2016) RCEP IP Chapter Leaked 15 Oct 2015 - Weatherall Section by Section Comments in Brief Working paper (2016), University of Sydney

West FJ, Allison Hoppert B. Extending the life of a patent in the United States. https://www.oblon.com/A11960/assets/files/News/125.pdf. Accessed 5 Mar 2021

White B et al (2017) Canada's Patent Linkage Regulations get long-awaited makeover, OSLER. https://www.osler.com/en/resources/regulations/2017/canada-s-patent-linkage-regulations-get-long-await. Accessed 5 Mar 2021

WHO (2011–2016) Regional Framework for Action on Access to Essential Medicines in the Western Pacific (2011-2016). https://apps.who.int/iris/bitstream/handle/10665/207519/9789290615705_eng.pdf. Accessed 5 Mar 2021

WHO (2020) Coronavirus disease (COVID-19) advice for the public: Mythbusters, 23 November 2020. https://www.who.int/emergencies/diseases/novel-coronavirus-2019/advice-for-public/myth-busters?gclid=EAIaIQobChMIjoGlirH06wIVhzMqCh3ISAVnEAAYASABEgKMz_D_BwE. Accessed 5 Mar 2021

Winkler AM, David Weingarten M, Cyr SK (2018) Requirements, benefits, and possible consequences of listing patents in FDA's Orange Book. July 3, 2018, BNA's Pharmaceutical Law & Industry Report. https://www.finnegan.com/en/insights/requirements-benefits-and-possible-consequences-of-listing-patents-in-fdas-orange-book.html. Accessed 5 Mar 2021

Zhang H, Li R, Min D, Yuxin J (2018) China is to establish patent linkage, Kluwer Patent Blog. http://patentblog.kluweriplaw.com/2018/04/03/china-establish-patent-linkage/. Accessed 8 Mar 2021

The manufacturer's authorised representative in the EU is Springer
Nature Customer Service Centre GmbH, Europaplatz 3, 69115 Heidelberg,
Germany. If you have any concerns regarding our products, please
contact ProductSafety@springernature.com

Printed and bound by CPI Group (UK) Ltd, Croydon, CR0 4YY
30/09/2026
02225287-0013